VOGUE SEWING

B

The Butterick® Publishing Company
161 Avenue of the Americas
New York, NY   10013

This work was previously published under the titles:
New Vogue Sewing Book and Vogue Sewing Book

Library of Congress Cataloging in Publication Data
Main entry under title:
Vogue Sewing.

Rev. ed. of Vogue Sewing 1985
Includes Index.
1. Dressmaking. 2. Sewing
TT515.V625 1982   646.4'04   97-077515

ISBN 1-57389-016-2

First Edition

10 9 8 7 6 5 4 3 2 1

The Butterick® Publishing Company
161 Avenue of the Americas
New York, New York 10013

Contents

Acknowledgments

The Vogue Sewing Book has long been the inspiration and "bible" to those of us who sew. The original book, launched in 1970 by Patricia Perry, and then in later versions, contained all the information we needed to know to create professional, fashionable-looking garments.

The changes in basic fashion sewing techniques have been minor over the years but much has changed in regards to sewing equipment, notions and supplies now available to the general sewing public. Quicker, faster ways of completing certain techniques, the broader use and production of high-quality fusible interfacings, and the introduction of brand new fibers to sew with are just some of the changes today. It was the editors' intent to provide you with this updated sewing information while still keeping the spirit of the original Vogue Sewing Book for you to use.

Throughout the years, it has taken the contributions of many people to make this book as viable as it still is today. We would like to thank them all for their hard work and generous giving of their time to make this new version possible. **Butterick Publishing**

Vogue Sewing (2000)

Editorial: JoAnn Pugh-Gannon, Caroline Politi, Stephanie M. Marracco, Nicole Pressly, Beth Baumgartel

Art: Elizabeth Berry, Debra Pantaleo, Jelena Bogavac, Juan Rios, Karen Longato, Greg Kopfer

Cover Photograph: Brian Kraus

Production: David Joinnides, Matt Dojny, Julia Dubrovich

Technical Support: Winnie Hinish and staff, Jim Kingsepp, Ben Ostasiewski, Diane Clark

Technical Advisors: Gail Wheeler, Kathy Marrone, Janet DuBane, Reg Fairchild, Penny Payne, Shirley Asper

Vogue Sewing (1982)

Editorial: Ada Cruz, Hewitt McGraw

Art: Sidney Escowitz, Kathryn Florentz

Production: Hugh MacDonald, Ron Ferguson, Renee Ullman

Staff at Harper & Row: Carol Cohen, Helen Moore, Mary Chadwick

The New Vogue Sewing Book (1980)

Editorial: Elizabeth Rice, Jeanette Weber, Linnea Leedham

Art: Phoebe Gaughan

Production: Maryanne Bannon

Technical Advisors: Margaret Lange, Timothy Healy, Carolyn Galante, Shirley Asper, Robin Harding

The Vogue Sewing Book (1975)

Editorial: Janet DuBane, Elizabeth Musheno, Betty Faden, Ellen Kochansky, Jeanne Johnson, Sheila DiBona, Barbara Trujillo, Caroline Dill, Marion Bartholomew

Art: Tony Serini, Lynne Perrella, Elaine Poprovsky, Dorothy Martin, Janet Lombardo, Susan Frye, Gisela Sachs

Production: Paul Milbauer, Grace Guerrera, Doreen Williams

Technical Advisors: Joe Molko, Alfred Raphael, Leopoldo Hinds, Helen Nemeth

The Vogue Sewing Book (1970, first edition)

Editorial: Patricia Perry, Janet DuBane, Betty Faden, Betty Musheno, Ellen Kochansky, Jeanne Johnson, Gisela Sachs, Sheile DiBona, Susan Frye, Doreen Williams, Grace Guerrera

Art: John Nicodemo, Mel Skriloff, Ed McGloin

Illustration: Dorothy Martin, Janet Grieshaber, Elaine Poprosky, Lynne Perrella

Technical Advisors: Joe Molko, Helen Nemeth

Production: Don Feder, George Keith-Beattie

Marketing and Distribution: Barbara Lolley

Fashion Information Service: Russ Norris, Herman Phynes, Donna Lang

1

The Fashion Game

Fashion Sewing as an Art Form

Fashion sewing can be compared, in some ways, to the classic art of sculpture. The sculptor is involved with the medium—manipulating clay or carving stone into a form. Sewing demands the same involvement with a medium—touching, appraising, and working with fabric that will be molded and shaped into a three-dimensional design.

The creative forces necessary to make flat, two-dimensional fabrics take on strong, structural three-dimensional shapes are no less important than those required to chip marble or mold clay. Just as a sculptor expresses dynamic ideas with plaster, bronze, or stone, the seamstress uses fabric to manifest her ideas about fashion.

Inspiration, as both artists know, comes only after attaining a good working knowledge of one's craft, and after a period of deliberation on the specific project. The end result must be firmly in mind before you begin. A sculptor wouldn't tap idly on a piece of marble with a chisel until inspiration came, and it makes no more sense for you to unwrap a length of fabric with your scissors poised until you've considered the relationship between the style and the fabric.

First, the sculptor carefully selects the basic material; it must be just right for the planned creation. No less consideration should be given to the selection of fabric. The silhouette you desire, the mood to be created, the type of body being covered—all are important to the proper fabric selection.

If ten seamstresses were given the same fabric and pattern, probably none of the finished garments would be exactly identical. With an eye to her own pluses and minuses, each would select, adapt, and embellish. The result would be what looks best on her. *A person who sews is a creative artist because she individualizes fashion to her own special preferences and requirements.*

The same principles that make a sculpture visually pleasing apply as well to clothing for the human body. A fashionable woman is aware that she is a three-dimensional form that can be seen from all angles. She must create a pleasing total visual impact by discriminating among colors, textures, and lines to discover the combination that is best suited to her own individual features. She is more than just a seamstress—she is an artisan, too. She draws upon her talents as artist, decorator, and designer to make unique creations which far surpass average ready-to-wear standards. She has, in other words, a good fashion sense.

Like creativity, good fashion sense is not limited only to designers and editors, but is a quality most women have in some degree. If you possess a strong sense of professionalism; if fine workmanship, good lines, and quality impress you; if you find shopping for patterns, fabrics, and trims irresistible; if the world of fashion intrigues and excites you; if you have good personal taste—then you are already on your way to attaining good fashion sense.

One of these qualities, personal taste, is especially important. It is, most broadly, the ability to relate fashion to yourself—your needs, figure, and preferences. Basic to that ability is being able to recognize which clothes and accessories will best accentuate natural good features. Any woman who truly cares about her appearance is very much aware of her figure's limitations, as well as those of her coloring. She analyzes her feelings about clothes—why she never wears pink and loves red; why she feels comfortable in a scoop neckline but not a high one. She forces herself to be open to change, simply for the sake of improving the way she looks and feels.

Just as a sculpture communicates a certain mood or message, a woman's clothes convey much about her. What's your fashion image? Do you picture yourself as a certain type? If not, what image would you like to convey: elegant sophisticate, sweet romantic, perky gamin, tailored classicist, avant garde dazzler? Since there is more than one side to every woman, your wardrobe will undoubtedly reflect the many facets of your personality, with all its feelings and moods. But a woman with strong fashion sense and personal taste relates her various looks to form a unified image, which conveys the confident air of a woman who knows who she is and enjoys being herself. How does one achieve this? Pick up ideas from your pattern catalogues, magazines, advertising, window displays, and other well-dressed women. Even though styles and colors shift seasonally, an awareness of your personal fashion identity will enable you to discriminately choose and select among them to organize your particular look.

The Fundamentals of Your Art

Every artist has had to absorb and apply the basic principles of design to achieve the desired artistic effect. You should do the same; once firmly grounded in them, you may confidently choose to follow them with a strict interpretation or with artistic license to achieve your exact fashion effect.

HARMONY is achieved when all elements are working together in a pleasing manner. It refers to elements of likeness, but not necessarily sameness; the key here is appropriateness and relativity.

PROPORTION requires all parts to be related to one another in size, length, and bulk.

BALANCE is achieved by maintaining equal amounts of interest in either direction from the natural center of interest.

RHYTHM is created by the eye moving smoothly and easily, connecting points of interest without jerking from point to point.

EMPHASIS means attracting the eye to one feature and subordinating all others.

Every fashion idea you have should be backed with an understanding not only of these principles, but also of the artistic components of color, print, texture, line, proportion, and balance. Just as the sculptor must understand the qualities of the raw material, whether it be rock, clay, or metal, you must understand the qualities of your fabric—color, print, and texture. Then you transform it into a design with the same components the sculptor uses to transform the material into a sculpture—line, proportion, and balance. Our aim in the next few pages is to provide guidelines in hopes that you'll find inspiration to create a prettier, newer, and more fashionable you.

Color

What is the first thing noticed about a garment? Invariably the answer is its color. We talk about "the woman in the blue dress" or "my brown suit"; only a designer would refer to "the slim low-waisted dress with inverted pleats and bateau neckline." This fact alone makes color quite worthy of consideration and a power to be placed at your disposal. Thus a fashion-conscious woman must be aware of the language and principles of color, immersing herself in all the thrilling effects that color can produce. Color know-how combined with a comprehension of her own needs and requirements can make the difference between being "sensational" or just "well-dressed."

Elements of Color

This is the technical language commonly used to describe color; learn it well, referring to the diagram and the color wheel in the first section of color photographs.

HUE, a term often used interchangeably with color, is the quality or characteristic by which we distinguish one color from another. The **primary** hues—red, yellow, and blue—are the basic building blocks of color from which all others are blended. The **secondary** hues, produced by mixing two primaries, are orange, green, and violet (purple). The tertiary hues (often called intermediates) stem from various combinations of the basic six; they are the "double-name" colors, such as yellow-green and blue-violet.

VALUE is the lightness or darkness of a color. Hues with white added are called tints and are higher in value than the original colors. To produce lower values, black is added to hues to create **shades**. Hues differ in their inherent value as well; yellow, for example, is higher in value than blue.

INTENSITY refers to the brightness or dullness of color. Again, certain hues have a higher intensity than others—orange is higher than violet, for example. **Tones** are hues with their complementary color or gray added, which reduces their intensity.

COLOR SCHEMES are many in number, but three of them are most common. A **monochromatic** color scheme uses various values and intensities of one color, or one color with black and white. These are sure and easy schemes to achieve, but the danger of monotony lurks if the variations are too similar. Use both ends of the spectrum to add contrast, such as beige to chocolate brown. An **analogous** color scheme utilizes hues which are closely related on the color wheel, or in other words, that contain similar components, such as blue, blue-green, and green. These are the real "mood makers" and are often the most pleasing and restful combinations. A **complementary** color scheme is one which involves direct opposites on the color wheel, such as red and green or blue and orange. These are exceedingly strong, bold combinations. To truly enhance each other, judgment must be used with variations in value and intensity, as complementaries used in combinations make each other look stronger. Remember that colors should never be seen as isolated entities, but in relation to each other.

Now, armed with an understanding of the basic concepts of color, turn your attention to what color can do for you. As every artist and advertising expert knows, color has profound psychological effects on all of us, as evidenced by such expressions as "seeing red," "green with envy," "black mood," "yellow streak," and "feeling blue." Some colors are cheering, compelling, vivacious, frivolous, active, and just plain fun, while others are restful, serene, relaxed, subtle, and dignified. Some lift the spirits, others subdue them; they can be soft and fresh or brassy and bold. It is not merely by chance, therefore, that we may reach into the closet for our brightest dress on a rainy day, or slip into a pastel dressing gown to relax after a hectic day.

But color can do far more for you than reflect or influence your multitude of moods and images. The skillful use of color can help present you at your loveliest. Too often women are led merely by whim, pure preference, or simple prejudice in their color selection, and not enough by what looks best on them. Always take your personal coloring into consideration. Before you buy any fabric, hold it up to your face and take a long, thoughtful look into the mirror. How does it relate to the color of your hair, eyes, and complexion? Don't mistakenly think that just because that jade green dress looks so good on you, kelly green will be just as becoming; often even a slight variation in value or intensity can make all the difference in the world. Always let your eye—or the helpful eye of a reliable friend— be the final judge.

Play tricks with color by discovering the optical illusions they can create. They can create impressions of size; cool colors of blue, green, and violet make the figure appear smaller, warm colors of red, yellow, and orange increase the apparent size of the figure. The degree of brightness or dullness can also affect size appearance—brighter colors make you look larger, duller colors make you look smaller. Boldly contrasting colors will create an impression of greater size; a more subtle color scheme will appear more compact. Another thing to note is that the eye will be attracted first to the brightest of contrasting colors; use this principle to draw your viewer's eye to or from particular areas.

Accessories can be the answer to many of your color quandaries. Use a gaily colored scarf or belt to add new spark to a dull dress, or dark shoes and bag to bring a boldly colored dress a bit closer to earth. If your figure demands subtle coloring, don't say goodbye to bright colors forever—use them in a scarf, bracelets, or a necklace. Let a bright sash riding on the hipline of your dress distract from bulk above the waist, or use a bright necklace to coax the eye away from excess width through the hipline.

The manipulation of color is not only one of the most artistic elements of fashion sewing but one of the most exciting. Experiment with it—contrast, complement, combine, or go solid. Don't be afraid of new colors or let yourself be boxed into a one-color wardrobe. Go on a creative fling to create a more colorful you.

Light, warm, or bright colors advance.   Dark, cool, or subdued colors recede.

Print

Vivid Print   Subtle Print   Large Plaid   Small Plaid

From plaids to paisleys, stripes to florals, dots to borders, prints are fashion's fun, and often its beauty as well. To create a truly harmonious effect, however, they must be carefully related to all the other design elements of your garment.

Prints are first and foremost combinations of colors, and the same rules apply to them as to solids. Vividly contrasting colors or bright shades will appear larger than subtle combinations or calmer shades. Prints can give you an advantage you may miss with solids; if you love a color that is unflattering on you, you may be able to wear it combined in a print with a more suitable color. Most prints will have a dominant color, and that is the one to consider in relation to your coloring; it will usually be either the brightest shade or the one that occupies the largest area (such as the background). Another thing to keep in mind is that colors used in combination may affect each other's apparent hue—red and blue used together, for example, may appear purple.

Also consider garment lines when selecting a print. While a solid color may require intricate lines for interest, they may be overwhelmed or appear cluttered in a print. Be aware that plaids, stripes, and many other prints have lines of their own, and make sure they are flattering to your build. Also relate the direction and shape of the various lines; a curved bodice seam would only work against an angular print and be lost.

Last and most importantly, relate the print to your own figure. A print that is greatly out of scale with the wearer and the garment will emphasize the contrast, making their size only more obvious. Use the placement of your print to direct attention to or from your pluses and minuses. A border print placed at the hemline will distract from the bodice or hips and draw attention to your legs. A dominant plaid or stripe will attract the eye, so place it only at attractive locations. Placing a dominant large-scale motif at the bust or derriere is definitely to be avoided.

Texture

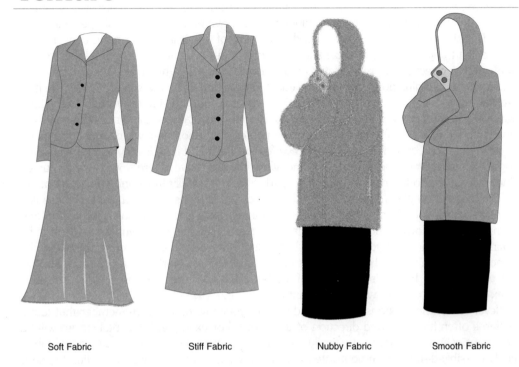

Soft Fabric   Stiff Fabric   Nubby Fabric   Smooth Fabric

The texture of your fabric is created by the characteristics of its fiber (wool, silk, etc.) and the manner of its construction (knitted, woven, etc.). All too often overlooked or taken for granted, it can be a special asset in the business of illusion-making.

The object is to create fluid eye movements in which the eye stops to rest at attractive, predetermined points of emphasis. Stiff textures hang straight without draping and thus will slide the eye smoothly up and down the lines of a sleek silhouette. One figure problem can be concealed this way, but overall roundness cannot. On the other hand, clingy fabrics rendered in straight or very simple designs do just one thing—reveal. If your figure is less than perfect, use them only in softly draped styles. And, of course, gauzy transparency should never reveal an unattractive body area.

Textural effects also contribute to an impression of size. Rough, thick textures always seem more bulky than they really are. If you adore chunky tweeds but wish to avoid their bulk, use them just at a slender section of your body, perhaps in a vest or skirt. Shiny, lustrous fabrics reflect more light and thus make you appear larger; just the opposite is true of rougher, duller textures. In other words, velvet, which absorbs light, may be a better choice in an evening dress than glittering sequins for a heavier woman.

Line

Line, as it applies to fashion, is often used synonymously with style. Every design is a carefully conceived structure of lines and shapes. The final garment will present three major sets of lines to the viewer's eye: body lines, silhouette lines, and detail lines. The ability to relate them to one another and to you in a pleasing and flattering manner will require, therefore, a basic understanding of the visual element of line. Set out to discover what line can do for you. Realize that lines influence eye movements, establish shape, and form moods, just as color does. Direction and placement of line will be your main concern.

The first thing you should realize about line is that our eyes are conditioned to move naturally in the direction we read—left to right, top to bottom. While there is a certain "pull" between the two directions, if given two equal intersecting lines, the eye will follow the horizontal more readily than the vertical. This leads us to another important concept— lines rarely are equal, as there are several factors that tend to make certain lines dominant. If a line is longer, wider, brighter, or more often repeated than another, it will be more dominant. A final point to keep in mind is that the eye follows a straight line directly and rapidly, making it the most severe and architectural line, while the eye moves more slowly along a curved line, making it a softer, relaxed line often used to lead gracefully from one point to another.

Thus lines often play tricks with our eyes and create illusions, and you want all those illusions to work for and not against you. Your primary target: to be a master of illusion and camouflage by knowing the rules of the fashion game. First, be your own best inspiration by taking a realistic look at yourself. What has nature given you that is worth emphasizing or concealing? Then follow the suggestions below to put line to work to make a more appealing you. After all, beauty is in the eye of the beholder, and the clever use of line can subtly coax the viewer's eye just where you want it.

Never forget the relationship of your design to your raw material. Remember that fabric patterns often have line and direction of their own. For example, horizontal stripes will be dominant even if the dress is vertically seamed, and even a less obviously directional fabric could possibly distract from your intentions. And when buying a plaid, check first to see if the plaid lines are dominant in a particular direction.

These are the basic "rules" for using line, but don't be misled into thinking they are necessarily hard and fast. The relationship of several lines is invariably greater than the direction of one of them. You need not do without unflattering lines entirely; simply do not use them as **dominant** lines. Regardless of your figure or the direction of the line, always be sure that the garment lines do not draw attention to an unattractive portion of the body; a horizontal across too-large hips will not look any better on a tall woman than on a short one.

Horizontal Lines   Vertical Lines

Verticals

Choose the strong classical effect of a vertical line to appear taller and thinner by leading the eye in an up and down direction. Single verticals give the strongest impression of height; when they are repeated at even intervals across the garment, the illusion of length is blunted because our eyes tend to move sideways from line to line as well. A straight or long unbroken silhouette also creates a vertical impression.

Horizontals

It is common knowledge that horizontal lines emphasize width, especially when two are used together. Placing a single horizontal line above or below the median of the body can, however, create an illusion of length throughout the longer area. Since horizontals are the strongest lines, avoid placing them at unflattering locations on the body. You can distract attention from a horizontal by using an opposing vertical, by placing it at other than the center, or by modifying it in the form of a diagonal or curve.

Diagonals

The modifying effect of diagonals depends primarily upon the angle and length of the line. As shown, the shorter diagonal line will lead the eye from side to side, giving an impression of width, while the longer line leads the eye equally downward and sideways for a longer, narrower look. And remember that the line should always move in the same direction as our eyes, from left to right, for the most pleasing effect. Diagonals possess both the discipline of straight lines and the softness of curves.

Curves

Whether they are created by shaped seaming or edges or soft draping, curved lines perform the same function of illusion as straight lines but in a less obvious manner. Curved lines also emphasize the curves of the feminine form by repetition, making them more defined. Many times a line that would be unflattering if straight can be nicely worn if modified by a curve. A curved bodice seam or front closing will be softer visually than a horizontal or vertical seam.

Curved Lines

Diagonal Lines

Proportion and Balance

Have you ever changed the hem on the skirt of a suit, and suddenly the jacket and skirt no longer seemed to go together quite the way they did before? Or seen a woman in a top and skirt that seemed to coordinate in almost every visible way but somehow didn't look quite right together? Perhaps you've stood before a mirror wondering why the style that looked so great on your best friend looks so odd on you. All of these problems may very likely be caused by an error in proportion and balance. The skillful use of the color, print, and texture of your fabric and the lines of your garment will all be for naught unless they are artfully related by these two elements. That beautifully coordinated, "well put together" look that accompanies a truly well-dressed woman is in large part due to an eye well-trained in the subtleties of proportion and balance.

Proportion   Balance

Proportion

This applies to the space relationships within a design, and involves relating such measurements as size and bulk. The most visually pleasing division of an area is one that creates the two aesthetic qualities of unity and variety—in other words, one that creates areas that are similar but not so alike as to be dull. Areas of identical size or exact divisions of space like halves, fourths, or thirds used together, while not displeasing, are often less interesting than divisions that are just far enough away from basic dimensions that the eye does not catch them immediately. Thus the most pleasing relationships, in mathematical terms, are two to three, three to five, five to eight, and so on, rather than two to two, two to four, two to six, etc. **Scale** is a term that also refers to size relationships; similar sizes are in scale with each other, widely disparate sizes are not and are visually jarring.

Balance

A design is balanced when an equal amount of interest is maintained in either direction from the natural center of interest. There are two kinds of balance: formal and informal. Formal balance is achieved when two halves of a design are exactly the same. If two halves are visually balanced but are not identical, it is called informal or asymmetrical balance. This is accomplished by shifting the center of interest with **emphasis.** Emphasis attracts the eye to one feature or area and subordinates the others.

Your Fashion Analysis

On the previous pages we have discussed the basics of artistic theory. As you know, these elements take a very active part in the overall visual impact of clothing. As important as it is to relate the various parts or areas of your garment to one another, several other elements need to be considered in order to establish a total, "put together" look.

Of course, the most important thing is to relate everything to you. Don't forget that you have proportions of your own as well. Thus, a garment that is beautifully balanced and proportioned on the hanger may not be so on you. The next step is to learn how to use art principles in relation to the individual needs of your figure.

Height

To help you learn more about your figure, we, as a pattern company, have done extensive surveys of the possible figure variations that may occur. The results of these studies indicate that **height** is the single most important factor when trying to camouflage a figure problem or trying to emphasize a particularly positive feature.

Automatically, three basic height divisions come to mind: short, average, and tall. But we believe there are really only two true groupings—**Short** and **Tall**. Even though a woman's height in inches (centimeters) may seem to make her average, this designation is misleading. Actually, average is a statistic, not necessarily the ideal. Due to their bone structure, build, and individual features, most women appear to be either short or tall. Described on the following pages are the important principles that the short woman, 5'4" (1.63 M) and under, and the tall woman, 5'7" (1.70 M) and over, should follow when selecting garments. If you fall somewhere in between, study yourself to determine the category into which your bone structure places you and the impression of height you wish to convey—delightfully small or gracefully tall. You will find that once you have established yourself as either one or the other you will have a fresh approach toward the clothes that are right for you.

Short

Don't consider being short a figure problem. Your attitude toward yourself is crucial; you must consider your height an advantage and boldly proceed with that very important outlook. Of course, there are some practical tips to follow before you can fool the observer into thinking that you are actually more petite or slimmer or perhaps taller than you really are. Above all, dress to your own scale. At this point, if you have not done so already, read Proportion and Balance, on page 16, as small women should be particularly concerned with these principles. For example, a short woman, especially if she is not model-slim, will do well to avoid very large prints; they will be greatly out of scale with her build and the size of her garment, making her seem even shorter and wider.

You should concentrate on an uncluttered appearance with everything in proportion to your height. Begin by avoiding the unnecessary bulk of billowing skirts or very heavy fabrics. Short, fitted jackets, gently flared silhouettes, and delicate detailing are your best choices. The scale of accessories should be appropriate as well. They can help pull an outfit together into a neat, fashionable picture or completely destroy all your devoted efforts. Don't let yourself look overwhelmed by massive jewelry or overpowered by a tremendous handbag.

Line, in both fabric and garment design, will be one of your most valuable tools. If you want to add inches (centimeters) to your height, no matter what your weight, depend upon the illusions vertical lines will provide. One-piece dresses with shoulder-to-hemline seaming will give the strongest, most immediate impression of height. Lengthening details such as long sleeves, V-necklines, pleats, or raised or lowered waistlines will all tend to heighten your appearance. Stay away from anything that may cut your figure by interrupting the up and down movement of the eye, such as wide belts, tight waists, very short skirts, or repeated horizontal construction.

Should you not be as slim as you would like, a little extra thought is required. On the whole, vertical lines are perfect slenderizers, but the appropriate ones for you should be chosen with discretion. Avoid gathers or pleats unless they are stitched down to the hip. Wear simple lines. Use a single vertical line or the repeated vertical seaming of a princess silhouette to whittle away the inches (centimeters) while adding to your height.

Color should be a very influential factor when dressing. In general, one-color outfits or monochromatic costumes will contribute to elongating your appearance. Color-coordinated accessories, such as belts or shoes, can be most helpful to your illusion. Warm colors and bright colors will tend to increase your stature visibly. Subtle colors may seem to diminish your size, but be sure they do so in a beguiling feminine fashion rather than making you blend unnoticed into the background.

If you are slim, your color range is almost unlimited, although you will find that solid colors, neat textures, and small prints are best for your body build. The same is true for the slightly heavy woman, but the use of vivid colors or shiny fabrics should be restricted to well-placed splashes for accent.

Tall

If you are tall, you have an immediate fashion edge. You are the fortunate woman who can carry the exotic prints or dramatic designs that can only be draped over a taller frame. Even though you have this head start, you must be as concerned with proportion and balance as short women. You will need to make an effort to wear clothes that are right for your size. Very tiny prints on a tall, large woman will emphasize the contrast between their delicacy and the size of the woman wearing them. You should take advantage of your size; select colorful prints, nubby fabrics, and bold stripes. Balance your height with horizontal divisions to present an impression of equality to the observer's eye. Wide belts, medium--long jackets, and crosswise stripes will contribute toward your goal of optical equilibrium.

Accessories should also warrant your concern when trying to maintain proper proportion and balance. Work with your height and lean toward large jewelry and handbags, and do indulge in some of the more daring fashion accents.

Line, in both garment and fabric design, should be consistently utilized to your advantage. Should you have a full figure, lean toward easy fitting, unfussy silhouettes, and curved or diagonal vertical lines. Gently lowered necklines with ties or collars will emphasize a pretty face while balancing a heavier figure. Orderly prints will be better looking than splashy plaids or repeated horizontal stripes. If you are extremely tall and you wish to appear shorter, cut your height dramatically with wide colorful cummerbunds, crosswise yokes, and other horizontal construction lines. Of course, if you are tall and willowy, the world of fashion is open to you. Try using frills to fill out your curves or be dramatic with yards (meters) of drapey, clinging fabric in unusual patterns. Appreciate your capacity to follow the whims of fashion or to branch out on your own.

Color can also be cleverly used to your advantage. Remember that cool colors as well as the duller hues make the figure appear smaller. Make your color selections according to your weight and width. As always, to appear more slender, wear medium to dark color values in your solids and soft shades for prints, plaids, and textures. To add bulk and roundness to the slim figure, select bright colors with shiny or chunky textures. Contrasting separates are always recommended for the tall woman. They will cut your height no matter what your girth and successfully balance your appearance. The degree of contrast and the division of the areas will influence the final effect. A note of caution before you get carried away with your use of color: make a conscientious effort to keep your total silhouette in mind and avoid a busy look.

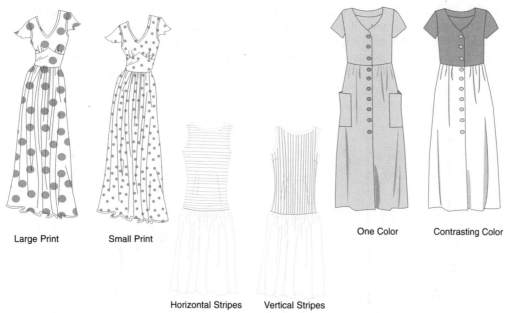

Large Print　　　Small Print

Horizontal Stripes　　Vertical Stripes

One Color　　Contrasting Color

Figure

In addition to the basic concepts related to height, your individual physical characteristics also deserve special consideration. Bosom size, width of hips, length of waist, posture and weight—all are prime problems for many women, and the solution is closely related to height.

Your adult height and bone structure are relatively constant, but your weight and shape may shift, depending on your age, diet, body chemistry . . . and your undergarments. Before beginning to sew, you might consider changing two important things that may cause fitting problems. If you are ten or twenty pounds overweight, it is probably within your control to do something about it. Even a loss of five pounds would help to reduce your bulk and eliminate potential fitting problems. If your posture is not good, you can try to improve it with the proper exercising. Most well-dressed women "walk tall." Being aware that you can stand straighter and taller anytime you wish is good medicine. A small weight loss and any improvement in your posture might lead to a noticeable change in the way you look even before you start to sew. Let's take the time now to see how your posture "stands up" to scrutiny.

Posture

Good posture is natural in that it is comfortable and healthful for the body. The rigid or extremely erect figure produces tension and strain, especially in the knees and back muscles. It shortens the distance from back of neck to shoulder blades, and lengthens the distance from base of neck to apex of bust thereby causing fitting problems. The opposite of this rigid posture is the slump, which is all too familiar. Slumping with the chin thrust forward, the chest sunken, and the stomach protruding will produce rounded shoulders, fatigue, and backache. Dowager's hump, sway back, and protruding abdomen are fitting problems which may evolve from slumping.

Naturally, you are wondering how your posture compares to the illustration of good posture. To test this, stand with your back against a wall and your weight resting on your feet. If posture is correct, your head, shoulder blades, and buttocks should touch the wall; you should barely be able to insert your hand between the wall and the small of the back. If only your shoulders touch the wall, your posture is too erect. If only your shoulder blades touch, you are round-shouldered. A woman with large buttocks might appear to have bad posture when in fact she does not; her derrière touches the wall sooner than her shoulders and shoulder blades. For reasons like this, use judgment with this guide.

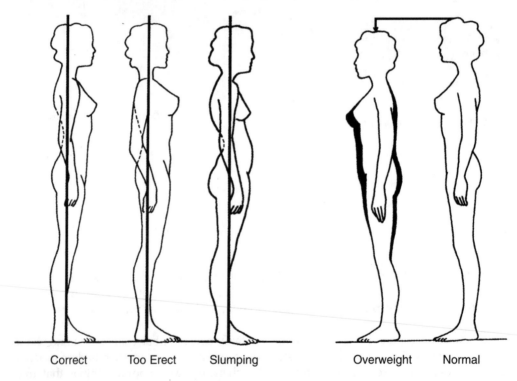

| Correct | Too Erect | Slumping | Overweight | Normal |

The pull of gravity causes additional posture and health problems to the woman who is overweight. Being overweight causes redistribution of the weight so that it does not fall in a plumb line over the knee cap and the arch of the foot. This can cause foot problems as well as backache. Excess weight also strains the muscles so that they cannot hold the chest, stomach, and buttocks in their proper positions; these areas then sag. The strain on the entire frame can cause a reduction in height, since the excess weight is pulling down and straining the muscles which are unable to hold the body erect against the pull of gravity. This downward pull on the body reduces height and inevitably leads to slumping. The compact figure without excess weight can maintain the muscular tension necessary to hold the organs and their surrounding flesh in place without strain, and can thus stand at full height comfortably. The overweight woman must work harder to stand up straight and often succeeds less because of her bulk. Undergarments will help support her weight, but will not eliminate the problem.

Do not be disheartened if the preceding test pointed out the fact that you have bad posture, for it can be corrected and improved by the following exercises. Walking is excellent for improving posture. Get into the habit of walking instead of hopping into the car or onto a bus for those fifteen-minute trips! When sitting and doing hand work, sit as tall as possible with your feet flat on the floor and your weight evenly distributed. Do not twist or wrap your leg around the chair leg. Because your lower back should be supported by the chair, a chair with a hard back is best. When at the sewing machine, lean forward from the hip. Good posture at the machine increases efficiency by giving you more visibility and more leverage for manual dexterity, and reduces strain on neck and shoulders. Get up and stretch now and then to ease strain and fatigue. When standing and fitting at your dress form, stretch your body upward against the pull of gravity.

But do not get carried away! Trying to do posture exercises at the sewing machine or when you are fitting may make you unable to concentrate on the job at hand. In the long run, thinking posture is almost certain to improve posture to some extent.

What if, after all your efforts to lose a few pounds, to pull in that stomach, and tuck in that derriere, nothing happens, and you are still facing that sagging you in the fitting mirror? Since it is easier to fit a figure that you like, rather than one that you dislike, try this last resort to eliminate that sagginess. Those wonderful people who invented undergarments must have known that the spirit may be willing, but the flesh is certainly weak. Purchase well-fitted undergarments for a controlled or more youthful figure. You are not the first to do so and will not be the last!

Undergarments

The flora and fauna of the undergarment world are so abundant that one would be hard put to keep track of all the newest ones. In the age of the no-bra bra and the ungirdled girth, there are still dozens of bra styles, endless girdle variations, and all-in-one foundation garments. With all these to evaluate, how can you decide which undergarments are meant for you? The decision is directly related to the function and fit of the undergarments with your figure and the clothes you'll be wearing.

A **youthful, firm** figure needs only a soft bra and panties of nylon or tricot. For a figure that **needs a little support** due to sagging busts or abdomen, or hip or thigh bulge, choose a bra to fit and support the breasts, and a girdle to firm up the problem area. If a panty girdle is preferred, make sure the crotch and buttocks shaping will be comfortable and not flatten the derriere, especially in pants. A **mature, heavier** figure looks best in an all-in-one foundation which eliminates midriff bulge.

To choose the correct bra size, measure snugly around the rib cage just under the bust, and add 5" (12.5 cm) to that measurement; for figures measuring more than 38" (96.5 cm), add 3" (7.5 cm). For cup size, measure above the breasts, then subtract that figure from the bra size. If the difference is 1" (25 mm) or less, wear an A-cup; 1¼ " to 2" (3.2 cm to 5 cm), B; 2¼" to 3" (5.7 cm to 7.5 cm), C; 3¼" to 4" (8.2 cm to 10 cm), D. If your rib cage is disproportionately smaller than your bust development, there will be variations from the above formula when measuring cup size. Complete instructions for taking your body measurements are on pages 74-75, but be aware that determining your bra size is different from measuring your bust.

Do not select undergarments when you are in a hurry or when you intend to lose a few pounds. Do not be satisfied until you have arrived at your most comfortable and sleek look, even though it may take endless trying on and patience.

When you have chosen undergarments which will minimize your figure flaws, make sure they do not create other problems for you when fitting—excessively tight bras or girdles cause rolls of fat to ripple unbecomingly above or below them. Two bras may seem alike to you but they may not be: one may have a soft, smooth apex, while the other may have more lift and a pronounced shape. During every fitting, **you must wear the same undergarments** that will be worn with the completed garment to avoid repeated changes in the placement of bust darts, over-the-bust seaming, waistline seams or darts, and darts at hip.

A Personal Interpretation

Frequently, the tides of fashion change so rapidly that it is difficult to discover the styles that are right for your figure. To tell you what is best for your body build, Vogue Patterns has prepared a visual dictionary illustrating the fundamental components that comprise most garment designs, accompanied by valuable information to help you determine your body shape. This information is designed to help you select the most flattering styles for your particular figure.

Read through all of the variations before deciding which shape your figure falls into and then select the appropriate patterns from the catalog that appeal to you. Choosing the correct pattern style is as important as choosing the correct size. Learn what styles are most appropriate for your body shape to avoid unnecessary mistakes or time-consuming alterations. How many times have you selected a style because it was a current trend only to discover that style was just not right for your body shape? By knowing your body shape you can proceed with confidence knowing your pattern adjustments will be minimal and your finished garment will flatter your figure.

The Vocabulary of Fashion

This list of fashion terminology was collected to give you a firm grasp of the language used by designers and fashionable women everywhere. It includes terms commonly used to describe the silhouettes, styles, and details of clothing design as well as fabric qualities, notions, and construction procedures. We have also included French terms that have become part of our fashion vocabulary. A knowledgeable and conversational use of the words listed here will certainly increase your fashion confidence.

a

A-line Dress or skirt resembling shape of an A.

accessories Articles of apparel that complete a costume, e.g., shoes, jewelry, etc.

allonger (a-lohn-zhay) Fr. To lengthen, to give clothing a longer appearance.

amincir (a-men-seer) Fr. To make thin; to give a slender look.

appliqué (a-plee-kay) Fr. Motif applied to cloth or garment.

ascot Broad neckscarf; tied so that one end falls over the other.

asymmetrical One-sided, not geometrically balanced.

atelier (a-te-lyay) Fr. Dressmaking establishment; work room or studio.

au courant (oh-koo-rahn) Fr. Up to the moment; to know all about it.

avant-garde (a-vahn-gard) Fr. Ahead of fashion or trend.

b

backing Fabric joined to wrong side of garment or garment area, typically for reinforcement or opacity.

balmacaan Loose overcoat.

band Strip used to hold, ornament, or complete any part of garment or accessory.

bateau Neckline following curve of collar bone.

bell sleeve Full sleeve, flaring at lower edge like a bell.

bias Diagonal direction of fabric. True bias is at a 45° angle to grainlines.

binding Strip encasing edges as finish or trim.

bishop sleeve Sleeve that is full in the lower part, either loose or held by band at wrist.

blind hem Hem sewn invisibly with hand stitches.

blouson Bloused effect of fullness gathered in at and falling over a seam, typically bodice over skirt.

bodice Portion of garment above the waist.

bodkin Sharp, slender tool used to pull fabrics through narrow enclosed space, such as casing.

bolero Short jacket that ends above waist; Spanish origin.

bolt Unit in which fabric is packaged and sold by manufacturer. Usually contains 12-20 yards.

boning Flexible strips used to stiffen seams or edges.

border Strip of self-fabric or commercial trimming used to finish edge.

boutique A small retail store in which accessories and miscellaneous fashion items are sold. Often part of a couture house.

c

caftan Long, coat-like garment fastened with long sash, having extra long sleeves.

camisole Short, sleeveless underbodice; often joined to skirt and worn under jacket. Also, lingerie-like outer garment worn as a blouse.

cap sleeve Short sleeve just covering the shoulder and not continued under the arm.

cape Sleeveless outer garment hanging loosely from shoulders, covering back and arms.

cardigan Close fitting collarless jacket, sweater, or bodice with center front closing.

cartridge pleat Rounded pleat that extends out rather than lying flat.

chemise Dress or undergarment styled like a loose slip or long undershirt.

Pointed Flat — Peter Pan — Puritan — Jabot — Tie — Mandarin — Ruff — Tuxedo — Funnel — Turtleneck — Wing — Sailor — Chelsea — Convertible — Shawl — Notched — Shirt

chesterfield Plain coat usually having velvet notched collar.

chevron V-shaped stripes.

chez (shay) Fr. At home, shop of; as chez Dior, Lanvin, etc.

chic (sheek) Fr. Originality and style in dress.

clip Cut in fabric to allow ease on curves or corners.

closure That which opens or closes a garment (buttons, etc.), or area on which they are placed.

coatdress Dress with coat-like lines and front closing.

collection All apparel exhibited at fashion showing. Spring and fall are the two major periods each year when collections are shown to trade and clientèle (customers).

colorfast Refers to fabric that will not fade or run during cleaning or laundering.

contrasting Opposing; showing off differences of color, fabric, shading, etc.

convertible Notched collar that can be worn either buttoned at neck or open with lapels.

couture (koo-tur) Fr. Sewing or needle work. Product of a seamstress; seam.

couturier (koo-too-ryay) m. or couturière (koo-too-ryare) f. Fr. Dressmaker; designer; head of a dressmaking house.

cowl Soft drape of fabric at neckline.

cravat Necktie folded or tied at front with ends tucked inside garment.

crew Round neckline that hugs the throat.

culotte Trouser-like garment with flaring leg portions to simulate a skirt.

cummerbund Wide sash worn around the waist.

cut-in-one Two or more sections cut in one piece, such as sleeve and bodice.

d

décolleté (day-kawl-eh-tay) Fr. Cut low at neckline, exposing neck and back or cleavage of bosom as in formal evening dress.

démodé (day-maw-day) Fr. Old-fashioned, out-of-style, unfashionable.

dernier cri (dern-yay-kree) Fr. The latest fashion; the last word.

dickey Detachable shirt front.

dirndl Garment with full gathered skirt.

dolman Sleeve set into a deep armhole so as to resemble a kimono sleeve.

double-breasted Front closing

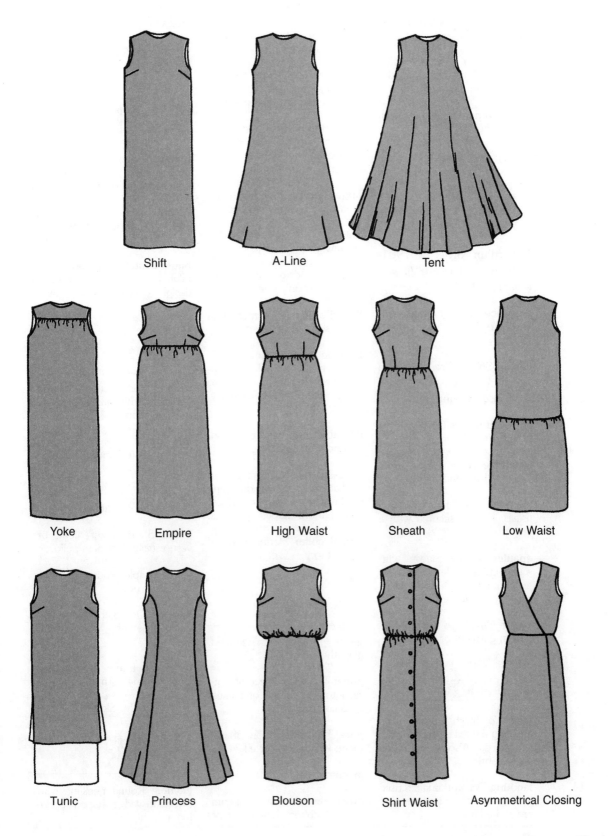

Shift   A-Line   Tent

Yoke   Empire   High Waist   Sheath   Low Waist

Tunic   Princess   Blouson   Shirt Waist   Asymmetrical Closing

that overlaps enough to allow two rows of buttons.

dressmaking Art of sewing dresses, skirts, etc., distinguished from tailoring.

drum lining Lining not sewn into garment seams.

e

edgestitch Topstitching placed very close to finished edge.

Edwardian Style of 1901-1910 when Edward VII was king of England.

elegance (ay-lay-gahns) Fr. Quality of being elegant; tasteful luxury.

empire Style of French empire period; high waistline, décolleté, loose, straight skirt.

enclosed seams Concealed by two garment layers.

ensemble The entire costume. Usually, dress and coat.

epaulet Shoulder trimming usually a band secured with a button.

epaulet sleeve Sleeve with square-cut shoulder section extending into neck in form of yoke. Strap sleeve.

eyelet Small, round finished hole in garment or fabric.

f

face To finish an edge by applying a fitted piece of fabric, binding, etc. Also, the right side of the fabric.

fagoting Decorative stitch used to join two fabric sections that are spread apart.

fancy work Hand embroidery and needlework.

favoring Rolling one garment section slightly over another at the edge to conceal the seam.

feathering Removing stains by rubbing lightly in a circular motion from the outside edge of the stain to its center.

finger press Pressing small area by creasing with fingers.

finish Any means of completing raw garment edge.

flap Shaped garment piece attached by only one edge.

flare Portion of garment that spreads out or widens.

fleur de lis (fler-de-lee) Fr. Lily flower; heraldic emblem of former French royalty. Used as design in fabric, embroidery, jewelry, etc.

fly Fabric used as lap to conceal opening in garment.

full-fashioned Garments knitted flat and shaped by dropping stitches, in contrast to circular knits that are shaped by seams.

funnel collar Flaring outward at the top.

g

garni (gar-nee) Fr. Trimmed, garnished.

godet Triangular piece of cloth set into a garment for fullness or decoration.

gore Tapered section of garment; wider at lower edge.

grommet Large metal eyelet.

grosgrain Fabric or, most commonly, ribbon having heavy crosswise ribs.

gusset Fabric piece inserted at underarm to give ease in sleeve area.

h

halter Neckline having band around neck, attached to front of a backless bodice.

harem pants Garment with legs softly draped and gathered to narrow lining or ankle band.

haute couture (oht-koo-tur) Fr. High fashion, creative fashion design. Couturier houses as a group.

i, j

inset Fabric section or trim inserted within garment for fit or decoration.

interlining Layer of fabric between lining and underlining for warmth.

jabot Ruffle worn down front of bodice and fastened at neck.

jerkin Short jacket, coat, or vest; usually sleeveless pullover.

jewel Simple, round neckline at base of neck.

jumper One-piece sleeveless garment with loosely cut bodice.

jumpsuit Pants and bodice joined in one garment.

jupe (zhup) Fr. Skirt.

k

keyhole Round neckline with inverted wedge-shaped opening at front.

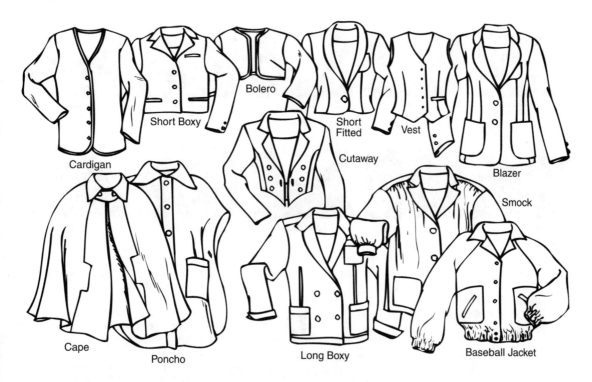

Cardigan
Short Boxy
Bolero
Short Fitted
Cutaway
Vest
Blazer
Smock
Cape
Poncho
Long Boxy
Baseball Jacket

kick pleat Pleat used for ease in a narrow skirt; may be a knife, inverted, or box pleat.

kilt Pleated, plaid skirt with un-pleated panel in front.

kimono Loose, wide-sleeved robe, fastened at waist with obi; also used to describe style of sleeve cut in one piece with the bodice.

l

lantern sleeve Bell sleeve with wrist section joining at bottom, creating a shape resembling a lantern.

lap Any edge that extends over another edge, as on a placket.

lapels Part of garment that turns back, especially front part of garment that folds back to form continuation of collar.

layout Cutting chart on instruction sheet showing placement of pattern pieces.

line Style, outline, or effect given by the cut and construction of the garment.

lingerie Women's lightweight underclothing.

longuette Style derived from below-knee hem lengths.

m

macramé Bulky, knotted lace woven in geometrical patterns.

maillot (my-yo) Fr. One piece, tight-fitting bathing suit.

maison de couture (me-zohnde-koo-tur) Fr. Dressmaking establishment.

mandarin Small standing collar that hugs neck.

mannequin (man-eh-kin) Fr. Dressmaker form, dummy. Person wearing new clothes to present at fashion show or collection.

marking Transfer of construction symbols from paper pattern to fabric.

martingale A half-belt or strap, generally placed on the back of a garment.

matelasser (ma-tla-say) Fr. To pad or cushion.

middy Slip-on blouse with typical sailor collar.

mini Hem length falling at midthigh.

miter Diagonal seaming at a corner.

mode (mawd) Fr. Fashion, manner, vogue.

motif Unit of design; used as decoration or pattern.

Jewel   Scoop   U-Neck   V-Neck   Square

Bateau   Cowl   Sweetheart   Keyhole   Halter

mounting Term sometimes used for underlining. Two layers of fabric are basted together and sewn as one.

n

nap Soft surface with fibers that lie smoothly in one direction.

negligée Decorative dressing gown, worn indoors by women.

notch v, Cutting wedges from seam allowances. n, Pattern symbol transferred to fabrics to indicate matching points.

notions Items other than fabric or pattern required to complete garment.

o

obi Broad Japanese sash.

opening Synonymous with closure; also, fashion showing of apparel for season.

overblouse Blouse not tucked in at waistline.

overskirt Decorative skirt worn over another garment.

p

pantsuit Women's suit consisting of jacket with pants instead of skirt.

passementerie (pahs-mahn-tree) Fr. Trimming, particularly heavy embroideries or edgings.

peasant sleeve Full sleeve set into dropped shoulder and usually gathered into wristband.

peignoir (pain-nwahr) Fr. Originally, a robe of terrycloth worn instead of a towel; now, a robe that matches a nightgown.

pelt Skin of animal with fur intact.

peplum Small flounce or extension of garment around hips, usually from bodice.

peter pan Flat shaped collar, with round corners.

piece Specified length of goods as rolled from loom.

piece goods Fabric sold in pieces of fixed length or by the yard.

pin basting Pinning seams before stitching.

pinafore Sleeveless apron-like fashion worn over a dress or other garment.

pinking Cutting raw edge with pinking or scalloping shears to retard raveling.

pivot Stitching around corner by leaving needle in fabric, raising presser foot, and turning fabric in new direction.

placket Hidden garment opening fastened with zipper, snaps, buttons, or hooks and eyes.

plunge Neckline cut so low as to reveal curve of breasts.

prefold Folding and pressing garment section or binding before applying to garment.

preshape Shaping fabric into curves like those of area to which it will be applied; done with steam before stitching to garment.

preshrink Contracting fabric before construction.

prêt à porter (pret-ah-portay) Fr. Ready to wear; more current than "confection."

princess line Garment fitted with seams instead of darts.

purl Stitch made by bringing needle out across thread so as to hold it; also looped edge of embroidery, lace.

r

raw edge Unfinished edge of fabric.

remnant Unsold end of piece goods, leftover piece of cloth.

répertoire (rep-e-twar) Fr. Collection of works by a designer.

right side Finished side of fabric, outside of garment.

rip Removing stitches improperly placed; also, tearing fabric along straight grain.

roll Desired curve and fold (commonly on a collar); shaping established by pressing, pad stitching, etc.

s

sash Ornamental band or scarf worn around the body.

scalloped Cut into semicircles at edge or border.

scoop Deep neckline cut to shape of U.

seam allowance The width of fabric beyond seamline, not including garment area.

seam binding Ribbon-like tape used to finish edges.

secure Fasten permanently by means of knot, backstitching, etc.

self Of same material as rest of garment.

selvage Lengthwise finished edges on all woven fabrics. ·

semi-fitted Fitted to conform partly, but not too closely, to shape of figure.

shank Link between button and fabric to allow for thickness of overlapping fabric.

shawl Triangular piece of fabric worn around shoulders.

sheath Close-fitting dress with straight skirt.

sheer Transparent fabric; comes in varying weights. shift Loose-fitting dress.

shirtwaist Dress with bodice details similar to shirt.

shrinking Contracting fabric with steam or water to eliminate excess in specific area.

silhouette Outline or contour of figure or garment.

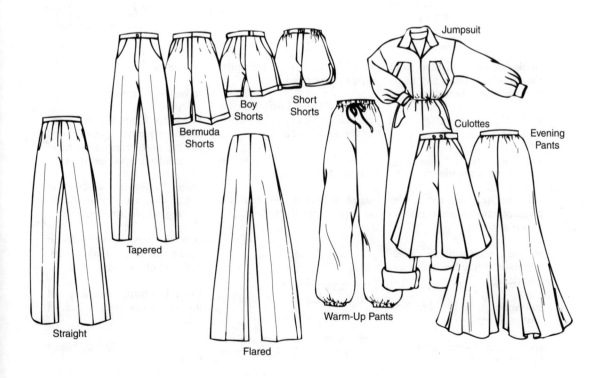

Straight

Tapered

Bermuda Shorts

Boy Shorts

Short Shorts

Flared

Warm-Up Pants

Jumpsuit

Culottes

Evening Pants

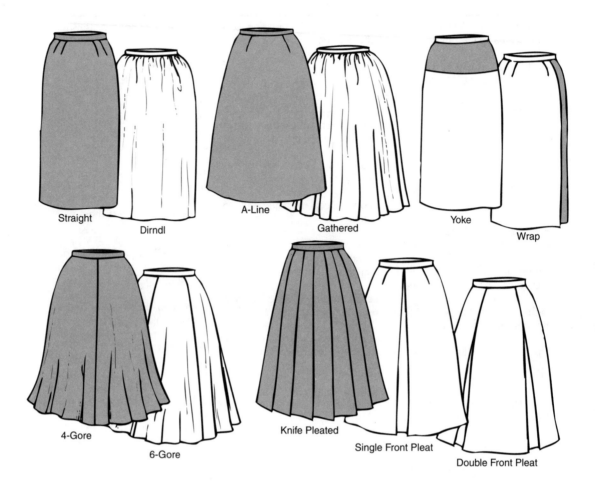

Straight

Dirndl

A-Line

Gathered

Yoke

Wrap

4-Gore

6-Gore

Knife Pleated

Single Front Pleat

Double Front Pleat

single-breasted Center front closing with enough flap to allow one row of buttons.

slash Cut taken in fabric to facilitate construction.

slit Long, narrow opening; also, to cut lengthwise.

soft suit Dressy suit with a minimum of inner construction also dressmaker suit.

soigné (swa-nyay) Fr. Well-groomed, highly finished, carefully done.

soutache (soo-tash) Fr. Narrow braid trim.

sportswear Garments meant for informal or casual wear.

stay Means of maintaining shape of garment area.

stiletto Pointed instrument for punching holes in fabric; smaller version called awl.

stole Long scarf wrapped around shoulders.

surplice Bodice with one side wrapping over the other side.

tab Small flap or loop attached at one end.

tack Joining two garment layers with small, loose hand stitches or thread loop.

taille (tie-y) Fr. Size, waist.

tailoring Construction technique requiring special hand sewing and pressing to mold fabric into finished garment.

taper Cutting or stitching at slight diagonal, generally to make gradually smaller.

tension Amount of pull on thread or fabric during construction of garment.

thread count Number of threads in one square inch of fabric.

tissu (tee-su) Fr. Textile, fabric; texture.

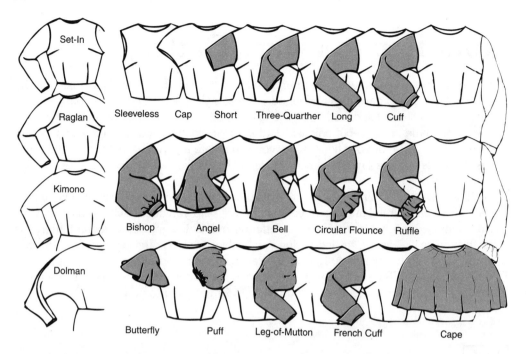

Set-In

Raglan

Kimono

Dolman

Sleeveless Cap Short Three-Quarther Long Cuff

Bishop Angel Bell Circular Flounce Ruffle

Butterfly Puff Leg-of-Mutton French Cuff Cape

toile (twahl) Fr. Linen or cotton cloth. Also muslin copy of a design, purchased by firms to copy original. Sometimes made by dressmakers to show customers garments that they are prepared to copy.

topstitching Machine stitching parallel to seam or edge, done from right side of garment.

train Extended part of garment, usually wedding dress which trails at back.

transfer pattern Commercial pattern having design stamped on paper, usually transferred to fabric by iron.

trim To cut away excess fabric.

trimming Feature added to garment for ornamentation.

tunic Long top, worn over another garment.

turnover A garment section, usually collar or cuff, which folds back upon itself.

turtleneck High turnover collar that hugs throat.

twill tape Firmly woven tape.

u

underlining Fabric joined in garment seams to give inner shape or support.

v

V-neck Neckline shaped in front like the letter V.

vane Web or flat extended part of a feather.

vendeuse (vahn-doos) Fr. Saleswoman. In Paris dressmaking houses, the saleswoman is an important staff member.

vent Faced or lined slash in garment for ease.

vest Short, close-fitting gar-

ment without sleeves, similar to man's waistcoat.

volant (vaw-lahn) Fr. Flounce.

w

welt Strip of material stitched to seam, border, or edge.

wrap-around Garment or part of a garment wrapped around person, as cape or skirt.

wrong side Side of fabric on inside of garment.

y

yardage block Guide on back of pattern envelope; includes garment description, measurement, yardage, notions, etc.

yoke Fitted portion of garment, usually at shoulders or hips, designed to support rest of garment hanging from it.

Your Key to Figure Flattery

If you are like most sewers, you love to browse through the pattern catalogs looking at the many beautifully styled garments and wonder if that style will look good on you. Chances are your figure will not fall directly into the tall, slender category of most models but may be any other shape or size—but uniquely you! By analyzing your body shape and selecting the right pattern style for your figure type, you can create a garment that is as flattering to you as the styles you see on those lovely models. The challenge is to select a style that will flatter you personally.

The first step in determining the correct style for you is to map your personal body profile. A realistic and careful analysis of your shape will help you decide which category your body falls into. Your goal is to achieve a flattering overall image. Since Vogue Patterns is in the fashion as well as the sewing business, our objective is to offer you insight into what looks are flattering to your body type as well as instructions on fitting. By using the KEY TO FIGURE FLATTERY symbols (shown below) in the pattern catalog, you will save yourself hours of frustration when selecting the style most flattering to you.

The Inverted Triangle
large bust and/or broad shoulders with narrow hips

The Triangle
small bust and/or narrow shoulder with full hips and/or thighs

The Rectangle
balanced on top and bottom, but boxy, with little or no waist definition

The Hourglass
equally balanced on top and bottom, with a trim waist

Your Body Profile

Use this chart to describe your figure accurately. Wearing only your undergarments and a leotard or slip, evaluate yourself from all angles in a full-length mirror. Be realistic in all your assessments and measurements!

1. HEIGHT _____Short _____Average _____Tall
[A female between 5'4" and 5'6" (1.63m and 1.68m) is considered average.]

2. BODY FRAME _____Small-boned _____Medium-boned _____Large-boned
[A wrist measurement of 5 ½" to 6" (14 cm to 15 cm) indicates a medium frame.]

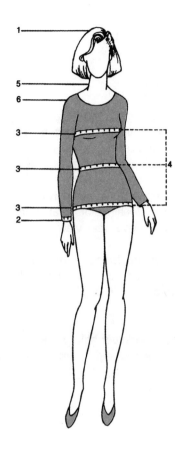

3.WIDTH PROPORTION

[On the ideal figure, the bust and hips measure almost the same and the waist is approximately 10" (25.5 cm) smaller.]

Measurements: _____Bust _____Hips _____Waist

_____Small Bust _____Average Bust _____Large Bust
_____Small Waist _____Average Waist _____Large Waist
_____Small Hips _____Average Hips _____Large Hips
_____Slim Arms _____Average Arms _____Heavy Arms
[The circumference of your arms is a visual judgment. Sometimes, very heavy or very thin upper arms can give the illusion of wide or narrow upper body proportions regardless of bust size.]

4. LENGTH PROPORTIONS

Waist:_____Short _____Average _____Long
[On the ideal figure, the waist falls halfway between the underarm and the hips.]

Arms: _____Short _____Average _____Long
[Your arm length is ideal if your elbow falls at your waistline and your fingertips reach the middle of your thighs.]

5. NECK _____Short _____Average _____Long

6. SHOULDERS _____Narrow _____Average _____Broad _____Sloping
_____Square
[Your neck and shoulder length, width and shape are based on your personal observation and experience.]

Using this new information, determine which of the following four basic body profiles best describes you. A description of each figure type, the triangle, inverted triangle, rectangle, or hourglass, is discussed here. Along with the knowledge you now possess about color, line, balance, and proportion, you can select the styles, which will provide you with the most attractive and flattering appearance.

TRIANGLE: Also known as the pear shape, the characteristics of this, the most common figure type, indicate shoulders narrower than the hips or a small bust with large hips.

DO'S
1. Minimize the hip area
2. Add fullness above the waist, using gathers, yokes, wide collars, or wide necklines
3. Keep sleeve hems simple
4. Use a high-waisted or A-line silhouette—draw the eye away from the hip area

DON'TS

1. Avoid horizontal lines (jacket hems) that fall direcxtly across the hips.
2. Avoid raglan sleeves which accentuate narrow shoulders.
3. Avoid sleeves with ruffles or French cuffs.
4. Avoid in-seam or patch pockets or any seams ending at the hips.

Your height and weight are also important factors when determining a balanced, pleasing appearance. If you are tall with a triangular body shape, you can wear larger, bolder prints, more dramatic styles, and textures on top keeping the bottom in darker hues or small, subtle prints. For the shorter figure, choose dark hues, small prints and smooth textures for your overall look.

The key to working with a triangular figure is to draw the eye up or down away from the widest hip area. Pins or jewelry above the waist, scarves, textured stockings or great shoes will help you achieve this effect. Too short or tight skirts will widen your rear view.

INVERTED TRIANGLE: The opposite of the triangle, this figure type has a large bust or broad shoulders and narrow hips. This body shape may be curvy and voluptuous or very athletic in build.

DO'S

1. Minimize the bust and waist areas.
2. Add pocket details, drop waists, peplums to lower half of body.
3. Emphasize the vertical line on top with v-necks, seams, turtlenecks, and simple jewelry.
4. Gathers and pleats at the hip add fullness.

DON'TS

1. Avoid high waistlines and empire seams.
2. Avoid pockets or ruffles on bodice.
3. Avoid extended or dropped shoulders, leg of mutton sleeves, gathered sleeve caps or wide collars.
4. Avoid large-scale prints or bulky textures on top.

Create vertical lines in the bust and shoulder areas and add horizontal lines to the hips. Darker hues and dull or matte textures are best on top. To appear taller, select one-piece styles or a one-color scheme for a continuous line from top to bottom. Avoid short shirts, Capri pants and narrow silhouettes which make you appear top-heavy.

RECTANGLE: This "boxy" shape measures with little difference between the bust, waist, and hips. The shoulders and hips are balanced but there is no curve to identify the waistline.

DO'S

1. Create a vertical line from top to bottom.
2. Add interest to the top with horizontal gathers, tucks, pleats or yokes.
3. Extended, dropped, tucked or flanged shoulders or dolman or cap sleeves with shoulder pads draw the eye upwards.
4. Dropped waists or skirts with center seams draw the eye away from the waist.

DON'TS
1. Avoid horizontal lines at the waist such as contrasting colored belts, waist-length jackets or prominent seamlines.
2. Avoid fullness that leads directly to the waist.
3. Avoid sleeves that end at the elbow or waist or are blousey.
4. Avoid waist-tied scarves, obis, peplums or fitted waists.

The key to the rectangular shape is to draw the attention away from the waist area or camouflage it. A long line created from a longer jacket and pleated skirt draws the eye down from the top and makes you look taller in the process! If you have a shorter torso, one-piece dresses with a vertical feel will make you appear taller too. Flared skirts, bias cuts and wide gores add more curves to your shape. Matching colored shoes, stockings and skirt also draw the eye away from the waist.

HOURGLASS: This figure type is equally balanced on top and bottom with the waist approximately 10" (25 cm) smaller. As the ideal fashion figure type, the choice of styles is almost unlimited.

DO'S
1. Use vertical lines to elongate your torso.
2. Maintain one focal point highlighting your best feature.
3. Try contrasting colors, bold textures and brighter colors.
4. Show off your narrow waist, if you have one.

DON'TS
1. Avoid large patterns or over-sized styles on a petite frame (under 5'4"/1.63m).
2. Avoid empire styles if you have a large bust.
3. Downplay heavy legs with opaque hosiery and shoes matched to the color of your fashion.
4. Avoid boxy, bulky styles that hide your figure.

With an hourglass figure you can wear almost any style as long as you keep it in proportion with your height and weight. You can experiment with colors, textures, prints, and drapeability. To appear taller, choose matte textures, small prints, monochromatic colors and vertical styling for an unbroken line. The same fabric choices and styles will work if you also want to appear slimmer. Horizontal lines or details, color-blocking or contrasting colored textures or patterns will make you seem shorter.

To show off your waist, select styles with waistline details such as ties, tucks, wide belts, darts, midriff insets or unique closures. Full skirts play up a narrow waist and short skirts highlight great legs!

No matter your body shape, be aware of how fashion influences the fit of your garments. Watch the trends but remember, no matter the style—loose-fitting or a closer more revealing fit—poor-fitted garments accentuate your figure flaws and make you appear unkempt and can even add years to your appearance. With the proper tools, it is now up to you to select the most flattering style and fabric, interpret the information on the pattern envelope and use your technical fitting skills.

The
Wonderful World
of Fabrics

Fabrics are a delight to the senses. The artist in fashion finds the material she uses a thrill and an inspiration, for she is aware that every aspect of a fabric will influence her finished garment, and she knows how to use it with her own personal flair. Her most valuable asset is that elusive sixth sense that can successfully match style line with fabric texture, color, and character to form a harmonious, pleasing, and flattering whole. While this sense is to some extent instinctive, it can benefit by experience and an understanding of the structure and origin of textiles. They are not made by magic, though some of the procedures they undergo may seem mysterious.

Every aspect of a fabric's history influences its character and hand—the things that have most to do with its success or failure as the medium for you sewing endeavors. Fluid, stiff, crisp, rough, soft, thick, or shaggy, it will lend its personality to the design. From fiber to yarn to cloth, from the loom to the finishing mill to the fabric shop, each detail of its past is a fascinating clue to the way it ultimately looks, acts, and feels. But its characteristics are not limited to tactile and visual ones; among the considerations most important in your busy contemporary world are those of care and performance. New developments in fibers and finishes have placed at your disposal fabrics that lighten your laundry chores and keep you looking your most impeccable self. Ask for the information on fiber content and finishing treatments that will help you choose and care for the fabric on which you will spend so much effort and time. Learn to distinguish quality fabric not by prices, but by a thorough understanding of the components that lend durability and the unmistakable touch of luxury. Fiber content, the tightness of the weave, the amount of twist and the structure of an individual yarn, and the performance of finishes and color treatment all have a bearing on its quality. These factors determine the amount of wear a fabric can withstand, how it will drape and fold, and whether it is worthy to serve as your fashion signature.

Fibers

Where does fashion begin? The realization of a concept of silhouette, texture, and color depends on the basic stuff of fabric—the fiber of which it is made. Especially since the advent of synthetic fibers, textile classification has developed into a bewildering maze of technical subtleties and chemical terms. Few consumers will need to be familiar with the quirks of the anhydroglucose molecule, but a basic understanding of the general fiber categories is an invaluable aid in the practical business of buying and caring for fabrics. Although its properties may be altered by yarn and fabric structure and by finishing treatments, ultimately a fabric's origin and chemistry are its soul. The primary distinction in fiber types is a very simple one—a fiber is either natural or man-made.

Wool

Silk

Cotton

Flax

Natural Fibers

Fibers exist in nature in many guises. Animal, vegetable, and mineral substances all provide the raw material for cloth. The wool of the sheep, the hair and fur of other creatures, and the fine filament from which the silk worm spins his cocoon are animal fibers composed of protein. Dozens of plants produce usable fiber in cellulose form. For example, linen is made from the fibrous stalk of the flax plants. The familiar cotton fiber grows as a puff protecting the seeds of the cotton plant, and grasses and leaves provide many other textile fibers. Minerals yield asbestos, which occurs naturally in fiber form and is used for fireproof fabrics, and metals that can be pounded into foils and cut into strips for luxury fabrics.

The unmistakable characteristics of the natural fibers are born in their structure. The familiar warmth of wool, the downy softness of cotton, the rich, dry texture of silk, and the crisp sheen of linen originate in the plant or animal that made them, and from the fact that natural things can never be quite uniform. The irregularities in their formation give them their distinction and explain many of their peculiar properties, such as the ability of wool to lock into felted constructions, the generally high absorbency of natural fibers, and the wide variation in quality among fibers of the same type.

WOOL is among nature's masterpieces. The fuzzy coat of the sheep possesses several remarkable and unique properties that make it especially adaptable to textile use. The wool fiber, which varies in length from 1½" to 15" (3.8 cm to 38 cm), has a natural crimp that facilitates the spinning of yarns and increases elasticity. The fiber itself is covered with minute scale. When wool is subjected to heat and pressure, these scales interlock, holding the fibers together and creating wool's unique felting capacity. The protein molecule of which wool is composed is spiral, or spring-shaped, contributing great resiliency, "loft," and shape-keeping ability. The fabric is highly absorbent and consequently very receptive to dyes but, in contrast, the surface tends to shed water. The hair and fur of other animals contribute fibers that are also classed as wool, and possess these properties in varying degrees.

SILK has a romantic history shrouded in regal legend, and the silk worm's life cycle is itself an exciting drama. A moth lays eggs which, after an incubation period, hatch into tiny, hungry silk worms. In about a month, each worm eats thousands of times its weight in mulberry leaves, growing rapidly and shedding its skin several times. Then it spins its cocoon. If allowed to continue the cycle, the worm transforms itself into a moth, which emerges from the cocoon to mate and lay more eggs. If the cocoon is to be used for silk, however, the worm is baked and dried in its blanket, and the fine protein fiber is unreeled in a continuous filament, which may be from 1500 to 4000 feet (450 m to 1200 m) long. A stiff natural gum called sericin is boiled away, and silk filaments are combined to form very fine threads. Silk is extremely strong, absorbent, warm, resilient, and highly elastic.

COTTON is a vastly popular, versatile, and relatively inexpensive fiber that produces durable, comfortable fabrics. Magnified cotton has a ribbon-like appearance and is of fairly uniform thickness. The many types of cotton fibers range in length from ½" to 2½" (13 mm to 6.5 cm). It is naturally soft and easily spun into a variety of textures. The cellulose of which cotton is composed is an inert substance, and as a result untreated cotton may have little resiliency and wrinkle easily. However, its normally high strength increases when wet, making it exceptionally easy to launder, and its natural absorbency makes it receptive to a variety of treatments, such as mercerization, color application, and wrinkle-resistant and easy-care finishes, which add to its desirability.

FLAX is the plant from whose stems linen is made. By a process developed at the dawn of civilization, the outer woody portion of the stalk is rotted away, leaving long, soft, strong fibers composed of cellulose. The magnified fiber has a jointed structure similar to that of bamboo, and the thickness may vary widely. Length ranges from 5" to 20" (12.5 cm to 51 cm). Because of their similar composition, linen resembles cotton in many ways, including its ability to withstand high temperatures and its easy launderability and low resistance to wrinkling. In addition, it is extremely durable and, if stored properly, will withstand years of use. However, the flax fiber tends to be stiffer than cotton, and linen fabrics are subject to abrasion and wear along edges and creases.

Man-made Fibers

For thousands of years, natural fibers were the only materials available for the creation of fabric. Then, in the middle of the nineteenth century, scientists began to experiment with the production of "artificial silk" from regenerated cellulose. The resulting fiber, rayon, heralded a new era for the textile industry. Rapid developments have greatly increased the number and refined the properties of man-made fibers, which have become indispensable in the contemporary world.

Each type of man-made fiber has a generic name, such as nylon or polyester. In turn, fiber producers have trademarks or brand names for the various fibers they manufacture. Often a fiber producer has several trademarks for one fiber, indicating one or more variations in its manufacture.

The chemical complexities of man-made fibers are endless, but one of the distinctions among them is the fact that some fibers are derived from *natural* materials such as cellulose or protein, while others are completely *synthesized* or developed from basic chemical sources. In either case, the production involves similar steps. A chemical solution is formed that contains the basic components of the fiber. The solution is forced through the tiny holes of a *spinneret* into a chemical-coagulating bath or air chamber that hardens the substance into filament form. A continuous "rope" of unlimited length is produced, and goes on to be textured and processed. The same solution can produce filaments with varying properties, depending on the size and shape of the holes in the spinneret and the nature of the hardening procedure.

Great advances have been made in the development of man-made fibers since their inception. Today, man-made fibers can be engineered specifically to impart the performance feature required by the end use of the fabric.

Yarns

Yarn is the medium of fabric construction. However the fabric is formed, its character is determined to a great degree by the type of yarn from which it is made.

Before they are formed into yarn, fibers are referred to as either staple or filament. Silk and all the man-made fibers originally exist as long continuous strands, or **filaments,** which simply require a small amount of twist to form yarn. All the natural fibers except silk occur in short lengths, or **staple** form; man-made fibers may also be cut into short staple lengths to imitate them. These require more complex yarn-making techniques. A mat of random fibers is first sorted, cleaned, and blended into a uniform mixture and then subjected to several procedures that align the fibers and impart twist. Carding produces a loose strand of more or less parallel fibers about an inch (25 mm) in diameter. Further **combing** eliminates shorter fibers and produces a strand of higher quality. (**Woolen** and **worsted** yarns are, respectively, the wool counterparts of carded and combed, yarns in other fibers.) The strand is then further stretched, twisted, and finally spun.

Yarn as it comes from the original spinning frame is called a **single.** Twisting several singles together produces a **ply yarn** and improves uniformity and strength. The character of a yarn is also influenced by the degree of twist. Low-twist yarns, soft and relatively weak, are used for napped fabrics. Higher twist increases strength and crispness. Very high twist is used for crepe effects, as the tension causes puckering.

COMPLEX OR NOVELTY YARNS include several types, most of which are produced primarily for appearance value since they are seldom strong. They may be single or ply, and often contain components of several colors or fiber types for visual variations. Novelty single yarns, called **slub** yarns, vary along their length in thickness and amount of twist. The typical novelty ply yarn illustrated here is composed of a strong base yarn that forms the support and determines the length, combined with an effect yarn that is held in place by a binder. Examples of this type are **bouclé, ratiné, spiral,** and **knot** yarns.

TEXTURED YARNS are produced from man-made fibers that possess the useful characteristic of thermoplasticity, which means they will melt when subjected to heat. Through the use of this property, filament yarns can be heat-set in interesting textured effects. Several manufacturing methods can change the contour of the filament to a **coiled, crimped,** or **looped** formation from its original rod-like shape. Yarns from such filaments may be lightweight, have great bulk, or have a high degree of stretch.

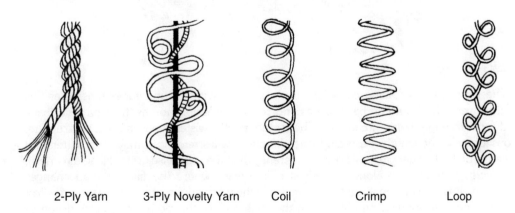

| 2-Ply Yarn | 3-Ply Novelty Yarn | Coil | Crimp | Loop |

Fabric Structure

The thread of textile weaves through history, touching each civilization since the dawn of man and creating a tapestry of variety and excitement. Each culture has made its unique contribution, and the panorama of fabric designs and types provides deep insight into the development of artistic achievement. Despite these subtle cultural distinctions and mechanical developments that have vastly increased the speed at which textiles can be produced, the basic principles involved in textile construction have remained essentially the same for centuries. Weaving, knitting, knotting, felting, and a recent innovation called Malimo are among the techniques by which fabric is formed.

Weaving

A woven fabric is easy to recognize by the fact that it is composed of two sets of yarns at right angles to each other. The loom that produces it, while it may be an extremely complex device, works on a fairly simple principle. A frame holds a series of yarns called the **warp** taut between two rollers, one each at the front and back of the loom. Arranged in a specific order and extending the width of the projected fabric, these yarns are each drawn first through a **heddle**, which has an eye like that of a needle and may be raised to alter the position of its yarn, and then through a space in the **reed**, which is a comb-like device at right angles to the warp yarns, serving to keep each thread straight and in its proper place. The heddles are raised in a specific sequence as the design dictates, and a single crosswise or **filling** yarn or **pick** is drawn between the warp yarns with a **shuttle** and beaten into place against the previous filling threads by the reed. Then the warp yarns are lowered, a different series is raised, and another filling yarn is drawn through and packed in place. This series of crosswise threads forms the **weft** or **woof**. As the fabric is completed, more yarn is released from the back **warp beam** and the fabric is rolled toward the front of the loom and wound on the **cloth beam**.

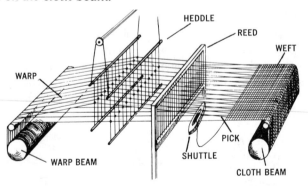

The warp must withstand considerable strain in weaving. It undergoes tension as it is held between the front and back beams and considerable abrasion as the reed slides back and forth through it. Its threads must be strong, tightly twisted, and uniform in structure. Consequently, the lengthwise grain (warp direction) will stretch less, may wear better, and because of its stronger yarn, will drape differently than the crosswise grain (filling direction). The **selvage** is formed along the edges of the warp where the filling thread changes direction. It is likely to be a tighter weave, since the warp edges must support the greatest strain. One indication of durability is in the "balance" of the cloth, or the proportion of warp to filling yarns. Fabric with nearly an equal thread count in both directions often gives longer wear.

BASIC WEAVES

There are several fundamental weaving structures that account for a vast majority of the fabrics we use. All the basic weaves can be produced on a simple loom, requiring no special attachments.

PLAIN WEAVE, true to its name, is the simplest and most common of weaves. Also called *tabby*, it is the prototype of woven structure: each yarn in both the warp and filling directions runs alternately over one and under one of the yarns it crosses. Though basically sturdy, this weave may vary in strength according to the weight of the yarn and the compactness of the weave. Cotton percale, voile, calico, and gingham; linen crash; silk organza and chiffon; synthetic organdy and taffeta; and wool challis are familiar fabrics in plain weave.

The *rib* variation occurs when the yarn in one direction of a plain weave are heavier or closer together than those in the other. Examples of ribbed fabrics, in order of fine to heavy rib, are broadcloth, poplin, faille, grosgrain, bengaline, and ottoman.

When the same alternating construction employs paired or multiple threads, it is called a *basket* weave. Such fabrics tend to be softer and less stable than fabrics of similar weight in single-thread plain weave, and may pose the problem of seam slippage. Examples you may be familiar with are oxford cloth, monk's cloth, and hopsacking.

TWILL WEAVE is often used to produce strong, durable fabrics such as denim and gabardine. A handsome weave characterized by a diagonal ridge usually running from lower left to upper right, its appearance depends to a large extent on the yarn weight and specific twill construction. A frequent variation in the twill weave is the *herringbone*, in which the diagonal ridge switches direction back and forth, creating a zigzag design.

SATIN WEAVE has a characteristic luxurious shine. The surface is composed of *floats*, or warp yarns, which pass over many filling yarns before being caught under one. The surface yarns, usually of filament fibers, intersect cross threads at points randomly spaced so the smooth texture appears unbroken. A variation called *sateen* has similar surface floats, but they run in the filling direction and are usually of a spun staple yarn.

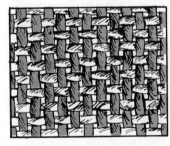

Plain Weave

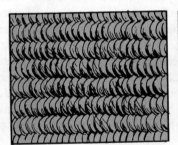

Rib Weave

Basket Weave

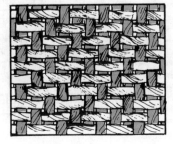

Twill Weave

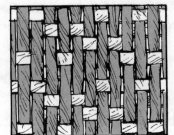

Satin Weave

DECORATIVE WEAVES

There are two basic types of fabric designs—those that are a product of the fabric's woven construction, and those that are applied to the fabric by such processes as printing or embossing. To create woven designs, the basic weaves may be varied and combined, surface floats may form involved designs, and complex mutations of the age-old loom may produce elaborate fabrics whose beauty wins constant attention.

PILE WEAVES provide soft, thick, textured fabrics for many purposes. Several different constructions may be employed to emphasize specific characteristics such as absorbency in terry, density and durability in carpeting, or texture in velvet. Extra warp yarn may be woven over wires, which cut the loops as they are withdrawn. In terry cloth, some of the warp yarns are woven with slack tension and forced up into loops as the filling is beaten back. Corduroy is woven with long filling floats that are cut after weaving to produce wales or cords. Some velvets are woven face to face, sharing warp yarns between two layers which are slashed apart when completed.

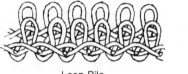
Loop Pile

Cut Pile

PATTERN WEAVES are the glory of the weaver's art. Delicate traditional coverlet designs can be created on a simple loom by an intricate order of threading. Other pattern weaves, such as crisp piqués, filmy curtain gauze, and patterns of flowers and scrolls in rich, deep brocades owe their existence to more complex variations of the loom.

Leno weaves are used most effectively in lacy, open fabrics. A special attachment twists the warp yarns around each other in a figure eight as the filling passes through, imparting stability to fabrics with widely spaced yarns. The leno construction is often combined with other weaves in a decorative effect for casement fabrics and may be especially attractive when designed with novelty yarns. Small figured and textured designs such as birdseye piqué are *dobby weaves,* produced on a more complicated loom. Usually a geometric pattern in a small repeat, these designs frequently employ heavy "stuffer" yarns in the filling to float on the back of the fabric and add texture to the weave. Further elaborations on the basic weaving process produce *jacquard weaves,* some of the most complex and beautiful fabrics available. These include huge repeats, detailed brocades, damasks, and tapestry effects. The jacquard loom controls each warp yarn individually with a series of punched cards like a computer deck. Since one card determines one filling pick, the repeat in the design can include as many threads as there are cards in the deck, permittng an unlimited range of design possibilities.

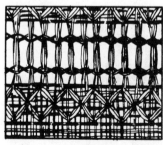
Leno Weave

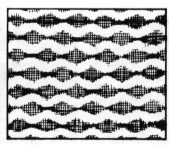
Dobby Weave

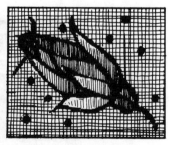
Jacquard Weave

Knitting

A relatively recent development in the history of cloth, knitting has grown through technical advancements from a tedious hand construction to a fast, economical means of producing comfortable, packable, and beautiful fabrics. Knits owe their many advantages to their structure. While the yarn in a woven fabric is in a straight position, the knit construction arranges a continuous yarn into interlocking loops. Since these loops can straighten out under tension without straining the yarn, knit fabrics are inherently stretchy and flexible.

Several terms are used to describe knit goods. The **gauge** of a knit refers to the number of needles in 1" to 2" (25 mm to 5 cm) of fabric, depending on the type of knit. **Denier** is a term dating from Roman times, when the weight of a coin by that name was used as a standard for buying and selling silk. It describes the weight of the yarn per unit length. A **wale** or **rib** is a column of loops running parallel to the long measurement of a knit fabric, corresponding to the lengthwise grain of a weave, and a **course** is a crosswise row.

WEFT KNITTING

The first knitting machines were designed to reproduce the type of knitting done by hand. Called weft or filling knit, this construction uses a continuous single thread to form a crosswise row of loops which links into the previous row and is in turn linked into the row that follows it. Two stitches, **knit** and **purl**, are the basis for all knitting constructions. The knit stitch is a loop drawn through the front of the previous one, the purl is drawn through the back. Simple weft knits are uniquely fragile, since all the loops in a vertical row are dependent on each other. A broken loop will release all the others in the row, marring the fabric with a run. Wool knits tend to have greater resistance to runs because of the capacity of the wool fibers to cling together, locking the stitches. Weft knitting produces fabric in both tubular and flat form.

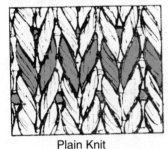
Plain Knit

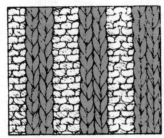
Rib Knit

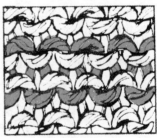
Purl Knit

PLAIN KNITS, found in the familiar fabric known as jersey, have a flat surface and a back characterized by short, horizontal loops. The right side exhibits the appearance of the knit stitch, and the loops on the back are the purl stitch. This structure is a common feature of hand knitting, where it is called **stockinette.**

RIB KNITS are made by alternating sets of knit and purl stitches in the same row, forming pronounced vertical ridges. The purl stitch tends to recede while the knit stitch advances, creating a fabric with a wavy cross-section and superior crosswise stretch. Rib knits have good insulation properties, and provide a snug fit.

PURL KNITS also have pronounced ridges, but in a horizontal direction. Entire rows are formed alternately of knit and purl stitches, yielding a fabric which has considerable crosswise stretch. It is completely reversible, since the appearance of the face is identical to that of the back, and similar to the reverse side of the flat knit.

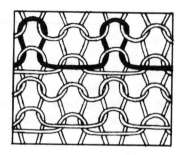

Pattern Knit

Double Knit

PATTERN KNITS are produced from the two basic weft knit stitches by re-arranging, dropping, adding, alternating, and crossing them. The beautiful "fisherman knits" are prime examples of the vast variety of patterns that owe their depth of texture to the fact that the knit stitch tends to advance and the purl stitch to recede. The machines that produce these fabrics, while they are not very economical to operate, can recreate hand-knitted structures with great fidelity.

DOUBLE KNITS, a versatile form of weft knitting, resist runs and have great stability. Produced by the interlock stitch, a variation of the rib stitch that can only be done by machine, double knitting employs two yarns and two sets of needles that draw loops through from both directions. It yields a heavy, firm, easily handled fabric that has the same rib-like appearance on both sides. Jacquard-type machinery has been adapted to produce highly decorative double knits.

WARP KNITTING

The technique of warp knitting, unlike that of simpler weft knitting, employs many yarns. Wound parallel to each other on a warp beam, the yarns are fed into the knitting machine and form loops in a lengthwise direction. Each yarn is controlled by its own needle and follows a zigzag course, interlocking with its neighbors along the length of the fabric. Warp knitting produces several varieties of durable and relatively run-proof fabrics whose low cost and vast design potential have won them enthusiastic consumer acceptance and a secure place in the future of the textile industry.

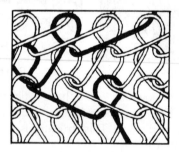

Tricot

Raschel Knit

TRICOT is used extensively for lingerie because of its good permeability and comfort. Available in a variety of weights, it is suitable for dresses, loungewear, and linings. This strong, drapable fabric can be recognized by a fine crosswise rib that appears on the wrong side, and by the fact that it will stretch much more in the crosswise direction than in length. It is resistant to both running and fraying. The name tricot is taken from the French "tricoter," meaning "to knit."

RASCHEL KNITS are becoming increasingly familiar as they are being produced in a wide variety of fabrics. While tricots and many weft knits are best suited to fine, uniform yarns, raschel knits can take advantage of every conceivable texture and fiber type because of a specially designed latch needle. Raschel knits range from fragile tulles to coarse fur cloths. They may often be identified by a chain of fine yarn, which restrains and stabilizes a heavier textured yarn in a lacy, open construction.

Other Fabric Constructions

Beautiful fabrics are produced by many methods other than weaving and knitting. Some have been developed from old hand processes, while others are strictly a product of modern technology. They may be limited to specific uses by their character or cost.

NETTING is the fabric construction that encompasses both the strong, simple, burly texture of fishnet and the delicate and complicated tracery of lace. Knots may secure sets of threads together where they cross each other, or continuous coils of thread may loop through each other, forming the hexagonal mesh that can create a background for further embroidery. The most elaborate machines in the textile industry can reproduce laces in many styles and weights.

CROCHETING is adapted from a hand process that involves the use of a hook to form a chain of loops from a single continuous yarn.

BRAIDING forms fabric whose yarns lie at acute angles to the edges in a bias-woven structure, usually a narrow strip. All the yarns originate from the same direction.

FELTING is a time-honored method for producing warm, versatile, though not very durable, fabrics of wool or fur fibers by the application of heat, moisture, friction, and pressure. This economical construction doesn't require spun yarn or weaving, but depends on the natural ability of wool fibers to shrink, coil, and lock together to form a mat. As there are no yarns to unravel, edges of felt fabrics require no finishing techniques. Since they do not depend on looped yarns, however, they have little or no elastic recovery. When stretched, they will not return to their original shape. Felt exists in many weights and qualities, from fine garment fabric to heavy industrial padding. Wool may be mixed with a certain proportion of cheaper non-felting fiber and still retain its felting capacity.

FUSING produces a non-woven fabric or a web by using an adhesive or bonding agent to join or fuse together a mat of textile fibers other than wool. The fibers are distributed on a belt and made into fabric by one of two methods. An adhesive may be applied directly to the web of fibers, or the fiber mixture may contain some fibers that melt at a very low temperature, fusing the fabric together when heat is applied. Many different characters of fabric may be produced by this method, depending on the length, concentration, and orientation of the fibers. Non-woven fabrics are generally used for interfacing, and the webs are used as a fusing agent on other fabrics.

BONDING is a term that has come to include those textiles which are technically called *laminated* fabrics. These are composed of two separate layers of knitted or woven cloth that are joined together with a bonding agent to improve stability, opacity, or handling ease. Sometimes a thin sheet of plastic foam is laminated between the face and backing fabrics to add texture and insulation. Plastic film may be given greated durability and made suitable for apparel use by bonding it to a base of woven or knitted fabric. Simulated leather and patent vinyl fabrics are produced this way. Bonding may change the "hand" or draping qualities of the face fabric, and off-grain or impermanent bonding may be unsatisfactory.

MALIMO is a textile process that produces extremely stable fabrics at great speed. Three sets of yarns are used—warp yarns, filling yarns laid across the warp, and a third set of yarns that stitches them together with a chain stitch.

Finishes

Fabrics as they come off the loom bear little resemblance to those that reach your sewing machine. Before they are sold they may have been washed in chemical solutions, brushed, pressed, beaten, and polished. Substances and treatments may alter their texture and appearance and improve their resistance to moths, static electricity, spotting, staining, shrinking, sagging, wrinkling, and burning. All the processes undergone by the fabric after its initial transformation from yarn to cloth are called *finishes.*

Texture Finishes

CALENDERING is a process in which the fabric is passed between heated rollers under pressure. Like a large iron, a calender may simply press the fabric flat. However, there are several variations. Smooth, high-speed metal rollers and a resin application produce a finish called *glazing.* When two layers of a ribbed fabric are calendered slightly off grain, a *moiré* effect results. Thermoplastic fibers, or those which melt in sufficient heat, can be permanently textured by *embossing* with rollers engraved with a raised design. A super-glossy finish, called *ciré,* is obtained by applying a wax or other sheen-producing substance to the fabric before it is rolled.

NAPPING is a common finish by which short fiber ends of spun yarn are raised to the surface of a fabric by a series of revolving wire brushes to create flannel or fleece.

BRUSHING is similar to napping except that long fiber ends are mechanically pulled out of the fabric to produce a mohair-look.

PLISSÉ is a process of printing untreated cotton fabric with a caustic soda solution to shrink the fabric in certain areas creating a puckered effect.

FULLING takes advantage of the natural shrinkage capacity of wool. Subjecting the cloth to moisture, heat, and pressure compacts the yarns, strengthens the weave, and imparts warmth, body, and stability. It is similar to the *felting* of non-woven fibers.

BEETLING, applied to linen or cotton, involves prolonged pounding with wooden blocks to flatten the yarns, fill out the weave, and impart an elegant luster to the cloth.

TENTERING straightens the fabric, setting the width and grain, and dries it in the set position. The conveyor-like frame is lined with pins that hold the fabric's selvages and stretch it into shape. An electronic or hand-operated mechanism controls the two belts of pins, keeping filling yarns at right angles to the warp. Off-grain fabric is a result of improper tentering. If it has been heat-set off grain during tentering, it cannot be straightened.

Temporary Finishes

Several finishes may be added that improve the fabric's hand and appearance, but which are quickly removed by normal wear and care. Some substances may temporarily alter the character of a fabric in such a way that poor quality is disguised.

SIZING, or *dressing,* provides body, weight, and luster. Fabrics are stiffened with glue, clay, or wax, which is not fast to laundering. Starch may restore this finish, but if fabric is of poor basic quality (low thread count) it will wear out quickly.

SOFTENERS give a lighter, fluffier, softer hand to fabrics and can be re-applied during the laundering process.

WEIGHTING is a process most often applied to silk to restore the weight that is lost when the natural gum is removed. Metallic salts are absorbed, which allows heavier fabrics to be produced but weakens the fiber. Weighted silk water-spots easily. Cottons and wools can also be weighed.

Performance Finishes

Manufacturers have been increasingly conscious of the consumer demand for fabrics with improved and specialized characteristics. Finishes can counteract the inherent disadvantages of certain untreated fibers, and give them texture and aesthetic appeal as well as safety, durability, and adaptability to special purposes.

Keep in mind the fact that "permanent," as used in the textile industry, is only a relative term. So-called "permanent" finishes would more accurately be called durable, since they are only designed to withstand normal wear, and must be treated and laundered as the manufacturer recommends. Here is a list of terms that you will find on hangtags, bolt ends, and labels.

ANTI-BACTERIAL Finish that checks growth or effect of bacteria and perspiration.

ANTI-STATIC OR CLING FREE A finish to help dissipate static electricity and thus reduce clinging.

COLORFAST Color in fabrics so labeled will not fade with normal use if laundered as recommended.

FLAME-RESISTANT Fabrics that have been treated to prevent the spread of flame once its source has been removed.

MERCERIZED A term for cotton and linen fabrics that have been immersed under tension in a solution of caustic soda to swell the fibers for increased strength, luster, and affinity for dyes.

MILDEW-RESISTANT Fabrics that have been treated to resist the growth of mildew and other molds.

MOTH REPELLANT Fabrics that have been treated to repel moths.

PERMANENT-PRESS or **DURABLE-PRESS** Indicates fabric will wash and dry by machine, shed wrinkles, and retain shape without ironing.

PRESHRUNK Fabrics that have undergone a preliminary shrinking process. Residual shrinkage, or the percentage of possible shrinkage remaining in a fabric, must be declared.

SANFORIZED® Ensures that fabric will not shrink more than one percent despite repeated washing. It is applied to mostly cotton and blends.

SHRINKAGE CONTROLLED Fabrics that have undergone compressive shrinkage in manufacturing; increases durability by compacting the weave.

SOIL RELEASE Treatment that makes possible the removal of stains from fabrics faster. Color brightness and soil release properties maintained after laundering.

STAIN- AND SPOT-RESISTANT Fabric finished to repel water- and oil-based stains.

WASH-AND-WEAR Fabrics that can be washed and re-worn with little or no ironing. This property may be produced by heat-setting or resin treatment and varies in permanence. Also termed easy care and minimum care.

WATERPROOF Fabrics that have been made non-porous so that water will not penetrate them.

WATER-REPELLENT Fabrics that have been treated to reduce their affinity for water yet remain porous.

WRINKLE- OR CREASE-RESISTANT A term applied to fabrics that have been treated to resist and recover from wrinkling caused by normal wear.

Color and Fabric Pattern

We can be sure that when cave men first began painting hunting scenes on walls of caves, the first textile designer was also painting the animal skins he wore. Though the content, construction, and finishing of a fabric provide all of its essential properties, richness of color and pattern have always held the most primary appeal. For centuries, special formulas for color and fabric have been jealously guarded secrets. Vast industries have developed on the basis of changing tastes and new technical developments in color and applied textile design in order to satisfy our unquenchable decorative instinct.

Dyeing

The complex science of dye chemistry has developed in response to demand for fast, vivid color that will withstand wear, sunlight, and the rigors of modern laundering.

Natural fibers, which frequently have distinct colors of their own, often require bleaching before they can be dyed. Many fibers naturally resist color, and among the chief advantages of such innovations as mercerizing is the improvement of a fabric's affinity for dyes. With the advent of synthetic fabrics and the increased importance of the chemical industry in textiles, the number and quality of synthetic dyes has grown by leaps and bounds since their inception in 1856.

Dyes are classified in several ways, including the chemical category and fibers to which they can be applied, the hue produced, and the method of application. The appearance of a fabric is often determined by the stage in manufacturing at which the dye is applied.

STOCK DYEING is used to produce color in a mat of fibers before they are spun into yarn. Colors penetrate the fibers thoroughly, and are likely to be fast. This method is commonly used on wool; hence the expression "dyed in the wool." It permits the spinning of tweed and mottled yarns from several batches of variously colored fibers.

SOLUTION DYEING is a procedure for coloring man-made fibers by introducing pigment into the chemical spinning solution before it is formed into filaments. Since the color is an inherent part of the fiber, it is extremely permanent.

YARN DYEING is one of the oldest methods of coloring textiles. The spun yarn is dyed in a skein, or it may be wound on a cylinder known as a *package*, which is then dyed from the inside out in a machine similar to a pressure-cooker. Typical yarn dyed fabrics are ginghams, plaids, checks, stripes, and those with iridescent effects.

PIECE DYEING is the most common and economical means of coloring fabric. It involves immersing the woven goods in a dye bath. The procedure is practical because it permits manufacturers to store a volume of undyed goods and dye to order as preferences in color change. Piece-dyed fabrics are usually a solid color, but an exception to this rule occurs with *cross dyeing*. Fabrics to be so treated are woven of a combination of fiber types, each with a different affinity for certain dyes. Those dyes which are accepted by one fiber are rejected by others, resulting in fabrics that can resemble either yarn-dyed or fiber-dyed fabrics. Difficulties may be encountered in attempting to dye fiber blends a solid color, and many must be dyed twice to impart the same color to both fibers.

Applied Design

The surface of a fabric provides enticing stimulus to an artist's creative imagination. An infinity of surface patterns can be reproduced in many ways.

TRANSFER PRINTING is the process of applying the print to paper and then transferring it to the fabric by the use of heat and pressure. Fine sharp registry of the design can be achieved by this method as well as the ability to obtain multiple colors and tones. Transfer printing is less expensive than roller printing.

ROLLER PRINTING, or direct printing, is a simple procedure used to produce large quantities of a design that is engraved on a series of rollers, one for each color to be used. These print rollers are arranged around a large drum in exact positions, and color is applied to them. When the fabric feeds between the rollers and the drum, the areas of color coincide to form the complete design. *Discharge printing* uses a bleaching paste to bleach out the design on a solid color fabric. *Resist printing* uses a dye-resistant paste to print the design. The fabric is then dyed and the paste removed, leaving a lighter print. *Burnt-out printing* uses chemicals to dissolve one of the fibers in the fabric, creating a raised motif on a sheer ground. *Flocking* adds textural interest by printing a design on the fabric with an adhesive and then applying short fibers to the surface. The fabric can also be completely flocked to give the appearance of a velvet or velour.

SCREEN PRINTING is a sophisticated version of the stencil process. The design is cut out of a thin sheet of film, which is then adhered to a frame covered with a fine, strong mesh fabric. The fabric to be printed is stretched out on a table, the screen laid on top, and the pigment or dye is forced through the screen in the areas where the non-porous film does not act as a barrier. Adapting photographic processes to cutting the film has allowed screen printing to produce fine gradations of tone and delicate detail. Though it is slower than roller printing, it is often used to produce limited quantities of a print.

TIE DYEING is an ancient craft that produces interesting and varied textile designs. Puffs of fabric are wrapped in waxed thread or sewn and tightly gathered, then dipped in dye, creating intriguing sunburst effects as the dye penetrates the fabric unevenly. The blending of several colors and the combining of techniques contribute to the unique effect. The technique has been copied effectively by a machine process.

BATIK is a process that can be used to create striking and delicate designs. It is a method of resist dyeing in which wax is applied to the cloth in areas that are not to receive color. After dyeing, the wax is boiled off, and the process repeated for each color to be used. It has now been adapted to machine printing.

EMBROIDERY was originally a hand technique executed on a base fabric with thread, yarn, or other materials and a needle. The production of eyelet embroidery, mechanized with the invention of the Schiffli machine, involves punching holes into the fabric as the edges are finished by machine.

Surface design on fabric has evolved dramatically over the years. With the introduction of the computer and very sophisticated home sewing machines, the average seamstress can literally create her own embellished fabric before construction of a garment. Printing and dyeing processes are available to anyone possessing a little imagination and time.

Fiber and Fabric Facts
Natural Fibers

	Fabrics	Properties	Care
Cotton	Extremely versatile in weight, texture, and construction. Found in fabric such as organdy, broadcloth, poplin, terry, corduroy, seersucker, denim, tweed. Used widely for summer wear, work clothes, and in heavier weights, for warm transitional garments.	Quite strong, even stronger when wet. Not susceptible to pilling or seam slippage. Comfortable and absorbent; carries heat from body. Free from static electricity, with good affinity for dyes. Will deteriorate from mildew; weakened by sunlight. Tendency to wrinkle.	Wash 10 minutes in hot water at regular speed with any good detergent. Can use chlorine bleach on white cottons; however, some finishes react to chlorine bleach and turn yellow (see label). Color safe bleach can be used on dyed cottons. Fabric softener will reduce wrinkling. Check the label for any wrinkle-resistant finish. Tumble dry on regular heat setting but don't over-dry. Press with hot iron while damp until completely dry or use a steam iron with a slightly dampened press cloth.
Linen	One of the oldest textiles known. Beautiful, durable, and elegant; has a luster. Can be made naturally into sheer, medium, or even heavyweight fabrics. Used commonly for dresses, blouses, and suiting.	Tendency to wrinkle unless treated. Exceptionally strong, but stiff; may show wear at the edges and along folds. Comfortable; excellent absorbency; carries heat away from the body. Poor affinity for dyes; bright colors may bleed when laundered. Fabric will shrink unless treated. Will deteriorate from mildew but not from moths. Does not lint.	Usually dry cleaned, but launders well if preshrunk. Wash 5-8 minutes in hot water at regular speed with any good detergent (see label). Can use chlorine bleach but over bleaching may weaken fiber. Tumble dry on regular heat setting, but remove and iron while still very damp. Iron at high setting (unless treated with special finishes; see label). For maximum durability, creases should be finger pressed, not ironed into the garment.
Silk	Beautiful, luxurious to touch; has a deep luster. Available in a variety of weaves and weights from sheer drapable chiffon to stiff rich brocades in brilliant colors and beautiful prints for dresses, suits, blouses, linings, lingerie. Found in fabrics such as crepe, brocade, satin, jersey, tweed.	Good wrinkle resistance. Builds up static electricity, may cling. Exceptionally strong for its fineness. Is very absorbent; will hold in body heat. Excellent affinity for dyes, but may bleed.	Usually dry cleaned. If marked washable, use mild suds in lukewarm water; can also machine wash for 3 minutes at gentlespeed. Chlorine bleach should never be used. Tumble dry at low setting for short time or hang up to dry, but avoid prolonged exposure to light. Iron on wrong side while damp with a low heat setting or use a steam iron; how-ever, silk is easily water spotted so you may need to protect the fabric with a thin cloth.

| **Wool** | Versatile in weight, texture, weave, and color. Unique properties of wool permit constructions not possible in any other fiber. Tailors well because of ability to be molded into shape. Used for coatings, suitings, crepe, tweeds, knits, gabardine, flannel, jersey. | Excellent wrinkle resistance and elasticity. Limited abrasion resistance. Weakens and stretches when wet. Exceptional absorbency, holds a large amount of moisture before it feels damp. Traps air in fibers, providing great natural warmth. Has good affinity for dye. Weakened by sunlight. Requires moth proofing; may be attacked by mildew if damp or soiled. Susceptible to shrinking and pilling if not treated. | Should be brushed between cleanings. Use a damp sponge on knits and finer fabrics. Usually dry cleaned. For hand washables, use mild suds in cool water; can also machine wash for 2 minutes at gentle speed, interrupting the agitation time for 10 minutes to let the fabric soak, and then completing the cycle. Do not tumble dry; block to shape on a flat surface away from heat. If labeled "machine wash- and-dry," wash 3-8 minutes in warm water at gentle speed with mild suds. Tumble dry at regular heat setting but remove while slightly damp. Do not use chlorine bleach; it will weaken and yellow the fibers. To avoid stretching, press gently at low heat setting on the wrong side using a damp press cloth or steam iron. |

Synthetic Fibers

| **Acetate**

Celanese Acetate® from Celanese Acetate Corp. | Silk-like appearance, luxurious soft feel, deep luster, excellent draping qualities. Found in fabrics such as satin, jersey, taffeta, lace, faille, brocade, tricot, and crepe, and often in blends with other man-made fibers. Used for dresses, foundation garments, lingerie, linings, and blouses. | Tendency to wrinkle. Accumulates static electricity. Takes colors well, but some dyes are subject to atmospheric fading. Relatively low in strength. Resistant to mildew and moths. Weakened by light. Moderately absorbent; holds in body heat. Resistant to stretch and shrinkage. | Usually dry cleaned. To hand wash, gently squeeze suds through fabric and rinse in lukewarm water. Do not twist or wring. Do not soak colored items. Iron while damp with light pressure on wrong side at lowest temperature; a hot iron may melt the fabric. Place strip of brown paper between garment and seam allowances or darts. Do not use acetone (as in nail polish remover) or other organic solvents. |
| **Acrylic**

Microsupreme®, Cresloft™, Creslan®Plus, BioFresh™, WeatherBloc™ from Sterling Fibers Inc.
Dralon™ from Bayer Inc.
Acrilan®, BounceBack®, Duraspun®, Pil-Trol®, Sayelle®, The Smart Yarns®, Wear-Dated®, Wintuck from Solutia Inc. | Commonly soft, light, fluffy fabric construction. Available in sheer fabrics, knits, fleece, fur-like and pile fabrics, and blends with natural and man-made fibers. Used for sweaters, dresses, suits, sports and work clothes. | Good wrinkle resistance and wash-and-wear performance. Lightweight. May accumulate static electricity. Low absorbency; quick drying. Good affinity for dyes; colorfast. Quite strong. Excellent resistance to mildew, moths, chemicals, and sunlight. Heat sensitive. May pill. Holds shape well, good pleat retention. | Remove oily stains before cleaning. May be dry-cleaned or hand washed. Wash on warm water setting with any good detergent. Add fabric softener to the final rinse cycle to reduce static electricity. Dries quickly, may be tumble dried at low heat setting or hung up to dry. (Sweaters, however, must be dried flat.) Seldom requires ironing if removed from dryer as soon as cycle is completed; otherwise, use moderately warm iron, never hot, on wrong side. |

Synthetic Fibers

	Fabrics	Properties	Care
Lyocell Tencel® from Acordis Cellulosic Fibers Lenzing Lyocell® from Lenzing	Fabrics have a soft hand and excellent drape. Extremely strong fiber both wet and dry. Absorbs dyes readily. Can be found in both woven fabrics and knits with a luxurious peach-skin surface. Often combined with other fibers such as cotton, wool or polyester producing a variety of fabrics from crepes to corduroy. Commonly used for dresses, suits, sportswear, upholstery fabrics, and home furnishings.	100% natural in origin. Produced from the cellulose of wood pulp in a process which is environmentally friendly. Shrink and wrinkle resistant. It has the breathability and absorbency of a natural fiber. Is washable and quick drying.	Can be laundered or dry cleaned. If blended with other fibers, check care of those fibers (e.g. silk or cotton) for cleaning. Machine wash at low temperature. Remove from cool dryer as soon as garment is dry. Use moderately warm iron.
Metallic Not currently produced in the United States.	Fibers glitter in gold, silver, and other colors; used in blended fabrics and trims.	Non-tarnishing if plastic coated. Not affected by salt water, chlorinated water, or climatic conditions.	Can be laundered or dry cleaned if plastic coated. Iron at low setting. Mylar polyester covering withstands heat better than acetate covering
Modacrylic	Available in deep-pile, fleece, and fur-like fabrics; used chiefly in blends and no-iron fabrics for deep-pile coats, trims, and linings.	Good wrinkle resistance. May accumulate static electricity Non-allergenic. Quick drying. Retains shape well, has an excellent elasticity. Resistant to moths, mildew, chemicals, and sunlight. Very heat sensitive; softens at low temperatures. Flame resistant.	Fur-like deep-pile garments are most safely cleaned by a furrier; other fabrics may be dry-cleaned or laundered If washable, follow same care directions as for acrylic. If ironing is absolutely necessary, iron at lowest temperature to prevent any stiffening or glazing. Finger press fur-like deep pile fabrics. Do not use acetone, as in nail polish remover.
Microfibers Silky Touch™ nylon, Sportouch® nylon from BASF Corp. Microsupreme® acrylic from Sterling Fibers Inc. Dacron® polyester microfiber, Supplex® Micro nylon, Micromattique™ polyester, Tactel® Micro nylon from DuPont Trevira Finesse® polyester, Trevira Micronesse® polyester, Trevira Micro® polyester from KoSa Micro Modal® rayon from Lenzing MicroSpun® from Wellman	Available in acrylic, nylon, polyester, and rayon. Defined as a fiber that has less than 1 denier per filament. Finer than the most delicate silk and very drapeable. Luxurious hand, often silken or suede-like touch.	Shrink resistant with excellent pleat retention. Great insulation from wind, rain and cold. Very strong fiber, with the exception of rayon. Found often in hosiery, blouses, dresses, sportswear, ties, scarves, swimwear, intimate wear and outerwear as well as curtains, upholstery, sheets, towels, and blankets.	Clean according to the instructions given for washing or dry cleaning fabrics made from these particular fibers (acrylic, nylon, polyester and rayon).

Nylon

Anso-tex® air textured, Capima®, Caplana®, Caprolan®, Caprolan-RC®, Captiva®, Crème de Captiva®, Hydrofil®, Patina, SeaGard®, StayGard® from Allied Signal Inc.
Crepeset®, Matinesse®, Resistat®, Shimmereen™, SilkyTouch™, Vivana®, Zeflure®, Zefsport® 200, 500 and 2000 from BASF Corp.
Type 6 and 6.6 from Cookson Fibers Inc. Antron®, Antron® III, Cordura®, Jentell®, Supplex™ Micro, Supplex®, Tactel®, Tactel® Aquator, Tactel®Micro, DyPont Nylon from DuPont FiberSet™ from Solutis Inc.

Several types of nylon produce a wide variety of fabric textures, from smooth and crisp to soft and bulky. Available in wide range of fabrics, both woven and knitted. Nylon 6 and 6.6 often found in blends. Used for dresses, blouses, shirts, skirts, sweaters, lingerie, ties, sock, swimwear, and rain-wear.

Very good wrinkle resistance. Exceptional strength. Washes easily. Low absorbency; holds in body heat. Good affinity for dyes; may fade in sunlight. Can be heat-set to hold shape, pleats, and embossed effects. High resistance to moths, mildew. Very elastic. Does not soil easily; may pill. Melts under high heat. Resistant to non-oily stains.

Remove oily stains before cleaning. Machine wash for 3-5 minutes on regular for sturdy fabrics, using warm water. Use gentle cycle or handwash delicate fabrics. For bright colors use cool water. Fabrics may yellow; bleach frequently with sodium perborate bleaches. A fabric softener in the rinse water will reduce static electricity. Tumble dry on wash-and-wear setting or drip dry; dries quickly. If removed from dryer immediately, may not require ironing; otherwise use low temperature on the wrong side. Never use a hot iron.

Polyester

Dacron®, Dacron® Microdenier, Thermax®, Thermastat®, Hollofil®, Hollofil® II, Hollofil® 808, Thermolite®, Thermolite ® Plus from DuPont Trevira®, Trevira Finesse®, Trevira Micronesse®, Trevira Micro®, ESP®, Polarguard HV®, Polarguard 3D®, Serene® from KoSa. Fortrel® ComFortrel®, Fortrel Spunnaire®, Fortrel Spunesse®. Microspun®, Fortrel EcoSpun® from Wellman

Available in many weights, textures, and weaves; often used in blends and minimum care fabrics. Used for durable press (perma-nent press), fiber fill, fleece, and knit fabrics found in suits, shirts, slacks, dresses, blouses, lingerie, and thread.

Excellent wrinkle and abrasion resistance. Accumulates electricity. Wash and wear, quick drying. High strength. Resistant to stretching and shrinking. Low absorbency; may hold in body heat. May yellow, but is otherwise color-fast. Retains heat set pleats and creases. Exceptional resistance to mildew and moths. Occasional seam slip-page. May pill and pick up lint.

Remove oily stains before cleaning. Machine wash for 3-5 minutes with regular agitation for sturdy fabrics, and gentle agitation for delicate fab-rics, using warm water. For bright colors use cool water. A fabric soft-en-er in the rinse water will reduce static electricity; rinse well. Chlorine bleach can be used for whites before the spin cycle; others can be tumble dried at wash-and-wear or low set-ting. If removed from dryer immedi-ately, may not require ironing; other-wise use a medium warm setting or steam iron.

Polyolefin (Olefin)

Alpha Olefin™, Essera™, Kermel™, Innova®, Marvess™, Ryton™, Trace™ from Amoco Salus™, Telar® from FFT Inc. Herculon®, Nouvelle® from Hercules Inc.

Wool-like hand and slightly waxy feel. Its light weight makes it especially good for deep pile and fake fur con-structions. Adaptable for activewear , sports-wear, jeans, socks, lin-ing fabrics, carpets, upholstery and wall cov-erings.

Excellent elasticity and resiliency. Lightest of textile fibers, will float on water. Virtually non-absorbent; quick drying. Will not shrink unless overheated. Very sensi-tive to heat; melts easily. Non- allergenic. Resists pilling, staining, and insects. Difficult to dye.

Machine wash in lukewarm water; add a fabric softener to final rinse. Machine dry only on very low set-ting, and remove immediately after cycle has stopped. Preferably drip dry. Iron on lowest possible temper-ature setting, or not at all. Stains may often be blotted away with absorbent tissue. Olefins should not be dry-cleaned if perchlorethylene is the solvent used.

Rayon
Modal by Lenzing, filament by North American Rayon

Comes in a wide range of qualities; can be made to resemble natural fibers; can be lightweight or heavy constructions. May have smooth surfaces or bulky napped textures. Soft hand drapes well. Used for dresses, suits, blouses, coats, lingerie, slacks, linings, nonwoven fabrics, and blends.

Soft and comfortable. Absorbent; holds in body heat. Good affinity for dyes; generally colorfast. Low resistance to mildew. Relatively low in strength; weaker when wet. Wrinkles unless specially finished. May shrink or stretch if not treated. Weakens in prolonged exposure to light.

Usually dry-cleaned; if wet may weaken, ravel, or shrink. If washable, use mild detergent in warm water at gentle speed for 3-5 minutes. When hand washing use mild lukewarm suds, gently squeeze them through fabric, rinse in lukewarm water. Do not wring or twist. Do not soak colored fabrics. Chlorine bleaches or the peroxygen type can be used; some finishes may be sensitive to chlorine bleach. Tumble dry; if hung to dry, avoid direct sunlight. Iron while damp at a moderate setting, on wrong side to prevent shine.

Spandex
Lycra® from DuPont Cleerspan®, Glospan® from Globe Manufacturing Co.
Dorlastan™ from Bayer

Found in stretchable, flexible, supple fabrics as used for foundation garments, swimwear, ski pants, other athletic apparel and elastic banding.

Lightweight; great elasticity. High in strength and durability. Nonabsorbent so it repels body oils. May yellow with exposure to light.

Hand or machine wash in lukewarm water for 3 minutes with gentle agitation. Do not use chlorine bleach, which will cause permanent yellowing. Use oxygen or sodium perborate bleach. Rinse well. Drip dry or tumble dry at cool setting, being careful not to over-dry. Can be ironed at a low temperature.

Triacetate
Not currently produced in the United States.

Often found in blends, fabrics such as tricot, sharkskin, flannel, and taffeta. Used for garments that require pleat retention, sportswear.

Good resistance to wrinkling and shrinking. Antistatic finish can be built in. Low strength. Good affinity for dyes; colorfast. Can be permanently pleated; holds heat-set shape and texture. Easily washed.

Machine wash; tumble dry, except permanently pleated garments which should be hand washed and hung to dry. Usually requires ironing; can withstand higher temperature than acetate. Do not use acetone, as in nail polish remover, or any other organic solvent

2

Your
Pattern
Profile

Pattern Design

When you flip through the Vogue catalogue in a store or unfold a Vogue pattern at home, have you ever wondered how pattern designs are created and patterns made? How do the latest couture fashions by your favorite designers become a part of the Vogue pattern collection? The creation of a pattern is a complex process involving many steps in planning, development, and testing before the pattern is finally presented to you. Working six months ahead, Vogue Patterns check and double-check every detail to guarantee that each pattern will serve as an expert guide to sewing.

The Creation of a Pattern

Four times a year, Vogue's design representatives attend the collections in Europe and America to purchase garments for pattern reproductions.

Back in New York City, the designer garment along with its flat pattern goes to the pattern maker who drapes a line-for-line copy of the garment, including all interfacings, linings, and details down to the last hook and eye. This muslin copy is compared with the original garment to make sure that all the design lines and details are identical.

For patterns created by Vogue's own designers, the pattern maker first makes a basic silhouette pattern using the designer's sketch or "croquis" along with notes on construction. She then cuts and drapes the muslin.

Next a "master pattern block" is traced from the muslin and marked with all the construction symbols such as darts, seams, and notches. From this master pattern, a dressmaker constructs the garment using a home sewing machine and dressmaking, rather than manufacturing, construction techniques. The pattern is tested for its suitability for striped, plaid, diagonal, and napped fabrics; then a model tries on the garment to check the fit and mobility of the design.

The master pattern block must next be "graded" or scaled up or down for all pattern sizes. The difference between sizes is based on standardized measurements and the style of the garment. The grading is done by a computer that adds a carefully predetermined amount to certain areas to achieve the different pattern sizes.

The pattern pieces are then measured for layout diagrams. Again the computer determines the pattern piece arrangement and the yardage (metrage) requirements and prints out a picture of the pattern layout. Meanwhile the Sewing Guide instructions are written from the original muslin and construction notes, and the illustrations are drawn to scale using the muslin. Photographs, sketches, yardage (metrage) requirements, and fabric recommendations are gathered together for the pattern envelope. Everything is checked one last time before being sent to the Vogue Pattern manufacturing centers throughout the world for printing.

All the pattern pieces are printed on a continuous roll of tissue paper. A band saw is used to cut around the pattern pieces cutting through 1300 layers of tissue paper at one time! The tissue paper patterns are folded by machine and inserted into the envelope with the Sewing Guide Sheet. From there the completed patterns are distributed to stores around the world for your selection.

The Vogue Catalogue

The Vogue Pattern catalogue offers an abundance of fashion designs to satisfy the desires of women—and men—to be beautifully dressed for every mood and occasion. We literally go to the ends of the earth to bring you the most complete selection of designs—from the great European collections, New York City's Seventh Avenue design centers, to our own design rooms. Great care is taken to feature the finest photography and the most realistic illustrations in order to convey both the fashion concept and the construction details of every design.

The introductory section of the catalogue is a photographic highlight of the very latest fashion trends in styles, fabrics, and colors. The rest of the catalogue is organized into sections to enable you to quickly find whatever style you are seeking. Most of the sections are divided according to the type of garment—dresses, separates, coordinates, sportswear, lingerie and sleepwear, loungewear, and evening wear.

The designers show up everywhere in the catalogue—*Vogue Paris Original, Vogue Designer Original, and Vogue American Designer Original*—to offer you the height of the European and American fashion markets. Some designers contribute elegant and dramatic fashions with the intricate detailing of haute couture. Others offer young, sophisticated, contemporary, and easy-to-wear designs. Vogue Patterns' own designers complete the vast selection of garments for every occasion.

In addition to the broad range of fashions included in the catalogue, there are several special categories of patterns. *Very Easy Vogue Patterns* couple fabulous style with simple, easy-to-follow construction and few pattern pieces. *Vogue Bridal Designs* offer an outstandingly beautiful selection of designs for the entire bridal party. *Vogue Maternity Designs* for the mother-in-waiting give her the very latest in fashion trends. *Vogue For Me* caters to the carriage set and on up to the school age crowd with marvelous party dresses, sporty separates, and special occasion creations.

Vogue Men, created by American and European designers as well as Vogue's own designers, include fashions to suit the most discriminating male. Whether his tastes are classic or innovative, Vogue offers a choice of patterns to reflect his particular needs and preferences. Last but not least, *Vogue's Craft and Accessories* patterns offer a wide range of creative ideas for gift items, fashion accessories, children's toys, and home and holiday decorations.

Although the Vogue catalogue is a wealth of fashion ideas, it also contains some very important information to assist you in your pattern and sewing selections. The caption for each pattern clearly describes all the views and construction details. Information about yardage (metrage) requirements, fabric suggestions, and notions are also listed. Located on the back, you will find a numerical index for every pattern included in the catalogue, a measurement chart, and instructions for taking body measurements and selecting the correct pattern size.

There is a world of fashion at your fingertips in every Vogue catalogue and a fantastic look in each pattern. Whatever your age, size, life-style, or personal taste, there is something there for you. The choice is yours . . . the Vogue choice.

Choosing the Pattern for You

Choosing the correct pattern size avoids wasting money and effort—not to mention time. Just imagine how many more creations you can turn out if you don't have to spend time needlessly adjusting an incorrect pattern size. To be sure you are buying the correct pattern size, you should consider figure changes that may have taken place. How many women do you know who plunge directly into cutting the same size they've worn for the last five years, only to discover that those few pounds added or subtracted make an irreversible difference in fit once the fabric has been cut? Even if you have maintained the same weight, it is possible that certain body areas may have become fuller while others have become more slender. These small body changes may require a careful re-evaluation of the silhouettes that are most becoming on you rather than necessitating the purchase of a larger or smaller pattern size. Also be aware of how fashion influences the fit of your garments. There are years or seasons when the trend is toward a closer, more revealing fit as opposed to a looser, freer line.

To determine your correct pattern size, follow these three easy steps: measure precisely, select your correct figure type, and gain an understanding of ease. With this knowledge, you can approach your next sewing project with confidence.

Your Body Measurements

Accurate measurements are the starting point in selecting your correct pattern size. When taking your measurements wear properly fitted undergarments or a leotard and your usual shoes so that your posture will be normal. Never measure over an outer garment.

Although it is easier if a friend can help you, measurements can be taken unassisted by working in front of a full-length mirror, though back waist and arm length measurements may be difficult to take alone. Make sure the tape measure is held straight and snug, but not tight, against the body. Check in the mirror to be sure the tape is always parallel to the floor for the circumference measurements; do not let it slide down in the front or back. Double-check your measurements for accuracy.

Review your body measurements periodically so you can be aware of any possible changes in your figure. Record your measurements, along with the date, on the convenient chart for your easy reference. Even though your weight remains stable, your body contours may shift, and you may find it necessary to change your pattern size or even figure type in the future.

First, tie a piece of narrow elastic around your waist to use as a reference point in taking other measurements. Bend from side to side until it settles in at your natural waistline. Stand comfortably, look straight ahead and maintain your normal posture.

The first four measurements are the keys in determining your pattern size. The remaining measurements will assist you in making any necessary length adjustments.

CHEST: Measure around the body, under the arms above the fullest part of the bust (1).

BUST: Measure around the fullest part of the bust, keeping the tape straight across the back (2).

WAIST: Measure around the body, over the elastic (3).

HIPS: Measure around the fullest part of the hip (4) or around the thighs if they are fuller than the hip. The distance from the waist to the full hip, called the hip length (5), is 9" (23 cm) for Misses' sizes, and 7" (18 cm) for Misses' Petites.

BACK WAIST LENGTH: Measure from the prominent bone at the base of your neck to the elastic at your waistline (6).

ARM LENGTH: With your arm slightly bent, measure from the bone at the top of your arm to your elbow (7) and from your elbow to your wristbone (8). Adding these measurements gives you your shoulder to wristbone measurement (9).

HEIGHT: Remove your shoes and stand in your stocking feet against a wall. Standing erect, place a ruler on top of your head, parallel to the floor. Mark its position on the wall and measure the distance to the floor with a tape or yardstick (10).

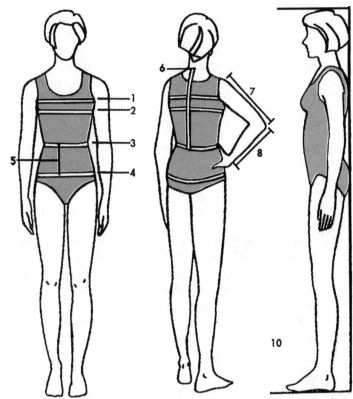

Personal Body Measurements				
PERSONAL ADJUSTMENTS		Measurements		Adjustments
		Standard	Personal	+ or −
1	Chest			
2	Bust			
3	Waist			
4	Hip			
5	Hip Length			
6	Back Waist Height			
7	Shoulder to Elbow			
8	Elbow to Wrist			
9	Shoulder to Wrist			
10	Height			
Name:	Date:	Weight:	Pattern Size:	

Your Figure Type

Once you have taken your body measurements and recorded them on the chart given here, it is time to select your pattern size. Since almost no one is a perfect pattern match, and it is usually easier to increase or decrease body circumference in the waist and hip area, use your upper body measurements to determine your correct pattern size.

Vogue Patterns are designed for the B cup figure, therefore, it is important to determine your personal cup size. Subtract your chest measurement from your bust measurement. If the difference is:

1" (2.5 cm) or less	A cup
1 ¼" to 2" (3.2 to 5 cm)	B cup
2 ¼" to 3" (5.7 to 7.5 cm)	C cup
3 ¼" to 4" (8.2 to 10 cm)	D cup
4 ¼" (10.7 cm) or larger	Larger than a D cup

Now, using the Standard Body Measurement Chart, select your pattern size. If you are an "A" or a "B" cup, use your bust measurement to determine your pattern size. If you are a "C" cup or larger, use your chest measurement to select your pattern size. This ensures a better fit across your shoulders, neckline, chest and upper back. The bust area can be adjusted for a larger cup size if necessary.

If your chest or bust measurement falls between two pattern sizes, your bone structure will be your determining factor. Choose a smaller size if you are small-boned; choose a larger size if you are large-boned.

Pattern Sizes

Because women vary greatly in size and shape, average figure types of varying proportions are the basis for the "grading" or sizing of pattern sizes. Figure type is a matter of proportion, not age. Your pattern is your sewing blueprint, from which you build your exact dimensions for a perfect fit.

Here is where your height comes in to play. Misses', Misses' Petites and Women's sizes are designed to allow for your specific height. Shortening or lengthening the pattern is easy to do and will become automatic once your adjustments are determined.

MISSES': The Misses' size patterns are designed for a figure 5'5" to 5'6" (1.65 to 1.68 M) tall without shoes, well-proportioned and developed. The standard full hip measurement is 9" (23 cm) below the waist.

MISSES' PETITES: A shorter figure, the Misses' Petites size patterns are for a person approximately 5'2" to 5'4" (1.57 to 1.63 M) tall without shoes, and who has a back waist length 1" (2.5 cm) shorter than the Misses' figure. The distance between the waist and full hip measurements is 7" (18 cm). As a rule, the Misses' Petite figure also has shorter shoulder-to-elbow and elbow-to-wrist measurements.

WOMEN'S: The Women's figure stands 5'5" to 5'6" (1.65 to 1.68 M) without shoes, but is a somewhat larger, more fully mature figure than the standard Misses' figure.

You should also consider the type of garment you are intending to make when selecting a pattern size. For dresses, blouses, tops, jackets, coats and vests, select the size closest to your bust or chest measurement. Adjust the pattern at the waist and hips as necessary. For skirts, pants, shorts or culottes, choose the pattern size closest to your waist measurement, particularly if there is detailing such as tucks, pleats or darts at the waist area. However, if your hips are proportionately larger than your waist—by 13" (33 cm) or more—use your hip measurement to select your pattern size. For coordinates including both tops and bottoms, select your correct size by using your bust or chest measurement. For maternity styles, the pattern size is based upon your measurements before your pregnancy.

Many women are a combination of two or more pattern sizes. If this applies to you, look for Vogue Multi-Size patterns, which combine two to three sizes in one pattern. The multiple cutting lines on the pattern enable you to change the sizes at the bust, waist, or hip, according to your figure. If the Multi-Size grouping for your pattern includes the pattern size you need for differences found on the top or bottom, pattern adjustments can be kept to a minimum. Simply choose the appropriate cutting line in each fitting area. Merge the sizes by drawing new lines that gradually blend different cutting lines.

Measurement Charts

Mearsurements are shown in inches (centimeters)

MISSES' PATTERNS are designed for a well proportioned and developed figure, about 5'5" (1.65 M) to 5'6" (1.68 M) without shoes. Misses' Petites are designed for the shorter figure; about 5'2" (1.57 M) to 5 4" (1.63) without shoes.

SIZE	X-Small 6	Small 8	10	Medium 12	14	Large 16	18	X-Large 20	22	XX-Large 24
Chest	28½ (73)	29½ (75)	30½ (78)	32 (81)	34 (87)	36 (92)	38 (97)	40 (102)	42 (107)	44 (112)
Bust	30½ (78)	31½ (80)	32½ (83)	34 (87)	36 (92)	38 (97)	40 (102)	42 (107)	44 (112)	46 (117)
Waist	23 (58)	24 (61)	25 (64)	26½ (67)	28 (71)	30 (76)	32 (81)	34 (87)	37 (94)	39 (99)
Hip	32½ (85)	33½ (??)	34½ (88)	36 (92)	38 (97)	40 (102)	42 (107)	44 (112)	46 (117)	48 (122)
Back Waist Length	15½ (39.5)	15¾ (40)	16 (40.5)	16¼ (41.5)	16½ (42)	16¾ (42.5)	17 (43)	17¼ (44)	17⅜ (44)	17½ (44.5)

TODAY'S FIT patterns are designed for the changing proportions of today's figure; about 5'5" (1.65 M) without shoes. The waist and hips are slightly larger than Misses' and the shoulders narrower.

SIZE	X-Small A	B	Small C	D	Medium E	F	Large G	H	X-Large I	J
Bust	32 (81)	34 (87)	36 (92)	38 (97)	40½ (103)	43 (109)	46 (117)	49 (124)	52 (132)	55 (140)
Waist	26½ (67)	28½ (72)	30½ (78)	32½ (83)	35 (89)	37½ (95)	41½ (105)	44½ (113)	47½ (121)	50½ (128)
Hip	34½ (88)	36½ (93)	38½ (98)	40½ (103)	42½ (108)	45 (116)	48 (122)	51 (130)	54 (137)	57 (145)
Back Waist Length	15¾ (40)	16 (40.5)	16¼ (41)	16½ (42)	16¾ (42.5)	17 (43)	17¼ (44)	17¼ (44)	17¼ (44)	17¼ (44)

WOMEN'S PATTERNS are designed for the larger, more fully mature figure; about 5'5" (1.65 M) to 5'6" (1.68 M) without shoes; Women' s Petites patterns are designed for the shorter women's figure; about 5'2" (1.57 M) to 5'4" (1.63) without shoes.

SIZE	X-Small 14W	Small 16W	18W	Medium 20W (38)	22W (40)	Large 24W (42)	26W (44)	X-Large 28W (46)	30W (48)	XX-Large 32W (50)
Bust	36 (92)	38 (97)	40 (102)	42 (107	44 (112)	46 (117)	48 (122)	50 (127)	52 (132)	54 (137)
Waist	29 (73)	31 (78)	33 (83)	35 (89)	37 (94)	39 (99)	41½ (105)	44½ (112)	47½ (118)	50½ (124)
Hip	38 (97)	40 (102)	42 (107)	44 (112)	46 (117)	48 (122)	50 (127)	52 (132)	54 (137)	56 (142)
Back Waist Length	16½ (42.5)	16¾ (42.5)	17 (43	17¼ (44	17⅜ (44)	17½ (44.5)	17⅝ (45)	17¾ (45)	17⅞ (45.5)	18 (46)

Understanding Ease

Each Vogue Pattern takes into consideration your need for comfort and mobility by building in **wearing ease** to allow you freedom of movement without restraint. **Design ease** is an integral part of many styles and will have additional dimensions added to the pattern beyond the wearing ease, as dictated by the garment's design lines.

BODY MEASUREMENTS	+	WEARING EASE	+	DESIGNER EASE	=	FASHION SILHOUETTE

The pattern caption in the catalogue and on the back of the pattern envelope describes how the garment is intended to fit. Some women prefer loosely fitting clothes while others prefer clothes fitted more closely to the body. Use this information to help you select the type of fit in your garments that is most flattering to your figure.

WEARING EASE

Wearing ease is additional inches (centimeters) necessary in a garment, over and above the body measurements. Never use this ease to accommodate a larger size or eliminate it when making pattern adjustments. Refer to the information below for wearing ease for your figure type.

	MISSES'	MISSES' PETITES	WOMEN'S
BUST	3" (7.6 cm)	3" (7.6 cm)	4" (10.2 cm)
WAIST	1" (25 mm)	1" (25 mm)	1 ⅓" (32 mm)
HIP	2" (5.1 cm)	2" (5.1 cm)	4" (10.2 cm)

Some patterns may have little or no wearing ease at all. Halter-neck, extremely cut-away armholes, and strapless bodices must fit very closely to the body. If your bust or hips don't match the standard body measurements for your pattern size, you will probably need to adjust the pattern to maintain the original amount of ease.

DESIGN EASE

The extra fullness added to a garment by the designer, over and above the wearing ease, to create a wide variety of silhouettes is called the design or fashion ease. The different silhouettes are described in the pattern descriptions as close-fitting, fitted, semi-fitted, loose-fitting and very loose-fitting.

A chart outlining the Misses' Ease Allowance, including both wearing and design ease, can be found on page 76. For dresses, blouses, shirts, tops, vests, jackets and coats, each silhouette describes the fit across the bust. For skirts, culottes and pants, each term describes the fit through the hips.

TODAY'S FIT Patterns

To meet the changing proportions of the American woman, a new pattern category was developed in 1999 at Vogue Patterns, called *Today's Fit*. Spearheaded by Sandra Betzina, syndicated sewing columnist and host of the cable TV show, "Sew Perfect," in conjunction with Reg Fairchild, Design Director of Vogue Patterns, a new pattern sizing program was established.

It was Betzina's belief that many people shy away from sewing because of fitting problems rather than sewing problems. Using data gathered from a study conducted at the University of Arizona in 1991 by Ellen Goldsberry and Naomi Reich, "ten" new sizes were created. The survey showed that the measurements taken from 7000 women in 38 states differed greatly from the current standards being used by the ready-to-wear and pattern industry.

Given letter designations, rather than a number reference, the Today's Fit pattern sizes can't be confused with standard pattern or ready-to-wear sizes. Rather than assuming you know your size, it is critical that you measure yourself and compare your measurements before selecting you "letter" size.

TODAY'S FIT SIZING BY SANDRA BETZINA

	A	B	C	D	E	F	G	H	I	J
bust	32"/81cm	34"/86.5cm	36"/91.5cm	38"/96.5cm	40½"/103cm	43"/109cm	46"/117cm	49"/124.5cm	52"/132cm	55"/140cm
waist	26½"/67cm	28½"/72cm	30½"/77.5cm	32½"/82.5cm	35"/89cm	37½"/95cm	41½"/105cm	44½"/113cm	47½"/121cm	50½"/128cm
hips	34½"/87.5cm	36½"/92.5cm	38½"/98cm	40½"/103cm	42½"/108cm	45"/116cm	48"/122cm	51"/130cm	54"/137cm	57"/145cm
back waist length	15¾"/40cm	16"/40.5cm	16¼"/41cm	16½"/42cm	16¾"/42.5cm	17"/43cm	17¼"/44cm	17¼"/44cm	17¼"/44cm	17¼"/44cm
cup size	B	B	B	C	C	C	D	D	D	D
height	5'3"/185cm	5'4½"/190cm	5'5"/192cm	5'6"/193cm	5'6¼"/194cm	5'6½"/194cm	5'6½"/194cm	5'6½"/194cm	5'6½"/194cm	5'6½"/194cm

The goal with this new pattern category is to reduce the number of pattern adjustments. Realizing some adjustments may be needed for a perfect fit, special adjustment lines have been printed on pattern tissue and special sewing instructions with up-to-date fitting tips and time-saving methods for garment construction are included.

Whether this new pattern sizing will revolutionize home sewing is yet to be seen. However, if you love to sew, this may be the first step in eliminating fitting frustration so you can concentrate on what you like to do best—sew!

Color

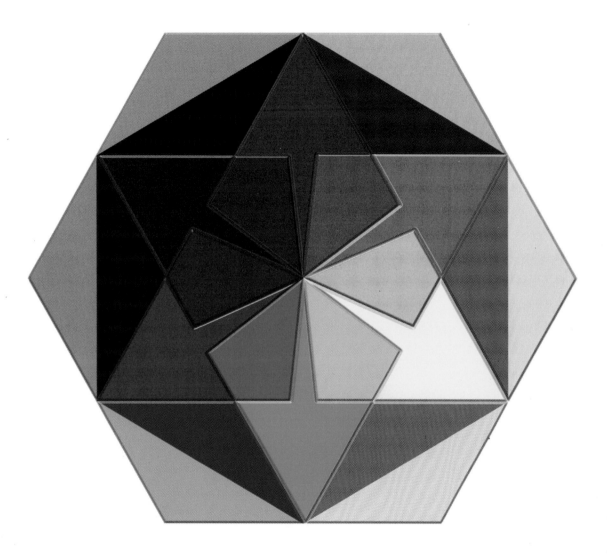

1-Primaries The three basic colors of red, yellow and blue that are combined to create other colors.

2-Secondaries Colors created by mixing equal parts of each primary color, e.g. red and yellow combine to make orange.

3-Tertiaries Color combinations created by mixing primary and secondary colors, e.g. yellow-orange or blue-green.

4-Tints White is added to create a lighter, pastel value of a color. Pink is a tint of red; lavender is a tint of purple.

5-Shades Black is added to create a darker value of a color. Navy is a shade of blue.

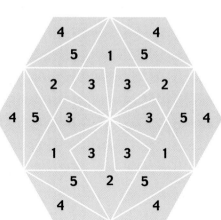

Dramatic Black and White

Black and white are grand, strong colors all on their own. Dramatic showstoppers, they create an impact every time you wear this clean combination, or let them stand proudly on their own. Designers use bold black and white to make a straightforward impression that is both sophisticated and contemporary. Whether you choose elegant velvets and satins, or crisp gabardines and suitings, mixing black and white always makes a statement.

Illuminating Brights

Wearing vivid, exciting colors adds panache, and a true sense of adventure to your wardrobe! Clear reds, yellows and blues, and their secondary combinations, remind us of exotic flowers, tropical birds and precious stones. Add show-stopping red, royal purple, electric blue or bright yellow to black for a dramatic mix. Follow the designers' lead in finding new combinations to brighten up your day!

Serene Pastels

Elegant pastel colors evoke images of romantic idylls, soft music and gentle breezes. Any color lightened with white becomes softer and more feminine. Wear a soft pastel to create the sense of a relaxed lifestyle, or to present a delicate, innocent appearance. Pastels in your wardrobe are like a breath of fresh air.

Refined Neutrals

Grey and beige are the neutral colors in the palette. Subtle and refined, neutrals provide a solid base to build upon. Add shades and tints as well as fine pastels to create a sophisticated yet understated element in your wardrobe. Add an exciting accent, such as a brightly colored scarf. Or, dress in all neutral tones for a refined look in today's hectic world.

Pattern Particulars
Envelope Front: Fashion

The pattern envelope presents the total fashion concept originally created by the designer. Through artwork and sometimes photography, the flair of the design as well as the construction details of the garments are shown. The pattern may be shown in different views to give you a wider selection of styles. The fabrics are carefully selected for illustration to show the types of fabric, suitable for different seasons, that are recommended for this particular pattern. Even the accessories are chosen to complement the design and to show the fashion concept.

Envelope Back: Information

The envelope front was instrumental in your pattern selection. Now use the envelope back to your advantage. All envelopes contain the complete information you will need to make the proper selection of fabric and notions.

1 **Style Number, Size, and Price:** Buying information is found on the envelope back.

2 **Descriptive Caption:** Sizing category, type of garment, and a detailed explanation describing the silhouette, pertinent details not visible in the sketch, and any additional instructions included in the pattern are stated.

3 **Body Measurements:** Patterns are computed for these measurements. Included in the pattern tissue are wearing ease and style ease as dictated by the design.

4 **Notions:** All required and optional notions with recommended sizes for your garment are listed here. They were chosen in the correct proportion to complement the garment design as featured.

5 **Fabrics:** Suggestions listed in this area are well-known fabric types suitable for the design to give you a wide choice.
Fabric Design Suitability: This important information tells if the pattern is not suitable for stripes, plaids, or diagonal fabrics. When these fabrics are suitable you'll find a line stating "No Allowance Made for Matching Stripes and Plaids" because the additional yardage (metrage) needed varies with the size of the fabric design.

6 **Yardage (Metrage):** Sizes are across the top. Garment type and/or version letter are just above fabric widths, including interfacing, lining, underlining, and trims needed for each version. Fabric widths have nap indications alongside them.
***/**:** This key indicates whether the yardage (metrage) shown is for fabrics with or without nap. Fabrics with nap (*) have layouts with all pattern pieces placed in the same direction, as required for directional fabrics. Layouts for fabrics without nap (**) may have pattern pieces placed in any direction; additional yardage (metrage) would be required for directional fabrics.

7 **Width at Lower Edge:** This measurement will tell you the hem circumference of a skirt, dress, shirt, or coat, or the width of the pant leg.
Finished Back Lengths and Side Lengths: These lengths are used as starting points for pattern tissue length adjustments.

8 **Back Views:** These drawings show styling and construction details for all design versions that were not visible in the fashion illustration.

9 **Labels:** This is a reminder to ask at the pattern counter for your *Vogue Paris Original, Vogue American Designer Original, or Vogue Designer Original* label. Call Consumer Services if the retailer does not have them.

10 **Vogue Pattern Service:** The truly international aspect of Vogue Patterns is reflected by its representative offices in several countries.

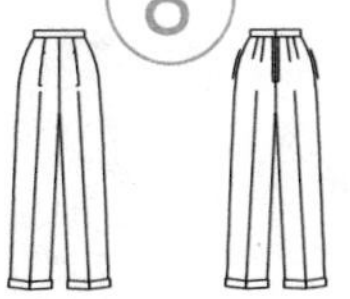

VOGUE PATTERN SERVICE

NEW YORK ● LONDON ● PARIS ● MILAN ● TORONTO ● SYDNEY ● www.voguepatterns.com
161 AVENUE OF THE AMERICAS, NEW YORK 10013 ● © 1998 BUTTERICK COMPANY, INC. ● PRINTED IN U.S.A. ALL RIGHTS RESERVED
THIS PATTERN IS TO BE USED FOR HOME SEWING ONLY● CE PATRON EST CONÇU POUR L'USAGE EXCLUSIF DE LA COUTURIÈRE AU FOYER

SIZE/TAILLE
2188

SIZE/TAILLE	6	8	10	12	14	16	18	20	22	24
Bust	30½	31½	32½	34	36	38	40	42	44	46
Waist	23	24	25	26½	28	30	32	34	37	39
Hip	32½	33½	34½	36	38	40	42	44	46	48
T. de poitrine	78	80	83	87	92	97	102	107	112	117
T. de taille	58	61	64	67	71	76	81	87	94	99
T. de hanches	83	85	88	92	97	102	107	112	117	122

VOGUE PATTERNS

U.S.	$ 22.50
CAN.	$ 29.95
AUST. *	$ 24.00
N.Z. *	$ 25.50
S.A. *	R 34,80
U.K.	ORANGE

* recommended price
* prix suggéré ●

2188

EASY/FACILE

MISSES' JACKET & PANTS Very loose-fitting, self-lined, below hip jacket has raised neckline, extended shoulders, shoulder pads, front bands, inset, pockets with fold-back flaps, side slits, fly button closing and long, two-piece sleeves with slit. Straight-legged, lined, cuffed pants (loose-fitting through hips) have waistband, front tucks, side pockets and back zipper. Purchased top.

NOTIONS: Jacket: ½" (13mm) Covered Raglan Shoulder Pads of Vogue #8817 and Six ⅞" (22mm) Buttons. **Pants:** 7" (18cm) Zipper, One Pkg. of 1¼" (3.2cm) Waistband Interfacing and One Hook and Eye Closure.

FABRICS: Lt.wt. Melton, Lt.wt. Wool Flannel and Wool Crepe. Unsuitable for obvious diagonals. Allow extra fabric to match plaids or stripes. Use nap yardages/layouts for pile, shaded or one-way design fabrics. *with nap. **without nap.

VESTE & PANTALON (Jeune femme) Veste au-dessous des hanches, ample et doublée même tissu, fendue aux côtés, avec boutonnage sur bandes partiellement dissimulé sous patte, incrustation, encolure montante, carrure élargie, épaulettes et manches longues 2-pièces fendues aux bords inférieurs; poches plaquées formant rabats. Pantalon doublé ample aux hanches, à jambes droites à revers, zippé dos, avec ceinture, plis-pinces devant et poches aux côtés. Haut non compris.

MERCERIE: Veste: Epaulettes recouvertes de 13mm (raglan), ou faites avec le patron Vogue 8817 - 6 boutons (22mm). **Pantalon:** Zip (18cm) - 1 paquet d'entoilage-ceinture (3.2cm) - 1 agrafe plate.

TISSUS: Drap ou flanelle de laine fins - Crêpe de laine. Grandes diagonales ne conviennent pas. Compte non tenu des raccords de rayures/carreaux. *avec sens. **sans sens.

FRONT
DEVANT

FRONT
DEVANT

SIZE	(6	8	10)	(12	14	16)	(18	20	22)
Fabric widths given in inches.									
JACKET									
45"/**	4½	4½	4⅝	5	5⅛	5¼	5½	5½	5⅝
60"/**	3⅜	3½	3½	3⅝	3⅝	4	4	4⅜	4⅜
PANTS									
45"/**	2½	2⅝	2⅝	2⅝	2⅝	2⅝	2⅝	2⅝	2⅝
60"/**	1¾	1¾	1¾	1¾	2¼	2¼	2¼	2¼	2¾
LINING (Pants)									
45	2⅛	2⅛	2⅜	2⅜	2⅜	2⅜	2⅜	2⅜	2⅜
WIDTHS Lower edge									
Jacket	40	41	42	43	45	47	49	51	53
Pants	18	18	19	19	20	20	21	21	22
LENGTHS Finished back from base of your neck									
Jacket	28¼	28½	28¾	29	29¼	29½	29¾	30	30¼
Finished side from waist									
Pants	40½	40½	40½	40½	40½	40½	40½	40½	40½

TAILLE	(6	8	10)	(12	14	16)	(18	20	22)
Largeurs des tissus données en centimètres.									
VESTE									
115 */**	4.2	4.2	4.3	4.6	4.7	4.8	5.1	5.1	5.2
150 */**	3.1	3.2	3.2	3.4	3.4	3.7	3.7	4.0	4.0
PANTALON									
115 */**	2.3	2.4	2.4	2.4	2.4	2.4	2.4	2.4	2.4
150 */**	1.6	1.6	1.6	1.6	2.1	2.1	2.1	2.1	2.2
DOUBLURE (pantalon)									
115	2.0	2.0	2.2	2.2	2.2	2.2	2.2	2.2	2.2
LARGEURS à l'ourlet									
Veste	102	104	107	109	115	120	125	130	135
Pantalon	46	46	48	48	51	51	54	54	56
LONGUEURS dos, votre nuque à l'ourlet									
Veste	71.5	72	73	73.5	74	75	75.5	76	77
côté, taille à ourlet,									
Pantalon	103	103	103	103	103	103	103	103	103

ASK FOR THIS LABEL
AT THE PATTERN COUNTER

DEMANDEZ CE RUBAN
GRIFFE AU COMPTOIR

Vogue
American
Designer
Original

Pattern Pieces: Blueprints

Pattern pieces are like blueprints. The master plans of any dressmaking project, they guide you by including all the construction symbols needed to make your sewing easier and more accurate. Every symbol has been printed on your pattern for a very specific and necessary purpose. Get acquainted with them; learn to recognize the markings on each piece and to understand their uses. Then all you will have to do is follow them faithfully.

1 Grainline: This heavy solid line with arrows at either end indicates the direction of the grain. Most often it runs parallel to the fabric selvage, along the lengthwise grain. When the pattern is illustrated in border prints, scallop-edged laces, etc., the tissue will state, "place on lengthwise or crosswise grain."

2 Cutting Line: Multiple cutting lines are indicated on Multi-Size patterns. The solid outer line is the largest size; broken inner lines are cutting lines for the smaller sizes. A "cut off" line for a style variation may also be found.

3 Adjustment Line: Double lines are printed to indicate areas where lengthening or shortening must be done before cutting, if necessary.

4 Center Front or Center Back Lines: These solid lines indicate where garment is to fall at the center of the body.

5 Fold Line: This solid line marks where the garment is to be folded during its construction.

Roll Line: A solid line shows where the pattern piece is to be softly creased to make a soft, rolling fold.

6 Buttons and Buttonholes: These symbols give you the length of the buttonhole, size of button, and precise location for each.

7 ⊕ This symbol indicates the Bust Point, Waistline and Hipline measurements.

Note: All seam allowances are ⅝" (15mm) and included on the pattern piece. However, a separate seamline is not usually indicated on multi-size patterns.

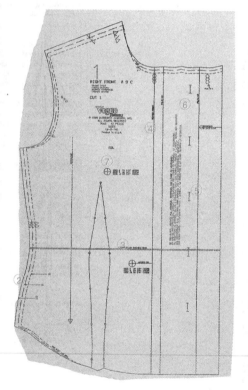

8 *Place-on-Fold Bracket*: Brackets shown on the center front or center back line indicate that a pattern piece is to be placed on the fold of the fabric before cutting.

9 *Notches:* Used for accurate joining of seams, notches are numbered in the order in which seamlines are matched.

10 *Symbols* oO△◊ ⊡ These symbols are printed on the tissue pattern for matching seams and construction details such as pocket placement.

11 *Dart:* Corresponding symbols that are to be carefully matched are placed on solid lines that meet at a point to comprise the dart marking.

12 *Zipper Placement:* This symbol indicates the placement of zipper on seamline. Pull tab at top and stop at the bottom indicate the exact length of zipper to be used.

13 *Hemline:* This line states the depth of the hem for optimum drape of design and weight of fabric.

14 *Pattern Piece and Version:* Name and letter identifies pattern piece. The numbers relate to you the order in which each garment is to be constructed.

Special Cutting Instructions: Any information on the cutting of inter facing, lining, or underlining pertaining to the pattern piece will be found in this enclosed area to highlight its importance. It also states when a piece is to be cut other than twice.

Vogue Pattern Trademark: Your guarantee of fine styling also includes the pattern style number and size. Everything is clearly marked to make identification simple.

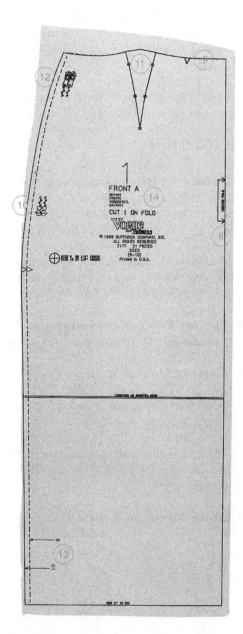

Pattern Cutting Guide

In your Vogue Pattern envelope you will find a Cutting and Sewing Guide along with the actual pattern pieces which, if followed thoroughly and consistently, can answer almost any question you might have about the general planning, pinning, cutting, and construction of your garment.

The information available in the Cutting Guide is everything in capsule form that you will need to know before you begin to actually sew. Spend time studying the correct procedure for preparing your fabric and laying out your pattern. Then no tears will be shed because you've run out of fabric by not placing your pattern pieces correctly or another equally avoidable mistake.

1 Fabric Cutting Layouts: Helpful hints are given for preparing fabric, arranging fabric for cutting layouts, and for cutting and marking the pattern. Instructions are given for cutting with or without nap, fabrics with pile, shading, or one-way designs. Right and wrong sides are shown for pattern pieces and the fabric.

2 Pattern Pieces: Pattern pieces show fronts and backs, grainlines and piece numbers. Recognition of the actual pattern piece is made simpler by noting this section first. The particular pieces needed for each style are listed.

3 Layout Piece Requirements: All pattern pieces needed for each version of the garment and for underlining, interfacing, and lining are listed.

4 Cutting Guide: The garment cutting layouts are divided into style versions and then into sizes and fabric widths. Each layout is also marked as to suitability for nap. Underlining, interfacing, and lining layouts are also given in the same manner. Pattern pieces to be placed with the printed side up are shown without shading, while those that are to be placed printed side down are shaded. Carefully follow the illustrations when you fold your fabric. If any pattern pieces extend beyond the fold, they are to be cut on a single thickness after all the other pieces are cut. Circle the layout you are using for easy reference.

5 Body Measurements: Complete measurements are given for all sizes for Bust, Waist, Hip and Back Waist Length.

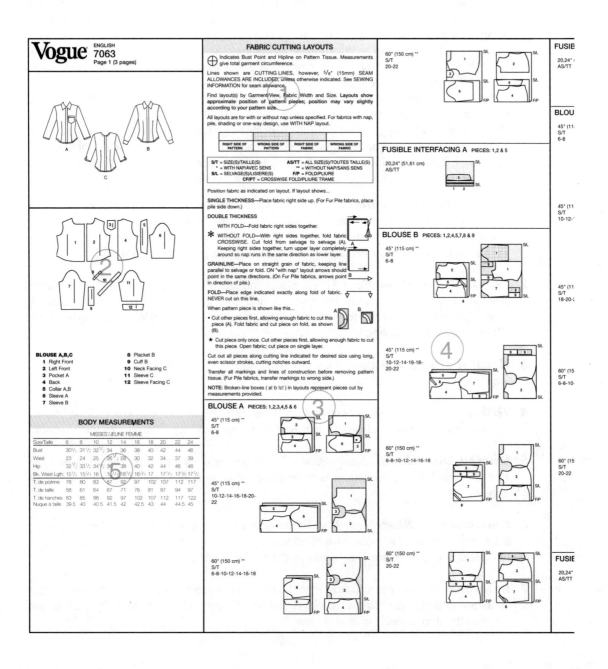

Vogue 7063

ENGLISH
7063
Page 1 (3 pages)

BLOUSE A,B,C
1 Right Front
2 Left Front
3 Pocket A
4 Back
5 Collar A,B
6 Sleeve A
7 Sleeve B
8 Placket B
9 Cuff B
10 Neck Facing C
11 Sleeve C
12 Sleeve Facing C

BODY MEASUREMENTS

MISSES/JEUNE FEMME

Size/Taille	6	8	10	12	14	16	18	20	22	24
Bust	30½	31½	32½	34	36	38	40	42	44	46
Waist	23	24	25	26½	28	30	32	34	37	39
Hip	32½	33½	34½	36	38	40	42	44	46	48
Bk. Waist Lgth.	15½	15¾	16	16¼	16½	16¾	17	17¼	17⅜	17½
T. de poitrine	78	80	83	87	92	97	102	107	112	117
T. de taille	58	61	64	67	71	76	81	87	94	97
T. de hanches	83	85	88	92	97	102	107	112	117	122
Nuque à taille	39.5	40	40.5	41.5	42	42.5	43	44	44.5	45

FABRIC CUTTING LAYOUTS

Indicates Bust Point and Hipline on Pattern Tissue. Measurements give total garment circumference.

Lines shown are CUTTING LINES, however, ⅝" (15mm) SEAM ALLOWANCES ARE INCLUDED, unless otherwise indicated. See SEWING INFORMATION for seam allowance.

Find layout(s) by Garment/View, Fabric Width and Size. Layouts show approximate position of pattern pieces; position may vary slightly according to your pattern size.

All layouts are for with or without nap unless specified. For fabrics with nap, pile, shading or one-way design, use WITH NAP layout.

RIGHT SIDE OF PATTERN	WRONG SIDE OF PATTERN	RIGHT SIDE OF FABRIC	WRONG SIDE OF FABRIC

S/T = SIZE(S)/TAILLE(S)   AS/TT = ALL SIZE(S)/TOUTES TAILLE(S)
* = WITH NAP/AVEC SENS   ** = WITHOUT NAP/SANS SENS
S/L = SELVAGE(S)/LISIERE(S)   F/P = FOLD/PLIURE
CF/PT = CROSSWISE FOLD/PLIURE TRAME

Position fabric as indicated on layout. If layout shows...

SINGLE THICKNESS—Place fabric right side up. (For Fur Pile fabrics, place pile side down.)

DOUBLE THICKNESS

WITH FOLD—Fold fabric right sides together.

* WITHOUT FOLD—With right sides together, fold fabric CROSSWISE. Cut fold from selvage to selvage (A). Keeping right sides together, turn upper layer completely around so nap runs in the same direction as lower layer.

GRAINLINE—Place on straight grain of fabric, keeping line parallel to selvage or fold. ON "with nap" layout arrows should point in the same directions. (On Fur Pile fabrics, arrows point in direction of pile.)

FOLD—Place edge indicated exactly along fold of fabric. NEVER cut on this line.

When pattern piece is shown like this...

• Cut other pieces first, allowing enough fabric to cut this piece (A). Fold fabric and cut piece on fold, as shown (B).

★ Cut piece only once. Cut other pieces first, allowing enough fabric to cut this piece. Open fabric; cut piece on single layer.

Cut out all pieces along cutting line indicated for desired size using long, even scissor strokes, cutting notches outward.

Transfer all markings and lines of construction before removing pattern tissue. (Fur Pile fabrics, transfer markings to wrong side.)

NOTE: Broken-line boxes (a! b !c!) in layouts represent pieces cut by measurements provided.

BLOUSE A PIECES: 1,2,3,4,5 & 6

45" (115 cm) **
S/T
6-8

45" (115 cm) **
S/T
10-12-14-16-18-20-22

60" (150 cm) **
S/T
6-8-10-12-14-16-18

60" (150 cm) **
S/T
20-22

FUSIBLE INTERFACING A PIECES: 1,2 & 5

20,24" (51,61 cm)
AS/TT

BLOUSE B PIECES: 1,2,4,5,7,8 & 9

45" (115 cm) **
S/T
6-8

45" (115 cm) **
S/T
18-20-2

45" (115 cm) **
S/T
10-12-14-16-18-20-22

60" (150 cm) **
S/T
6-8-10-12-14-16-18

60" (150 cm) **
S/T
20-22

FUSIB
20,24"
AS/TT

FUSIB
20,24"
AS/TT

BLOU
45" (11
S/T
6-8

45" (11
S/T
10-12-

45" (11
S/T
18-20-

60" (15
S/T
6-8-10-

60" (15
S/T
20-22

Pattern Sewing Guide

On the reverse side of the Cutting Guide you will find a step-by-step Sewing Guide arranged by garment versions with numbered and outlined instructions for fast reading and comprehension. The large and precise technical sketches that accompany the written instructions are easy to understand and as informative as having a sample of your garment in front of you. At the top of the sheet is the illustration key and suggestions on stitching, trimming, and pressing, which can serve as excellent reminders.

A glossary of sewing terms are listed. Definitions of each term help you understand the sewing technique used in the construction.

The Cutting and Sewing guides are indispensable ingredients in achieving the perfect fit and finish to your Vogue pattern. Whether you're a nervous beginner or a highly skilled seamstress, following the instructions diligently to the completion of your garment can only help to make the most professional looking garment possible.

1 Pattern Identification: The pattern number is given along with the page number. To give you the benefit of couture construction in designer patterns and comprehensive directions for multiversion styles, you may find several instruction sheets in the envelope. Pages are numbered consecutively as well, stating the amount you will find.

2 Fabric Illustration Key: This explains the use of shading and texture in technical sketches: underlining is shown by crosshatching, interfacing by dots, lining with shading lines, right side of fabric by tone. *We follow the same distinctions throughout the illustrations in this book.*

3 Helpful Hints: Important points to remember on stitching, trimming, and pressing are shown and explained for your benefit.

4 Titles: The construction procedures for different parts of the garment and the individual versions are presented separately. A title in large bold type introduces each section.

5 Sewing Directions: Construction of each garment section is explained individually as it is needed. Every procedure is outlined and numbered consecutively for quick reference.

6 Construction Sketches: Many sewing techniques are easier to understand when they are shown in comprehensive illustrations. They are meant to be used with the written instructions, since some procedures cannot be sketched.

7 Enlarged View: You will find that details of important and/or difficult construction areas are enlarged and circled to clarify the sewing procedure involved. Be sure to pay special attention to each enlarged view.

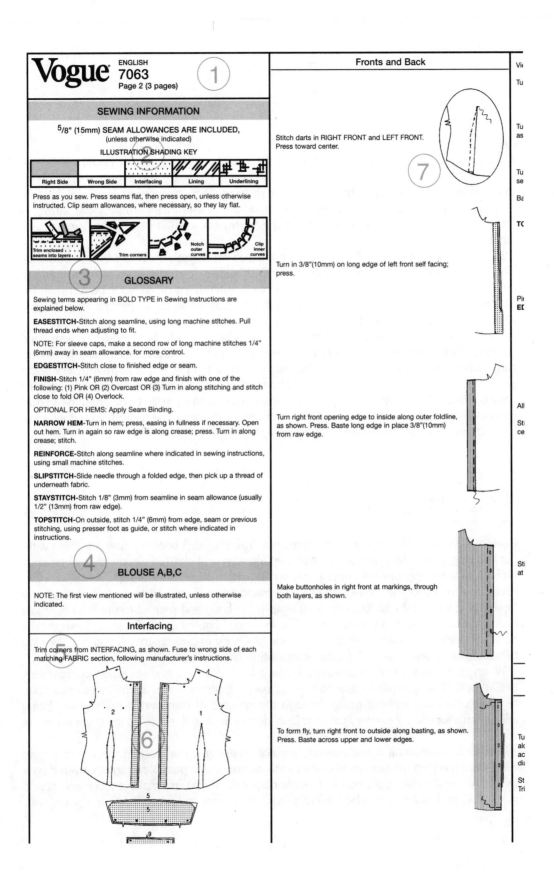

SEWING INFORMATION

⁵/₈" (15mm) SEAM ALLOWANCES ARE INCLUDED,
(unless otherwise indicated)

ILLUSTRATION SHADING KEY

Right Side	Wrong Side	Interfacing	Lining	Underlining

Press as you sew. Press seams flat, then press open, unless otherwise instructed. Clip seam allowances, where necessary, so they lay flat.

Trim enclosed seams into layers.

Trim corners

Notch outer curves

Clip inner curves

③

GLOSSARY

Sewing terms appearing in BOLD TYPE in Sewing Instructions are explained below.

EASESTITCH-Stitch along seamline, using long machine stitches. Pull thread ends when adjusting to fit.

NOTE: For sleeve caps, make a second row of long machine stitches 1/4" (6mm) away in seam allowance. for more control.

EDGESTITCH-Stitch close to finished edge or seam.

FINISH-Stitch 1/4" (6mm) from raw edge and finish with one of the following: (1) Pink OR (2) Overcast OR (3) Turn in along stitching and stitch close to fold OR (4) Overlock.

OPTIONAL FOR HEMS: Apply Seam Binding.

NARROW HEM-Turn in hem; press, easing in fullness if necessary. Open out hem. Turn in again so raw edge is along crease; press. Turn in along crease; stitch.

REINFORCE-Stitch along seamline where indicated in sewing instructions, using small machine stitches.

SLIPSTITCH-Slide needle through a folded edge, then pick up a thread of underneath fabric.

STAYSTITCH-Stitch 1/8" (3mm) from seamline in seam allowance (usually 1/2" (13mm) from raw edge).

TOPSTITCH-On outside, stitch 1/4" (6mm) from edge, seam or previous stitching, using presser foot as guide, or stitch where indicated in instructions.

④

BLOUSE A,B,C

NOTE: The first view mentioned will be illustrated, unless otherwise indicated.

Interfacing

⑤

Trim corners from INTERFACING, as shown. Fuse to wrong side of each matching FABRIC section, following manufacturer's instructions.

⑥

Fronts and Back

Stitch darts in RIGHT FRONT and LEFT FRONT. Press toward center.

⑦

Turn in 3/8"(10mm) on long edge of left front self facing; press.

Turn right front opening edge to inside along outer foldline, as shown. Press. Baste long edge in place 3/8"(10mm) from raw edge.

Make buttonholes in right front at markings, through both layers, as shown.

To form fly, turn right front to outside along basting, as shown. Press. Baste across upper and lower edges.

Achieving
Perfect Fit

Achieving a perfect fit depends on more than just buying the correct pattern size. The standard body measurements compiled by the pattern industry are simply average body measurements of women within a particular size range. Since individuals within that size may vary in any number of ways from the standard measurements, they serve simply as starting points from which you must make adjustments and alterations to fit your own dimensions.

All Vogue patterns, regardless of style, are based on the same standard measurements. Thus, once you have determined how your body differs from the basic pattern figure in your size, you can make the same adjustments or alterations on all your patterns. If, for example, you need to take in ½" (13 mm) on the shoulder seams of a basic pattern, you will also take in ½" (13 mm) on the shoulder seams of a blouse, a dress, a suit, or a coat.

The first step for achieving a perfect fit is to take complete body measurements and compare them with the actual pattern measurements. Most differences in length and circumference can be made directly on the pattern, using flat pattern adjustments. For some people, it may be necessary to make additional changes in a pattern to allow for specific body contours. These alterations must first be worked out in a muslin or gingham basic shell because they affect a specific dimension of the body. All adjustments and alterations must be made in your pattern *before* you cut out your fabric.

Accurate Measurements

Custom fit begins with accurate measurements. You shouldn't begin to alter a pattern without knowing your exact contours, so make up a convenient chart of all your measurements. Be sure to wear appropriate undergarments and shoes when measuring.

Whether you take the measurements or a friend takes them—be honest; make sure the tape is held snug and taut (but not tight) against the body and parallel to the floor for most circumference or width measurements. The illustrated figures and the text on the opposite page will guide you in taking accurate, meaningful body measurements. If you are planning to make pants, see page 111 for the measurements to take.

When your chart is completed, keep it ready for adjustment and alteration comparisons at all times. Then you will be able to transfer your adjustments and alterations to most patterns automatically without going through the process of discovering the specific fitting adjustments for each and every pattern. Don't forget to note the date on the chart for future use.

To be sure that small figure changes are not creeping up on you unnoticed, take your bust, waist, and hip measurements often to be aware of any possible changes. Even if your weight remains stable, your measurements may shift. If you are making too many adjustments and alterations, it may be preferable to change sizes and possibly figure types as well.

TAKE COMPLETE MEASUREMENTS

Select the same undergarments you normally wear, a leotard or a full slip, panty hose and comfortable shoes with the heel height you usually wear. Tie a narrow piece of elastic snugly around your waist. Move and bend until the elastic fits on your natural waistline.

Bust: Measure around the fullest part of the bust with the tape straight across the back (1).

Chest: Measure around the body above the fullest part of the bust (2).

Waist: Measure around body over the elastic (3).

Hip: Measure around the fullest part of the hip approximately 7"-9" (18 cm-23 cm) below the waist (4). If the circumference of your thighs is larger than the circumference of your hips, record the thigh measurement for the hip measurement.

Bicep: Measure around the upper arm approximately 1" (2.5 cm) below your armpit (5).

Hip Length: Measure the distance from the waist to the full hip at side (6).

Arm Length: With the arm slightly bent, measure from the shoulder to the elbow (7) and from the elbow to the wrist bone (8).

Front Length: On the front, measure from the base of the neck, around the neck to the bust point (9) and from the bust point to the center front waistline (10).

Back Length: Measure from the back of the neck to back bustline (11) and from the bustline to the waist (12).

Skirt Length: Measure from the center front waistline to desired point on your leg for the length (13). Refer to the back of the pattern envelope for a description of the length.

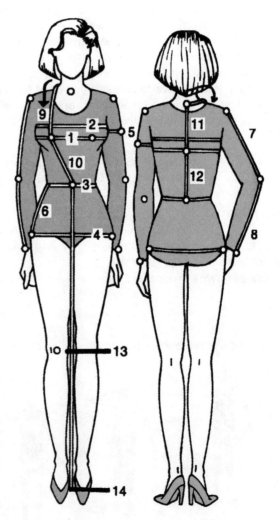

Once you have selected the correct pattern size for your figure, it is now important to evaluate how that pattern is **supposed** to fit and if it will fit that way on you. Then you can determine whether it is necessary to adjust the pattern before you cut out the fabric or start to sew.

To make it much easier for you to determine the ease allowed on the particular pattern you have chosen we have done the measuring for you, at the bustline and the hipline. Each pattern has the bust point and hipline marked with a target symbol ⊕ on the main front pattern piece showing you exactly where the shaping and fullness for the bust and hip are, so there's no confusion about where to make any necessary adjustments. The total garment measurement—the measurement of the finished garment around the bust or the hips if sewn as the pattern comes out of the envelope without any adjustments—is also given for you. Any details such as seam allowances, darts, pleats or tucks are not included in this measurement.

The total amount of ease will vary from one pattern to the next. It's important to read the full description on the envelope back to understand the designer's intent for the fit.

To evaluate how much ease the garment will have on your figure, subtract your bust and hip measurements from the total garment measurements. This tells you how much ease the garment will have when you wear it. Compare with the amount of ease the pattern is supposed to have to decide if you need to make some pattern adjustments.

Use the ease allowance chart and drawings below to better understand the descriptions of fit that appear on the catalog page and the back of the pattern envelope.

	DRESSES, BLOUSES, SHIRTS, TOPS, VESTS	JACKETS (Lined or Unlined)	COATS (Lined or Unlined)	SKIRTS
CLOSE-FITTING	0-2⅞" (0-7.3cm)	Not Applicable	Not Applicable	0-1⅞" (0-4.8cm)
FITTED	3"-4" (7.5-10cm)	3¾"-4 ¼" (9.5-10.7cm)	5¼"-6¾" (13.3-17cm)	2"-3" (5-7.5cm)
SEMI-FITTED	4⅛"-5" (10.4-12.5cm)	4⅜"-5¾" (11.1-14.5cm)	6⅞"-8" (17.4-20.5cm)	3⅛"-4" (7.9-10cm)
LOOSE-FITTING	5⅛"-8" (13-20.5cm)	5⅞"-10" (14.8-25.5cm)	8⅛"-12" (20.7-30.5cm)	4⅛"-6" (10.4-15cm)
VERY LOOSE-FITTING	Over 8" (Over 20.5cm)	Over 10" (Over 25.5cm)	Over 12" (Over 30.5cm)	Over 6" (Over 15cm)

*Ease allowances given are not applicable to garments designed for stretchable knit fabrics.

The following silhouettes show the body in relation to the five fit descriptions for dresses in the above chart.

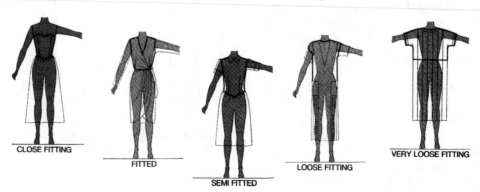

CLOSE FITTING FITTED SEMI FITTED LOOSE FITTING VERY LOOSE FITTING

The bodice is crucial to a good fit. Compare your bust, waist, and back waist length measurements to those listed on the pattern envelope for your size. If the measurements differ, you must make the proper adjustments. The shoulder seam of the pattern and your shoulder length should correspond. Also compare neck circumference. To locate the bust point, find the target symbol on the main front pattern piece. Compare your personal measurements with the pattern. Bust darts should point directly toward the bust point and end ½" to 1" (13 mm to 25 mm) from the point.

For sleeves it is important to determine both the proper sleeve length, including any cuffs, as well as the correct elbow dart placement. It may be necessary to alter the sleeve length either above or below the elbow or in both locations. Sleeve circumference should allow for wearing ease of about 2" (5 cm), with a greater allowance for heavier arms than for thin ones.

For skirts, both the waist and hip measurements can be compared with the measurements on the envelope. The hipline is established on a pattern at 9" (23 cm) below the waistline for Misses' and Women's sizes and at 7" (18 cm) below the waistline for Misses' Petites. It is essential for a comfortable and attractive fit that you have the right hip fit in the exact spot. Find the target symbol for the hipline and compare the measurement to your measurements.

Usually the garment's finished length is given on the pattern envelope or you can measure the actual pattern pieces along the center back. Compare it with your personal skirt length measurement.

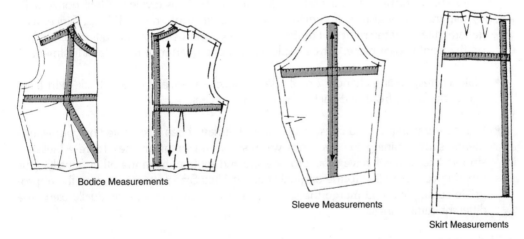

Bodice Measurements

Sleeve Measurements

Skirt Measurements

On the following pages are explained all the specific procedures you will need for personal fitting. The changes you will make are divided into two categories. **Adjustments** are minor changes that are made "in the flat" on your pattern tissue before you cut your muslin. **Alterations** are major changes that are made on the muslin fitting shell to ensure they will relate to your body contours.

All the changes are clearly illustrated for you. *Only the front pattern pieces are shown for adjustments, since equal changes are made for the front and back pattern pieces. Alterations, which are more localized, may not require changes on both front and back pieces, and thus only the affected pieces are shown.* So that you may relate your adjustments and alterations to everything you sew, we will also show you how to make them on other basic shapes (princess lines, raglan sleeves, etc.) when applicable.

Flat Pattern Adjustments

Let us help take the mystery out of pattern adjustments. You need not be reluctant to try an original idea to get a better fit as long as you remember this principle: since all patterns and fabric are flat, any change you make must be done in such a manner that the pattern tissue will also remain flat after it is adjusted.

Flat basic pattern pieces are essential tools of the pattern and clothing industries for maintaining consistency in sizing. Use your adjusted fitting patterns the same way to achieve a personalized and perfect fit.

When making the flat pattern adjustments on the following pages, follow these rules:

- Keep grainlines, center front, and center back foldlines straight.

- Make adjustments with discretion to carefully preserve style lines of design.

- Maintain wearing ease built into pattern.

- Use adjustment lines provided for lengthening and shortening. Make sure you have made your length adjustments the same amount along the entire adjustment line.

- When making circumference adjustments, keep in mind that each major pattern piece represents a quarter of your body. Think of your body as divided in half horizontally by the waistline and in half vertically by the center front and back lines. Since, as a general rule, only the right half of the pattern is given, the amount of adjustment taken on the front bodice piece, for example, is only one quarter of the total adjustment.

- Make corresponding changes on all related pieces—bodice front and back, skirt front and back, facing front and back, lining front and back, etc.

- When re-drawing printed construction lines that have been interrupted by your adjustments, simply joining the two ends will result in an irregular line. To re-establish a smooth line, you will have to add to one line and subtract from the other equally, thus tapering your new line to the original line. On Multi-Size patterns, choose the appropriate cutting line and merge the sizes by drawing new lines that gradually blend the different cutting lines.

The cutting line and dart corrections of the pattern pieces on the following pages are indicated by **bold lines.** Correct seamlines accordingly.

Remember that only the front pattern pieces will be shown for all flat pattern adjustments. Be sure to make the comparable adjustments on the back pattern piece.

Length Adjustments

While making pattern length adjustments for your figure, you may find yourself an interesting sizing statistic. You may be long-waisted with a shorter than average hipline, or your arm may be longer from shoulder to elbow and average from elbow to wrist; thus you must adjust the pattern lengths to your personal needs. Shortening or lengthening your pattern pieces is an easy adjustment to make and is crucial to correcting many fitting problems.

SHORTENING PATTERN PIECES: There are areas indicated on every Vogue pattern piece where shortening may be made to adjust the pattern lengths to your personal needs. Two adjustment lines, placed close together, are shown within the body area, and a note is placed at the lower edges of skirts. The hipline may also need to be raised to the correct position. Remember to make equal changes on front and back pieces.

To **shorten the bodice and sleeves,** crease the pattern between the adjustment lines within the body area and make a fold half the amount needed to be shortened. Secure the change with transparent tape.

To **raise the skirt hipline,** crease just above the hipline of the pattern. Make a fold half the amount needed to bring the hipline into position. Secure the change with tape.

To **further shorten the skirt at the lower edge,** simply cut away excess pattern tissue, following the shape of the pattern.

Correct the seamlines, dart lines, and cutting lines as shown on the pattern pieces.

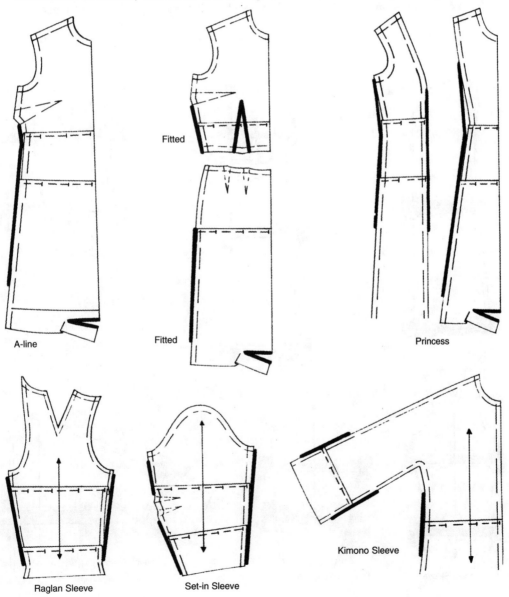

A-line

Fitted

Fitted

Princess

Raglan Sleeve

Set-in Sleeve

Kimono Sleeve

LENGTHENING PATTERN PIECES: On every Vogue pattern piece there are areas indicated where lengthening may be made to adjust the pattern to your personal needs. Within the body area are shown two adjustment lines, placed close together, and a note is placed at the lower edge of skirts. The hipline may also need to be lowered to the correct position.

To *lengthen the bodice and sleeves,* cut the pattern along adjustment lines within the body area. Tape tissue paper to the cut edges of one section. Spread the cut pattern edges apart the required amount and secure the changes with tape.

To *lower the skirt hipline,* cut the pattern along the hipline. Place tissue paper underneath; lower the hipline into the correct position and secure the other edge with tape.

To *further lengthen the skirt at the lower edge,* extend the pattern with tissue paper and fasten with tape. Extend the seamlines and cutting lines at the sides, and draw the cutting line across lower edge, retaining the original curve.

Correct all necessary seamlines, dart lines, and cutting lines on the pattern pieces.

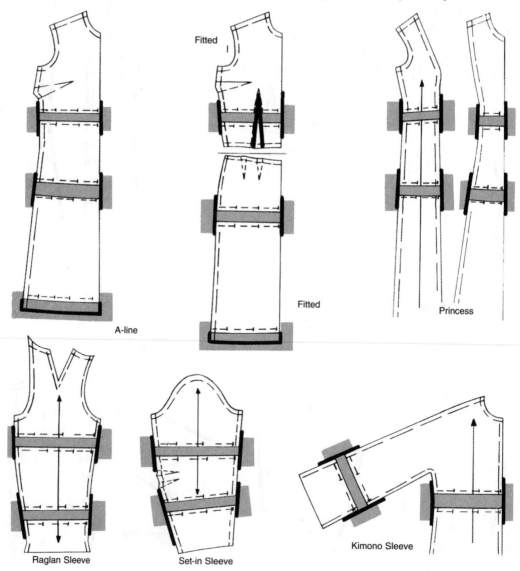

A-line

Fitted

Fitted

Princess

Raglan Sleeve

Set-in Sleeve

Kimono Sleeve

80

Circumference Adjustments

Changing the pattern to coincide with your body contours allows you to make the fitting pattern personally yours. You will be amazed how much better your garment will actually flatter your figure when your own curves are really built into the pattern before you ever cut your fabric. Be sure to make equal adjustments on front and back pieces.

REDUCING WAIST AND HIPS: For adjustments *less than 1" (25 mm),* draw in new seamlines and cutting lines at the sides. First mark ¼ of the amount to be reduced at the waist and hipline and pin the bust dart along the dart lines. Connect markings and draw new seamlines and cutting lines, tapering from waist to bustline. Remove pins and press tissue.

For adjustments *larger than 1" (25 mm)* in the fitted style with a waistline seam, it will be necessary to slash the pattern as indicated and lap the edge ¼ of the amount required. Clip the seam allowance where necessary for the pattern to lie flat.

For a princess style, adjust each seam, dividing the amount by the number of seams.

A-line styles should not be reduced more than 1"(25 mm) or the style lines may become distorted.

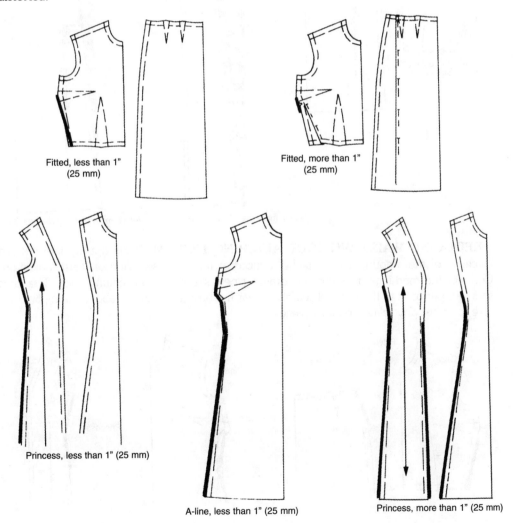

Fitted, less than 1" (25 mm)

Fitted, more than 1" (25 mm)

Princess, less than 1" (25 mm)

A-line, less than 1" (25 mm)

Princess, more than 1" (25 mm)

ENLARGING WAIST AND HIPS: For adjustments of *less than 1" (25 mm)* (not shown), mark ¼ the amount needed to be enlarged at the waist and hipline and pin bust darts together along the seamline. Connect the markings by drawing new cutting lines and seamlines, tapering above the waist to the bustline.

Correct all necessary seamlines, dart lines, and cutting lines on pattern pieces.

For adjustments *larger than 1" (25 mm),* slash the pattern as indicated. Place tissue paper underneath. Spread slashed pattern edges ¼ of the amount needed at the waist and hipline. Secure with tape. For a fitted style, make sure you have slashed enough to allow the pattern to lie flat. A small pleat will form in the seam allowance or hem area. For princess styles, divide the amount needed by the number of seams and adjust each seam as indicated.

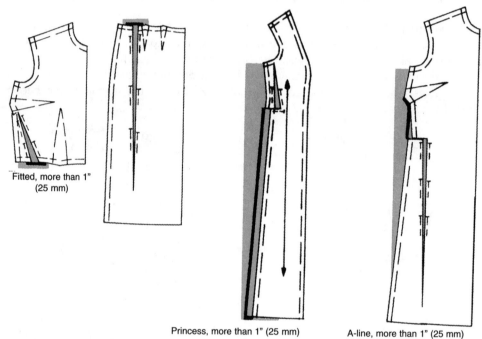

Fitted, more than 1"
(25 mm)

Princess, more than 1" (25 mm)   A-line, more than 1" (25 mm)

REDUCING WAIST WITHOUT ALTERING HIPS: Mark the appropriate pattern pieces ¼ of the amount needed to be reduced at the waist seamline or waist indication. Connect the markings by accurately drawing new seamlines and cutting lines. The lines should taper back to the original seamline near the bust dart and just above the hipline. Be sure to adjust any related pattern pieces.

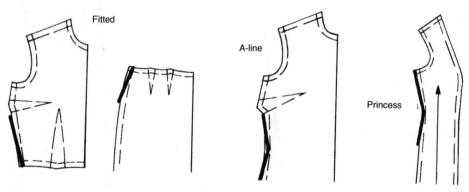

Fitted

A-line

Princess

ENLARGING HIPS: If the adjustment required is *2" (5 cm) or less,* place the tissue paper under the side edges. Mark ¼ of the amount needed at the hipline and hemline. Draw new seamlines and cutting lines, connnecting the marks, and taper to the waist.

For adjustments of *more than 2" (5 cm),* slash the pattern parallel to the grainline or center fold. For skirts, slash from top to bottom. For A-lines, slash to hipline and then cut across hipline to side seam. Over tissue paper, spread each piece ¼ of the amount needed at hipline and secure with tape. Taper seamline and cutting line to bust dart or bust area. For princess styles, be sure to divide the amount needed by the number of seams and adjust each seam as indicated.

Take out excess circumference at the waist by adding darts near the side seam or reducing the pattern along the side edges, retaining hip adjustment.

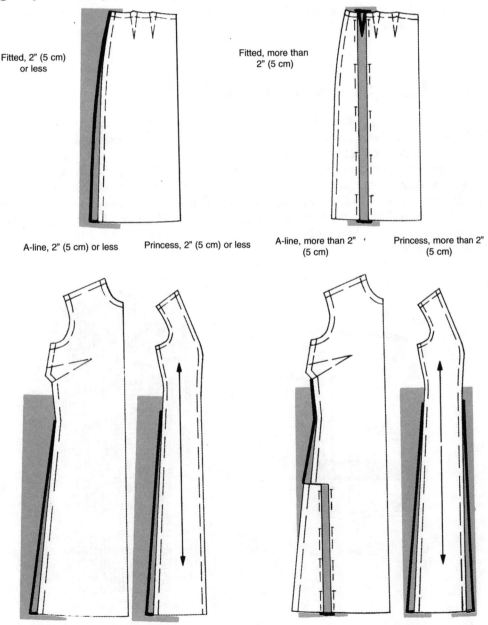

Fitted, 2" (5 cm) or less

Fitted, more than 2" (5 cm)

A-line, 2" (5 cm) or less   Princess, 2" (5 cm) or less   A-line, more than 2" (5 cm)   Princess, more than 2" (5 cm)

Vogue's Personal Fit Patterns

Vogue's personal fit patterns allow you to experiment successfully while working toward your ultimate goal—a perfect fit. Fit is what separates an average garment from a truly superior one. Exquisite fabric and couture sewing techniques cannot make up for an ill-fitting garment that sags, pulls, and wrinkles.

Probably every seamstress has had the bitter experience of painstakingly constructing a garment only to find her time and effort wasted because her lovely creation doesn't fit. More often, the pleasure of a garment may be blunted by a minor fitting problem—tight hipline or baggy neckline—which keeps it from being as comfortable and attractive as it should be.

Vogue, understanding this frustration, has developed two patterns to help you better understand all your personal fitting needs.

Basic Fitting Dress or Pants Shell

Vogue's Basic Fitting patterns for dresses and pants enable you to understand how your body differs from Vogue's average pattern figure as you fit a basic bodice, sleeves, and skirt or pants shell that you cut from gingham fabric.

Each pattern is designed with extra allowances or "outlets" in common problem areas such as shoulders, waist, hip, abdomen, sleeve cap, and hem. This enables you to make the pattern larger as well as smaller; the stitching lines are normal. The dress pattern includes three bodice front pattern pieces in bra cup sizes B through D. Since commercial patterns come sized only for a B cup, this gives you the opportunity to select the bodice front that will fit you perfectly.

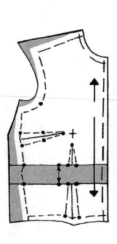

Basic Fitting Shell

Gingham Check Shell

The basic pattern is cut out and constructed preferably in woven gingham check fabric or muslin. When trying on the gingham shell, you can immediately see any problem areas—wherever the gingham checks are not square on the body.

The pattern includes a comprehensive guide sheet that covers many common fitting problems. Drawings are used to indicate the fitting problems and their simple solutions. After the gingham has been fitted to your body, you can follow the instructions for transferring the changes made on the gingham back to the pattern pieces.

To achieve a proper fit, it is extremely important to begin with the correct size pattern. To determine what size to purchase, measure your chest and your full bust, and compare measurements. If the difference is 2 ½" (6.5 cm) or more, select the size of your Vogue Basic Fitting Shell pattern by the chest measurement. If your bust measurement falls between two sizes, select the smaller size pattern.

Once the basic pattern has been customized to fit your figure, you will understand how to fit any pattern to your body. Instructions are given for transferring changes made on the dress or pants basic fitting shell to the fashion patterns included in the pattern or to any Vogue dress, blouse, skirt, vest, or jacket pattern. Thus, if you have to make a bust adjustment on this pattern, you can automatically make the same adjustment on all other Vogue patterns, except perhaps for very loose-fitting styles.

The Basic Fitting Shell patterns are truly educational tools for learning how to obtain a perfect fit as well as a permanent personal reference to be used for pattern adjustments and alterations.

Use Your Basic Pattern

With both Basic Fitting patterns, try on the gingham or muslin shell periodically to see if your measurements have changed at all, and adjust accordingly. When constructing a garment with unusually shaped pattern pieces or complex seaming details that cannot be compared with your basic pattern, you may wish to construct that portion of the garment in muslin before cutting out the fashion fabric. Machine baste this muslin together and fit it carefully to your figure, restitching as necessary. When satisfied with the fit, rip the muslin apart and transfer the changes to your pattern.

To preserve your basic pattern, press an iron-on pattern saver or interfacing to the back of the tissue pattern. You will have an easy, handy, and permanent record for achieving perfection each and every time you sew.

Personal Fitting Alterations

The alterations in this section pinpoint areas where you may need further changes to accommodate your body contour or bone structure. Make the necessary alterations as directed, being careful not to over-fit; too precise a fit will tend to accent a figure fault.

Transfer the changes to your pattern pieces, using the same techniques as for flat pattern adjustments. If you find it too difficult to translate any adjustments, take your muslin fitting shell apart to use as a guide. When you have recorded all necessary alterations, they can be transferred to every pattern you use. If ever in doubt about the accuracy of a pattern adjustment, test it by first constructing the section in muslin.

Necklines

The neckline of the muslin fitting shell (called a jewel neckline by our designers) should encircle the body at the base of your neck. All necklines are raised or lowered from this point to give you many variations. For styles other than a jewel neckline, the back pattern piece will have a note stating exactly how much lower or higher it is at the base of neck.

When a neckline pulls, is too large, or does not hug your body in a flattering manner it will need further alteration. Choose one of the following procedures to help you achieve a perfect fitting neckline.

TIGHT NECKLINE: Neckline pulls uncomfortably around neck. To correct this, draw a line on the garment at the correct neckline location. Stitch along this line. Clip to the new seamline at ½" (13 mm) intervals until it is comfortable. Adjust the front and back pattern pieces of the bodice and facing in equal amounts by drawing in new seamlines and cutting lines.

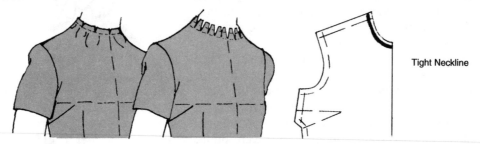

Tight Neckline

LARGE NECKLINE: Neckline is too big and does not reach to the base of neck. To correct, fill in the neckline to the base of the neck with a folded, shaped bias strip of fabric: baste. Adjust the front and back pattern pieces of the bodice and facing in equal amounts by extending the seamlines and cutting lines as indicated by the strip.

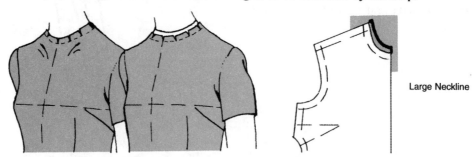

Large Neckline

GAPING NECKLINES: This problem is caused by the wrong bust cup size, too small a pattern, a hollow chest, or a pigeon chest. Even though you bought your pattern by bust measurement, the pattern may not allow enough room across the garment front for your bust cup size or body contour. Therefore, the bodice will not drape smoothly over the body contours, causing gaping and distortion of lower necklines. Cut the bodice in muslin. Try on the bodice to find your problem area. Gaping and pulling can be caused in the same neckline. You may need only one of the alterations listed below or a combination of two. The changes will be the same for square, V-, or U-necklines.

Excess fabric causes the neckline to wrinkle above the bust and to stand away from the body. Pin out the wrinkles, tapering to the armhole seam. Transfer the alteration to the pattern front by lowering the cutting lines and seamlines at the shoulder and neck and by shortening the amount needed at the center front.

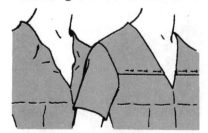

Excess fabric at neckline

Pulling at the armhole distorts the neckline above the bust. Slash from the neckline to the armhole seam. Spread as needed. Insert strips of fabric; baste to the cut edges. Transfer the alteration by slashing the pattern front in the same way. Spread as needed and fasten with tape. Correct the shoulder, armhole, and neckline seams and cutting lines.

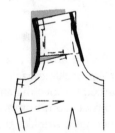

Pulling at the Armhole

DECOLLETE OR LOW NECKLINES: Cut your neck facings in muslin and stitch them together. Stitch along the neck seamline; turn the seam allowance to the inside along the stitching, clipping at ½" (13 mm) intervals; baste. Try on facing and see where it rests on your body. Fill in a very low neckline to desired depth. Transfer the alteration to facing and front pattern pieces before you cut fabric. Correct cutting lines and seamlines.

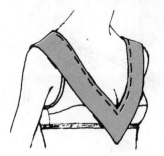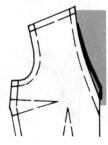

Shoulders

Since your shoulders support the hang of the entire garment, it is essential that they are fitted properly with the fabric smoothly molded over the body. Be sure the shoulder seams rest directly on top of the shoulders and end at the arm hinge and at the base of the neck.

SLOPING SHOULDERS: Wrinkles appear near the bust dart at armhole and across the end of the shoulder in back because the shoulder and armhole seams are not placed at the angle needed for your figure. To correct this, first try shoulder pads. If wrinkles remain, remove the sleeves. Pin out the excess fabric at the shoulders, tapering to the neckline. Lower the armhole seamline and adjust sleeve cap the same amount (see Sleeve Cap Too Deep). Transfer the alteration to the pattern.

For raglan and kimono sleeves, transfer the alteration to the pattern pieces as illustrated.

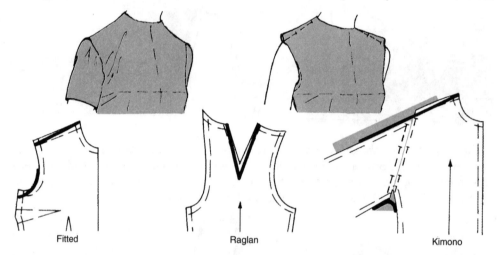

Fitted   Raglan   Kimono

SQUARE SHOULDERS: Pulling around the shoulders and armhole creates wrinkles across the back and front near the neckline because the shoulder area is not wide enough for your bone structure. To correct, remove the stitching in armhole above notches. Slash the front and back near the shoulder seam from the armhole edge to the neckline. Spread the cut edges the amount needed until wrinkles disappear. Insert strips of fabric under cut edges and baste. Transfer the alteration to pattern pieces.

For raglan and kimono sleeves, transfer the alteration to the pattern pieces as illustrated.

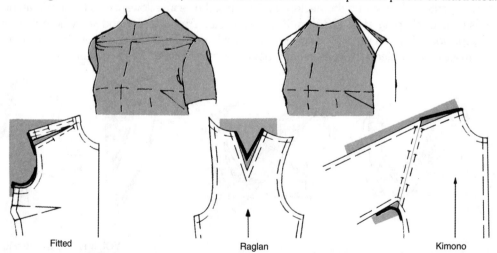

Fitted   Raglan   Kimono

NARROW SHOULDERS: The armhole seams fall beyond the end of the shoulder for set-in sleeves. Other sleeve types wrinkle across the upper arm and sometimes pull and restrict movement. To correct the muslin garment, pin the dart in front and back deep enough to pull the armhole seam into place. Adjust the bodice pattern pieces the same amount.

The muslin fitting shell covers only the basic style with a normal shoulder seam and a set-in sleeve. To transfer the alteration to style variations, adjust the pattern pieces as shown below and·test in muslin *before* cutting into the fashion fabric.

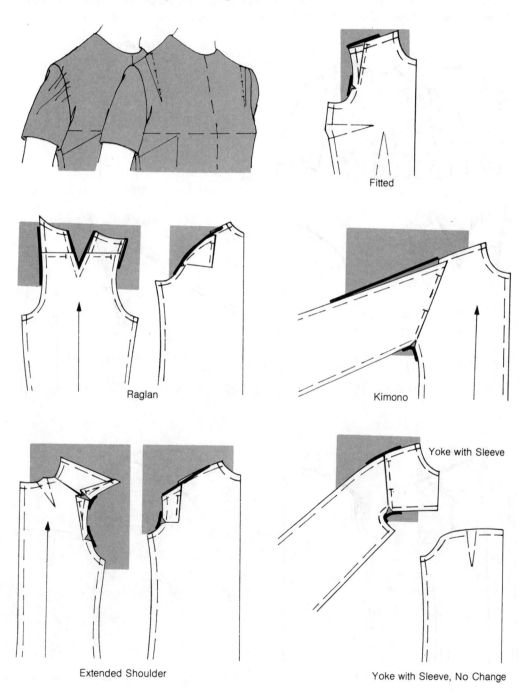

Fitted

Raglan

Kimono

Extended Shoulder

Yoke with Sleeve

Yoke with Sleeve, No Change

BROAD SHOULDERS: The armhole seams draw up over the shoulder, causing wrinkles and pulling in a set-in sleeve. Other sleeve types pull and do not have enough ease in the shoulder area for movement. To correct the muslin garment, slash the front and back from the shoulder seam to the armhole seam. Spread the cut edges the amount needed until wrinkles disappear. Insert strips of fabric under the cut edges; baste. Adjust the bodice pattern pieces the same amount.

The muslin fitting shell covers only the basic style with a normal shoulder seam and a set-in sleeve. To transfer the alteration to other style variations, adjust the pattern pieces as shown below and test in muslin *before* cutting your fashion fabric.

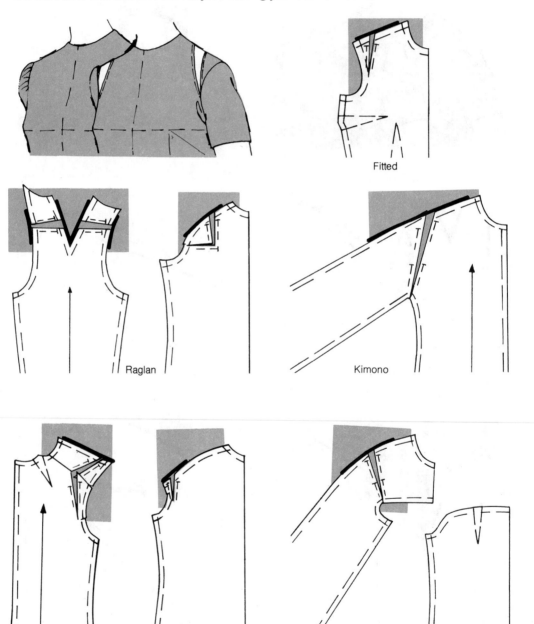

Fitted

Raglan

Kimono

Extended Shoulder

Yoke with Sleeve

Yoke with Sleeve, No Change

Sleeveless Armholes

There is nothing less attractive than an armhole in a sleeveless garment that does not lie correctly on the body. An armhole that is too small will bind and cut. When the armhole is too big it will gap, exposing your undergarments. Stitch along the seamline at the armhole; turn the seam allowance to the inside. Clip at ½" to ¾" (13 mm to 20 mm) intervals; baste. Try on the bodice. The underarm portion should be 1" (25 mm) below the armpit and the garment should fit smoothly around the armhole. It should not bind, pull, or restrict arm movement.

TIGHT ARMHOLE: Draw the correct line at the armhole. Stitch carefully along the line and clip to the new stitching at ½" (13 mm) intervals until the armhole seam is comfortable. Transfer the alteration to both the bodice and the facing pattern pieces.

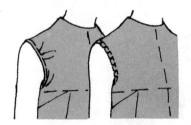
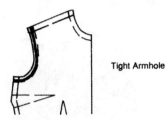

Tight Armhole

LARGE ARMHOLE: To correct a large armhole, insert bias strips of fabric to fill in the amount needed around and under the arm. When placed accurately, baste securely and transfer the alteration to the bodice and facing pattern pieces.

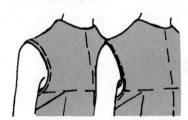
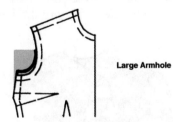

Large Armhole

GAPING ARMHOLE: Pin out excess fabric at the shoulders to bring the armhole into place, tapering to the neck. If the alteration is extensive, you may have to raise the underarm further by inserting a bias strip of fabric; baste. Transfer the alteration to bodice and facing pattern pieces. If gaping still occurs, the pattern is too small at the bust or back and you will need to alter the bodice. Make alteration for bust with a large cup, page 99, rounded back, page 101, or large back, page 103.

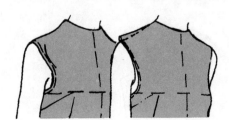
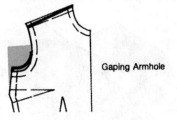

Gaping Armhole

Sleeves

The ease needed in a sleeve cap has traditionally been a stumbling block for many, since the pattern pieces and their markings are designed for the standard figure. Many times the only thing wrong with your sleeve is improper distribution of ease due to your body contour or bone structure. However, these same figure problems can affect the length of the sleeve cap, too.

IMPROPER DISTRIBUTION OF EASE: Diagonal wrinkles will form, starting at the sleeve cap and continuing across the sleeve, distorting the lengthwise grain. When this occurs, remove the sleeve cap from the armhole between the notches. For wrinkles that start at the front of the sleeve cap, re-distribute the ease, moving it forward until the wrinkles disappear. For wrinkles that start at the back of the sleeve cap, re-distribute the ease, moving it backward until the wrinkles disappear. Baste the sleeve into the armhole and check the appearance.

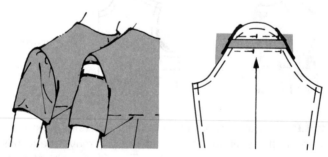

SKIMPY SLEEVE CAP: Sleeve cap pulls and collapses, causing wrinkles. To correct, slash across the top of the sleeve cap. Insert a strip of fabric under the cut edges. Spread the amount needed to increase the ease around the upper armhole seam and baste. Adjust the sleeve cap area of the sleeve pattern the same way.

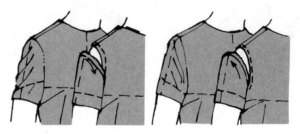

SLEEVE CAP TOO DEEP: The sleeve cap wrinkles across the top of the sleeve just below the seam. Reduce the amount of ease by pinning out excess fabric. Adjust the sleeve cap area of the sleeve pattern the same way.

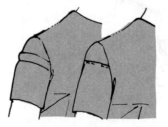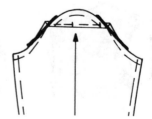

EXCESS EASE IN SLEEVE CAP: The sleeve cap wrinkles around armhole seam. To correct, release the stitching. Smooth the sleeve cap and pin in a shallow vertical dart at the top; baste the sleeve in place. At the shoulder marking, make a slash of 3" to 4" (7.5 cm to 10 cm) into the pattern. Overlap the edges the amount to be decreased (pattern will bubble slightly). Make 1½" (3.8 cm) clips at each end of ease so that the seam allowances lie flat. Be sure to maintain the girth across the sleeve cap where the ease ends and to shorten the sleeve cap slightly as indicated.

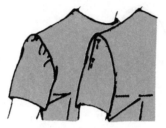 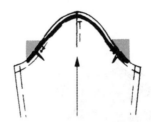

LARGE ARM: The sleeve pulls due to a lack of wearing ease. To correct, slash the sleeve along the lengthwise grain. Insert a strip of fabric under the cut edges and spread the amount needed, tapering to the shoulder seam and sleeve edge. If the sleeve cap still pulls, remove the stitching, add a piece of fabric to extend the cap, and baste. Add ease thread to the strip and insert in the armhole. Adjust the sleeve pattern the same amount, folding the pattern so that it lies flat. Re-draw grainlines.

For raglan and kimono sleeves, transfer the alteration to the pattern pieces as illustrated. Test in muslin *before* cutting the fashion fabric.

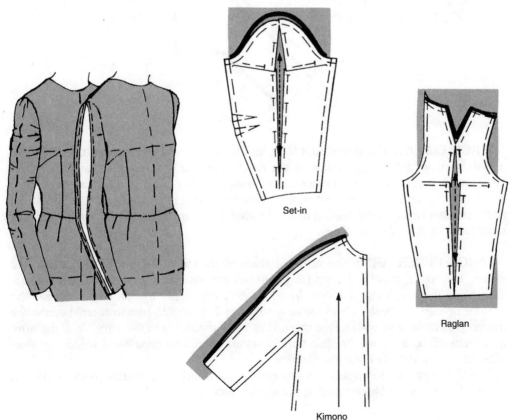

Set-in

Raglan

Kimono

THIN ARM: The sleeve wrinkles and sags. To correct, pin out excess fabric by making a lengthwise fold from the sleeve cap to the lower edge, tapering the fold at the lower edge if necessary to provide room for the hand to slip through. Adjust the sleeve pattern piece in the same way. The sleeve cap will have less ease.

For raglan and kimono sleeves, transfer the alteration to the pattern pieces as illustrated. Test in muslin *before* cutting the fashion fabric.

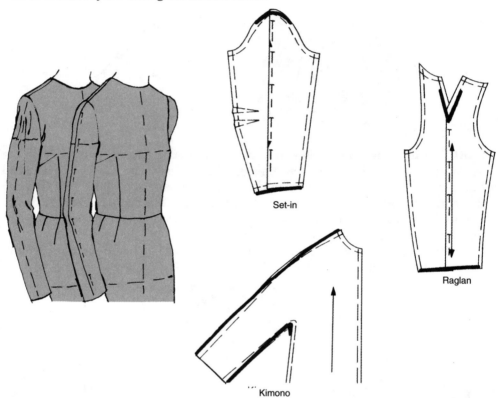

Set-in

Raglan

Kimono

THICK ELBOW: The sleeve pulls from the shoulder and is snug around the elbow. To correct, remove the stitching between the notches on the sleeve seam. Slash the sleeve between the darts to the lengthwise grain marking and then slash to the sleeve cap edge. Insert strips of fabric under the cut edges. Spread the amount needed and baste. Make an additional dart between the existing darts. Re-stitch the seam. Adjust the sleeve pattern the same way. Re-draw the grainlines.

LARGE UPPER ARM: The armhole seam binds and the sleeve is snug above the elbow. To correct, remove the stitching between the notches on the sleeve cap. Make a slash along the lengthwise marking. Insert a fabric strip under the cut edges. Spread the amount needed and baste. Continue ease stitching 1" to 2" (25 mm to 5 cm) beyond the markings to make a smooth sleeve cap and re-baste the sleeve in the armhole. If the armhole seam still binds, make the alteration for square shoulders, page 88. Transfer the alteration to the pattern. Re-draw the grainlines.

To make alterations for raglan and kimono sleeves, transfer the alterations to the pattern pieces. Test in muslin *before* cutting the fashion fabric.

THICK ELBOW

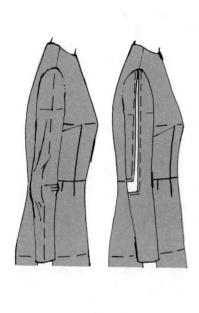

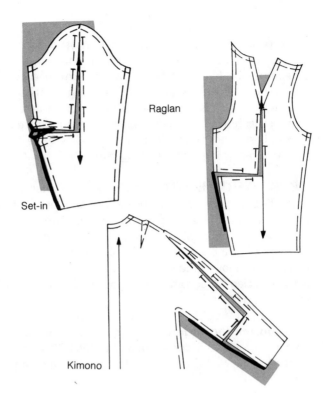

Set-in

Raglan

Kimono

LARGE UPPER ARM

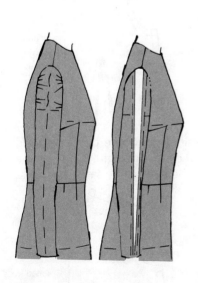

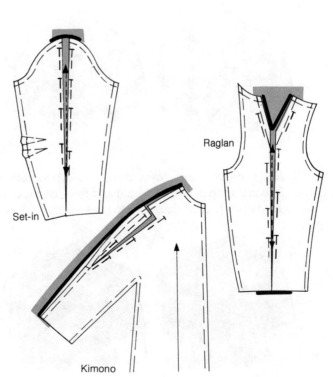

Set-in

Raglan

Kimono

Bust

Because the bust area is the most difficult portion of the pattern to alter, purchase appropriate patterns according to your bust measurement. This should give you the circumference needed in this area. In some cases, however, the contours of the body or bone structure across the **back** can take away the girth needed and the fabric will not lie smoothly over the bust. For these alterations, see pages 101 to 103. Sometimes the only alteration needed is the re-positioning or re-shaping of the darts, but frequently other situations, such as a bust with a large cup or a small cup, can require detailed alterations to fit the contour of your bust. Once you make them, you will see the difference immediately and be on your way to constructing a better fitting garment.

BUST DART LENGTH: This is the most important feature in creating a smooth, flattering fit over your bosom. The proper dart lengths will vary with every woman, as they are dependent on the shape as well as the size of your breasts. The underarm bust dart should end ½" (13 mm) from the apex and the front darts should end ½" to 1 " (13 mm to 25 mm) below the apex so fabric will cup smoothly over bosom. Refer to page 75 to determine the location of the apex of your bust. If, however, lengthening or shortening the dart is not sufficient to accommodate your body contour, refer to the alterations listed on the following pages

To *shorten the underarm dart,* mark the muslin with a pin where the dart should end. To correct, open the side seam and re-stitch the dart the proper length. (Do the same for front darts if included in your pattern.) Adjust the pattern the same way.

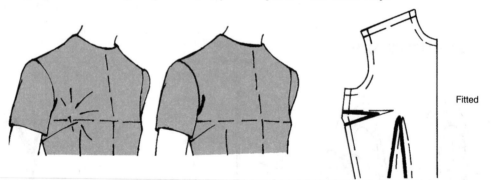

Fitted

To *lengthen the underarm dart,* mark the muslin with a pin where the dart should end. To correct, open the side seam and re-stitch the dart the proper length. (Do the same for front darts if they are included in your pattern.) Adjust the pattern the same way.

Fitted

HIGH BUST: The bust darts do not fall in line with the fullest part of the bust and need to be raised. Make a line on the muslin where the dart should be. To correct, open the side seam and re-stitch the dart in the proper position. Adjust the position of the dart on the pattern as shown. This alteration is applicable to **all** underarm bust darts, regardless of their angle. Lengthen the front darts as indicated, if necessary.

To alter styles that have bust shaping without the use of darts, place your adjusted fitting pattern underneath the pattern pieces to use as a guide. Above the armhole notch, make a fold ½ the amount needed to be raised and secure with tape. Slash through the pattern below the bust area and spread over the tissue paper, adding the amount the bust was raised to maintain your bodice length. Secure with tape. Make new seamlines and cutting lines for the armhole below the notches.

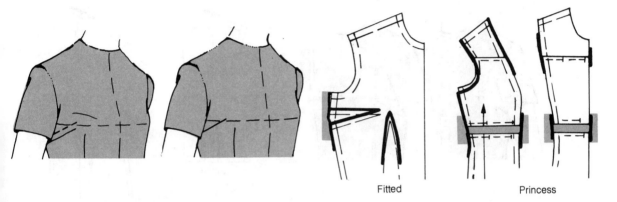

Fitted

Princess

LOW BUST: The bust darts do not fall in line with the fullest part of the bust and need to be lowered. Make a line on the muslin where the dart should be. To correct, open the side seam and re-stitch the dart in the proper position. Adjust the position of the dart on the pattern as shown. This alteration is applicable to **all** underarm darts, regardless of their angle. Shorten the front darts as indicated, if necessary.

To alter styles that have bust shaping without the use of darts, place your adjusted fitting pattern underneath the pattern pieces to use as a guide. Slash through the pattern pieces at the armhole notch. Spread over the tissue paper, lowering the bust shaping area into position. Secure with tape. Make a fold below the bust area ½ the amount the bust was lowered to maintain your bodice length. Secure with tape. Make new seamlines and cutting lines for the armhole below the notches.

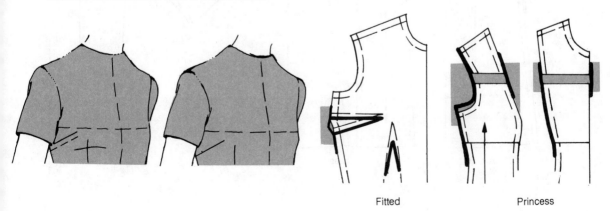

Fitted

Princess

BUST WITH SMALL CUP: The bodice wrinkles over the point of the bust. To correct the muslin garment, pin out excess fabric; taper horizontal folds to the side seams. Taper vertical folds to the waist seam (lower for A-line style garments). Transfer the alterations to the front pattern piece. When the tapering extends into skirt portions, be certain to add the amount taken out to the seams. For A-line styles, slash through the center of the dart to allow these edges to overlap. The darts will become shorter and narrower; adjust their length to your figure. Correct cutting, seam, and dart lines.

To transfer this alteration to garments without darts, place your adjusted fitting pattern underneath the front pieces to use as a guide. Reduce the pattern sections for the bust as indicated. Test in muslin *before* cutting out of the fashion fabric.

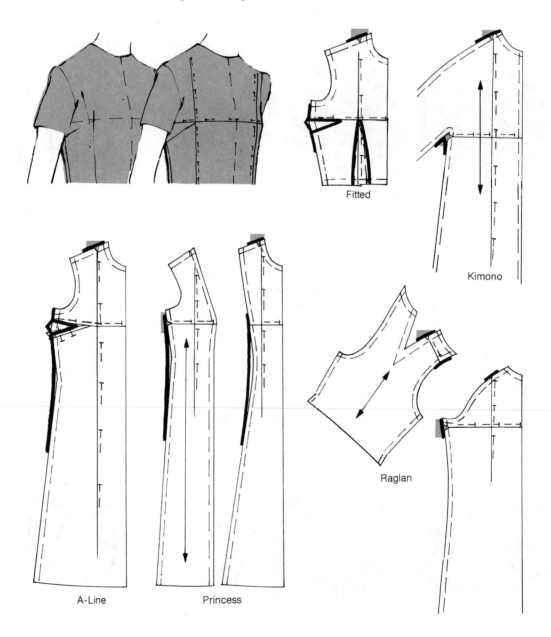

Fitted

Kimono

A-Line

Princess

Raglan

98

BUST WITH LARGE CUP: The bodice pulls over the bust, flattening the bust at the apex. To correct the muslin garment, slash through the bust darts and across the front. Slash down the front from the shoulder to the waist seam (lower for A-line style garments). Spread the edges the amount needed until the bust is not flattened. Insert strips of fabric under the cut edges and baste. Transfer the alteration to the pattern front. When enlargement extends into the skirt portion, be certain to take out the amount spread at the side seams. Correct cutting, seam, and dart lines. Darts will become deeper, adjust their length to your figure. Trim darts to within ½" (13 mm) of stitching if necessary to reduce bulk; press cut edges open.

To transfer this alteration to garments without darts, place your adjusted fitting pattern underneath the front pieces to use as a guide. Enlarge the pattern section for the bust as indicated. A dart will be needed in raglan and kimono styles. Test in muslin **before** cutting out of your fashion fabric.

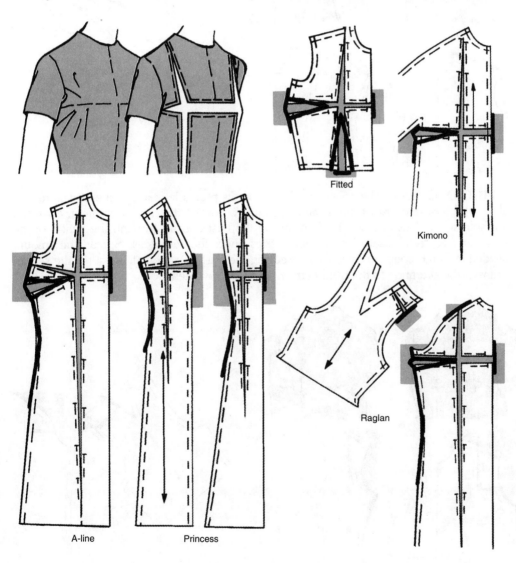

Fitted

Kimono

A-line

Princess

Raglan

Chest

The upper portion of the chest above the bust would seem to be an area of little concern when fitting a garment. The bone structure of the rib cage and collar bone controls the bodice length along the center front, however, and may create a need for alterations.

HOLLOW CHEST: The bodice wrinkles above the bust and below the neckline. To correct the muslin garment, pin out the wrinkles, tapering to the armhole or shoulder seams. Adjust the front pattern pieces at the neck and shoulder edges the amount needed.

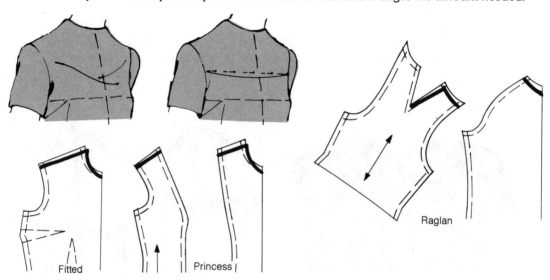

Fitted

Princess

Raglan

PIGEON CHEST: The collar and breast bones protrude, causing the bodice to pull above the bust and distort the armhole seam. To correct the muslin garment, open the armhole seam. Slash across the front above the bust and up through the center of the shoulder area to the seam. Insert fabric strips under the cut edges. Spread the amount needed to fit the body contour. Baste, keeping the slashed edge flat. Re-stitch the seams. Transfer the alteration to the front pattern pieces as indicated.

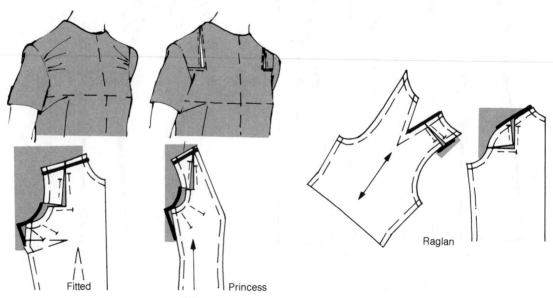

Fitted

Princess

Raglan

Back

The entire garment back should mold smoothly over your body contour from the neck to the hem edge. There should be no wrinkles or pulling and the hem must be even. Adjusting the pattern to your measurements will give the girth needed, but the fabric may not drape evenly due to bone structure or posture and will require alteration.

VERY ERECT BACK: The bodice back has parallel wrinkles across the back above the shoulder blades. To correct, pin out the wrinkles, tapering to the armhole or shoulder seams. Adjust the bodice pattern the amount needed at neck and shoulder edges.

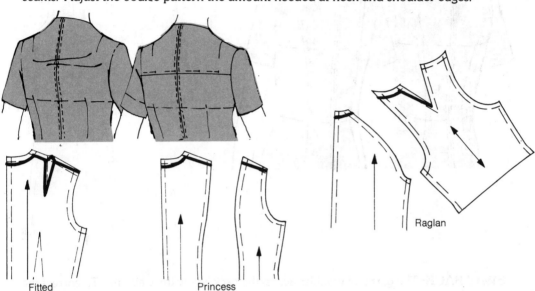

Fitted

Princess

Raglan

HIGH, ROUNDED BACK (DOWAGER'S HUMP): The bodice wrinkles and pulls across the shoulders and near the sleeve tops. To correct the muslin garment, slash across the back between the armhole seams. Remove the stitching from the zipper above the slash. Insert strips of fabric under the cut edges and spread them the amount needed. Baste, keeping the slashed edges flat and allowing for the center back opening. Pin darts in neck edge to fit the contour. Add strips to extend the back edges to the center opening. Adjust bodice back pattern piece same amount, adding a dart at neck edge as indicated.

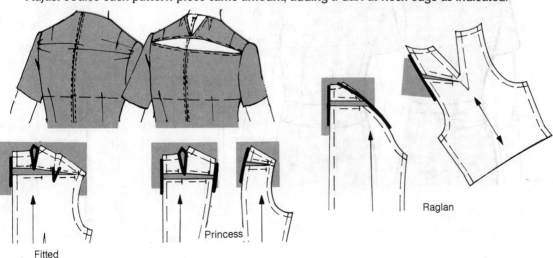

Fitted

Princess

Raglan

NARROW BACK: The bodice is loose through the shoulder area. A garment with a waist seam may have extra fullness above the seam, while an A-line garment may be longer in the back at the hemline. To correct, pin out excess fabric between the shoulder darts and waistline. Transfer the alteration to the pattern back as indicated. For a princess style, simply take a deeper seam.

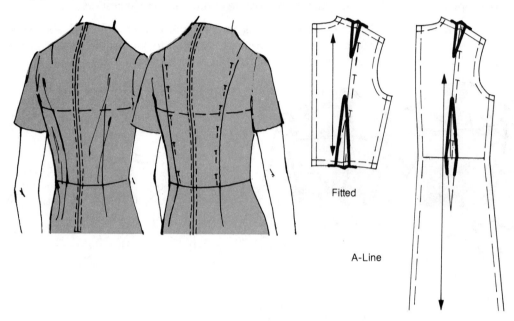

Fitted

A-Line

SWAY BACK: The garment wrinkles across the back below the waistline. To correct the muslin garment, pin out the wrinkles, tapering to the side seam. Transfer the alteration to the pattern back by removing the excess length along the center back seam the necessary amount. The darts will become shorter.

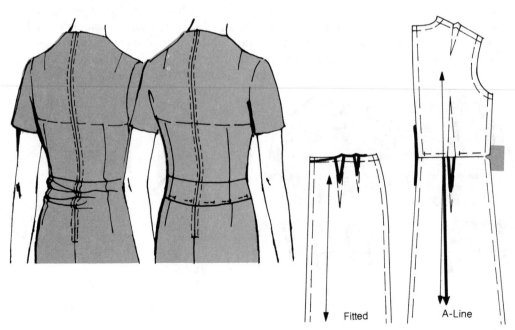

Fitted

A-Line

LARGE BACK OR PROMINENT SHOULDER BLADES: The bodice wrinkles and pulls across the fullest part of the back and is tight when raising the arms. To correct, remove the stitching at the shoulder seams, darts, and side seams. Slash across the back below the armhole and up through the center of the shoulder dart. Spread the edges the amount needed. Insert strips of fabric under the cut edges and baste. Make the existing dart deeper or add a dart to fit the contour and then re-stitch the seam. Transfer the alteration to the pattern back.

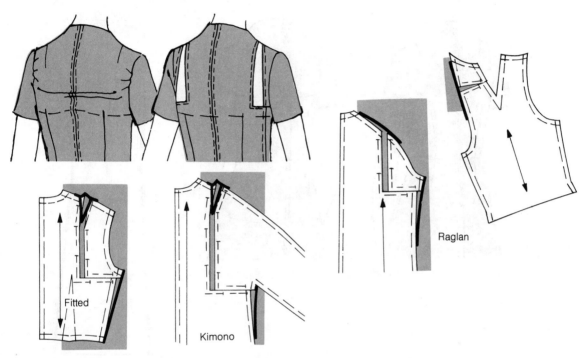

Raglan

Fitted

Kimono

Hips

Since the hip circumference was already taken care of before making the muslin fitting shell, you now must be concerned about the effect your bone structure or posture has on the garment. The fabric should mold smoothly over the buttocks and hip bones without wrinkles or pulling.

PROTRUDING HIP BONES: This is usually noticeable only in fitted garments. The bones protrude, causing pulling across the front. To correct, remove the stitching from the darts and seams. Pin the darts to fit the contour. If this makes the waistline smaller, add to the side seams. Re-stitch darts and seams. Transfer the alteration to the pattern front.

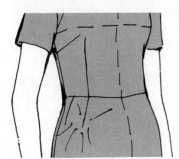

Fitted

FLAT BUTTOCKS: The skirt area wrinkles and sags at the back, causing an uneven hemline. For both styles, release the darts. Pin the darts, making them shorter to fit the body contour and narrower to retain the same waist measurement. To correct an A-line garment, release the zipper below the back bustline. Pin out the excess fabric at the side and center back seams. To correct garments with a waist seam, pin out excess fabric across the hips. Pin out any sag, making the hemline even.

Transfer the alteration to the pattern back as indicated.

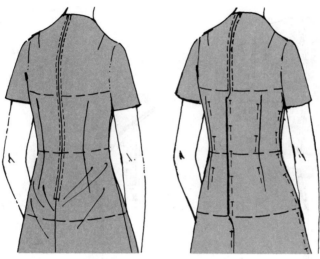

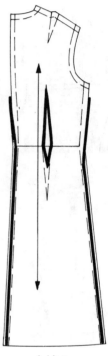

Flat Buttocks, A-Line

A-Line

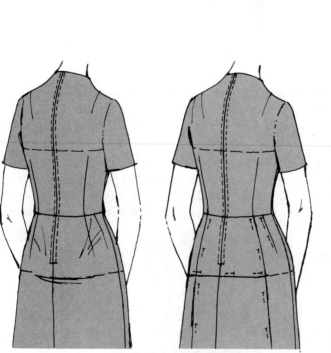

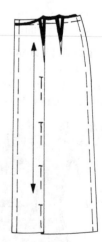

Flat Buttocks, Fitted

Fitted

LARGE BUTTOCKS OR HIGH ROUNDED BACK: Wrinkles form between the waist and hipline with pulling that distorts the side seams. The hemline is shorter in the back. To correct an A-line garment, release the darts, seams, and zipper below the back bustline. Place strips of fabric under the center back and side seams. Make equal adjustments at each seam to bring the side seams into position; baste. Pin the darts to fit the contour. To correct a garment with a waist seam, release the darts below the waist and remove the stitching from the waist seam. Pin the darts to fit the contour.

Transfer the alteration to the pattern back as indicated.

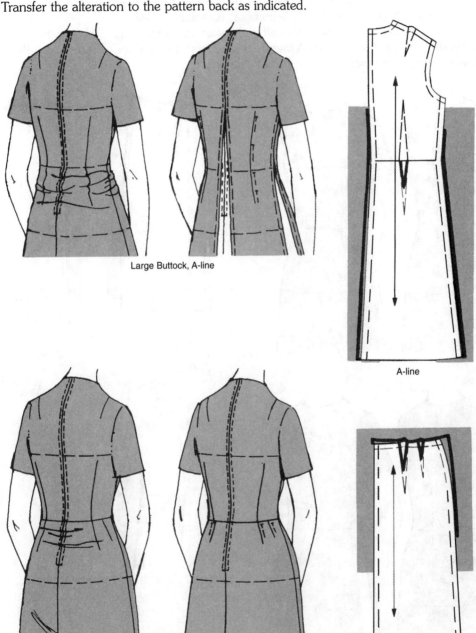

Large Buttock, A-line

A-line

Large Buttock, Fitted

Fitted

ONE LARGE HIP: The skirt pulls up on one side of the front and back, causing an uneven hemline. It is most obvious in fitted garments, but may also show up in other garments.

To correct a garment with a waist seam, remove the stitching from the side seam, waist seam, and darts on the shorter side. Drop the skirt until the grain and hem are straight. Insert strips of muslin at the sides and top; baste. Pin darts to fit the contour. Re-stitch the seams. For A-line garments, remove the stitching from the side and darts on the shorter side. Spread the edges until the grain and hem are straight. Insert muslin strips at the sides; baste. Pin back the dart to fit the contour. Re-stitch the seam.

Make a paper pattern for the other half of the skirt and transfer the alteration to the side that needs to be enlarged. You will then have a record of both sides of your skirt. (Shown below are the pattern pieces for the altered side only.)

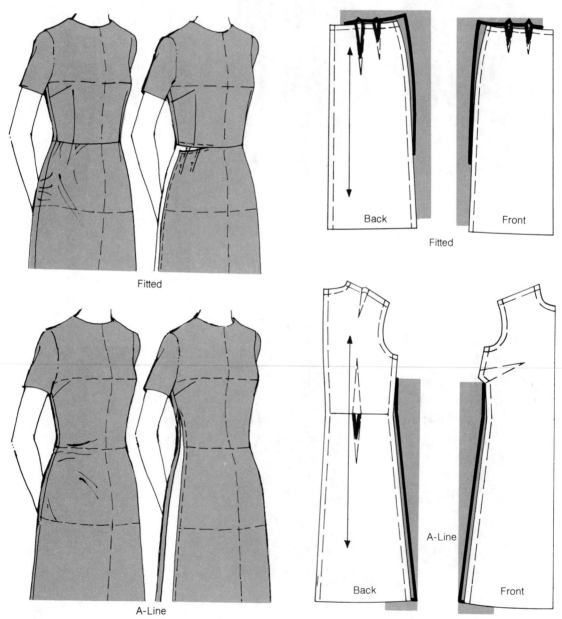

Fitted

Back

Front

Fitted

A-Line

A-Line

Back

Front

106

Abdomen

The hip circumference measurement allows for the girth of this area, but will not compensate for wrinkles and pulling caused by posture and body contour. As with all figure flaws, fabric molded smoothly over this area will minimize rather than accent it.

LARGE ABDOMEN: The skirt front rides up, pulling the side seams forward and causing the waist and hipline to pull up. To correct a garment with a waist seam, release the front waist seam and darts. Drop the skirt front until it hangs evenly. Baste a fabric strip to the top of the skirt. Pin darts to fit the contour. If this makes the waistline smaller, add to the side seams. Re-stitch the darts and seams. Transfer the alteration to the pattern as indicated.

To correct an A-line garment, slash the front up to the bust area. Spread the edges the amount needed until the side seams, waistline, and hipline fall into position. Place strips of fabric under the slashed edges and baste. Transfer the alteration to the pattern front as indicated, slashing through the bust dart to make the pattern lie flat, and let the edges overlap.

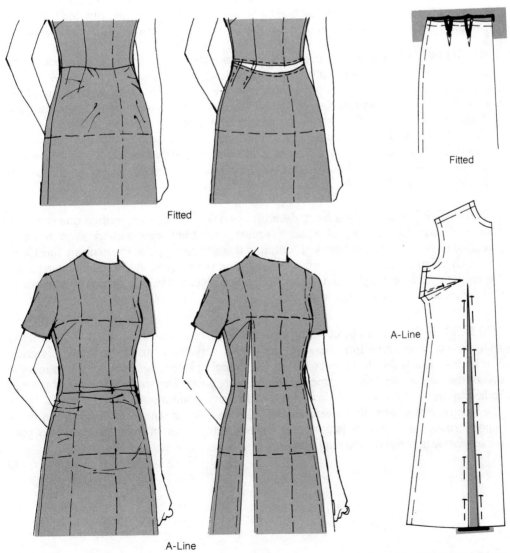

Fitted

Fitted

A-Line

A-Line

Combine Two Patterns

How many times have you wished your pattern had longer sleeves or a different neckline than the one shown? Perhaps you've even passed up a pattern style that you loved because it had a design feature that was not flattering on you. With some initiative and practice, you can avoid such compromises by using parts of different styles to create a garment that is truly custom-designed for your particular taste and figure. This information is intended to allow you to exercise your designer instincts and to provide some guidelines that will help you combine patterns successfully.

Within each size range of a Vogue pattern, the structural body relationships of shoulder to neck, bust to waist, etc., never change—for example, a size 12 bodice from one style number will fit a size 12 skirt from another style number if they both have waistlines and the styles are similar. To achieve the preferred silhouette for your needs, it is possible to combine necklines, collars, and other features from two different style numbers if the structural features of the two are the same.

Most people who understand the alterations required for their particular figure flaws will also know what style lines will minimize them. This knowledge can reduce your style selection at times because either the bodice or skirt is not right for you. But don't let these limitations discourage you. Combining two patterns can expand your fashion horizons.

NECKLINES: The shape of your neckline can either reveal or camouflage your neck and upper body, and you should be aware of which function you wish it to serve. When you have a limited number of flattering necklines to choose from, you must be aware of the bodice style. A bodice with raglan or kimono sleeves requires a different style of draping and shaping to achieve the proper fit than does a bodice wiih a set-in sleeve, so the necklines of the two styles cannot be interchanged. Empire and low-waisted seaming or dropped shoulders are also very stylized and need careful evaluation of the neckline before you cut into your fashion fabric. Do not be afraid to experiment, however, as long as you test your proposed adaptations in muslin.

COLLARS: Do not make a hasty decision when you decide to substitute one collar for another. Even if two collars look alike, you must check the bodice pattern pieces to make sure they match line for line before substituting them. The shape of the neckline must vary with each different collar style in order to get the proper shaping in the collar. Interchange the collars of different styles only when the bodice pieces match closely. Also make sure that the location of the closings is the same.

SLEEVES: While it is obvious that radically different sleeve styles, such as raglan and set-in sleeves, cannot be interchanged, very subtle variations can make a big difference. The bodice style is the deciding factor in interchanging sleeve versions, for it controls the size of the sleeve cap and the amount of necessary ease. The shoulder seams of the two bodices must be at the same angle and end at the same point where the arm joins the body. The lengths of the armhole curvatures must also be alike. If you wish to stray from these general rules, be very sure to test your experiments in muslin before cutting into your fashion fabric to avoid disappointing results.

Combine Two Sizes

Let's face it! Very few of us have perfect figures. Instead, many women are actually two sizes—one on top and one on bottom. Vogue Multi-Size patterns are ideal for such figures because three sizes are included in one pattern. If your size changes at the bust, waistline, or hip, simply use a combination of the cutting lines to accommodate those changes.

If the pattern you select is not available in multi-size patterns, it is often easier to use two pattern sizes rather than alter a bodice or skirt drastically. The secret to combining these two areas is in making the waistline a transitional area.

Note the difference in inches (centimeters) between the waist measurements of the two sizes listed on the back of your pattern envelope. If your waist measurement is the same as one pattern size, adjust the waist of the other pattern to correspond. If the waist needs to be adjusted on both patterns, determine how much to enlarge or reduce the waist of each piece, dividing the amount to be changed by the number of seams involved. Adjust each piece accordingly.

Keep center fronts, center backs, and grainlines straight. For fitted styles with a waist seam, adjust the waist area of the bodice and skirt so the waistlines match when joined. Adjust the position of the darts in the skirt so they will meet the bodice darts at the waist, retaining the distance across the centers of the garment between the darts. For A-line styles, cut both patterns apart and join the sections needed with transparent tape. Shown below, in both styles, are the situations that may require two sizes—the smaller size bodice combined with a larger size skirt and the larger size bodice combined with the smaller size skirt. Mark ¼ the amount needed for the waist at the side seam for both front and back pattern pieces. Draw new side seams from the bust to the hip, simulating original curves as much as possible.

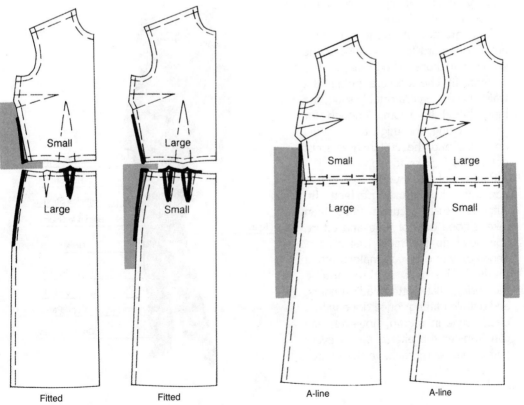

Small	Large	Small	Large
Large	Small	Large	Small
Fitted	Fitted	A-line	A-line

Pants, Pants, Pants

A wardrobe including casual, tailored, and luxurious pants will always be an important part of the fashion scene. They can be worn from morning to after dark—on the street, out to dinner and the theater, entertaining at home, or for active sports. Not to be forgotten are shorts: they too can be the basis of a smart ensemble costume.

The length of your pants or shorts is important to your total look. Full-length pants that are too short can have a skimpy, "out-grown" look, and pants that are too long can be clumsy and troublesome. Make sure your shorts do not end at an unattractive point on your leg; sometimes even an adjustment of ½" (13 mm) in length can make a world of difference in their attractiveness.

At all times you should strive toward a balanced silhouette. A long jacket, tunic, or top can camouflage those few extra pounds or inches (kilos or centimeters) or give an illusion of height. You may prefer a shorter top with a shorts costume or if you are short-legged. Consider your accessories; the same ones you wear with dresses may not be appropriate or in correct balance with pants.

Select the pattern for your pants carefully, choosing the type of pants that are best for your figure type. If you have prominent hips, a hip-hugging style with fitted thighs would not only be hard to fit, but would also be unflattering. If you have heavy thighs, pants that are wider and straight-legged from the hips down are a good choice because they will not cling or accent the thighs.

Choose your pants by waist measurement unless your hip measurement is much larger or smaller than that shown with the waist size; if so, select your size by hip measurement and adjust the waistline.

Pants are not difficult to construct, but can be hard to fit because of the endless variations in body shapes. For accurate fit, check several points: the waist should be comfortably snug, the hips should be roomy enough for ease in sitting, the thigh area should not bind, and the crotch area must not be too tight or too loose

Pants, of all your garments, demand the most perfect fit. Although such accurate fitting can take a good deal of time and effort, you need do the most major alterations only once if you make a fitting muslin. This will require precise measuring, flat pattern adjustments, and detailed fitting; once done with a classic style in muslin, however, you can transfer the alterations to every pair of pants you make in the future.

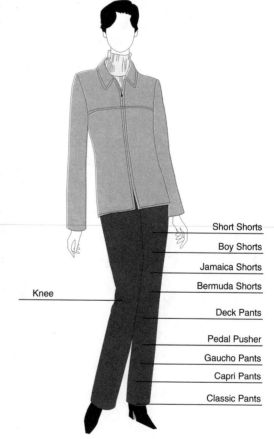

Short Shorts
Boy Shorts
Jamaica Shorts
Bermuda Shorts
Deck Pants
Pedal Pusher
Gaucho Pants
Capri Pants
Classic Pants

Knee

Precise Measurements

MEASURE YOURSELF: Be sure to wear the proper undergarments with your pants. Some can flatten the contour and give a "stuffed sausage" look. Be sure they do not cause unsightly indentations or bulges over the fullest part of your hips or thighs. Wearing the correct undergarments and shoes, take the following measurements.

Tie a narrow piece of elastic around the thinnest part of your waist. Bend and twist until the elastic lies on your natural waistline. Take measurements on your right side only unless there is a dramatic difference between both sides (one large hip, for example.) If this is true, measure and record both sides of your body. Keep the tape measure parallel to the floor when taking any circumference measurements and snug but not tight against your body.

Waist: Measure around your body over the elastic (1).

Hip: Measure around the fullest part of the hip, approximately 7-9" (18-23 cm) below your waistline (2).

Thigh: Measure around the fullest part of the upper leg, approximately 1" (25mm) below the crotch (3).

Crotch Depth: Sit straight on a hard, flat chair. With a straight ruler, measure from chair to waist at side seam (4).

Pants Length: Measure from the waist at side seam to middle of ankle bone (5).

Crotch Length: The crotch length is measured from the waistline to the center back waistline between your legs. Using a string and a narrow length of ribbon, tie a key or pencil to one end of the string. Tie the other end of the string around the ribbon so it can slide. With a friend's help, place the ribbon under the elastic in the center front, through your legs, and under the elastic in center back.

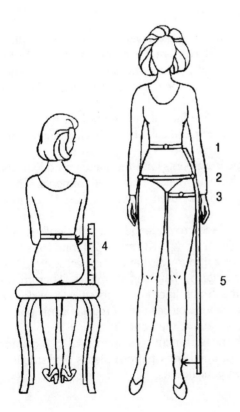

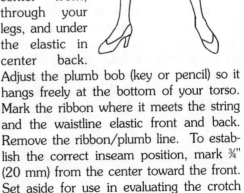

Adjust the plumb bob (key or pencil) so it hangs freely at the bottom of your torso. Mark the ribbon where it meets the string and the waistline elastic front and back. Remove the ribbon/plumb line. To establish the correct inseam position, mark ¾" (20 mm) from the center toward the front. Set aside for use in evaluating the crotch length.

COMPARE MEASUREMENTS: Ater you have taken your personal measurements, compare them with the actual pattern measurements, taking into account ease (see page 63), to determine if any adjustments have to be made in the pattern. Measure pattern pieces only from seamline to seamline, excluding any darts or tucks. If pants have side front slanted pockets, be sure to include the side front pattern piece.

SIZE	6	8	10	12	14	16	18	20	22	24	
Waist	23 (58)	24 (61)	25 (64)	26 1/2 (67)	28 (71)	30 (76)	32 (81)	34 (87)	36 (92)	38 (97)	inch cm
Hip	32 1/2 (83)	33 1/2 (85)	34 1/2 (88)	36 (92)	38 (97)	40 (102)	42 (107)	44 (112)	46 (117)	48 (122)	
Thigh	17 7/8 (45.5	18 1/2 (47)	19 1/8 (48.5)	20 (51)	21 (53)	22 (56)	23 (58)	24 (61)	25 (64)	26 (66)	
Crotch Depth	10 7/8 (27.5)	11 1/8 (28)	11 3/8 (29)	11 5/8 (29.5)	11 7/8 (30)	12 3/8 (31.5)	12 3/8 (31.5)	12 3/4 (32.5)	13 1/8 (33)	13 1/2 (33.5)	
Pants Length	37 3/4 (96)	37 3/4 (96)	37 3/4 (96)	37 3/4 (96)	37 3/4 (96)	37 3/4 (96)	37 3/4 (96)	37 3/4 (96)	37 3/4 (96)	37 3/4 (96)	

Mark adjustment and fitting lines on your pattern tissue. Start with the front pattern piece and extend the grainline the full length of the pattern. Draw lines perpendicular to the grainline for hip and thigh, measuring down from the waistline the same amount as when you took your measurements. For slim pants, it may also be necessary to indicate the knee and calf positions.

Lay the back pattern over the front, matching sides. Indicate the end of each line from the front piece along the side seamline. Draw lines perpendicular to the back grainline from these locations.

For waist and hip, first compare your body measurements with the standard body measurements listed here. If these differ, you will have to make pattern adjustments. Thigh measurement of the pattern should equal your thigh measurement plus at least 1" (25 mm) for wearing ease.

Compare measurements for both crotch depth and crotch length. Crotch depth should exactly equal your crotch depth measurement plus ½" to ¾" (13 mm to 20 mm) for sitting ease. For pants that may be attached to a yoke or contour waistband, it is necessary to first pin the yoke or waistband pattern to the pants pattern, matching seamlines. Then measure from the waistline marking or seamline to the crotch line. For pants styles that do not extend up to the natural waistline, compare the pattern pieces with a regular pants patten to determine where the natural waistline is located above the pattern.

Crotch length should equal your crotch length measurement plus up to 1 ½" (3.8 cm) for ease. Adjustment can be made equally to the front and back pattern pieces or distributed more to one piece than the other, depending on your figure.

Flat Pattern Adjustments

The most critical step in achieving perfectly fitted pants is to adjust the crotch. Unless the crotch is in the correct position, no amount of adjustment made later can overcome a poor fit. Crotch adjustments should be made first because they can affect other adjustments.

Be sure to keep grainlines straight and connect the seamlines and cutting lines in a smooth, gradual line, tapering to the original lines as indicated on the pattern pieces.

CROTCH DEPTH: The crotch depth should exactly equal your measurement plus ½" to ¾" (13 mm to 20 mm) for sitting ease. If not, it must be adjusted by lengthening or shortening the pattern pieces. Be sure to make equal changes on the front and back pattern pieces.

To shorten this area, make a fold ½ the amount needed at the adjustment line on each pattern piece. Fasten with tape. *To lengthen,* cut the pattern along the adjustment line, place tissue paper underneath, and spread the amount needed. Fasten with tape.

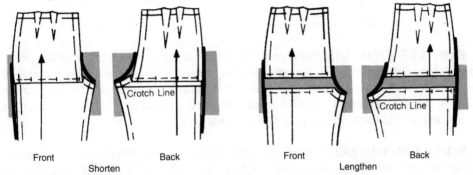

| Front | Back | Front | Back |
| Shorten | | Lengthen | |

CROTCH LENGTH: The crotch length can be adjusted either at the waistline or inner leg. Your body contours determine the best location. Both types of adjustments affect only the crotch seam and do not change the side seam.

Increases or decreases can be made equally to the front and back pattern pieces or distributed more to one piece than to the other. Altering at the inner leg will also affect the upper thigh measurement. Altering along the crotch seam enables fullness to be added or subtracted across the abdomen or the derriere.

To *decrease* crotch length at the inner leg, slim the pattern the required amount. To *increase* crotch length, add to the crotch seam. Remember to retain the crotch curve shaping and gradually taper new lines back to meet the original leg seams.

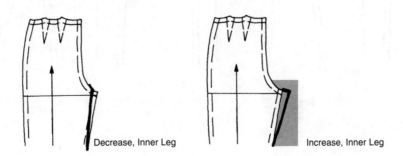

Decrease, Inner Leg   Increase, Inner Leg

To **decrease** crotch length along the crotch seam, fold the pattern on the adjustment line the amount needed, tapering the fold out to the side seam. To **increase** crotch length, cut the pattern along the adjustment line just to, but not through, the side seam. Place tissue paper underneath and spread the amount needed.

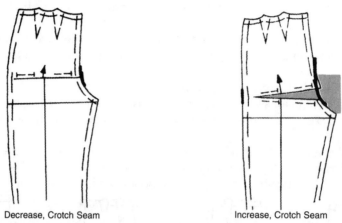

Decrease, Crotch Seam

Increase, Crotch Seam

PANTS LENGTH: After the crotch adjustment is done, check the total length of the pants along side seamline. If they are **too long,** make a fold ½ the excess amount above hemline across the leg of pattern front and back; fasten with tape. If they are **too short,** slash across the leg above hemline on pattern front and back. Place tissue paper underneath and spread the amount needed. Fasten with tape.

WAIST CIRCUMFERENCE: If your waist is **smaller,** first determine the amount needed to be decreased. Then take away ⅛ of this amount from the pattern front and back at each center and side seam. If your waist is **larger,** add ⅛ the necessary amount to the pattern front and back at each center and side seam. Be sure to make corresponding adjustment on the waistband or facing pattern pieces.

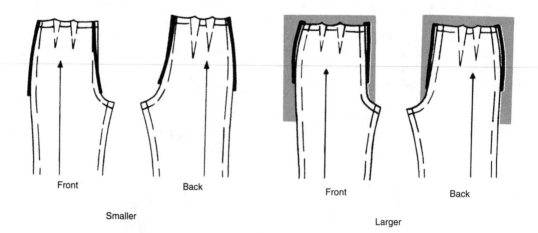

Front

Back

Smaller

Front

Back

Larger

HIP CIRCUMFERENCE: If your hips are much larger or smaller than your waist measurement, be sure to purchase your pattern by your hip measurement. However, adjustments of 2" (5 cm) or less in hip circumference can be made along the side seam. Mark ¼ of the amount needed to be increased or decreased at the hipline and hemline of the pattern pieces. Using a curved ruler, draw new seamlines and cutting lines, connecting the marks, and taper to the waist. See skirt adjustments, pages 103 to 106.

THIGH CIRCUMFERENCE: If the pattern measurement is close to that of your thigh plus 1" (25 mm) for wearing ease, no adjustment is necessary. To make the thigh **smaller,** slim the pattern ¼ the amount along each leg seam. To make the thigh **larger,** add ¼ the amount to each leg seam. Using a curved ruler, draw new seamlines.

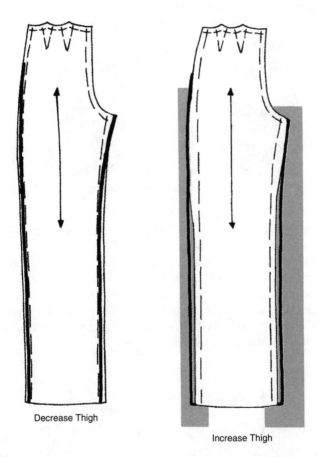

Decrease Thigh

Increase Thigh

If you are making tapered, slim-fitting pants, it would also be wise to check the knee, calf, and instep measurements. If your measurements (plus at least 1" (25 mm) for wearing ease) are larger or smaller than the pattern measurements, adjust the leg seams accordingly.

Fitting Adjustments

Some minor fitting adjustments can be made in pants after they are constructed. If you are unsure of the fit, cut your seam allowances 1" (25 mm) wide to allow for any later fitting problems.

If the pants wrinkle at the high hipline, release the darts. Pin to fit body contour, lengthening or shortening the darts as needed. Restitch.

If the waist pulls downward at center front or back when you sit or stand, release the waistband. To correct, set waistband higher at the center seam, tapering to the side seams.

Often pants have wrinkles that either point up or down from the crotch line in either the front or the back, indicating that the crotch depth, crotch length, or crotch curve needs adjustment. If the problem is major, alterations can only be done on the pattern before the garment is cut out. Refer to adjustments for crotch depth and length, pages 113 and 114.

Wrinkles Caused by Poor Fit at Crotch

If the problem is minor, adjustments can be made in the crotch seam and at the waistline. If the wrinkles point up toward the waistline, the crotch must be lengthened. Remove the waistband and let out the waistline seam up to ⅜" (10 mm). Make a deeper curve in the crotch seam by lowering the seam at the bottom of the curve and letting out the center front and center back seams, tapering to the original seamline below the waist.

If the wrinkles point down away from the waistline, the crotch must be shortened. Remove the waistband and take in the waistline seam. To shorten the curve, raise the seam at the bottom of the curve up to ⅜" (10 mm), and take in the center front and center back seams, tapering to the original seamline below the waist.

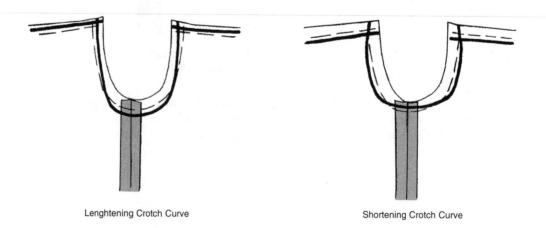

Lenghtening Crotch Curve   Shortening Crotch Curve

Vogue's Personal Fit Pants Pattern

The Vogue Basic Fitting Pants Shell is a specially designed pants pattern with extra fabric allowances in common problem areas such as abdomen, sides, thigh, length, and crotch depth. These "outlets" have been included to enable you to make a pattern larger, in addition to making it smaller. The stitching lines are normal.

The pattern is cut out and sewn in woven gingham check fabric, or muslin. When trying on the pants, you can easily identify any problem areas because the gingham checks will not be square on the body.

The pattern includes a comprehensive guide sheet that covers the most common fitting problems for pants. Drawings are used to indicate the fitting problems and their simple solutions. Directions can be followed for transferring the changes made on the shell back to the pattern.

Once this pants pattern has been customized to fit your figure, you know how your body differs from the average pattern figure. Thus, if you have to make a crotch depth or length adjustment on this pattern, you can automatically make the same adjustment on all other Vogue patterns. To compare a new pattern to the basic for a quick analysis of problem areas, simply lay the new pattern on top of the basic pattern, aligning crotch lines. Remember that some pants patterns will include more ease as part of the fashion design and thus will be larger than the basic pattern which fits close to the body. Be careful not to overfit and eliminate the fashion ease.

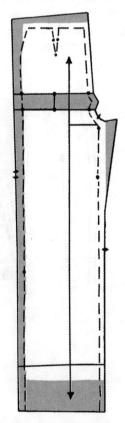

Basic Fitting Pants Shell

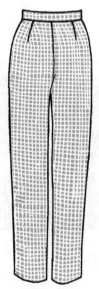

Gingham Check Pants for Fitting

Pants-Fitting Muslin

A pants-fitting muslin can be made from any basic pants pattern. Alter the pattern, cut out the muslin, and transfer all seamlines and markings with a tracing wheel and dressmaker's carbon. Also trace your hipline and your thigh line to the right side of the muslin. Machine baste the pants together. Baste a temporary waistband of grosgrain ribbon to the waist seamline to support the pants while fitting.

Take a critical look in a full-length mirror to spot problems due to bone structure or body contour. The side seams should be perpendicular to the floor. The traced lines should be parallel to the floor. If they are pulled or distorted or if wrinkling occurs, you will need further fitting and pattern adjustments to compensate for your figure flaws. If minor adjustments do not correct the problems to your satisfaction, you may need one of the more specialized alterations on the following pages. For comfort and attractiveness, avoid fitting pants too tightly.

Personal Alterations

These fitting alterations can only be accomplished by fitting your muslin and cannot be made after the fashion fabric has been cut. Since the alterations are quite individualized, the same changes are not always required on both the front and back pattern pieces.

FOR LARGE ABDOMEN: Release the darts and stitching in front waist seam. Lower the top of the pants until the side seams hang straight and the wrinkles disappear. Baste a strip of fabric to the top and add to the front inner leg seam until the pants hang without wrinkles. Pin darts to fit the contour. Transfer the changes to your pattern.

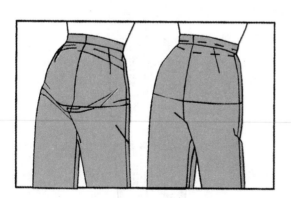 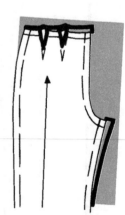

PROTRUDING HIP BONES: Release the darts and stitching from the front waist seam. Pin to fit the contour. This may include widening or shortening the dart. If this makes the waistline smaller, add to the side seams, then transfer the alteration to the pattern.

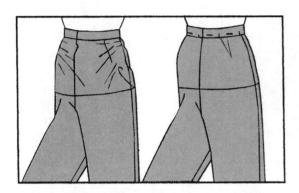
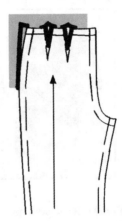

FULL HIPS: Buying your pattern by hip measurement will give you girth for a large derrière. However, you may need more length at the center back in order to fit the contour and to let the side seams fall into position. Release the darts and back waist seam stitching. Drop the top of the pants until the side seams fall into position. Baste strips of fabric to the top and add to the back inner leg seam until the pants hang without a wrinkle. Pin darts to fit the contour. If the waistline measurement is not large enough after this alteration, add to the side seams. Transfer the alteration to your pattern piece.

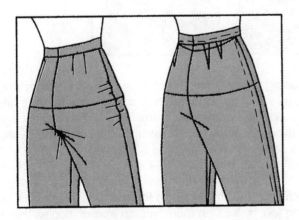

FLAT BUTTOCKS: Eliminate the wrinkles on the muslin by removing stitching in back waist seam and darts. Reshape the darts and pin to fit the contour, taking out the excess waistline measurement at the side and center back seams. Transfer these adjustments to the back pattern piece, clipping seam allowances to lie flat.

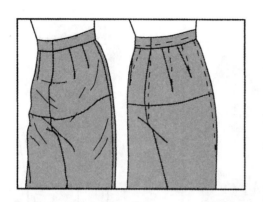 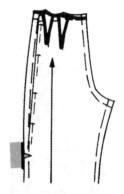

SWAYBACK: If you have a swayback, wrinkles appear across the back just below the waist. Remove stitching in back waist seam. Raise waist seam at center back until excess fullness disappears. Reshape and pin darts, if necessary. Transfer new darts and waist seam to back pattern piece.

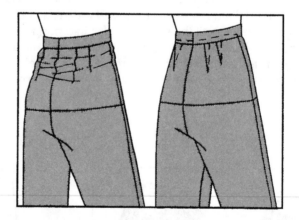

FINAL STEPS: When constructing pants, baste and fit to see how your fabric drapes over your body contours, making minor fitting adjustments to compensate for your fabric. Since the crotch area receives considerable strain, use a smaller straight stitch or a very small zigzag stitch when stitching the curve of the crotch seam. Clip the seam at the top of the curve and press open. Add a second row of stitching ¼" (6 mm) from the first row between the clips. Then trim and overcast this edge. This portion of the seam remains unpressed.

Armed with the knowledge you have gained by making a fitting muslin, make your pants pattern pieces a permanent sewing tool by backing them with an iron-on non-woven. Use them as a guide to alter any style of pants, shorts, culottes, pantskirt, or jumpsuit you plan to make. You will find it is a handy, time-saving device.

Fitting As You Sew

You should always try on your garment after completing each unit of construction to check the fit. But what exactly is good fit? Clothes that fit well are clothes that allow enough ease for comfort and freedom of movement, hang smoothly without wrinkles or bulges, and flatter the figure. If a garment does not conform attractively to your contours, all your efforts at fine construction will have been wasted.

There might seem to be a fine line between fitting and alterations. In reality, however, alterations or adjustments are those significant changes that should be made on the pattern tissue before you even reach for the fabric, while fitting involves those minor changes necessary to perfect and finalize the garment. Tissue pattern alterations alone may not guarantee a flawless fit, since paper, by its very nature, will behave differently than your fabric.

First Fitting

This fitting should tell you how your fabric will mold into the style you have chosen. It should include only the garment areas that constitute the basic outer layer; omit the collar, cuffs, facings, sleeves, and any other details such as pockets. Baste the darts and press them lightly with the fingers. Pin or baste the major seams at the shoulders, sides, and waistline along the seamlines. Pin shut any openings where the zipper, buttons, or plackets will later be placed. For the best fit, the garment should always be tried on as it will be worn, with the right side out.

Before you attempt to fit any garment, wear the undergarments, shoes, and belt intended for that garment, and work before a full-length mirror in a well-lighted room. Stand naturally and look into the mirror. Make sure the garment provides enough ease for comfort. Sit, bend, walk, and move your arms. The garment should look balanced, with adequate length

from the neck to the waist and from the waist to the hem. Keep in mind that most figures are not perfectly symmetrical. Do not allow yourself to fit so closely that figure flaws such as a high hip or low shoulder become noticeable. Check the placement of closures and fastenings, the number of buttons, and so on to be sure that the closings will not gap. Don't become alarmed by high necklines and armholes; they will be smaller during the first fitting stages because the seam allowances are not turned in the proper direction until these edges are finished.

CONCENTRATE ON THE FABRIC: Learn to use your hands to lightly smooth the wrinkles, easing the fabric into the correct position. Grainlines and remaining wrinkles will tell you how the fabric is reacting to your figure. Check the placement of darts, necklines, armholes, and seams for any indication that the basic structure of the garment does not agree with the basic structure of your body.

SEAMLINES – GRAINLINES – WRINKLES: All lines are very important guides in fitting. Note the positions of your seamlines and grainlines. They should divide the body as intended by the designer. Grainlines should be parallel to the floor if they are crosswise and perpendicular to the floor if vertical (unless a section has been cut on bias grain as part of the design). When you are cutting out and marking your pattern, thread trace the grainlines on the fabric to indicate crosswise and lengthwise grainlines on each of your main garment pieces.

Wrinkles are the telltale signs of a grain distortion or of areas that are too tight or loose. If a vertical seam or grainline is not perpendicular to the floor or does not hang as your pattern envelope illustrates, look at the adjoining horizontal (or approximately horizontal) seams to see whether reducing or increasing their depth will sufficiently correct grainline and seam positions. Changes may have to be distributed between both the horizontal and vertical seams to bring the fabric into position. For these changes, you may open and re-pin seams on your figure, but it is faster to pin or chalk mark new seamlines and then make the change after you remove the garment. Fitting problems should be solved by the least complicated changes possible to avoid unnecessary work and unintentional disruptions of

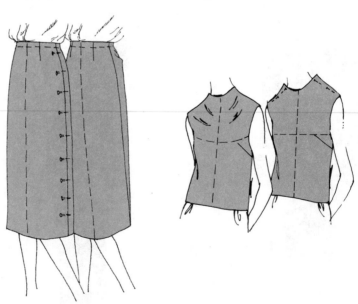

the design. Be aware that moving seamlines will mean that corresponding changes will have to be made in the adjoining garment sections.

Horizontal straining--stress at seams--indicates that a garment is too snug. Even after pattern alterations have been done, heavy or tightly woven fabric may require more wearing ease. Release all your seams slightly in even amounts to produce the needed ease.

DARTS: If the point ends in an unattractive location, remove the basting and adjust length of your dart. Relocate the point end first. You can adjust the depth of the dart to compensate for the thickness of your fabric.

NECKLINES: Necklines often require minor corrections. To remedy tight or high necklines, deepen the neck seamline an even amount around entire neckline to avoid distorting the line. If your neckline is a little large, slightly increase the shoulder seam or the center back seam at the neckline, tapering to the shoulder. Remember, straining at the neckline may be caused by the seam allowance that has not yet been turned under.

TO COMPLETE FITTING: Baste garment sections together along the new seamlines established during the first fitting, stitching any darts or seams that did not require fitting changes, and press. Press basted seams open with fingertips. Try on the garment again, testing the fit before stitching these areas together permanently.

Second Fitting

The second fitting takes place after sewing the darts and major seams, attaching the facings, and basting the sleeves or armhole facings into position. Test a jacket over a blouse, or a coat over a dress or jacket for really precise fit. Turn up the proposed hem. Review the appearance of your garment critically in the mirror. Side, back, and front seams should be straight and perpendicular to the floor by now. Diagonal wrinkles are often the result of fabric slippage as you sew. Smooth fabric perpendicular to the wrinkles to discover where to open and restitch the seam. Then check the new seamline. It is important to machine stitch directionally, generally sewing up from the hemline and down from the neckline. If you are letting out seams in fabric that frays easily, extend seam allowances with ribbon seam binding to ensure durability.

CLOSINGS: Pin the closings in position, matching center markings. Asymmetrical closings by their very nature need additional care and handling to prevent stretching any bias edges. Center markings should be anchored securely before you proceed with the fitting, or the additional weight of the closing details may distort grainlines and seams.

SLEEVES: The fit of the sleeve affects the entire garment. Raise your arms; freedom of movement is vital. Alterations should be handled during the tissue stage, as in the pattern adjustment section. For set-in sleeves, review pages 284 and 285. Kimono sleeves and gussets can only withstand very minor fitting adjustments.

Make sure that the fabric grainlines on the set-in sleeve cap are at right angles to prevent rippling toward the front or back of the armhole. Minor fitting adjustments can be done at the upper portion of the armhole. Remove the basting between notches. Raise or lower the sleeve cap until it is positioned correctly, taking a deeper or narrower seam allowance on the bodice at the shoulder; do not change the sleeve seam allowance.

The underarm seam below the notches will be trimmed after the sleeve has been permanently set in. About 1" (25 mm) below the armpit is ample room for movement.

Contrary to what may seem logical, the lower the underarm part of the armhole, the more the sleeve or armhole facing may resist movement, causing pulling and straining. Remove the basting across the underarm. Raise or lower the sleeve, taking a deeper or narrower seam allowance on the bodice at the underarm as needed.

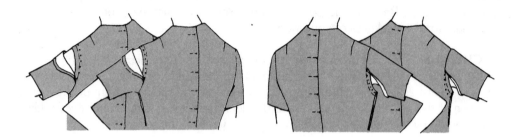

Final Fitting

After the garment has been completely sewn and pressed (except for the hem), try it on to determine the length. Review the final pressing to be sure that your seams are flat.

In the second fitting, the hem is pinned up to establish the most flattering length. Experiment with the estimated hem length. Once a length has been chosen, the actual measurement with a pin or chalk hem marker can take place in the final fitting.

Essentially, fashion dictates hem lengths; but the type of garment, the nature of the fabric, and the height of the wearer determine the depth of the hem. Usually the hem allowance is 3" (7.5 cm), which adds weight and therefore influences the drape of the garment. Of course, if the hem is for a very full skirt or a sheer fabric, the depth will vary--1" (25 mm) for a circular skirt and as narrow as ⅛" (3 mm) or as wide as 6" (15 cm) for a chiffon overskirt.

It is always more accurate to have someone else mark your hem for you. Make sure you are wearing the same height heels you plan to wear with the finished garment. Stand erect, look straight ahead, and have the person doing the marking move around you. For longer length garments, stand on a stool or a low table. Garments with bias or circular hems should always hang for at least 24 hours to allow the bias to set and prevent the hemline from sagging after it is hemmed.

After the hemline has been marked, pin up the hem and examine it carefully from all angles. Is the length flattering to your figure? Are the proportions of the garment pleasing to the eye? Is the hem parallel to the floor? Sometimes only a small change in length makes the difference between a hemline that is flattering and one that is not. For plaids, checks, and horizontal stripes, it may be necessary to change the curve of the hemline so that it follows the design of the fabric.

Once the best hemline has been accurately established, turn to page 340 for the ideal hem finish to select for your individual fabric and design.

Your honest, objective, critical awareness is vital if you want to improve your sewing with each item you make. We hope that these suggestions have encouraged you to try to solve your individual fitting enigmas undaunted. If the most orthodox solutions don't work for you, don't be afraid to invent others. Be intuitive, flexible, and creative and you'll see how effortlessly you can accomplish a more perfect fit.

3

Planning Your
Fashion Approach

(continued on next page)

Choosing the Correct Fabric

Perhaps the most critical phase of any sewing project is that moment in the fabric store when, pattern in hand, you make your fabric decision. Be careful not to make it lightly, for the success of each sewing venture hinges on the quality and the suitability of the fabric you use. Quality is an elusive factor that does not depend on high price. Learn to recognize it by touch, not necessarily by cost, and don't skimp. Sleazy fabric never justifies the time and effort you spend on it. The suitability of the fabric to the pattern design is all-important—a crisp fabric will never create soft, flowing lines just as a soft, fluid fabric cannot be crisply tailored. The best judgment is based on experience, but these guidelines will also help prevent disasters due to a poor fabric choice:

- Let the back of your pattern envelope be your guide. The fabric suggestions reflect the designer's recommendations. Are crisp or soft fabrics listed? Is the design suitable for plaid, striped, or obvious diagonal fabrics?
- Look at the photographs or sketches on your pattern envelope to determine the silhouette of the garment. Does it stand away from the body or fall closely against it? Is it crisply tailored or softly gathered? Is the design detailed or does it have only a few seams?
- Feel the fabric's weight, bulk, and texture. Does it lend itself to your pattern's silhouette and line? Will it drape or gather effectively? Unwrap a length of fabric from the bolt, gather it up in your hand, and see how the fabric hangs.
- Analyze the design of the fabric. A dramatic print or highly textured fabric is best for a garment with simple lines, while a plain fabric allows the design lines of a garment to be highlighted. Will the fabric require matching? Does it have a nap or pile, shading, or a one-way design?
- Test the fabric for wearability and performance. Crush it. Is it wrinkle-resistant? Stretch it. Does it give? Does it spring back? Crease it. Is it suitable for pleats? Read the label on the bolt end for fiber content, finishes, and care information.
- Examine the fabric closely. Hold it up to the light. How strong and close is the weave? Loose weaves ravel easily and require more finishing details. Will it require any special sewing techniques? Is the fabric finished off-grain? Are there any imperfections in the weave or uneven streaks? For a printed fabric, does the design correspond to the grain?
- How will the fabric look on you? Unfold some and hold it up to your face before a mirror. Do the color and scale suit you? Will the fabric be appropriate for the garment's intended use and care? Carry with you snips or color swatches of other wardrobe items which must coordinate with your new garment. Above all, will you enjoy wearing this fabric?

Special consideration must also be given to the stretchability of knitted fabrics and to the additional yardage (metrage) requirements of certain fabrics, as explained on the following pages.

Stretchability of Knits

Knitted fabrics have a wide range of stretchability. Some are very stable and can be handled like a woven fabric, while others have considerable stretch in either one or both directions. It is very important to determine the amount of stretch in a knit before you make your pattern and fabric selection.

Many patterns recommend both woven and knitted fabrics as suitable for that particular design. For these patterns, the stretchability of the knit is not as important as the weight and texture of the fabric. Double knits can be tailored for suits, coats, and dresses while single knits are best for softer designs that drape and flow. For loose or bulky knits, patterns that are simple in design are recommended.

However, some patterns have been designed specifically for use with stretchable knits. These patterns have very little wearing ease and rely on the stretchability of the fabric to provide ease for movement and comfort. Thus only stretchable knits can be used for these patterns—regular fabrics or stable knits would result in a garment that fits too tightly. These patterns are marked in the Vogue catalogue and on the pattern envelope with "use only stretchable knits."

Vogue Patterns has developed a Stretch Gauge to assist you in determining the stretchability or "give" of an individual knit. The weight or texture of a knit is not an indicator of its stretchability. Some lightweight knits are very stable, just as some heavyweight knits are very stretchy. The Stretch Gauge appears on the inside back cover of the Vogue catalogue and on the individual pattern envelopes for your convenience.

To use the Stretch Gauge, fold the fabric 4" (10 cm) from the crosswise edge and place it in a relaxed state on the Stretch Gauge. Firmly hold the left edge of the fabric in place at the end of the gauge and gently stretch the fabric to the right. If the fabric design is distorted or the upper edge curls, the fabric is stretched too much. To be considered a stretchable knit, your fabric should stretch easily to the right end of the gauge, indicating that 4" (10 cm) of the fabric will stretch to at least 5⅜" (13.7 cm).

Now release the fabric end in your right hand to observe its ability to recover. If it springs back immediately, you are assured of a garment whose shape will not change. If the fabric does not recover well, you will have to control the stretch during construction to avoid a misshapen garment.

Some patterns, such as swimwear, require a two-way stretch fabric that must stretch equally in both directions. For these patterns, be sure to check the stretchability in both the crosswise and lengthwise directions to determine if the fabric is a two-way stretchable knit.

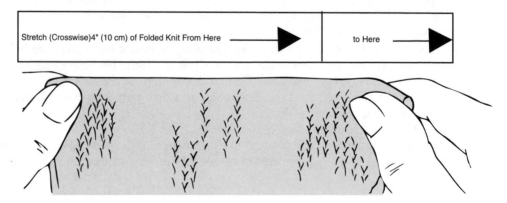

Stretch (Crosswise)4" (10 cm) of Folded Knit From Here ⟶   to Here ⟶

Vintage Vogue

Everlasting allure…There is something undeniably glamorous about the fashions of the 1930s, 40s and 50s. The timeless look of tailored suits, exquisite gowns and handsome jackets, with all the details of custom couture, never go out of style. Original dresses, jackets and skirts from these past decades have returned to the pages of the Vogue catalogue--showing that fashion truly does come full circle.

The 1930s

The 1940s

The 1940s

The 1950s

Fabrics Requiring Extra Yardage

Some fabrics, due to their construction or pattern design, require additional yardage (metrage) for the fabric layout. Refer to the back of your pattern envelope for special yardage (metrage) requirements and information. However, for some other fabrics, you will have to make your own calculations.

If your fabric is directional with a nap or pile, shading, or a one-way design, use the separate "with nap" yardage (metrage) requirements. Always read the envelope carefully. For some patterns, the yardage (metrage) for certain fabric widths is the same for both "with nap" and "without nap" fabrics, while for other fabric widths the amount differs. If you are uncertain of either the construction or design of your fabric, purchase the "with nap" yardage (metrage) amount so that you will be able to follow a nap layout if necessary.

If your fabric is a plaid, stripe, or geometric design, allowance for matching the pattern is usually not included in the yardages (metrages) given. To calculate the amount of additional yardage (metrage) required for matching, you must measure the length of one repeat, which is one complete motif of the design. Then multiply this measurement by the amount of yardage (metrage) required. For example, if the repeat measures 4½" (11.5 cm) and 4 yards (3.8 M) of fabric are required--you will have to purchase an additional 18" (46 cm) or ½ yard (0.5 M) of fabric for a total of 4½ yards (4.15 M).

A large-scale print may require additional yardage (metrage) in order to balance the design appropriately on the figure. Use the same calculations as for plaids.

Some fabric designs may fall into more than one category when determining yardage (metrage). For example, a large uneven plaid will require a "with nap" layout, matching, and design placement on the figure. Thus, consider all aspects of your fabric to be certain that you will have enough yardage (metrage) when you start to lay out your pattern pieces. For complete accuracy, some fabric stores will allow you to make a trial layout on the fabric before it is cut for purchase.

Fabric Width Conversion Chart

We have provided this guide to help solve those quandaries that occur when the width of the fabric you've chosen is not included on the pattern envelope. It is strictly an estimate, and does not include changes in your fabric requirements caused by pattern alterations, large-scale fabric designs, directional fabrics, and garment designs with unusually shaped or large pieces. In these instances, it's best to exercise your own judgment about how much fabric you'll need.

Fabric Width	**32"** (81 cm)	**35"- 36"** (90 cm)	**39"** (100 cm)	**41"** (104 cm)	**44"- 45"** (115 cm)	**50"** (127 cm)	**52"- 54"** (140 cm)	**58"- 60"** (150 cm)
Yardage (Metrage)	1⅞ (1.8m)	1¾ (1.6m)	1½ (1.4m)	1½ (1.4m)	1⅜ (1.3m)	1¼ (1.2m)	1⅛ (1.1m)	1 (1.0m)
	2¼ (2.1m)	2 (1.9m)	1¾ (1.6m)	1¾ (1.6m)	1⅝ (1.5m)	1½ (1.4m)	1⅜ (1.3m)	1¼ (1.2m)
	2½ (2.3m)	2¼ (2.1m)	2 (1.9m)	2 (1.9m)	1¾ (1.6m)	1⅝ (1.5m)	1½ (1.4m)	1⅜ (1.3m)
	2¾ (2.6m)	2½ (2.3m)	2¼ (2.1m)	2¼ (2.1m)	2⅛ (2.0m)	1¾ (1.6m)	1¾ (1.6m)	1⅝ (1.5m)
	3⅛ (2.9m)	2⅞ (2.9m)	2½ (2.3m)	2½ (2.3m)	2¼ (2.1m)	2 (1.9m)	1⅞ (1.8m)	1¾ (1.6m)
	3⅜ (3.1m)	3⅛ (2.9m)	2¾ (2.6m)	2¾ (2.6m)	2½ (2.3m)	2¼ (2.1m)	2 (1.9m)	1⅞ (1.8m)
	3¾ (3.5m)	3⅜ (3.1m)	3 (2.8m)	2⅞ (2.9m)	2¾ (2.6m)	2⅜ (2.2m)	2¼ (2.1m)	2 (1.9m)
	4 (3.7m)	3¾ (3.5m)	3¼ (3.0m)	3⅛ (2.9m)	2⅞ (2.9m)	2⅝ (2.4m)	2⅜ (2.2m)	2¼ (2.1m)
	4⅜ (4.0m)	4¼ (3.9m)	3½ (3.2m)	3⅜ (3.1m)	3⅛ (2.9m)	2¾ (2.6m)	2⅝ (2.4m)	2⅜ (2.2m)
	4⅝ (4.3m)	4½ (4.2m)	3¾ (3.5m)	3⅝ (3.4m)	3⅜ (3.1m)	3 (2.8m)	2¾ (2.6m)	2⅝ (2.4m)
	5 (4.6m)	4¾ (4.4m)	4 (3.7m)	3⅞ (3.6m)	3⅝ (3.4m)	3¼ (3.0m)	2⅞ (2.9m)	2¾ (2.6m)
	5¼ (4.8m)	5 (4.6m)	4¼ (3.9m)	4⅛ (3.8m)	3⅞ (3.6m)	3⅜ (3.1m)	3⅛ (2.9m)	2⅞ (2.9m)

Reprinted courtesy of New Jersey Cooperative Extension Service, Rutgers, The State University

Fabric Terminology

Before preparing and cutting your fabric, it is important to understand the terminology for woven and knitted fabrics.

Grain is the direction in which the threads composing the fabric run. Every woven fabric consists of crosswise threads worked under and over the more sturdy lengthwise threads. The narrow, flat, woven border resulting at both lengthwise sides when the crosswise threads reverse direction is called the **selvage**. The threads composing it are strong and densely woven. This border is a prefinished edge, and may be used to advantage in center back seams, waistbands, etc. The direction of the lengthwise threads running parallel to the selvage is known as **lengthwise grain**, or sometimes "straight-of-fabric." These threads are very strong and stable, since they must withstand great tension during weaving. For this reason, garments are usually cut with the lengthwise grain running vertically for durability. The direction of the crosswise threads, running from selvage to selvage at right angles across the lengthwise threads, is known as the **crosswise grain**. In most fabrics it has a very slight amount of give.

A third term used to describe direction on woven fabric is **bias**. Bias is any diagonal intersecting the lengthwise and crosswise threads. Fabric cut on the bias grain possesses much greater elasticity than that cut on the crosswise grain. Maximum stretchability occurs on the **true bias**, which is obtained by folding your on-grain fabric diagonally so the crosswise threads are parallel to the selvage. Thus, true bias exists at any 45° angle to any straight edge of a fabric whose lengthwise and crosswise threads are perpendicular.

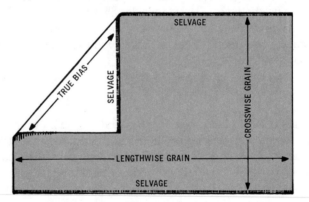

Knitted fabrics are structured of interlocking loops of yarn. **Wales** or **ribs** are columns of loops running parallel to the long measurement of a knitted fabric. They correspond to the lengthwise grain of a woven fabric. **Courses** are the crosswise rows of loops.

Fabric as sold in stores is folded or rolled lengthwise on a cardboard or metal form. In this packaged state it is known as a **bolt**. You will find that on the bolt the selvages may be located at the top and bottom of the retainer, or both selvages may be at one end with a fold at the other. Knitted fabrics come either flat or tubular. Tubular knits can be cut open along one edge.

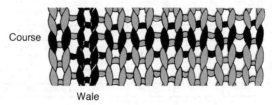

Preparing Your Fabric

You're excited about your new project, and anxious to start sewing immediately. Hang onto your enthusiasm, but don't be so eager to begin cutting that you neglect the all-important preparation. Fabric and pattern may both need attention before you do the final layout, and the success of your finished garment depends on care in these preparatory steps.

First, turn your attention to your fabric. Carefully steam-press it to remove wrinkles and fold lines. If the fabric has been long in the store, this may reveal a soiled mark along the fold, which must be washed out or dry-cleaned before you proceed. In some fabrics, such as knits and permanent-finish fabrics, the crease may not always be removed by pressing. For these fabrics, avoid layouts where pattern pieces are placed on the fold. If no other layouts are included in your pattern, place the pattern pieces so that the crease will not appear in a conspicuous place on your garment.

Straightening Fabric Ends

Straighten the ends of a woven fabric to coincide with the crosswise threads by snipping close to the selvage, pulling a crosswise thread until the fabric puckers, then cutting along that puckered line across the entire width. This is the most time-consuming method, but also the most accurate. If a crosswise thread is readily visible, you may omit pulling threads and cut directly.

Tearing the fabric is the quickest means, but should be used only with extreme caution. The pulling action may throw the first several inches off grain at both fabric ends, or if the tear is not done swiftly and accurately, the cloth may suddenly split along the lengthwise grain.

For a knitted fabric, cut along a course or crosswise line of loops to straighten the fabric ends. If the loops are not easily seen, it may be necessary to first mark the course with chalk or thread tracing. These markings can also be used for determining if the knit is on-grain or not. A tubular knit can then be cut open lengthwise following a rib or lengthwise row of loops.

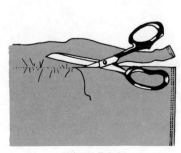

Woven Fabric

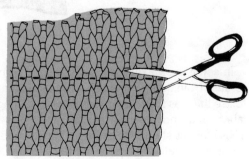

Knitted Fabric

Straightening Grain

We cannot emphasize strongly enough how vital the correct grain is to the final appearance of your garment. Your fabric is on grain when crosswise and lengthwise threads or loops are at perfect right angles to each other.

Check the grain after the ends of your fabric have been evened. Fold the fabric lengthwise, matching selvages and fabric ends. If the edges do not align along all three sides, the fabric is off-grain and must be straightened. If the edges are even, check also to see if the corners form right angles by aligning a corner of the fabric with a corner of your cutting surface. For knitted fabrics, match only the ends of the fabric; unlike the selvages of a woven fabric, the lengthwise edges of a flat knit are not always straight.

If the fabric is only slightly off-grain, it can be straightened by steam-pressing the threads into proper alignment. With the fabric folded lengthwise, right sides together, pin every five inches along the selvages and ends. You may need to pin the fabric to the ironing board to keep it square. Press firmly, stroking from the selvages toward the fold.

 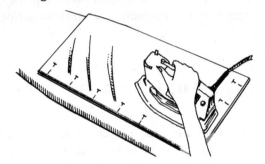

Fabric that is very much off-grain can be straightened by pulling the fabric gently but firmly in the opposite direction from the way the ends slant until a perfect right angle corner is formed. If the fabric is washable, place it in warm water for a few minutes to help relax the finish before pulling the fabric ends. Then pin a selvage to a taut clothesline every few inches or lay on a flat surface, and allow to dry. Repeat if necessary.

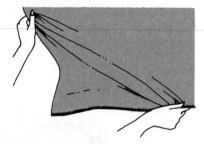

In some cases you may have to try a combination of the above techniques for the best results. Note that permanent-finish fabrics can never be straightened. It is perfectly all right to use them as they are, matching and pinning the selvage only, not the ends. Some printed fabrics may not be off-grain, but the print design does not coincide with the grainline. These fabrics should be avoided. If you should wish to use them, you must allow the print design to dictate the layout, not the grain.

Preshrinking

Many fabrics on today's market are "ready for the needle" and require no preshrinking. Always read the label on the fabric bolt to determine the specifics on shrinkage and whether the fabric is washable or dry cleanable. If the fabric has not been shrunk by the manufacturer or if it will shrink more than one percent according to the label, you must shrink your fabric before cutting it out. If you are unsure, it is always safer to preshrink your fabric rather than discover a shrinkage problem after the garment is completed. Washing or dry-cleaning can also help to remove resins used for finishing some knitted and woven fabrics that can cause skipped stitches.

For washable fabrics, you can launder and dry the fabric following the same methods that you will use with the finished garment. Or fold the fabric evenly and immerse it in hot water for thirty minutes to an hour. Gently squeeze out the water and dry according to the fabric care instructions.

Dry cleanable fabrics such as woolens should be shrunk by a professional dry cleaner if possible. To do it yourself, first straighten fabric ends, snip selvages at intervals, and fold in half lengthwise. Baste across the ends and along the selvages. Place a very damp sheet on a flat surface and lay the fabric on the sheet. Fold carefully, keeping the sheet on the outside. Leave the fabric folded overnight in a tub or basin. Unfold, smooth and stretch the fabric into shape and on grain. Let the fabric dry and press lightly with a steam iron. Then test for grain perfection before cutting, as previously discussed.

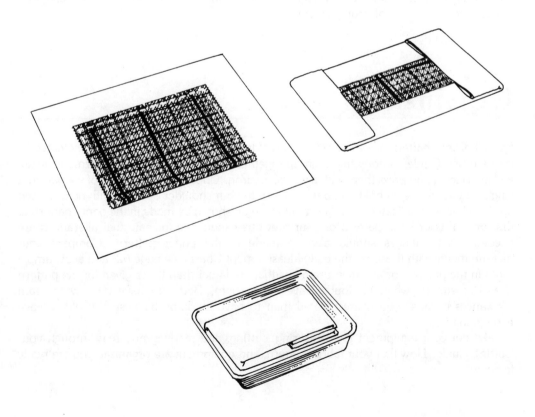

Identifying Right Side of Fabric

Occasionally the right side of the fabric is not readily discernible from the wrong. The way the fabric is displayed on the bolt can be an excellent clue in distinguishing the right and wrong sides, for you will find that certain fabrics are usually wound on the bolt in a consistent manner. For example, cottons and linens are almost always folded in half with their right sides out, then placed on the bolt. Wools can be packaged either prefolded with the right side in and wrapped on a rectangular bolt or rolled unfolded on a tube with the right side toward the inside. Many easily marred, delicate fabrics and imported fabrics are also rolled with their right side on the inside as protection against damage.

If you've purchased the fabric in a state other than its usual packaging, or forgotten which side is which, try the following procedures to differentiate the right side from the wrong side. Look at the center fold, which is parallel to the lengthwise grain or selvages, and refer to the usual packaging procedures mentioned above. Examine the selvages for slubs, nubs, and other irregularities. In general, the selvages will look less finished on the wrong side of the fabric. You can also examine the fabric surface itself to see if the finish used will indicate the right side. The finished side may be shinier, flatter, more brushed, or the weave more pronounced.

For knitted fabrics, the cut edge usually rolls toward the right side when pulled in the direction of the greatest stretch. The right side also may be more decorative or textured.

As a last resort, pick the side you like best! There is no reason why you cannot use either side of many fabrics. Just be very certain to use the same side consistently when laying out your pattern on the fabric. If you neglect to do so, the slightest variation in shading can destroy the good looks of your garment.

Organizing

Sort all of your pattern pieces, selecting those for the view you have chosen, as indicated by your Cutting Guide. Among these, group together the pieces for the main garment, lining, and interfacing and press them with a warm, dry iron. Check the proportion of the garment length to your figure by holding up the pattern to your shoulder or waist, with hems folded up. If a change is indicated, an adjustment in length should be made in the paper pattern at this time. If your basic pattern or your previous experience indicate that alterations are needed, such changes should also be made in the paper pattern. Compare your measurements with those on the body Measurement Chart (see page 62) and allow ample room in the pattern for any measurements that are larger than those given for the pattern size. Remember—when in doubt, leave extra room! Better to have nice, wide seam allowances because you overestimated than to have to skimp because you didn't leave enough fabric.

Take out your equipment for measuring, cutting, and marking and read through your Cutting Guide. Now that your fabric, pattern, and equipment are organized you are ready to begin!

Cutting with Care

Assuming your pattern alterations are double-checked and your fabric is fully prepared, circle the correct layout for your version, size, and approximate fabric width on your Cutting Guide. Be sure to use the "with nap" layout if your fabric is a knit or has a nap or pile, shading, or a one-way design. The pattern layout provides you with a completely reliable guide for laying out your pattern swiftly and economically. If you think you can bend the rules by laying some pieces a little off grain to fit, don't. A simple maneuver like this can jeopardize all your future efforts on that garment—one side of the skirt may flare more than the other, the entire bodice section might ripple and pull, and facings cut off-grain will pucker.

Here are some ideas used by professionals—suggestions to follow as you lay out and cut your pattern for perfect results every time.

Layout

- Pin fabric every three inches (7.5 cm) or so on indicated foldline and along all ends and selvages. The selvages may have to be clipped every few inches (centimeters) so that the fabric will lie flat. For knitted fabrics, match straightened ends or thread trace along one rib near center of fabric to use as lengthwise foldline or for aligning crosswise fold.
- Extend a short grainline to pattern ends with pencil, and measure often to be sure that the pattern is placed on the correct grain.
- Double-check all alterations to see that seam and cutting lines are redrawn and all corresponding pieces are altered, including facings.
- Lay out all pattern pieces before you begin cutting to be sure you have enough fabric.
- Place pattern pieces printed side up unless otherwise indicated by the Cutting Guide.
- Place pattern pieces right side up unless otherwise indicate on the Fabric Cutting Layout. All layouts are for with or without nap unless specified.

RIGHT SIDE OF PATTERN	WRONG SIDE OF PATTERN	RIGHT SIDE OF FABRIC	RIGHT SIDE OF FABRIC

S/T = SIZES(S)/TAILLE(S)	**EAST**= ALL SIZES/TOUTES TAILLES
* = WITH NAP/AVEC SENS	** = WITHOUT NAP/SANS SENS
S/L = SELVAGE(S)/LISIERES(S)	**F/P** = FOLD/PLIURE
CF/PT = CROSSWISE FOLD/PLIURE TRAME	

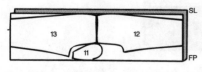

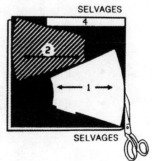

With Fold--fabric is folded in half on the lengthwise grain, right sides together, matching selvages.

Without Fold--fabric is folded in half with right sides together on the crosswise grain of the fabric, matching selvages. Cut from selvage to selvage. Turn the upper layer completely around so nap runs in same direction as lower layer.

Double Fold—fabric is folded twice along the lengthwise grain, right sides together, with the selvages usually meeting in the center.

Single Layer—fabric is opened up to single thickness and placed right side up. For fur pile fabrics, place pile side down.

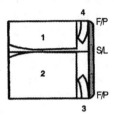

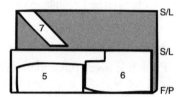

Partial Fold—fabric is folded with right sides together on lengthwise grain, only wide enough to fit the width of the pattern piece or pieces on the fold. Other pattern pieces are placed on the single layer of fabric above the folded portion.

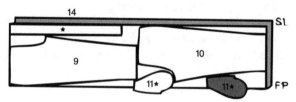

- When your layout shows a pattern piece extending beyond the fabric fold, cut the other pieces first, then unfold the fabric, and cut out the remaining pattern piece.

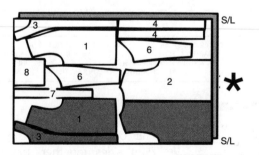

- Stars are used to indicate that the pattern piece is cut only once on a single layer of fabric.

- If the layout is marked with a large asterisk, the fabric must be folded as Without Fold (see page 138).
- If the fabric design must be matched, always take care to match seamlines, not cutting lines. See next section on Special Fabric Layouts.

Cutting

- Pin first along lengthwise grainlines and foldlines.

- Place pins perpendicular to and ¼" (6 mm) inside the cutting line and diagonally at the corners of the pattern, spacing them about every three or four inches (7.5 cm or 10 cm) apart, or closer for sheer or slippery fabrics.

- Use long, bent-handled shears, and cut with steady, even slashes. Never cut out a pattern with pinking shears. Use them only to finish seams during construction.

- To avoid distorting the fabric, cut "directionally" with the grain.

- Never lift the fabric from the table. Keep one hand flat on the pattern piece while cutting.

- Use the point of the scissors to cut notches outward. Cut groups of notches in continuous blocks for easier matching.

- Be sure to use each pattern piece the correct number of times. Such details as pockets, cuffs, welts, and belt carriers are likely to need more than the usual two pieces.

- Fold the cut pieces softly and lay them on a flat surface.

- Save fabric scraps left from cutting. They are often needed for such things as bound buttonholes, sleeve plackets, and other sections not cut from pattern pieces; or for testing tension, stitch length, and pressing techniques.

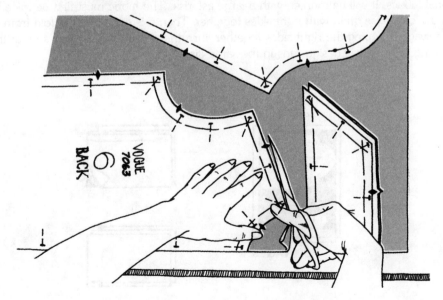

Special Fabric Layouts

If you have been avoiding fabrics that require special layouts, such as napped or pile fabrics, diagonals, plaids, stripes, and border prints, let us dispel your fears by providing a reassuring supplement to your Fabric Cutting Layout. You can usually use the same methods for preparing, pinning, and cutting, but do give more than average attention to laying out your pattern pieces and basting the garment together.

If you haven't had any experience with the special demands of an unusual fabric, arm yourself with our suggestions and a spirit of adventure. Choose a fairly simple design until experience bolsters your confidence, and sew ahead.

Directional Fabrics

Fabrics with nap, pile, shading, or one-way designs must be cut with all pattern pieces placed in the same direction. If your pattern suggests these fabrics, your Fabric Cutting Layout includes a "with nap" layout, which you must follow.

Napped fabrics, such as fleece, are those which are brushed after weaving to produce a directional, fuzzy surface on one side. Pile fabrics, such as velvet, are actually constructed so some of their component yarns rise at an angle from the woven surface of the fabric. Both give a different impression in color and texture according to the direction of the nap or pile. Cut with nap running down for a lighter, shinier look; with nap running up for a deeper, richer color. The fabric will feel rough when you move your hand against the direction of the nap, and smooth when with the nap. With piles and naps, pin the pattern to the wrong side of the fabric so that the pattern tissue does not shift.

Knits and textured fabrics, such as satins and brocades, also have to be treated as one-way fabrics because of the way light is reflected off their surface, causing a shading effect.

For fabrics with a one-way print, be sure that the print will be right side up when the garment is completed.

Sometimes a special cutting layout is included in your Fabric Cutting Layout for directional fabrics. It will be marked with a large asterisk. The fabric must first be folded in half on the crosswise grain with right sides together. Then it is cut along the fold from selvage to selvage. Keeping the right sides together, turn the upper layer around so that the nap, shading, or one-way design runs in the same direction.

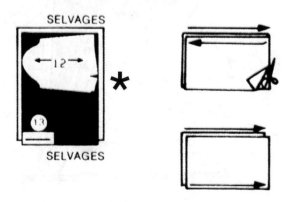

Diagonals

Diagonal fabrics require special care in pattern selection and pattern layout in order that the direction of the diagonal remains consistent in the garment and does not create any unusual optical illusions. Twill weaves, such as flannel, serge, and gabardine, have a diagonal ridge running from either the lower left corner to the upper right, or from the lower right to the upper left on the fabric. Sometimes the diagonal is hardly noticeable unless the fabric is napped. Other times, it is very distinct because of different colored or heavy yarns used in the fabric. Diagonally striped fabrics are usually printed, not woven, and are treated the same as twills.

Select your pattern carefully, choosing a simple design with set-in sleeves, straight underarm darts, and a slim skirt. If your pattern has the warning "obvious diagonal fabrics are not suitable," it is an indication that diagonal stripes or prints will be difficult or impossible to match. However, many diagonals are less obvious when draped into a garment than lying on a flat surface. Always drape a length of fabric on yourself in front of a mirror to determine how prominent the diagonal will be.

Certain design features are to be avoided with diagonals. Collars cut on the fold and roll-back lapels will have the diagonal pattern running in different directions on the left and right sides. Strange illusions will be created by V-necklines, long bias darts, and any sleeve cut-in-one with the bodice-the diagonal pattern will be parallel to one side of the neckline, dart, or sleeve and will be perpendicular to the other. Garments with bias-cut side seams will have the diagonals meeting each other perpendicularly.

When working with a diagonal fabric, you must plan your layout carefully so that the diagonal is consistent in both front and back. Cut out your fabric single thickness with all the pattern pieces running in the same direction as in a "with nap" layout. If your collar is cut on a fold, change the foldline to a seamline and add a ⅝" (15 mm) seam allowance. Lay out the collar on the bias with the diagonal running parallel or perpendicular to the original foldline. (For printed fabrics, the diagonal may not be exactly on the true bias.) Or you can lay out the collar on the bias and flip at the foldline to avoid a seam. Now the collar will match on both the left and right sides. For the rest of the garment, match the diagonal at the notches and dots along the seamline.

Features to Avoid
with Diagonals

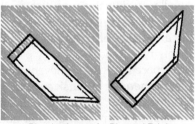

Planning Layout for Diagonal Fabric

If your fabric is identical on both the right and wrong side, the pattern can be laid out so that the diagonal forms a chevron. Cut the fabric into two equal lengths and place one length on top of the other with the right side of one against the wrong side of the other, matching the diagonal. The pattern, which must have a center front and center back seam, can be cut double thickness.

When a diagonal fabric is cut on the bias, the design will run horizontally or vertically. You can use this contrasting effect for pockets, cuffs, and bindings.

Plaids

Plaids present an additional design dimension in any garment. When sewing with plaids, therefore, the idea is to avoid extremely complicated fashions and let the plaid tell the story. Also keep in mind that the size of the plaid should be in scale with both the garment and the person wearing it if it is to flatter rather than overwhelm. For the best results, plaid garments should be made only in designs recommended for plaids by your pattern catalogue or the back of the pattern envelope. If "Not Suitable for Plaids," it is because they cannot be properly matched at the seams.

There are several things to keep in mind when purchasing a plaid fabric. First, always remember to buy extra yardage (metrage) for matching. The actual amount will be determined by the size of your pattern, the size of the plaid repeat, and the number of lengths of major pattern pattern pieces required by your Fabric Cutting Layout. Secondly, never purchase your plaid from a small sample, as it seldom shows the repeat. A strong vertical or horizontal movement in the fabric, which might easily affect your choice of fabric, can only be noted from looking at a large piece of fabric. Thirdly, if you decide on a printed rather than a woven plaid, check carefully to see that the stripes of the plaid are on grain. If the plaid is printed just slightly off grain, match the plaid since it is more noticeable than the grain in this particular instance. Do not buy an extremely off grain printed plaid, since it will not drape or mold satisfactorily when made into a garment.

For the most attractive and professional looking results, be concerned with the placement of the lines of your plaid, especially the dominant stripe. The lines should always be continuous from front to back and from neck to hem. This also holds true for two-piece dresses and suits; the plaid lines of the jacket or top should match those of the skirt. Horizontally, avoid placing a heavy, dominant stripe at the bustline or waistline. It is generally preferable to place it at the hemline; this means, of course, that you must determine the finished length of your garment and mark it on the pattern tissue before you cut. On an A-line or other curved hem, the horizontal lines will appear to arc slightly downward toward the side seams if the center fold or seam is on the straight grain. In such a case, ignore the traditional rule and place your fabric's least dominant section along the garment's lower edge, thus drawing a minimum amount of attention to the distortion of the plaid design at the hemline. Vertically, place the dominant line of the plaid at center front if possible. Always make all your fitting adjustments on the pattern before you cut out your fabric, or you may destroy all your careful placement and matching efforts.

Since the kind of plaid you buy will determine your layout, you should understand the elements of a plaid design. A plaid is composed of stripes crossing each other at right angles, spaced evenly or unevenly, and repeated in sequence. All manufactured plaids consist of a *repeat* or a foursided area in which the pattern and color of the design are complete. These units, arranged continuously side by side, form the fabric pattern and determine whether the plaid is even or uneven. In an *even plaid,* the stripe arrangement is the same in both the lengthwise and crosswise directions, creating a perfectly square repeat. When folded in any direction through the center of any repeat, the halves must form a mirror image. In an *uneven plaid,* the design and spacing are different in the lengthwise, crosswise, or both directions.

Plaid test: To test the plaid, first fold the fabric diagonally through the center of any repeat. (Plaid must be perfectly on-grain.) If spaces and colors match, test further by folding the plaid vertically or horizontally through the center of any repeat.

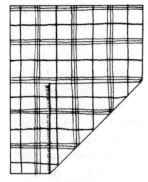

In an even plaid the spaces and colors match in both directions.

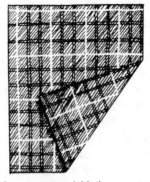

In an uneven plaid, the spaces and colors do not match in both directions.

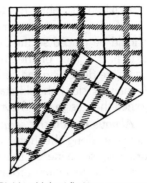

Plaids which at first appear even may, in reality, be uneven.

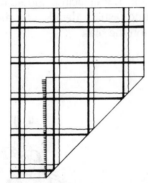

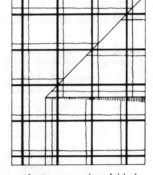

The design in this plaid does form a perfect square when folded diagonally, but does not make a mirror image when folded vertically or horizontally through the center of any repeat.

Slip basting: Slip basting will help to ensure a perfectly matched plaid. To slip baste, work from the right side of the fabric. Crease and turn under the seam allowance along one edge. Lay the folded edge in position on the corresponding piece, matching the plaid at the seamline, and pin. Slip the needle through the upper fold, then through the lower layer using a single long stitch. Continue this stitch for the entire length of the seam. You can now machine-stitch the seam in the normal manner from the wrong side.

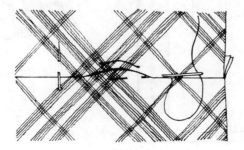

EVEN PLAIDS

Even plaids are relatively easy to match. Prepare your fabric according to the cutting layout. Since the fabric is not always folded correctly on the bolt, make sure the fold is at the center of the dominant line or the center of the plaid design. The selvages will not be even when the fabric has to be refolded. The "without nap" layout can be used, but often the shading or coloring makes the "with nap" layout most effective. The pattern pieces should be placed so the notches and the symbols along the seamline are matched at the side and center of the front and back pieces. Center seams must be placed with the seamline directly in the center of the plaid repeat for a straight seam, while a shaped seam (center or side) should start out in the center of the plaid repeat. When the seams are joined the design will chevron—the angle will depend on the shape of the seam.

Always match the seamlines, not the cutting lines. Start by placing the predetermined hemline along the dominant line of the plaid. Plaids should be matched at the front armhole seamline at the notch, but the curve of the sleeve cap may make the plaid impossible to match around the rest of the armhole seam. You will also have difficulty matching diagonals—darts, shoulder seams, etc. The side seams will not match above the bust dart. With two-piece garments, remember that the plaids should be continuous from the top to the bottom when worn. Always match design details such as cuffs and pockets to the plaid portions they cover on the finished garment. Lapel facings should be cut from the same part of the plaid as the bodice. For interesting fashion details, you may wish to cut pockets, yokes, cuffs, and bound buttonhole strips on the bias.

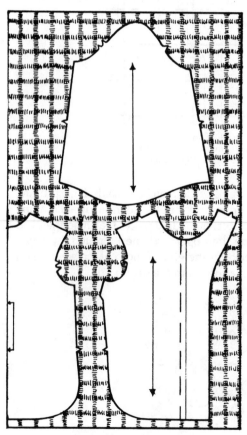

Layout for Even Plaid Fabric

UNEVEN PLAIDS

To be realistic, we must admit that sewing with uneven plaids is not for the novice. But it can be a rewarding experience if you remember to choose a pattern with as few construction lines as possible to reduce the number of matching points.

The matching and placement concepts are the same as for even plaids with the following exceptions. Uneven plaids cannot be matched in both directions. Pick the stripes of the plaid design that you want to be emphasized, both vertically and horizontally, relative to your figure. Choose the desired plaid stripe for the center front. Fold the fabric, matching two desired stripes for front sections. Pin at intervals, matching the plaid lines of both layers. Next, pin the front pattern pieces to the fabric, placing the center front on the desired line. Match the plaid lines for the front sections, either vertically or horizontally as the fabric dictates. When the front pattern pieces are placed satisfactorily, place the back pieces, matching the side seamlines to those of the front. You may need to refold your fabric. Always use a "with nap" layout. Some plaids and fabric widths necessitate planning and cutting the garment on a single thickness, using the same methods as explained above. Be sure to turn the pattern pieces over (printed side down) to cut the left side of garment sections.

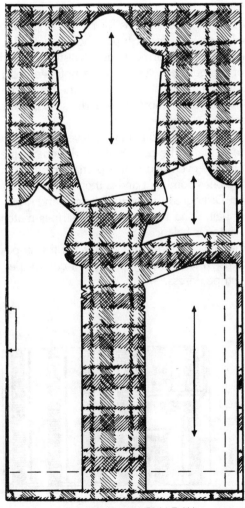

Layout for Uneven Plaid Fabric

CHECKS

In matching checks, let the scale of the pattern be the deciding factor. Checks ½" (13 mm) square or larger are usually matched, following the same principles as for even plaids. Smaller checks do not require matching unless they would be visually disturbing in the finished garment if left unmatched.

Stripes

Sewing with stripes should definitely influence your pattern selection. Designs illustrated in stripes are especially suitable; if your pattern is marked "Not Suitable for Stripes," it is because they cannot be matched properly or will distract from the design lines. It would also be wise to read *Your Fashion Analysis*, pages 17 to 35, to help you decide which stripe and direction-balanced or unbalanced, horizontal or vertical-will be best suited to your figure. The amount of extra fabric required for matching horizontal or unbalanced vertical stripes will depend upon the size of the stripe repeat and the number of pattern lengths in the Fabric Cutting Layout. The principles for working with stripes also apply to wide wale corduroy and other obviously wide-ribbed fabrics.

While the methods for laying out stripes are basically the same as for plaids, stripes are easier to match because the design runs in only one direction. Stripes should run in the same direction throughout the garment. Other parts of the garment-cuffs, waistbands, and pockets-must be adjusted to match the body of the garment. Stripes on a notched collar should match those on the lapel. Set-in sleeves should match at the notch of the front armhole seamline. Buttonholes should be aligned with the direction of the stripes and, if the stripes are very large, they should match the color of the stripe.

You will have to discover which stripe is dominant in order to plan your layout. Squint at the fabric to see whether the widest stripe, the stripe at the center of the design, or the stripe with the strongest color is dominant. You may even find that a particular group of stripes, acting as a part of the overall design, becomes dominant and is then treated in the layout the same way as a single dominant stripe. Distinguish between balanced and unbalanced stripes by folding the dominant stripe in half along its length. If the stripes match when a corner of the fabric is folded back, the stripe is balanced.

Once you've become familiar with the principles involved in stripe layouts, let the stripes suggest creative visual effects. Don't be afraid to use a bias binding, pocket, or cuff, or perhaps a horizontally striped yoke on a vertically striped dress.

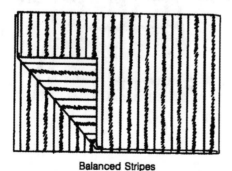

Balanced Stripes

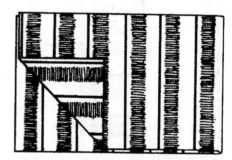

Unbalanced Stripes

BALANCED STRIPES

Horizontal: Matching a balanced stripe horizontally is the easiest of the stripe layouts. The lengthwise grainline arrow should run perpendicular to the stripe. The general rule is to place the dominant stripe at the hem foldline, so you must predetermine the hemline before you cut. There are two exceptions, however; if you have an obviously curved hemline or if thus placing the dominant stripe will also place it at the bustline or hipline, place the hemline at a less dominant location. If you do place the dominant stripe at the hemline, center a portion of it at the hemline in the center front and back of the garment to obtain the proper optical illusion. Match the stripes at center seams and at side seams below the bust dart, and make sure they are continuous from neck to hem, especially with two-piece garments such as suits.

Vertical: With the lengthwise grain arrow of your pattern parallel to the stripes, center the dominant stripe at the center front and back for the best-looking results. For a center fold, simply fold the fabric through the dominant stripe. If the center is on a seam or opening, pin two dominant stripes together and place the center seamline (not cutting line) through the center of the dominant stripe. If the pattern has a straight center front or back seam, you will have to plan carefully to allow for the seam allowances and for matching the stripes. If you are making a two-piece garment, make sure that the dominant stripe is at the centers of both pieces and runs continuously from the top or jacket to the skirt. Place the sleeve so that it matches on the front armhole seamline at the notch.

For an A-line skirt, a chevron will form at the side seams, the angle of which will depend on the fullness of the skirt. Note: Do not use styles for striped fabric that state specifically "not suitable for stripes," as this designation was made because you will not be able to match the stripes at the seams.

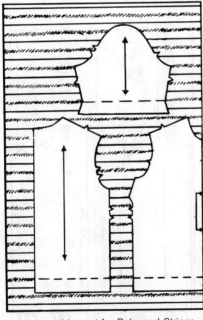

Horizontal Layout for Balanced Stripes

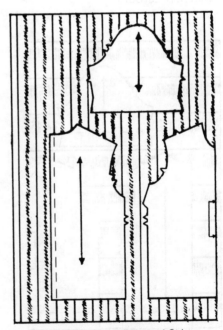

Vertical Layout for Balanced Stripes

UNBALANCED STRIPES

Horizontal: To plan for an unbalanced horizontal stripe, place the dominant stripe in the same manner as for a balanced stripe on the previous page. Be sure the lengthwise grainline arrow is perpendicular to the stripe. Predetermine and mark the hem lengths of all the garment sections before you cut your fabric. Then, using a "with nap" cutting layout, lay all your garment pattern pieces in the same direction. Use the notches and symbols to adjust the layout until the side seams match and the sleeve matches the bodice at the front armhole seamline. Also take care to lay the pieces so that the stripe design will be continuous and running in the same direction from neck to hem, especially with two-piece garments such as suits. For example, the stripe on a jacket hem should be a continuation of the stripe on the skirt.

Vertical: To use an unbalanced stripe vertically, the lengthwise grainline arrow should correspond with the stripe. To have the stripes move in the same direction around the body, use a "with nap" layout. Choose the desired stripe for the center front. Next, fold through the center of the stripe for a center front fold or pin two matching desired stripes together for a center front seam. Pin the pattern to the fabric, placing the center front on the desired stripe. Place the back pieces with the same stripe at the center. Refold the fabric if necessary. Depending on the design repeat, you may be able to plan side seams so stripes are continuous around the garment, but shoulder seams will not match. With shaped seams, sides will not chevron nor is it likely the stripes will match. Some designs may necessitate cutting fabric in a single thickness.

To have both sides of the garment form a mirror image, the center seam must be straight and parallel to the grainline. Place left-side pattern pieces in the opposite lengthwise direction as the right-side pieces. (This treatment cannot be used with fabrics requiring a "with nap" layout.)

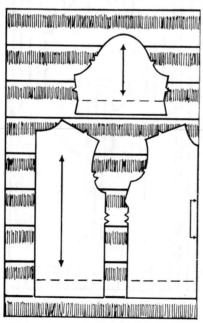

Horizontal Layout for Unbalanced Stripes

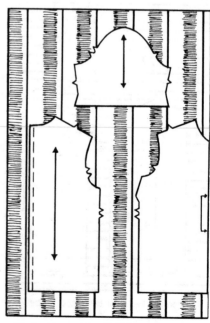

Vertical Layout for Unbalanced Stripes

Bias-cut Plaids and Stripes

Some of the most attractive design effects are brought about by cutting the plaid or stripe on the bias. The final result is a chevron, which is two sets of stripes meeting at identical angles. The specific angle of the chevron will depend upon the angle of the seams in relation to the lengthwise grainline. When selecting your fabric for a bias-cut garment, choose an even plaid or a balanced stripe without a pronounced diagonal weave. (Some plaid and striped fabrics are actually printed or woven on the bias; these are cut on the straight grain and matched as for a bias-cut fabric. See diagonals, page 139.)

Unless your pattern is specifically recommended for bias-cut fabrics, you will need to establish a bias grainline on each of the pattern pieces by drawing a long line at a forty-five-degree angle to the lengthwise grainline. Lay the pattern out on a single thickness of fabric to make sure that the plaid will chevron properly. Cut the right and left sides individually, turning the pattern pieces over (with the printed side down) for the left side. With each pattern piece, be sure that the plaid or stripe design corresponds at the symbols and the notches before cutting the fabric. This will ensure you a perfectly matching design once the seams are joined. To prevent the bias seams from stretching, pin strips of tissue paper to the wrong side of the layer that will remain flat while you are slip basting. Also place the tissue paper under the fabric on the machine bed when stitching the bias seams.

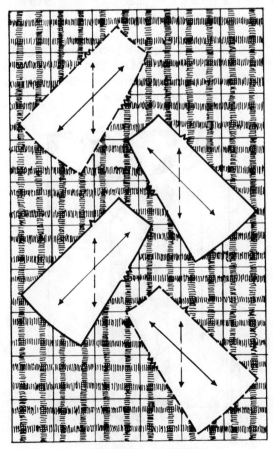

Layout for Bias-Cut Plaid Fabric

Prints

BORDER PRINTS

Special layouts are included with patterns illustrated in border prints; for others, you will need additional yardage (metrage). For your initial attempt, choose a fabric with the border running along one lengthwise edge and place it where the hem will fall. When the pattern is laid out along the crosswise grain, the garment can only be as long as the width of the fabric unless you seam it at the waist or bodice. Place the predetermined hemline at the border and the lengthwise arrow along the crosswise grain of the fabric. The pattern hem should be perpendicular to the center front and back and as straight as possible; if the hem is not straight, follow the edge of the border to create the best optical illusion. Avoid obviously A-line patterns. Match the motif at the side seams where feasible; if fabric has a dominant motif, place it at the center front and back.

LARGE-SCALE PRINTS

Carefully place the motifs of a large-scale print. Your goal should be a totally harmonious effect in the finished garment, where nothing stands out as visually disturbing. Large flowers and bold crosswise or lengthwise designs should be placed so that major body curves are avoided. For a pleasing visual balance, it is best to center large-scale designs vertically. You should definitely avoid placing large flowers or circles, etc., directly on the bust or derrière. Some large-scale prints have a definite vertical or horizontal direction, and thus fall into the category of one-way prints. If this is true of your fabric, use the "with nap" layout, letting your own judgment guide you in deciding whether the motif is prominent enough to require matching. It would be wise to analyze critically the scale of the print in relation to the scale of your figure. Very large prints are most effectively presented in styles with few design lines or in long garments, such as evening clothes or loungewear.

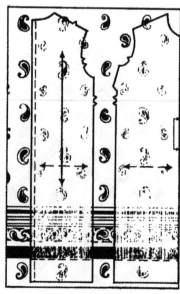

Layout for Border Print Fabric

Layout for Large-Scale Print Fabric

Marking
with Accuracy

Accurate marking of every notation on your fabric makes sewing that much easier. All those symbols and lines are put on the pattern piece for a reason, each having its separate purpose, which ultimately helps to create the shape of your garment. Happily, you will know exactly where to stitch on a curve, where ease should be adjusted, and whether corners will match perfectly.

All markings on pattern pieces should be transferred to the wrong side of the fabric as soon as the garment sections are cut and before pattern tissues are removed. Markings include construction symbols, seamlines, foldlines, darts, center front and center back lines, grainlines, and position marks. Always transfer these markings from your pattern pieces because they serve as continuous reference points for making your garment through all stages—pinning, stitching, fitting, even sewing on buttons. After you've completed marking the wrong side of your fabric, remove your pattern tissue and transfer position marks, foldlines, and any other long lines to the right side of your fabric, temporarily, with thread tracing. At this time, thread trace lengthwise and crosswise grainlines on the right side of each of your main pattern pieces, as special guidelines for fitting. If underlining is being used, you may want to mark it instead of your fashion fabric. Pin it to your fabric with the wrong sides together and then thread trace all necessary markings through both layers of each piece.

The tremendous variety in weights and types of fabric available means that you will need to use more than one method of marking in your sewing projects. Determine the fastest, most accurate, and most appropriate way to mark your particular fabric from among the following methods.

TRACING WHEEL and **DRESSMAKER'S TRACING PAPER** are used with hard-surfaced fabrics and all underlinings. First, test the color that you intend to use on a scrap of fabric. Steam-press the scrap to see if the tracings disappear. You may not have realized it, but white is best for white as well as light colors; red, yellow, or blue are better for dark colors. **Never** use vividly contrasting colors unless you know that they will disappear during pressing or cleaning.

If your garment is not underlined, trace markings on the wrong side of your fabric, one piece at a time. The carbon side of the paper should be next to the wrong side of the fabric when you trace.

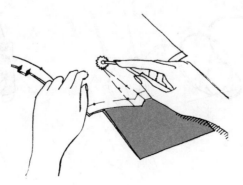

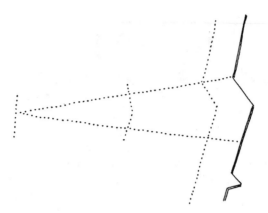

If your garment is underlined, mark only the underlining, not the fabric. Insert double layers of dressmaker's tracing paper around both layers of underlining, with the carbon side next to the underlining. With the fingers of your left hand holding the layers in place, trace over all markings, using just enough pressure on the tracing wheel to make light lines.

Use a ruler to guide tracing of straight lines. Trace through the center of any symbols. Indicate small symbols on seamlines with a short line perpendicular to the seamline. Also indicate the ends of darts, the points of slashes, and other small symbols which do not cross any seamlines with short horizontal lines; mark large symbols with an X; and so on, until you have developed your own shorthand for delineating the differences between the various construction symbols. Refer to the marking equipment section, page 189, if you need information on the types of tracing wheels and tracing paper to buy for your particular fabric.

TAILOR'S TACKS are used on delicate fabrics that might be marred by other methods of marking. They are especially necessary for soft-surfaced fabrics, such as velvet or spongy tweeds with napped or nubby faces. The technique is always the same whether you mark the fabric as a single or double layer. Using a long double strand of thread *without* a knot, take a single small running stitch through the tissue and fabric at a bold symbol. Then, sew another stitch crossing over the first, pulling the thread until a large loop is formed. As you go on to the next symbol, leave a loose thread, as shown. Clip the loops and the long threads connecting each tack. Raise the pattern tissue carefully, roll the upper fabric back gently, and cut the threads between the layers, leaving tufts on either side. When you are marking a single layer at a time, the tufts will appear on the right side, the short stitches on the wrong side. Use the fabric as soon as possible, or fold it carefully to prevent the clipped threads from slipping out of position.

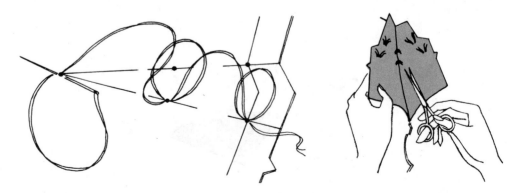

TAILOR'S CHALK or **MARKING PENCIL** are used on soft- or hard-surfaced fabrics. Place pins through the pattern and both layers of fabric at symbols, construction markings, and corners of pattern. Turn the piece over and chalk the wrong side of the fabric at each pin. Turn the piece back to the pattern side. Starting at the edge and working toward the center, hold the pins as you remove the pattern by forcing the pinhead through the tissue, and chalk the fabric. Remove pins as you work. Run thread tracing along the chalk lines if the chalk tends to rub off.

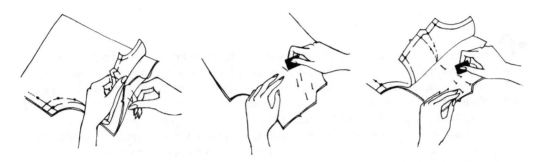

THREAD TRACING is uneven basting for quick marking of grainlines on all garment fabrics and for transferring necessary position marks to the right side of your garment fabric. Using a single thread (do not use knots), begin by taking a small backstitch. The type of uneven basting stitch to use as you thread trace is a matter of personal choice; it should be one that you find works best for you. With very little practice you will be able to develop a rhythm that makes this procedure a simple routine. Use silk thread or a basting thread on napped fabrics, piles, and light colors to avoid leaving an imprint. After all symbols and construction lines are transferred to the wrong side of your fabric or underlining by one of the previous methods, remove the pattern tissue. Pin underlining to fabric where necessary. Thread trace center front and back lines, foldlines, and grainlines on *one* section at a time.

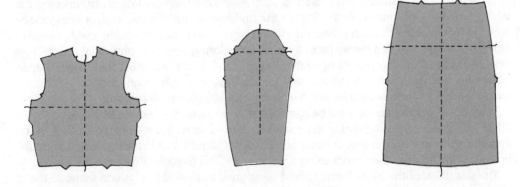

We suggest that you thread trace a lengthwise grainline on sleeves, starting at the shoulder and ending at the elbow, and a crosswise grainline at the bust, hip, and sleeve cap. These lines will save you much guesswork in fittings. With one glance in the mirror, many needed adjustments will become obvious, as distortions in these long, thread tracing lines appear immediately.

Inner Construction: The Undercover Story

Designers' styles require fabrics to take many different shapes. They depend on either the fabric's natural ability to flare into a silhouette or hidden inner components that support the fabric in its desired shape. Underlining and interfacing, when chosen and used correctly, will help achieve the designer's intended effect with relative ease. They are the concealed elements that help garments retain their shape and wear longer. In lining a garment, the designer uses only fabrics that will comply with the drape of the style and will be attractive, comfortable, and smooth. The use of these hidden components, correctly executed, is one of the hallmarks of fine couture.

As fashion styles and silhouettes change from year to year, so do the fabric preferences of designers. Some seasons crisp silhouettes executed in firm fabrics predominate; other seasons the fashion pendulum swings to soft, fluid styles with lightweight, flowing fabrics. Therefore the type, weight, and amount of inner construction used in garments varies according to the styles and fabrics highlighted by current fashion.

When choosing underlining, interfacing, and lining, consider the style of your garment, the weight of the fashion fabric, and the type of care required by the fashion fabric. For crisp or tailored garments, an underlining may be necessary to maintain the silhouette, while for soft, woven fabrics and knits, an underlining would inhibit the drapability or stretchability of the fashion fabric. However, interfacing is needed to shape detail areas such as collars, cuffs, and buttonholes in almost all garments regardless of the silhouette or weight of fabric.

To achieve best results when selecting your inner construction fabrics, try draping the fabrics together—placing outer fabric over the underlining, interfacing, and/or lining to see how the fabrics relate to each other. Interfacing fabrics are now available in a wide range of types and weights—from heavy hair canvases for tailoring coats to lightweight interfacings designed with a certain amount of stretch to use with knits. Remember that heavy fashion fabrics do not necessarily require heavy interfacings, nor lightweight fabrics, lightweight interfacings. Also, fusible interfacings may become a little stiffer after fusing.

Inner construction fabrics must be compatible in care with the fashion fabric. A washable outer fabric necessitates washable inner fabrics. A residual shrinkage of less than 1% in the underlining, interfacing, lining, or outer fabric will not require preshrinking. When in doubt, however, preshrink all the fabrics using a suitable method described on page 133.

The durability of the inner fabric should be as great as that of the fashion fabric so that it will last the life of the garment. There is nothing more annoying than having to replace a lining that has weakened and torn from normal use, pulled away from the seams at points of stress, and crumbled at the armholes from moisture and wear; or to have a crisp stand-up collar lose its stiffness after the garment has been laundered.

Inner construction is never seen, except for a beautifully lined coat or jacket, yet its proper selection and application often determine the final appearance of your garment—not only when it is first constructed, but long after it has been worn and cleaned many times. Inner construction should never be overlooked.

Underlining

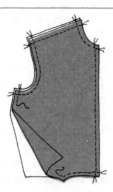

Underlining helps to impart a sculptured look to your garment. It is cut from the same pattern pieces as the garment fabric. Then the underlining and fashion fabric are basted and sewn together to act as one layer throughout construction.

Underlining adds body and durability to your garment by supporting and reinforcing the fabric and seams. It also helps to reduce wrinkling and prevent stretching. Underlining can act as a foundation for the garment so that the interfacings, facings, and hems can be sewn without stitches or ridges appearing on the right side of the garment. With sheer and lightweight fabrics, underlining can be used for opaqueness in certain areas of the garment. When used for crisper shaping, it can give support to the outer fabric to maintain a silhouette that otherwise could not have been achieved.

Underlining helps to facilitate the marking and stitching of your garment. All markings are made on the underlining, which is then pinned to the wrong side of your fashion fabric. Slight changes or adjustments can be recorded on the clearly marked underlining without overhandling the garment.

When selecting underlining, test it with the fashion fabric by draping both together over your hand to make sure they relate well to each other. A tightly woven fabric is best for preventing stretching and preserving the shape of your garment. Test the tightness of the weave by scratching the fabric with your thumbnail. If the threads spread apart or slide, the fabric generally will not wear well.

To achieve different effects in different areas of the same garment, more than one kind of underlining is often necessary. A lightweight wool dress with a soft bodice and A-line skirt will need a soft, lightweight underlining for the bodice and a crisp underlining for the skirt.

Special underlining fabrics are available in a wide selection of colors and fiber blends and may be labeled for softness or crispness. Or you can use other light and mediumweight fabrics such as batiste, China silk, marquisette, organdy, organza, muslin, and taffeta. In general, the underlining should be lighter in weight and as soft or softer than the outer fabric so as not to affect the appearance of the garment, except in cases where subtle shaping is desired. To aid you in your selection, refer to the chart of underlinings and linings, pages 160 to 162.

Method of Underlining

Transfer all markings to underlining fabric only. Center the marked underlining over the unmarked fabric, checking to be sure that the traced grainlines and center fold lines coincide with the grain of your fabric. Pin together along the traced lines and around the raw edges. Your cut edges will not always be exactly even, but that is to be expected since the two layers were cut separately.

To make your underlining and fashion fabric relate to each other the way they will when curving around your body, it may be necessary to make the underlining slightly smaller than the fashion fabric. Remove all pins except those along the center lines, and fold both layers along this pinned center line with your fashion fabric uppermost. Insert a thick newspaper, large magazine, or cardboard between the folded fabric. Smooth the fashion fabric over the underlining, keeping crosswise grain aligned, and pin where it lies along all raw edges and at all construction lines. The underlining will extend slightly beyond the edges of the fashion fabric. The difference between the seam allowances will increase with the thickness of your fashion fabric. After repositioning, trim away the excess underlining. Use a seam gauge to mark the new underlining seamlines so they will align with the fashion fabric seamlines.

From the underlining side, run a line of thread tracing along all markings through both layers of fabric. Baste next to, **not on**, the traced seamlines so the basting threads will be easy to remove later. Or staystitch ½" (13 mm) from the edge through both layers so that the fabrics can be handled as one throughout construction.

To stitch darts, hand or machine baste along the foldline of each dart through both fabrics, beginning 2" to 3" (5 cm to 7.5 cm) beyond the point of each dart. Fold dart along center, matching markings, and stitch. Remove basting that extends past dart point. Darts can also be stitched separately in the fashion fabric and underlining before basting the two fabrics together; then handle the two fabrics as one.

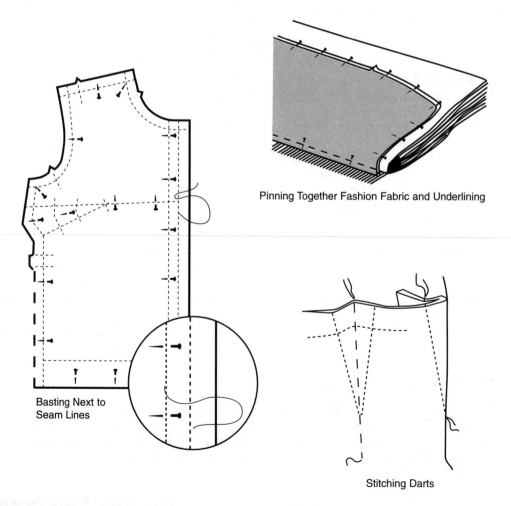

Pinning Together Fashion Fabric and Underlining

Basting Next to
Seam Lines

Stitching Darts

154

Interfacing

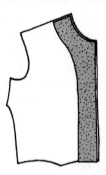

Interfacing is used to shape detail areas in a garment. It can maintain a gentle roll in collars and lapels; add body without bulk to garment edges, cuffs, and pockets; prevent stretching of necklines and buttonholes; and add crispness and stability to waistbands and belts. Almost all garments, regardless of their style or type of fabric, require some interfacing—a tailored jacket may have many areas interfaced while a simple knit dress may have interfacing only in a V-neckline.

Interfacings are available in a wide range of fibers, weights, and degrees of crispness. They are categorized according to their method of application: *sew-in* interfacings are stitched by hand or machine to your garment; *fusible* interfacings have a resin coating on the back that will fuse to fabric when steam, heat, and pressure are applied. Both types can be woven, non-woven, or knitted and are available in white, black, and neutral colors.

Woven interfacings are made of synthetic, cotton, or a blend of fibers; canvases may include wool or goat hair. They are available in different weights and crispness from lightweight polyester to heavyweight hair canvas. Woven interfacings must be cut on straight grain, or they can be cut on the bias for softer shaping in rolled collars and hems. *Non-woven* interfacings are made of synthetic fibers bonded together in weights from sheer to heavy. Pattern pieces can be laid in any direction for stable or "all-bias" non-wovens; however, for those that have crosswise stretch and lengthwise stability, the pattern pieces must be laid out as for woven fabrics. *Knitted* interfacings are tricot knit, tri-dimensional, weft insertion, or warp insertion construction, providing flexibility for lightweight knits and wovens. Other fabrics such as organza, cotton batiste, and lightweight underlining fabrics can also be used as interfacings.

The selection of the appropriate interfacing depends upon the weight of the fashion fabric, the area in which it will be used, the amount of shaping or stiffness desired, and the type of care the fabric will receive. Sheer or featherweight interfacings are designed for lightweight woven and knitted fabrics; lightweight interfacings for dress weight fabrics; mediumweight interfacings for suitings and medium to heavyweight fabrics; and heavyweight interfacings are recommended only for accessories and crafts.

In general, your interfacing should not be heavier in weight than your garment fabric, although it can be crisper. Some fabrics may require an interfacing with a certain amount of stretch or flexibility to achieve subtle shaping. With sheer fabrics, a piece of self-fabric can act as interfacing. To determine a compatible weight of interfacing, drape it and your fabric into a shape that resembles how they will be used, such as a cuff or hem edge, and check for the crispness and shaping you desire. Remember that fusible interfacings may be slightly crisper after fusing. Do not hesitate to mix different types and weights of interfacing within your garment in order to produce the desired fashion effect with your fabric.

Finally, most sew-in interfacings can generally be preshrunk in the same manner as the outer fabric. However, fusibles require pre-treating in a different manner.

For washable wovens, wefts, and tricot knits, fold the interfacing loosely and immerse in a tub of hot water. Let sit until the water cools to room temperature (approximately 15 to 20 minutes). After rolling in a towel to remove excess moisture, let air dry. When you are ready to use the interfacing, "steam shrink" as you would nonwoven and dry-clean only interfacings. With the resin side down over the wrong side of the garment piece (collar, cuff, etc.), hold the iron about 1" to 2" (2.5 to 5 cm) above the pieces and steam for 5-7 seconds. Do not place the iron on the fabric. Smooth out the pieces and fuse as usual.

Applying Sew-in Interfacings

Two different methods can be used for stitching interfacing to a garment, depending primarily on the weight of the interfacing fabric. Light and mediumweight interfacings have very little bulk so they can be stitched into the seams. Heavier weight interfacings and all hair canvases are too bulky or rigid to extend past the seamline, so the seam allowances must be trimmed away before the interfacing is attached to the garment.

Interfacing is usually cut from the facing pattern pieces. Separate interfacing pieces are usually provided for tailored jackets and coats that have a large portion of the garment interfaced. Follow your pattern directions for the correct placement of the interfacing on the garment sections. For almost all garment areas, the interfacing is applied to the garment or outer layer of fabric, not to the facing. For most collars, however, it is attached to the undercollar for better shaping.

Interfacing is applied to each separate section of the garment, and then the interfaced sections are stitched together. This method helps to reinforce the seamlines and prevents an outline of the seam allowances from showing on the outside of the garment.

LIGHT AND MEDIUMWEIGHT INTERFACING

Cut out the interfacing, being sure that the pattern pieces are placed correctly if interfacing has grainlines or stretchability. Pin interfacing to wrong side of fabric, matching seamlines and markings. Baste next to the seamline in the seam allowance, or staystitch ½" (13 mm) from the edge. Trim interfacing close to stitching. Stitch seams; trim and grade fabric seam allowances (1).

When interfacing a garment section that has a foldline along one edge, such as a collar, cuff, waistband, or front edge with extended facing, the interfacing should be trimmed at the foldline if the edge will be topstitched or edgestitched. Catch-stitch the interfacing to the garment along the foldline (2). For a softly rounded edge, extend the interfacing approximately ½" (13 mm) beyond the foldline. Secure interfacing to garment along the foldline with long running stitches spaced about ½" (13 mm) apart, with only a tiny invisible stitch catching the garment fabric (3).

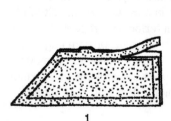

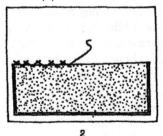

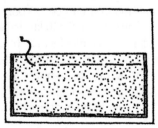

1   2   3

HEAVIER WEIGHT INTERFACING

Cut out interfacing, checking on pattern placement as for light and mediumweight interfacings. Stitch any darts or center back collar seam in the interfacing as shown on pages 423 to 426.

Trim away all seam allowances. Pin interfacing to wrong side of fabric, aligning cut edges of interfacing with seamlines of garment; baste in place. Catchstitch interfacing to garment along seamlines. Then pin, baste, and stitch interfaced garment sections together.

To attach interfacing along a foldline, use either catchstitches or long running stitches as shown above.

For additional information on interfacing a jacket or coat, refer to pages 432 to 444 in chapter 8.

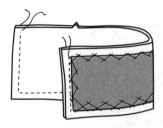

Applying Fusible Interfacings

Fusible interfacings, although very easy to apply, do require the proper combination of steam, heat, and pressure for a specific amount of time in order to achieve a lasting bond. Always follow the manufacturer's instructions precisely, and pretest on a scrap of your fabric before beginning to fuse. Also check the crispness of the fused sample-the fusing process sometimes adds a little body or stiffness to the fabric.

Fusible interfacings are usually applied directly to the garment, not to the facing, just as for sew-in interfacings. However, with lightweight fashion fabrics, you may wish to fuse the interfacing to the facing if the edge of the fused interfacing creates an outline or imprint visible on the right side of the garment. For small detail areas, such as cuffs and pocket flaps, fusible interfacings are always applied to the outer fabric sections.

Cut out fusible interfacing, being sure grainline or stretch direction is positioned as you desire. Trim away ½" (13 mm) of seam allowances to reduce bulk; for heavier-weight fusible interfacings, you may wish to trim away the entire seam allowance. Make a diagonal clip at any corners to further reduce bulk.

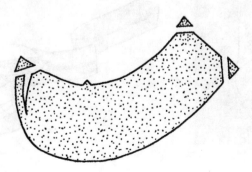

Place interfacing with adhesive side down against wrong side of fabric, aligning seamlines. Hold in position by steam-basting-pressing lightly with the tip of your iron in several places. To fuse, press down firmly using a steam iron and/or damp press cloth for 10 to 15 seconds, depending on manufacturer's directions. Press one area, then lift up iron and press again, overlapping the previous area. Do not slide iron along fabric or you may form wrinkles. Turn the piece over and, using a press cloth, repeat the fusing process again from the right side of the fabric.

If you make an error, most fusible interfacings can be removed by repressing with steam until the two layers of fabric can be gently pulled apart. However, the interfacing cannot be refused.

Fusible interfacings can be used to stabilize small areas such as buttonholes, slashes, and plackets. If the edge of the interfacing creates a visible outline on the right side of the fabric, try pinking the edges of the interfacing before fusing.

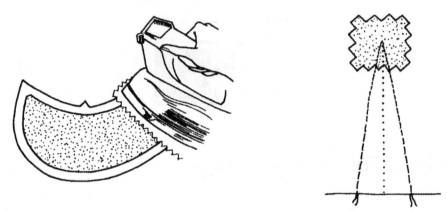

Fusing Agents

A fusing agent is used to hold two layers of fabrics together. They can be used in detail areas such as hems, cuffs, pocket flaps, and belts to add body simply by fusing the layers of fabric together. Unlike interfacing, fusing agents cannot be used to stabilize an area to prevent stretching but are used to hold fabric pieces in place. For information on different types, uses, and methods of application, see Notions, page 171.

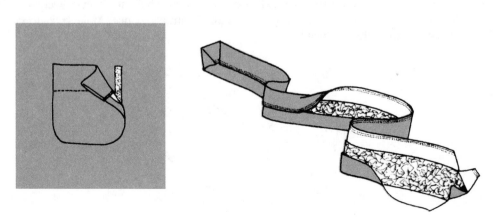

Lining

Lining gives your garment a smooth, luxurious feeling for added comfort as well as a quality finished, custom-made look. It is either cut from the same pattern pieces as the garment or from separate lining pieces, if provided; it is assembled separately, then sewn into your garment by hand or machine. A lining prolongs the life of the garment by covering the inner construction details and protecting the fashion fabric from abrasion during wear. It prevents stretching, helps preserve the shape, reduces wrinkling, and adds body to limp fabrics when desired.

The lining fabric should not affect the fit or characteristics of the outer fabric. Generally it should be softer and lighter in weight than the outer fabric, but not so lightweight as to reveal ridges and bumps from construction details. A lining fabric that is too firm for your fashion fabric may distort the silhouette of your garment.

A lining should be static-free; otherwise it might cling to the wrong side of the garment or to your undergarments. It should also be smooth and slippery to help your garment slide easily over your other apparel, especially in a jacket or coat.

Color is important in choosing a lining fabric, especially in a jacket or coat where the lining may show when the garment is opened. Matching lining and fabric colors are best if the jacket will be worn over different colored blouses and sweaters. Or select a colorful print or snappy stripes to add excitement and verve to a garment that will be worn over a matching dress or top. If the lining fabric is darker in color than the fashion fabric, make sure it does not show through to the outside of the garment.

When selecting a lining fabric, consider how often you plan to wear and clean the garment. Delicate fabrics such as China silk can be used for lining a velvet dress that will be worn occasionally for elegant evenings, but will not last in a garment worn or dry-cleaned often. Lining fabrics, like interfacings and underlinings, must be able to receive the same care as your outer fabric. For example, for a garment made of a permanent-press fabric, be sure to choose a lining that is washable and requires no ironing. When shopping for a lining, note the special characteristics of the fabric listed on the bolt in addition to its fiber content. The majority of trade-name linings are colorfast, perspiration-proof, wrinkle-resistant, and have non-cling finishes, as well as other desirable atttributes. To insert a lining by hand, refer to pages 438 to 441.

Interlining

Interlining is a separate layer of wool, fuzzy cotton, or non-woven polyester fleece placed between the lining and underlining or fashion fabric for additional warmth, especially in coats. For application, see page 442. Some linings designed for coats and jackets are backed with wool, a metallic reflective finish, a napped finish, or a foam-type insulation. Since the wool or foam types add more bulk than a plain lining, you must make an allowance for this added thickness when cutting the pattern.

Guide to Underlinings and Linings

Fabric Name	Fiber Content	Weight	Color	Use
Ambiance* Cupra-RayonŒ	100% Bemberg™ cupromonium rayon	Woven Light	Range of colors	Lining for all weights of fabrics
Armo Press® Σ	50% polyester/ 50% cotton	Woven Soft; firm	White and black	Underlining for light to medium-weight wovens; permanenet press wovens and stable knits
Armo® Fleece Plus Σ	100% polyester	Fleece	White	Underling for quilted projects, coats and heavier suitings
Armo® Rite Σ	70% polyester/ 30% rayon	Woven	Cream	Underlining for neckties, sleeve heads, and general tailoring
Batiste Breezy Batiste ø	100% cotton Cotton/poly-	blends Woven Light	Range of colors	Underlining for all weights of fabric
Brocade	Silk or man-made fibers	Woven Medium to heavy	Range of colors	Elegant lining for fur coats and evening wear
Charmeuse$f$ Interlude∞	100% silk or 100% polyester	Woven Medium to heavy	Range of colors	Lining for jackets or suits; also used for fashion fabric for blouses, dresses, lingerie
China silk$f$ Polyester china silkŒ Exotica∞	100% silk 100% polyester	Woven Light	Range of colors	Lining for all weights of fabrics
Cintilla Satin\	100% acetate	Woven Medium	Range of colors	Satin lining for coats, jackets, medium-weight dresses
Crepe de chine$f$	100% silk	Woven Light to medium	Range of colors	Lining for medium to heavy weight fabrics; also used as fashion fabric for blouses and dresses
Designer Touch\	100% celanese acetate	Woven Medium	Range of colors	Jacquard lining for coats, jackets, and suits
Deluxe Acetate Twill\	100% celanese acetate	Woven Medium to heavy	Range of colors	Lining for coats, jackets and suits

160

Guide to Underlinings and Linings *(continued)*

Fabric Name	Fiber Content	Weight	Color	Use
Duet ø	100% polyester	Woven Light to medium	Range of colors	Lining for all weights of fabrics
El Dorado\	100% polyester	Woven Light to medium	Range of colors	Lining for all weights of fabric
Fake fur	Man-made fibers	Woven or knit Heavy	Range of colors	Pile lining for coats and jackets
Gloriosa II‡	100% polyester	Woven Medium	Range of colors	Lining for all weights of fabrics
Hang Loose*	100% polyester	Woven Light to medium weight	Range of colors	Lining for all weights of fabrics
Lawn	100% cotton or cotton blends	Woven Light to medium	Range of colors	Underling or lining for lightweight fabrics
Lexus II‡	100% polyester	Woven Medium to heavy	Range of colors	Crepe-like lining for medium to heavier fabrics
Lexus II‡	100% polyester	Woven Medium to heavy	Range of colors	Crepe-like lining for medium to heavier fabrics
Mayfair¥	100% nylon Woven	Light	White	Crisp, crinoline finishing or underlining
Mesh	Cotton or man-made fibers	Woven or warp-knitted Light	Limited colors	Underlining for sheer fabrics
Muslin	100% cotton or cotton blends	Woven Medium	Natural or white	Underlining for coats and suits
Organdy or organza	100% cotton or man-made fibers	Woven Light	Range of colors	Fine, crisp underlining for sheer and lightweight fabrics
Percale	Cotton or cotton blends	Woven Light to medium	Range of colors	Lining especially for cotton fabrics
Pima Cotton	100% cotton	Woven Light	Range of colors	Very fine cotton for underlining
Pongee	100% polyester	Woven Light	Range of colors	Lining for mediumweight fabrics
Silk broadcloth or surrah	100% silk	Woven Light	Range of colors	Lining for lightweight fabrics

Guide to Underlinings and Linings *(continued)*

Fabric Name	Fiber Content	Weight	Color	Use
Swimwear Lining Ω	100% stretch nylon or 78% nylon / 28% lycra Knit	Light	Nude, white and black	Lining for swimwear and bodysuits; lining with Lycra™ has more stretch
Taffeta∞	100% acetate	Woven	Medium Range of colors	Lining for medium to heavyweight fabrics
Thermolite®^ Thermoloft® Plus^	100% polyester	Light to medium	White	Insulation fabric for coats and jackets
Tricot Ω	100% nylon Knit	Light	Range of colors	Lining for laces or mesh/netting
Satinette® §	Celanese acetate	Woven Light to medium	Range of colors	Reversible crepe-back satin lining for coats, jackets, and suits

*	Logantex, inc.
Σ	HTC Inc.
\	Balson-Erlanger / The Balson Hercules Group, LTD.
§	David Textiles
^	DuPont
∞	Pago Fabrics
Œ	Berenstein Textiles
‡	Rosebar Textiles Co.
ø	Robert Kaufman Co., Inc.
¥	Blank Textiles
ƒ	Exotic Silks
Ω	Sew Easy

Guide to Interfacings
Sew-in-Interfacings

Fabric Name	Type and Weight	Fiber Content and Care	Color	Use
Acro Σ	Woven, washable canvas Medium to heavy	54% polyester/ 27% hair/ 12% cotton / 7%wool Machine wash, warm delicate cycle; tumble dry low.	Natural	Medium and heavy-weight coatings and suit fabrics
ArmoFlexxx® Σ	Woven Medium	62% nylon / 19% polyester/19% rayon Washable and dry cleanable	White	Sew-in stabilizer for waistbands, self-fabric belts and straps
ArmoFlexxx® Σ	Woven Medium	50% nylon / 50% polyester Washable and dry cleanable	White	More flexible sew-in stabilizer for waistbands, belts and straps
Armo® Intra-Face Bias Lightweight and Featherweight Σ	Non-woven Light to medium	50% polyester / 50% rayon Machine wash, warm; tumble dry, remove promptly	White	Light to medium-weight bias cut or stretch wovens and knits
Armo Press®Soft Σ	Woven Light and soft	50% polyester / 50% cotton Machine wash, warm; tumble dry, remove promptly.	White and black	Light to medium-weight wovens, linens and broadcloth
Armo Press®Firm Σ	Woven Medium	50% polyester / 50% cotton Machine wash, warm; tumble dry, remove promptly.	White and black	Light to medium-weight permanent press woven and stable knits
50/50 Durable Press[a]	Woven Medium	50% polyester / 50% rayon Machine washable and dry cleanable.	White and black	Crease-resistant for all permanent press fabrics
Fino II Σ	Woven Medium canvas	35% wool /30% cotton/1% rayon /16% goat hair Dry clean only	Natural	Medium to heavy-weight fabrics

Fabric Name	Type and Weight	Fiber Content and Care	Color	Use
Form-Flex™ Woven Σ	Woven Medium	100% cotton Machine wash, warm; tumble dry, remove promptly.	White	Light to medium-weight wovens
HTC Intra-face™ Lightweight Σ	Non-woven Light	75% rayon / 25% polyester Machine wash, warm; tumble dry, remove promptly.	White and black	Light to medium-weight bias cut or stretch wovens
HTC Intra-face Mediumweight Σ	Non-woven Medium	75% rayon / 25% polyester Machine wash, warm; tumble dry, remove promptly.	White	Light to medium-weight wovens, heat-sensitive fabrics
HTC Intra-face Heavyweight Σ	Non-woven Heavy	80% polyester / 20% rayon Machine wash, warm; tumble dry, remove promptly.	White	Structured support in medium to heavyweight coating and suit fabrics
Pellon #905 Sew-In•	Non-woven Light, soft	100% polyester	White	Lightweight fabrics such as sheers, voiles, gauzes
Pellon #910 Sew-In•	Non-woven Light	100% polyester	White	Mediumweight fabrics such as chambray, challis, jersey, linen.
Pellon #930 Sew-In•	Non-woven	100% polyester	White	Active sportswear such as corduroy, chino, poplin, rainwear.
Sewin' Sheer™ Σ	Knit Light	100% nylon stabilized tricot, not stretch Machine wash, warm; tumble dry, remove promptly.	White, black and champagne	Sheers, laces, beaded fabrics and those that can't be fused
Sew-Shape™ Featherweight Σ	Non-woven Light, and soft	100% polyester Machine wash, warm; tumble dry, remove promptly.	White	Sheers, batiste, georgette, chiffon

Fabric Name	Type and Weight	Fiber Content and Care	Color	Use
Shaping Aid, light weight[a]	Non-woven Light	100% polyester machine wash or dry cleanable.	White and black	Non-stretch, light weight fabrics
Shaping Aid, medi-umweight[a]	Non-woven Medium	100% polyester Machine washable or dry cleanable.	White and black	Non-stretch, medi-um to heavyweight fabrics
Shaping Aid, heavyweight[a]	Non-woven Heavy, firm	100% polyester Machine washable or dry cleanable.	White	Non-stretch, heavy-weight fabrics, stiff-ening for crafts
Shaping Aid, feath-erweight bias[a]	Non-woven Light	100% polyester machine washable or dry cleanable.	White	Lightweight fabrics such as jerseys, crepes, gauze, voile for flexible shaping
Shaping Aid, light-weight bias[a]	Non-woven Light	100% polyester machine washable or dry cleanable.	White	Light to medium-weight fabrics for soft shaping
Shirt Maker, Lightweight[a]	Non-woven Light	100% spunbonded polyester Machine washable and dry cleanable	White	Lightweight wovens and knits for shirts, blouses and leisure wear
Shirt Maker, mediumweight[a]	Non-woven Medium	100% spunbonded polyester Machine washable and dry cleanable	White	Mediumweight sportswear fabrics such as denim, flan-nels, wools, knits
Sta-Form™ or Ver-Shape™ Σ	Woven Medium, Firm	50% polyester / 50% rayon Machine wash, warm; tumble dry, remove promptly.	White and black	Light and medi-umweight perma-nent press wovens and stable knits. Bodice support in bridal and special occasion fabrics
Stretch & Bounce[a]	Non-woven Light, soft	50% polyester / 50% rayon Machine washable and dry cleanable.	White and charcoal	Crosswise stretch for knits, bias stretch for wovens
Tailor's Pride™ Σ	Woven Medium	41% acrylic / 19% hair / 16% poly-ester / 15% vis-cose / 9% cotton Dry clean only.	Natural	Medium to heavy-weight coating and suit fabrics. Woolens, velve-teen, corduroy.
Woven durable Press[a]	Woven Medium	50% polyester / 50% rayon Machine washable and dry cleanable.	White and black	Crease-resistant for all permanent press fabrics

Fusible Interfacings

Fabric Name	Type and Weight	Fiber Content and Care	Color	Use
Armo® Fusi-Form Σ	Non-woven Light to medium	70% polyester / 30% rayon Machine wash on warm; tumble dry, remove promptly.	White and charcoal	Structured support in medium to heavy coating and suit fabrics.
Armo®Weft Knit Σ	Light	60% polyester / 40% rayon Machine wash on warm; tumble dry, remove promptly.	White, black and grey	Moderate support for general tailoring of wools, linens, double knits, suiting
Bi-Stretch Lite™•	Woven Light	100% polyester Machine washable and dry cleanable	White	Lightweight sheer interfacing with two-way stretch that drapes like a knit. Light to medium-weight knits, wovens, stretch wovens
Designer's Sheer™•	Non-woven Light		White and black	Sheer to light-weight knits and wovens such as voile, rayon, fine cotton. Support without weight.
Designer's Lite™•	Non-woven Medium		White and black	Light to medium-weight knits and wovens such as gabardines, twills, wool crepe.
Easy-shaper®•	Non-woven Light	100% polyester Machine washable or dry cleanable	White and grey	Stable fusible for light to medium-weight tailoring
Flex Weave™ Σ	Woven Light	34% polyester / 33% modal (acrylic) / 33% cotton Machine wash warm on delicate cycle, tumble dry; or dry clean.	White and charcoal	Crosswise give and flexible support for newer "hi-tech" fabrics and blends
Form-Flex™ All Purpose Σ	Woven Medium	100% cotton Machine wash on warm, delicate cycle; tumble dry.	White and black	Mediumweight sportswear fabrics such as denim, poplin, flannel, duck

Fusible Interfacings *(continued)*

Fabric Name	Type and Weight	Fiber Content and Care	Color	Use
Form-Flex™ All Purpose Σ	Woven Medium	100% cotton Machine wash warm, on delicate cycle; tumble dry.	White and black	Mediumweight sportswear fabrics such as denim, poplin, flannel, duck
Form-Flex™ 50/50 Σ	Woven Medium	50% polyester / 50% cotton Machine wash, warm; tumble dry, remove promptly.	White	Mediumweight sportswear fabrics such as poplin denim, flannel, duck, double knits
Form-Flex™ Non-woven Σ	Non-woven Light to medium	75% rayon / 25% polyester Machine wash on warm; tumble dry, remove promptly.	White	Light to mediumweight fabrics such as shirtings, oxford cloth, broadcloth, chambray
French Fuse[a]	Woven Light to medium	Machine washable and dry cleanable	White, black and beige	Use as interfacing, lining and seam binding for knits and wovens
Fusi-Form™ Lightweight and Suitweight Σ	Non-woven Light to medium	100% polyester Machine wash on warm; tumble dry, remove promptly.	White and charcoal	Light to mediumweight knits and wovens
Fusi-Knit™ Σ	Knit Light to medium	100% nylon tricot Machine wash on warm, delicate cycle; tumble dry.	White, black, ivory, and grey	Knits and wovens where drape and flexibility are desired
Fusible Acro Σ	Woven Medium	54% polyester / 27% hair / 12% cotton / 7% wool Washable canvas	Natural	Medium to heavy-weight coating and suit fabrics, woolens, corduroy and velveteen
Fusible Shirt Maker[a]	Non-woven Medium	100% spunbonded polyester Machine washable and dry cleanable	White	Mediumweight fabrics
Jiffy Flex, Lightweight[a]	Non-woven Light	80% polyester / 20% nylon Machine washable and dry cleanable	White and charcoal	Crosswise stretch for all lightweight knits and wovens
Jiffy Flex, Suitweight[a]	Non-woven Medium	80% polyester / 20% nylon Machine washable and dry cleanable	White and charcoal	Flexible shaping for all mediumweight wovens and knits

Fusible Interfacings *(continued)*

Fabric Name	Type and Weight	Fiber Content and Care	Color	Use
Jiffy Flex, super lightweight[a]	Non-woven Light	100% polyester Machine washable and dry cleanable	White	Very light fabrics such as lightweight jersey, batiste, gauze, blouse-weight knits and wovens
Non-Woven Fusible[a]	Non-woven Light to medium	100% rayon Machine washable and dry cleanable	White and black	Light to medium-weight fabrics
Pel-Aire®• Non-woven	Medium	85% polyester / 15% nylon machine washable and dry cleanable	White and oxford grey	Medumweight wovens and knits
Pellon® #906 Fusible•	Non-woven Light	100% polyester Machine washable and dry cleanable	White	Light to medium-weight wovens for soft shaping
Pellon® #911 Fusible•	Non-woven Medium	80% polyester / 20% nylons Machine washable and dry cleanable	White and grey	Mediumweight wovens
Pellon® #931 Fusible•	Non-woven Medium to heavy	50% polyester / 50% nylon machine washable and dry cleanable	White	Medium to heavy-weight wovens
Perfect Waist Shaper<	Non-woven Medium	60% polyester / 40% rayon Machine washable and dry cleanable	White	Pre-cut waistband interfacing
Perfo-Fuse™ Non-woven Σ	Light to medium	75% polyester / 25% rayon Machine wash, warm delicate cycle, tumble dry	White	Pre-cut strip perfo-rated interfacing strip for waistbands, shirt plackets, cuffs
Poly-O[a]	Non-woven Light	100% polyester machine washable and dry cleanable	White, charcoal and beige	Sheerest fabrics, printed and raw silks, all silk-types
Satin Weave™ Woven Σ	Medium	78% viscose / 22% polyester Machine wash, warm, delicate cycle; tumble dry or dry cleanable	White and charcoal	Better suitings such as crepe, wools, sueded surfaces
Sheer D'Light™ Featherweight and Lightweight Σ	Non-woven Light	100% polyester, thermal bonded Machine wash, warm; tumble dry, remove promptly.	White and charcoal	Very sheer and lightweight fabrics such as single knits, challis

Fusible Interfacings *(continued)*

Fabric Name	Type and Weight	Fiber Content and Care	Color	Use
Shir-Tailor®•	Non-woven Medium to heavy	100% polyester Machine washable and dry cleanable	White	Mediumweight fabrics
Shirt-Shaper™ Σ	Non-woven Light	75% rayon 25% polyester Machine wash, warm; tumble dry, remove promptly	White	Light to medium fabrics
Sofbrush™ Σ	Knit, Cool Fuse™ Medium	100% polyester, warp insertion with all-bias stretch Machine wash, warm, delicate cycle; tumble dry.	White, black, ivory, and grey	Mediumweight drapable fabrics such as knits, micro-fibers, suede textures, natural and blended suitings
Sofknit™ Σ	Knit, Cool Fuse™ Light	100% nylon tri-dimensional knit with all-bias stretch machine wash, warm, delicate cycle; tumble dry	White, black and champagne	Knits and wovens where complete drape is desired
Sof-Shape®•	Non-woven Light	80% nylon / 20% polyester Machine washable and dry cleanable	White	Soft and flexible for drape in medi-umweight knits and wovens
Sof-Tailor™•	Non-woven Light	30% polyester/ 70% nylon machine washable and dry cleanable	White and black	Light to medium-weight knits and wovens
Softouch™ Σ	Non-woven, Cool fuse™ Light	100% nylon, ther-mal bonded with brushed surface machine wash, warm, delicate cycle; tumble dry.	White and charcoal	Subtly textured fab-rics such as sueded synthetics and sand-washed silks
So Sheer™ Σ	Knit Light	100% polyester tri-cot, crosswise stretch Machine wash, warm delicate cycle, tumble dry.	White, black and ivory	Lightweight wovens, knits, laces, organza
Stacy Easy-Knit®•	Knit Light	100% nylon Machine washable and dry cleanable.	White and black	Soft drapable tricot knit for light to mediumweight wovens and knits

Fusible Interfacings (continued)

Fabric Name	Type and Weight	Fiber Content and Care	Color	Use
Stacy Shape-Flex® •	Woven	100% cotton Machine washable and dry cleanable.	White and black	Light to medium-weight fabrics such as oxford cloth, chambray, poplin, calico
Suit Maker[a]	Knit, weft insertion Light	85% rayon / 15% polyester Machine washable and dry cleanable.	Natural and charcoal	Light fabrics for soft tailoring
Tailor's Elite™ •	Non-woven with stitch reinforcement lengthwise Light	90% polyester/ 10% nylon Machine washable and dry cleanable	White and black	Loosely woven or stretchy knits in medium to heavy weights benefit from stitch reinforcement lengthwise but still have some movement crosswise
Tailor's Lite™ •	Non-woven Light	30% polyester / 70% nylon Machine washable and dry cleanable	White	Lightweight fabrics such as batiste, shirtings
Tailor's Touch™ •	Non-woven Medium	90% polyester / 10% nylon Machine washable and dry cleanable	White	Medium to heavy-weight fabrics for firm support and shape, especially for napped or hairy fabrics
Textured Weft™ Σ	Knit, weft insertion Light to medium	100% polyester machine wash, warm; tumble dry, remove promptly.	White and charcoal	Maintains or adds loft to tweeds, boucles, hand knits, handwovens
Touch O' Gold™ Σ	Woven, Cool Fuse™ Light	100% rayon, Machine wash, warm, delicate cycle; tumble dry.	White, black and ivory	Temporary bond during construction then releases for light support
Ultra Weft™ •	Knit, weft Insertion Light	85% rayon / 15%polyester Dry clean only.	Natural and black	Lightweight wools, cashmere, camel hair, crepe
Whisper Weft Σ	Knit, weft insertion Medium	60% polyester / 40% rayon Machine wash, warm, delicate cycle, tumble dry.	White, black and grey	Moderate support for general tailoring

Fusing Agents

Fabric Name	Fiber Content and Care	Weight and Color	Width
Jiffy Fuse[a]	100% polyamide web Machine washable and dry cleanable	Light Clear	20" (51cm) wide
Heat 'n Bond® Lite ◊	Polymer resin Machine washable NOT dry cleanable	Light Clear	17" x 1 yard (43.2 cm x 91.4 cm)
Heat 'n Bond® Hem, Lite, Regular and Super Weight ◊	Polymer resin Machine washable, dry cleaning NOT recommended	Light to medium Clear	⅜" to ⅞" (1 to 2.2 cm)
Hot Stitch Fusible Web Δ	100% polyamide web Machine washable and dry cleanable	Light Clear	16" (40.6 cm) wide
Stitch Witchery®—	100% polyamide web Machine washable and dry cleanable	Light Clear	20" (51 cm) wide
Steam-A-Seam® and Steam-A seam 2® ≈	Hot melt adhesive Machine washable and dry cleanable	Light Clear	¼", ½" and 12" (0.6 cm, 1.3 cm. And 30.5 cm)
Thread Fuse™< Stitch n Fuse * Fusible '	Polyester / nylon thread Machine washable and dry cleanable	Light Clear	Thread
Trans-Web™ Σ	100% polyamide web Machine washable and dry cleanable	Light White	16" (40.6 cm) wide
Ultra Hold Fusible Web Δ	100% polyamide web Machine washable and dry cleanable	Light Clear	Sheets 16" x 36" (40.6 cm x 91.4 cm)
Wonder-Under® And Heavy-Duty Wonder Under®•	100% polyamide web Machine washable and dry cleanable	Light Clear	17" (43.2 cm) wide
Wonder Web®•	100% polyamide web Machine washable and dry cleanable	Light Clear	15" (38 cm) wide

Σ	HTC Inc.	≈	Prym-Dritz Corporation
[a]	Staple Sewing Aids Corp.	Δ	Aleene's
•	Pellon Consumer Products Division, Freudenberg Nonwovens	◊	Therm O Web
		W	The Warm Company
—	Registered trademark of Bostik; distributed under this name by HTC Inc. and Prym-Dritz® Corporation	*	Coats & Clark
		'	Gutermann of America, Inc.

Notions: Your Sewing Accessories

Having chosen your fabric, you must now remember to stop at the notions counter and pick up those little necessities that might otherwise cause another trip back to the store. Generally, it is a good idea to keep on hand a supply of the more standard notions, such as pins, needles, snaps, and hooks and eyes, to save yourself the frustration of having to continually interrupt your sewing to purchase some small item you have forgotten. There are some notions, however, that you will have to buy each time you purchase fabric to ensure that they will match and be appropriate to your particular fabric and style; buttons, thread, zippers, and bindings or tapes are perfect examples. Still other notions are so specialized that you will need to purchase them only as they are called for by a specific garment, such as horsehair braid for the hem of an evening gown. Special shaping notions, such as shoulder pads, boning, and weights, are described in The Shapekeepers, pages 446 and 447.

Couture finishing requires the proper sizes and types of notions. Since the notions counter contains a seemingly endless array of gadgets, use the back of your pattern envelope and the following descriptions to guide your selection.

Pins

Pins vary in size and type. Pin size is stated in sixteenths of an inch according to length: a size 16 is $^{16}/_{16}$" or 1" (25 mm) long, a size 8 is $^{1}/_{2}$" (13 mm) long. For general sewing, #17 (1 $^{1}/_{16}$" or 26 mm) dressmaker pins are most commonly used. These are slender pins of medium diameter. For fine sewing and delicate fabrics, choose #17 silk pins, very slender with fine points; #16 pleating pins, extra fine; #20 super-fine sharps, for microfibers; or #22 glasshead pins, super-fine with a .5mm shaft. Ball point pins should be used on knitted fabrics as their rounded tips slip between the yarns to avoid snags. Larger, longer pins are ideal for home decorating, craft or quilting projects. T-pins are good for deep pile fabrics, slipcovers, upholstery and craft projects.

All pins must be rustproof brass, nickel-plated steel or stainless steel. Plastic or glassheaded pins are available in various sizes and are easy to see on the fabric. Glassheaded pins are extremely heat resistant.

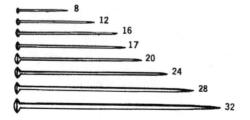

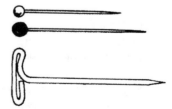

Hand Sewing Needles

Hand sewing needles are classified by the shape of the eye, the length and the point, each designed for a specific use. Choose the type of needle according to the job it will be doing, and the size of needle according to the thread it will be pulling through the fabric. The finer or sheerer the fabric, the sharper and more slender the needle should be.

Two size scales are generally used for needles—1 through 10, and 14 through 22. For each needle type, the smaller the size number, the longer and thicker the needle. Sizes 7 through 10 are best for most dressmaking, while the other sizes are for heavier or specialized sewing.

Dressmaking Needles

SHARPS are all-purpose medium-length needles with small, rounded eyes used for general sewing.

BETWEENS are shorter needles with small, rounded eyes used for detailed handwork and quilting requiring short, fine stitches.

MILLINER'S needles are long with small, rounded eyes used for long basting stitches, gathering, and millinery work.

EMBROIDERY needles are medium-length with long oval eyes; generally used for embroidery and crewel work, they can also be substituted for sharps.

Needles are also available with ball-point tips for use with knitted fabrics. The slightly rounded tip slips between the yarns to help prevent snagging the fabric. Easy threading, self-threading or calyx eye needles have a slot on the outer eye for easy threading.

Sharp

Between

Milliner's

Embroidery

Specialty Needles

BEADING needles are extremely long and fine with a small round eye; generally used for beading due to their flexibility, they can also be used to sew fine, lightweight fabrics.

CHENILLES are short, thick needles with long, oval eyes and sharp points for ribbon embroidery and crewel work on coarse fabrics.

TAPESTRY needles are short and thick with large eyes and blunt points for use with tapestry or needlepoint.

COTTON DARNERS are long needles with long eyes and sharp points which can be used for darning or basting.

YARN DARNERS are very long, coarse needles with large eyes used for darning with heavy or multiple yarns.

Beading

Chenille

Tapestry

Cotton Darner

Yarn Darner

GLOVER'S OR LEATHER needles are medium length with a wedge-shaped point, designed to penetrate leather and plastic without splitting or tearing.

SAILMAKER'S needles are long, coarse needles with a wedge-shaped shank and sharply tapered point designed for use on heavy coating, canvas, and heavy leather.

DOLLMAKER'S needles are extra-long with long eyes for doll making, soft sculpture and crafts.

CURVED needles are semicircular with a large oval eye and sharply tapered point, ranging from 2" to 3" (50 mm to 75 mm) in length; used for upholstery, lampshades, mattresses, braided rugs, and wherever a straight needle is impracticable.

Sewing machine needles are selected according to the type and weight of fabric to be sewn and the thread used. They vary according to the type of point and thickness of the needle--the larger the number, the larger the needle. Refer to *The Sewing Machine* on pages 186-187 for more detailed information.

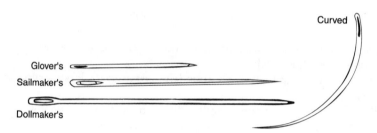

Thread

A quality thread is strong, smooth, and consistent in thickness, and it resists tangling. Select the proper thread according to fabric weight, purpose, and color. Thread should be the same color or slightly darker than the fabric. For multicolored prints and plaids, select thread colors according to the predominant hue in the fabric.

POLYESTER THREAD, either 100% polyester or cotton covered, provides strength and elasticity for sewing on fabrics made of synthetic, natural, or blended fibers. It is especially desirable for knit, stretch, and permanent-press fabrics because of its stretch and recovery, and its non-shrinkage. 100% polyester thread can be made from strands of long staple polyester multifilaments or spun short staple multifilaments, which are then twisted tightly together. Cotton-covered polyester cord thread is formed by twisting together two or more strands of polyester multifilaments wrapped with mercerized cotton. The cotton sheath provides resistance to heat, while the polyester cord gives strength and elasticity. Polyester thread is available in different weights for specific uses: extra fine for lightweight fabrics; all-purpose for general sewing; topstitching and buttonhole twist for decorative stitching and hand-worked buttonholes; button and carpet thread for hand sewing buttons and extra strength; and machine and hand quilting thread.

MERCERIZED COTTON THREAD is strong and lustrous, without any stretch or give, for use on woven natural fiber fabrics. It is formed by twisting together two or three strands of spun staple cotton fibers that have been mercerized for added strength, luster, affinity for dye, and color fastness. Size 50, a medium diameter thread, is suitable for hand and machine sewing on light and mediurnweight fabrics. Size 40, a heavier thread, is used for heavier fabrics, slipcovers, and draperies as well as machine embroidery.

Other types of cotton thread are: fine machine embroidery and sewing thread; button and carpet thread for hand sewing buttons and heavy fabrics; soft basting thread, which breaks easily under tension; and quilting thread for hand and machine quilting.

SILK THREAD is durable, pliable, and lustrous for sewing silk and woolen fabrics. It is formed by tightly twisting two or more strands of silk fibers together. It is excellent for tailoring and basting because it can mold permanently with the fabric and leaves no imprint or lint when pressed. Silk thread can be used for hand sewing and on your sewing or overlock machines. Heavier silk thread is used for decorative topstitching or quilting, hand-worked buttonholes, machine embroidery and applique.

NYLON THREAD is a very strong thread with twice the tensile strength of the same size cotton thread. Used for upholstery and home decorating, this heavy-duty machine or hand sewing thread can be used for both indoor and outdoor applications as it is rot-proof and abrasion resistant. Another type of nylon thread is made from one continuous filament of 100% transparent nylon or polyester and available in clear and smoke. This finer *monofilament* thread is often used for machine quilting, applique, crafts, and home decorating as it is strong with little stretch. It is excellent for overlock sewing.

SPECIALTY THREADS are used for all types of decorative details for both hand and machine work. Metallic, multicolor, rayon, woolly nylon, ribbon floss, and specialty bobbin thread are just a few of the many threads and fiber combinations available today. Whether couched, embroidered, or wound on the bobbin of your sewing machine, unique threads create surface texture and detail interest to your fabric.

Thread can also be waxed or conditioned for a more pliable, smoother surface allowing it to glide through the fabric with little drag and no tangling. Most types of threads are wound either on spools or cones for your convenience.

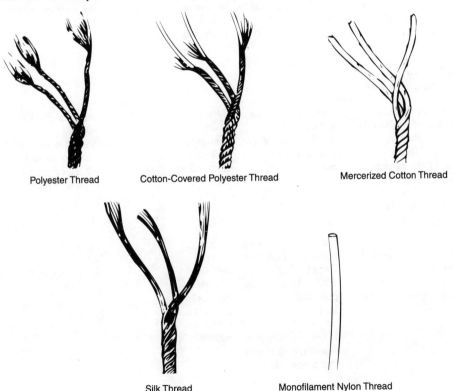

Polyester Thread   Cotton-Covered Polyester Thread   Mercerized Cotton Thread

Silk Thread   Monofilament Nylon Thread

Needle and Thread Chart

FABRIC WEIGHT AND TYPE	THREAD	HAND NEEDLES	MACHINE NEEDLES
Very Light: 100% cotton batiste, chiffon, china silk, gauze, georgette, lingerie, organza, net, , tulle, voile	100%cotton — extra fine + < @ Cotton-covered polyester—extra fine*Silk ' <	9, 10, 11, 12 Sharps Betweens Milliner's Beading	Universal 60/8 or 65/9
Light: Cotton/polyester blend batiste, handkerchief linen, lace, lawn, silk crepe de chine, silk jersey	100% cotton — extra fine + < @ Cotton-covered polyester—extra fine* Silk ' <	9, 10 Sharps Betweens Milliner's Beading	Universal 65/9 or 70/10 Ballpoint or stretch 70/10 or 75/11
Medium Light: Calico, challis, cotton single knit, crinkle cotton, eyelet, lycra knit, microfiber, polyester silky, seersucker, silk charmeuse, silk noil, spandex, taffeta, tricot	Cotton-covered polyester * D 100% long staple polyester + ' @ Silk ' <	8, 9 Sharps Betweens Milliner's Embroidery	Universal 70/10 Ballpoint or stretch 70/10 or 75/11 Microtex 70/10 Jeans/denim 70/10
Medium: Broadcloth, chambray, chino, chintz, cotton/cotton blend, cotton knit, faille, flannel, lame, linen, moire, muslin, pique, poplin, rayon, satin, shantung, silk dupioni, stretch velvet, wool boucle, challis or crepe, vinyl, viyella	Cotton-covered polyester * D 100% long staple polyester + ' @ Silk ' <	6, 7, 8 Sharps Betweens Milliner's Embroidery	Universal 70/10 or 80/12 Ballpoint or stretch 75/11
Medium Heavy: Brocade, camel hair, corduroy, denim, duck, fleece, gabardine, leather, quilted fabric, sequinned fabric, sweatshirt fabric, suede, terrycloth, tweeds, twill, velvet, velveteen, vinyl-coated fabric, wool and wool blends	Cotton-covered polyester * D 100% long staple polyester + ' @ Silk ' <	5, 6 Sharps Betweens Milliner's Embroidery Glover's	Universal 80/12 or 90/14 Jeans/Denim 90/14 Ballpoint or stretch 80/12 or 90/14 Leather 90/14
Heavy: Boiled wool, canvas, coating, double-faced wool, drapery fabrics, faux fur, heavy-weight denim, leather, sailcloth, wool melton	Cotton-covered polyester – Button & Carpet * D 100% long staple polyester – extra strong + ' Silk ' < 100% nylon Upholstery & Home Dec thread * D	4, 5 Sharps Betweens Milliner's Embroidery Darners Glover's Sailmaker's	Universal 90/14 or 100/16 Jeans/Denim 90/14 or 100/16

FABRIC WEIGHT AND TYPE	THREAD	HAND NEEDLES	MACHINE NEEDLES
Very Heavy: Canvas, duck, upholstery fabrics	Cotton-covered polyester – Button & Carpet * D 100% long staple polyester – extra strong + ' 100 % nylon Upholstery & Home Dec thread * ' D	1, 2, 3 Sharps Betweens Milliner's Embroidery Darners Glover's Sailmaker's	Universal 100/16, 110/18 or 120/19 Jeans/Denim 100/16 or 110/18 Leather 100/16 or 110/18

Special Uses

Uses	Threads	Needles
Basting	100% cotton basting * + Silk ' <	HAND: Milliner's, Darner's, Sharps MACHINE: Universal or Ballpoint 70/10 or 80/12
Beading	Silk ' < ' 100% Nylon Monofilament < Ç D @ '	HAND: Beading MACHINE: Universal 60/8
Bobbin Filler for embroidery	100% nylon < 100% polyester ' @ D Ç	N/A
Buttonholes	Silk < ' ' Cotton covered polyester – Topstitching and Buttonhole Twist * D ' 100% long staple polyester + <	HAND: Embroidery 6, 7 MACHINE: Topstitching 80/12, 90/14, or 100/16
Buttons and Fasteners on heavier fabrics	Silk < ' ' Cotton covered polyester – Topstitching and Buttonhole Twist * D ' 100% long staple polyester + <	HAND: Embroidery 6, 7 MACHINE: Universal 90/14 or 100/16
Embroidery and Other Decorative Stitching	Silk < ' ' Rayon Embroidery @ ' ± * D + Ç 40% wool /60% acrylic < Acrylic embroidery < 100% polyester filament @ Metallic < @ ' + Ç 100% cotton @ + BOBBINWORK: Rayon Cord < @ Metallic Cord, Braid ' @ Metallic, yarn-like < @	HAND: Sharps, Embroidery 9, 10 MACHINE: Embroidery, Metafil or Metalica 70/10, 80/12, or 90/14

Special Uses Chart *(continued)*

Uses	Threads	Needles
Quilting	HAND: 100% cotton < ' * D 100% cotton covered polyester, waxed + MACHINE: 100% glazed cotton < 100% mercerized cotton + Cotton covered polyester * D	HAND: Betweens 7 MACHINE: Universal or Quilting 80/12 or 90/14
Topstitching	Silk < ' ' Cotton covered polyester – Topstitching and Buttonhole Twist * D ' D 100% long staple polyester + < '	HAND: Sharps, Betweens, Milliner's, Embroidery appropriate to fabric weight MACHINE: Topstitching 80/12, 90/14, or 100/16

*	Coats & Clark
±	Brewer Sewing Supplies
D	Gutermann of America, Inc.
'	Kreinek Mfg. Co.
@	Madeira
+	Mettler
<	YLI Corporation
D	Signature from American & Efird, Inc.
Ç	Sulky of America

Buttons

Make your buttons work as an accent to your garment. Buy them to enhance your creation, not merely to finish it. Although buttons are available in a wide range of shapes and contours, there are basically only two types. A sew-through button has two to four holes for attaching the button to the garment. A shank button has a metal, plastic, or fabric shank behind the button through which the button is attached. The shank allows room for the overlapping fabric so that the button rests on top of the buttonhole. You can cover your own buttons using a two-piece button form or mold. See pages 325 to 327 for a detailed discussion of buttons and how they may be used.

To determine button size, use the button gauge below. Technically, buttons are sized in "lines"—40 lines equal one inch (25 mm). When the size is known in inches (millimeters), refer to the chart to convert the size into lines.

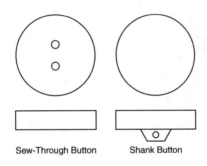

Sew-Through Button   Shank Button

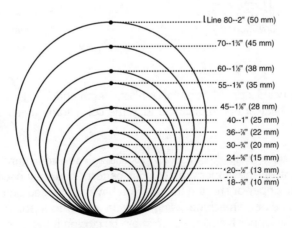

Line 80--2" (50 mm)
70--1¾" (45 mm)
60--1½" (38 mm)
55--1⅜" (35 mm)
45--1⅛" (28 mm)
40--1" (25 mm)
36--⅞" (22 mm)
30--¾" (20 mm)
24--⅝" (15 mm)
20--½" (13 mm)
18--⅜" (10 mm)

Zippers

Zippers are available in a variety of colors, sizes, and weights for almost any conceivable fastening task. Choose a zipper according to the style needed for your garment opening and a weight that is compatible with your fabric. The conventional zipper, the most common type, can be used for most standard zipper applications on most garments. Specialty zippers designed for specific openings or garments are also available.

The weight of a zipper is determined by its construction and the type of tape used. A coil-constructed zipper is made from a continuous strand of nylon or polyester twisted into a spiral and attached to a woven or knitted synthetic tape. It is lightweight and flexible, yet very strong, and is ideal for light and mediumweight fabrics and all types of knits. A coil zipper can be easily repaired if fabric catches in the zipper. Just bend the zipper in half, pinch the fold tightly, and twist to open. Pull the slider down past the opening and then up again to close.

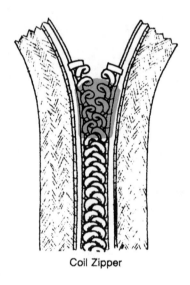

Coil Zipper

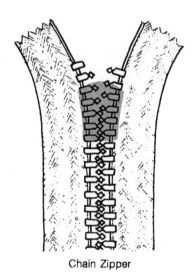

Chain Zipper

A chain-constructed zipper has metal or plastic teeth attached to a cotton or cotton-blend tape. It is a little heavier and more rigid than the coils; some metal styles are excellent for heavy-duty use.

Your pattern will specify the proper zipper length for your garment. If you make any length adjustments in the zipper area of your pattern, you may need to either purchase a longer or shorter zipper or shorten the one you have as directed on page 329. Zippers can be inserted by hand or by machine, using a special zipper foot, for any type of zipper application. Protect the zipper from excessive strain by closing it before laundering or dry-cleaning. If the zipper seems stiff and sticky to operate after laundering or cleaning, run a piece of beeswax or soap over the teeth or coils or use a zipper lubricant.

The **CONVENTIONAL ZIPPER** is designed so that one end opens at the edge of a garment and the other end has a bottom stop to prevent the slider from running into the seam. It can have synthetic coils or metal teeth and is available in 7" to 22" (18 cm to 55 cm) lengths. Shorter lengths, 4" to 6"(10 cm to 15 cm), and extra long lengths are usually available only in limited colors.

The **SEPARATING ZIPPER** opens at both ends for use on coats, jackets, parkas, vests, and detachable hoods and linings. Lightweight types with metal or nylon teeth range in length from 12" to 22" (30 cm to 55 cm). Heavyweight types have heavy brass or molded teeth in 18" to 24" (45 cm to 60 cm) lengths. The separating zipper is also available in a reversible version that has a pull tab on both sides of the slider and comes 18" to 30" (46 cm to 77 cm) long.

The **TWO-WAY ZIPPER** has two identical sliders on both the top and bottom of the zipper, enabling the garment to be opened from either end. Two-way separating zippers are ideal for parkas, ski pants, and snowsuits. Two-way zippers closed at the bottom can be used for jumpsuits and coveralls. Lengths range from 26" to 48" (66 cm to 122 cm).

The **TROUSER ZIPPER** is a heavy-duty variation of a conventional zipper with metal teeth, special bar supports on the slider to withstand frequent laundering, and extra wide tapes for double reinforcement stitching. It is available in 9" and 11" (22 cm and 28 cm) lengths.

The **BLUE JEAN ZIPPER** is a variation of the trouser zipper with a brass finish for use on jeans, skirts, and work pants. It is available in 5" to 9" (13 cm to 22 cm) length.

The **DECORATIVE OR INDUSTRIAL ZIPPER** has large metal or plastic teeth, matching or contrasting tape, and a big ring pull. It is available in both conventional and separating types in limited lengths. It is usually applied with the zipper teeth exposed for added emphasis.

The **INVISIBLE ZIPPER** is designed so that the teeth or coil is totally concealed behind the tape when the zipper is closed, and the completed application looks just like a seam. The zipper must be applied before the seam is stitched, using a special invisible zipper foot. It is available in lengths of 9" to 22" (23 cm to 55 cm).

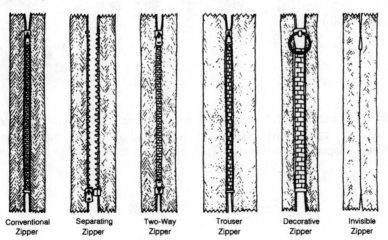

| Conventional Zipper | Separating Zipper | Two-Way Zipper | Trouser Zipper | Decorative Zipper | Invisible Zipper |

Fastenings

SNAPS, used for closing and anchoring garments, are available in many sizes and types. Snaps come in nickel or black enamel-coated metal with the smaller sizes, 4/0 to 1 (6 mm to 11 mm), being the most popular. The larger sizes, 2 to 4 (13 mm to 17 mm), are suitable for heavy-duty use. Large silk-covered snaps, ideal for suits and coats, are available in neutral colors. You may cover your own for special color combinations (see page 449) or purchase see- through nylon snaps to blend with the color of your garment. For casual clothes and children's wear, snaps prespaced on cotton tape and no-sew snap fasteners applied with special pliers or attaching tool can be used. Fur snaps are perfect for attaching fur collars and other accessories to your garment.

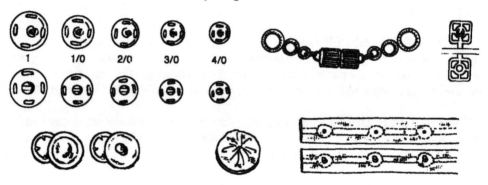

HOOKS AND EYES come in a variety of designs for special holding purposes. The standard type is made with brass, nickel, or black enamel finish, and comes in sizes 00 to 2 for lightweight fabrics and sizes 3 to 5 for bulky and heavyweight fabrics. The eye can be curved or straight.

Large hooks and eyes, either plain or silk-covered, make sturdy fastenings for coats or other items, especially fur. Specially shaped hook and bar closures, both sew-on and prong, make practical fasteners for waistbands on skirts and pants. Hooks and eyes are also available prespaced on cotton tape.

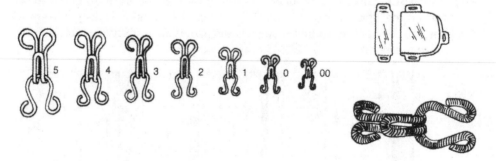

HOOK AND LOOP TAPE consists of two strips, one with tiny hooks and one with a looped pile, that intermesh when pressed together and open when peeled apart. It is available in precut shapes and by the yard.

BUCKLES are available in a wide variety of shapes and sizes, with or without prongs. They come in all types of materials such as metal, wood, plastic, and leather; or they may be covered with fabric for a custom finish. They can be purchased singly or in kits with belting. Eyelets are available with a nickel, gilt, or colored enamel finish and are applied with special pliers or attaching tool. They can be used for belts, lacing, and decorative ties.

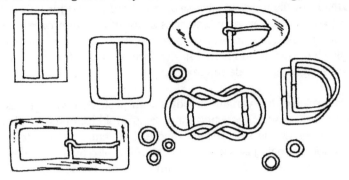

Elastics

Elastics are available in many different types and widths to be used in casings or applied directly to the garment. Elastics are made from a rubber or stretchable synthetic core that is wrapped with cotton, synthetic fiber, or a blend of fibers. Elastic thread is a very thin, covered core that is used for shirring. Elastic cord is a round or oval covered cord in varying diameters that can be sewn directly to the garment or used for loop closings.

Elastic braid, ribbon, and ribbed elastic are made of several covered cores woven, knitted, or braided together. They range in width from ¼" to 3" (6 mm to 75 mm) and are available in soft and hard stretch. Woven and knitted elastics retain their original width when stretched and thus can be sewn directly to the garment or inserted into a casing. Because braided elastics become narrower when stretched, they are recommended only for casings.

Special purpose elastics are available for pajamas, lingerie, intimate apparel, and swimwear. They are usually constructed of a softer strip or band, sometimes with a decorative edge, so that they are more comfortable when worn next to the skin. Do not use rayon elastic for swimwear because it stretches when wet. Special elastics are also designed for stretchable waistbands on both men's and women's wear.

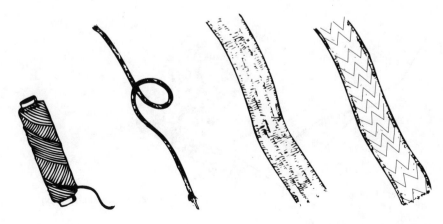

Tapes and Trims

Completing the inside of your garment in an aesthetic manner will result in a finished garment that is a delight to wear. Tapes, laces, and bindings in matching colors will give the inside of your garment a custom-made look--not to mention perfectly finished edges!

SEAM BINDING, a truly indispensable sewing notion, is used for finishing hem edges and straight facing edges. Ribbon seam binding is a woven tape approximately ½" (13 mm) wide, which can also be used to reinforce or extend seams. Lace seam binding can be used for a decorative finish on seams and hems; stretch lace is suitable for use on knitted fabrics. It is available prepackaged, in a wide range of colors.

BIAS TAPE is available in a variety of widths with prefolded edges to use for binding curved or straight edges, casings, ties, and trims. Single-fold bias tape is ½" (13 mm) wide with edges folded to the wrong side and meeting at the center. Double-fold is ¼" (6 mm) wide and has been folded again just slightly off-center; it is also available in an extrawide ½" (13 mm) width. Wide bias tape is ⅞" to 1" (22 mm to 25 mm) wide with edges folded ¼" (6 mm) to the wrong side. Bias tape is prepackaged in a wide range of colors and prints. Stretchable lace binding, prefolded to 112" (13 mm) width, can be used as bias tape for binding edges, seams, facings, and hems.

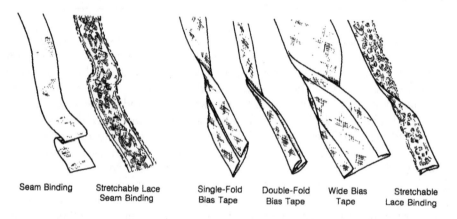

| Seam Binding | Stretchable Lace Seam Binding | Single-Fold Bias Tape | Double-Fold Bias Tape | Wide Bias Tape | Stretchable Lace Binding |

HEM FACING is a 2" (50 mm) wide bias tape or lace strip used for facing hems and binding edges. Bias hem facing has both edges folded to the inside and is available in both a polyester and cotton fabric and a taffeta. Stretchable lace hem facing has a decorative lace design. Both are prepackaged in many colors.

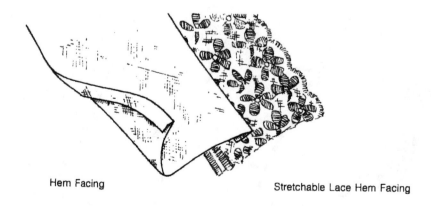

Hem Facing   Stretchable Lace Hem Facing

TWILL TAPE is a very firmly woven tape used in tailoring and for reinforcing seams. It comes in black, natural and white in ¼", ½", ¾", and 1 " (6 mm, 13 mm, 20 mm and 25 mm) widths.

GROSGRAIN RIBBON is a firmly woven, ribbed ribbon used for staying waistlines, facing waistbands and belts, and for decorative trims. It is available in a wide range of widths, colors, geometric patterns, and prints.

PIPING is a narrow, corded, bias strip with a ¼" (6 mm) seam allowance, which is inserted into a seam for a decorative accent. It comes in several colors in prepackaged lengths.

CABLE CORD is used as a filler for piping, cording, tubing, and trapunto and for making corded buttonholes and tucks. It is sold by the yard (meter) in ⅛" to 1" (3 mm to 25

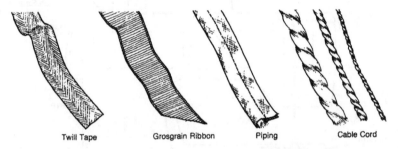

Twill Tape   Grosgrain Ribbon   Piping   Cable Cord

mm) diameters.

FOLD-OVER BRAID is a knitted braid with finished edges that is folded in half, sometimes with one edge slightly wider than the other. It is used for binding and trimming an edge without a hem or facing. It is available in different colors and designs, both prepackaged and by the yard (meter).

RIBBING is a knitted band with a variety of types, weights, and widths that is used to finish the neckline, armhole, sleeve, pants leg, or waistline of a garment. The stretchability of ribbings varies, depending upon the knit- some are quite stable while others are very stretchy. Ribbing is available prepackaged or by the yard (meter).

HORSEHAIR BRAID is used to stiffen hem edges, especially on evening and bridal wear, so they will softly flare. A stiff, bias braid woven of transparent synthetic yarns, it may have a heavy thread along one edge for easing. It is available in different widths.

BELTING is a very stiff band used to reinforce self-covered belts and waistbands. Available in both regular and iron-on types, it is sold in prepackaged lengths or by the yard (meter) in ½" to 3" (13 mm to 75 mm) widths. Specially designed waistband strips, used to finish the inside of a waistband, are also available.

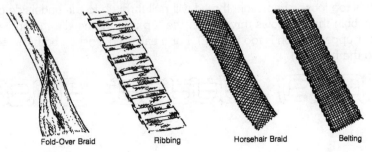

Fold-Over Braid   Ribbing   Horsehair Braid   Belting

The Sewing Machine

Sewing machines have become very sophisticated today with the advancement of the computer age. With the introduction of new fabrics, new needles and presser feet have been designed to meet the demands of the fashion sewer. When buying a new machine, it is important for you to analyze what type of sewing you currently do and what you would like to do in the future.

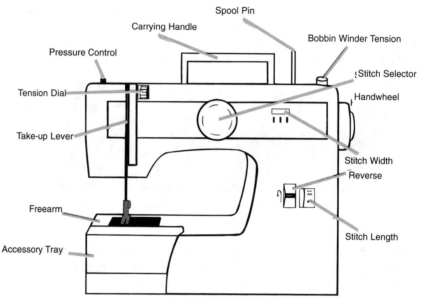

Even the most basic model sewing machines offer a broad range of built-in stitches to select from—from utilitarian to decorative—for your use. And with the increase in technology, your sewing machine can even be hooked up to your personal computer for unlimited stitching capabilities. Many machines also accept "cards" or "discs" to increase their stitch selection.

All sewing machines share one important feature, no matter the number of stitches they offer—***the thread tension.*** The strength of your seams depends on the correct thread tension. Before stitching on any garment, you should test the tension on a scrap of fabric on both the lengthwise and crosswise grains. Before adjusting your tension, check your thread choice and needle size for the fabric you sewing on. For normal sewing, you should be stitching with the same type thread through your needle and on your bobbin. A too large or too small needle will affect your stitch quality also.

As a general rule, your should only adjust your upper tension. In most cases, the bobbin tension has been factory set. The upper tension controls the thread that passes through the needle. If it is too loose, the needle thread will pull through to the underside of your fabric (1). If the bobbin thread shows through on the top and the needle thread lies flat on the surface, your upper tension is too tight (2). For a balanced tension, both threads are drawn equally into the fabric (3).

| 1 | 2 | 3 |

If you continue to experience tension problems with your machine, have it checked by the authorized sewing machine dealer for your brand. They have been trained to adjust your make of machine. Remember that sewing should be a pleasurable experience so don't fight with your machine to achieve the results you desire! Proper care of your machine will provide you with years of sewing enjoyment.

MACHINE EQUIPMENT

It is as important to select the proper sewing machine equipment as it is to choose the correct interfacing or marking tools to use on your fabric.

NEEDLES

Needles should be selected according to the weight and type of the fabric used as well as the thread selected. Many decorative threads require the use of special needles to reduce the amount of thread breakage during sewing. Needle sizes range from very fine (7/60) for delicate fabrics to larger sizes (19/120) for heavyweight fabrics. Refer to the needle chart on pages 172 to 174 for the specific needle size recommended for your weight of fabric.

Many types of needles are available based on the type of sewing you will be doing. Select the correct needle by the point, the shape and size of the eye and the overall size suitable for your fabric. A **universal** point (130/705H), appropriate for most all woven and knit fabrics, has a modified ball point to slip through the fabric easily. A **sharp or Microtex** (130/705 H-M) needle is recommended for wovens or microfibers. A **ball point** (130/705 H SUK) needle has a medium rounded point that will not damage knit fabrics whereas a stretch (130/705 H-S) needle is suitable for elastic, spandex and other knitwear. The **denim or jeans** needle has an acute point and strong shaft for sewing through tightly woven, dense fabrics. A **leather** needle has a wedge-shaped point designed to cut through leather and vinyl. **Topstitching** (130N) needles have a larger eye to accommodate heavier topstitching threads. **Machine embroidery** (130/705 H-E) needles are used for rayon and specialty embroidery threads. **Metafil or Metallic** (130 Met) are specially designed with a large polished eye and large groove for use with metallic threads to prevent shredding, snagging or breakage. **Quilting** (130/705 H-Q) needles have a special taper to the point to allow stitching through different densities of fabric without skipping stitches.

SHANK
needle portion that is inserted into machine, rounded in front and flat in back

SHAFT/STEM
center needle section with long groove to guide thread

GROOVE
holds the thread in place

EYE
hole for thread

POINT
penetrates the fabric and carries the thread

Double and triple needles, mounted on a crossbar from a single shaft, can be used for decorative as well as functional stitching. **Single and double wing** needles are also another type of decorative-use needle as they produce "holes" in the fabric similar to traditional hemstitching.

It is recommended that you change your needle every time you begin a new sewing project. Many stitching problems are the result of dull or blunt needles, needles not inserted correctly, or the wrong size needle being used for the fabric and thread.

PRESSER FEET

Your sewing machine will come with a variety of presser feet designed to perform numerous tasks more easily for you. By learning what each foot does, various sewing techniques will become much easier and faster to accomplish. Let the machine and feet assist you in achieving the specific task at hand.

A **general-purpose foot and general-purpose needle plate** are standard with all sewing machines. They have a wider hole and needle opening to accommodate the sideways motion of all the zig zag-type stitches

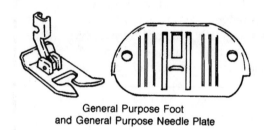

General Purpose Foot
and General Purpose Needle Plate

A **straight stitch foot and straight stitch needle plate** is available for most all machines. Use this foot and plate when straight stitching on very light, spongy-type fabrics or where extra fabric control is needed. The small hole will prevent the fabric from being pulled down into the machine while stitching.

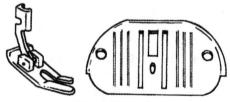

Straight Stitch Foot
and Straight Stitch Needle Plate

The **zipper foot** is designed to stitch very close to the raised teeth during zipper insertion. The foot itself may slide side-to-side or the needle position may need to be adjusted to stitch both sides during insertion. This foot is also often used for covering cords and applying piping into seams.

Zipper Foot

The **blindhem foot** is used for machine hemming. The bar, often adjustable, allows the needle to just penetrate the hem fold for an invisible hem finish. (See page 423.)

Blindhem Foot

An indispensable foot, often similar in appearance to the blindhem foot, is the **edgestitching foot**. This bar on this foot acts as a guide for straight, even topstitching and edgestitching.

Edgestitching Foot

Hemmer feet turn a narrow hem and stitch it in one operation using either straight or decorative stitches. These feet are available in a number of sizes based on the weight of the fabric being hemmed.

Hemming Foot

The **embroidery foot** is used when satin stitching or stitching any of the decorative stitches on your machine. The wide groove on the bottom of the sole allows the more densely stitched patterns to move easily under the foot. These feet are also often available in clear plastic and with cutout opening between the toes for better visibility while sewing.

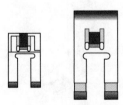

Embroidery Feet

An **overedge or overcasting foot** is designed to hold knit fabrics flat while using an overedge stitch to sew a seam and overcast the edge at the same time.

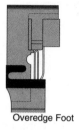

Overedge Foot

Most sewing machines today have a built-in buttonhole stitch. In fact, many models have more than one type of buttonhole stitch to select from—standard, stretch, or keyhole, to name a few. A **special buttonhole foot** is used to sew these stitches to ensure that multiple-sewn buttonholes are exactly the same size. Whether your machine sews electronically sized buttonholes or the presser foot measures the size of the button while sewing, the results are the same—the buttonholes are all the same size.

After sewing your buttonholes, you can sew on the buttons with your **button sew-on foot**. Designed to hold any two- or four-hole button securely, a zig zag stitch is used to attach the button to the fabric. Some machines even have a stitch designated solely for this purpose.

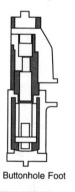

Buttonhole Foot

Button Sew-on Foot

The **gathering foot** is used to gather or shirr with every stitch. It can also be used to attach the gathered piece to a flat piece at the same time.

Gathering Foot

SPECIAL ATTACHMENTS

Even Feed Foot

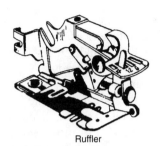

Ruffler

Binder Foot

The **walking or even-feed foot** is used to sew hard-to-feed napped or pile fabrics, stretch fabrics, plaids and stripes, slippery fabrics, or multiple layers of fabrics that may shift or hang up on each other. The top layer of fabric is helped along at the same rate as the bottom fabric.

A **ruffler** can make uniform gathers or tiny pleats on light- to mediumweight fabrics: it can ruffle one layer and stitch it to a flat fabric, lace can be inserted while ruffling, and tiny pleats can be sewn in intervals.

The **bias binder** attachment or foot is used to apply purchased or self-fabric bias binding to a cut edge. The binding is rolled around the edge, or pre-folded tape may be used.

Teflon™ feet have a coated sole that is helpful in stitching on leathers, vinyl, suede and other "sticky" fabrics. Another foot designed to handle these same difficult fabrics is the **roller foot.** Designed with one or more rollers, the upper fabric is kept from slipping while stitching.

Pintuck feet, also available in sizes based on the weight of the fabric, are used in conjunction with the double needle. The grooves on the bottom of the foot create tiny raised tucks in the fabric.

Braiding, cording, felling, free-motion or darning, and quilting or patchwork feet are just a few of the many other specialty feet available.

There are many more specialty feet available designed to make your sewing projects easier. Ask your local authorized sewing machine dealer for a list of those made for your brand machine. Take classes to learn more about the feet and what they will do for you.

Be sure to use the correct bobbins for your model machine. Bobbins can be either made of plastic or metal so consult your sewing machine's manual before purchasing additional ones. It is recommended to keep several on hand, wound with your basic colors. Avoid winding one color thread over another or using damaged or knicked bobbins, as they may cause stitching problems.

Keep your sewing machine tools handy as they are an important part of your machine. Needles and some presser feet may need to be removed and attached with a small screwdriver. If your machine needs to be oiled, do so prior to beginning your sewing project rather than when you are finished so the oil gets worked through the machine's moving parts while you sew. And, keep your bobbin area and around the feed dogs free of lint for a smoother-working machine.

The Overlock Machine

The overlock machine, or serger, as it is often called, has become almost commonplace in everyone's sewing room today. Used in factories for almost 100 years, this handy machine was introduced to the sewing public in the mid-1960's. It immediately appealed to those that sew because it produced a stitch "just like ready-to-wear". The serger trims the fabric while overcasting the edges at the same time.

Most sewers thought, at first, that the serger was only for sewing knits but we all soon came to realize how versatile this machine really is. Numerous models with a variety of stitch formations are now available from most sewing machine manufacturers. Sophisticated top-of-the-line machines have such features as computerized stitch selection and tension control. Less expensive models may offer color-coded threading, differential feed or snap-on presser feet. The serger can be used to sew seams just as easily as it can finish fabric edges or apply decorative trims.

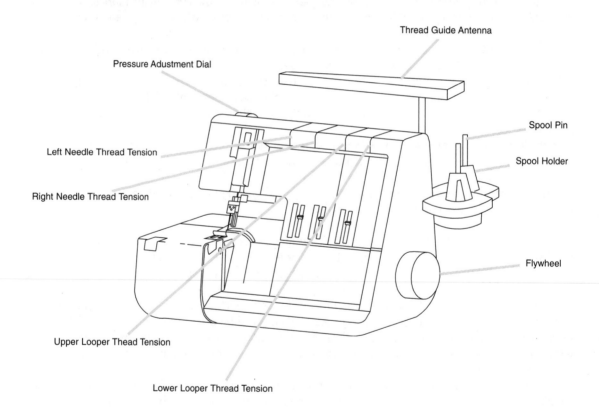

Stitch Types

A variety of stitch types are available depending on the number and position of the needles on your machine. Rather than working with a bobbin as on a sewing machine, the serger uses "loopers" to form the stitch. The needle thread(s) holds the looper threads in place as the stitch is being formed. As this stitch has somewhat a zigzag appearance, it will have built-in stretch in the seam.

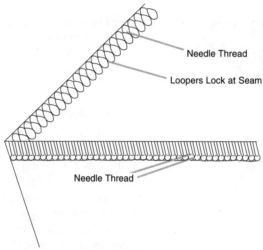

Needle Thread

Loopers Lock at Seam

Needle Thread

The choice of the stitch is based on the type of fabric selected, the end-use of the garment, and the location of the seam. Many stitch formations may work in any number of seam locations however, one stitch is usually the most appropriate for the end use of the garment. Listed below are a number of the common stitches available on many overlock machines.

2-THREAD Overlock Stitch: Using one needle and one looper, this stitch is best used for an edge finish particularly on fine fabrics. It is not strong enough for a seam.

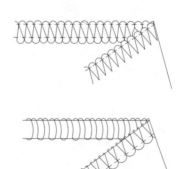

2-THREAD Rolled Hem: The fabric edge is rolled by the stitch formed by the needle and one looper. When stitched with lightweight threads, this edge finish is a very elegant finish on fine silk, wool, and cotton.

3-THREAD Overlock Stitch: This stitch is formed using one needle and two loopers. Used on medium- to heavy weight fabrics, this balanced stitch is suitable as the seam on knitwear or an edge finish on raveling fabrics.

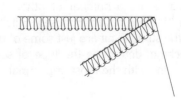

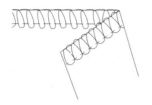

3-THREAD Rolled Hem: Sturdier than the 2-thread rolled hem, this stitch is often used as a hem finish on skirts, scarves, ruffles, or on home decorating projects. It can also be used to make pintucks as a decorative technique.

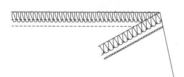

4-THREAD Overlock Stitch: This stitch is formed using two needles and two loopers. It is a sturdy stitch often used as a seaming stitch on medium to heavy weight fabrics.

5-THREAD Overlock Stitch: This stitch is actually a combination of two stitches—a 2-thread chainstitch and a 3-thread overlock stitch. It used as a seaming stitch on medium- to heavy weight woven fabrics and has very little stretch because of the chainstitch. If you have this stitch on your machine, you may or may not be able to stitch a 2-thread chainstitch alone. This stitch is often used for home decorating.

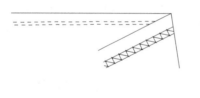

Cover Hem: This stitch looks like a double row of topstitching on the right side and an overlock stitch on the wrong side of the fabric. Formed with two needles and the chainstitch looper, it is used to hem or topstitch garments. This stitch may vary in width depending on the brand of machine you own.

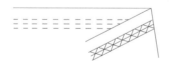

Triple Cover Hem: Similar to the cover hem, this stitch uses three needles and the chain looper to form the stitch. The outward appearance is of three rows of parallel straight stitching. It is also used for hemming, topstitching or making belt loops.

There are a number of other stitch formations available depending on the brand of machine you have purchased. Stitches like stretched wrap or super stretch, wrapped edge, or the stretch knit are just some of the names they possess. Before purchasing an overlock machine, determine the type of sewing you will be doing most often so you can buy a machine with the most appropriate stitch combinations for you.

Serger Thread Tension

Thread tension on the serger is very different than the tension on your sewing machine. Often one of the biggest concerns for the sewer just learning to use her serger is dealing with the tension adjustments as most overlock machine have 4 to 5 tension dials or knobs to adjust (see picture on page 192). At first, these adjustments seem somewhat intimidating but become less so once their function is completely understood. Each tension dial or knob controls the thread for its corresponding needle or looper. The higher the number or a move to the +(plus) side means there is more tension on the thread—less thread will pass through the machine. The lower the number or a move to the –(minus) side means that there is less tension on the thread—more thread will pass through the machine.

The trick is to find the perfect balance between all the threads. The upper and/or lower looper threads should lay on the fabric with the needle thread(s) looking like a straight stitch on the right side of the fabric. The looper threads should meet equally along the trimmed edge of the fabric. You will immediately know if the tension is incorrect by the appearance of your stitch.

There are many factors that can effect the thread tension such as the type of thread you use, the weight of the fabric, the stitch length and the stitch width. As with all sewing projects, it is also important to start with a new needle and double check your threading before starting to turn dials. Be sure to test your stitch on a swatch of fabric before starting any garment.

Most sergers today use standard sewing needles as described on page 183. As the serger can accommodate a variety of decorative threads it is equally important to use the correct needle for the thread. A special needle is recommend by some overlock machine manufacturers if you are experiencing difficulties with your cover hem stitch.

There are a number of special presser feet and accessories available for your serger. Check with your sewing machine dealer to learn more about them.

Special Serger Notions

There are a few notions that are important when using your serger. They make your serging experience easier and more pleasant. We have listed just a few for your use.

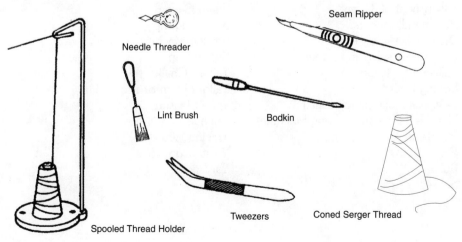

Needle Threader

Seam Ripper

Lint Brush

Bodkin

Tweezers

Coned Serger Thread

Spooled Thread Holder

Tools
for Every
Sewing Need

A vast assortment of tools and sewing aids have been manufactured to serve the woman who sews. Each one has been carefully designed to save time and simplify construction. You should begin by acquiring tools according to your immediate needs (shears, steam iron, etc.) and then start to purchase those extra, handy time-savers that are constantly appearing on the market. The more basic items will be your only expenditure in the very beginning, while the more complicated tools will become necessary as your skill and interest increase. Thus, your purchases will be spread out as you go along.

Because your equipment is essential to your sewing success, it must be of good quality and always kept in the peak of working order. Experiment with various types of equipment and see which one is best for you. If possible, it is wise to test the tool before you purchase it to be sure the parts are working smoothly. Most importantly, give each tool the same scrupulous attention you would give any other household appliance and there will be no need to buy replacements.

To save yourself time and confusion, have your equipment stored systematically in categories, making each item readily accessible at all times. Keep together all your marking equipment, your fastenings, your thread, and so on. Having them handy will accelerate your work and increase your accuracy. If you follow this advice, it will be easy to get into the habit of using the right tool at the proper time.

Use the following guide as a reference when purchasing your equipment. We have carefully sorted through the extensive variety of tools sold, creating a list of those you should have to sew correctly without needing to improvise.

Assortment of Thread	Seam Gauge
Bent-handle shears	Sewing Lamp
Dressmaker's Silk Pins	Sewing Machine
Dressmaker's Tracing Paper	Steam Iron
Full-length Mirror	Tailor's Chalk
Ironing Board	Tailor's Ham or Press Mitt
Overlock Machine (optional)	Tape Measure
Needles (Hand and Sewing Machine)	Thimble
Pincushion	Tracing Wheel
Press Cloths	Waste Container
Ruler	Yardstick
Scissors	

Measuring Tools

Measuring tools are among the most important items in your sewing box. Good quality equipment and correct usage will assure you a better-fitting garment. Be sure to have a variety available to avoid the temptation to guess or the need to substitute. The key to success is to measure often and accurately.

Tape measures are indispensable. They should be 60" (152 cm) long with metal tips and made of a material that will not stretch. It will be most helpful if the numbers, in inches or centimeters, are printed on both sides. (1)

Rulers are necessary for all your sewing projects. You should have at least one 12-18" (30.5-46 cm) long, and one 5-6" (12.5-15 cm) long. They can be found in a variety of materials. If you select wood, keep in mind that it may warp. It should have a metal edge for accuracy. The plastic see-through type easily retains its straight edges, is well suited for buttonholes, pleats, etc. and can readily serve all your needs. The numbers should be clearly indicated. (2)

Yardsticks are invaluable for general marking purposes. They should be made of shellacked hard wood or metal. Those made of metal are sturdiest.

A *sewing gauge* is a 6" (15 cm) metal or plastic ruler with a sliding indicator. It is ideal for quick, accurate measurements of hems, buttonholes and pleats. (3)

A *hem gauge* is generally made of lightweight metal with one gradually curved edge designed to accommodate the shape of your hems. The different hem depths are clearly indicated on it surface. The straight edges are also marked in inches or centimeters to provide another measuring tool. (4)

A *French curve* is a marking tool that is sharply curved along one side. Use it to redraw curved areas such as armholes, necklines, and princess seams when altering patterns. (5)

T-squares can be made of either clear plastic or metal. Use it for straightening grain, locating opposite grains, altering your pattern tissue, or for other marking tasks. (6)

A *skirt marker* is the quickest, easiest and most accurate way to mark hems. There are several types: pin, chalk and a combination of both. The pin marker is more precise but does require the assistance of another person, which is not necessary for the chalk variety with a blower on a tube. A skirt marker that combines pin and chalk allows you to have the best qualities of both. Be sure the base is heavy and steady and that the marker extends high enough to be suitable for all your fashion lengths. (7)

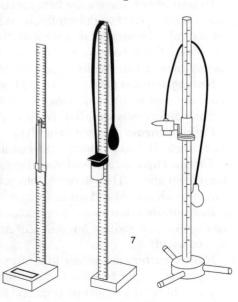

EZY-HEM GAUGE

Cutting

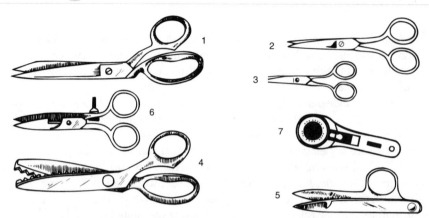

It is vital to be accurate when cutting out the individual pieces of your garment. An even edge, an obvious notch, and a true curve will make sewing much simpler. With that in mind, your cutting tools become some of the most important pieces of sewing equipment you will own.

When purchasing shears or scissors, look for high-quality steel scissors with either smooth (knife-edge) or serrated (small notches along one edges—ideal for cutting silks or other slippery fabrics) blades. Test the mechanism to be sure the scissors fit your hand, work smoothly and cut sharply from the back of the blades to the point. There are a number of shears and scissors that have been ergonomically designed to make cutting more comfortable for those with arthritis or other hand problems.

Many shears and scissors are made with an adjustable screw to allow the user to adjust the "run" of the shears to her particular feel. Your sewing shears and scissors should be used for cutting fabric only as cutting paper will quickly dull the blades. Wipe the blades with a soft cloth after each use and keep your scissors sharpened using a professional sharpening service to prolong their life. Never use an electric knife sharpener to sharpen your scissors.

Dressmaker's shears are bent-handle shears with 7"or 8" (18 or 21 cm) blades hinged with a screw. The two differently shaped handles accommodate more fingers and yield better control. The bent handles are preferred because the fabric can rest flat on the table when being cut. Some have a serrated edge on the blade that helps control the cutting of lightweight fabrics. Left-handed shears are also available. (1)

Sewing scissors have small round handles and range from 4" to 6" (10-15 cm) in length. They are used for more delicate cutting and trimming. (2)

Embroidery scissors, 3-4" (7-10 cm) long, are used for buttonholes and detail work. (3)

Pinking shears are used to finish raw edges of fabrics that do not ravel easily. Select 7½" to 9" blades (19-23 cm) with a ball-bearing pivot. (4)

Thread clips are a scissor variation with short blades and an inner spring mechanism to keep them apart. They fit neatly into your hand and are used with a clipping motion to cut stray threads quickly and easily. (5)

Buttonhole scissors are constructed to allow you to begin cutting within the body of the fabric. A screw and nut arrangement makes it possible to set the blades to cut only a prescribed length. (6)

Rotary cutters are similar to a pizza cutter and are used with a special self-healing mat and plastic ruler for accurate cutting. Replaceable blades are available.(7)

The cutting area should be large and flat, perferably about 38" (97 cm) high, and at least 36" (92 cm) wide, and 6 to 8 feet (1.83-2.4 M) long. Ideally the area should be accessible from all four sides.

Marking

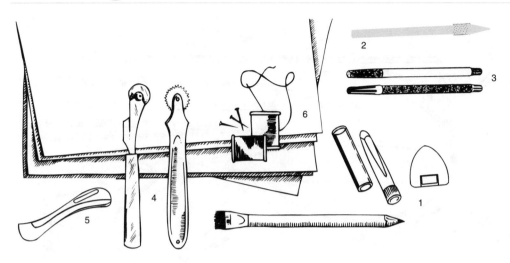

Marking plays an important role in the construction process. Haphazard stitching of seams and darts or arbitrary placement of collars, pockets, etc. cause by incorrect markings will unquestionably yield unfavorable results. The pattern tissue has specific construction lines and symbols printed on its surface for you to transfer to your garment pieces. If you have been accurate in marking these guidelines, construction will be greatly simplified and errors kept to a minimum.

Since you will be working with many varieties of fabric, from lush woolens to transparent voiles, you should have on hand the accompanying types of marking equipment.

Chalk is ideal for marking most fabrics. Easy to use it comes in many forms such as clay chalk wedges or squares, chalk wheels, chalk marking pencils, and wax chalk. (1) Do not use wax chalk on synthetic fabrics because it will be difficult to remove by any method. Chalk wheels can be refilled and chalk marking pencils sharpened with a pencil or cosmetic sharpener. A small brush is useful for erasing pencil marks. A soapstone marker is an alternative to chalk pencils and can easily be removed.(2)

Fabric marking pens work well on most washable fabrics. There are two types of pens, air- and water-soluble. Air-soluble disappears in the air within 12 to 48 hours. Water-soluble pens rinse away with water. Do not press over either of these types of marking pens as the marks may become permanent.(3)

Tracing wheels and dressmaker's tracing paper is suitable for most fine fabrics. The wheels, available in a single or double wheel format, have serrated, smooth, blunt or stiletto edges. The wheels are used to mark with wax-free tracing paper, which can be single- or double-sided or of a disappearing type (4).

A *hera* marking tool is a Japanese tool that marks the fabric when pressure is applied leaving an indentation. It works best on natural fiber fabrics (5).

Thread tracing is used to mark pockets, garment center lines, tailor tacks, grainlines or for general basting. Silk thread is recommended for fine fabrics and when basting stitches are not to be removed before pressing. Choose thread in a slightly contrasting color for easier removal (6).

Sewing Aids

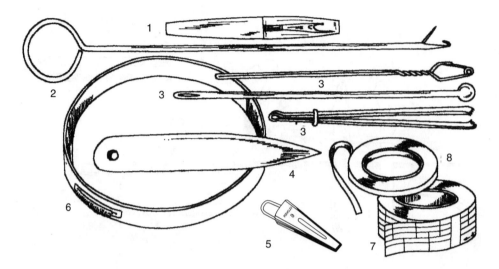

These additional sewing aids help contribute to fine workmanship. They enable you to perform your hand tasks more quickly and easily.

A ***seam ripper*** is a simple and safe pen-like device that allows careful ripping of adjustments and mistakes. Never, never use a razor blade as a substitute. (1)

A ***loop turner*** is a specially designed tool with a latch-hook device at one end. It is used to turn tubing or bias cording to the right side. (2)

A ***bodkin*** is used to draw elastic, belting and cording through casings. Gripper teeth or a safety pin closing hold the elastic or cording. Another type has an eye for threading and can be used for turning bias tubing. (3)

A ***pointer and creaser*** is a flat wooden tool approximately 4" (10 cm) long. One end is pointed, the other is rounded. The pointed end is used for pushing out small corners; the rounded end is used in conjunction with an iron to flatten seamlines or to assist finger pressing. (4)

A ***bias tape maker*** with the aid of an iron makes single-fold bias tape. Bias tape makers are available in ¼" to 2" (6 mm to 50 mm) sizes. (5)

An ***embroidery hoop*** is a two-part frame. One hoop fits snugly over another to hold a section of fabric taut for embroidery or beading. It can be purchased in both metal and wood, and in a variety of shapes and sizes. Select a hoop with a screw mechanism that permits adjustment for various weights of fabric. (6)

Sewing tape is measured on one side to use as a stitching guide, especially when topstitching. One type can be separated into various widths. (7)

Basting tape is very narrow and has adhesive on both sides. Use it to hold a zipper in place or two layers of fabric for stitching. Do not stitch over tape and be sure to remove it after sewing the seam. (8)

Tissue paper should always be on hand. Use it when stitching those fabrics that may need special treatment to go through the feed dog and presser foot of your machine. The tissue is also used when lengthening your pattern tissue, making alterations, or transferring monograms and designs.

More Sewing Aids

Liquid seam sealant prevents fabrics from fraying. Use it to secure thread ends on buttonholes, serger seams, prevent fraying on seam allowances, or ends of ribbons. It's also great for controlling runs in pantyhose. (1)

A *magnetic seam guide* attaches to the bed of the sewing machine next to the needle plate. Adjust it easily to ensure uniform stitching and seam allowances. (2)

A *pocket curve template* is used as a guide for pressing and stitching perfectly shaped pockets. Four pocket corners are on each template. (3)

Pincushions are essential tools in any sewing room, be they used on the tabletop or on your wrist. We suggest having as many as you desire. At least one should be filled with fine emery for sharpening and removing rust from your needles and pins. Magnetic pin-cushions are available both for table and wrist use. They are useful when picking up loose pins that have fallen to the floor. (4)

Beeswax should be kept handy in a holder to coat your hand sewing threads. It strengthens the thread and reduces tangling, knotting and breaking. (5)

A *needle threader* is a small device to help you on those frustrating days when you just can't thread your needle. (6)

Iron cleaner is used to remove any residue left on the bottom of your iron after working with fusibles . (7)

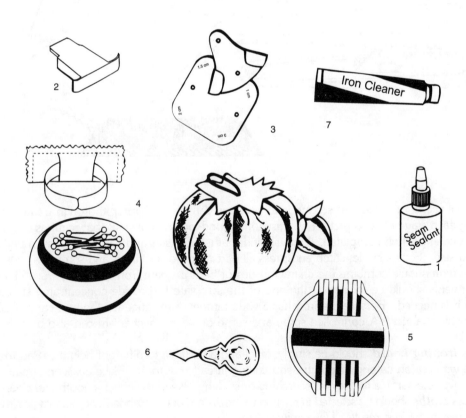

Pressing

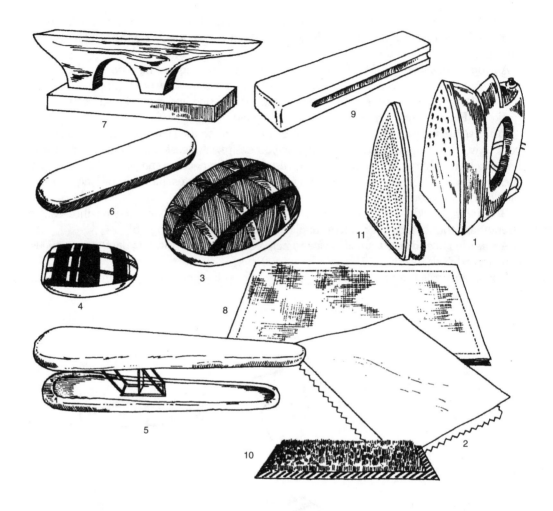

The real secret of success in sewing is to press as you sew. Careful, thorough treatment during each stage of construction will result in a good-looking garment that requires only a light touch-up when completed. You will find that it is quicker and easier to press in units as you sew. For example, stitch and press all darts and pocket flaps, and so on.

The **iron** should combine the characteristics of both a steam iron and a dry iron. The steam vents should be located at the end of the soleplate to provide concentrated steam when it is needed. Be sure the iron has a wide temperature range for the best care of all you fashion fabrics. A controlled spray and surge of steam mechanism can also be helpful. (1)

The **ironing board** should be sturdy, level and adjustable to different heights. Pad the board with cotton batting or purchased padding already cut to fit. Place a silicone-treated cover over the surface to prevent scorching or sticking. Keep the cover smooth and clean.

Press cloths should be selected in relation to the weight of your fabric. They should be similar in weight for best results. Have at least three on hand: a transparent variety for seeing details, a two-part wool and cotton type for most general pressing needs, and a non-stick or Teflon™ type for fusibles. For pressing on the right side, use a scrap of the garment fabric as a press cloth. Keep cheesecloth available for ready use as a press cloth (2).

A *tailor's ham* is an oblong, firmly stuffed cushion with subtly rounded curves. It is designed for pressing the curved areas of your garment such as darts, sleeve caps, princess seams, or any place that requires a rounded, curved shape pressed in. There are no substitutes for this item as it simulates actual body curves. Hams come in different sizes and should be covered in half cotton and half wool. One version has a concave as well as a convex section (3).

A *press mitt* is similar to a tailor's ham, but small enough to fit over your hand. It has pockets on either side to protect your hand. The mitt is good for small hard-to-reach areas or it may be slipped over the end of a sleeve board for sleeve caps. It also may be covered on one side with wool and on the other with cotton (4).

A *sleeve board* is actually two small ironing boards attached one on top of the other. They are designed for pressing small or slim areas, such as sleeves or necklines, that do not fit over your regular board. It should have a silicone cover and padding (5).

A *seam roll* is a long, firmly stuffed, tubular cushion that is rounded at each end. It is used to press small, curved areas and long seams in hard-to-reach areas such as sleeves. Because the roll is rounded, you press only the seam and not the surrounding fabric. This prevents ridges from forming on the right side. Again, one side should be covered with wool and the other side with cotton. To make a seam roll, cover a tightly rolled magazine with scraps of fabric (6).

A *point presser* or *pressing board* is made of wood and provides many differently shaped surfaces for pressing points, curves, and straight edges. The different sizes of curves and narrow straight edges allow you to press seams flat and open without wrinkling the surrounding area. The board can be used as it is for firm fabrics and sharp edges, or covered with a contoured pad for softer edges (7).

A *pressing pad* is three or four thicknesses of soft fabric stitched together to make a padded surface for pressing monograms, buttonholes, sequined fabric, and other raised surfaces. Place the raised surface face down on the pad and press on the wrong side. The pad prevents puckers and flattening of the decoration. A heavy turkish towel may be substituted (8).

A *pounding block* or *clapper* is a block of wood used with steam to flatten seam edges. It was originally designed to be used on hard-finished woolens and linens, but it may be used to form soft rolled hems. It is a must for tailoring. First make as much steam as possible with a steam iron and a damp press cloth. Remove the iron and cloth and pound firmly, regulating your pressure and slapping motions to suit the desired edge (9).

A *needleboard* is a bed of needles mounted on a flat surface that is placed between your fabric and the ironing board to prevent flattening pile fabrics. When the fabric is placed face down on the board, the pile falls in between the needles. It is essential for pressing velvet and other high-piled fabrics and very useful when pressing easily marred woolens. Also available with a stiff, high-pile fabric surface instead of needles (10).

An *iron cover* is placed over the soleplate of your iron and is used instead of a press cloth to prevent shine and scorching. One type is made of pre-formed heat-resistant fabric stretched over a metal frame and attaches to the iron with a spring; another is made of wool or canvas and has a drawstring for adjustment (11).

Brown paper is essential. Strips should be placed under the folds of darts or the edges of pleats, etc., to avoid unsightly ridges from appearing on the right side.

Dress Form

Have you ever had to compromise on fit because you could not reach that puckered seam or extra back fullness? Such compromises could lead to disappointing results. As every fine seamstress knows, an accurate fit is as vital as good workmanship to the lovely look of a finished garment. The perfect solution to these and other tricky fitting problems is a dress form, which duplicates your figure and allows you to fit and alter from all angles.

Whichever type you choose, it should have a heavy, sturdy base and be adjustable for figure changes, different heights, and convenient storage. Compressible shoulders are also a definite plus, as they allow you to slip your garment on and off the form easily.

A *foam form* is covered with a fabric shell that can be individually fitted to your contours. It can be adjusted by altering the fabric shell, and will not be harmed by pinning fabric to its surface. It is also available in pants forms (1).

A *molded, sectional form* can be adjusted both horizontally and vertically in several places to correspond to your own measurements, but it cannot duplicate your figure variations (2).

A *wire mesh form* can be slipped on and shaped to your own body and posture. It is then unsnapped and attached to a stand. Although easily adjustable, it does not have a smooth contour. It is also available in pants forms (3).

A *fabric-covered cotton batting form* is smoothly shaped, takes pins, and is good for working with very heavy fabrics or garments. However, it can be adjusted only by adding padding to the outside of the form (4).

Remember to check your measurements occasionally to make sure your dress form is still accurate, and adjust accordingly if necessary.

Once you begin using a dress form as part of your sewing equipment, you will be happily surprised at its many uses and the convenience it provides. Fitting, of course, will be quicker, easier, and more accurate. You will be able to see and understand more completely the reasoning behind darts, structured seams, and built-in ease. It will help you check such details as the fall of a hem or the roll of a collar before it is too late to easily make any necessary adjustments. You can steam press directly on the dress form to perfectly set design lines. Most importantly, you can stand away from your garment and see it as others will, giving you greater objectivity and a three-dimensional view you can't get in a mirror.

1   2   3   4

4

CONSTRUCTION BASICS

Your Complete Sewing Handbook

Now you're about to begin your adventure into the actual creation of fashion. Let's suppose that you have already made your fabric selection and chosen your pattern. Thread, bindings, trims, interfacings, all the things you need to shape fabric into fashion are at hand, and you are ready to make your first move. This is the time for you to consult your sewing handbook.

Since your pattern instructions cannot possibly elaborate on every variation of your particular garment, we've designed chapters 4 and 5 to be used along with your pattern instruction sheet. They provide step-by-step guidance that will help you to understand **why** certain procedures should be followed, and **how** to put these procedures to use. These chapters will help you to sew creatively with a minimum of effort and a maximum of fun. Turn to them often, and the results you achieve will be worth every minute you invest.

Here you will find a multitude of different sewing techniques that represent the most practical approach to good dressmaking.

Since making your sewing quicker and easier is our job, let us point out a time-saving plan that should serve as a guide for every project you sew:

- Do all preparatory steps first-cutting, marking, and basting the underlining to your fabric-as these operations definitely require a large, flat, clean surface that may be difficult to find once you've begun sewing.

- Complete sewing of small details, such as pocket flaps and buttonholes, on each garment section **before** it is joined to the other sections, as the weight of the entire garment can be extremely cumbersome when you are trying to be so precise.

- Make all buttonholes at one work session to assure consistent results.

- Organize yourself by attempting to finish a complete stage of construction at each sitting.

- Spend your extra moments on those often envied finishing details such as overcasting seams, attaching lingerie straps, etc.

- And, as a final word of professional advice, be sure to press seams as you finish each section.

Hand Stitches

With the advent of the sewing machine, the drudgery of making clothes was eliminated and fine hand sewing was elevated to the position it so rightly deserves. Hand sewing plays such an important part in the construction of clothes that no properly made dress can be completed without it. It is the attention paid to the hand-sewn details that determines the quality of your finished garment. As hand sewing becomes less of a necessity, it becomes an increasingly desirable luxury. Whether you love hand sewing or regard it as a necessary evil, there are ways you can do it quickly yet precisely enough to pass the closest scrutiny.

Choose a needle size in accordance with your fabric and thread, consulting the thread and needle chart on pages 176 to 178. Use a single 18" to 20" (46 cm to 51 cm) length of thread, coated with beeswax for added strength and slipperiness. It may seem elementary, but learn to wear a thimble on the second finger of your sewing hand. You'll be able to sew hard-surfaced fabrics more quickly and easily and with greater assurance.

THREADING THE NEEDLE: Cut the thread at an angle; never break, bite, or tear the end; pass the cut end through the needle eye, then knot the same end you put through the eye like this: using the left hand, hold the thread between the thumb and first finger (1). With your right hand, bring the thread over and around the fingertip, crossing it over the thread end, as shown (2). With your thumb over the crossed threads, and the longer thread taut, gently push the thumb toward the fingertip, causing the thread end to roll around the loop (3). Slide the loop off the fingertip and, lightly pinching the rolled end between the thumb and second finger, pull the longer thread in the right hand taut to set the knot (4).

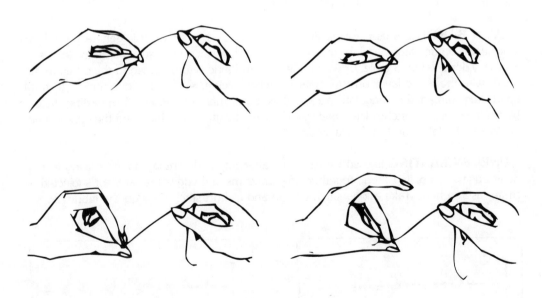

FINISHING STITCHING: To end your hand stitching, you have two choices-several backstitches (page 210) or a knot. Begin the knot by taking a tiny stitch on the wrong side of your fabric, directly over your last stitch. Pull the thread until a small loop remains. Run your needle through the loop, pulling the thread a second time, until another small loop is formed. It is through this second loop that you insert your needle for the last time. Pull the thread taut, forming an inconspicuous knot at the base of your stitches.

Basting

Basting is a **temporary** stitch used in the preparatory phase of your sewing. Whether matching plaids, indicating markings, attaching interfacing, or holding fabric pieces together for stitching, the trick is to use the right stitch in the right place and to follow these common sense principles. Always work on a flat, smooth surface. Pin your garment pieces together **before** basting, and use contrasting colored thread. Begin with a knot or a backstitch, and always remove basting **before** pressing permanent stitching. Silk thread is recommended for fine fabrics or when basting stitches are not to be removed before pressing, as in the case of pleats or hems. Always baste alongside the seamline within the seam allowance for easy removal of your basting threads.

EVEN BASTING is used for basting seams subjected to strain. It is generally used for long seams on any fabric and for areas that demand close control, such as set-in sleeves. It is usually done flat on a table, or when one layer of fabric is to be eased to the other, in the hand, with the eased layer on top. Space stitches evenly, ¼" (6 mm) long and ¼" (6 mm) apart, beginning and ending with backstitches rather than a knot. For firm basting, take a backstitch every few inches (centimeters). Gear the length of stitching and the type of needle to suit the fabric and probable strain (1).

UNEVEN BASTING is used for marking, attaching underlining and interfacing to fabric at edges, or holding fabric together only at seams and edges that are not subjected to strain, as in a hem. Take a long stitch on top and a short stitch through the fabric (2).

1

2

DIAGONAL BASTING or **TAILOR BASTING** is used for holding facings, interfacings, and linings in place during fitting. Take short stitches through the fabric at a right angle to the edge, spacing them evenly. This results in diagonal stitches on the upper side and short horizontal stitches on the underside.

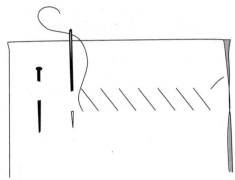

SLIP BASTING is used for matching stripes, plaids, and prints; intricate curved sections; and for fitting adjustments made from the right side. Crease and turn under the seam allowance on the edge. Right sides up, lay the folded edge in position on the corresponding piece, matching the fabric design at the seamline; pin. Slip the needle through the upper fold, then through the lower garment section, using a stitch ¼" (6 mm) in length. The result is a plain seam with basting on the wrong side.

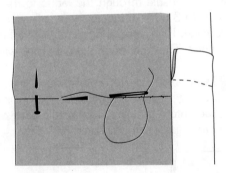

MACHINE BASTING is used for firm fabrics that won't slip or show needle marks. Set your machine for the longest stitch and loosen the upper tension slightly so thread is easily removable. To remove, clip the top thread at intervals and pull out the bobbin thread. Most brands of machine may have a built-in basting stitch.

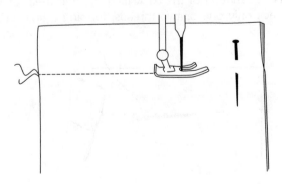

Hand Sewing

Hand sewing means to stitch **permanently** in place by hand. Keep stitches fairly loose to avoid a puckered, strained look. Work from right to left unless otherwise stated, reversing direction if you are left-handed. To secure the thread in the fabric, start with a few small backstitches or make a knot at the end and conceal it in the wrong side of your fabric.

The **RUNNING STITCH** is the most basic of stitches. It has many uses--easing, gathering, tucking, mending, and sewing seams that are not subjected to much strain. Take several small forward stitches, evenly weaving the needle in and out of the fabric before pulling the thread through; pick up as many stitches as your fabric and needle will allow. For permanent seams, use stitches $\frac{1}{16}$" to $\frac{1}{8}$" (2 mm to 3 mm) long; for easing and gathering, $\frac{1}{16}$" to $\frac{1}{4}$" (2 mm to 6 mm) long.

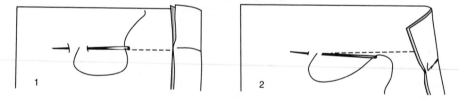

The **BACKSTTICH** is one of the strongest hand stitches. It is especially useful for repairing hard-to-reach seams that have ripped. It has the appearance of a machine stitch on the right side, but the stitches overlap on the wrong side. With right sides together, following the seamline, bring the needle through the fabric to the upper side. Take a stitch back about $\frac{1}{16}$" to $\frac{1}{8}$" (2 mm to 3 mm), bringing the needle out again $\frac{1}{16}$" to $\frac{1}{8}$" (2 mm to 3 mm) forward on the seamline. Keep inserting the needle in the end of the last stitch and bringing it out one stitch ahead. The stitches on the underside will be twice as long as those on the upper side (1).

The **HALF-BACKSTITCH** is suitable for any seam. It is also used to understitch finished facings to prevent the edge from rolling toward the outside of the garment. Follow the same method as the backstitch, but carry the needle back only half the length of the last stitch while continuing to bring it out one stitch ahead (2).

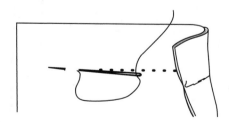

1   2

The **PRICKSTITCH,** a variation of the backstitch, is often used for inserting zippers. The needle is carried back only one or two threads, forming a tiny surface stitch with a reinforced understitch.

The **HAND PICKSTITCH** is used as a decorative finish and has the same appearance as the prickstitch. The only difference is that the bottom layer of fabric is not caught when backstitching. The thread should not be taut, and should lie beadlike on the fabric surface.

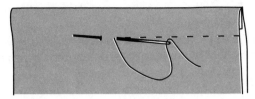

The **HEMMING STITCH,** used for all types of hemming, is most often used for hems finished with seam binding, especially when the garment is not underlined. Take a tiny inconspicuous stitch in the garment, then bring the needle diagonally up through the edge of the seam binding or hem edge. Continue in this manner, spacing stitches about ¼" (6 mm) apart (3).

The **SLIPSTITCH** is used to hem, attach linings, and hold pockets and trims in place, and it provides an almost invisible finish. Slide the needle through the folded edge and at the same point pick up a thread of the under fabric. Continue in this manner, taking stitches ⅛" to ¼" (3 mm to 6 mm) apart; space the stitches evenly (4).

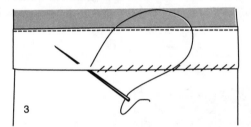

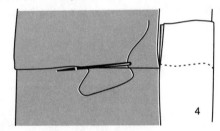

The **CATCHSTITCH** is used for holding two layers of fabric together in place while still maintaining a degree of flexibility. Its most common uses include attaching raw edges of facings and interfacings to the wrong side of garment sections, sewing pleats or tucks in linings, and securing hems in stretchy fabrics such as knits. Working from *left* to *right,* make a small horizontal stitch in the upper layer of fabric a short distance from the edge. Then, barely outside the edge of the upper layer, make another stitch in the lower layer of fabric diagonally across from the first stitch. Alternate stitching along the edge in a zigzag fashion, keeping threads loose (5).

The **BLIND CATCHSTITCH** is good for hemming heavy fabiics. Finish the raw edge of the hem and roll the hem back about ¼" (6 mm). Make catchstitches between the two layers of fabric, keeping stitches loose (6).

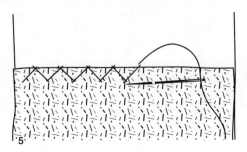

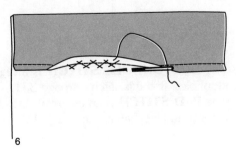

The **BLINDSTITCH**, used for hemming and holding facings in place, is inconspicuous on both sides of the garment. First, finish the raw edge of the hem or facing. Roll this edge back on the garment about ¼" (6 mm); make a small horizontal stitch through one thread of the garment or underlining fabric, then pick up a thread of the hem or facing diagonally above. Do not pull the stitches tight (7).

The **OVERCAST STITCH** is the classic stitch used to finish raw edges to prevent them from raveling. Working from either direction, take diagonal stitches over the edge, spacing them evenly apart at a uniform depth (8).

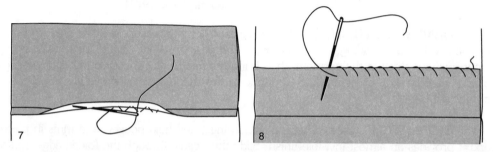

The **OVERHAND STITCH** holds two finished edges together with tiny, straight, even stitches. It is primarily used to join lace edging or to attach ribbon to a garment. Insert the needle at a diagonal angle from the back edge through to the front edge, picking up only one or two threads each time.

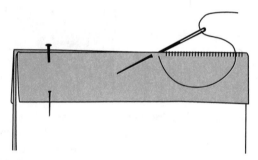

The **WHIPSTITCH** is a variation of the overhand stitch. It may serve the same purpose, differing in that the needle is inserted at a right angle to the edge, resulting in slanted stitches.

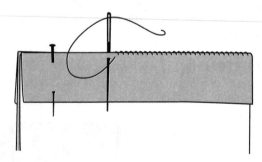

The **BUTTONHOLE STITCH** is a highly specialized stitch for making hand-worked buttonholes; find this stitch on page 331.

The **PAD STITCH** is an essential stitch in tailoring used to precisely shape and control the collar and lapel areas; see page 438.

The **BLANKET STITCH** is used for a wide variety of hand-finished details. Always work from left to right with the edge of the fabric toward you. Anchor your first stitch at the edge. For the next stitch and each succeeding one, point the needle toward you and insert it through the right side of your fabric, approximately ¼" (6 mm) above the edge and ¼" (6 mm) over from the preceding stitch. Keep the thread below your work and under the needle, as shown. A variation of the blanket stitch is generally used to form inconspicuous thread eyes, loops, and belt carriers (9).

The **BAR TACK** is used to reinforce points of strain, such as pocket corners or the end of a slit. It is formed by working a blanket stitch over two or three long stitches (10).

The **FRENCH TACK** is used to hold two parts of a garment together, such as the hems of a lined garment, and is constructed the same way as a bar tack (11).

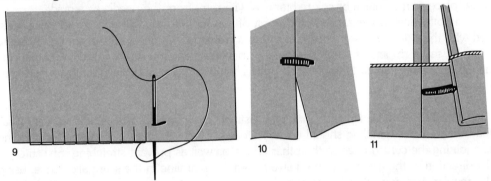

9   10   11

The **CHAINSTITCH** is a substitute for the blanket stitch when making thread loops and fastenings; see page 324.

The **CROSS-STITCH TACK** is used to hold two layers of fabric together. A single tack can be used to hold a facing edge in place at a seamline and is usually stitched several times (12). A series of cross-stitches is used to hold folds of a jacket lining in place at the center back or at the shoulder (13).

The **FAGOTING STITCH** is a decorative stitch used to join two fabric sections across an open seam; see Decorative Seams, page 223. Stitch through folded edge and diagonally across opening, entering material from underneath. Place needle under the thread, creating a twist, and stitch diagonally across opening again, spacing stitches evenly (14).

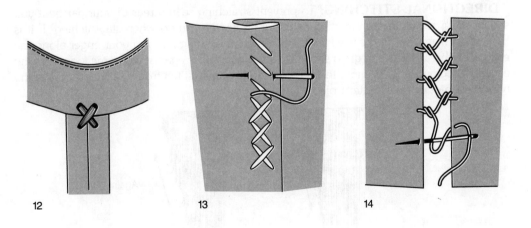

12   13   14

Seams and Seam Finishes

Be it plain or fancy, the mark of professional sewing is a perfect seam--a seam that is never puckered, never stretched, never wobbling, and is finished without a tangle of ravelings or crooked edges.

To stitch a perfect seam, always adjust the machine tension, pressure, and stitch length to suit the fabric texture and weight. See Chapter 6 for additional hints on handling of special fabrics, and pages 176 to 178 for thread and needle sizes before you begin. The usual seam allowance set by the pattern industry is ⅝" (15 mm) unless otherwise specified. If your machine doesn't have a seam guide attachment or stitching lines marked on the needle plate, place a small piece of colored tape ⅝" (15 mm) from the needle as a guide.

A smooth, sleek appearance is the result of careful seam handling. If you are not satisfied with the way your seam looks, it is easy to remedy. Simply rip the seam out by using a pin, a seam ripper, or small scissors--but never a dangerous razor blade. Correct any unhappy results at an early stage, and you will be rewarded by a professionally finished garment.

STAYSTITCHING: Prior to pinning, basting, and permanent stitching, curved areas that require extra handling should be staystitched. This will act as a guideline for clipping and joining the curved edge to the other edges, as well as prevent stretching. Staystitch in the direction of the grain ⅛" (3 mm) away from the seamline in the seam allowance, using the regular machine-stitch length suited to your fabric. For zipper openings, stitch ¼" (6 mm) from the cut edge.

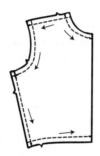

DIRECTIONAL STITCHING: To prevent stretching seam areas of your garment you should stitch seams in the direction of the grain just as you do when staystitching. If it is hard to tell from the cut piece which is the direction of the grain, run your finger along the edge. The threads with the grain should lie smoothly; those against will come loose and the edge will begin to fray. Without testing, you can generally stitch from the widest part to the narrowest part of each pattern piece.

 With Grain

Against Grain

Constructing a Seam

The main purpose of all seams is to hold your garment sections together.

JOINING SEAMLINES: When pinning the edges of your fabric together, place the pins at right angles to the seamline with the heads toward the seam allowance. Your seams will be held in place accurately. It is not recommended to sew over pins. If you hit one with your needle you will most likely knick or break the needle, and you could possibly harm yourself. You may wish to baste next to the seamline in the seam allowance.

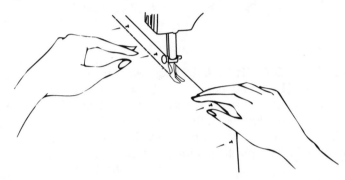

STITCHING: Begin to stitch ½" (13 mm) from the end, backstitch to the end, and then stitch forward. Keep stitching along the seamline, following the seam guidelines on the needle plate of your machine. Keep the cut edges of the fabric even. Secure by backstitching at other end of seam. Some machines have a lockstitch which may be used instead of backstitching.

The seam may also be stitched from end to end without backstitching and the ends secured by tying a knot. Hold the thread in your left hand. Form a loop (1). With your right hand, bring the thread ends around and through the loop from the back (2). Holding the loop in your left hand, work the intertwined thread down to the base and hold in place with your left thumb (3). With your right hand, begin pulling the thread taut until the loop disappears and forms a knot (4).

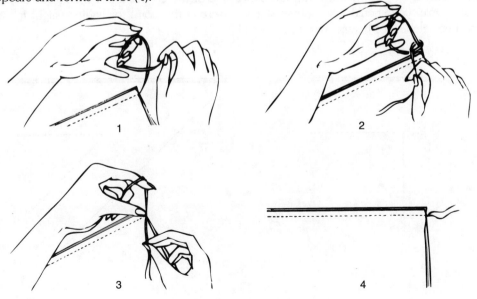

If you must end your stitching before reaching the edge, pull one of the thread ends through to the other side with a pin (5). Then tie both thread ends together (6).

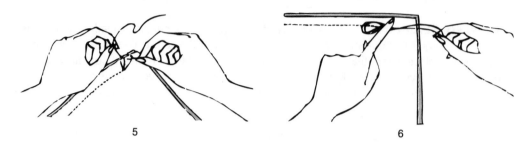

5   6

REINFORCING A CORNER SEAM: Whenever you stitch a seam with a corner, use reinforcement stitches [15 to 20 per inch (6-8 per cm) depending on your fabric] to strengthen the point. If it is a corner that will need to be clipped for easy sewing, reinforce it before joining in a seam. Just inside the seamline, stitch for about an inch (25 mm) on either side of the point (1). Clip to the point. Pin both sections right sides together with clipped section up and stitch, pivoting at the point (2).

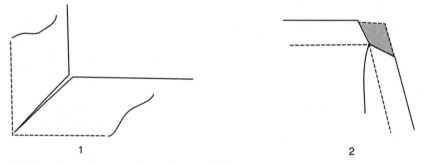

1   2

When joining two corresponding pieces of fabric, as in a pointed collar, use reinforcement stitches for an inch (25 mm) on either side of the corner (3). If the corner is at an acute angle, you should take one small stitch *across* the point for lighter-weight fabrics, and two stitches for heavier-weight fabrics (4).

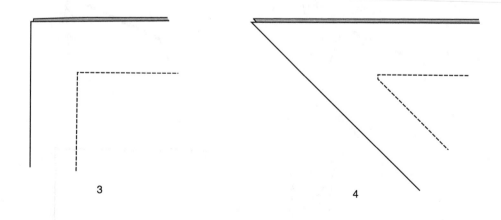

3   4

TRIMMING: Seam allowances should be trimmed only where less bulk is desired. In general, enclosed seams call for ¼" (6 mm) seam allowances, but if the fabric is very light you may want to trim less. Cut diagonal corners from the ends of the seams, especially if they will later cross other seams (1).

For corners of an enclosed seam, trim across the point close to the seam. Then trim diagonally along either side of the point to eliminate any bulk when the corner is turned (2).

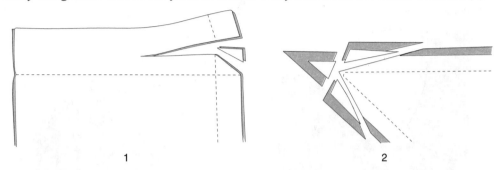

GRADING: When seam allowances are turned together in one direction, they must be graded to avoid making a ridge and to make seams lie flat without bulk. Grading is especially important when the fabric is heavy or if there are more than two layers of fabric. Each layer should be trimmed to a different width. Enclosed seams may be trimmed a little narrower than exposed seams. Generally the garment seam allowance is left widest (1).

NOTCHING and **CLIPPING:** Curves must be graded first and then trimmed in a special way in order to lie flat. On an outward curve, cut small wedges or notches from the seam allowance at even intervals; on an inward curve, clip into the seam allowance at even intervals. These intervals should be about ½" to 1" (13 mm to 25 mm), depending on the sharpness of the curve. Be very careful not to clip past the seamline (2).

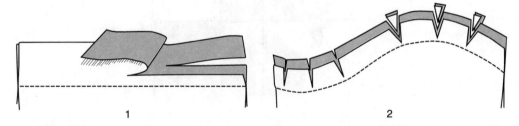

PRESSING: Pressing any seam is a two-step operation. First press the stitching line flat to blend the stitches into the fabric; then press the seam open (1). For enclosed seams in collars, cuffs, and pocket flaps, press the seam open with a point presser so that the seamed edges will be sharp (2).

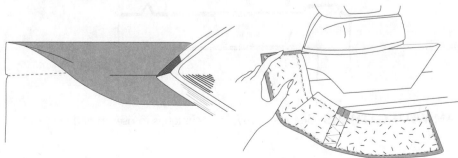

UNDERSTITCHING: When a seamline is pressed to form an edge that encloses the seam allowances, the underside should be understitched. This technique is often used for facings to prevent them from rolling to the outside of the garment. Grade both seam allowances and press toward the facing. Be sure to clip or notch curved edges when necessary. From the right side of the facing, work the half-backstitch (1) or machine-stitch (2) close to the seamline and through all the seam allowances. Turn the facing in and press the seamed edge.

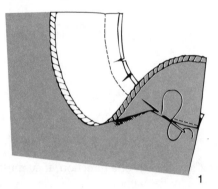

1

2

Special Seam Situations

INTERSECTING or **CROSSED SEAMS:** Stitch one seam and press open. Stitch the second seam in the same manner. Pin the two seams with right sides together, using a pin point to match the crossed seams exactly at the seamline. Then pin on either side of the seams and stitch. Trim corners diagonally as shown.

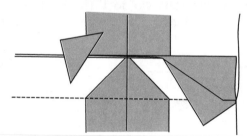

SEAM WITH EASE: To ease, stitch close to the seamline with long machine stitches extending the stitching slightly beyond markings. Pin the two layers right sides together with the eased side facing up. Pull up the ease thread between the markings and distribute the fullness evenly. Baste carefully to control the extra fabric and stitch.

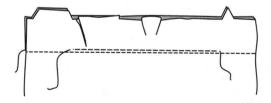

SEAM WITH GATHERS: See page 237 for techniques to use on gathers.

TAPING A SEAM: A seam may be stayed or taped to strengthen and prevent stretching in the finished garment by using twill tape or woven seam binding. This technique is often used at waistline and shoulder seams. The tape should be placed over the seamline of one garment section, with the edge extending ⅛" (3 mm) into the seam allowance. Baste next to the seamline and sew the tape on permanently as the seam is machine-stitched (1).

TISSUE PAPER UNDER SEAMS: You may have discovered that some lightweight fabrics are inclined to stretch or shift during sewing, creating uneven seams. To prevent mishaps, try placing tissue paper on the machine bed under the seams. Stitch through both the fabric and the paper, then tear the paper away (2). Tear-away stabilizers are also available for the same purpose.

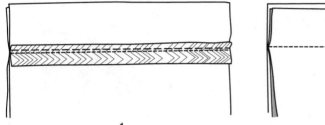

1

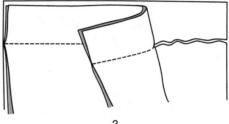

2

BIAS-CUT SEAMS: If you are joining a bias edge to a straight edge, pin and baste the bias edge to the straight edge. When stitching, be sure to always keep the bias side up in order to control the stretch of the bias and to avoid puckers (3).

If you are joining two bias edges, stretch the fabric slightly as you stitch over tissue paper so that the finished edge will hang correctly. Otherwise the seam may pucker and the threads will break when the garment is worn.

If it is a lengthwise seam, baste the fabric together, and let the garment hang for 24 hours to allow the bias to stretch before stitching the seam.

PRINCESS SEAM: Staystitch both curved edges ⅛" (3 mm) from the seamline within the seam allowance. Clip the inward curved seam allowance on the center panel of the garment to the staystitching. Pin the seamline, spreading the clipped edge so that it will lie smoothly. Make any additional clips if necessary. With clipped side up, stitch the two edges together, being careful to keep the underside smooth. Press seam open over a tailor's ham, notching the seam allowance on the side panel until it lies flat. Wherever possible, stagger the position of the clips and notches (4).

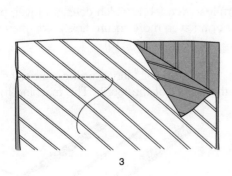

3

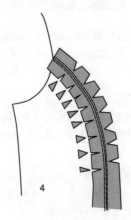

4

SCALLOPS: Stitch the curved scallop seam with small reinforcement stitches [15-20 per inch (6-8 per cm)]. Take one stitch across each point to make turning easier later. Now clip into each point, being careful not to cut through the stitching. Grade the seams and notch all the curves (5).

JOINING NAPPED FABRIC TO NAPLESS FABRIC: First pin, then baste closely using small stitches along the seamline. Always stitch in the direction of the nap with the napless fabric uppermost. This procedure will help to reduce any slippage caused by the nap (6).

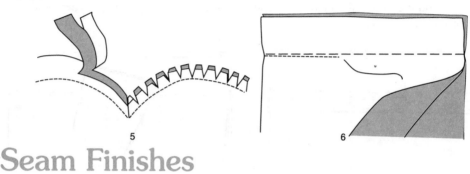

5

6

Seam Finishes

Since the inside story is as important to fine couture as the outside, all seams should be finished by the most suitable method if they are not covered by a lining. A seam finish helps the seam allowances to support the garment shape, ensures durability, prevents raveling, and contributes to the overall neatness of the garment.

HAND OVERCAST: This finish is suitable for most fabrics. For a seam pressed open, stitch ¼" (6 mm) from each raw edge, then trim to ⅛" (3 mm). (For firm fabrics, stitching and trimming may be omitted.) Overcast the edge by hand, using machine stitching as a guide (1).

MACHINE ZIGZAG or **RUNNING STITCH:** For fabrics which tend to ravel easily, use a zigzag or running stitch to reinforce each raw edge. Use a smaller stitch for lightweight fabrics and a larger stitch for heavy, bulky fabrics, pretesting for the best results (2).

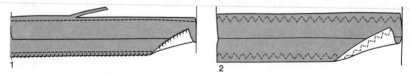

1

2

PINKED: If you are working with a firmly woven fabric which does not ravel, pink the edges with pinking or scalloping shears. For an even more secure finish, you may wish to stitch 1/4" (6 mm) from each edge before you begin to pink (3).

SERGED: This edge finish is appropriate for nearly all fabrics, as it can be sewn in a 2- or 3-thread configuration depending on the weight of the fabric. The machine trims the fabric while it overcasts the edges (4).

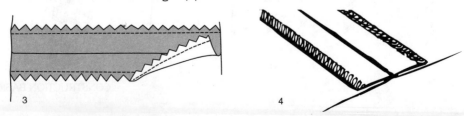

3

4

TURNED UNDER: Use this method for lightweight fabrics and plain-weave synthetics. It is not suitable for fabrics with bulk. Turn under the raw edges of the seam allowances, press if necessary, and stitch close to the edge (3).

BOUND EDGE: For heavy, bulky, easily frayed fabrics, especially in unlined jackets or coats, encase each raw edge in purchased double-fold bias tape. Use purchased tricot tape or strips of organza on lace fabric or nonravelling fabrics (4).

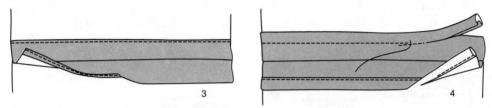

HONG KONG FINISH: For a couture touch, see page 460.

Self-Finished Seams

Some seaming techniques enclose the seam allowances as the seam is stitched. This gives a very neat appearance to seams that are visible such as in sheer fabrics and in unlined jackets.

FRENCH SEAM: This seam is well suited to sheer fabrics. It looks like a plain seam on the right side and a small, neat tuck on the wrong side. It is used on straight seams. Pin wrong sides together and stitch ⅜" (10 mm) from the seamline in the seam allowance. Trim to within ⅛" to ¼" (3 mm to 6 mm) of stitching. Right sides together, crease along the stitched seam; press. Stitch along the seamline, encasing the raw edges (1).

SIMULATED FRENCH SEAM: This seam can be made after first making a plain seam. Do not press it open. Instead, turn both of the seam allowances toward each other ¼" (6 mm) and press. Now edgestitch the folded edges together (2).

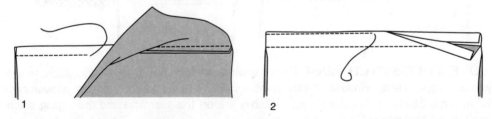

FRENCH WHIPPED SEAM OR DOUBLE-STITCHED SEAM: For lace and embroidered fabrics or curved seams on sheer fabrics, stitch a plain seam, then stitch again ⅛" (3 mm) away in the seam allowance. Trim to ⅛" (3 mm) from this stitching and carefully overcast the raw edges by hand or with a narrow, short zigzag stitch.

FLAT-FELL SEAM OR FELLED SEAM: A sturdy seam often used on sportswear and menswear. With wrong sides together, stitch a plain seam, and press toward one side. Trim the lower seam allowance to ⅛" (3 mm). Turn under the edge of the other seam allowance ¼" (6 mm) and fold over the narrow seam allowance. For non-bulky fabrics, machine-stitch close to the folded edge; for bulky reversible fabrics, slip-stitch the fold in place. Many machines have feller feet to guide the fabric in stitching this seam (3).

SELF-BOUND SEAM: Trim one seam allowance of a plain seam to ⅛" or ¼" (3 mm or 6 mm), depending on your fabric. Turn the edge of the other seam allowance under and slip-stitch or machine-stitch over the seam, encasing the trimmed seam allowance (4).

3   4

HAIRLINE SEAM: For sheer fabrics where there is no strain, place a narrow row of zigzag stitching along the seamline, then trim away the seam allowances as close to the stitching as possible (5).

DOUBLE-STITCHED SEAM: This seam can be used on soft knits which have a tendency to curl at the edges. Stitch a plain seam, then stitch again ⅛" (3 mm) away within the seam allowance using either a straight stitch or a narrow zigzag stitch. Trim seam allowances close to stitching (6).

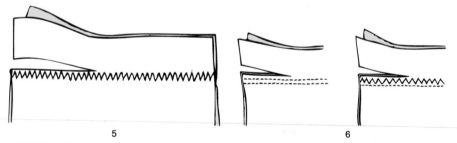

5   6

OVEREDGE-STITCH SEAM: If your sewing machine has an overedge stitch, you can join and finish a seam on knit or stretch fabrics in one operation. Trim seam allowances to ¼" (6 mm). Stitch so that the straight stitches are on the seamline and the zigzag stitches enclose the raw edges (7).

3- OR 4-THREAD OVERLOCK SEAM: An overlock machine or serger sews the seam and trims the fabric all at the same time. Using one or two needles, these stitches are good for knits but are suitable for wovens also (8, 9).

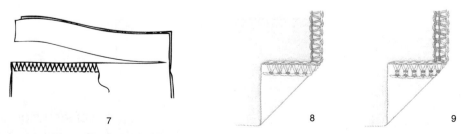

7   8   9

Decorative Seams

You can be creative in your sewing by letting your seams show. Topstitching on the right side of the fabric adds a special decorative touch. Choose one as a design feature in your garment and be inventive-your finished product will be an original!

TOPSTITCHED SEAM: Press a plain seam to one side as indicated on the pattern. Topstitch the desired distance from the seam on the right side of the fabric through all thicknesses (1). See Stitchery, page 473, for further instructions.

DOUBLE TOPSTITCHED SEAM: First press a plain seam open. Topstitch the desired distance from each side of the seam on the right side of the fabric. Be sure your stitches go through both thicknesses of the fabric (2).

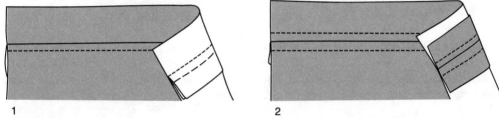

1   2

WELT SEAM: Stitch a plain seam and press it toward one side. Trim the lower seam allowance to ¼" (6 mm). Then stitch through only the upper seam allowance and garment close to the trimmed edge, encasing the lower seam allowance (3).

DOUBLE WELT SEAM: When completed, this seam gives much the same appearance as a flat-fell seam. First construct a welt seam as directed above. Then topstitch close to the seam on the right side of the fabric, as shown (4).

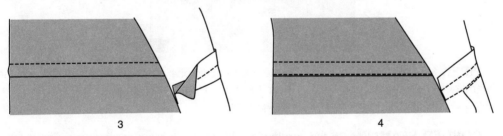

3   4

SLOT SEAM: Machine or hand-baste a plain seam; press open. Cut a strip of fabric as long as the seam and slightly wider than both seam allowances. From the right side, topstitch the same distance on each side of the seam. Remove basting threads (5).

FLATLOCK SEAM: A 2- or 3-thread serger seam where the two layers of fabrics are pulled open and flattened (6, 7).

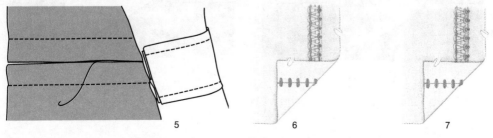

5   6   7

LAPPED SEAM: Turn in the edges of the overlapping section along the seamline and press. Working from the right side, pin the folded edge over the remaining section with the fold along the seamline. Stitch close to the fold through all thicknesses (5).

TUCKED SEAM: Follow the directions for a lapped seam and slip baste the fold in place. To form the tuck, stitch the desired depth from the fold through all thicknesses, stitching no closer than ¼" (6 mm) from the raw edges. Remove the basting (6).

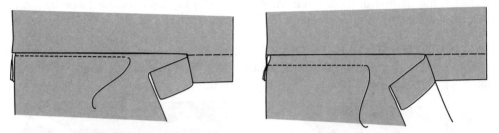

FAGOTED SEAM: Turn the seam allowances under and press. Pin the edges to strips of heavy paper, spacing edges ⅜" (10 mm) apart and baste through all the thicknesses. Stitch between the two edges using a fagoting stitch, page 213, or machine embroidery stitches. After finishing stitching, remove the basting, and trim the seam allowances to ⅛" (3 mm).

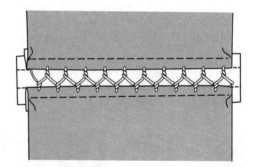

PIPED SEAM: Baste the piping to the right side of one of the fabric sections along the seamline. Place the second section over the piping right sides together and baste; then stitch on the seamline through all thicknesses (7).

CORDED SEAM: Encase the cording in a bias strip, using a cording or a zipper foot. Attach the cording and baste the fabric sections together, like the piped seam. Stitch along the seamline through all thicknesses, using a cording or zipper foot (8).

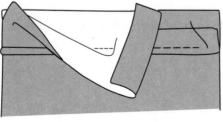
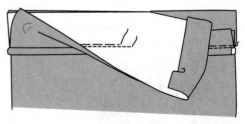

7

8

Darts

Darts create the difference between the flatness of fabrics and the curving third dimension of the feminine form. They rank highly among the basic sewing concepts that must be understood before you can construct a garment with any degree of fit. Their function is to provide carefully shaped fullness. Although the fitting of darts is dealt with on pages 96 to 99, it is always wise to keep a few working axioms in mind. A low bustline will detract from what otherwise could be a youthful appearance. For this reason, if you have an inkling that a low bustline is the cause of your fitting problems, adjust the straps of your foundation garments before you adjust your patterns or fit your garment. Then make certain that the dart position provides fullness that conforms with the lengthwise and crosswise contours of your figure. The dart should point to the fullest part of the body-to the point of the bust, to the curve over the pelvic bone, and so on. Since the length of all darts has been designed for a person of average height, you may have to adjust the dart length to agree with your own proportions--for a short figure, slightly shorter darts; for a tall figure, slightly longer darts. If the vertical bodice darts require relocating, the skirt darts should be realigned to match.

Constructing a Dart

MARKING: Transfer the dart markings to your fabric, using the most suitable method. You may not notice until the dart is folded that the subtle styling of many designs requires concave or convex curves as opposed to straight darts. Use your tracing wheel or tailor's chalk to make short horizontal lines indicating the bold symbols for matching sides, as well as the end of the dart. Always have the darts on the left and right sides of the garment mirror each other in length and placement.

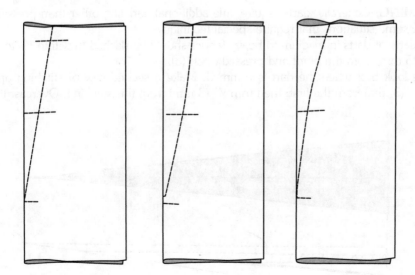

STITCHING: Begin sewing all darts at the wide end. About ½" (13 mm) from the point., shorten your stitch length to 12 to 14 stiches per inch (25 mm) and sew to the point. The thread ends of all darts, particularly at the point, should be secured with a knot rather than by backstitching. Tie the knot, as shown, working it to the end of the dart using the point of a pin. Backstitching often results in an unsightly bubble or pucker because the previous line of stitching was not duplicated exactly (1).

PRESSING: Always press darts before the major seams are stitched or before they are intersected by seams. The dart fold and stitching line should be pressed flat first to blend the stitches together. Be careful not to crease the fabric beyond the end point. Next, spread open the garment and press each dart over the curved surface of a tailor's ham or press mitt to maintain the built-in shape. Once you've steamed the dart into its proper position the area around the dart may become slightly wrinkled. Touch up this area while the dart is still on the tailor's ham with a dry iron (2).

Vertical darts should be pressed toward center front or center back, depending on their location. Horizontal darts are pressed downward unless otherwise specified. Deep darts, however, are pressed open with the point pressed flat.

Place brown paper between the dart and garment to prevent ridges if your fabric mars or use a presscloth to protect your fabric and avoid any shininess.

TRIMMING: Generally, darts require little additional handling other than pressing, but there are some situations that require special techniques.

Deep darts or darts in medium to heavy fabrics should be slashed to within ½" to 1" (13 mm to 25 mm) from the point and pressed open (3).

Sheers look best when the dart is trimmed. Make a second row of stitching approximately ⅛" (3 mm) from the first; then trim ⅛" (3 mm) from this stitching. Overcast the raw edges (4).

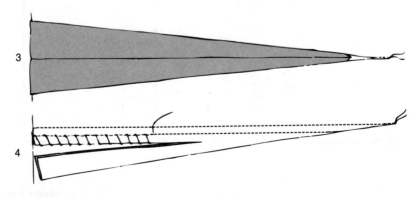

French Dart and Contour Dart

French darts and contour darts are both long darts that help to shape the waistline area of a garment without a waistline seam.

The French dart begins at the side seam and extends diagonally from the hip to the bust. Staystitch ⅛" (3 mm) away from stitching line, ending about 1" (25 mm) from point. Slash through center of dart up to end of staystitching. (Some patterns trim away center of dart when the pattern is cut out.) Pin stitching lines together, matching lines carefully. Stitch dart from end to point; knot thread ends securely. Clip seam allowances to allow dart to curve smoothly.

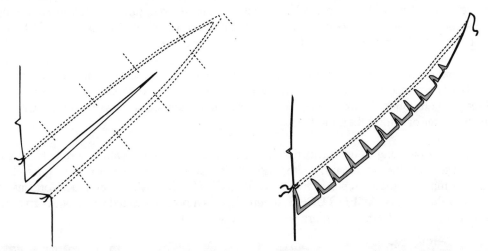

The contour dart tapers upward toward the bust or back and downward toward the hip. Fold dart along center line and pin stitching lines together. Stitch from the waist out toward each point, overlapping the stitching at the waist and knotting the thread ends at the points. Clip dart at waistline and at several places along the fold, if necessary, to relieve strain.

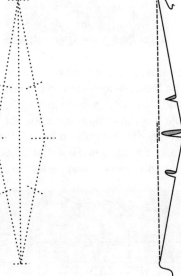

Tucks

The tuck is a versatile element in the designer's repertoire and fulfills a multitude of structural and ornamental needs. Each tuck is a slender fold of fabric that can be stitched along all or part of its length. Tucks are usually folded on straight grain, and, if chosen for decoration, the fold is generally formed on the outside of the fabric.

When tucks are used to control fullness and shape the contour of the design, the fold is formed on the inside, stitched to a designated point, and then released. In this case they may be stitched on- or off-grain and either straight or contoured, like darts. Or they may be just small pleats of fabric secured by a seam. These released tucks, or dart tucks as they are sometimes called, are found at the shoulder line and waistline of a bodice or skirt, and should point toward the fullest part of the body in those areas.

Decorative tucks, stitched on the right side of the fabric, require very careful selection of needles and thread to coordinate with the fabric. Generally you should try to match your thread to your fabric. However, you may achieve interesting effects by using thread just one shade lighter or darker than the fabric.

If you are planning to add tucks to a garment, choose a design with few style lines and be sure to have the placement, width, and spacing of the tucks relate to your figure. The three commonly known types of tucks are: **BLIND TUCKS,** where each tuck touches or overlaps the next, **SPACED TUCKS,** where there is a predetermined space between each tuck, and **PIN TUCKS,** which are very narrow spaced tucks.

 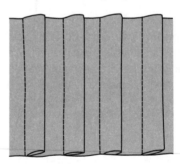 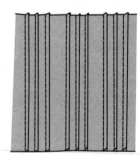

ADDING TUCKS: If you would like decorative tucks on a garment, and the pattern does not call for them, tuck the fabric before cutting the pattern piece. To determine the amount of additional fabric width needed, multiply the width of a tuck by two to allow for both thicknesses. Then multiply this figure by the number of tucks you plan. Because the extra width required may interfere with the pattern layout, you may need additional fabric to lay out your pattern. A rule of thumb: purchase the amount of fabric required on the back of the envelope plus the length of one main pattern piece.

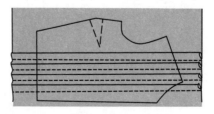

Making Uniform Tucks

Tucks are usually made on the straight grain. Do be sure to make the fold of the tucks parallel to the threads in the fabric.

MARKING AND BASTING: Mark stitching lines of each tuck on either the outside or inside of your fabric. Remove the pattern, fold the tucks either to the inside or outside of the garment, matching stitching lines. Baste in place.

Or eliminate marking your tucks by making a cardboard measurement gauge, cutting a notch for the depth of the tuck and a second notch to indicate the space from fold to fold. Place the top of the gauge along the fold of the first tuck. Using the first notch as a guide, make a row of basting stitches parallel to the fold, sliding the gauge as you stitch. For the next tuck, move the gauge so that the second notch is now even with the first fold, and make your next fold at the top of the gauge. Continue this procedure for each consecutive tuck (1).

A louvered pleating board or stainless steel pleating bar are two very handy tools that help you mark and press even tucks or pleats into your fabric before stitching (2).

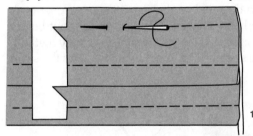
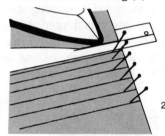

STITCHING: To control the finished look and the evenness of the stitching, be sure to stitch from the side of the tuck that will be seen. For narrow tucks, from ¼ to ¾ (6 mm to 20 mm), you can use the needle plate on your machine as a guide for stitching. Use the quilting bar attached to your machine or presser foot for wider tucks. Tucking may be pieced, if necessary, by carefully lapping, then stitching the tucks.

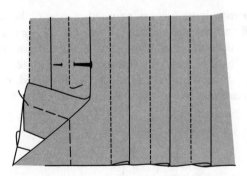
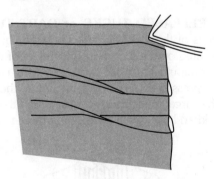

PRESSING: Press tucks as you stitch each one, or directly after stitching the series. First press the crease in the tuck from the right side of your fabric but on the underneath side of the fold. This step makes the final pressing much easier. Press the entire tucked area from the wrong side. Use very little steam to prevent puckering or the tuck fold from making unwanted indentations in the fabric. To prevent the latter problem in some fabrics, you may have to use strips of brown paper under the fold of each tuck as you press. Touch up the right side of the tucks as necessary.

Special Tucks

CROSS TUCKS are done before the fabric is cut into pattern sections. Measure, baste, and stitch the base rows first. Press carefully before dealing with the crossing tucks. Again measure, baste, and sew with these new tucks at right angles to the base set. The earlier rows of tucks should lie with the folds facing downward as you stitch. Press all the tucks in the proper direction. Cut out the garment and staystitch around the seam allowances of the tucked area to keep the tucks in place and lying in the right direction (1).

MACHINE PIN TUCKS are sewn using specially designed pin tuck feet which have narrow grooves on the sole. Available in a variety of sizes depending on the weight of the fabric being sewn, the tiny tucks are sewn using corresponding sized double needles. These tucks may be corded or left uncorded. Refer to your sewing machine manual for specific instructions on setting up your machine for this technique (2).

SHELL OR SCALLOPED TUCKS are generally ¼" (6 mm) wide. Baste each tuck. To form the scallop by hand, lightly mark every ½" (13 mm) with small dots along the length of the tucks. Sew tiny running stitches between dots and, at the same time, sew over each tuck at the designated intervals using two overhand stitches. Draw the thread taut before making the next set of running stitches (3). If you prefer a quicker and more sturdy method, stitch the tucks by machine using an all-forward stretch stitch (---^---^) which sews the seam and draws in the fabric at the same time.

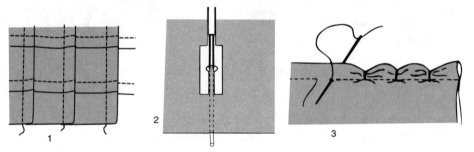

RELEASED TUCKS or DART TUCKS may have fullness released at one or both ends of the tuck. Construction techniques will vary greatly according to where the tuck is located on the garment. Regardless of construction, the most significant factor to remember about all released tucks is that the released fullness below the stitched fold should never be pressed flat. The stitching line at the point of releasing fullness can be backstitched, or the thread ends tied securely. When the tucks are pressed to one side, stitch across to the fold and backstitch or knot the thread ends.

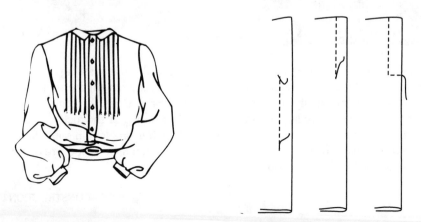

Pleats

Pleats are always in style, adding a special swing to your fashions whether they're crisp, sharp pleats in a tailored skirt or supple, rolled pleats in a soft dress. Pleats are, quite simply, folds of fabric which provide controlled fullness where you want it. The time and patience required to make them perfect will seem well worthwhile as soon as you see yourself in your new pleated creation.

Although there are many variations, basically pleats are of just two types: folds in the fabric made by doubling the fabric over on itself, and folds with an underlay or separate piece stitched to the pleat extensions on the underside of the garment. There are four well known variations, used either singly or in series: **KNIFE** or **SIDE PLEATS** with all folds turned to one side; **BOX PLEATS** with two folds turned away from each other and underfolds meeting at the center; **INVERTED PLEATS,** box pleats in reverse, with folds turned toward each other and meeting; and **ACCORDION PLEATS,** always pressed along the entire length with folds resembling the bellows of an accordion.

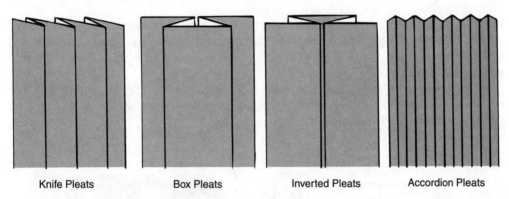

| Knife Pleats | Box Pleats | Inverted Pleats | Accordion Pleats |

Whether the pleats are pressed or hang freely, they look best when executed in fabrics that have good resiliency and drape, such as wool, wool blends, cotton blends, silk, and most synthetics. Some of these can be more crisply pleated than others. If you want a sharp edge on permanent-press fabrics or other fabrics that have been treated with a crease-resistant finish, try edgestitching both the front and back edges of the pleats.

Fabrics and completed garments can be professionally pleated with knife pleats or accordion pleats. To find a firm that does commercial pleating, refer to your yellow pages, check fashion magazines, or inquire at the notions counter of a fabric store.

The proper pattern size for a pleated skirt should be determined by your hip measurement, because the waistline is easier to adjust. All pleats should be shaped with precision. Complete mastery depends on transferring the pleat markings accurately, basting pleats to keep them in place during preparation, fitting with care, and pressing correctly.

Before you begin, it is important to be aware of and understand the three "line" indications in pleat patterns. The *roll line* used in unpressed pleats is meant to alert you to the fact that the pleats will form soft rolling folds, not creases, while the *foldline* used for pressed pleats indicates a sharply creased fold that can be edgestitched. The placement *line* indicates that the rolled edges or folded edges are brought to this line.

Straight Pleats

It's best to do pleating on a surface large enough to hold the entire pleated garment. For multiple pleats, the hem should be completed before making the pleat folds. Your length can then be adjusted from the waistline after the pleats are formed. For treatment of hems in pleats, see page 352.

Marking

Your pleats can be made either from the right or wrong side, depending upon the designer's intended appearance of the garment and the method that works best for you. Whichever method you choose, be sure to transfer your markings to the right side of the fabric when forming pleats on the right side, or to the wrong side when pleating on the wrong side of the fabric.

Use different colors of thread to key the various "line" indications.

Pleating

Pressed and unpressed pleats are both made the same way; pressing makes the difference.

From the wrong side: Bring the indicated markings for each pleat together and baste. Press or turn pleats in the direction indicated for your type of pleat. Baste pleats in place along waistline edge (1).

From the right side: Following your markings, turn the fabric in along foldline or roll line. Bring the edge to the placement line and pin. Starting at the hem edge and working upward, baste each pleat in place through all thicknesses. Baste pleats in place along waistline edge (2).

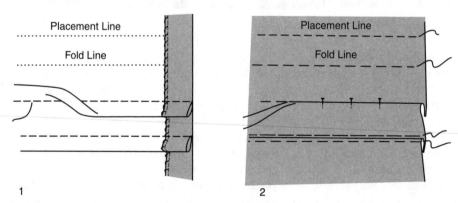

Fitting

After basting the pleats in place, and before trying on your garment, baste a temporary belt of grosgrain ribbon at the waistline on the inside to ensure that the pleats will be supported and hang properly as you fit your garment.

When fitting you may find that the waistline is too large or too small if you have adjusted your pattern to accommodate your hip measurement. Distributing the change evenly between the pleats, make a hairline adjustment on the placement line of each pleat at the waistline. The tiny dotted lines on each side of the placement line indicate the small change needed to make the difference in fit. On straight pleats it is very important to maintain the straight grainline on the outside fold of each pleat by carefully controlled tapering of the placement line. If you adjust the waistline area, be sure to retain ½" to 1" (13 mm to 25 mm) extra for ease.

After pleats and hems are completed, retain the basting only at the upper edge. Baste grosgrain ribbon to the skirt again. Try it on before attaching to the garment or waistband. If your pleats do not fall straight to the hem but tend to open up, raise the skirt at the waist until the hem is even, using a larger waistline seam allowance. However, if the pleats overlap, drop the waist until the hem is even, using a smaller waistline seam allowance.

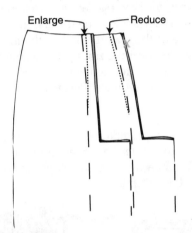
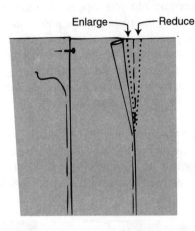

Pressing

For pressed pleats, make certain the pleats are accurately measured, marked, and basted. Pin them to the ironing board at their edge and steam them on both sides just enough to set them. Use a press cloth on the right side to avoid shine. Support overhanging fabric by a chair or table to prevent the weight of the fabric from pulling the pleats out of shape.

If you discover that light pressing creates an unattractive ridge or line on your fabric, insert strips of brown paper under the fold of the pleat before you press. To assure yourself of a sharp, lasting press, iron on both sides of the pleats. Unpressed pleats may require a very slight steaming just to set the shape and fall of the pleat as the designer intended. This can be done most effectively as the garment hangs on your dress form.

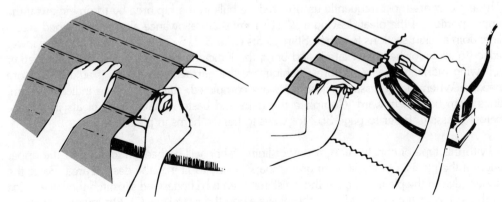

Zipper Applications

A zipper is the easiest and most secure way to close a pleated garment.

For box or inverted pleats, the zipper is usually placed at the left side or center back seam, where the folds of the pleats meet. Use the centered zipper application on page 340.

For a knife-pleated skirt, the placket opening is usually located at the center back or the left side and is the last seam to be stitched. Stitch this last seam, leaving an opening for the placket. (Your last pleat is made *after* this seam is stitched.) Be sure to have the seam at an inside fold so that it will not show and that the underfold of the pleat will be deep enough to accommodate your zipper. To make your last pleat, turn the overlapping section to the inside along the pleat foldline and baste. Clip the seam allowance of the undersection at the placket marking, as shown. Turn the seam allowance of the undersection to the inside ⅛" (15 mm) and baste (1). Place the edge of the undersection over the zipper tape with the bottom stop even with end of the opening. Have the edge close to the teeth with just enough room for the pull tab to slide easily. Baste carefully, then stitch the undersection to the zipper tape near the zipper teeth (2).

Place the remaining side of the zipper face down on the underlay of the overlapping section. The zipper teeth will extend beyond the seamline. Baste the zipper to the underlay, keeping the rest of the skirt free. Then stitch ⅛" (3 mm) away from the zipper teeth, continuing across the end of the zipper below the stop; backstitch (3).

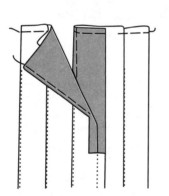 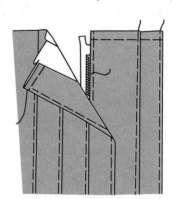 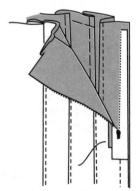

Shaped and Stitched Pleats

These pleats are most frequently used to reduce bulk in the hip area by trimming away the upper portion of the pleat, leaving a ⅝" (15 mm) seam allowance along the stitched seamline. Join all skirt sections together. Start pleats 6" to 8" (15 cm to 20.5 cm) from the lower edge (to allow for hemming later), and bring the indicated pleat and/or seamlines together following markings; baste. Before stitching, try the garment on to see if adjustments are needed. When the necessary adjustments are completed, stitch along the indicated seamlines from bottom upward. Complete the hem and baste remainder of pleats into place before pressing. Refer to page 352 for ways to handle hems in pleats (1).

With this type of construction, a stay of lining fabric will be needed to support the upper edge of the pleats. On the straight grain, shape a stay to fit into the desired area. Baste the upper edge to the pleated area at the waistline; then turn under and slipstitch the lower edge of the stay over the upper edge of the pleats along the seamlines (2). On inverted box pleats, a self-stay can be formed by trimming away only half of the top of the pleat, leaving a seam allowance of ⅝" (15 mm). The remaining pleat fabric can then be basted across the upper edge for support (3).

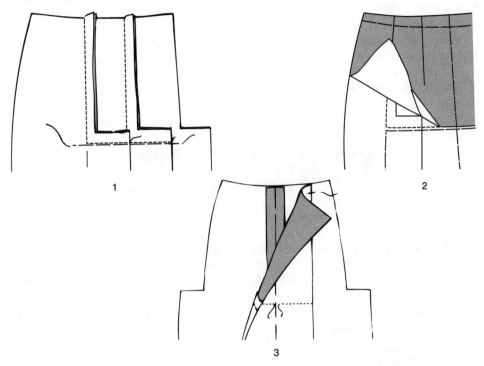

1
2

3

Pleats with a Separate Underlay

These pleats are made from the inside and are often used singly. Bring the coordinating markings together and baste. Open out the pleat extensions. Stitch the pleat underlay to the pleat extensions and baste in place across the upper edge.

Press the seam allowances flat, not open. Check the fit for necessary adjustments. Then join all seams and prepare your hem. For ways to handle hems on pleats, see page 352.

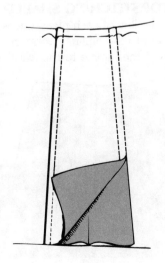

Edgestitching & Topstitching Pleats

When you are certain that your pleats fit and hang properly, are well pressed, and are hemmed evenly, the folds can be edgestitched to keep creases sharp. The pleats can also be held in place by topstitching through all thicknesses from the hip area to the waist. Both edgestitching and topstitching should be done before the skirt is permanently attached to the garment or waistband.

EDGESTITCHING STRAIGHT PLEATS: Stitch close to the outside creased edge of each pleat from the hem up toward the waistline. You may also want to stitch the inside folds on the wrong side. Your edgestitching foot is ideal for straight stitching.

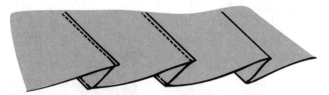

TOPSTITCHING STRAIGHT PLEATS: Always stitch on the right side of the garment, through all thicknesses, from the hip area to the waist. Mark each pleat where the topstitching will begin. For knife or side pleats, stitch along the fold upward to the waist (1). For inverted pleats, topstitching is done on both sides of the pleat. Make 2 or 3 stitches across the pleat, pivot, and stitch along the fold to the waist. Repeat on other side of pleat (2). Pull thread ends to inside and tie.

1

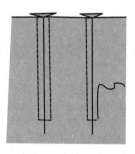

2

EDGESTITCHING AND TOPSTITCHING SHAPED PLEATS: Release the stitching for about 1 " (25 mm) at the hipline of each pleat. Edgestitch the creased edge of each pleat on the outside from the hem to the hipline. Connecting stitches, topstitch along the seam through all thicknesses from the hipline to the waistline. Then pull the thread ends to the inside and tie.

Gathering and Shirring

Softness and suppleness will always be associated with the graceful fullness produced by gathering and shirring. Gathers are small, soft folds made by drawing fabric up on a line of hand or machine stitching. Shirring is formed by numerous rows of gathers and is both decorative and functional. It can be used to achieve varied surface effects such as smocking and may be used at waistline, yokes, and sleeves.

Use a stronger thread in the bobbin to make it easier to pull up gathers without breaking the threads. (The bobbin thread can be pulled more easily by loosening the upper tension.) In order to have small, even folds when stitching for gathering and shirring, do not use a longer stitch than necessary. First, try approximately 8 stitches per inch (3 per cm). If the fabric still does not gather easily, lengthen the stitch accordingly. Normally, thick and closely woven fabrics need longer stitches than lightweight and sheer fabrics.

Gathering

With the right side of the fabric up, stitch along the seamline and again ¼" (6 mm) away in the seam allowance. To form the gathers, pin the edge to be gathered to the corresponding edge at notches, centers, and all remaining markings. Draw up the bobbin threads at one end until almost half of the gathered edge fits the adjoining straight edge. Fasten gathers by winding threads around a pin in a figure-eight fashion. Draw up the remaining half and again fasten the threads. Adjust gathers evenly between pins; then stitch on the seamline with the gathered side up. Press the seam, taking care not to flatten the gathers, and then lightly press in the desired direction.

When you are using a gathering stitch on heavy, bulky fabrics, try to avoid stitching across your seam allowances. When applying your gathering stitch, stitch up to the seamline and stop; then begin on the other side of the seamline (1).

If you have a zigzag machine, you may gather by using a large zigzag stitch over fine strong cording (see page 405). Gathering by hand is done with small, even running stitches, the same length on both sides of the fabric. Sew at least two rows. For hand-gathering it is best to work on an individual fabric piece before the pieces are joined to each other.

STAYING GATHERS: Seam binding or twill tape can be used as a stay to reinforce and finish off a gathered seam. Place seam binding or tape with one edge right next to the seam line. Stitch along lower edge through all thicknesses.

Trim seam allowances even with top edge of stay. If fabric has a tendency to fray, zigzag or serge along the top edge of the stay and seam allowances (2).

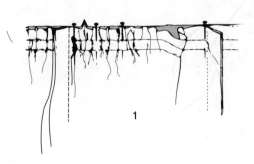

1

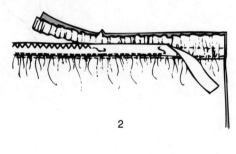

2

Shirring

Shirring is formed by several rows of gathering, requiring **absolute accuracy** for best results. Make as many rows as you desire, using only soft or very lightweight fabric that has been steam-pressed to eliminate any stiffness and to soften the finish. Gather on the bias or crosswise grain for the most satisfying effect. Never press directly on the shirred area, but work the point of the iron into the area below the shirring. When using more than two rows of shirring, secure each row separately with a knot and stitch over knots. If rows of stitching are not further secured by a seam, fold fabric,on the wrong side and stitch narrow pin tucks over knotted ends to hold them securely. A gathering foot will eliminate the need to pull the threads to produce the gathers.

Stay shirring by placing a strip of self-fabric over the wrong side of the shirred area; turn in the raw edges of the strip and slipstitch it in place.

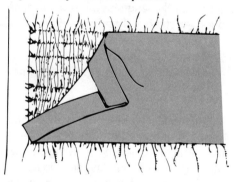

ELASTICIZED SHIRRING is used to snug fabric into place comfortably and prettily. It consists of multiple rows of flexible gathering stitches. Wind elastic thread on the bobbin by hand, stretching it slightly and winding it firmly until the bobbin is almost full. Then set your machine for a long stitch [about 7 stitches per inch (3 per cm)] and use a scrap of your garment fabric to test the tension, which might have to be loosened. Mark the location of the shirring with thread tracing or tailor's chalk clearly visible on the right side of your fabric. Now stitch from the right side, holding the fabric taut as you stitch. Continue to stretch the elasticized fabric in each of the preceding rows as you sew so that the shirring will be evenly distributed. You may use the previously stitched row as a guide along with your markings to keep the lines straight. Be sure to knot all the thread ends and, in addition, stitch over the knots in a seam or encase them in a narrow pin tuck, as explained above.

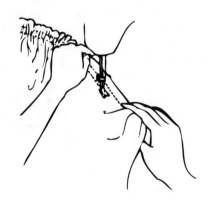

Ruffles

Whether they are eyelet, organdy, or self-fabric, gathered or circular, ruffles always lend a graceful touch. Let them frame your face, border your hem, or become the perfect ending to a graceful sleeve. The effect can be soft or pert; the mood, sophisticated elegance or spring-like freshness. However you choose to use the ruffle, let your fabric and your mood inspire this softer, more romantic look in fashion.

If you do not have a pattern piece for a ruffle or if you want to estimate its fullness, remember that you will need a fabric strip three times the length of the edge to which it will be joined for a very full ruffle; a fabric strip twice the finished edge length for minimum fullness. Wide ruffles should have more fullness than narrow ones to keep them from looking skimpy. The sheerer your fabric is, the fuller the ruffle should be. You should realize that inward corners will require less fullness and outward corners more fullness than the rest of the ruffle. Always keep in mind the proportions of the ruffle and the garment so that neither overwhelms the other. There are two types of ruffles: the straight ruffle, whose fullness is created by gathering a rectangular strip of fabric; and the circular ruffle, whose fullness is created when the inner curve of the circle is straightened.

Straight Ruffle

A straight ruffle is gathered and constructed from a continuous strip of material. It can be cut either on the straight grain or on the bias. If the ruffle must be seamed, the seam should be made on the straight grain. Bias ruffles applied to a small area, such as a sleeve, are the exception--in this case, make the seam of the ruffle on the bias to match the seam of the garment.

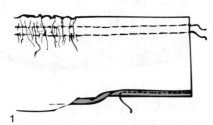

1

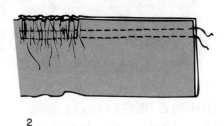

2

A straight ruffle may be constructed of a single layer of fabric with a narrow hem at the lower edge (1). Or the ruffle may be self-faced by folding the fabric in half lengthwise with wrong sides together (2). For gathering a ruffle, always stitch two rows of long machine stitches-one on the seamline and the other ¼" (6 mm) away in the seam allowance. The two rows will help to distribute the fullness evenly and will protect each other, should one break during the ruffling process. Use a strong thread in the bobbin to reduce the chance of the thread breaking under tension.

Draw the gathers to the proper length. When adjusting gathers over a short distance, secure both threads at one end and gather from the opposite end. For longer distances, begin gathering from one end, secure the threads, and then gather from the other end. For very long ruffles, gather it in quarters. After you have attached the ruffle, remove any gathering stitches that might show.

Pin the ruffle to the garment edge, matching seamlines. Adjust the gathers until they are evenly distributed and baste in place (3). To make machine stitching and turning easier, press the basted seam allowances flat, holding the tip of your iron parallel to the seam, not on the ruffles (4). With ruffle up, stitch along seamline. Finish the application with a bias facing as directed on page 242.

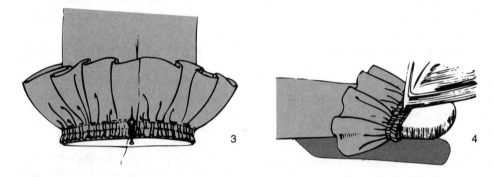

To sew a ruffle into a seam or along a faced edge, pin the ruffle to the right side of garment. Check to see if the gathers are distributed evenly and the ruffle is facing the desired direction after the seam is completed. With ruffle side up, stitch a scant ⅛" (3 mm) within seam allowance. When rounding a corner, be sure to provide extra fabric at the corner (5). Pin to second garment section so that the ruffle is between the right sides of the fabric. Stitch just beside the first row of stitching so that no stitches will show on the right side of the garment or ruffle (6).

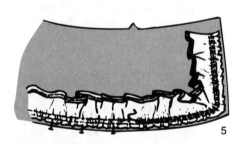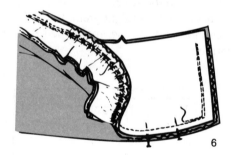

DOUBLE RUFFLE: A variation of the straight ruffle, the double ruffle has two free edges and is gathered in the center or off-center for a more asymmetrical took. When gathered off-center it is also known as a ruffle with a heading. Both types can be easily applied by simply stitching them on to the garment rather than having to sew them in during construction.

Make a narrow hem along the two free edges. The fabric can be doubled for a self-facing, having the raw edges meet directly under the gathering line. If the ends will be left hanging free, finish with a narrow hem, or seam and trim ends that are to be joined.

Stitch two lines of long machine stitches ¼" (6 mm) apart, one on either side of the gathering line.

To apply the ruffle to a finished edge, pin it wrong side down on the right side of the garment. Baste, adjusting the gathers. Topstitch twice, stitching close to both rows of gathering stitches, as shown on next page (7).

To apply the ruffle to a raw edge, trim garment seam allowances to ¼' " (6 mm). Pin wrong sides together with the ruffle side up. The bottom row of gathering stitches should be even with the seamline of the garment. Baste, adjusting the gathers and stitch close to the bottom of gathers.

Press the garment away from the ruffle. Baste the ruffle to the right side of the garment, enclosing the raw edge; stitch close to the top row of gathers. Remove basting (8).

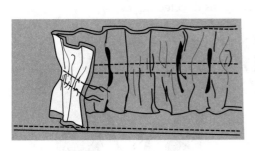

7

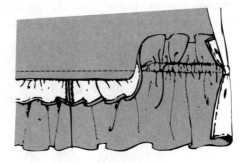

8

Circular Ruffle

A circular ruffle can be added to any edge--cuffs, V-neckline, rounded neckline--wherever you wish. It is cut from several circles that are first slashed and then joined along the straight grain. This method produces a maximum amount of fullness. Exert great caution when laying out, pinning, and cutting the ruffle sections. You will find that exact location and maintenance of the grainline is most important if the circular ruffle is to drape correctly.

You may staystitch each ruffle section ⅛" (3 mm) from the inner seamline in the seam allowance before joining (1).

The edge of a circular ruffle may be faced with self-fabric or it may have a narrow hemmed or rolled serger edge. Should a narrow or serger hem be required, join the circles and complete the hem before basting the ruffle to its proper edge. If your ruffle has a facing of corresponding circles, stitch the seamed facing and ruffle sections together along the outer edges. Trim seam allowance to ¼" (6 mm) (2). Turn the ruffle and press. Baste the raw edges of the ruffle and facing together for handling ease.

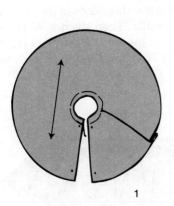

1

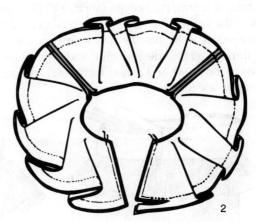

2

If you are applying ruffles to a neckline or any other curved edge, first stay the seamline so that its shape will not be distorted by the weight of the ruffle. Whether the ruffle is cut single or is faced, the inner circle should be staystitched and then clipped where necessary as you pin the ruffle to the garment in order to fit smoothly on the seamline. As a rule, deep curves require a clip at almost every ½" (13 mm) up to the line of staystitching; shallow curves will, of course, require fewer clips. If the ruffle does not lie flat, do not cut through the staystitching; merely clip more frequently. Then baste the ruffle in place (3). Finish the ruffle application with a shaped facing, as directed below (4).

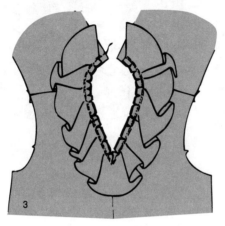
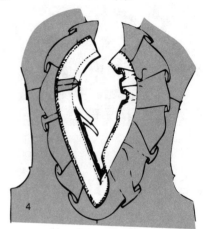

Finishing Ruffles

SHAPED FACING: For ruffles contained by a facing, pin the facing to the garment edge over your ruffle. The ruffle is now sandwiched between the two layers, right sides together. Stitch along the seamline. Trim, grade, and clip the seam allowance so that the facing will lie flat when turned. Turn the facing to expose the finished ruffle. Press, being careful not to press over the ruffle. Understitch the facing by hand through all thicknesses to prevent it from rolling to the outside. If you are using a zipper, insert your zipper and slipstitch the facing along the zipper tape. Blindstitch the facing to the garment or underlining.

BIAS FACING: For a fine finish on ruffles at the hemline, cut a bias strip of your fashion fabric, or a firm, lightweight fabric, 1¼" (3.2 cm) wide and ½" (13 mm) longer than the length of the seam to be faced. Stitch a ¼" (6 mm) seam at the short ends of the strip. With the raw -edges even, pin the bias strip over the basted ruffle. Then stitch a ⅝" (15 mm) seam through all thicknesses, trim, and if necessary, grade the seam allowances (1). Turn the bias to the inside and press. Turn the raw edge under ¼" (6 mm) and slipstitch it to the garment or underlining (2).

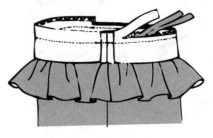

1

2

Mitering

Like the use of wine in cooking, mitering is a subtle art. When successful, it merely enhances the total effect; it is noticeable only when incorrect. Mitering is a neat and easy means of eliminating bulk at corners. Since your goal is to achieve a flat, neat-looking miter, you must concentrate on trimming at just the right moment in your mitering plan. Also remember that most miters involve folds, either at right angles or 45° angles to the seam or strip being mitered. The method you use to miter depends on many factors--whether you are working with garment areas, binding, or continuous strips of trim, and whether the miter is made as you attach the trim or before application.

Continuous Strips

If your band or trim has seam allowances, press them to the inside before you begin mitering. To miter the band before it is applied, pin the band to the garment for an accurate measurement of where the miter should be made. Measure to the outermost point where the corner will be formed, and mark with a pin.

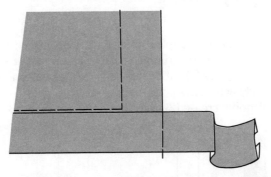

Remove band and fold it with right sides together at marked point (1). Turn the fold diagonally to meet the turned-back edges of band, as shown, and press (2). Open the diagonal fold and stitch along the pressed crease. Since it is important that the knots do not show once the miter is finished, pull the thread ends to one side of the band and knot. Trim to ⅛" (3 mm) and press the seam open (3). Then attach the strip (4).

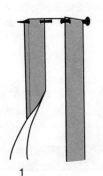
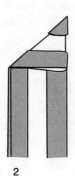
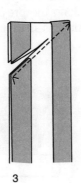
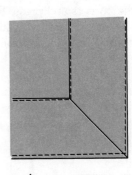

1 2 3 4

To miter while you are attaching the trim, use trim with a finished edge such as ribbon or braid. Pin the trim in position, then edgestitch or hand-sew the inner edge (5). Fold the band back on itself, then diagonally to the side, making a right angle; press.

Again fold the band back on itself and stitch on the diagonal crease-through the band and garment. Since it is important that the knots be invisible once the miter is finished, pull the thread ends to one side of the band, as shown, and knot (6). If trim is bulky, you may trim the small corner close to the stitching. Press flat from the right side, miter remaining corners, and edgestitch or hand-sew outer edge in a continuous motion (7).

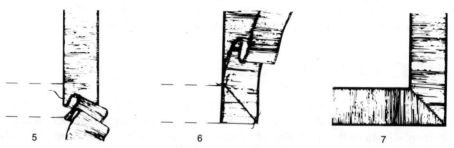

Square Corners

Pockets, appliqués, or any other applied areas requiring square corners, need to be mitered so the excess fullness can be easily trimmed away. Pressing is the key feature. Turn all seam allowances to inside and press (1). At the corners, open the seam allowances and turn them to the inside diagonally across the point, as shown, and press. Trim corner to ⅜" (10 mm) from the pressed diagonal crease (2). Slipstitch to fasten miter (3).

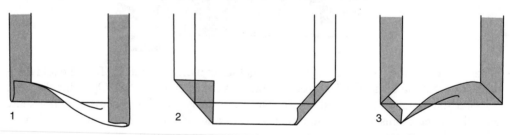

For a quick sturdier method, make a diagonal fold in the turned-back seam allowances at the corners and press. Stitch along the pressed diagonal crease (4). Trim the seam to ⅜" (10 mm) or less for bulkier fabrics, as shown. Press diagonal seam open (5), then turn the corners to the inside (6). Press.

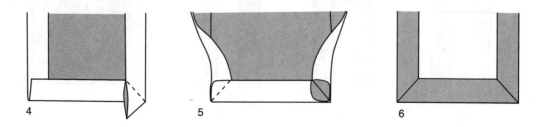

5

Construction Techniques

(continued on next page)

Facings
and Other
Edge Finishes

The edge of a garment can be finished in a variety of ways—either inconspicuously with a facing that is concealed on the inside, or accented with cording, piping, binding, banding, or a casing. Whatever finish you choose, apply it carefully and smoothly to achieve that custom-made look. Never take shortcuts or you may sacrifice the appearance of the entire garment, no matter how much loving attention you have given to other details.

Facings

A well-applied facing does much for the look and comfort of your new garment. The purpose of a facing is to neatly finish and conceal a raw edge by turning it to the wrong side of your garment. Your facing will always perform this task beautifully if you consistently strive for a smooth, flat appearance.

Although the shape and actual construction of facings vary stylistically, they fall into three basic categories—a *shaped facing,* an *extended facing,* or a *bias facing.* Let your fabric and the edge to be faced determine the most suitable method.

There are some construction procedures that can be used on all types of facings to produce the best results, as well as to simplify the work at hand. The garment edge is usually stabilized or reinforced in some manner, either by small stitches, interfacing, or ribbon seam binding. Except for the bias facing, one edge of most facings must be finished since it will be exposed on the inside of the garment. A sturdy way of finishing many facings is to stitch ¼" (6 mm) from the unnotched edge, trim to ⅛" (3 mm) and overcast, zigzag or finish with your serger.

For a more attractively finished appearance with added fashion interest, you may try enclosing the edges with bias binding, stretch lace, or other lightweight, flexible trims. When the facing is attached, press the seam or foldlines carefully before you turn and tack the facings to the inside of the garment. To prevent any shaped facing or variation of it, such as the combination facing, from rolling to the outside, open out the facing and understitch it to the seam allowances. If the facing edge is at a visible area, you can favor the garment slightly along the seamline so that the facing does not show. You should, however, use caution or you may destroy the clean line of the edge.

Always tack the facing to the inside of the garment to keep it in place. Blindstitch the facing to the underlining only, or if the garment is not underlined, sew it to the inner seam allowances. Tack loosely; many short, tight stitches will give your garment a strained or puckered appearance. When making adjustments and alterations on your garment, don't forget the facings! They must be changed to conform to the new lines of the garment.

Shaped Facing

A shaped or fitted facing is the most commonly selected method used to finish necklines and sleeveless armholes. It is a separate piece provided with your pattern and cut to match the shape of the area to which it will be applied.

Prepare the facing by stitching, trimming, and pressing the seams. The outer edge of the facing must be finished since it will be exposed on the inside of the garment. Stitch ¼" (6 mm) from the unnotched edge, trim to ⅛" (3 mm), and overcast or zigzag stitch the raw edges(1); or, trim and serge with your overlock machine.

Pin and baste the facing to the garment, matching the seams and markings. Then, with the facing side up, stitch the facing to the garment. Trim, grade, and clip the seam allowances. Press the seam allowances toward the facing (2).

To keep the facing from rolling to the outside, open out the facing and understitch it to the seam allowances, pulling it taut as you stitch. Understitch by hand on custom clothes, using small backstitches close to the seam through the seam allowances and facing. On casual clothes this can be accomplished by machine stitching. Turn the facing to the inside and press. Tack the facing to the inner seams, or blindstitch the free edge to the underlining (3).

For a neckline facing with a zipper opening, insert the zipper first. Turn the facing ends under to clear the zipper teeth and slipstitch the ends in place. Tack the facing at the shoulder seams or blindstitch facing edge to underlining. Fasten with a hook and eye at top of placket (4).

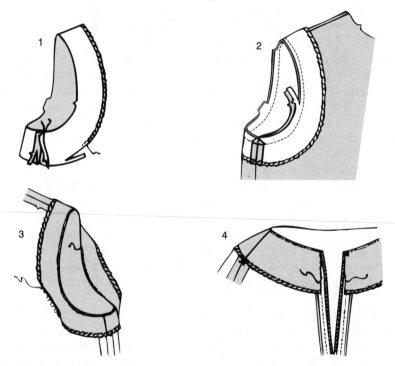

When working with soft or loosely woven fabrics that tend to stretch, stabilize the garment edge with interfacing or ribbon seam binding. Attach either reinforcement to the wrong side of the garment, not to the facing which must be able to mold to the garment edge. Necklines that are cut on the bias must also be reinforced to prevent stretching of the curved or bias edge.

SEAM BINDING: Center the ribbon seam binding over the seamline on the inside of your garment, fold out any fullness at points or corners and baste in place (1).

Pin and baste the facing to the garment edge. Stitch, pivoting at any points or corners. For sharp corners such as those on a V-neckline or a square armhole, reinforce with small stitches [15-20 stitches per inch (6-8 per cm)] on the seamline for an inch (25 mm) on either side of the point and take one stitch across the point. Grade and clip the seam allowances carefully. Press the seam toward the facing and understitch (2). Turn the facing to the inside and press.

1

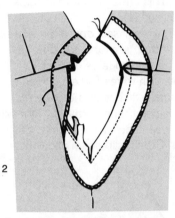

2

INTERFACING: If your pattern doesn't include an interfacing pattern piece, cut the interfacing the same as the facing and trim ⅜" (10 mm) from the inner edges. Pin the corresponding interfacing sections to the front and back garment pieces and stitch them in place (1). Stitch the garment sections together and press open.

For a slashed neckline, pin and baste the facing to the garment along the stitching lines of the opening and neck edge. Stitch the opening to within 2" (5 cm) of the point. Then change to smaller stitches [15-20 per inch (6-8 per cm)] for 2" (5 cm) on either side of the point and take one stitch across the point. Stitch remainder of opening and neck edge, pivoting at corners. Slash opening to machine stitching, being careful not to cut through it. Trim opening edges if necessary for firmly woven or heavy fabrics. Trim, grade, and clip the neck seam so that the garment seam allowance is left widest (2). Complete facing as above.

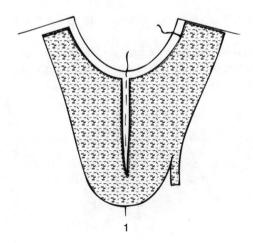

1

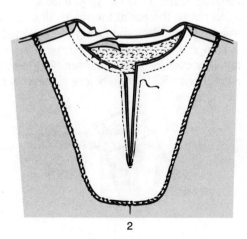

2

Combination Facings

This is a variation of the shaped facing in which the neckline and armhole facings are cut and applied as one piece. It is often used on garments with narrow shoulder seams, as a dress with cutaway armholes. You will find it quite simple to apply if you remember one rule; do not sew the shoulder seams of either the garment or the facing until after the facing is stitched to the garment.

Prior to pinning the facing to the garment, pin a minute tuck in both garment shoulders, as shown. This ensures that the seams and facing will not show on the right side once the facing is turned (1).

Join the garment sections at the side seams, leaving the shoulder seams open, and press. Join the facing sections together in the same manner and press. Then, finish the unnotched facing edge as desired.

You may wish to reinforce a curved neckline with ribbon seam binding, or a square neckline with small stitches at the corners.

Pin the facing to the garment, right sides together. Since the raw edges will not be even, follow the seamline of the facing. Stitch to within ⅝" (15 mm) from shoulder edges and backstitch. Grade; clip seam allowances (2).

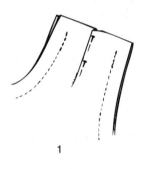

1

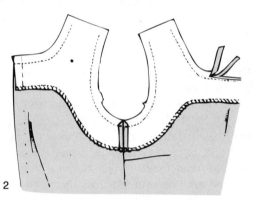

2

Unpin the tuck in the garment shoulders. Turn the facing to the inside and press. To prevent the facing from rolling to the outside, understitch it to the seam allowances close to the seam. Fold the facing seam allowances back and stitch the garment shoulder seams, carefully keeping the facing free (3).

Do not tie threads at the seam edge. Bring both threads to one side and tie so the knots will not show when the facing is completed.

Trim and press open the garment seams. Turn in the facing edges and slipstitch them together over the garment seam (4). On bulky fabric you may wish to trim the facing seam allowance to ¼" (6 mm) before turning them in.

3

4

Extended Facing

An extended facing is cut in one piece with the garment, and folded to the inside. It is used for finishing edges cut on straight grain which can simply be extended to create a fold at the edge rather than a seam.

Because extended facing edges are usually overlapped, be sure to transfer position lines with thread tracing. Interface for reinforcement, especially if a buttonhole closing is intended. Your pattern will usually include a pattern piece for the interfacing.

If your pattern doesn't include an interfacing piece, cut the interfacing from the facing portion of the garment pattern, plus a ⅝" (15 mm) extension at the foldline for a softly rolled edge. Trim ⅜" (10 mm) from the edge opposite the foldline. Attach the interfacing to the garment, using long running stitches to hold the interfacing along the foldline (1). For a garment that will be topstitched, trim the interfacing at the foldline and catchstitch the edge in place.

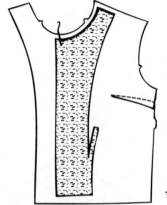

If additional facing sections are to be joined to the extended facing, such as the back neck facing, attach these sections before stitching the facing to the garment.

Turn facing to the right side along the foldline of the garment so right sides are together. Pin and baste the facing to the garment along the neck seamline. Stitch the seam; trim, grade, and clip the seam allowances (2). Turn the facing to the inside and press. Understitch close to the neckline seam through the facing and the seam allowances just as you would a shaped facing. Finish the raw edge and tack the facing in place at the shoulder seam.

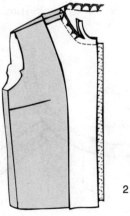

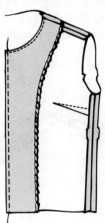

Bias Facing

Ease of handling and versatility make a bias facing a suitable replacement for your regular shaped facing. It is particularly useful when you do not want to use your garment fabric (if it is scratchy or bulky) or where a wide facing may be objectionable (as in sheers).

Cut a bias strip from your lining or underlining fabric four times the desired width plus ¼" to ⅜" (6 mm to 10 mm) to allow for shaping (or use double-fold bias tape with folds pressed open) and the length of the garment edge plus 2" (5 cm) to allow for finishing the ends.

Fold the strip in half lengthwise with wrong sides together . Press the strip lightly, steaming and stretching it into curves corresponding to those of the garment edge. As the bias takes shape, its width will become distorted. Equalize the width of the bias facing by measuring from the folded edge the desired facing width plus a ¼" (6 mm) seam allowance, marking the strip as you work. Trim away excess fabric along markings.

Your closure should be completed before you apply your bias facing. If you have a zipper, trim the zipper tape away below the seamline. Trim the garment seam allowance to ¼" (6 mm). With raw edges even, place the folded strip on the right side of the garment with 1" (25 mm) extending beyond the closing edges. Pin, baste, and stitch directionally with grain continuing to the ends of the bias strip (1).

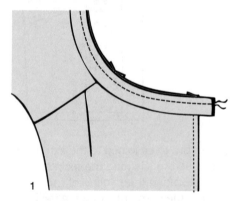

Clip the seam allowances, and trim the two extending bias ends to ¼" (6 mm). Turn the bias strip to the inside, **favoring** the garment edge slightly so that the binding is inconspicuous. Turn the bias ends in (2). Pin the bias strip in position and slipstitch the folded edge to the underlining (3). Finally, fasten the closing edges with a hook and eye.

If the facing ends meet, as on an armhole, fold in the ends ¼" (6 mm). Trim the excess length and slipstitch free ends together to finish.

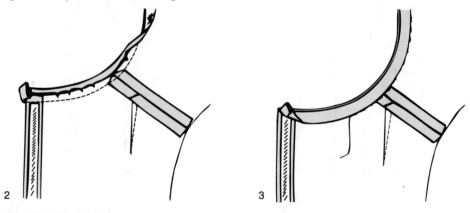

Cording and Piping

This finish can be added to any edge--a neckline, armhole, or hemline--before the facing is applied. The distinction between piping and cording refers to the size of the filler used: piping is thin; cording is thick. First cut a bias strip the size of the filler plus ¼" to ⅜" (6 mm to 10 mm) and two ⅝" (15 mm) seam allowances. Allow at least ⅝" (15 mm) for finishing the ends. Bring the bias strip around the filler, matching the raw edges. With your zipper foot and using 8-10 stitches per inch (3-4 per cm), stitch close to, but not on, the filler.

Baste the corded or piped strip to the right side of the garment, matching seamlines.

To finish ends at a closing, pull the bias back, removing stitches for 1½" (3.8 cm), exposing the filler. Cut the filler off just inside the end of the opening, leaving the empty bias strip. Fold in the bias ends (1). Slipstitch the ends and restitch the bias, enclosing the filler. Using a piping or zipper foot, apply a shaped facing (2). For thick cording, apply snaps to the ends (3). Narrow cording or piping requires a regular hook and eye closure on the garment.

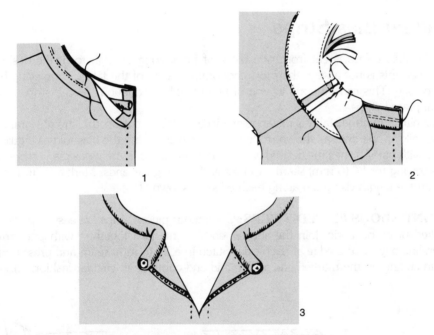

On an edge without a closing, place the joining at an inconspicuous location. For narrow piping, pull the bias back, removing a few stitches from the bias so you can cut the filler off where the ends cross. Overlap the two empty bias ends, easing the ends of the bias slightly toward the seam (4). For thick cording, do not enclose the filler with bias until you have stitched one edge of the bias to the garment and pieced it. Then, using the proper length of filler for the edge, enclose it in the bias, using a piping or zipper foot (5). Apply a facing over all piping or cording with a piping or zipper foot.

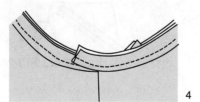
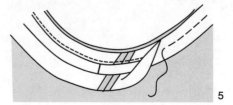

Bindings

The versatile bias binding was designed to enclose raw edges, thus providing a finish that both conceals and strengthens. A binding can be beautiful as decorative trim around closure edges—whether you use self-fabric or a contrasting fabric. It can be helpful around a neckline or armhole when used in place of facings. One of the great satisfactions of sewing is a bias binding that turns smoothly and evenly over an edge with nary a twist, a pull, or a ripple to mar its flat surface. To achieve a perfect binding, cut strips of fabric evenly on the true bias, join them on the grain, and press and shape them before application.

You can also purchase bias strips ready-made in a variety of colors and a choice of several widths. Whether single- or double-fold, the edges are usually pressed under for your convenience. Depending upon your needs, the folds can be pressed open and the full width of the bias made available. The techniques used for applying or piecing the commercial bias strips are the same as those suggested for bias-cut strips you have made yourself.

Cutting Bias Strips

The ideal bias strip is cut from one piece of fabric long enough to fit the desired area. However, this is not always the most economical usage of the fabric, so piecing becomes a necessity. This can be done in one of two ways-by continuous pieced strips or by individual pieced strips.

For either method, take a rectangular piece of fabric cut on the straight grain. Fold it diagonally at one end, as shown, to find the true bias. Using the bias fold as a guide, mark fabric with parallel lines the desired width of the bias strips, marking as many strips as needed, allowing for ¼" (6 mm) seams. Cut away the triangular ends. Mark a ¼" (6 mm) seamline on the lengthwise grain along each edge as shown (1).

CONTINUOUS PIECED STRIPS: Continuous pieced strips are easy to make. On the marked piece of fabric, join the shorter ends, right sides together, with one strip width extending beyond the edge at each side. Stitch in a ¼" (6 mm) seam and press it open (2). Begin cutting on the marked line at one end and continue in circular fashion (3).

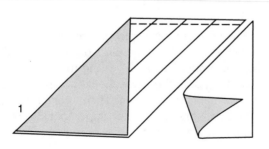

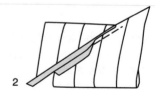

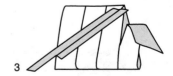

INDIVIDUAL PIECED STRIPS: Individually pieced strips are more time consuming. Cut along the markings for the bias strips. The short ends, previously cut on the grain, will appear diagonal. Mark a seamline ¼" (6 mm) from each end. With right sides of the strip together, match the seamlines (not the cut edges), pin, and stitch. Press the seam open.

Preshaping the Binding

To preshape the strip and to take out the extra slack, the bias should first be pressed, steaming and stretching it gently (1). You will then have a slightly narrower, taut strip to work with, eliminating the problem of a wobbling seamline. Fold the strip in half lengthwise, wrong sides together, and press again lightly (2). For single binding: open, fold cut edges toward the center, and press lightly (3). A bias binder maker is a helpful notion for pressing single binding (see Sewing Aids, page 200). Lastly, shape the tape into curves that correspond to those on the garment by positioning it on your pattern piece and steam pressing (4). Since one folded edge of the finished binding will be even with the seamline of the garment, you must always trim the seam allowance from the edge to be bound. When applying the bias strips to the garment, try to place the piecing seamlines at inconspicuous locations wherever possible. Also, leave 2" (5 cm) extra on the bias strip free at the beginning of any application for finishing. (Note: Commercial binding can be shaped, but the slack has already been removed by the manufacturer.)

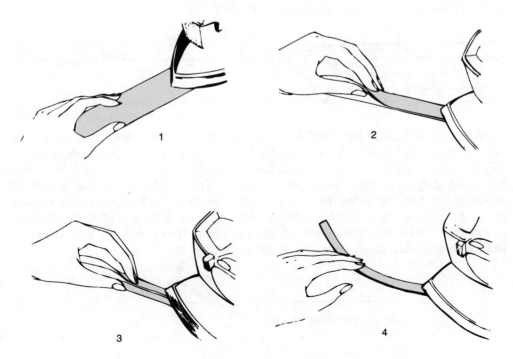

Applying the Binding

SINGLE BINDING: Trim the seam allowance from the garment edges to be bound. Cut bias strips four times the desired finished width plus ¼" to ⅜" (6 mm to 10 mm), depending on your fabric. This will give you ample width for stretching and turning. Preshape your bias strip with a steam iron, as shown earlier, to match the curves of the garment edge. Open out the bias strip and, with right sides together and the raw edge of the strip even with the raw edge of the garment, pin it to the garment. Baste the strip at a distance from the edge slightly less than the width of the finished binding. Stitch next to but not on the basting, so that the basting threads can be easily removed (1). Turn the bias over the seam allowance. Pin and slipstitch over the seamline (2).

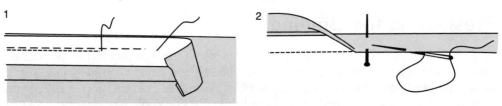

DOUBLE BINDING or **FRENCH BINDING:** This method makes an attractive finish for sheers. Trim the garment seam allowances. Cut bias strips six times the desired finished width plus ¼" to ⅜" (6 mm to 10 mm) to allow for stretching and turning. Fold the strip in half lengthwise with wrong sides together, and press lightly. Preshape the bias to match the garment edge. Trim raw edges so entire strip can be folded equally. Divide it into equal thirds and press again. Open out the folded edge of the strip. With raw edges of strip and garment even, pin the strip to the right side. Baste the strip at a distance from the edge slightly less than the width of the finished binding; stitch next to the basting (1). Turn the strip over the seam allowances and slipstitch in place (2).

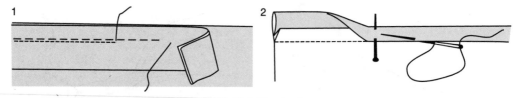

MACHINE-APPLIED BINDING: This is a speedy, one-step method in which success depends upon careful pressing. Preshape the bias strip as mentioned previously, with one very notable exception. Instead of folding the tape equally in half lengthwise, fold the bottom half slightly wider than the top half, as shown. This overlap on the bottom half will ensure its being caught by the machine stitching. With the wider edge on the wrong side, encase the trimmed garment edge with the folded bias strip. Edgestitch through all layers, as shown, and your binding is completed. Many machines have bias binder attachments or feet that help guide the pre-folded or flat bias strips while sewing.

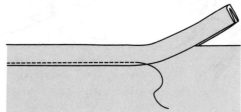

Special Techniques

When bias bindings are used as trim, they often have to be applied around corners, joined together, or ended at a seam or opening.

OUTWARD CORNERS: Open out one prefolded edge of your bias strip; then pin or baste it in place as for single or double binding. Stitch from one end to the corner and back-stitch for reinforcement (1). Fold the strip diagonally, as shown, to bring it around the corner. Pin or baste, then stitch the adjoining edge through the corner from one end to the other end (2). Fold to form a miter at the corner on the right side and turn the bias over the seam (3). To finish the wrong side, form a miter (with the fold of the miter in the opposite direction from the one formed on the right side, so that the bulk of the miter will be evenly distributed). Turn, pin, and slipstitch the binding over the seamline, fastening the miter at the corner, if desired (4).

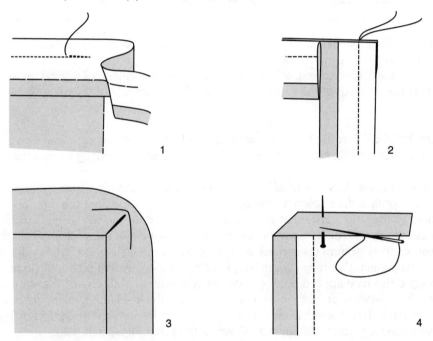

INWARD CORNERS: Reinforce the corner along your planned seamline, as instructed on page 216 (1). Open out one prefolded edge of your bias strip; then pin and baste it to the garment, pulling the corners so the binding remains straight. Stitch from the wrong side of the garment, keeping the binding straight (2).

Form a miter on the right side (3). Pull the fold of the miter to the wrong side through the clip, and form a miter on the wrong side in the reverse direction from the one on the right side (4). Turn, pin, and slipstitch the binding over the seamline, fastening the fold of the miter at the corner, if desired (5).

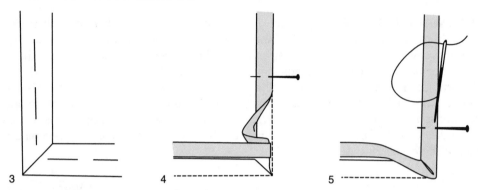

When making machine-applied binding for an outward or inward corner, pin and baste the bias strip to the edge as for single or double binding. Form a miter at the corner, as above. For machine-stitching, follow the directions for machine-applied binding, page 246, remembering to pivot at the corners. If desired, fasten the fold of the miter with slipstitches.

JOININGS: When the binding is applied to a long or continuous edge, such as a front closure or hem, a joining is often required. Try to locate the joining in an inconspicuous place.

A binding applied as described in single our double binding is joined by stopping your stitching slightly before reaching the area of the joining. Open out the strip and fold the garment so the strip ends are at right angles as they are for piecing, page 255. Stitch the ends close to the garment, but without catching the garment in the stitching. Trim the seam allowances to ¼" (6mm) (1) and press open. Complete stitching the strip to the garment across the joining. Finish by slipstitching the strip to the garment across the joining.

To lap a machine-applied binding, edgestitch to within 2" (5 cm) of the starting point, leaving extra binding on both ends. Fold one end to the inside on straight grain, and trim to ¼" (6 mm). Trim the other end as shown, also on the straight grain. Pin or baste and continue stitching across the joining. Slipstitch the joining if desired (2).

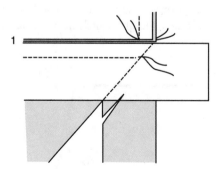

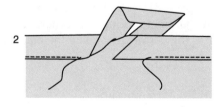

ENDINGS: Binding an edge which ends at a seam or opening requires a special finishing technique. In any of the following cases, the facings should be completed and the seam allowances turned under or the zipper inserted before the binding is applied.

To finish a single or double binding, pin, baste, and stitch the binding to the garment through all layers and to the ends of the bias, which extends about 1" (25 mm) past the garment opening edge on both ends (1). Trim the bias ends to ¼" (6 mm) beyond the garment edge. Then trim the garment seam allowance on a diagonal at the corner and fold the extending bias ends back. Turn the strip over the seam allowance, matching the folded edge with the line of machine stitching. Slipstitch the open ends; then pin and slipstitch the folded edge to the garment (2).

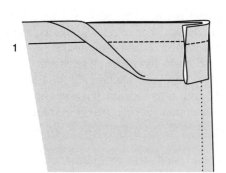
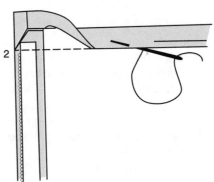

A machine-applied binding, since it is applied and stitched in one step, requires care in trimming and stitching the ends to achieve a tidy finish. Fold in about ½" (13 mm) at one end on the bias grain and trim, as shown. To encase the raw edge of the garment with binding, make sure the under edge is deeper than the top edge and that the ends are even (3). Starting at one end, edgestitch in place through all layers to about 3" (7.5 cm) from the other end. Measure and cut off the binding ½" (13 mm) past the garment fold. Trim; fold in the binding end. Complete stitching; finish the open ends with slipstitching (4).

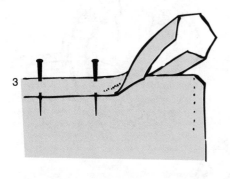
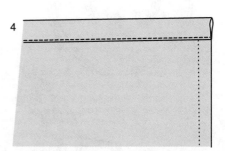

Bandings

Fabric bands can be an important design feature of a garment as well as finish the edge of a neckline, armhole, sleeve, center front opening, or hem. They can take many shapes, such as square, round, keyhole, V-neck, or straight. Sometimes the band will extend only part way down the garment front to form a placket. Knit bands can be used for neckline or sleeve finishes on knitted garments. Subtle in self fabric or bold in contrasting colors, fabric bands can accent any edge.

Applied Band

An applied band is usually cut from a shaped pattern piece. The two layers are stitched together and then the band is applied to the garment edge. For a hemline, the band may be cut on the bias with an extended facing, which is turned up along the fold line.

Staystitch the edge of the garment directionally and insert the zipper, if necessary. Stitch or fuse the interfacing to one band section and trim close to the stitching. (If the band sections have seams, stitch them before you join the band to its facing.) Then pin and baste the band sections together, leaving the notched edge open. Stitch; then trim, grade, and clip the seam allowances, leaving the interfaced band seam allowance widest (1). Turn the band and press it flat.

Pin and baste the outer edge of the interfaced band section to the garment, matching markings at shoulder seams and clipping the garment seam allowance. Stitch from the band side for the best control, then trim and grade the seam, leaving the garment seam allowance the widest (2).

Notch the band seam allowances to eliminate extra fullness so that all seam allowances can be pressed toward the band. Turn the band, rolling the seam just slightly to the inside to prevent it from being seen on the finished garment; pin.

Turn the remaining free edge under where it falls over the stitching and baste close to the edge. Trim away any excess seam allowance close to the basting. Slipstitch the band over the seamline (3). Fasten the band with hooks and thread eyes.

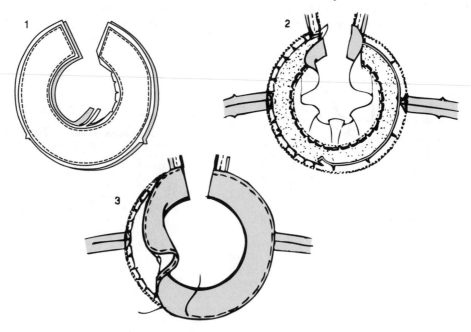

When a flat finish is desired for the band, finish the free edge with a stitch-and-overcast, zigzag or serger treatment. Do not turn the edge under, however. Just blindstitch the free edge where it falls, covering the band seam completely (4).

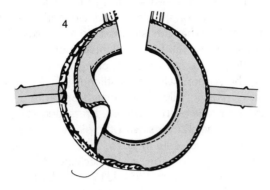

Topstitched Band

If a band will be topstitched, it is often constructed in a slightly different method—the inner band or facing is stitched to the garment and then the outer band is folded over and top-stitched in place.

Interface the band as previously described and stitch any seams in the band sections.

Turn in the seam allowance on the notched edge of the interfaced band and baste close to the fold. Trim seam allowance to ¼" (6 mm) and press.

Pin the two band sections with right sides together; stitch. Trim and clip the seam allowances. Turn the band and press (1).

Pin the right side of the band without interfacing to the wrong side of the garment, matching markings, and baste. Stitch seam, trim, and press seam toward band (2).

On the outside, pin the basted edge of the band over the seamline and baste. Topstitch close to the inner and outer edges of the band (3).

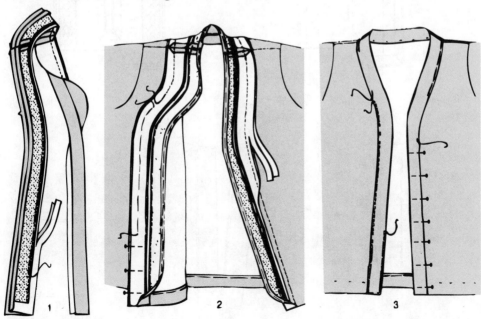

One-Piece Placket Band

A placket band is a variation of the applied band and is used for an opening extending only part way down a garment. Baste or fuse the interfacing sections to the wrong side of the band. Turn in the seam allowances on the sides and lower end of the front band, as shown, folding in the fullness at the corners; baste close to the folds. Trim the basted seam allowances to ¼" (6 mm) and press (1). Pin the right side of the band to the wrong side of the garment front, matching all markings. Stitch along the stitching lines, pivoting at the corners, and reinforcing the corners with small stitches [15-20 stitches per inch (6-8 per cm)] along the seamline. Clip diagonally to the corners and trim the seam allowances (2).

Turn the placket to the right side of the garment. Press long seams toward the band and the triangular end down. Fold the shorter side of the placket along the foldline, placing the basted edge over the seamline, and baste in place. Stitch close to the basted edge, ending at the marking. Baste upper edges together at the neckline (3).

Fold the other side of the placket along the foldline, and baste in place as above. Stitch close to the basted edge ending at the marking, being sure to keep the other side of the placket free. Baste upper edges together (4).

Place lower end of the placket band along the placement line and topstitch in place (5).

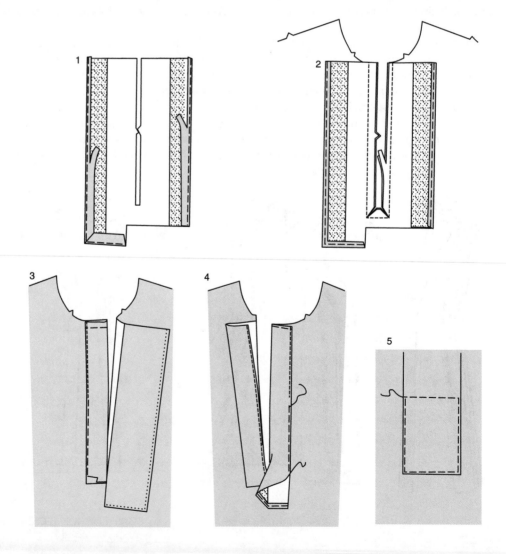

Two-Piece Placket Band

The two-piece placket band must be used at curved areas when the neck and placket bands are combined. Reinforce the front opening corners on the garment with small stitches on the seamline, pivoting at corners. Clip to corners (1). Stitch shoulder seams, then staystitch the neck and front edges of garment. Insert your zipper, if necessary. Interface and construct each band as for the applied band, page 260, stitching along the curved unnotched edges and center back. Leave the lower ends free. Trim and grade the seam allowances, clipping and notching where necessary to allow the bands to lie flat (2). Turn the bands and press them flat.

Leaving the lower end free, baste the interfaced edge of the left neckband to the left half of the garment, clipping where necessary. Stitch with the neckband up. Trim, grade, notch, and press the curved seam allowances toward the band. Turn the free edge of the band under, and baste close to the fold, clipping as necessary for the band to lie flat; slipstitch (3). (Or, for bulky fabrics, use the flat finish for applied bands, page 261.) Do not turn the band under at the lower edge. Just stitch across the end through garment and band (4). Press the lower end toward the garment.

Apply the right neckband to the right half of the garment as above, ending stitching at the right front corner (5). Finish the lower end by turning in and grading the seam allowances and slipstitching them together (6).

Lap the right band over the left band, matching centers. You may wish to slipstitch the lower edge in place along the seamline.

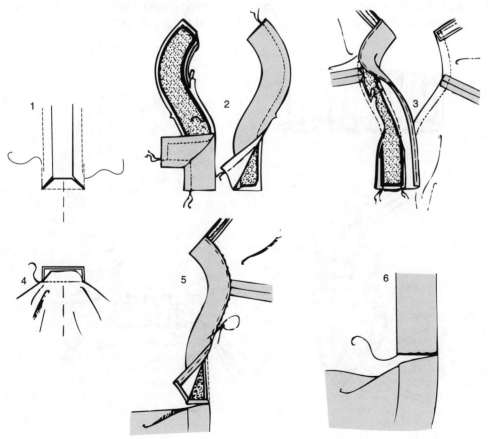

Knit Bands

Knit bands give a professional look to the edges of a knitted garment and allow you to take advantage of the stretchability of the fabric. The band can be cut from self-fabric or you can use purchased ribbing, which is sold by the yard (meter) or prepackaged.

A knit band is always cut a little shorter than the edge to which it is applied. Then the band is stretched slightly as it is stitched to the garment, resulting in a smooth, unpuckered seam.

With right sides together, seam the band to form a tube, if necessary. Trim and serge or double stitch the seam and trim close to the second row of stitching. Fold the band in half lengthwise, wrong sides together (1). (Some purchased ribbings have only one layer of fabric.)

Divide the band into fourths and mark with pins. Pin the band to the right side of the garment, matching the pins with center front, back and shoulder markings. With band side up, stitch the band to the garment, stretching the band between the pins, but being careful not to stretch the garment edge. Stitch again ⅛" (3 mm) away from the first row of stitching with either a straight or zigzag stitch, or use an overedge stitch if your machine has one. Trim seam allowances close to the second row of stitching (2). A 3- or 4-thread overlock serger stitch is the ideal seam treatment for knit fabrics (3). (See Seams, page 212.)

Holding the iron above the seam, steam the band gently to allow it to return to its unstretched state. Press seam allowances toward the garment (4).

For a self-fabric band, your pattern may include instructions for stitching a narrow piece of elastic between the two rows of stitching or for stitching a seam binding stay to the seam, depending on the amount of stretch in your fabric and the shape of the band.

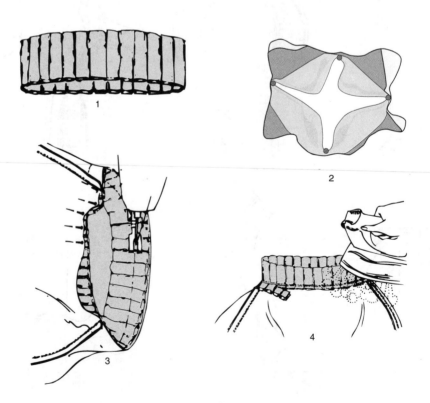

Casings

Casings, which often go unnoticed, are significant in that they enable fabric to be snugged into place with elastic or pulled into graceful folds with a drawstring. Most important, they provide comfort while adapting to the body shape. One essential principle to be remembered is that a casing must always be wide enough to allow the elastic or drawstring to be pulled comfortably. It should be equal in width to the elastic or drawstring, plus ⅛" to ¼"(3 mm to 6 mm) for their thicknesses, plus another ½" (13 mm) for seam allowances. It should be equal in length to the area to which it is to be applied, plus ½" (13 mm).

Applied and SelfCasings

A selfcasing is formed by an extension of the garment that has been folded to the inside (forming a hem) and edgestitched. An applied casing is a separate strip of fabric cut on the straight or bias grain or like a shaped facing. You may use prepackaged bias tape for a quick applied casing. Trim garment seam allowances to ¼" (6 mm) wherever casing is to be applied. For the selfcasing, allow an extra ¼" (6 mm) seam allowance on the long edge. Allow ¼" (6 mm) seam allowances on all edges for an applied casing. Either type can be used on a finished edge, such as the lower edge of a sleeve; at the waistline, to create a blouson effect or with a heading, which extends beyond the casing to form a ruffle.

AT FINISHED EDGE: For a selfcasing, mark and then turn in the fabric along the foldline; baste. Turn in raw edge ¼" (6 mm) and edgestitch to the garment, leaving the desired opening (1). Selfcasings used on a slightly curved edge most be extremely narrow. The stitched fold may need to be stretched or gently eased while stitching. For an applied casing, cut the casing as indicated above. Right sides together, pin one edge of the strip to the garment, turning ends to inside. Stitch in ¼" (6 mm) seam, turn to inside, and press. Finish as selfcasing (2).

WITH A HEADING: The extension for a heading requires extra fabric. For a selfcasing, extend the garment edge, twice the desired width of the heading, plus the casing and a ¼" (6 mm) seam allowance. Mark heading foldline. Turn fabric to inside and baste close to fold. Mark casing seamlines. Stitch, leaving desired opening (3). For an applied casing, extend the garment edge twice the width of the heading plus a ¼" (6 mm) seam allowance. Mark heading foldline. Turn fabric to inside: baste along foldline. Cut casing as instructed in introduction. Turn all edges under ¼" (6 mm) and press. From the wrong side, baste casing in place, matching raw edge of casing with raw edge of heading. Edgestitch bottom and top edges of casing to garment, leaving desired opening (4).

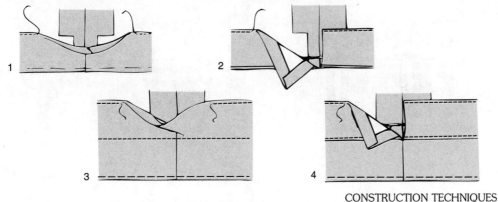

Elastic

Using elastic in a casing will ensure regularity in fit. Unlike the drawstring tie, an elastic pull is not adjustable. It will breathe and move with you, but will not change from the specific measurement you give it. Elastic is used most commonly in sleeves and waistlines. The opening for its insertion is inside the garment. The length of elastic depends upon its stretchability and should be slightly less than the measurement of the body at the casing position, plus ½" (13 mm) for lapping. Usually, the narrower the elastic, the shorter it will have to be. Pull elastic through casing with a bodkin or a safety pin, being careful not to twist it. Lap the ends ½" (13 mm) and stitch securely (1).

Close the opening at the edge of the casing, stretching the elastic as you stitch (2). For an opening across the casing, slipstitch the opening edges together securely (3).

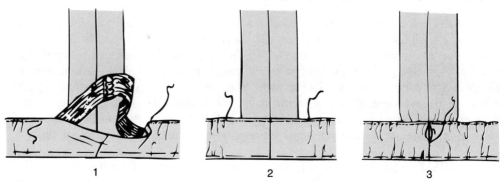

1   2   3

Drawstring

Cord or tubing knotted at the ends, braid, leather strips, ribbon–anything that captures your fancy can be used as a drawstring. Its length should be equal to the measurement of your body at the casing position plus an extra amount to allow for tying a knot or bow. Often quite decorative, the openings for the drawstrings are usually made on the right side of the garment before you make the casing.

There are two types of casing openings for drawstrings. The first, the eyelet or button-hole type, is made in the outer fabric between the casing placement lines before the casing is applied. From the wrong side, stitch casing in place. When the casing is completed, pull drawstring through the casing with a bodkin or safety pin (1). The second type of opening is in a seam. Stitch seam, leaving an opening the width of the drawstring; reinforce each end (2).

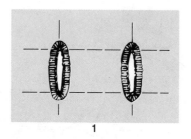

1

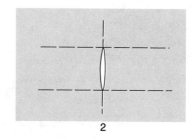

2

Collars

A visible mark of quality workmanship on a garment is its collar. Regardless of style, the collar is a detail that requires careful handling in every stage of construction in order to retain its quality appearance. When you're browsing through a fashion magazine or pattern catalogue, you'll find the variation in collars can be quite staggering. But however exotic the collar shape may seem, three basic shapes–**flat, standing,** and **rolled**–are the starting point for all variations.

The deeper the curve on the collar neck edge, the flatter your collar will lie, especially as the curve corresponds more closely to that of your garment neck edge. A flat collar is almost identical to the garment in the shape of its neck edge; while the opposite extreme, the standing collar, will have a straight or very slightly curved neck edge. The neck edge of a rolled collar can vary in shape from straight to a curve opposite that of the garment. This collar gently rises from the neck seam and turns down to create a rolled edge around the neck. The line along which the collar is turned is called the **roll line** or **roll**.

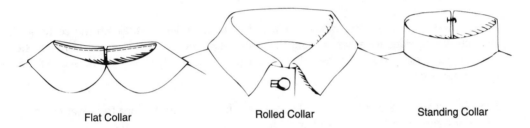

| Flat Collar | Rolled Collar | Standing Collar |

Here are some guidelines for determining whether or not a collar is well made. All collars with corners and center front or back openings should be symmetrical-with identically shaped curves or points, and the inside edge should smoothly encircle the neck without straining or rippling. The underside, or **undercollar**, should never show, nor should seams at the finished edge. Your collar should hug the garment closely without the corners flipping up or the neck seams showing unintentionally at the back or front of the garment.

To achieve these results, always stitch the collar sections together directionally then trim and grade the seam allowances. Corners should be reinforced with tiny stitches [15-20 stitches per inch (6-8 per cm)], trimmed diagonally, and turned gently. Careful pressing will shape the collar as well as prevent the undercollar or outer seam from showing. For detailed information, refer to page 270-273.

The necessary body and shape of the collar are maintained by interfacing, which is usually cut from your collar pattern. Lightweight interfacing can be stitched into the collar seams and then trimmed close to the stitching. For heavier-weight interfacings, the seam allowances are first trimmed away, then the interfacing is catchstitched to the collar along the seamlines. For fusible interfacings, the seam allowances and corners are trimmed away before fusing to the undercollar. A collar meant to be softly rolled, made of a soft or sheer fabric, or part of a very soft style (as in many blouses), may not require interfacing. For more information about interfacing selection, see pages 163 to 167.

Flat Collar

The flat collar with curved edges and angular or curved corners is unquestionably the easiest collar to make. Often called a Peter Pan collar, it has very little roll because it is cut on straight grain with a neck edge curved like the garment neck edge. Both the upper and undercollar sections are cut from the same pattern piece. The collar itself may be one- or two-piece, with or without a front or back opening.

Attach the interfacing to the section that will be your undercollar. Stitch the collar sections with wrong sides together, leaving the neck edge open. Trim, grade, and notch the seams (1). Then turn and press the collar, favoring the outer edge seam of the section that is to be your upper collar.

Even collars with very little roll need some help from you if they are to be set correctly on the garment. With the upper collar on top, work your collar into the shape shown on the pattern envelope: roll the neck edge, as shown, then pin along the roll and just above the neck seam (2). To make attaching the collar easier, baste the neck edges as they fall together along the seamline of the undercollar. If your collar is made in two sections, baste the sections together at the center front neckline.

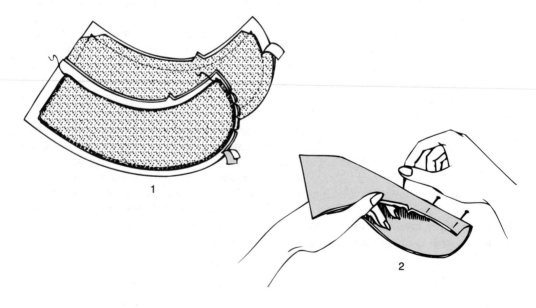

For either a front or back opening, prepare a buttonhole closure by checking the buttonhole placement; then attach your interfacing to the garment and make the necessary buttonholes. If using a zipper, you may insert it before or after attaching your collar.

With the interfaced section of the collar next to the garment, pin the collar in place. matching markings, and baste (3). The upper collar will bubble slightly, but that is as it should be, since you've shaped the collar over your hand.

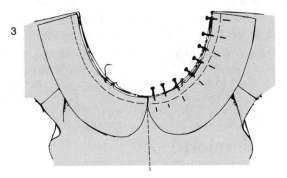

If you are finishing the collar seam with a shaped facing, prepare the facing and finish the unnotched edge. Pin or baste the facing to the neck edge over the collar: again match markings, and stitch. Trim, grade, and clip the seams. Turn the facing to the inside an,press. Understitch the facing to the neckline seam allowance (4).

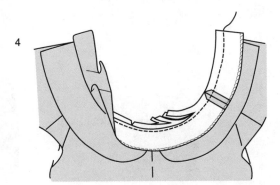

For a zipper closing, turn under the ends of the facing to clear the zipper after it has been turned to the inside. Anchor the facing and fasten the closing with a hook and eye. For a buttonhole closing, turn the facing to the inside, anchor the facing, and complete the back of the buttonholes.

There are other means of finishing the collar and garment seam. You can also use a standard bias facing application (found on page 252) when you wish to reduce bulk in a heavy fabric. Or, for one-piece collars, you may stitch the undercollar to the garment neck edge, keeping the upper collar free to be turned in and slipstitched over the seam.

Rolled Collar

Any molded collar with a pronounced roll around the neck is considered a rolled collar. It is usually cut with a one-piece upper collar and a two-piece bias undercollar that is slightly smaller. The center back seam brings the collar close to the neck, giving excellent control and fit. The standaway version of the rolled collar is cut in one piece on bias grain and folded at the outer edge. The rolled collar can be applied with or without a back neck facing.

The method of construction for a rolled collar depends upon the weight of the garment fabric. For light and mediumweight fabrics, the collar can be stitched to the garment and then the facing attached, as illustrated for Version I. For heavier weight or bulky fabrics, the undercollar should be stitched to the garment and the upper collar to the facing, so as to divide the bulk at the neckline between the two seams. For this method, see Version II, page 272, or the tailoring section, pages 440 to 441.

Rolled Collar, Version I

This version is suitable for light and mediumweight fabrics as the collar is attached to the

neckline before the facing is applied. The collar is usually cut with a two-piece bias undercollar and a slightly larger one-piece upper collar cut on crosswise grain. For the one-piece version, the collar is cut on bias grain for a smoother roll, Both types of collars are applied in the same manner. Careful molding and handling of the roll helps to shape the collar.

Attach interfacing to wrong side of each undercollar section. Stitch center back seam, press open, and trim. For one-piece collars folded at the outer edge, use long running stitches to sew interfacing to collar at the foldline.

Stitch collar sections together, stretching the undercollar to fit and using small stitches at the points. Trim corners carefully so the points will be sharp when turned (1). Turn and press the collar, favoring the upper collar at its outer edges so that the seam is on the undercollar side.

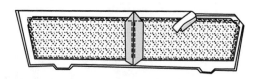

Now establish the **roll line.** Shape your collar until it looks like the pattern illustration, continuing to favor the outer edge of the upper collar. Baste raw edges together from the undercollar side as they fall, and thread trace the roll line (2).

Lap collar over garment, matching neck seamlines; baste (3).

Try the garment on or put it on a dress form to check the collar set and roll. The roll should be smooth, even, and unbroken from front to back. Be sure that the points lie symmetrically against the garment when closed (4). The finished edge of the collar should cover the back neck seam. Adjust the collar at the neck seamline until all of these features are correct. When satisfied with the appearance of your collar, transfer any adjustment lines and remove the collar. Attach garment interfacing and front facing, if necessary.

Staystitch the neck edge of the garment and the facing. Baste the collar to the garment, clipping the garment neck edge only where necessary, and stretching or easing the collar

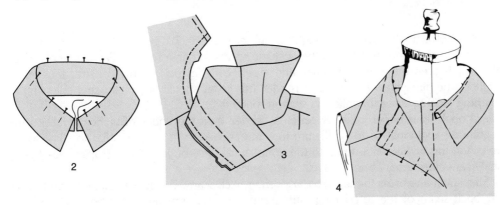

to fit as indicated on your pattern. The upper collar will bubble along the roll when opened out (5). Staystitch the neck edge of the back facing and join to the front facing. Baste the completed facing over the collar, matching markings. Clip the facing edge only where necessary. Stitch on the garment side. Then trim, grade, and continue clipping the seam through all thicknesses. Turn the facing to the inside, baste close to the folded edges, and press. Understitch the facing to the seam allowance close to the neckline seam and to within one inch (25 mm) of the opening edges (6). Or you can use a bias facing to finish the collar seam,

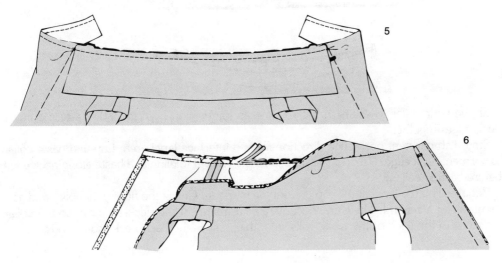

Rolled Collar, Version II

A rolled collar made of heavier weight or bulkier fabric should be constructed so as to eliminate as much bulk as possible in the neckline seams. When a rolled collar has lapels added, the notch area between the collar and lapels can be tricky. This construction version reduces the difficulties. For the best results, this collar should be constructed following the shaping techniques in the tailoring section, page 432.

Although your upper collar is generally larger than the undercollar, heavy fabrics may require an additional ⅛" to ¼" (3 mm to 6 mm) added to the upper collar to allow for the roll. Add this additional amount to the unnotched edges of your collar. Taper back to original seam allowances at neck edge.

First stitch and press the undercollar's center back seam. To reduce bulk, overlap the center back seam of the interfacing, stitch and trim. Or trim away the center back seam allowances, and place ribbon seam binding over the abutted edges and stitch. Attach interfacing to the undercollar (1).

Stitch collar sections together, stretching the undercollar to fit. Use small stitches at the points and trim corners carefully. Turn and press the collar, favoring the upper collar at its outer edges so that the seam, is on the undercollar side (2).

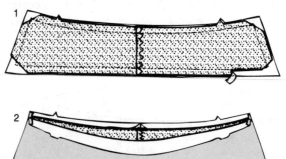

Shape your collar to establish the roll line as for Version I, page 270. Baste the collar neck edges together.

Staystitch garment neck edge directionally and interface lapel area. Lap and baste collar to garment neck edge. (Turn any extended facing back at foldline and baste along neck edge before basting collar.)

Begin rolling the lapel at the top buttonhole marking. Check the fit of your collar and garment, as for Version I. Make any necessary adjustments at the neckline seam so the collar sits close to the back of the neck, rolls smoothly, covers the back neck seam, and falls symmetrically. When you are satisfied with the collar, mark the roll line and transfer adjustment lines before removing it from the garment (3). If you are making bound buttonholes, do them next. (See page 325.)

Baste the undercollar to the garment, clipping the garment neck edge; stitch between the markings (4).

Prepare the facing and staystitch the neck edge. Baste the upper collar to the facing, clipping the facing. Stitch together between markings. Stitching from the garment side to eliminate bubbles that sometimes occur when the collar meets the lapel, join the facing to the garment. Start where it meets the collar, reinforce the corner, and continue around the facing. Trim, grade, and clip the seams (5).

Press collar and garment neck seams open. Turn the facing inside and press. Try on the garment to check the roll of the lapels. Favoring the outer edge of the upper collar and the garment edge below the top buttonhole, pin along the roll and again above the neck seam. Loosely blindstitch both neck seams together as they fall (6). Complete the facing side of buttonholes and anchor facings.

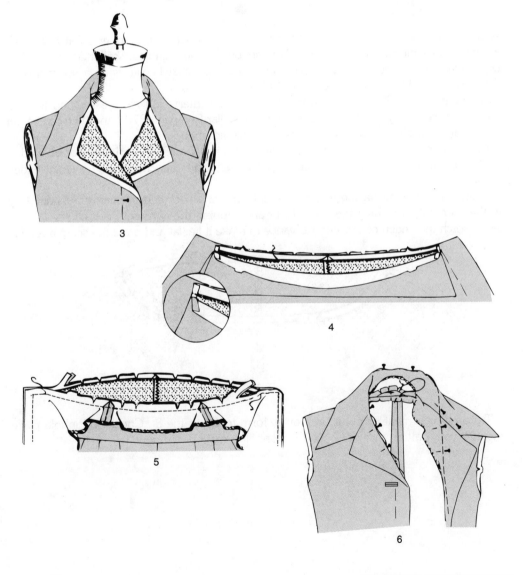

3

4

5

6

Shawl Collar

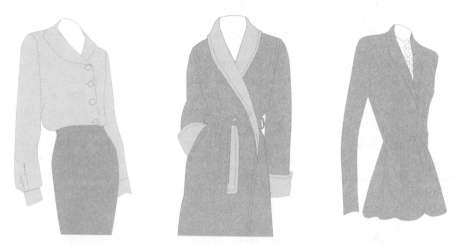

A shawl collar is a special version of the rolled collar in which the upper collar and lapels are cut as one piece. It can vary greatly in shape, having a curved, scalloped, or notched edge. Traditionally found on wrap coats and robes, the shawl collar is usually wrapped in the front and held with a sash, but it can also be buttoned.

For light and mediumweight garment fabrics, the interfacing can be stitched to each undercollar section as for Version I of the rolled collar (see page 270); and then the center back seam of the undercollar is stitched and pressed open.

For heavier weight and bulky fabrics, the interfacing should be overlapped or abutted as for Version II of the rolled collar (see page 272) and then attached to the seamed undercollar.

Then attach the interfacing to the garment front and neck edges. Stitch the undercollar to the garment, stretching the collar to fit and clipping the garment neck edge as necessary. Notch the undercollar seam allowance to make it lie flat and press the seam open (1).

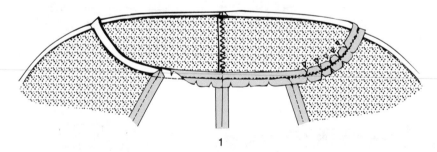

1

Try on the garment or put it on a dress form to check the fit. Check buttonhole placement. If your pattern includes bound buttonholes, make them now.

Before joining the collar/facing section to the garment, reinforce the inner corner with small stitches along the seamline, pivoting at the marking. Clip to the corner (2).

Stitch the center back seam of the collar/facing and press it open. Then pin it to the back facing along the neck and shoulder edges, clipping the back neck facing where necessary. Stitch, pivoting at corners. Press the seam open. Trim excess fullness at corners and catchstitch. Finish the unnotched edge of the facing. Stitch the collar/facing unit to the garment and undercollar, stretching the undercollar to fit. Trim and grade seams, leaving the garment seam allowance widest; notch curves (3).

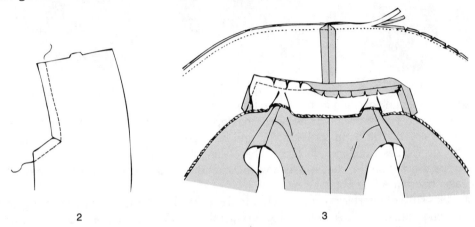

2   3

Turn the collar/facing to the right side and press. Favor the outer edge of the collar so that the seam is on the undercollar side. Below the place where the collar begins to roll, favor the front edge of the garment so that the seam is on the facing side.

Try the garment on again or put it on a dress form to set the roll of the collar. The roll should be smooth and unbroken and the collar should lie close to the back of the neck. When you have achieved the desired effect with the collar/facing in its proper position, pin the facing in place, continue to favor the collar and garment edges as mentioned previously. Blindstitch the facing seam allowances, as they fall, to the garment seam allowances at the neck edge. Also blindstitch the facing edges in place (4). Complete the underside of any buttonholes.

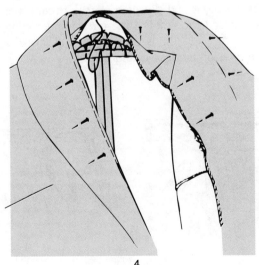

4

Standing Collar

Generally known as the Mandarin or band collar, this basically uncomplicated collar is able to take on many exciting forms. It can be a stiff and close military collar or a soft loose band, and it can be cut in one or two sections depending on whether the finished edge is straight or curved. The depth of the collar and how closely it is fitted to the neck greatly affect the overall design of your garment. This collar will always work and look better if you cut your interfacing on the bias. It will curve around your neck smoothly-without stiff cracks or breaks that mar a fine appearance.

Cut a bias strip of interfacing and attach it to the collar. If collar is cut in one section, use long running stitches to hold interfacing along foldline. Fold the collar with right sides together and stitch the ends to within ⅝" (15 mm) of the neckline edge. Trim and grade the seam allowances (1). Turn and press the ends only, **not** the foldline, or you may have an undesirable crease in the finished collar.

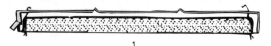

1

For either a front or back opening, insert your zipper or facings.

Baste and stitch the interfaced side of the collar to the garment neck edge, matching all markings and clipping the garment where necessary. Trim and grade the seams, leaving the garment seam allowance widest (2). Press the seam toward the collar. Trim and turn in the remaining edge of the collar and slipstitch over the seam. For hard-to-handle fabrics, you may want to baste close to the fold of the turned-under edge before slipstitching the edge in place (3). Fasten the collar ends with hooks and thread eyes. Complete the buttonholes and anchor the facing in place as required.

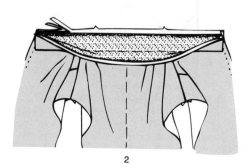

2

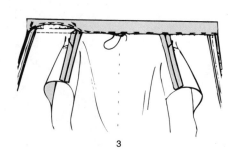

3

Foldover Bias Collar

A foldover bias collar, which is commonly known as a turtleneck collar and sometimes mis-named a rolled collar, is really a one-piece standing collar cut on the bias and rolled or fold-ed over to cover the neck seam.

Cut interfacing on the bias to extend ⅝" (15 mm) beyond the foldline of the collar; stitch or fuse to collar and sew along the foldline with long running stitches (1). Fold the collar with wrong sides together and stitch the ends to within ⅝" (15 mm) of the neck edge. Trim and grade the seams. Turn and then press the ends only; do not press the foldline. Staystitch the bodice neck edge and insert zipper or apply facings where needed.

Baste the interfaced collar edge to the garment, clipping the garment neck edge where necessary, and stretching or easing the collar to fit. Stitch, trim, and grade all seams, leav-ing the garment seam allowance widest (2).

Press the stitched seam allowances toward the collar. Lap the remaining raw edge in place at the seamline and baste loosely. To establish the roll on the garment, turn the fin-ished edge of the collar down to just cover the neck seam, stretching gently until it fits the contour. Thread trace the roll line through all layers. Remove basting, trim, and turn in remaining edge as it falls over seam; slipstitch (3). (For bulky fabrics, overcast edge and blindstitch in place.) Fasten the ends with hooks and eyes.

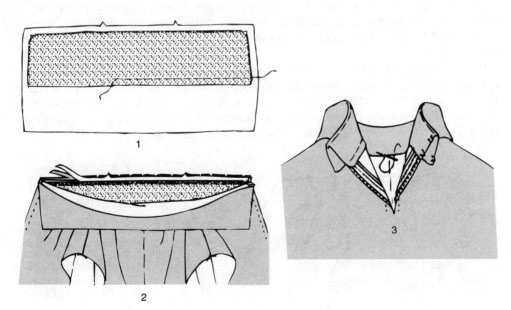

1

2

3

Tie Collar

This collar, basically a foldover or standing collar ending in a tie, adds a delightfully graceful touch to any garment. The difference between the two collar styles is only a matter of dimension; the tie will generally be wider on the foldover collar.

Attach the interfacing to the collar and sew along the foldline with long running stitches. Do not interface ties: added bulk would cause difficulty when tying. Reinforce the seamline at the point where collar and tie meet clip to the seamline. Fold the collar; stitch the tie along the ends and to, its termination points. (For a back opening, you have two collar sections. Stitch the back opening ends; then, stitch the tie ends to their termination points.) Trim and grade seams and corners (1). Turn the collar and tie ends; press the seams lightly.

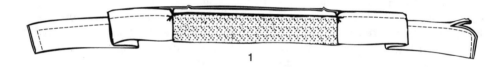

1

Staystitch garment neck edge. Stitch facing to the garment, stopping where the collar begins. Clip to the end of the stitching. Trim and grade the seam allowances. Turn and press. Baste facing and garment neck edges together and anchor the facing at the shoulders.

Baste one edge of collar to garment, clipping the garment neck edge where necessary. A space has been allowed between the termination point of the collar and center marking in order to knot the tie. Stitch, trim, grade, and clip the seam (2), Press the seam toward the collar. Turn in the remaining edge and slipstitch over the seam (3). Complete buttonholes. For a back closing, fasten the collar with hooks and eyes.

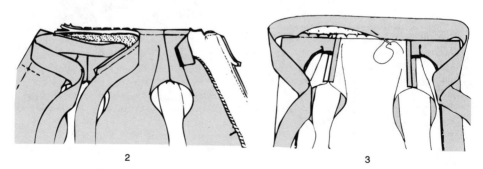

2   3

Collar with Stand

Many man-tailored shirts and jackets have collars with stands. Such a collar has practically no roll; it turns down at the top of the stand and nearly always has a front closure.

Prepare the collar the same as you would for a flat collar, page 268. Apply the interfacing to the wrong side of one collar stand section. (Sometimes the stand is an extension of the collar, and then the interfacing is applied to both the undercollar and stand in one piece.)

Pin the interfaced stand to the undercollar and the remaining stand to the upper collar, right sides together, and baste. Stitch the ends and upper edge to within ⅝" (15 mm) of the neck edges. Trim, grade, clip, and notch the seam allowances (1). Then turn the stand and press. The collar is now encased in the stand.

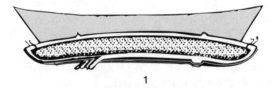

1

Complete the garment front opening. Staystitch the garment neck edge. Pin or baste the interfaced stand to the garment neck edge, clipping the garment as necessary. Stitch, trim, and grade the seams, leaving the garment seam allowance widest (2). Press the seam toward the stand. On the remaining free edge of the stand, trim and turn the seam allowance under and baste close to the fold. Slipstitch the folded edge over the seam (3). Topstitch if desired. Make machine-worked buttonholes.

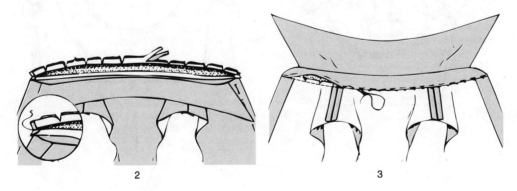

2   3

Cowls

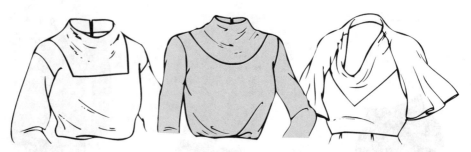

Cowls can drape softly around the face or plunge dramatically down the front or back of a garment. A cowl collar is simply a very wide foldover bias collar crushed down around the neckline. A cowl neckline usually consists of a yoke cut on the bias for draping ability and a stay cut on straight grain for reinforcement so that the cowl will drape as the designer intended.

Join the yoke sections at the shoulders. Press seams open and clip. Baste ribbon seam binding over the back seamlines of the yoke between the markings.

Prepare a narrow, shaped facing, finishing the inner unnotched edge as desired. Pin, baste, and stitch the facing to the yoke; trim and grade the seam, press it open and clip where necessary. **Roll** the facing to the inside.

Stitch the back and front stay at the shoulders. Press seams open. Finish the stay neckline with bias tape or a 2" (5 cm) wide bias strip of fabric, applied as a bias facing. Place the right side of the stay on the wrong side of the yoke. Baste the raw edges together, stretching the lower yoke edge to fit (1).

Baste and stitch the yoke to the garment. Insert your zipper and blindstitch the facing in place. If your fabric needs a weight in order to drape properly, cover a flat weight (page 457) and attach it to the cowl with a French tack (2). Experiment with the placement of the weight to determine its most functional position.

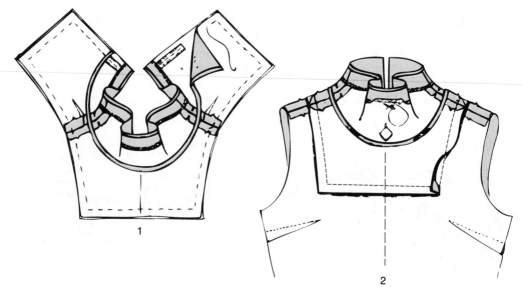

1

2

Detachable Collar

This category includes two types of collars–the first lies on top of an existing collar; the second fits inside a collarless neckline. You can use this collar to provide a removable, washable trim on a garment that requires dry cleaning.

The most familiar type of detachable collar forms a decorative overlay to your garment's original collar. It must be longer and wider in order to cover the existing collar. Unless your pattern is designed for a detachable collar, you will probably have to adjust its dimensions so that the decorative collar has the same shape and size as the garment collar when it is worn. Determine how much to add to the pattern by comparing the weight and depth of your garment fabric with the fabric for your detachable collar.

Construct the desired collar and stitch its neck edges together ⅛" (3 mm) from the seamline in the seam allowance. Clip the seam allowances to the stitching every ½" (13 mm) so the detachable collar neckline can spread to fit the garment neckline smoothly.

Extend the collar neck edge with bias binding to allow for fastening it to the garment (1). For a ½" (13 mm) finished binding, cut a bias strip 1¾" (4.5 cm) wide and the length of the neckline plus 1" (25 mm). Then apply the bias as a single binding to the collar neck edge, shaping the binding and clipped edge of the collar as you work so it will fit the garment neck edge (2). Grade seam allowances if necessary. Pin the collar to the neck edge of the garment, matching seamlines, and slip baste the binding to the neck facing (3).

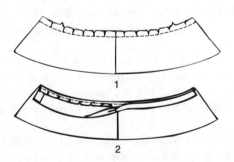

If you don't have a pattern for the second type of detachable collar, it is possible to use a collar from another pattern with the same neckline. Construct the collar and finish the edges with bias binding in the same manner as described above. Then attach it to your garment with snaps or slip basting. If the closure on your collar does not correspond to that of the garment, fasten the collar in place with snaps rather than slip basting.

If you wish to add matching detachable cuffs to complement your detachable collar, refer to Cuffs, page 303, for detailed instructions.

For a More Perfect Collar

Here are some professional techniques that contribute so much to the finished appearance of every collar.

Always stitch the collar sections together directionally, stitching with the collar grain. Start stitching at the center first, then stitch toward one end. Repeat for the other half, overlapping stitches ½" (13 mm). At corners use 15 to 20 stitches per inch (6-8 per cm) and one stitch across the point when the point is very sharp.

Any rolled collar should be characterized by a smooth roll with the neck seam completely covered. The pattern piece for the upper collar is usually larger than that for the under-collar. This ease allows the collar to roll and accommodates the depth of your fabric. However, only an average roll depth can be allowed on most pattern pieces, so you may have to add as much as ¼" to ⅜" (6 mm to 10 mm) to the upper collar to allow for very bulky or heavy fabric. Then be sure to ease or stretch the collar sections to each other when you stitch them together.

The importance of trimming to reduce bulk cannot be stressed enough as it can be the single contributing factor to an unattractive collar. Trim the seams, grading the ones to be enclosed so that the seam allowance of the upper collar is left the widest. Trim the corners diagonally as closely as possible without cutting into your stitching to ensure that the corner seams will miter once the collar is turned, You should not trim ravelly fabrics closer than ¼" (6 mm) from the seamline. Notch or clip curves so that the seam allowance will lie flat without pulls or bumps when the collar is turned.

There is a professional way to turn and press a collar swiftly and accurately. Prepress the collar **before** you turn it to the right side and you will not only obtain a more finished appearance, but eliminate problems with "shine" and handling of the fabric on the right side as well. Press the collar seam allowances open over a point presser or a tailor board. Then press the seam allowances toward the undercollar side. Holding the seam allowances together at one corner, turn the collar corner by pulling the upper collar over your hand. Repeat for the other corner. If necessary, use a needle or pin from the right side to pull the corners to a point. **Never** use the point of a scissors to poke corners out because you can easily poke a hole in your fabric.

Press the outer edge, using a press cloth. Carefully **favor** the upper collar edge by rolling the outer seam just slightly to the underside of the collar. This ensures that the seam will not be visible at the edge of the completed collar. For thick or resilient fabrics, flatten and smooth the outer edge with a pounding block.

The best way to ensure that your collar will look right is to fit it before you permanently attach it to the garment. Baste the collar to the neck edge, **lapping** the seams for easier fitting, rather than matching them right sides together. Then try on the garment or put it on a dress form and check the features mentioned above, as well as those mentioned in the preceding pages.

When you attach the collar, take special care to align the markings of the collar with those on the garment at the shoulders, front, and back. To help ensure a perfectly symmetrical collar, stitch the neck edge directionally.

Sleeves, Sleeve Finishes, and Cuffs

A sleeve should be a thing of beauty and comfort. It should look handsome, conforming to the shape of your arm without signs of pulling or straining. Since the arm is probably the most active part of the body, the sleeve should perform well in motion without causing discomfort or distorting the fit.

The comfort of a sleeve is determined mostly by the fit and ease of the two points of action–the upper arm and elbow. The sleeve cap must be neither too tight nor too loose, and in any long or three-quarter sleeve there must be room for the elbow to bend. When the arm is at ease, the sleeve should hang evenly and gracefully in a curve that corresponds to the natural curve of your arm.

Sleeve Types

A profusion of sleeves is at your disposal, in lengths and shapes to suit every whim. Most of them fall into three basic types. The first type is the **SET-IN SLEEVE,** which joins the garment in a seam that encircles the arm over the shoulder. The area of the sleeve at the end of the shoulder or upper arm, called the *sleeve cap,* must be shaped and eased to curve smoothly into the armhole.

The second type, the **RAGLAN SLEEVE,** joins the bodice in a diagonal seam extending to the neckline area, providing a smooth, round silhouette and a great degree of comfort. It tends to be a good choice for hard-to-fit shoulders, since the diagonal seam can be readily adjusted to accommodate differences in the individual figure. Shoulder shaping is achieved by a curved seam or a shaped dart.

The third type, the **KIMONO SLEEVE,** is cut in one with the garment or a part of it, such as a yoke. If it is loose-fitting or short, it may simply be reinforced in the underarm seam, but tighter versions frequently call for gussets or further refinements designed to combine greater comfort with a finer degree of fit.

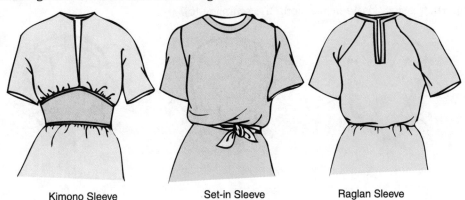

Kimono Sleeve   Set-in Sleeve   Raglan Sleeve

Set-in Sleeve

The one-piece set-in sleeve is the most classic and most popular of these sleeves, and allows for many variations in style. Slightly more refined in fit, the two-piece set-in sleeve is inserted in exactly the same manner, but often calls for the fairly sophisticated sleeve finishes explained in the tailoring section, page 443. If you are using heavy or bulky fabrics, such as boiled wool or velveteen, which cannot be eased, see page 92 as a guide to adjusting the pattern tissue.

To begin your sleeve, run a line of thread tracing, as shown, along the crosswise grain of the sleeve cap. Easestitch on the right side of the sleeve cap [about 8-10 stitches per inch (3-4 per cm)] just inside the seamline in the seam allowance between markings, as shown. An additional row of easestitching ¼" (6 mm) from the first row in the seam allowance will give you more control over the fullness and simplify the process of easing (1).

If the sleeve is long or three-quarter length and snug, elbow shaping is needed for comfortable movement, either by easing or using darts. To ease, stitch with large stitches along the seamline on the back edge of the sleeve between markings. Pin the sleeve seam, matching notches and markings; adjust ease (2). Where darts are indicated, stitch and press downward. Match markings; pin and stitch the sleeve seam (3).

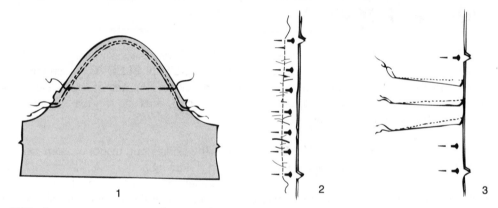

1   2   3

With the garment wrong side out, place sleeve in the armhole, right sides together. Pin together at the notches, markings, and underarm seam, being sure to use the stitching line at the underarm for the sleeve when indicated on your pattern (4). Pull the easing threads up until the sleeve fits the armhole; secure thread ends around a pin in a figure-eight fashion (5). Adjust the fullness and pin about every ½" (13 mm). If not indicated by markings, be sure to leave one inch (25 mm) of flat area at the shoulder seam where the grain will not permit easing. Baste firmly along the seamline (6).

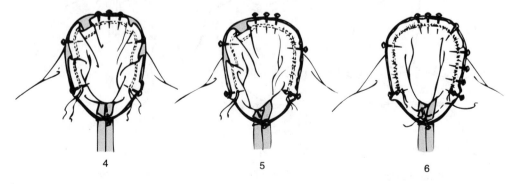

4   5   6

Now try on the garment. First check the line of thread tracing. If it is not perfectly parallel to the floor, you have an obvious indication that a slight adjustment is in order. If the grainline slants or ripples, you will find a quick referral to Sleeves, page 92, extremely helpful. Then check the length, allowing for the anticipated finish (hem, cuff, etc.) and any blousing in a full sleeve. Finally, be sure that the ease is located where it is needed, adjusting it for your particular upper arm shape and shoulder curve.

After fitting, tie the ease thread ends securely and remove the sleeve from the armhole. Holding the curve of the sleeve cap over a tailor's ham, shrink the fullness by using a steam iron. Begin by steaming the seam allowance to shape the sleeve cap, being careful not to press beyond the stitches (7).

Hold the sleeve in your hands, and turn in the seam allowance along the ease thread. You should have a smooth rolling sleeve cap without puckers or pulling. If dimples remain on the roll near the seamline, slide fullness along the threads until your problem has been eliminated and steam again. Do not be overly alarmed if your unattached sleeve still retains some puckering, as some fabrics do not respond well to shrinking and may need additional handling when the sleeve is being placed into the armhole for permanent stitching (8). Before you permanently set in the sleeve, complete the sleeve finish. The separate piece will be easier to maneuver than the entire garment. Replace the sleeve in the armhole, pinning and basting it in place. Try it on, checking the shoulder and arm shaping and the sleeve finish.

For a problem sleeve, place the garment on a dress form. Turn in the sleeve seam allowance along ease thread and, from the right side, pin into armhole. Pin and slip-baste in place, working with the sleeve cap until you have a smooth rolling shape (9).

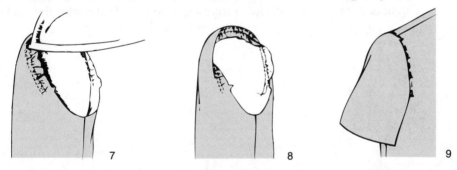

7   8   9

When the sleeve is set in to your satisfaction, start at the underarm and stitch the armhole seam with the sleeve side up, controlling the fullness as you work (10).

Stitch again in the seam allowance ¼" (6 mm) from the first row of stitching. To reduce bulk. trim close to this second row. If the garment is unlined. overcast or zigzag the seam allowances to prevent ravelling (11). Never press sleeve cap seam after the sleeve is set in. Simply turn the seam allowances toward the sleeve to give a smooth line to the seam and support to the sleeve cap.

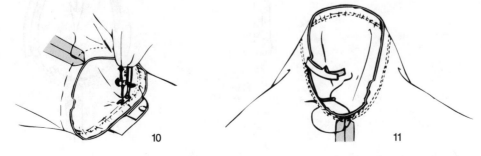

10   11

There are a few extreme instances when the sleeve cap seam is still not perfectly smooth and rounded–such as lightweight or limp fabrics, fabrics which do not ease, certain designs, and certain figure irregularities. These situations can prove difficult and may call for lambs-wool padding. We must stress that it is not a remedy for a poorly set-in sleeve. For detailed instructions on how to insert sleeve padding, put lining in a sleeve, or set in a two-piece sleeve, refer to the tailoring section, page 442.

Raglan Sleeve

This sleeve is well liked for its comfortable fit and relatively easy construction. Its diagonal seamline can lead into another seam or form part of a neckline. It can be cut on the straight or bias grain, with a one- or two-piece construction. The shoulder curve is part of the sleeve shape, and is created by a dart, a seam, or gathers.

First stitch the dart or shoulder seam and the sleeve seam. Press the seams open (1). Pin and baste the sleeve into the armhole, matching notches, symbols, and underarm seams (2). Try on the garment.

The curve of the dart or seam should conform to your own shoulder and upper arm shape, with the sharpest part of the curve neither above nor below the point of your shoulder. Test it, standing in a normal position with your arms down. Then swing your arms, making sure there is enough room for comfortable movement. Adjust if necessary, referring to the hints in the adjustment section, pages 93 to 95.

Stitch, then stitch again ¼" (6 mm) away in the underarm seam allowance between the notches. Clip at ends of the second row of stitching, trim close to this stitching, and overcast or zigzag the edge. Press the seam open above the clips (3).

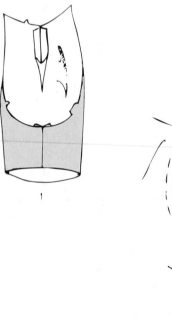

1

2

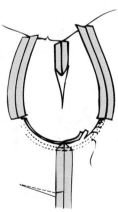

3

Kimono Sleeve

The classic kimono sleeve is a gem of simplicity. The T-shaped garment that every child has made for a favorite doll is a perfect example. However, arms are seldom at right angles to the body; when they are in a relaxed position, the T-shape creates folds. This draped effect can be a graceful design feature in a kimono sleeve with a large opening; however, as the arm opening becomes smaller and shaping adjustments are made to eliminate folds, further sewing refinements are necessary for comfort and strength.

INVISIBLE REINFORCEMENTS: If the sleeve is cut as an extension of the bodice, the main thing to remember is that the underarm area must be adequately reinforced, since it undergoes considerable strain with arm movements. Pin the back to the front at shoulders and sides. Center a piece of stretched bias tape over the seamline at the underarm. Baste both seams, then clip the curve, being careful not to cut the tape. Fit your garment, then stitch the seam, using a smaller stitch [15-20 per inch (6-8 per cm) according to your fabric] on the curves. Press the seam open (1).

An alternative method is to stitch the underarm seam, using smaller stitches on the curve. Clip the curve; press the seam open. Center a piece of stretched bias tape over the open seam and baste through the seamline. Stitch on both sides of the seamline as you spread the clips, catching only the tape and seam allowances (2).

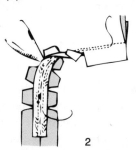

KIMONO SLEEVE CUT WITH YOKE: When the kimono sleeve is cut in one with a yoke, you will get a closer fit without the additional construction of a gusset. The seaming detail allows for easier shaping and fitting adjustments. Reinforce the inner corners at the point where the yoke ends and the sleeve begins; clip to markings. Stitch the yoke/sleeve front and yoke/sleeve back sections together along the shoulder and sleeve seams. Press the seams open (1).

With the yoke/sleeve section dropped into the dress section, place right sides together. Pin and baste the yoke/sleeve section to the dress along the bottom of the yoke and underarm, matching markings. Stitch from the yoke/sleeve side, pivoting at corners. At the underarm, stitch again ¼" (6 mm) away. Trim close to the second row of stitching and overcast. Press the garment seam toward the yoke. The underarm seam remains unpressed (2).

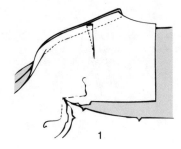

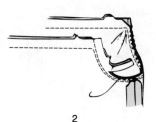

Gussets

Just the mere mention of the word "gussets" can cause panic if you aren't accustomed to sewing them. But don't despair–you can attain foolproof results with even the trickiest of gussets by using appropriate reinforcement and **very careful** stitching.

A gusset is a triangular or diamond-shaped piece of fabric set into a garment at a slash. Most commonly it will be found at the underarm curve of a kimono sleeve, set in a slash that cuts across the garment from front to back. It makes possible a longer, slimmer kimono sleeve with an armhole closer to the body–in general, a more sophisticated fit than the kimono sleeve without a gusset. Another by-product of the gusset is added comfort through increased flexibility of the sleeve. Because the area under the arm receives a maximum amount of strain and needs ease for movement, the gusset should always be cut on the bias.

The gusset can be one- or two-piece construction–with a seam joining the two sections. Occasionally the gusset is combined with a portion of the garment, such as the underarm section of the sleeve or a side panel of the bodice.

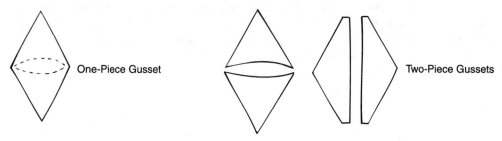

One-Piece Gusset Two-Piece Gussets

There is very little difference between the insertion of one- and two-piece diamond gussets. The gusset can be shaped by either a contour dart or a seam to eliminate bulk under the arm. The other variation, a triangular gusset, is quite simple to construct because the gusset and the garment side seams are continuous.

REINFORCING: Before you slash the garment. it must be very carefully reinforced. Cut 2" (5 cm) bias squares of underlining or 4" (10 cm) long pieces of ribbon seam binding for each slash point. Center them over the slash points and stitching lines on the right side of both front and back sections. Or, for fabrics that ravel easily, use a **very lightweight** fusible interfacing on the wrong side of your fabric at the slash point **before** you underline. For all reinforcements, stitch along the stitching lines, using short stitches [15-20 per inch (6-8 per cm)] and taking one stitch across the slash point (1).

Cut between stitching lines right up to the point. Turn reinforcement squares or seam binding to wrong side of garment so they can be treated as a seam allowance while you are pinning and stitching (2).

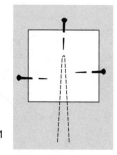

1

2

DIAMOND GUSSETS: Stitch all bodice seams, ending stitching at markings as shown on your pattern and leaving gusset area open. Press all seams open. Prepare gusset by stitching any dart or shaped seam, if necessary. Pin or baste gusset to garment, right sides together, placing stitching line of garment along seamlines of gusset.

From the garment side, stitch gusset to garment. Use small stitches and stitch on the garment along side the previous stitching, beginning at the seams or markings and pivoting carefully at the point, treating the reinforcement patch or seam binding as seam allowances. End stitching at seams or markings so that the side seam allowances of the garment are not caught in the stitching. Press all gusset seams toward the garment.

TRIANGULAR GUSSETS: Stitch shoulder seam only and press open. Right sides together, pin or baste the gusset pieces into their corresponding garment slashes, placing stitching lines of garment along seamlines of gusset. Stitch gussets in place the same as for the diamond gusset, being very careful at the slash points. Press gusset seams toward garment. Matching gusset seamlines of the garment front and back, stitch underarm seam of bodice and sleeve in a continuous seam. Press the side seam open, clipping where needed.

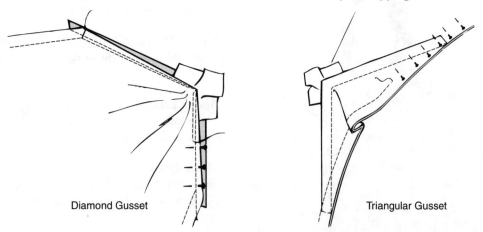

Diamond Gusset   Triangular Gusset

FINISHING: Pull all thread ends to wrong side of gusset and knot. If you used squares of underlining for reinforcement, trim the square of fabric to ³⁄₈" (10 mm). Press the gusset seam toward the garment (1). To further strengthen the gusset on sporty or casual clothes, topstitch close to the gusset seam on the outside, as shown (2).

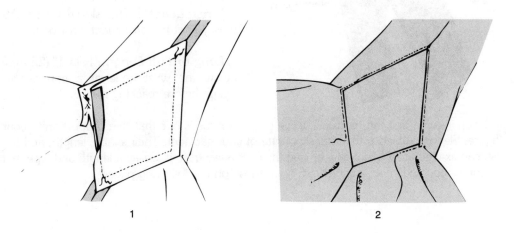

1   2

Sleeve Finishes

Let every gesture of the arm display a perfectly polished sleeve finish–tastefully suited to the overall design, neatly pressed, and flawlessly completed. Feel free to adapt the finish in accordance with the pattern design and your fabric.

The style description on your pattern envelope includes mention of the sleeve length preferred by the designer. Check the length of your sleeve when it is pinned into the armhole, referring to the diagram below for an explanation of the designer's length. If a cuff is a part of the design, be sure to take its depth into account in the total sleeve length. Also allow for blousing in a full sleeve.

Here are the suggested lengths that should be used for reference when you are adjusting your pattern or fitting your garment.

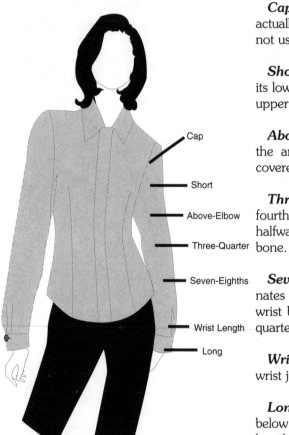

Cap: This is a very, very short sleeve, actually an extension of the shoulder and not usually continued under the arm.

Short: The typical short sleeve lies with its lower edge relatively straight across the upper arm.

Above-Elbow: As the name suggests, the arm above the elbow is completely covered by the sleeve.

Three-Quarter: This sleeve is three-fourths the length of the arm. It ends halfway between the elbow and the wrist bone.

Seven-Eighths: A sleeve which terminates approximately 2" (5 cm) above the wrist bone or halfway between the three-quarter and the long sleeve.

Wrist Length: This sleeve grazes the wrist just at the prominent wrist bone.

Long or Full Length: Falls 1" (25 mm) below the wrist bone at a comfortable length before reaching the hand.

Keep in mind that the "correct" sleeve length for you is one that is in proportion to your figure. Sleeves influence the total silhouette of your garment. Their shape, length, and finish can exaggerate a figure flaw or lead the eyes away from it. Select a length and type that becomes you and choose your finish from those on the following pages.

Finish a Sleeve with Finesse

A well-made finish enhances the sleeve and handsomely sets off the completed garment. Be precise–avoid sloppy plackets, uneven hems, and mismatched closures with half-sewn snaps. Consider the mood of your garment when choosing a sleeve finish, because varying the finish can give your sleeve an entirely different appearance. A shirt- sleeve placket is perfect for casual clothes, while a fragile thread loop and button closing would be more suitable for dressy or couture garments.

Try on the sleeve. For any of the lapped closures, check to see that the lap will open properly when finished. It should be in back of the sleeve (above the little finger) and open toward the body. Be doubly sure that the right and left sleeves open in opposite directions so that your careful work won't result in two left openings. Establish the location of any buttons or fastenings. Remember that a long sleeve without a closing needs to have an opening big enough for the hand to pass through, while the sleeve with a closing can have a smaller opening circumference. Allow ½" to 1" (13 mm to 25 mm) for ease between the circumference of the arm and the opening when the sleeve is fastened.

Fit the sleeve, then remove it from the garment for easier handling when you apply your sleeve finish. Use interfacing for a precise, well-shaped look that lasts through the rigors of wearing and cleaning. Careful matching, stitching, and trimming are natural steps toward achieving a sleeve finish with savoir-faire.

Straight Hem

Although it is the most basic and easiest of all sleeve finishes, the straight hem can be quite elegant as it gracefully circles the arm in a smooth curve. Careful construction and an appropriate interfacing are necessary for a hem that is to hold its curved line without "breaking." The interfacing you use should be determined by your fabric for the desired effect-whether it be a creased edge or a rolled edge. Cut the interfacing in bias strips equal in length to the circumference of the finished sleeve plus ½" (13 mm) and equal in width to the depth of the hem.

Stitch the underarm seam of the sleeve. Place the lower edge of interfacing ⅝" (15 mm) below the hemline; overlap ends ½" (13 mm) and sew, as shown. Sew the interfacing to the garment or underlining along the hemline with long running stitches and along the upper edge of the interfacing with long catchstitches. For a sleeve edge that will be topstitched or edgestitched, trim interfacing along foldline and catchstitch in place. Turn up the hem to cover the interfacing. Baste close to the fold. Check to see that the hem is an even depth all around, and trim if necessary. Finish the raw edge of your hem with a stitch and overcast, zigzag or serger finish. Blindstitch the edge to the underlining of your garment fabric.

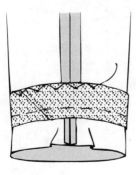
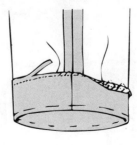

Facings

SHAPED FACING: Overcast the unnotched edge of the sleeve facing with hand or machine stitching. Stitch the facing ends together. Trim the seam allowances to ¼" (6 mm) and press open (1). Stitch the facing to the sleeve; then trim and grade the seam (2). Turn the facing to the inside, favoring the outside of the sleeve, and press. Blindstitch the free edge to the garment or underlining (3).

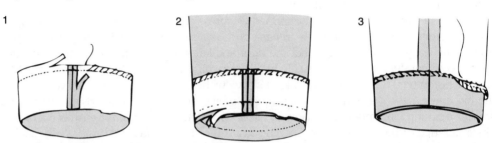

SELF-FACING WITH SLIT: This finish continues part way up the vertical seam and usually includes mitered corners. Interface the opening and hem before you stitch the sleeve seam. If you do not have an interfacing pattern piece, use your sleeve pattern as a guide, and cut the interfacing on the bias equal in width to the depth of the hem and equal in length to the circumference of the sleeve plus 1¼" (3.2 cm). Position the interfacing so that it extends ⅛" (15 mm) past the hemline and slit foldlines, as shown. Sew the interfacing to the sleeve or underlining with long running stitches along the hemline and slit foldlines and with catchstitches along the upper edges (1).

Miter the corners of your sleeve by turning the edges to the outside along the hemline and foldlines; then stitch to the corners (2). Trim and press the seams open (3). Stitch the long sleeve seam to the appropriate marking. Turn the corners and the facing to the inside along the foldlines and hemline; press. Baste close to the fold. Overcast the raw edges, by hand or machine. Blindstitch the free edges to the sleeve or underlining. Reinforce the end of the slit with a bar tack on the inside sleeve (4).

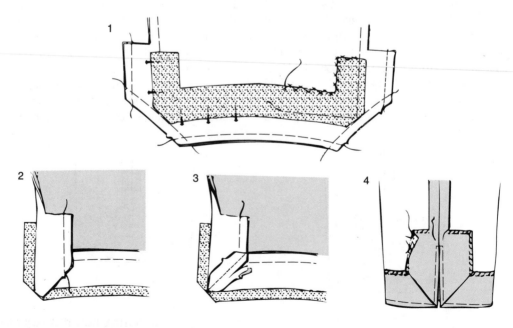

BIAS FACING: Cut a 1½" (3.8 cm) wide bias strip in a length equal to the circumference of the sleeve plus 2" (5 cm). With raw edges even, pin the bias strip to the sleeve, right sides together. Pin ends together on straight grain. Remove bias strip from sleeve and stitch ends in a diagonal seam; trim to ¼" (6 mm) and press open (1). Then stitch the bias to the sleeve; trim and grade the seam allowances (2). Turn the bias inside, favoring the right side of the sleeve, and press. Turn the raw edge under ¼" (6 mm) and slipstitch to the sleeve or underlining (3).

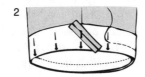

LAPPED CLOSING WITH ROLLED HEM: Generally used with a buttoned cuff, this closing allows for a cuff opening without the necessity of making a sleeve placket. Reinforce the area to be hemmed, using small stitches along the seamline through the markings; clip to the markings. Trim the seam allowance between the clips to ⅜" (10 mm); trim any underlining up to the stitching (1). Turn raw edge along stitching to form a rolled hem and slipstitch (2). Whipstitch the ends. Stitch underarm seam, add gathers, and apply cuff (3).

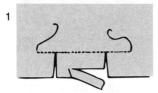
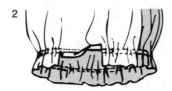

Casings

For a casing at the edge of a sleeve, turn up the fabric along the foldline and baste. Turn in raw edge ¼" (6 mm) and edgestitch to sleeve, leaving the desired opening (1). Or an applied casing can be formed from a separate strip of fabric or bias tape and applied like a shaped facing. Insert elastic into casing, overlap ends ½" (13 mm), and stitch securely. Complete edgestitching (2).

For a casing with a heading, which forms a ruffle at the edge of the sleeve, extra fabric is required for the extension. Turn fabric to inside along heading foldline and baste close to fold. Mark casing seamlines and stitch, leaving desired opening (3). An applied casing can also be used with a heading. Insert elastic and stitch securely. Stitch opening closed.

Refer to section on casings, page 265.

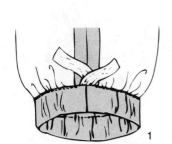

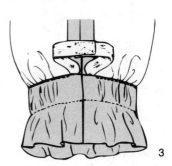

Placket Opening for Cuffs

For cuffs which fit snugly around the wrist, a placket must be inserted into the sleeve before the cuff is applied.

FACED PLACKET: For the placket facing, cut a 2½" (6.5 cm) wide strip of self-fabric the length of the opening plus 1" (25 mm). Finish the raw edge on the sides and one end of the facing with hand overcasting, zigzag, or serger stitching. Right sides together, center it over the slash markings with the raw edge at the bottom. Stitch along the stitching lines with small stitches, taking one stitch across the point. Slash carefully to the point, without cutting through the stitching (1). Turn the facing inside and press (2). Complete sleeve with a binding, cuff, or hem; then blindstitch the facing to the underlining or the garment (3).

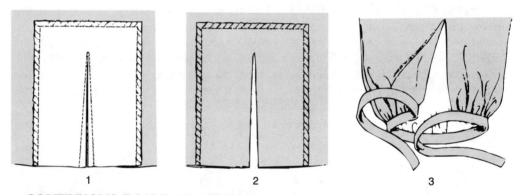

CONTINUOUS BOUND PLACKET: Inserted in a slash or a seam, the continuous bound placket can be an extremely durable and simple opening for sleeves. Since the edges of the placket overlap, it can be used with any lapped cuff.

TO INSERT IN A SLASH, reinforce the area to be slashed with small stitches along the stitching line, taking a stitch across the point. Slash to the point (1). Cut a straight strip of self-fabric 1½" (3.8 cm) wide and twice the length of the slash. Spread slash open and, with right sides together, place its stitching line ¼" (6 mm) from one long edge of strip. Stitch with small stitches on garment beside previous stitching (2). From the right side, press lap away from garment. Turn the free edge in ¼" (6 mm) and slipstitch over the seam (3). To keep the lap from turning to the outside, stitch a diagonal line at the top of the fold (4).

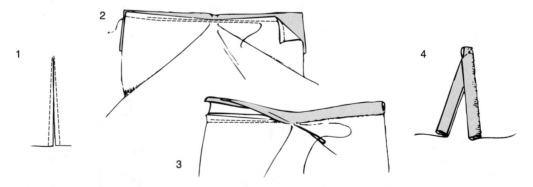

Bulk may be decreased by cutting 1 ¼" (3.2 cm) wide strip on a selvage. Use the raw edge for the first seam; then slipstitch the selvage over the seam allowance without turning it under. When a more durable finish is desired, substitute topstitching for slipstitching.

TO INSERT IN A SEAM, stitch the seam, leaving an opening for the placket at the end of the seam for reinforcement. Press the seam open, leaving the placket seam allowances unpressed. Clip the seam allowances at end of opening and trim the opening edges to ¼" (6 mm) (1). Cut a straight strip of self-fabric 1½" (3.8 cm) wide and twice the length of the opening. Spread the seam open and with right sides together, stitch the strip to the opening edge with small stitches in a ¼" (6 mm) seam. Grade the seam (2). Turn the free edge in ¼" (6 mm) and slipstitch over the seam (3). Stitch diagonally at top of fold (illustration 4, page 294).

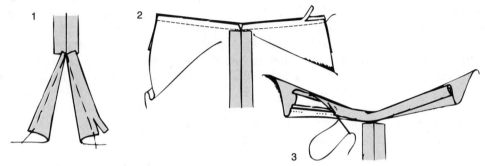

SHIRT-SLEEVE PLACKET: This sporty finish designed for a man-tailored shirt requires precision and care in its making for a fine professional look. First reinforce the sleeve opening by stitching along the seamlines, using small stitches. Slash between the stitches and carefully clip to the corners (1).

Stitch the right side of the underlap piece to the wrong side of the back edge of the sleeve (the edge nearer the underarm seam). Trim and press the seam allowances toward the underlap. Then turn under the remaining long edge of the underlap ¼" (6 mm) and press. Place the pressed edge over the seam allowances and edgestitch through all thicknesses (2).

Stitch the right side of the overlap piece to the wrong side of the remaining slashed edge. Trim the seam and press it toward the overlap. Stitch the base of the triangular end of the slash to the end of the overlap. Press the stitched end of the overlap up. Turn in the overlap at the seam allowances and along the foldlines; press and baste. Pin the overlap in place along the folded edges (3).

Keeping the underlap free, stitch the outside fold of the overlap to the top of the opening. Tie thread ends securely on the wrong side. Stitching through all layers, stitch across the placket, securing both the point of the slash and the top of the underlap in the stitches; pivot and stitch along the remaining edges of the overlap. Tie ends securely on the wrong side (4).

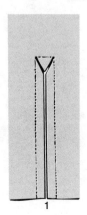
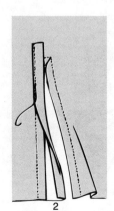
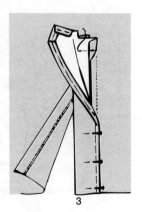
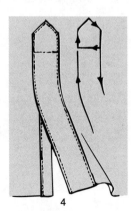

Special Sleeve Closings

Long, narrow sleeves tapering to the wrist are extremely elegant and graceful. They can be closed with snaps, thread loops and buttons, fabric loops and buttons, or a zipper.

SNAP CLOSING: Stitch the sleeve above the marking. Clip the back seam allowance ½" (13 mm) above the opening. Press the seam open above the clip, and the front edge to the inside along seamline. Turn up the lower edge of the sleeve along the seamline or hemline, and baste close to the fold. Finish the raw edge with ribbon seam binding, easing if necessary. Sew the hem in place. To finish opening edges, place ribbon seam binding ⅛" (3 mm) over the raw edges, turning under the top ends as shown and leaving ½" (13 mm) extending past the hem fold. Stitch close to the edge of the seam binding (1). Turn in the seam binding ends. Turn the front edge inside along the seamline; turn the back edge inside along the seam binding edge, as shown. Press. Slipstitch the lower ends and long edges of the seam binding in place. On the inside, lap the back seam allowance over the front below the clip, matching seamlines. Slipstitch the upper edge in place, taking care not to sew through to the right side (2). Fasten with snaps (3).

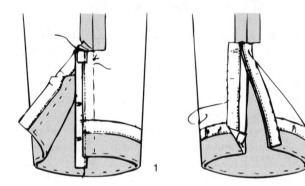
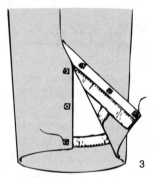

1   2   3

THREAD LOOP AND BUTTON CLOSING: This finish is perfect for the row of tiny buttons that is such an elegant touch on a sleeve. It eliminates the bulk of fabric loops, enabling you to use many small buttons spaced closely together. Finish the lower and opening edges of the sleeve with ribbon seam binding, as described above for the snap closing. Lap the opening and align the buttons on the undersection with the edge of the overlap. Space the loop markings evenly. Make the loops as instructed in Thread Loops, page 334. The loops should be uniform in size and shape and just large enough for the buttons to pass through. Secure the ends of the loops on the wrong side.

FABRIC LOOP AND BUTTON CLOSING: On the back edge only, clip the seam allowance ½" (13 mm) above the opening. Turn up the lower edge of the sleeve along the hemline and baste close to the fold. Finish the raw edge with ribbon seam binding, easing if necessary. Sew the hem in place. Make the fabric loops according to the instructions in Fabric Loops, page 332. Machine baste them along the seamline of the overlap, as shown, and check to see that they are just large enough for the buttons to pass through (1).

Press seam open above clip. Place ribbon seam binding along the seamline over the loop ends and ⅛" (3 mm) over the back raw edge, leaving extra seam binding at both ends. Stitch close to seam binding edge. Turn front edge to the inside along the seamline and back edge to the inside along the seam binding, turning under seam binding ends (2). Slipstitch upper and lower ends in place and blindstitch long edges to underlining or garment (3).

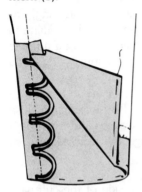  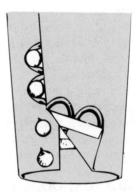

ZIPPER CLOSING: Stitch and press open the sleeve seam above the marking. Finish the hem edge. Baste and press open the remainder of the seam, clipping at the hemline (1). To shorten zipper, whipstitch several times over zipper teeth ¼" (6 mm) below desired new length and cut off excess. On the inside, center the closed zipper face down over the basted seam with the zipper tab just above the hemline; baste. Trim the zipper tape away below the hemline to eliminate bulk (2). On the outside, prickstitch the zipper in place along the sides and across the upper end.

Turn and pin the hem and baste close to the fold, turning in the ends to clear the zipper teeth. Slipstitch the ends to the zipper tape. Blindstitch sleeve hem to underlining or garment (3).

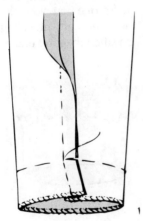 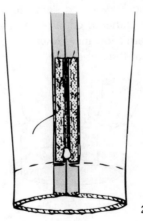 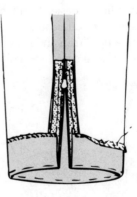

Cuffs

The cuff is one design detail that constantly changes, but never goes out of style. Of the two main categories, the primary function of the **EXTENDED CUFF** is to add length to the sleeve, whereas the **TURNBACK CUFF** rolls back to cover the base of the sleeve and often serves solely as a decorative feature. Both may control fullness. They can be straight bands folded in half, or may be shaped from separate fabric pieces. If a sleeve opening is used, a cuff should fasten closely around the wrist; but without an opening, a cuff must be big enough for the hand to pass through. Remember that trimming and grading of all seams is essential to a well-made cuff. For pressing tips, refer to page 354.

INTERFACING: The outer layer of the cuff should be interfaced. For a cuff cut in sections, use the cuff pattern piece and cut the interfacing on the bias for softer shaping. For a cuff made from one piece, cut the interfacing to extend ⅝" (15 mm) past the foldline to help maintain a smoothly rolled edge. Sew interfacing along the foldline with long running stitches. However, if this cuff is to be topstitched or edgestitched, trim the interfacing along the foldline.

Lightweight interfacing can be stitched into the seamlines. Pin interfacing to the wrong side of the outer cuff section and stitch ½" (13 mm) from the edge. Trim interfacing close to stitching. For heavier-weight interfacing, trim away the seam allowances and catchstitch the interfacing along the seamlines of the cuff. For fusible interfacings, the seam allowances and corners are trimmed away before fusing.

BUTTONHOLES: Transfer the placement markings to the right side of the cuff with thread tracing before applying interfacing. Make bound buttonholes before stitching the cuff sections together. Machine- or hand-worked buttonholes are made after the cuff is completed.

Extended Cuffs

BAND CUFF: This cuff is the simplest of all cuffs to make. Stitch the cuff ends together and press open. Stitch the gathered sleeve to the interfaced half of the cuff, right sides together. Trim and grade the seam (1). Press the seam allowances toward the cuff. Turn the cuff inside along the foldline, wrong sides together, and baste close to the fold. Trim and turn in the raw edge along the seamline; slipstitch it in place over the seam (2). You may find it easier to attach a thickly gathered sleeve to a band cuff **before** you close the sleeve or cuff seams. Stitch the gathered edge of the sleeve to the open cuff, matching markings. Trim and press the seam allowances toward the cuff. Then stitch the long underarm sleeve seam and cuff seam at the same time.

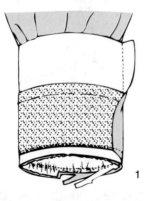

1

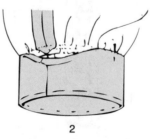

2

LAPPED CUFF WITH AN OPENING: A buttoned cuff is most often used on full-length, gathered or pleated sleeves with a continuous bound placket (see page 294). Make your bound buttonholes. Fold the cuff lengthwise, and stitch the ends from the fold to within ⅝" (15 mm) of the long edge. Trim, grading seams (1). Turn and press. Fold under the front lap of the sleeve placket so that the folded edge is even with the cuff edge. Place the back lap of the sleeve on the cuff at the marking. Stitch the gathered sleeve to the interfaced half of the cuff (2). Press, trim, and turn the cuff in the same manner as for a band cuff. Baste close to the fold. Trim and turn in the raw edge along the seamline and slipstitch it over the seam and extension end (3). Complete your button and buttonhole closure (4).

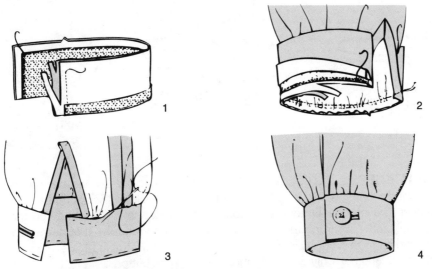

LAPPED CUFF WITHOUT OPENING: You will probably want to put a button trim on this cuff. Fold the cuff lengthwise. To form a finished extension, start stitching at the fold, pivot at the corner, and stitch as far as the marking. On the other end, stitch from the fold to within ⅝" (15 mm) of long edge. Clip the seam allowance to marking on the long notched edge. Trim and grade the seam. Turn to the right side and press (1). Stitch the gathered sleeve to interfaced half of the cuff. The end of the cuff section will meet the extension marking at the clip, as shown. Clip the sleeve seam allowance at the marking (2). Press, trim, and turn the cuff in the same manner as for a band cuff. Baste close to the fold. Trim and turn in the raw edge along the seamline; slipstitch (3). Fasten extension in place on the right side, as desired (4).

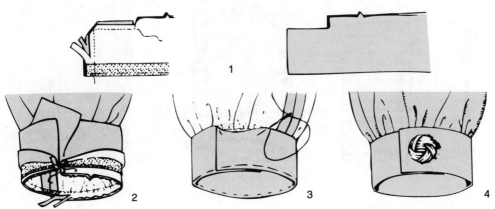

SHIRT-SLEEVE CUFF: A shirt-sleeve cuff is used with a shirt-sleeve placket and is usually topstitched. Stitch the cuff sections together, ending ⅝" (15 mm) from the long notched edge. Trim, turn, and press (1). Stitch the **_wrong side_** of the gathered sleeve to the non-**_interfaced_** section of the cuff, placing the placket edges even with the cuff edges. Trim and grade the seam (2). Press the seam toward the cuff. On the outside, turn in the remaining edge where it falls over the seam and baste in place. Topstitch close to all edges of the cuff and again ¼" (6 mm) away from the first line of stitching. Fasten with a machine-made or hand-worked buttonhole and button (3).

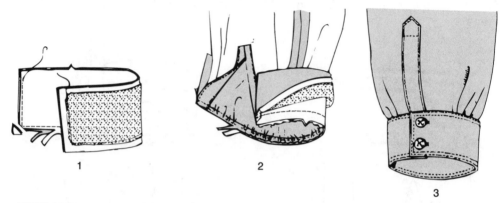

1   2

3

FRENCH CUFF or **BUTTON-LINK CUFF:** These cuffs are worn with the ends extending rather than lapping. The French cuff is folded back on itself and fastened by cuff links passing through four buttonholes. Bound buttonholes should be made on the outermost cuff only, after inserting the interfacing. The two buttonholes that do not show are machine-worked to prevent bulk. The button link cuff is constructed the same way, but is not folded back and has only two buttonholes for the link buttons.

For a French cuff, the inside layer of the cuff will be on the outside when turned back; therefore, apply the interfacing to the inside cuff section and sew it along the foldline with long running stitches. Stitch the cuff sections together, ending ⅝" (15 mm) from the long notched edge; trim, grade, turn, and press (1). Matching markings, stitch the gathered sleeve to the non-interfaced side of the cuff. Trim and grade the seam (2). Press the seam toward the cuff. Turn the raw edge under on the inside and slipstitch over the seam. Slipstitch the extended ends when applicable. Make any remaining buttonholes by hand or machine. Turn the lower edge to the outside along the roll line so that the buttonholes meet; press lightly. Fasten with link buttons or cuff links (3).

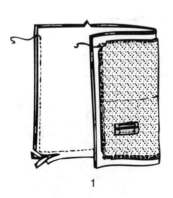
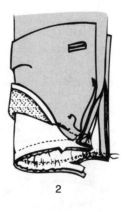
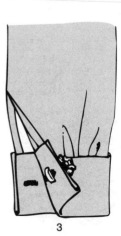

1   2

3

Turnback Cuffs

We have illustrated here only the most classic examples of straight and shaped cuffs. Their variations are unlimited, including scalloped, slashed, and sculptured design edges that may circle the sleeve in a continuous seam or stop at multi-shaped finished ends. They can be attached to the sleeve in many ways as well, and often serve a dual role as extended cuffs by simply not folding them back.

STRAIGHT TURNBACK CUFF WITH SELF-HEM: These cuffs should taper out slightly to be somewhat larger than the sleeve at the finished edge; this will ensure that the sleeve will not pucker when the cuff is turned back.

After you have determined the finished length of your sleeve, add twice the desired width of the cuff plus 1" (25 mm) for a hem to the finished length of the sleeve; be sure to taper the cuff out from the hemline to the cuff foldline. Interface the cuff area before stitching the seams. Cut the interfacing the same width as the cuff plus 1¼" (3.2 cm) and extend the interfacing ⅝" (15 mm) beyond the foldline and roll line for a softer edge. Sew interfacing to the cuff at foldlines and roll lines with running stitches. Stitch the sleeve seam and press it open (1).

To form the rolled cuff, finish the raw edge and turn the cuff inside along the foldline. Baste close to the fold (2). Roll the folded edge to the outside, forming the cuff. Baste through all thicknesses to hold the roll in place (3). On the inside, blindstitch the hem edge to the sleeve (4).

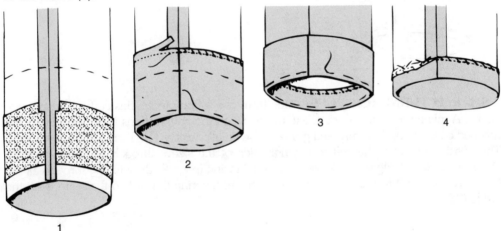

VARIATION WITH A SLIT: Prepare your cuff as in step 1, above. Finish the raw edge, then turn the interfaced side to the outside along the foldline. Mark the position of the slit and stitch along the markings, taking a stitch across the point. Clip the slit close to the stitching, and, using a sleeve board, press just the slit area. Turn the cuff to the inside and finish, as above.

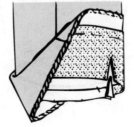

STRAIGHT TURNBACK CUFF: Usually a single rectangle cut on the bias or straight grain, a straight cuff can also be two fabric sections. This cuff should be slightly larger in circumference at its foldline than the sleeve to which it is attached so that it can turn back easily. Apply interfacing to one half of the cuff, extending ⅝" (15 mm) beyond foldline and roll line for a softer edge. Stitch the ends of the cuff together. Trim the seam allowances to the foldline as shown and press them open. Stitch the non-interfaced side of the cuff to the sleeve, right sides together; trim (1). Press the seam open. Finish raw edge with stitching, lace, or seam binding. Then turn the cuff inside along the foldline, wrong sides together; baste close to the folded edge. Blindstitch the hem to the sleeve or underlining (2). Roll the cuff to the outside over the sleeve (3).

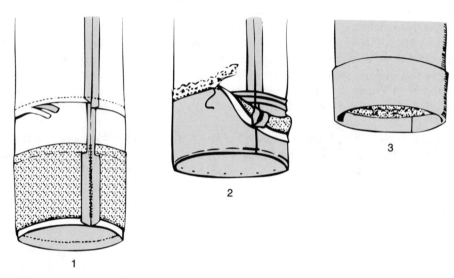

SHAPED TURNBACK CUFF: Made from two fabric pieces, this cuff has many variations. Apply interfacing to one fabric piece. Stitch the cuff sections together, leaving the notched edge open; then trim and grade the seam allowances (1). Turn and press the cuff. Then baste and stitch the cuff to the right side of the sleeve through all thicknesses (2). Finish the notched edges with a bias or shaped facing (page 292), stitching through all the layers. Roll the cuff to the outside along the seam, favoring the cuff so the seam is on the inside (3).

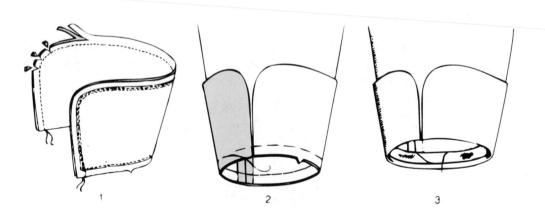

Detachable Cuffs

There are few fashion accents more elegant than the crisp, trim appearance of detachable cuffs. They can be straight or shaped. You can make them in a continuous band, open, or partially open with a slit or a slash. They may be designed to turn back over a sleeve or an existing cuff, or they can simulate a shirt cuff by extending below the hem of a jacket sleeve. They are often used to provide a removable, washable trim on a garment that requires dry cleaning.

Detachable cuffs that are designed to turn back must taper so that the finished edge, which fits over the sleeve will be somewhat wider than the inside edge, which slips inside the sleeve. Cuffs that are meant to extend below the sleeve will have to be made to fit just the inside measurement of the sleeve to which they will be applied.

BAND CUFF: This is usually made by stitching the ends of the cuff together and pressing the seam open. Fold along the foldline with wrong sides together. Turn in the remaining raw edges along the seamline and slipstitch (1), From the right side, lap the sleeve over the cuff the desired depth and pin. Turn to the wrong side and slipstitch or snap the cuff in place (2).

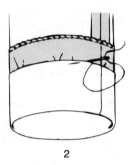

1   2

CUFF WITH A SLIT: Fold cuff, right sides together, and stitch each end. Grade seams, turn, and press. Join cuff by slipstitching ends together, leaving a slit. Baste raw edges together. Then encase them in a bias strip (self- fabric or commercial binding) cut to fit the inner circumference of the sleeve. Simply edgestitch the binding to the raw edges, overlapping the ends (1). From the right side, lap the sleeve over the cuff the desired depth and pin. Turn to the wrong side and slipstitch or snap the cuff in place (2). Roll the folded edge to the outside, forming the cuff, and anchor the corners with a bar tack if desired (3).

3

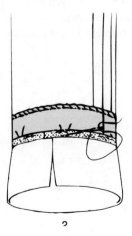

1

2

Pockets

If you are a novice at the art of sewing, or even if you've acquired a great amount of skill, you probably will be confused at the seemingly endless variations in pocket types and names. To help clear your mind, just remember that pockets branch out from two basic constructions–pockets of self-fabric applied to the garment, and pockets of lining pushed to the inside through a seam or slash, and sometimes covered by a flap or a welt.

Pockets can beautifully accent a professional seam or they can expose a poor construction job. A few simple but vital rules will bring about successful results: thread trace all pocket markings to the right side of all pocket and garment parts; pull pockets through openings very gently; keep all corners true; use interfacing for body—strive for even, balanced welts or flaps; and anchor the side edges of flaps and welts *invisibly* to the garment.

One excellent rule for positioning pockets below the waist is that they should be located at a level where your hands can slip into them naturally and comfortably. If placed too near the hem, they will look and feel awkward. However, there are instances when the rules are meant to be flexed a little. Pockets above the waist, and patch pockets anywhere, are so often meant to be strictly decorative that you should concentrate on whether their position is flattering, regardless of how accessible the pocket may be. When adjusting your pattern, the pockets may require relocating if you shorten or lengthen your garment.

All types of pockets made in lightweight or loosely woven fabrics need to be interfaced. Interfacing provides added strength, reinforces the opening, and preserves the pocket shape. Welts and flaps should be interfaced if their shape and resiliency are to be preserved. The interfacing is generally cut on bias grain to extend ⅝" (15 mm) past the foldline unless the welt or flap is going to be topstitched. Patch pockets usually need no interfacing, but are often lined for a custom finish. In-seam pockets will not require interfacing, but may need the reinforcement of a stay to keep the pocket edge from stretching.

As a decoration or means of emphasizing a design line, topstitching is superb. As a method of applying your pocket, however, topstitching is not generally recommended. The patch pocket in particular will have a neater appearance if the topstitching is done before the pocket and garment are joined. It will then be easier to topstitch a straighter, more even line than when you are trying to concentrate on connecting the pocket and the garment. The topstitched pocket is then sewn to the garment by hand. It is possible to topstitch your pocket in place on lightweight, closely woven fabrics, but stitching over many thicknesses of bulky fabric or napped fabric can become a problem.

Patch Pockets

Patch pockets are usually made from self-fabric and applied to the outside of the garment. They can be lined or left unlined. When constructing a pair of patch pockets, check carefully to be sure both pockets are the same size and shape and are attached to the garment evenly.

UNLINED: Turn under the top edge ¼" (6 mm) and stitch. Then turn the upper edge of the pocket to the outside along the foldline. Stitch ends and trim, as shown. If yours is a rounded pocket, easestitch the rounded area ¼" (6 mm) away from the seamline on the seam allowance to ensure a flat finish (1). Turn both the hem and the seam allowance to the inside. On a rounded pocket, pull in the easestitches to shape the pocket curve. If the pocket is square or rectangular, miter all corners (if you need mitering instructions, refer to page 243). Baste around the edges, notching away the excess fullness. Slipstitch the top hem to the pocket (2).

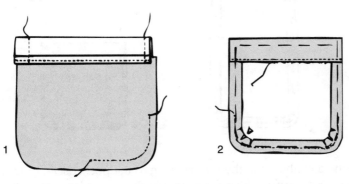

When topstitching is desired, do it before you attach the pocket. Then, from the right side, pin and baste the pocket in place. If the pocket is to be applied to a curved area of your garment, such as the front hip, place the garment over a curved surface such as a tailor's ham in order to pin the pocket in place. From the wrong side, work a small backstitch through garment and pocket. Be sure the stitches do not show on the right side. Or, you can slipstitch the pocket to the garment from the right side, taking care not to pull the stitches too tight, or the pocket will pucker.

SELF-LINED: Cut the desired pocket shape twice the length of the pocket plus seam allowances on all sides. Simply fold your pocket right sides together and stitch both sides and a portion of the bottom. Leave an opening for turning. Trim and grade the seam allowances (1). Turn the pocket, press it, and slipstitch the opening shut (2).

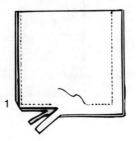

LINED: There are two methods for constructing a lined patch pocket. In the first method, the lining is slipstitched by hand to the inside edge of the pocket; in the second method, the lining is stitched by machine.

With right sides together, stitch the pocket lining to the pocket self-facing. Press the seam toward the lining. For rounded pockets, easestitch the rounded areas on both the pocket and the lining ¼" (6 mm) away from the seamline on the seam allowance. Turn in the edges of the pocket along the seamlines, drawing up the ease thread where necessary. Starting at the foldline, taper the seam allowances of the lining ⅛" (3 mm) so that the finished lining edge will fall ⅛" (3 mm) inside the finished pocket edge. Baste close to the edge (1). Turn the lining and self-facing to the inside along the pocket foldline. Slipstitch the lining in place around the inside pocket edge (2).

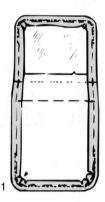 

For the machine method, pin the pocket lining to the pocket self-facing, with right sides together. Stitch seam, leaving a small opening in the center for turning the pocket. Press the seam toward the lining. To ensure that no lining will show at the edges of the completed pocket, trim ⅛" (3 mm) from around the lining edge. Fold pocket along pocket foldline with right sides of fabric together. Align bottom and side edges; stitch along pocket seamline. Trim and grade the seam allowances.

For a square pocket, trim diagonally across the seam allowances at the corners; for a rounded pocket, notch out the excess fabric in the curved areas (3).

Turn pocket to the right side by pulling it gently through the opening. Press pocket, rolling outer seam slightly to the lining side. Slipstitch opening closed (4).

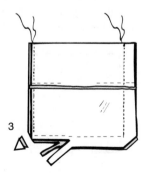 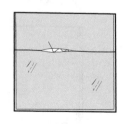

Pocket Flaps and Welts

Just about any type of pocket can be covered or set off by a flap or welt. Both may also appear by themselves as decorative fakes. The major distinction between a flap and a welt is that a flap hangs downward freely while a welt generally points upward and is securely attached along its sides.

The example shown is a decorative flap, but the same construction principles apply to any flap or wide welt. Interface the outer half of the flap so that the interfacing extends ⅝" (15 mm) past the foldline. Sew along the foldline with long running stitches. For flaps that will be topstitched, trim interfacing away at the foldline and catchstitch the edge in place (1). With right sides together, fold and stitch the gap ends to ⅝" (15 mm) from the flap base. Trim and grade the seam; clipping or notching will be necessary for a shaped flap (2). Turn and press.

When the direction of the seam allowance coincides with the direction of the finished flap or welt, you must establish the roll of the flap at the seamline so that it will lie flat. Turn the seam allowances of the flap down over your hand to establish the roll line, adjusting the flap or welt if more upper fabric is required (3). Pin and baste along the new seamline of the upper portion through both layers. Remember this treatment will be necessary only when the flap or welt turns over its own seam allowance.

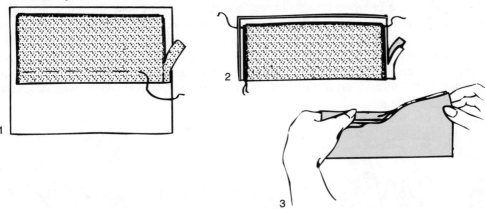

To attach the flap, place the new seamline along the placement lines on your garment and stitch through all thicknesses. Turn back the upper seam allowance and trim the lower one close to the stitching. Turn in ¼" (6 mm) on the long edge of the upper seam allowance, folding the ends in diagonally, and turn it down over the trimmed edge (4). Then edgestitch. Fold the flap down and press, being careful not to overpress or unsightly ridges from the flap edges will appear on the garment. To secure upper sides of corners, slipstitch to the garment from right side, or backstitch heavy fabrics from the wrong side (5).

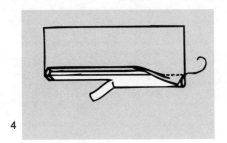

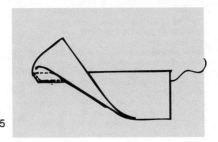

Welt Pockets

A welt pocket gives a very crisp, neat, and precise look to create an essentially tailored appearance. The construction of a welt pocket is similar to a bound buttonhole. It can be made with a single welt, a double welt, or covered with a pocket flap.

To make construction easier, mark precisely and stitch accurately. Use short stitches and begin and end your stitching exactly at the markings. Cut carefully when you are slashing the pocket open. Finally, take time to press after each step and you will be rewarded with a professional-looking welt pocket.

Single Welt Pocket

For this pocket the welt is pressed upward over the opening of a lining pocket. If your fabric needs more body, interface the welt in the usual way. Construct and press the welt. It will be easier to work with if you baste the raw edges together on the seamline and trim them to ¼" (6 mm) from the seamline. Always do any required topstitching before you attach the welt. Then pin the welt to the garment, placing the seamline of the welt over the lower stitching line on the right side of the garment; baste. Now pin and baste the lining pocket over the welt with the deeper portion above the welt. Stitch along the stitching lines, backstitching or using small knots at the ends (1). Slash between your stitching to within ½" (13 mm) of both ends; clip diagonally to the corners. Turn the pocket to the inside, turning the welt up. Overcast the raw edges of both narrow seam allowances (2). Press. Positioning the pocket and garment as shown, carefully stitch around the pocket edges, being very sure to catch the base of the small triangular ends in your sewing. Trim and overcast the pocket edges. The final step takes place on the outside; just slipstitch the ends of the welt in place (3).

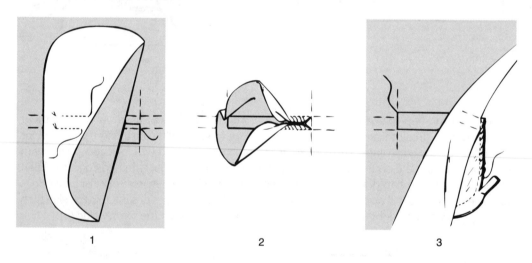

1   2   3

Double-Welt Pocket

This pocket opening looks like a large bound buttonhole. It has two very narrow welts that face each other and is the exception to the rule that welts point upward. Fold both long edges of the welt, wrong sides together, to meet at the center; press. With cut edges up, center folded welt over the pocket markings; baste. Slash through center of welt; do not cut the garment (1). Baste garment fabric section of pocket in place along upper stitching line over welt, matching markings. Baste lining section in place along lower stitching line in same manner. Stitch through all thicknesses along the indicated lines; backstitch or knot the ends (2). From the wrong side, slash through the center for pocket opening. Clip diagonally to ends of stitching, making triangular ends ½" (13 mm) deep. Pull pocket parts to inside through slash (3).

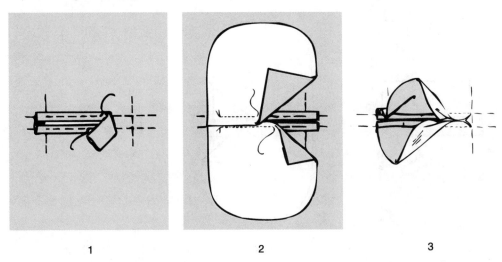

1   2   3

Press welts to meet in center of opening and whipstitch together loosely. Matching pocket edges and starting at the top, stitch side and lower edges together, catching base of the small triangular ends in stitches (4). Trim and overcast edges. To support weight of pocket, catchstitch upper edge to underlining (5).

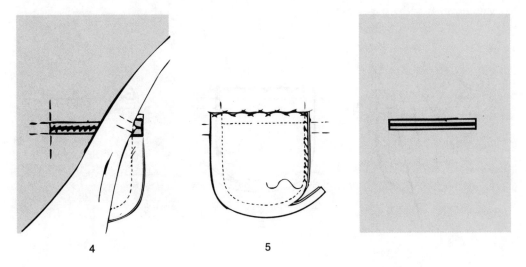

4   5

Welt Pocket with Flap

In this instance, the flap and a narrow welt are combined for a very tailored, precise appearance. Make flap according to directions on page 307, steps 1 and 2. Baste raw edges along seamline. To make welt, fold wrong sides together and baste along seamline on long raw edge. Trim basted seams of both flap and welt to ¼" (6 mm). On the outside of the garment, baste the flap to the upper stitching line and the welt to the lower stitching line; the long raw edges will meet (1). Matching markings, baste larger pocket section over flap and smaller section over welt. Stitch through all thicknesses along the indicated lines; backstitch or knot ends (2). From the wrong side, slash through the center to within ½" (13 mm) of end of stitching for pocket opening. Then clip diagonally to the ends of the stitching without cutting the flap or welt. Pull all pocket parts to inside (3).

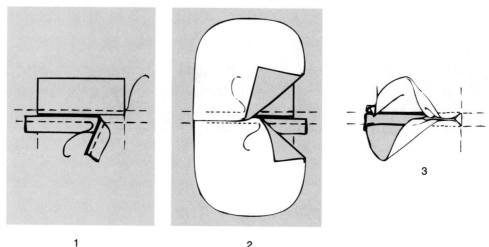

1   2

Press welt upward (over opening) and flap downward. Matching pocket edges and starting at the top, stitch side and lower edges together, catching the base of the triangular ends in your stitches (4). Trim and overcast these raw pocket edges by hand, machine or serger. To support the weight of the pocket, catchstitch the upper edge to the underlining (5).

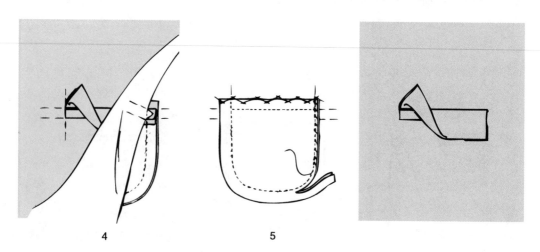

4   5

Side-Front Slanted Pockets

Side-front slanted pockets are constructed from two different size pattern pieces–a pocket section and a side front section. The pocket section can be of self-fabric or lining fabric, but the side-front section must be of self-fabric because it becomes a visible part of the main garment at the side seams and the waistline. If any hip or waist alterations must be made in the garment pattern pieces, be sure to include the pocket pattern pieces as well.

Because the pocket opening is in a slanted or bias seam, the garment front should be reinforced with a stay to prevent the pocket edge from stretching. Cut a piece of ribbon seam binding 2" (5 cm) longer than the pocket opening and center over the seamline on the wrong side of the garment front; baste (1). For pockets that have a curved, rather than a slanted seam, the pocket opening should be interfaced for reinforcement. Cut a strip of interfacing 2" (5 cm) wide and same shape as the curved seam; baste to wrong side of garment front along seamline.

Pin and stitch pocket section to slanted edge of garment front and trim seam to ³⁄₁₆" (5 mm), being careful not to cut the seam binding (2). Turn pocket to inside of garment and press. Understitch close to the seamline through pocket and seam allowances to prevent the pocket from rolling to the right side of the garment (3). Or you can topstitch along the finished edge.

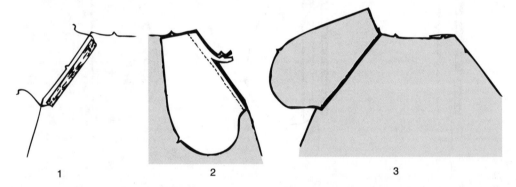

1   2   3

Pin side front section to pocket section, right sides together, and stitch around the seamline to the side of the garment, keeping the front free. Press and finish raw edges with overcasting or machine stitching (4).

Turn pockets down and baste pockets to the garment front along the upper and side edges (5). Pin and stitch front and back sections of garment together at the sides, catching pocket and side front in the seams; press. Treat the upper edge of the pocket as one with the garment when stitching the waistline seam.

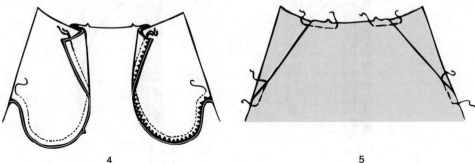

4   5

In-Seam Pockets

This inconspicuous type of pocket is concealed in side or front seams. The pocket top may be controlled from the inside by a waistline seam. An in-seam pocket is generally made of lining fabric and can be stitched to an extension of the pocket opening or directly to the seamline, depending upon your pattern.

With many fabrics, the seamline on the garment front should be reinforced with a stay to prevent the pocket edge from stretching. Cut a piece of ribbon seam binding 2" (5 cm) longer than the pocket opening and baste in place as shown below.

IN-SEAM POCKET WITH EXTENSION: Place stay on wrong side of garment front with one edge next to the seamline, as shown. Baste, then stitch by hand or machine ⅛" (3 mm) from edge of stay nearest seamline (1). Stitch one pocket piece to each front and back extension, with right sides of fabric together. Press seams open (2).

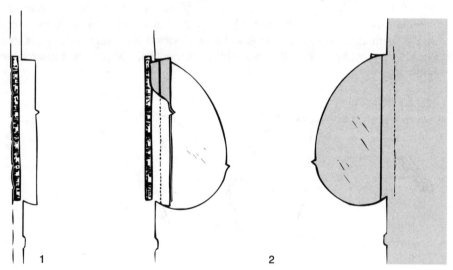

Baste the garment sections together at the seam and across the pocket openings; also baste the pocket edges together. Start stitching from the lower edge and continue around the pocket, pivoting at the corners. Use reinforcement stitches at all pivot points (3). Turn the pocket toward the front along the foldline or roll line. Clip the back seam allowance above and below the facing extension so you can press the seam above and below the pocket. Press lightly for a fold or steam for a soft roll (4).

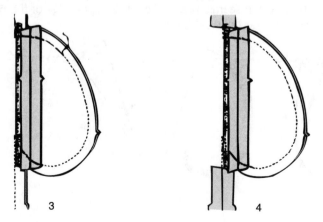

IN-SEAM POCKET WITHOUT EXTENSION: Center stay over seamline on wrong side of garment front; baste (1). Join pocket pieces to front and back garment sections, right sides of fabric together, matching pocket markings. Stitch a ¼" (6 mm) seam, and press seam toward pocket (2).

Baste the garment sections together at the seam and across the pocket openings. Then baste the pocket edges together. Start stitching from the lower edge and continue around the pocket, pivoting at the corners (3).

Turn the pocket toward the front and clip the back seam allowance above and below the facing extension. Press (4).

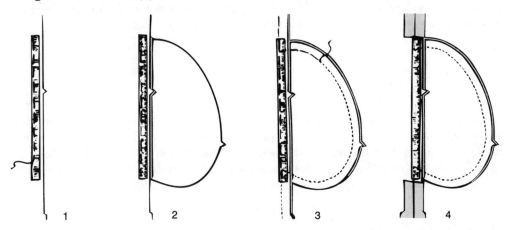

1   2   3   4

How to Add an In-Seam Pocket

You can add this type of pocket in lining fabric or self-fabric to your garment. The dimensions are given in scale. Seam allowances of ⅝" (15 mm) should be added to all edges. Cut two for each pocket. The pocket with a straight upper edge is the style suitable for waistline seams, the pocket without the straight upper edge is the style suitable for side seam pockets that are not caught in the waistline seams.

Just align the pocket opening edge with the seamline on your garment. being sure that the pocket is at the correct level for your hands. Then construct and press the pocket as described above. If desired, pocket and garment can be cut in one piece, eliminating the seam at the pocket opening (refer to Very Easy Vogue section, page 399).

Each Square Equals 1" (25mm)

Opening

Waistlines, Waistbands, and Belts

Fashion dictates the location of the garment waistline, which may or may not be at the natural waistline, and whether it is fitted closely or loosely or not at all. A waistline can be defined in many ways–with a seam, a casing, a waistband, or a belt.

Waistlines

Although in many garments the waistline falls at the natural waistline, other styles are highlighted by a waistline either above or below the natural waistline. The range is wide–from the Empire style with the seamline just below the bust, to the lowered waistline with the seam located at the hipline. A waistline seam is used to join the top and bottom sections of a garment together and may be straight, curved, or sharply angled.

Waistline Seams

Usually the skirt section is larger, if only slightly, than the top and must be eased onto the bodice section. Slip the bodice inside the skirt with right sides together. Carefully match all seamlines, notches, and markings. For a fitted skirt, distribute any fullness evenly around the waistline. With bodice side up, stitch along the seamline (1).

For a gathered skirt, pull up the gathering until the skirt is the same width as the bodice. Adjust gathers evenly. (See page 237 for gathering techniques.) With skirt side up, stitch waistline seam taking care that unwanted tucks or pleats do not form in the gathers (2).

Trim ends of darts and seam allowances diagonally. Press seam toward bodice and overcast or zigzag raw edges, if necessary.

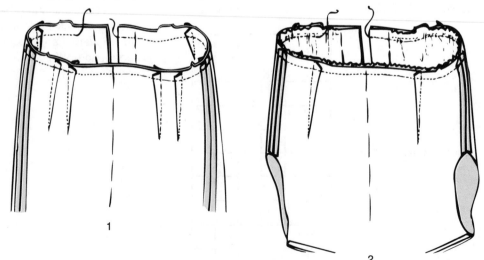

1

2

Waistline Stays

For some fabrics, it may be necessary to apply a waistline stay to prevent the seamline from stretching. Use ribbon seam binding, twill tape, or grosgrain ribbon ½" to 1" (13 mm to 25 mm) wide.

Cut the stay the exact measurement of the waistline from seamline to seamline. Pin and baste to the seam allowances on the skirt side with one edge along the waist seamline and the ends at each seamline. Machine-stitch through both seam allowance layers just above the stitched seam. Trim seam allowances to the same width as the stay; do not trim the stay.

For bulkier fabrics, the skirt seam allowance can be trimmed narrower than that of the bodice. For fabrics that ravel, stitch upper edge of stay and seam allowances together.

A second type of waistline stay can be applied inside a garment after the zipper is inserted to help relieve stress in the zipper area and to hold the waistline area in place. It is recommended for sheath or princess style dresses, delicate or stretchy fabrics, or when the skirt fabric is heavier than the bodice fabric. Refer to the couture section, page 456.

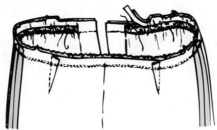

Waistline Casings

A casing enables fabric to be easily gathered at the waistline with elastic or drawstring. Casings are simple to construct and can be easily adjusted to your waistline measurement. For a waistline casing along the edge of a garment such as a casing at the top of a skirt or pants, or a casing at the bottom of a blouse or jacket, refer to edge finishes, page 265.

A waistline casing on a one-piece garment takes the place of a waistline seam. Use self-fabric (if lightweight), lining fabric, or single-fold bias tape. The width of finished casing must be ¼" (6 mm) wider than elastic or drawstring to allow either one to be pulled smoothly through the casing.

Cut the casing; turn in all edges ¼" (6 mm) and press gently. Mark the garment waistline and prepare an opening if drawstring is to be used. (See drawstring section, page 266.) From wrong side, place the bottom edge of casing along waistline markings. Stitch along both long edges. Insert elastic or drawstring and finish as required (1). If a zipper is used with a waistline casing, end casing at zipper seamline. Insert elastic or drawstring and sew raw ends securely to casing at each end, keeping garment free (2). Insertion of zipper will secure ends of casing and elastic or drawstring. After zipper is applied, whipstitch seam allowances securely to casing and elastic or drawstring (3).

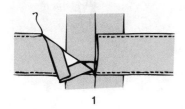

1

2

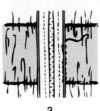

3

Dress Placket

This type of placket is usually placed in a side seam and centered at the waistline. It is an effective closing for lightweight, sheer, or lace fabrics, where a zipper tape would be unsightly.

Stitch the seam and press it open, leaving an opening between markings for the placket. Use two straight strips of self-fabric or lining fabric 2" (5 cm) longer than the opening for the placket. Cut front strip 1¼" (3.2 cm) wide and back strip 1¾" (4.5 cm) wide. Finish one edge of each strip as you plan to finish your garment seams. With raw edges matching and right sides together, center front strip between markings and stitch to opening edges along seamline. Trim and grade seam allowances, leaving garment seam allowances widest. Fold strip to inside along the seam; press (1).

Clip the garment back seam allowance ½" (13 mm) beyond each end of the opening. Right sides together, center and stitch the back strip to the opening seam allowance ¼" (6 mm) from the edge. Press small seam open. Lap back strip over front so that folded and finished edges cover garment seam allowances (2).

Stitch both strips to the front seam allowance at the upper and lower ends of the placket opening, keeping the garment free. Blindstitch long free edges in place on front and back placket. Catchstitch raw edges to garment seam allowances (3).

Fasten opening with snaps; place a hook and eye at waistline. When pressing, do not let the iron rest on the placket (4).

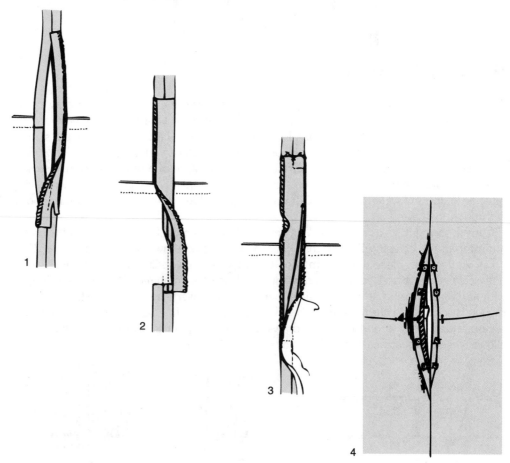

1
2
3
4

Waistbands

A properly sewn and fitted waistband is a joy to wear. It never stretches, wrinkles, or folds over as some waistbands have a way of doing, nor does it bind you or slip down on your hips. To attain this ideal combination of fit, good looks, and comfort, you must know a few general facts about waistbands.

Your preference and garment style determine waistband width. Most waistbands need the reinforcement and body of interfacing or ribbon seam binding to prevent stretching–particularly loosely woven fabrics and wide or contour waistbands. With knits, use elastic in the waistband to ensure the proper stretch and fit. Unless the garment is gathered, the skirt is usually eased to the waistband to accommodate the curve of your body directly below the waistband. For this reason, your skirt should be ½" to 1" (13 mm to 25 mm) bigger at the waistline than the finished waistline measurement of the garment. If the ends of the waistband overlap, the overlapping edge faces toward the left or the back. Side closings are on the left side. The underneath section usually extends at least 1¼" (3.2 cm) for the underlap. Put in the zipper before you apply the waistband, unless directed otherwise by the pattern instructions.

Straight Waistband

This waistband is cut on the lengthwise grain for the least amount of stretch, and can be constructed in many ways. Base your construction on the type of fabric, the style of the garment, and the wear that it will receive. If using a zipper, position the zipper stop ⅛", (3 mm) below the waist seamline.

Cut interfacing for the full width of waistband and baste or fuse to wrong side of fabric ½" (13 mm) from edge. Trim interfacing close to stitching. To hold interfacing to waistband along foldline, stitch through both layers on the facing side of the waistband ½" (13 mm) below foldline. Turn waistband, right sides together, along foldline. Stitch ends to within ⅝" (15 mm) of the edge. Grade seams and trim corners (1). Turn and press.

Pin and baste the waistband to the garment, matching markings. Ease the garment to fit the waistband; stitch. Trim and grade seams, leaving garment seam allowance widest. Press seam toward waistband. Turn in the remaining raw edge and slipstitch over the seam, continuing across the underlap (2). Fasten with hooks and eyes (3).

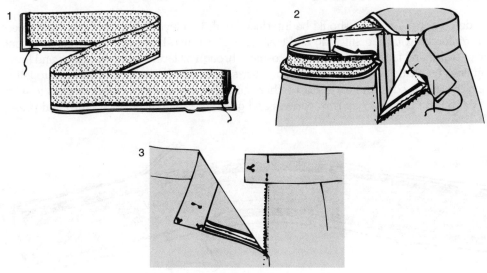

Variations on a Straight Waistband

If your fabric is fairly heavy or bulky, you may wish to use one of the following methods to eliminate bulk and make a flat, smooth waistband.

First, to reduce the ridge caused when all seam allowances at the waistline are turned in the same direction, lay the waistband pattern piece with *seamline* of the unnotched edge even with selvage. The selvage acts as a finished edge and is not turned under (1).

The second variation produces a thinner, less bulky appearance. Cut the waistband from your fabric equal to its finished width plus two seam allowances. Lap grosgrain ribbon (purchased in the same width as the finished waistband) over the upper seam allowance, even with the seamline; stitch ribbon close to edge (2).

Finish both waistbands by folding them right sides together along the upper seamline or foldline. Stitch across both ends. Trim corners and grade seam allowances. Turn and press. Attach them to the garment as usual. Slipstitch the selvage of the fabric or the edge of the grosgrain ribbon over the seam, continuing across the underlap. Be sure that the ribbon does not show on the outside.

The last variation is a quick, sturdy way to finish a waistband on a casual or sporty garment. Stitch the right side of the waistband to the *wrong* side of the garment. Press seam toward the waistband. Turn in the remaining edge and baste it over the seam on the right side of the garment. From the right side, topstitch close to basted edge through all thicknesses (3).

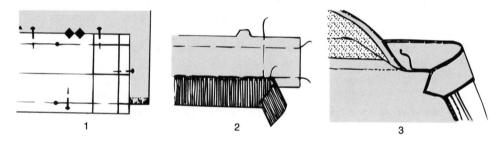

1   2   3

Contour Waistband

A wide contour waistband should be interfaced with two layers of interfacing for stiffness and reinforced with pad stitching and twill tape. Baste two layers of interfacing to wrong side of waistband facing and machine padstitch through all layers. Stay the upper and lower seamlines by basting ¼" (6 mm) twill tape over seamlines. Pin waistband sections together along the upper edge and ends. Baste, then stitch the upper edges and both ends to within ⅝" (15 mm) of the edge. Trim corners and grade the seam allowance. Turn and press.

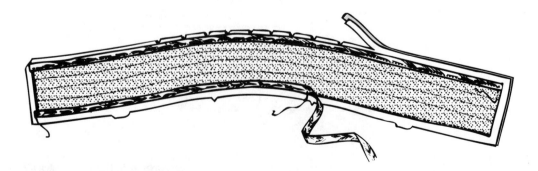

Pin the waistband to the garment with the right sides together, matching all markings. Adjust the ease; baste and stitch. Trim and grade seam; press toward the waistband. Turn in the remaining edge and slipstitch over the seam, continuing across the underlap. Fasten the end of the waistband with hooks and eyes. Be sure to keep hooks aligned with the edge of the waistband and eyes directly above the zipper opening.

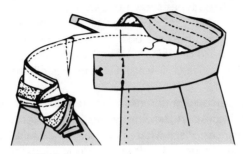

Faced Waistline

Skirts or pants without visible waistbands are usually finished with a facing made from lining, lightweight fabric, or ribbon to reduce bulk.

FABRIC: Cut and prepare facing. Stay the facing waist seamline with ribbon seam binding or twill tape, placing one edge ⅛" (3 mm) inside seam allowance; baste. Pin the facing to the garment, easing garment to fit. Stitch, trim, and grade seams. Understitch facing to keep it from rolling to the outside (1). Turn and press. Turn in ends; sew to zipper tape. Tack facing to garment at seams and darts. Add a hook and eye at top of closing (2).

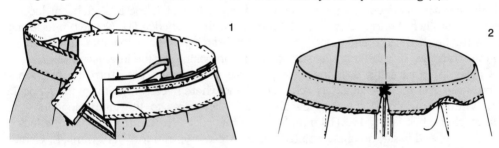

RIBBON: Shape a ¾"- 1" (20 mm-25 mm) wide strip of grosgrain ribbon by steaming it into curves corresponding to those of the waistline edge. Shape by stretching the edge that is to be left free; if you shrink the edge to be joined to the garment, it will stretch during wear. Fit ribbon to your body, allowing 1" (25 mm) for ends. Trim garment seam allowance to ¼" (6 mm). Place grosgrain over raw edge of garment with unstretched edge along seamline and ends extending ½" (13 mm). Because you are joining two opposing curves, pin or baste carefully, easing the garment to fit. Stitch close to edge of ribbon and complete as for a fabric facing above.

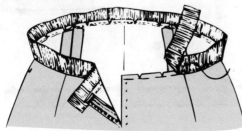

Belts and Carriers

Since ancient Grecian times, belts and belt carriers have been moving up and down fashion's silhouette in an amazing variety of shapes and widths. Modern belt-making techniques can best be exemplified by the basic types shown below.

If you are adding a belt and your pattern doesn't include one, you must plan the belt carefully. To find the proper length, encircle your body where the belt will be worn with belting or interfacing in the desired width; add 7" (18 cm) to this measurement for finishing your belt. Wider belts extending above your waistline require additional length.

TIE BELT or **SASH:** Your personal preference will determine the type–narrow or wide, bias or straight grain. Cut fabric twice the finished width and the desired length (long enough to tie) plus seam allowances. Piece where necessary, then fold the sash in half with wrong sides together lengthwise. Stitch the ends and the long edge, leaving an opening, as shown. Trim corners and grade seams. Turn and press the sash. Slipstitch the opening.

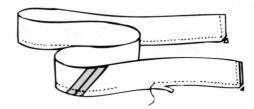

STRAIGHT BELT WITH INTERFACING: On the lengthwise grain, cut two strips of fabric the required length and width of the finished belt, adding ⅝"" (15 mm) seam allowances on all edges. Shape one end as desired. If your fabric is stretchy or loosely woven, staystitch the long edges ⅜" (10 mm) from the raw edge (1). Cut two interfacing strips the finished width and length. Stitch the interfacing sections together in rows at ¼" (6 mm) intervals, or substitute one strip of grosgrain belting for the interfacing (2).

Center the interfacing over the wrong side of the belt and pin. Turn the belt seam allowances over the interfacing. Notch pointed end where necessary to make the fabric lie flat. With long running stitches, sew the seam allowances to the interfacing only (3). Staystitch the belt facing 1½" (13 mm) from the raw edge. Turn in the edges of the facing ¾" (20 mm) and baste, notching pointed end as necessary; trim to ⅜" (10 mm) (4). Center and pin the facing over the belt, then slipstitch in place (5).

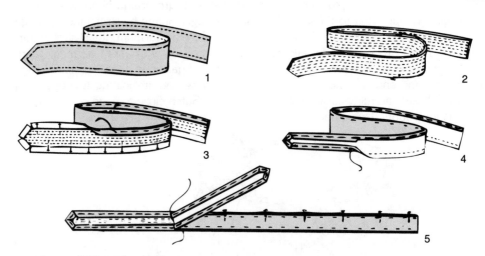

STRAIGHT BELT WITH COMMERCIAL BELTING: Follow manufacturer's directions, or cut one fabric strip on the lengthwise grain the required length and twice the width of the belting plus seam allowances. Shape one end of the belting as desired. Fold belt strip right sides together over the belting, and stitch with a zipper foot close to the belting. Do not catch belting in stitches. Trim seam allowances to ¼" (6 mm) (1). Slide the seam around to the center of belting, and press seam open with the point of your iron. Stitch the shaped end and trim (2). Remove belting and turn; do not press. Slip the belting into the belt, shaped end first, cupping slightly for easier insertion (3).

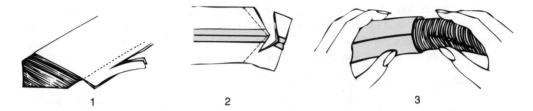

1   2   3

CONTOUR BELT: Follow the instructions for cutting the straight belt. Easestitch the shaped ends and outer curved edges. The interfacing will require some special handling. Pin two layers of interfacing together and trace an outline of your contour belt on them. Stitch the layers together within the outline at ¼" (6 mm) intervals along the lengthwise grain. Cut out belt along traced outline. For a stay, baste a strip of stretched bias tape to the inner curved edge of the interfacing and stitch in place directionally. Then construct the belt as you would a straight belt, adjusting the ease threads as necessary.

CUMMERBUND: Cut a bias rectangle the measurement ot your rib cage plus ½" (13 mm) and at least 9" (23 cm) wide. Stitch ¼" (6 mm) from the long edges and overcast. Turn in long edges 1" (25 mm); press lightly. Make a row of gathering stitches ¼" (6 mm) from each end for a back opening and two rows ¼" (6 mm) apart for gathers at sides of belt. Pull gathers to the desired depth and fasten threads on the inside. Check fit, respacing gathers if necessary to make it snug.

Cut four pieces of feather boning ¼" to ½" (6 mm to 13 mm) shorter than the depth of the belt; remove casing. For sides, cover boning with seam binding as shown (1). Center over gathers, and sew in place. For back opening edges, stitch ½" (13 mm) wide grosgrain ribbon along gathering stitches, extending ends ½" (13 mm). Catchstitch boning over gathers. Turn in ends, folding ribbon to wrong side; favor cummerbund. Sew ribbon securely to underside of gathers (2). Fasten with hooks and eyes so ends meet. Make and attach grosgrain or self-fabric underlap.

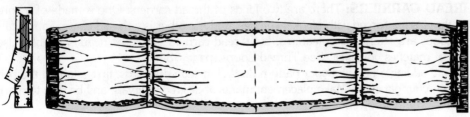

1   2

There are several ways to fasten a belt—with a prong and eyelet buckle, a clasp buckle, hooks and eyes, or snaps. Try on your finished belt. Mark the center front position on both ends for all fastenings but the clasp buckle. Trim the unfinished straight end to measure 2" (5 cm) from the center front line. Stitch ¼" (6 mm) from the trimmed end and overcast.

PRONG AND EYELETS: Pierce a hole for the buckle prong at the center front marking nearest the overcast end. Overcast the raw edges of the hole (1). Slip the buckle prong through the hole; turn back the end and sew securely in place (2). For a half buckle, make a fabric belt loop; slide it over belt close to the buckle and secure. Then secure the belt end (3). On the finished end of your belt, make one eyelet at the center front marking and one or more on both sides for adjustments. You may use commercial eyelets, which come in a variety of colors, or make hand-worked eyelets as instructed on page 331.

CLASP BUCKLE: Slip the ends of the belt through the buckle and bar fastener, folding the ends back along the bars, and try it on. Trim excess at ends to 1" (25 mm). Stitch ¼" (6 mm) from each end and overcast. Slip the ends through the bars; turn back and attach securely.

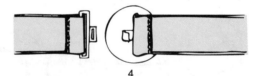

FABRIC CARRIERS or **BELT LOOPS:** The loops should be long enough to accommodate the belt width plus ¼" (6 mm) (possibly a little extra if your fabric is very thick). Cut a straight strip from a selvage edge three times the desired width, and make two folds with the selvage edge on top. Slipstitch the selvage in place (1). Bring ends together and whipstitch. Place the carrier over the markings and sew to the garment at both ends (2). For other methods of making loops, see page 332.

THREAD CARRIERS: There are two kinds of thread carriers. One is made of a core of long threads reinforced with blanket stitches, and the other is a thread chain. Fabric carriers or loops are often design features, but thread carriers should be nearly invisible. Use thread that matches your belt. See Thread Loops, page 334.

If you are adding a belt and your pattern doesn't include markings, first establish the belt position on your garment. Make placement marks at desired intervals, and be sure to mark the width of the belt for your carriers.

Closures

Although closures are primarily functional, their precision and workmanship can add a special dimension to your garments. From tailored, bound buttonholes to delicate thread loops–from decorative buttons to inconspicuous snaps– there is a wide variety of closures from which to choose.

Buttonholes

Let the design and the fabric determine your choice of buttonhole. Couturiers use bound buttonholes for a tailored, professional look on all garments, hand-worked buttonholes for soft or delicate fabrics, and machine-worked buttonholes for man-tailored and casual garments. Your pattern markings include exact placement and size of buttons and buttonholes as recommended by the designer.

Any changes from the designer's intended placement or size should be carefully planned. If you have adjusted the length of the pattern tissue, adjust the buttonholes by evenly spacing them between the top and bottom buttonholes. If you are adding buttonholes, the most important consideration in the placement is the size of your button. Remember that large buttons are placed farther apart than small ones. If your button is larger than recommended, do not move the buttonhole away from the edge, as this will change your center line; rather, extend the closing edge to accommodate the button. (Make this adjustment on the pattern **before** you cut your fabric so the underlap on the left side will be as wide as the overlap on the right side.)

Always test the buttonhole on a scrap of your fabric with the appropriate underlining and interfacing to discover any problems you might encounter. Refer to Pressing, page 358, for tips on pressing your buttonholes.

BUTTONHOLE SIZE: The size of the buttonhole should always be determined by the button. Minimum buttonhole length is equal to the diameter plus the thickness of the button. Add ⅛" (3 mm) to allow for the shank and slight size reduction due to fabric thickness (1).

To find the buttonhole length needed for a thick or ball button, wrap a ¼" (6 mm) wide strip of paper around the button and mark with a pin where the ends meet. Then fold the paper strip flat and measure between the pin and the fold to determine the correct buttonhole size. Add the ⅛" (3 mm) mentioned above (2).

In general, attractive buttonholes are slim, about ¼" (6 mm) wide with each lip ⅛" (3 mm) wide. They may be slightly narrower for lightweight fabrics and a little wider for bulky fabrics, but total width should not exceed ⅜" (10 mm).

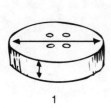

1

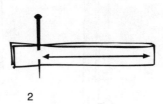

2

PLACEMENT MARKING: Make your buttonhole markings on the right side to make certain that the finished buttonhole will follow the fabric grainlines. First mark the position and length of your buttonhole with pins or chalk, then thread trace for precise markings.

Begin all *horizontal buttonholes* ⅛" (3 mm) to either side of the buttonhole placement line – the side nearest the closing edge to allow for the natural tendency of the garment to "pull" away from the closing. This "pull" is downward for *vertical buttonholes;* begin them ⅛" (3 mm) above the actual button placement and directly on the lengthwise placement line.

The reference point in placing your buttonholes is the garment center line; center lines must meet when your closing is fastened. Thus it should always be the first line marked. Next mark the short horizontal lines for the position of the buttonholes and, lastly. the long continuous vertical lines to indicate their length.

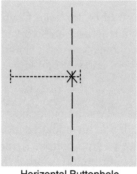 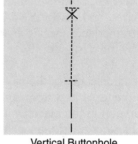

Horizontal Buttonhole   Vertical Buttonhole

For a center closing, the buttons are positioned on the underlap center line, the buttonholes in corresponding positions on the overlap center line (1).

The top buttonhole is generally placed below the neckline edge at least half the width of the button plus ¼" (6 mm). The last buttonhole should be 3" to 4" (7.5 cm to 10 cm) from the bottom, *never through the hem.* Buttonholes are not usually placed closer than ⅝" (15 mm) from a closing edge; for a large button, the extension should be no less than half the button's width plus ¼" (6 mm).

For a double-breasted closing with functional buttonholes, place each row of buttons an equal distance on each side from the underlap center line, and buttonholes in corresponding positions from the overlap center line. Remember the *buttons* are placed equal distances from the center line, not the buttonholes, and make certain both rows of buttonholes extend in the same direction from the buttons (2). For an asymmetrical closing, first make sure center lines match. Mark the short placement markings perpendicular to the edge and the long length lines parallel to the edge (3).

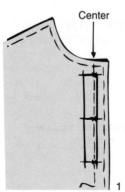 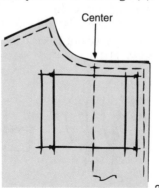 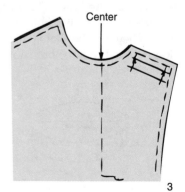

Center   Center   Center

1   2   3

Bound Buttonholes

Make bound buttonholes before attaching the facing. They are formed from strips of fabric cut on either straight or bias grain. Those cut on the bias can add an interesting design feature in plaid or striped fabrics.

There are several methods for making a bound buttonhole—choose the one that you prefer. There are, however, some techniques that are basic to all the methods.

STITCHING: Carefully stitch, using small stitches [15-20 stitches per inch (6-8 per cm)] and follow the buttonhole markings exactly for precise corners and even buttonhole lips.

SLASHING OPENING: After stitching, there are two methods of slashing your bound buttonhole. After securing your thread ends, cut through garment at the center of the buttonhole, cutting between stitching lines from the wrong side with small sharp scissors. Slash along the center of the stitching, stopping ¼" (6 mm) from each end, and clip diagonally to the ends of the stitching or into the corners, being careful not to cut the stitching. Or, you may cut diagonally through the center of the buttonhole, slashing directly to the ends of the stitching or corners.

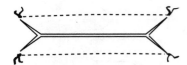 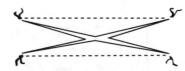

SECURING CORNERS: You must carefully secure the ends of your buttonholes if they are not to pull out or ravel when worn. With the garment placed right side up, fold garment back at each end of the buttonhole to reveal the strip ends with the fabric triangle on top. Then stitch back and forth across the base of each triangle several times with small stitches to square the corners and strengthen the ends. Trim ends to ¼" (6 mm) and catchstitch them to the underlining.

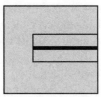

INTERFACING: If you are using lightweight interfacing, make the buttonholes through it so they will be reinforced and supported (1).

To reinforce the buttonhole area in fabrics or garment areas that may not need interfacing, cut a rectangle of interfacing 1" (25 mm) wider and longer than the buttonhole. Center it over the buttonhole markings and baste it in place before making the buttonhole.

Heavier-weight interfacing and all hair canvases are too stiff or bulky to be sewn with the buttonhole. Instead make the buttonholes through just the fabric and underlining and then attach the interfacing. Cut openings in the interfacing slightly larger than the buttonhole openings. Pull buttonholes through, and catchstitch the edges of the buttonhole to the interfacing (2).

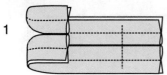 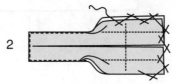

TO COMPLETE BOUND BUTTONHOLES: For a quick and easy finish, pin or baste facing to garment through all thicknesses. Hold buttonhole lips together with diagonal basting for hard-to-handle fabrics. Stick a pin from the outside through each end of the buttonhole opening. Be sure that the pins are in line with the grain of the facing. Slash the facing between the pins and turn in the raw edges. Hem around the buttonhole, as shown, taking a few stitches at each end for reinforcement (1).

To make a better-looking finish on garments to be worn open, establish the length of open buttonhole on the facing with pins. Then cut to within ¼" (6 mm) of each end and clip diagonally into the corners. An additional finish for a thoroughly professional look, or for extremely difficult fabrics, is presented in the couture section, page 458 (2).

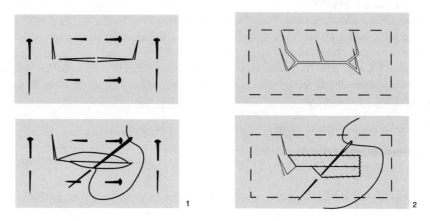

FIVE-LINE PATCH METHOD: This is a very easy method that enables you to measure the five rows of stitching for accuracy before you slash the buttonhole.

Cut a patch of garment fabric 3" (7.5 cm) wide and 2" (5cm) longer than the finished buttonhole. With right sides together, center the patch over the buttonhole markings and pin. Machine- or hand-baste through the center of the patch exactly on top of the buttonhole positon line. Baste again exactly ¼" (6 mm) on either side of the center line to form three parallel rows of basting (1).

Fold the top edge of the buttonhole patch down along the basting line and press. Using a short stitch, sew exactly ⅛" (3 mm) from the fold, beginning and ending exactly at the marking lines which indicate the length of the buttonhole (2).

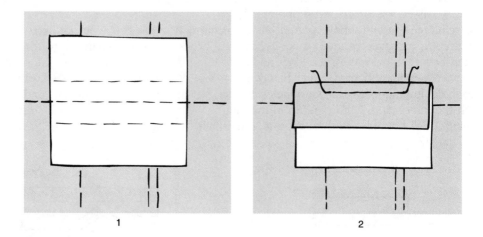

Fold the other edge of the patch up along the basting line to form the second lip of the buttonhole; press and stitch as below (3). On wrong side of garment, measure to see that the five rows of stitching are exactly ⅛" (3 mm) apart along their entire length. Restitch if necessary. Pull thread ends to wrong side of fabric and tie securely (4).

Remove three rows of basting. Cut through the center of the patch, being careful not to cut into the garment (5). On wrong side of garment, slash along the center line and diagonally into the corners, being careful not to cut the stitching (6). Turn patch through slash to the wrong side of the garment and press. Baste the buttonhole lips together (7). To cord your buttonhole, see page 330. Secure corners as on page 325. Trim fabric patch to within ¼" (6 mm) of stitching lines, rounding corners, and press.

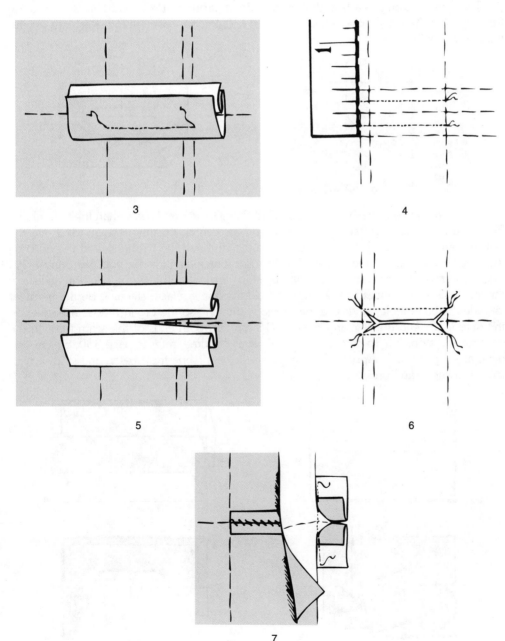

3

4

5

6

7

ORGANZA PATCH METHOD: This method is almost foolproof, and is especially suitable for fabrics that ravel easily or are bulky. Eliminate another problem with these fabrics by applying the interfacing *after* making buttonholes, rather than making them through all layers. Turn to page 325 for directions.

For your patch, always use a crisp, sheer fabric with the same qualities as organza. Cut patch 1" (25 mm) bigger than the buttonhole. Center the patch over the buttonhole marking on the right side of the garment; pin. If you find the markings difficult to see, emphasize them with tailor's chalk. Stitch ⅛" (3 mm) from each side of marking, using small stitches. Start at middle of the marking, pivot at corners, and carefully count the stitches at ends for accuracy. Overlap stitches where you began. Slash, being careful not to cut stitching (1). Turn patch through slash to the wrong side of garment. Press seam allowances away from opening. You now have a neatly finished hole in your garment the exact size of your finished buttonhole (2).

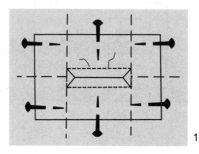

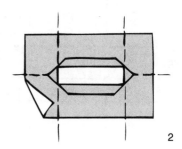

Cut two strips of your fashion fabric 1 ½" (3.8 cm) longer and wider than the buttonhole. Baste the two strips right sides together along the center, forming a seam (3). Press the basted seam open (4). Then accurately place the strips on the wrong side of the opening with the basted seam at the center. This forms the two even lips for your buttonhole. Pin the strips in place close to each end (5). Turn the garment to the wrong side. Pin and stitch the long seam allowances to the strips to hold the lips in place, stitching on the garment (outside the buttonhole) alongside the previous stitching so the organza does not show on the outside. Extend the stitching lines ½" (13 mm) on both ends of the seam through the organza and strips (6). To cord your buttonhole at this time, refer to page 330. Secure corners, as on page 325. Apply interfacing. Trim excess fabric from patch and strip, rounding out corners, and press.

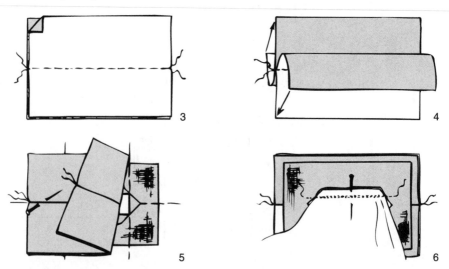

ONE-PIECE FOLDED METHOD: This method requires only one fabric strip per buttonhole and is suitable for light and mediumweight fabrics. Cut a strip of self-fabric 1" (25 mm) wide and 1 " (25 mm) longer than the buttonhole. Mark a center line along the length of the strip. With wrong sides together, fold edges so they meet at the markings; press (1). With the cut edges up, baste the center of the strip over the buttonhole markings. Stitch with small stitches ⅛" (3 mm) from each side of the center, starting at the middle of the side and going across the ends. Carefully count the stitches on the end for accuracy. Overlap stitches where you began (2). Slash, being careful not to cut through the stitching. Turn strip to the inside and press (3). If you wish to cord your buttonhole, refer to page 330. Fold back the garment and secure the corners as on page 325.

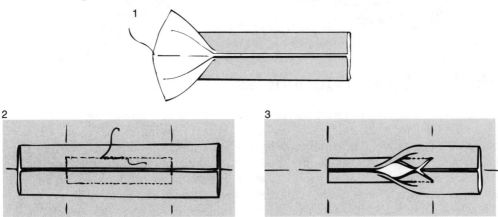

TWO-PIECE METHOD: This method is fast and easy for firm fabrics and textured knits. Cut a strip of self-fabric 1" (25 mm) wide and long enough for all the buttonholes. For the length of this strip, multiply the length of each buttonhole plus 1" (25 mm) by twice the number of buttonholes. Wrong sides together, fold strip in half lengthwise and press lightly.

Machine baste ⅛" (3 mm) from folded edge. Strip can be easily corded as you baste; see page 330. Cut the strip into sections the length of the buttonhole plus 1" (25 mm) and trim the cut edge to a scant ⅛" (3 mm) from the stitching (1).

Baste one strip to the right side, placing the cut edge along the thread-traced position line. Using small stitches, stitch the length of the buttonhole through all thicknesses directly over the stitching on the strip. Leave the thread ends long enough to tie. Repeat for the second strip on the opposite side of the thread-traced line so that the cut edges meet (2). Pull the thread ends through to the wrong side; tie. Slash, being careful not to cut through the strips. Turn the strips to the inside and press (3). Finish the corners as on page 325.

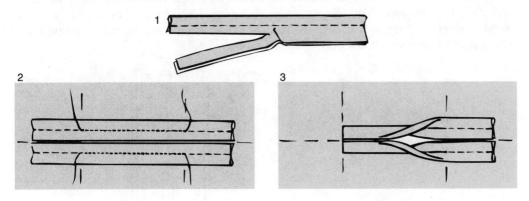

TO CORD BOUND BUTTONHOLES: Cording buttonholes reduces their elasticity, but adds body, strength, and durability. Their raised appearance also provides a finer finish. There are two methods for cording bound buttonholes. For the five-line patch, organza patch, and one-piece folded methods, draw a strand or two of string or yarn through lips just before stitching triangular ends (1). For the two-piece method, fold strip, wrong sides together, around cable cord or twine before you begin to construct the buttonhole. Machine baste close to the cord using a zipper foot (2).

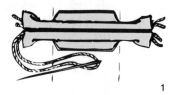
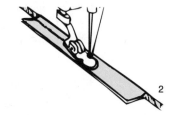

1   2

Machine-Sewn Buttonholes

There are a variety of styles of machine-sewn buttonholes available today. Traditional square-ended, stretch, keyhole, round-ended and buttonholes for fine fabrics are just some of the variations provided by current sewing machines. Refer to your sewing machine manual for your particular machine for the appropriate buttonhole foot to use for a specific buttonhole style and fabric. Some machines have a different presser foot for sewing automatic buttonholes which helps make a continuous series of same size buttonholes.

Machine-sewn buttonholes are suitable for casual, less-tailored garments. Attach any facings or interfacings and apply all markings prior to sewing the buttonholes. Carefully cut the buttonholes open after the stitching is completed. Machine-corded buttonholes add strength and eliminate stretching of the opening. Fine gimp cord is drawn along as the buttonhole is being stitched. Pull the cord ends to the wrong side and knot or clip the ends close and work them into the stitching.

Seam Buttonholes

These buttonholes are actually small openings in a seam. Mark buttonhole placement; pin and baste seam. Cut two strips of ribbon seam binding for each buttonhole 1" (25 mm) longer than opening. On one seam allowance, place strip next to seamline along markings and stitch close to each edge. Repeat on other seam allowance (2). Then stitch garment seam, ending stitching at markings; backstitch. Press seam open. Remove basting from opening. Add bar tacks at ends on wrong side (3).

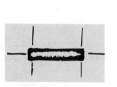
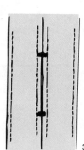
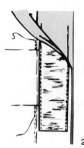

1   2   3

Hand-worked Buttonholes

These buttonholes are sewn through all layers after the facing is applied. Machine-stitch a scant ⅛" (3 mm) on either side and across both ends of the buttonhole marking. Carefully slash along the length marking.

    Take an 18" (46 cm) length of buttonhole twist and insert the needle at one end, anchoring the thread with backstitches on the wrong side. Work the buttonhole stitch by inserting the needle through the slash from the right side and bringing it out just outside the stitching line. Keep thread under eye and point of needle as shown (1). Draw up the needle so a purl (knot) is formed at the buttonhole edge (2). Repeat, keeping stitches even and each purl exactly on the edge of the slash. Fan stitches at the end closest to the finished edge as shown (3). Place a bar tack at the remaining end.

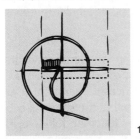

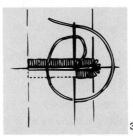

1   2   3

    BAR TACK: Finish both ends of the buttonhole with a bar tack. First take 3 or 4 long stitches across the width at each end of the buttonhole. Then work the blanket stitch over the core threads, catching the fabric underneath (4).

    KEYHOLE: If you prefer a keyhole buttonhole on man-tailored clothes, follow instructions for hand-worked buttonholes, with one exception: make a hole with an awl at end nearest opening edge to form keyhole. Then work buttonhole stitches around hole and slash; finish remaining end with a bar tack (5).

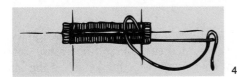
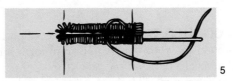

4   5

    CORDED: Hand-worked buttonholes can be corded by working the buttonhole stitch over buttonhole twist secured at one end with a pin. Add bar tack to end: clip cord (6).

    EYELET: This type of buttonhole is used with studs, cuff links, drawstrings, and belts. Sew around placement marking with small running stitches. Cut an opening the desired size or punch a hole with an awl. Bring needle up through fabric from the wrong side a scant ⅛" (3 mm) from edge of hole. Leave 1" (25 mm) of thread on the wrong side and work around the hole with buttonhole stitches. Fasten threads securely on the wrong side (7).

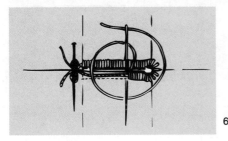
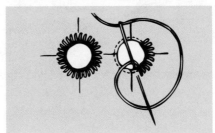

6   7

Fabric and Thread Loops

Some details, no matter how time-consuming, are those little touches that add greatly to the pleasure of wearing a garment you have made. Fabric and thread loops are perfect examples. With careful planning and accurate marking they can be easier to make than they look.

Fabric Loops

Fabric loops add an impressive touch to a simple style whether used with purchased buttons or formed into frogs and Chinese ball buttons. They can be made of self-filled or corded bias tubing, in contrasting or self-fabric, purchased braid; or other tubular material that complements your garment fabric.

SELF-FILLED TUBING: Cut a bias strip the desired length and the finished width plus enough seam allowance to fill the tubing. The additional seam allowance depends upon your fabric-the bulkier the fabric, the narrower the seam allowances. Experiment to determine the correct width for your particular fabric. Remember also that the strip will become somewhat narrower as it is stretched during stitching. Right sides together, fold bias in half lengthwise and stitch, stretching bias as you sew. At end, slant the stitching diagonally, making the tube wider. To turn, pass a heavy thread and a tapestry needle, eye first, through the bias or use a loop turner or bodkin. For a narrow tubing, turn in the raw edges, roll bias between your finger, and sew edges together, eliminating turning process.

 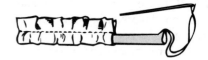

CORDED TUBING: Cut a bias strip of fabric the desired length and wide enough to fit around the cord plus ½" (13 mm) for seam allowances and stretching. If necessary, piece the bias as directed on page 255. Cut a piece of cable cord twice the length of the bias; the extra cord will facilitate stitching and turning. Fold the bias over the cord with right sides together and edges even. Place one end of the bias ¼" (6 mm) beyond the center of the cording. Using a zipper foot, stitch across the end at the center of the cording. Then stretch the bias slightly while stitching the long edge close to the cording. Trim the seam allowance (1). To turn right side out, slowly draw the enclosed cord out of the tubing; the free cord will be pulled into the tubing automatically (2). Cut off the stitched end and the excess cording.

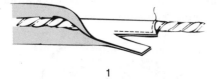 

| 1 | 2 |

There are several new tools or notions available that help turn tubing faster and easier.

ATTACHING LOOPS: Fabric loops can be applied singly or in a continuous row, depending on the fabric weight and spacing desired. Mark the seamline the length of the closure area on a strip of lightweight paper. Make a line for the distance that the loops are to extend (approximately half the diameter of the button, plus the thickness of the cording). Make spread of each loop equal to button diameter plus twice the cord thickness (1).

Single loops: Cut each loop the correct length to fit within the markings plus two seam allowances. Form each loop with the seamed side up and the loop pointing away from the edge, keeping the edges of the paper guide and the loops even. Use narrow masking tape to hold them in place. Using large stitches, stitch on the paper close to the seamline within the seam allowance. Then remove the masking tape, pin paper guide to the appropriate garment edge on the right side of the fabric, matching seamlines. Stitch close to seamline near first stitching (2). Tear away paper and apply facing.

Continuous loops: With a long strip of bias tubing, form a continuous row of loops on the paper guide within the markings, extending them ½" (13 mm) into the seam allowance. Tape and stitch them to the paper and then apply them to the garment in the same manner as single loops (3). The short looped ends in the seam allowance may be trimmed to ¼" (6 mm) to reduce any unnecessary bulk before applying facing.

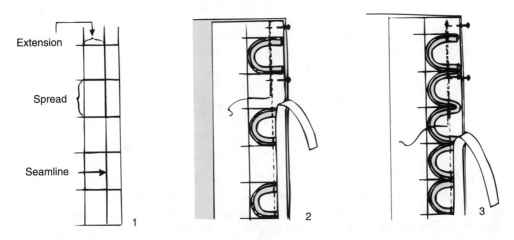

FROGS: Follow the diagram, using soutache braid, round braid, or self-filled or corded tubing. Keep tubing seamline on top while forming the frogs. Use small hand stitches to tack each successive loop as it is formed and tiny invisible stitches to attach the finished frog. You can vary the shape by changing the size of the loops, but remember to keep one loop large enough to extend beyond the garment edge and pass over the button. For intricate shapes, form the frog on paper with masking tape and basting, before stitching.

Thread Loops

Thread loops can be used for a variety of purposes in different locations, as indicated by their names. A thread loop is usually placed at the corner of a neck opening and fastens to a small button. It is also often used in place of a metal eye on delicate fabrics or in conspicuous locations. Its length should be equal to the diameter plus the thickness of the button. A longer loop is used to form a **belt carrier**. Usually placed at the side seams, it should be just large enough to let the belt slip through. A **thread eye** is often used with a metal hook in place of a metal eye, especially on delicate fabrics or in conspicuous locations. Relatively taut, it is the same length as the metal eye it replaces.

A **French tack** or **swing tack** holds two parts of a garment together, such as the two hems of a lined garment, and is usually placed at seams on the wrong side. All types can be formed by either a blanket stitch or a thread chain.

BLANKET STITCH: The blanket stitch is the classic stitch used for most thread loops. Use matching double thread or single buttonhole twist. Take 2 or 3 foundation stitches the desired length and depth of your loop, securing the ends with small backstitches. These stitches form the core of your loop, and it is essential that they be the correct size, if you are using a belt, button, or hook with your loop, make sure the loop size accommodates them and allows for ease. Then, with the same thread, work blanket stitches closely over the entire length of the foundation threads.

THREAD CHAIN: If you prefer, a thread loop can be made with the chainstitch. Use a double thread or single strand of buttonhole twist securely fastened to the garment with one or two small overlapping stitches (1). Form a loop on the right side by taking another short stitch. Slip the thumb and first two fingers of your left hand through the loop while holding the needle and thread end in your right hand (2). Using the second finger of your left hand, pick up a new loop and pull it through the first loop, tightening as you proceed (3). Continue to work the chain to the desired length. Place the needle through the last loop to form a knot and end the chain (4). Secure the free end with several small stitches.

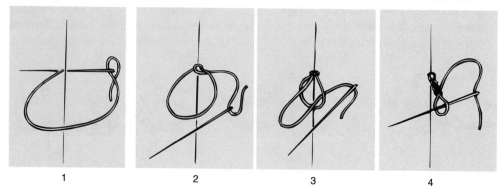

| 1 | 2 | 3 | 4 |

A chainstitch thread chain for belt loops or French tucks can be made on your overlock machine. Follow your machine manual for this technique.

Buttons

Buttons are an important finishing touch not only in their more practical sense as fasteners, but also as adornments and essential parts of the garment design. Gone are the days when buttons simply closed the front or back openings and cuffs of a garment. Today you will see them perching on shoulders, outlining seams, closing skirts and pants, fastening waistbands, attaching belts, ending sleeve vents. They can match, contrast, or complement; give a tailored, casual, or dressy look.

Think of the many different ways you can use them to close a garment–with buttonholes, loops, frogs, or a short chain between two buttons. You might care to group your buttons in clusters, space them irregularly, or use a row of small ones instead of a few larger ones.

However you use buttons, remember that they must relate to the fabric, the design of the garment, and especially to the wearer. Spacing and proportion are the keys to expert selection and placement. For example, a petite figure calls for many small buttons, or a few larger ones. It is best to remain with the button size recommended by the designer. If you prefer to experiment, the best way to find the correct size for your button is to pin on different sizes and see how they look *before* stitching your buttonholes. Refer to the button chart on page 179 to determine correct button sizes.

If you've lengthened or shortened your garment, you may need to adjust the number of buttons and the buttonhole placement accordingly. Be sure that there are buttons located at all points of stress. Place a button at the waist of a fitted jacket or coat to prevent gapping unless you have a belt. If you are using a belt or sash, place your buttons sufficiently above and below the belt so they won't interfere. It is also wise to have a button at the fullest part of the bustline for a large-bosomed figure. If your garment still gaps between buttons, close these spaces with covered snaps.

BUTTON PLACEMENT: The time it takes to see that your buttons are placed correctly is well spent, for it ensures that your garment will close in a straight line and lie flat. Pin the garment closed, matching center basting lines. For a horizontal buttonhole, push a pin through the end of the buttonhole near the finished edge of the garment. The center of the button should be sewn at this point and directly on the center front or center back line. Vertical buttonholes have the buttons placed ⅛" (3 mm) below the top of the buttonhole and on the center front or center back line. Place each button directly in line with the previous button.

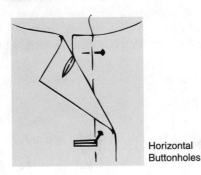

Horizontal
Buttonholes

Vertical
Buttonholes

THREAD: To sew on the button, use a double strand of polyester or cotton thread, heavy duty thread, or buttonhole twist. For buttons on heavier weight coats and jackets, button and carpet thread may be used. Drawing your thread through beeswax will prevent knots from forming in the thread while you sew. For easy handling, your thread should not be much longer than 18" (46 cm). Secure your thread with a couple of small backstitches on the right side under the button, rather than with a knot, for a neater application.

SEW-THROUGH BUTTONS: These should have a thread shank to allow the buttoned fabric to lie smoothly and not pull around the buttons. The length of the shank should equal the thickness of the garment at the buttonhole plus ⅛" (3 mm) for movement. Always begin sewing on the right side. Place a pin, matchstick, toothpick, or other object over the button and sew over the object when sewing on the button. Remove the object, raise the button to the top of the stitches, and wind the thread tightly under the button to form the thread shank. Backstitch several times into the shank for a secure finish. Buttons used for trim will not need a shank (1). Many sewing machines have a special presser foot and built-in button sew-on stitch

REINFORCED BUTTONS: For coats and suits, reinforced buttons are advisable. Place a small flat button on the back of the garment under the larger button. Sew directly through from one to the other for added stability. Use a small folded square of ribbon seam binding in place of the reinforcement button for delicate fabrics. Place it inside the garment directly beneath the holes where it cannot be seen when worn (2).

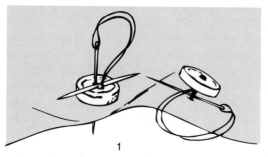
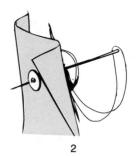

1

2

SHANK BUTTONS: Attach the button with small stitches sewn through the shank. If your garment fabric is very thick and bulky, a thread shank must be made as with the sew-through button. Remember that the direction of the shank should always be aligned with that of the buttonhole (3). To make your shank buttons detachable, insert them through eyelets and secure with toggles (4). Stud buttons are simply inserted through eyelets.

LINK BUTTONS: Link buttons are most commonly used with cuffs, but may also be used to close vests or capes. You may use either purchased or covered buttons. Run heavy thread through two buttons, leaving the thread long enough to form the link and to pass through the joined garment edges. Work over the thread with a blanket stitch (see page 324). Fasten thread securely (5). Buttons can also be sewn to the ends of a narrow turned fabric strip (6).

3

4

5

6

CHINESE BALL BUTTONS: These can be made of purchased braid or self-filled or corded tubing. (See page 332.) Cut a piece of tubing 16" (40.5 cm) long and follow the diagram for the loop formations. Keep tubing seamline on top and loops open while shaping the button. Then draw the ends to pull the loops closer together, easing and shaping the loops to form your button. Clip off any excess tubing and fasten the ends securely to the button.

COVERED BUTTONS: If you want your buttons to be inconspicuous or if your fabric is hard to match, buttons covered with self-fabric may be your answer. Use a commercially prepared kit available in many sizes and shapes or make your own with bone rings.

For a covered ring button, select a bone ring the size of the button you need. Cut a circle of fabric slightly less than twice the diameter of the ring. Gather the edge of the fabric with a small running stitch. Insert the ring, pull up the gathering thread, and secure. Add a special touch by sewing a small running stitch just inside the ring through all layers with buttonhole twist. Back can be covered with a smaller fabric circle, gathered around edge, and slipstitched in place. (See Finest Fastenings, page 459.) Attach with a shank.

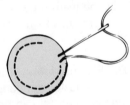

JEWELED BUTTONS: To use jeweled or rough-edged buttons on fabrics that might snag or pull, sew your button directly to the buttonhole, and use covered snaps underneath to secure the opening. This technique will give you the look of a buttonhole closing without the possible mishaps.

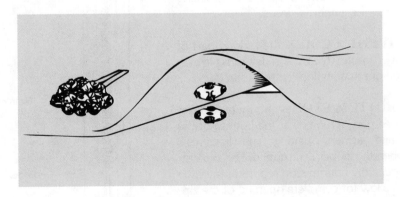

Zippers

Zippers are those mechanical wonders used to close an amazing variety of fashion features. They provide a fast, readily accessible means of getting in and out of your clothes, an asset so valuable in our busy, time-conscious days. Since their invention, zippers have grown lighter, less obvious, and more supple.

Zippers can be made of metal or synthetic teeth or coils and are available in a variety of sizes and wide range of colors to coordinate with your fabric. Specialty zippers, such as separating, invisible, and heavy-duty versions, can also be purchased; refer to the notions section in Chapter 3, pages 176 and 177, for additional information.

Know Your Zipper

For your own information and to unravel any difficulties you may have in use or application, you should be able to identify and understand the function of the various parts of your zipper.

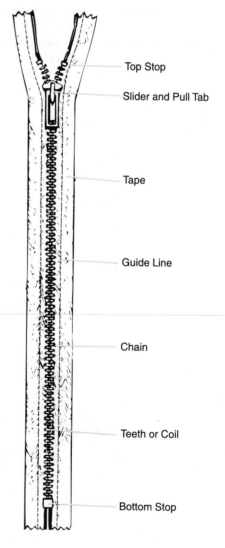

The **TOP STOP** is the small metal bracket or thread bar tack at the top of the zipper that prevents the slider from running off the tape and the teeth from pulling apart.

The **SLIDER AND PULL TAB** is the mechanism that enables you to work the zipper. It locks the teeth together to hold the zipper closed, and unlocks the teeth to open the zipper.

The **TAPE** is the fabric strip on which the teeth or coil are fastened and is the part that is sewn to the garment. It can be woven or knitted, and sometimes covers the back of the coil.

The **GUIDE LINE** is a raised line woven into some zipper tapes to act as a stitching guide.

The **CHAIN** is formed by the interlocking teeth when the zipper is closed.

The **TEETH** or **COIL** is the locking part of the zipper upon which the slider runs. It may be made of metal, nylon, or polyester.

The **BOTTOM STOP** is the metal bracket or bonded part of the coil at the bottom of the zipper and garment opening. The slider rests here when the zipper is unzipped. For separating zippers, the bottom stop separates into two parts to allow for complete opening of the zipper.

Top Stop

Slider and Pull Tab

Tape

Guide Line

Chain

Teeth or Coil

Bottom Stop

Basic Application Procedures

The length of the zipper and the specific type required, if any, will be indicated on the back of your pattern envelope. When you make your zipper selection, consider the weight of the zipper in relation to the weight of your fabric. For example, a synthetic zipper that is lighter in weight and more flexible than a metal zipper is preferable for lighter-weight fabrics.

Complete instructions for all of the major methods of zipper insertion are offered here. You will find that zippers won't be the least bit tricky if you follow the directions carefully and rely on these basic application tips:

- Close the zipper and press out creases before application. When pressing on the right side of the garment, use a press cloth to prevent any unsightly shine, puckers, or impressions.
- Always close the zipper before laundering or dry cleaning.
- Staystitch the zipper opening edges directionally in the seam allowance.
- Bias seams or stretchy fabric may require a stay before inserting the zipper. Cut two strips of seam binding the length of the opening, and baste to the wrong side along the seamline in the seam allowance.
- Extend seam allowances of the zipper opening with ribbon seam binding if they are less than ⅝" (15 mm) wide.
- For zippers with cotton tape, preshrink the zipper if it will be applied in a washable garment.
- Always pin the zipper from the top downward.
- Remember that plaids or stripes should match at the zipper closing as well as at other seams; baste the closing shut, matching the pattern of the fabric.
- A zipper foot is essential for machine-stitching and, if it is adjustable, permits stitching on either side of the zipper without turning the fabric.
- Always sew both sides of your zipper in the same direction.
- For an easier and a truly custom-tailored way to apply a zipper, use the prickstitch.

SHORTENING A ZIPPER: Zippers can be shortened from either end though many prefer to shorten the zipper from the top ensuring the zipper ends are sewn into the seams. To shorten from the top, place the zipper stop slightly above the bottom of the opening. Stitch the zipper and apply the waistband or facing before trimming the excess zipper tape from the top. Separating zippers should be shortened only from the top.

To shorten from the bottom, measure the desired length and whipstitch or bartack by machine across the teeth or coil to form a new bottom stop. Cut the zipper ½" (13 mm) below the stitching. Apply the zipper as usual.

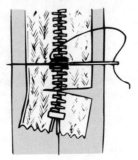

STITCHING A ZIPPER: For an attractive appearance, the final stitching that shows on the outside of the garment must be straight and an even distance from the zipper opening. For best results, topstitch from the right side of the garment using thread basting or sewing tape as a guide. Always begin your stitching at the bottom of the zipper placket and stitch to the top. To stitch past the slider, pull the tab up and turn the slider on its side, or leave the needle in the fabric, raise the zipper foot, and move the slider down before completing your stitching.

One of the easiest methods of achieving straight, even stitching is to use a tiny prickstitch and complete the final stitching by hand. This method is a custom technique and is especially desirable on delicate and pile fabrics. See the couture section, page 448, for complete instructions.

Centered Application

This application is the one most frequently used for center front and center back openings. Attach the facing before installing the zipper. Trim and grade the seam; understitch the facing to the seam allowances. Then turn and press the facing. Waistbands are applied after zipper is inserted.

Open out facings. Machine-baste opening edges together along seamlines, and press seam open. Face down, place closed zipper on opened seam allowances with zipper teeth centered over the seamline and the pull tab ¼" (6 mm) below neck or waist seamline; baste (1).

On outside, stitch by machine or hand across lower end and continue along one side, ¼" (6 mm) from basted seam (2). Begin again at lower end and stitch other side in same manner.

Completing the facing is both quick and easy. Simply turn the facings to the inside, folding in the ends to clear the zipper teeth. Slipstitch the ends in place. Anchor the remaining facing edge. Fasten the neck edge with a hook and eye on the inside of your garment (3).

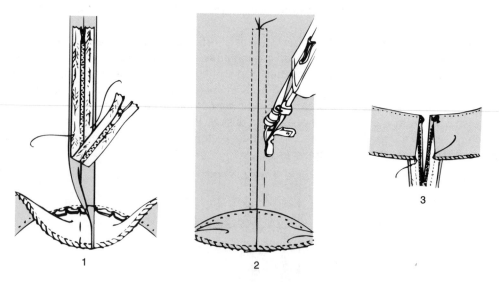

1   2   3

For another method of inserting a centered zipper before the facings are applied, refer to the Very Easy Vogue section, page 420.

Lapped Application

This method neatly conceals your zipper, making it particularly suited for zippers that do not match perfectly with the color of your fabric. It is also used for openings in the side seams of garments. When the garment edge is faced, the facing should be attached before the zipper is inserted. Because the facing may have a tendency to catch in the teeth of the closure and provide excess bulk over the zipper pull tab; we recommend a technique calling for special manipulation of the facing **before** it is stitched to the garment.

FACING: As you are pinning the facing in place, turn back 1" (25 mm) on the end of the overlapping side and trim to ⅝" (15 mm). Then stitch the facing to the garment, continuing to the very end of the opening. Trim, grade, and clip all seam allowances, stopping just short of the unfaced portion of the seam allowance (1). Understitch the facing to the neckline seam allowances, then turn and press (2). Insert zipper as directed below. Turn the facing and zipper tape to the inside. The overlapping facing end will automatically clear the zipper teeth. Turn in the other end to clear the zipper. Slipstitch the facing ends in place and the upper neckline edges together. Anchor the remaining facing edge (3). Complete with a hook sewn on the inside and an eye sewn to the outside of your garment (4).

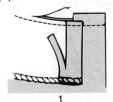

1

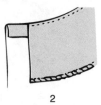

2

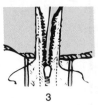

3

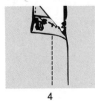

4

APPLICATION: Complete steps 1 and 2 if you are applying your zipper to a faced garment edge. Then mark the seamline on the underlapped opening edge with thread tracing. Turn in the edge ⅛" (3 mm) from the traced seamline in the seam allowance; baste and press. A tiny fold will appear in the seam allowance at the lower edge. Then turn in the full seam allowance on the other opening edge; baste and press (5).

Place the underlapped edge over the zipper tape with the bottom stop of the zipper even with the end of the garment opening. Baste close to the zipper teeth, leaving enough room for the tab to slide easily. Stitch close to the edge by hand or machine (6). Position the overlapping edge to just cover the stitching on the opposite side of the opening. Baste the remaining zipper tape in place to be sure it does not shift during stitching. Stitch by machine or hand across the lower end, pivoting at the corner and continuing along the side ⅜" (10 mm) from the edge (7).

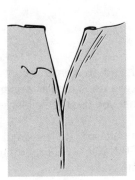

5

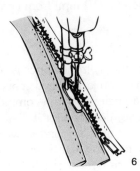

6

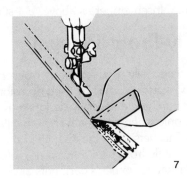

7

Separating Zipper

FACING: Begin by treating both sides of the facing as shown for the overlapping side of the facing in the lapped application. Follow steps 1 and 2 on the previous page.

APPLICATION: Machine-baste the opening edges together along their seamlines, keeping the facing and hem free; press open. Face down, center the closed zipper on the opened seam allowances with the zipper stop at the bottom of the opening. Turn down the tape ends at the top on each side of the pull tab; tack securely. Baste the zipper in place (1).

On the outside, stitch ¼" (6 mm) from each side of the center front by hand or by machine as you would a centered application, still keeping the facing and hem free. On the inside, turn the facing and hem ends in to clear the zipper teeth; slipstitch. Catchstitch the remaining facing and hem edges in place. Turn in any lining seam allowances, making sure the long edges clear the zipper teeth; baste close to the edge. Slipstitch in place (2).

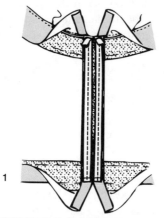

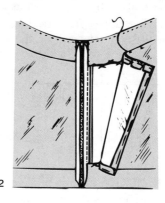

REVERSIBLE GARMENTS: Separating zippers with two pull tabs for reversible garments are available. The zipper area inside the reversible garment is finished so that it is identical in appearance to the outside. Baste zipper in place as above, keeping the long edges of the opening free on the inside. From the inside, turn under the seam allowances so the edges meet over the center of the zipper; baste. From the right side, stitch ¼" (6 mm) from each side of the center front through all thicknesses,

QUILTED OUTDOOR GARMENTS: To eliminate bulk in the zipper area, baste ¾" (20 mm) seam and trim away fiberfill in the seam allowances. Stitch ⅛" (3 mm) from each side of the center front through the fabric and the seam allowances to flatten the zipper area. Insert zipper as above, but stitch ⅜" (10 mm) from center.

Fly-Front Placket

Traditionally used for men's trousers, the fly-front zipper is often found on women's pants and skirts and may be used occasionally on jackets and coats. You can use a regular zipper or purchase a specially designed trouser zipper. We recommend that you use the fly placket only when your pattern is specifically designed for it.

This version is the simplified method usually found in women's patterns. For the traditional fly front with a fly shield, refer to Menswear Sewing, page 502. Remember that the placket in women's garments always laps right over left, just the opposite of men's.

Turn in both front extensions along the foldlines and baste close to the folds. Pin or baste the closed zipper under the left front, with the teeth close to the basted edge and the pull tab ⅛" (3 mm) below the waist seamline. Stitch close to the edge (1). Lap the right front over the zipper, even with the center front marking on the left front, and baste close to the fold through all thicknesses (2). On the inside, baste remaining zipper tape to the right front, through all thicknesses (3). On the outside, stitch on the right front along the stitching line, ending at the seamline marking. Pull threads to the inside and tie (4).

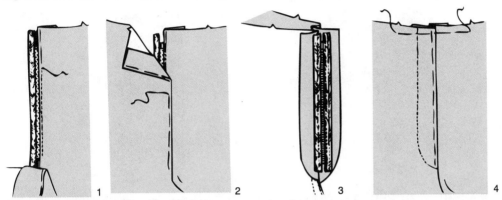

Special Applications

EXPOSED ZIPPER: The exposed zipper application can be used where there is no seam. A fabric patch is first stitched to the placket area to stabilize the opening, prevent raveling, and to eliminate bulk when sewing sweater knits. Use organdy, a lightweight interfacing, or a lining fabric for the fabric stay. Cut fabric stay 2 ½" (6.5 cm) wide and 2" (5 cm) longer than the zipper. Place center of stay strip over the center of the garment opening. With right sides of fabric together, pin or baste in place. Stitch ⅛" (3 mm) on each side of the center line and across the bottom at the end of the zipper marking. Slash along the center line between the rows of stitching and diagonally into the corners (1).

Turn fabric stay to the inside of the garment and press. Center the zipper under the opening with the bottom stop of the zipper at the end of the opening; pin in place. Slip baste the edge of the fabric to the zipper tape, exposing only the zipper teeth or coil. Using a zipper foot, stitch across the base of the triangle through the garment fabric, the stay, and the zipper tape as shown (2). Turn back one side of the garment opening and stitch the garment to the zipper tape along the reinforcement stitching line, beginning at the bottom (3). Repeat for the other side of the opening (4).

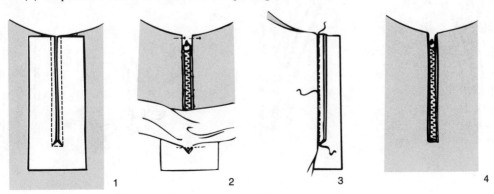

DRESS SIDE PLACKET: For a placket located on the side of a dress, the zipper is inserted in a seam that is closed at both ends. To make a top stop for the zipper, simply whipstitch the upper edges of the zipper tape together. Before inserting zipper, be sure the opening length is equal to the zipper length, with the bottom stop barely concealed. If the zipper is too long, shorten it as on page 339. Insert your zipper, using the lapped or centered application, ignoring facing instructions. As you complete the zipper, stitch across the bottom end, along the long edge, and across the top end by machine or by hand.

INVISIBLE ZIPPER: The invisible zipper, which has no rows of stitching on the outside of the garment, must be stitched with a special invisible zipper foot. Unlike other zippers, the invisible zipper is applied to the opening edges **before** the remainder of the seam is stitched. The facings are usually applied after the zipper is installed.

Open the zipper and place it face down on the right side of the fabric. Have the teeth lying on the seamline and the tape in the seam allowance. Lower the right-hand groove of the foot over the teeth, and stitch from upper edge to pull tab (1). Keep stitches as close to the teeth as possible. Close the zipper to position the other side on the opposite seam allowance. Pin or baste as desired. Open the zipper and stitch with the left hand groove of the foot over the teeth (2). Close the zipper. To finish the seam below the zipper, slide the zipper foot to the left. Lower the needle and begin stitching just slightly above and to the left of the last stitch. Stitch seam closed (3). To complete the application, stitch each end of the zipper tape to the seam allowances (4).

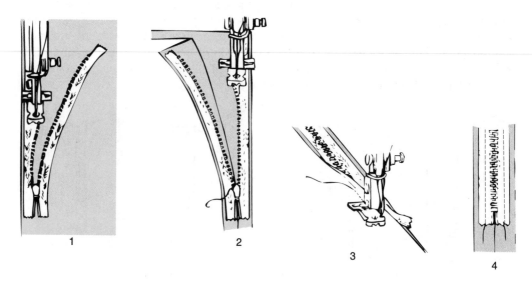

1   2   3   4

Fasteners

There are many commercial fasteners available. The key is to select the one best suited to your individual needs. These fasteners, to be truly functional, should be chosen in a size appropriate to the fabric weight, the amount of strain the closure will receive, and the type of cleaning and care the garment will require. For types and sizes of fasteners, refer to page 178. Choose a fastener that will also be inconspicuous while the garment is being worn. To simplify matters, we have divided the commercial fasteners into three basic categories *snaps, hooks and eyes,* and **hook and loop tape fasteners.**

Snaps

These fasteners are used on overlapping edges that receive a minimum of strain. The ball half of the snap is sewn on the underside of the overlap. The socket is sewn on the upper side of the garment section closest to your body. Sew the ball on first. Take several small stitches close together through each hole, picking up a thread of the garment with each stitch. Carry the thread under the snap from hole to hole. To mark the location for the socket, rub tailor's chalk onto the ball and position the garment as when fastened, or use a pin through the ball section.

For a couture finish, use fabric-covered snaps that are ready-made, or you can cover your own. To use a snap on garment edges that just meet, choose either an extended snap or a hanging snap application; refer to the couture section, page 459.

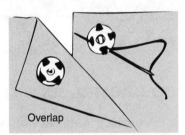

Overlap

Hooks and Eyes

Hooks and eyes are most frequently found at neck edges or waistbands. To attach the hook, work stitches around the circular holes, picking up a garment thread with each stitch. Secure the thread, but do not clip. Slip the needle through the fabric, surfacing to sew the hook end to the garment to hold it flat. To fasten straight or curved metal eyes, work stitches around the circular holes as for the hook. For curved metal eyes, continue to sew a few stitches on either side of the eye to hold it flat. For a thread loop, see page 334.

If the edges overlap, sew the hook even with the overlapping edge on the inside. Then sew a straight metal or thread eye on the outside of your garment on the underlap.

If the closing edges just meet, such as a neckline, sew a hook and a curved metal eye on the wrong side of the garment. Place and sew the hook ⅟₁₆" (2 mm) from one edge. The curved eye should be placed with the loop extending slightly beyond the other edge (1). Or make a thread eye, the same length as the metal eye it replaces (2).

Large or heavy-duty hooks and eyes are used on areas that receive excessive strain, such as waistbands. Position them as you would regular hooks and eyes and sew them on through the holes (3). In addition to the slide type shown here, large covered hooks and eyes are available for closures on heavyweight garments, such as furs and coats.

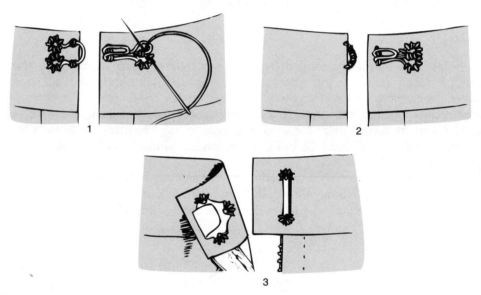

1   2

3

Hook and Loop Tape Fasteners

This fastener operates on the same principle as hooks and eyes. One strip is faced with tiny hooks, the other with a pile fabric serving as minute eyes. When pressed together, the two strips fuse until pulled apart. They are excellent on loose-fitting garments such as jacket fronts, belt overlaps, etc., but are not suitable on tight-fitting garments, on very lightweight fabrics, or whenever extra bulk is not desirable.

There are several effective methods of application. You may machine-stitch the lower strip in place through all layers and the upper strip through just one layer where it cannot be seen. This application must be done during the construction process. Another method is to apply the upper strip by hand, using a sturdy slipstitch through just one layer of fabric, and the lower strip by machine through all layers. Topstitching both strips through all garment layers is also popular as a design detail on casual clothes.

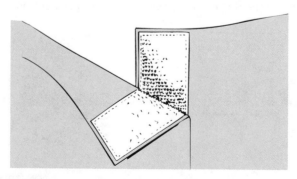

Hems

One of the most important fashion aspects of any garment is its hemline. Although the real purpose of the hem is to help your garment hang well by adding weight to the edge, variations in hem lengths will also change the silhouette and proportion of your garment. To be really complete, your wardrobe should include several different hemlines and the accompanying illustration will show you the principal lengths.

We wish to emphasize the fact that there is no standard hem length that is correct for every woman. Always let the lengths most becoming to you influence your choice of hem levels.

Although fashion and proportion dictate hem lengths. the type of garment, the nature of the fabric, and the height of the wearer determine the depth of the hem. Usually the hem allowance is 3" (7.5 cm), which adds weight and therefore influences the drape of the garment. This is suitable for straight garments and for medium and lightweight fabrics. Flared skirts, stretchy fabrics such as knits, and heavier-weight fabrics should have a narrower hem of 1 ½" to 2" (3.8 cm to 5 cm). Very full or circular skirts need only a 1" (25 mm) hem. Narrow-rolled hems only ⅛" (3 mm) wide or very deep hems up to 6" (15 cm) wide are suitable for sheer fabrics.

A well-made hem is always the least noticeable hem. Always take the time to eliminate bulk, reduce extra fullness, and press carefully to prevent ridges. Above all, never pull the stitches tightly as you sew.

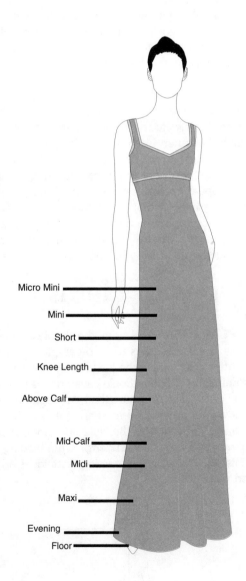

Micro Mini
Mini
Short
Knee Length
Above Calf
Mid-Calf
Midi
Maxi
Evening
Floor

MARKING HEMLINE: When preparing a hem, there are several fundamental steps to follow. As with any other phase of fitting, the proper undergarments and shoes must be worn when measuring the hem. If you plan to add accessories such as a belt, sash, or jacket, wear it while you are measuring. It will be a factor in determining the hem length in proportion to the total garment design and will affect the garment length considerably when worn.

For absolute accuracy, always have someone mark your hem for you. To avoid discrepancies, stand stationary and have the person doing the marking move around you, Pins should be placed every 3" (7.5 cm) for a straight skirt and every 2" (5 cm) for a flared skirt. If your garment has a bias cut or circular hem, let it hang for 24 hours before measuring, allowing the bias to set and preventing hemline sag.

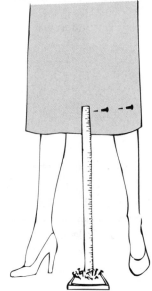

After the hemline has been marked, pin up the hem to see if it looks good. Insert the pins at right angles to the hemline, letting it fall in a natural manner. Regardless of length, the hem should look right. It should be parallel to the floor, but occasionally a perfectly straight hem will appear uneven, especially in garments with pleats, plaids, or that are biascut. If such a situation occurs, the hem must be changed to adapt to the optical illusion. Make the correction, using a carefully controlled, gradual change in the hem depth; then try the garment on again to see if the hemline appears to be even.

Types of Hems

PLAIN HEM: This hem, the simplest and most basic of all the hems, has little or no fullness. The procedures used to complete it are the preliminary steps for most hems.

After determining the length, trim any seam allowances below the hemline to ¼" (6 mm), eliminating bulk that could cause ridges when the hem is pressed. Then baste close to the fold of the hem, measure the hem depth, and trim evenly. Press the hem with brown paper between the hem and the garment, steaming out any fullness. Finish the raw edge in the maner best suited to the style and fabric. Sew the hem in place with a slipstitch or hemming stitch for turned-under or seam binding finishes and blindstitch for pinked or overcast finishes. Then use the pressing techniques applicable to the hem edge desired, as described on page 360.

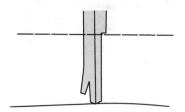

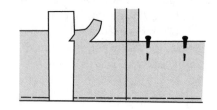

EASED HEM: When your hem has excess fullness that must be adjusted, an eased hem should be used. To ease, stitch ¼" (6 mm) from the raw edge, using long stitches. Pull up the ease thread every few inches (centimeters), then shrink out the fullness with a steam iron. Refer to Pressing, page 360, for detailed information on how to shrink hems. Finish the raw edge and sew as suggested for the plain hem.

CIRCULAR HEM: This hem should be about 1" (25 mm) in depth to eliminate bulk and excess fullness. Let the garment hang for 24 hours before marking. Then mark and complete hem, following the steps for the eased hem (1).

NARROW HEM: For blouses, lingerie, and accessories, use a narrow hem. Trim hem allowance to ½" (13 mm). Turn under raw edges ¼" (6 mm) and press. Turn up edge again and press. Stitch by machine through all thicknesses for casual clothes, or slipstitch to complete the hem (2). Silks and sheers require the couture touch of a hand-rolled hem; refer to page 451.

1   2

MACHINE-STITCHED HEM: A topstitched hem is suitable for garments in which topstitching has been used elsewhere. Fold hemline to desired width. For woven fabrics, turn under hem edge 3/8" (10 mm) and press. From right side of fabric, topstitch close to upper edge. If desired, a second row of topstitching can be placed ¼" (6 mm) below the first row (3).

For other machine-stitched hems, turn to the *Very Easy Vogue* section, page 413.

3

COVER STITCH HEMS: Two types of hem finishes for knit fabrics are sewn on the overlock machine besides a traditional serger blindhem. Using two or three needles, the cover hem resembles topstitching on the right side (4 and 5).

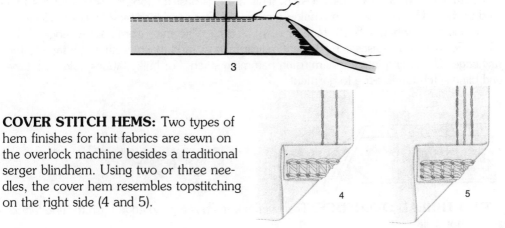

4   5

Hem Finishes

STITCHED AND OVERCAST: This method creates a very fine finish. The completed hem is inconspicuous from the outside after pressing, and the raw edges are finished securely without bulk. Stitch ¼" (6 mm) from raw edge, using a large stitch if your hem will be eased. Overcast edge, using this stitching as a guide. To ensure an invisible hem, turn the edge back ¼" (6 mm) and blindstitch (1).

STITCHED AND PINKED: Here is a quick and effective finish for fabrics that ravel slightly. Stitch ¼" (6 mm) from the raw edge; use a large stitch for an eased hem, Then pink or scallop the edge. Turn edge back ¼" (6 mm) and blindstitch to garment (2).

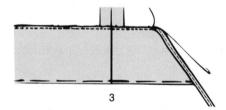
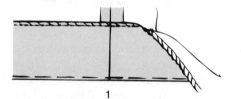

1

2

TURNED-UNDER: Use this finish for light and mediumweight fabrics, for sheers, and for limp hems. Turn in the raw edge ¼" (6 mm) and stitch close to the fold. (Omit this stitching for sheers.) Use hemming stitch to complete hem (3).

ZIGZAGGED: A fast, easy finish for fabrics of all weights. For heavier-weight or firmer fabrics, place zigzag stitches over the raw edge. For lighter-weight and softer fabrics, stitch about ⅛" (3 mm) away from the raw edge. Attach hem to garment with a catchstitch: use a blind-stitch for heavier fabrics (4).

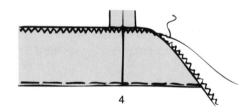
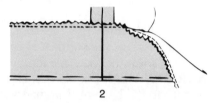

3

4

SEAM BINDING OR BIAS TAPE: This finish is best for loosely woven fabrics that tend to ravel. Use ribbon seam binding for straight hems and bias tape or flexible lace for eased and circular hems. Stitch tape or seam binding ¼" (6 mm) from the raw edge of the fabric. For bias tape, easestitch the hem, adjust fullness, and machinestitch the tape to the raw edge. Then complete the hem using hemming stitch. For bulky fabrics, fold back tape and blind-stitch fabric edge to garment.

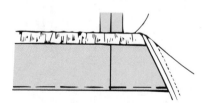
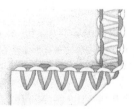

TWO THREAD OVEREDGE: This overlock stitch is a good edge fnish for fine fabrics as it is not bulky.

HONG KONG FINISH: A special couture finish for seams and hems; see page 460.

Special Hems

BIAS-FACED HEM: A facing constructed of a lightweight fabric will provide a smooth finish for garments with inadequate hem allowances, very full skirts, or very bulky fabrics. You may use either commercial bias facing or your own bias strip cut from a lightweight material the desired width plus ½" (13 mm) for seam allowances.

Mark your hemline, leaving at least ½" (13 mm) additional fabric at the bottom edge. For a very curved hemline, shape the bias to the garment. Match raw edges and stitch in a 1 ¼" (6 mm) seam, joining the ends of the facing as on page 258. Press seam open. Turn in raw edge ¼" (6 mm), turn facing up, and slipstitch (1).

DOUBLE-STITCHED HEM: This hem is ideal for unlined heavy fabrics and knits. Stitch and overcast the raw edge. Mark the hemline with thread tracing; shrink and adjust any ease. Baste along the center of the hem. Fold back the hem along the basting and blind catchstitch the hem. Do not pull the stitches too tightly; this line of stitching is for support only. Turn up the top edge of the hem and sew it with a second line of loose catchstitching (2).

1   2

INTERFACED HEM: Your garment style or fabric may require the control of an interfaced hem to create a smooth, unbroken line. Mark the hemline with thread tracing. Finish raw edge of hem.

For lined garments, the interfacing extends above the hem to prevent any impression of the hem on the right side of the garment. Cut interfacing 1 ⅝" (4 cm) wider than hem. For unlined garments, cut interfacing the same width as hem. Use regular interfacing fabrics for body or lamb's wool for a very softly rolled effect. Cut a bias strip long enough to lap the ends ½" (13 mm). Piece if necessary. For curved hemlines, preshape the interfacing to correspond with the curve. Place interfacing over hemline with one edge extending ⅝" (15 mm) below the thread tracing. For hems which will be topstitched or edgestitched, cut off interfacing at hemline.

Sew interfacing to garment with invisible catchstitches along both edges. Turn up hem and baste close to fold. For lined garments, catchstitch hem to interfacing only. For unlined garments, blindstitch hem, easing fullness if necessary. To press, steam the hem, never resting your iron on the fabric. Refer to Pressing, page 360, for additional information.

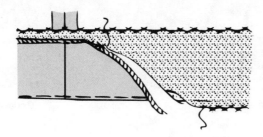

HEMS WITH PLEATS: Press open the seam within the hem area where it crosses the hem at the edge of a pleat fold. Finish the raw edge of the hem, then measure up from the hemline the width of the hem and clip the seam. Both seam allowances above the hem will face in one direction, helping to keep the pleat fold flat (1).

An effective way to ensure that any pleated hem stays creased is to edgestitch the fold of the pleat. Stitch through all thicknesses of the hem on the inside (2).

To handle fullness effectively in a pleated hem, restitch the seam below the hemline at a slant opposite that of the garment seam above the hemline. Remove previous stitching and trim the seam below the hemline to ¼" (6 mm) (3). Complete the hem.

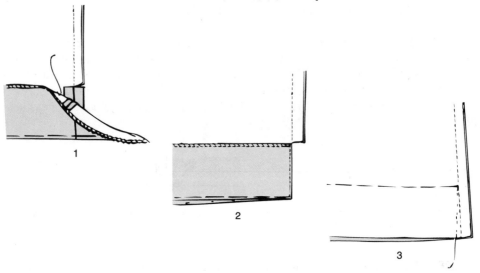

HEMS WITH GODETS: A godet can be used to give extra width to a hem. It can be inserted into a seam, dart, cut-out, or slash. A pie-shaped godet, (the most common shape) is usually cut with the straight grain down the center of the fabric, leaving bias edges on the sides.

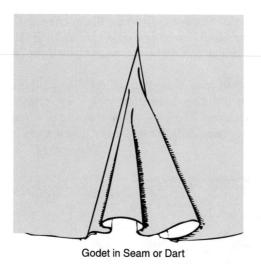

Godet in Seam or Dart

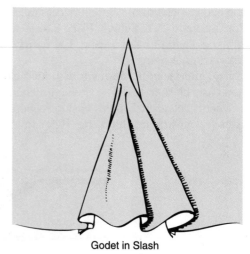

Godet in Slash

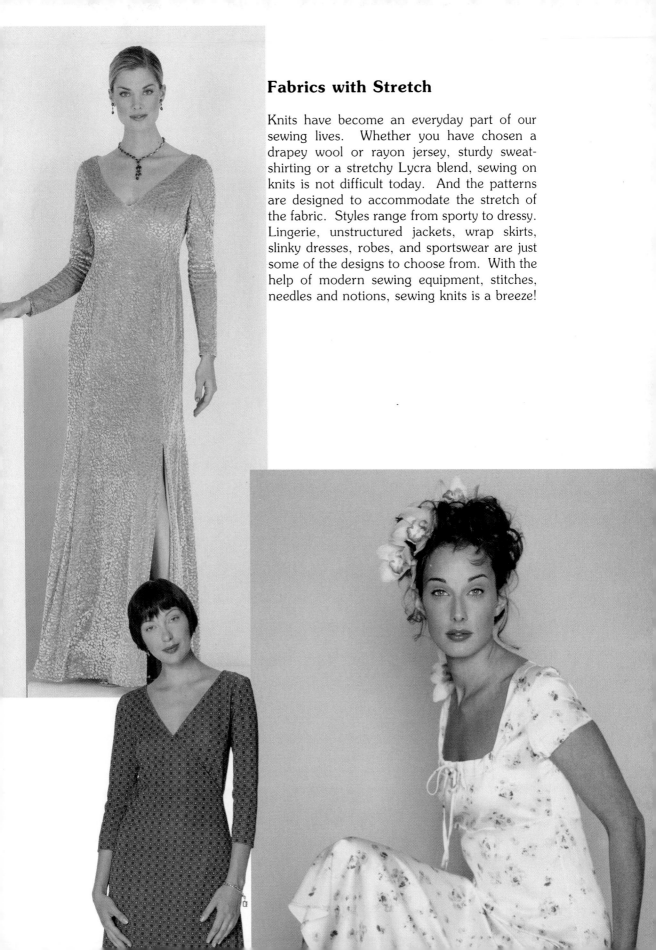

Fabrics with Stretch

Knits have become an everyday part of our sewing lives. Whether you have chosen a drapey wool or rayon jersey, sturdy sweatshirting or a stretchy Lycra blend, sewing on knits is not difficult today. And the patterns are designed to accommodate the stretch of the fabric. Styles range from sporty to dressy. Lingerie, unstructured jackets, wrap skirts, slinky dresses, robes, and sportswear are just some of the designs to choose from. With the help of modern sewing equipment, stitches, needles and notions, sewing knits is a breeze!

Faux Fur and Feathers

The luxurious feel of fur is indescribable! Soft and plush, it lends itself well to handsome cuffs and collars on jackets and coats. The choice of fur type is up to you--low or high pile, silky or stiff. Whatever your choice, it can add an element of opulence or pizzazz to your garments. Or you could add a feather trim on a shawl or jacket edge for an equally exciting look. Select a simple pattern when using either trim.

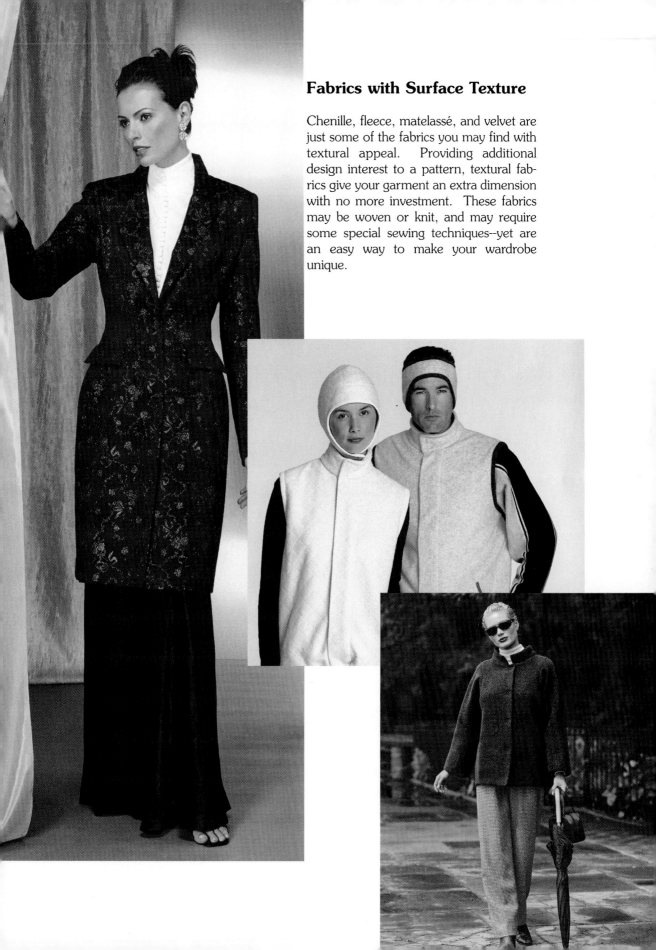

Fabrics with Surface Texture

Chenille, fleece, matelassé, and velvet are just some of the fabrics you may find with textural appeal. Providing additional design interest to a pattern, textural fabrics give your garment an extra dimension with no more investment. These fabrics may be woven or knit, and may require some special sewing techniques--yet are an easy way to make your wardrobe unique.

For insertion into a seam or dart, pin godet to garment, matching seamlines and markings. For heavy or stretchy fabrics, center ribbon seam binding over seamlines for support. Baste and stitch on either side from point to hem (1). Clip seam allowances 1" (25 mm) below the point. Press seam allowances open below the clip, toward the garment above the clip, and open again above the point (2).

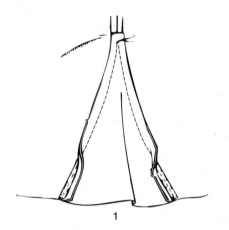

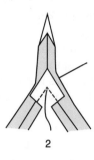

For insertion into a slash, reinforce the slash by sewing just inside the seamlines in the seam allowance, using small stitches [15-20 per inch (6-8 per cm)] on both sides of the point and pivoting at the point. If fabric is especially fragile, reinforce point with a patch of underlining. At point, clip exactly to stitching (3). Pin godet to slash, turning patch inside and matching the godet marking to the clipped point first. Baste and stitch, slashed side up, from point to hem (4). Press seam allowances toward garment (5).

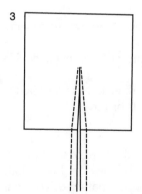

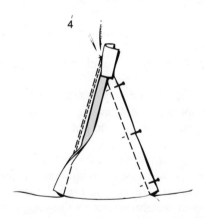

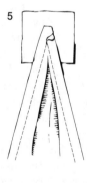

With heavy or loosely woven fabrics, stitch the godet to the garment for only a few inches (centimeters) on either side of the point and let the remainder of the godet hang free for 24 hours to allow the bias to set. Before hemming, allow all garments to hang 24 hours.

For other couture hem finishes—soft hems, extremely curved hems, and horsehair braid finish—see pages 461 and 462. To achieve a smooth corner when a facing folds back at the hemline, see the tailoring section, page 446. For an explanation of pressing techniques and equipment to use on hems, see page 360.

Pressing

That finely finished look every woman strives for is as much a product of good pressing as it is of careful construction. Do not ignore pressing directions in your haste and zeal. If you postpone your pressing until the garment is completed, it will be too late to accomplish well-defined edges and sculptured contours. Set up your pressing equipment near your sewing machine and use it faithfully.

The most important idea to remember is that pressing is not ironing. Pressing is the process of lifting the iron and setting it down in the proper position. You can use pressing to accomplish feats not possible with a needle and thread.

Specifically, pressing techniques depend on the particular fabric and garment construction, but there are some basic rules which should always be followed:

- Have an assortment of equipment available so that you can place the fabric in the most practical position for the area being pressed.
- Always test an odd scrap or an inconspicuous area to determine the best technique for your fabric. Test a piece large enough to allow a comparison between the pressed portion and the unpressed portion.
- Check your fabric's reaction to steam and moisture. Both should be used sparingly, or water marks, puckering, and dulling may result.
- Press with the grain of your fabric whenever possible; be very careful not to stretch edges or curves by pulling the fabric.
- Whenever possible, press on the wrong side of your fabric. If you must press on the right side, use a press cloth.
- Use brown paper strips to prevent impressions of seam allowances, darts, or pleats from appearing on the right side of your fabric. Cut strips at least 2" (5 cm) wider than the area to be pressed.
- Always press seams and darts before they are crossed with other seams to eliminate any extra bulk.
- Never press any sharp creases until the fit of your garment has been double-checked.
- Try to use only the tip of your iron and work in the same direction as you stitched.
- To avoid marring fabric, do not press over basting threads or pins.
- Above all, know your fabric, and do not over-press.

PRESS CLOTH: To prevent shine and protect your fabric from the heat of the iron and its impression, use an appropriate press cloth between the fabric and the iron. Press cloths are made of a variety of fabrics. The one you use depends upon the nature of your garment fabric. Select one of a weight similar to the weight of your fabric and use a size approximately 12" by 18" (30.5 cm by 46 cm). An extra scrap of your fabric makes an excellent press cloth. In general, a wool press cloth is best for preserving the spongy texture of woolens, while firm cotton is ideal for most flat-surfaced cottons and mediumweight blends. Cheesecloth, used singly or folded several times, will readily adapt to most of your needs because it is supple and you can see through it for pressing details.

You may use a dry press cloth with either a dry or steam iron. A uniformly damp press cloth may be necessary. If so, moisten it with a sponge, or immerse, wring, and press it until the proper dampness is achieved. To avoid shrinkage, **never** place a really wet cloth on your fabric and don't have the iron so hot that the cloth dries immediately. Keep in mind that there are several very suitable commercial press cloths in addition to making your own.

STEAM: The moisture of steam provides the slight amount of dampness needed to get truly flat seams or edges. Curved or softly draped sections of your garment may be "set" to hang correctly by steaming them into position. Steam is of special value for collars and lapels. They will always roll correctly if carefully steamed in position on a dress form or a rolled towel during construction.

Use a press cloth if you apply the iron directly. If the iron is held about 3" (7.5 cm) from the fabric, no cloth is needed. Let the steam do most of the work. Steam, then mold the fabric with your fingers while it is still damp. Allow the steam to dissipate and the fabric to dry before you resume working.

Seams

Initially, all seams are treated alike. Press along the stitching line in the same direction as the seam was sewn to merge stitches with fabric. Open the seam flat with the tip of your iron. Then let the shape of the seam dictate further handling.

FLAT SEAMS often leave ridges in the right side of your garment. Steam press with the garment over a seam roll or with brown paper under the seam allowances. To get some seams truly flat, you may have to steam the surface and use short quick movements with a pounding block on the seamline only (1).

CURVED OR ROUNDED SEAMS pose different problems. The seamline should be pressed flat, but the seam area should maintain its built-in roundness. Employ the techniques used for a flat seam, but vary the equipment. Use a tailor's ham or dressmaker's cushion, alone or with a sleeve board, as your pressing surface (2).

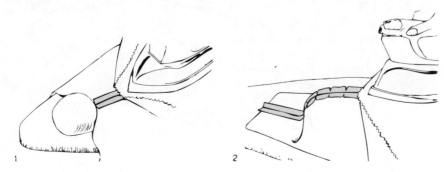

1

2

SEAMS AT FINISHED EDGES with allowances completely enclosed within parts of your garment (such as facings, cuffs, pocket flaps, and collars) should be pressed before turning. Due to the confined area, narrow seam allowances, and the necessity of precise pressing, you will find it easier to work without a press cloth. After stitching, place the seam over the edge of a point presser or tailor's board and open it with the tip of your iron to facilitate turning and ensure a flat seam that will not roll (1). Then lay the section flat on the ironing board with the underside up. Turn pressed seam allowances toward the section until the stitching line shows and press very lightly to make turning and favoring the outer edge easier (2). Turn right side out and press with a cloth from the underside; keep the seam on the underside (3).

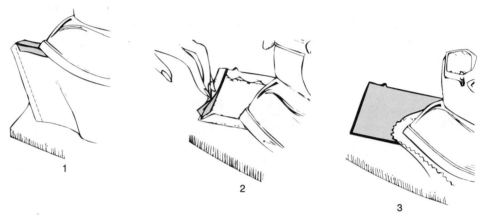

Darts

Darts require a subtly rounded pressing surface such as a tailor's ham or dressmaker's cushion. First press the dart flat, as it was stitched, being careful not to let your iron stray past the pointed end. Then open the garment and press the dart in the proper direction, working from the wider end toward the point. Do not give the dart a sharp crease until the garment has been fitted. In general, vertical darts are pressed toward center back or front and horizontal darts are pressed downward. Press contour or doublepointed darts like singlepointed darts, one half of the dart at a time, working from the middle to the pointed ends. Slash darts in heavy fabrics along the fold to within ½" to 1" (13 mm to 25 mm) of the point. Over a rounded surface, open the dart edges with the tip of your iron. Using a press cloth, press darts completely open. After pressing the dart, press the surrounding garment area.

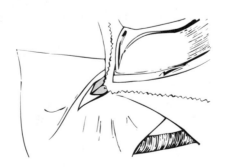

Tucks

First press tucks from underneath side of fold. To retain the soft fold of a released tuck, never press past stitching line. Be cautious with steam; too much may cause puckering. Press the fold of released tucks toward center front or back from wrong side. Tucks made on right side are pressed from stitching line toward folds; put brown paper under folds of wide tucks. Use a press cloth when pressing from right side (1).

Gathering and Shirring

Press from the wrong side wherever possible. Hold the gathering along the stitching as you work. Move your iron from the flat, ungathered area toward the rows of stitching. Use the tip of your iron to get between the folds of fabric. Repeat the procedure until no sharp creases remain. Press gathered seam allowances flat before stitching (2).

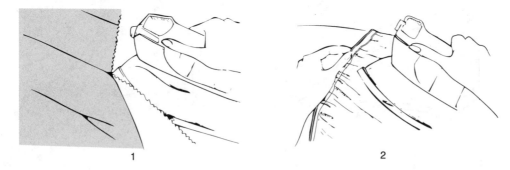

1   2

Pleats

When you are sure of fit, baste the length of each pleat; then press on both sides of the pleat, using a press cloth and very little steam. Press just enough to set the pleat. If the pleats fall correctly, press again to within 8" (20.5 cm) of the lower edge, setting the creases permanently; use strips of brown paper under the folds. Hem and set remainder of pleat creases. (Press the full length if the hem is already completed.) To prevent overhanging fabric from distorting the pleats, support with a chair or table.

Soft or unpressed pleats should be steamed gently into folds rather than sharp creases. Place the garment on a dress form so the folds fall naturally and steam thoroughly with your iron. If a dress form is not available, pin the pleats in place on your ironing board cover and steam them, holding the iron 2" to 3" (5 cm to 7.5 cm) from the fabric. Let the fabric dry completely before removing the garment from the board.

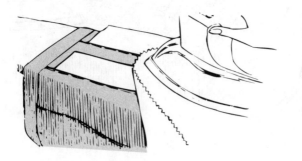
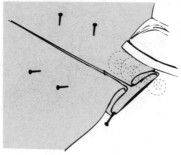

Plackets and Zippers

Because these features can be found in curved or flat areas, let the shape of the garment area determine the appropriate equipment to use. Position your placket right side down on a press pad, thick woolen scrap, or a heavy towel placed on your ironing board, or a tailor's ham. The padding will prevent unwanted ridges from appearing as you press. Work from the wrong side; use a press cloth and limited moisture since excess dampness may create puckers. Do not press directly on zipper teeth, hooks and eyes, or snaps to avoid marring them or the sole plate of your iron. Should you need to touch up the right side of your fabric, place brown paper between the placket lap and the fabric underneath and press, protecting the fabric with a press cloth. Again be especially sparing in your use of steam and moisture.

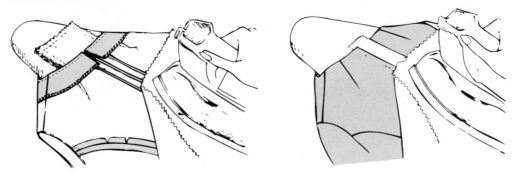

Buttonholes

Since buttonholes call for detailed construction techniques, you'll find that careful pressing applied at the appropriate times will greatly simplify the entire procedure. After stitching the buttonhole to the garment, use a press cloth and brown paper under the strip edges to press the buttonhole from the right side, merging fabric and threads. Then use a sleeve board, placing the wrong side of the buttonhole area on the larger side of the board to prevent the surrounding garment area from becoming wrinkled. Lift up the strips and touch up portions of the garment between the buttonholes, if necessary. Then lay garment flat on ironing board and press the surrounding garment area.

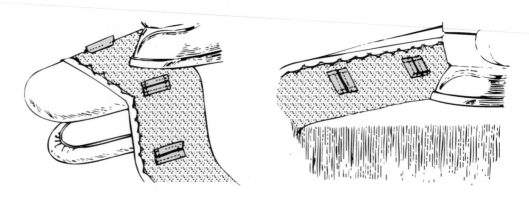

Pockets

The procedure for pressing pockets is quite similar to that of buttonholes. After stitching the pocket to the garment, press from the right side, using a press cloth. For welt or flap pockets, first put brown paper between the garment and the welt or flap. Then turn to the wrong side and press along seamlines, using a press pad. Then lift up the pocket and touch up the garment area underneath the pocket, using the moisture appropriate to your fabric.

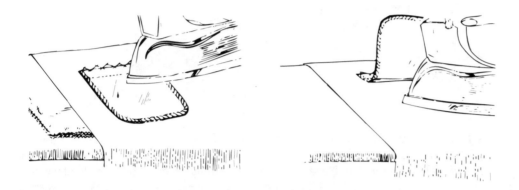

Sleeves

Start by pressing the sleeve seam open over a sleeve board. After easing and fitting the sleeve cap, remove the sleeve from the garment and place it on the narrow end of a sleeve board. Then use the tip and side of your iron to shrink the fullness from the seam allowance only. Be very careful not to press beyond the stitching line or flatten the sleeve cap. Some fabrics, such as permanent press and velvet, do not respond well to shrinking. If your fabric and sleeve cap need additional handling, see Set-in Sleeves, page 284. After the sleeve has been stitched into the garment, press along the seam over a tailor's ham to blend the stitches into your fabric. Avoid extending the iron into the sleeve cap and use steam sparingly.

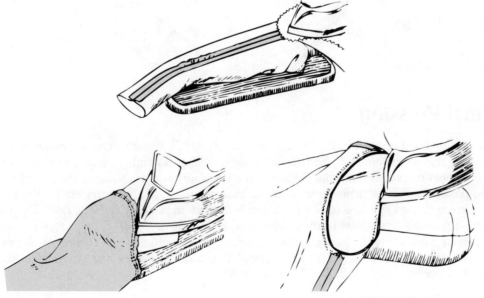

Hems

After marking, baste hems near the fold. Place brown paper between hem and garment and steam out any excess fullness. Avoid pressing over basting threads. For a great amount of fullness, easestitch along upper edge as directed on page 349. Then, holding iron above hem, steam it, shrinking as much fullness as possible. Once hem has been sewn in place, remove basting. Steam again. Use a pounding block if a crisp edge is desired.

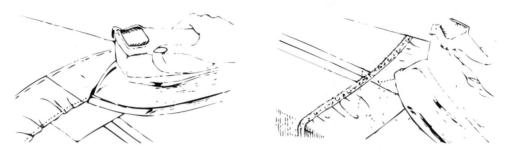

SOFT HEMS with a gently rolled edge may be preferred in place of a sharp crease. To achieve this finish, simply hold the iron 2" to 3" (5 cm to 7.5 cm) from interfaced hem, steaming the fabric thoroughly. Never rest the iron directly on the fabric. Pat lightly with a pounding block or ruler to mold the hem. Let the garment dry thoroughly before wearing (1).

PLEATED HEMS with seams at the fold must be pressed carefully before hemming. First clip the pleat seam at the top of the turned up hem before the raw edge is finished. Press seam allowances open below clip. Grade the seam allowances of bulky fabric. Finish the raw edge and complete the hem. Press a sharp crease in the underfold with the edge of your iron. If the folds still do not lie flat, stitch close to the edge of the fold (2). For more on pleated hems, see page 352.

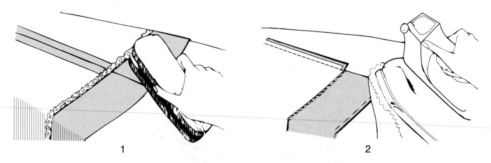

1   2

Final Pressing

The last pressing operation should be a mere touch-up job, never a cure-all for haphazard pressing during construction. Soft pleats, godets, collars, and other areas that need "setting" should be pressed with the garment on a dress form or hanger. Just steam and pat into position without touching iron to fabric. You may use tissue paper padding under collars, inside sleeve caps, and in other areas to hold them in place while fabric dries. Do not remove garment from dress form until fabric is completely dry.

Certain fabrics (satin, crepe, metallics, velvet, silk, synthetics) and trims (paillettes, sequins, beads, trapunto) will require special pressing techniques and equipment; see Special Handling, page 362, and Trims, page 463.

6

Fabrics Requiring Special Handling

Fabrics with Give

Comfort and good fit, two important criteria for clothing, are characteristic of fabrics with give. Whether knitted or woven, these fabrics offer a wide range of stretchability –from maximum stretch needed for active sportswear to minimum stretch used for shape retention of the fabric. New developments in fiber and fabric technology are creating interesting new fabrics for evening dresses, sportswear, lingerie, and swimwear. With the proper techniques, sewing with these fabrics can be easy and rewarding.

Knit Fabrics

The versatility of knits is almost unlimited since they are available in every weight, texture, color, and fiber. From soft jerseys and lacy raschels to firm double knits and bulky pattern knits, these fabrics are inherently flexible – resulting in comfortable, wrinkle-resistant, easy-care clothes.

Knits vary in stretchability; some are very stable and can be handled like a woven fabric, while others have considerable stretch in the crosswise direction or in both the crosswise and lengthwise directions. It is very important to determine the amount of stretch in a knit before you select your pattern, as the applicability of the design and the construction techniques to be used depend upon this fact. Use the Stretch Gauge printed on the inside back cover of the Vogue Catalogue or on the envelope of a pattern designed for stretchable knits; see page 128.

STABLE KNITS have a limited degree of stretch and retain their original shape well. Although they move with the body to a somewhat greater extent than woven fabrics, use the same construction techniques as you would for a woven fabric of similar weight.

STRETCHABLE KNITS have pronounced stretch and recovery characteristics and are perfect for the Vogue Patterns designed specifically for stretchable knits, as well as for regular patterns with soft styling. Construction techniques either maintain or limit the stretchability of the fabric depending upon the specific area of the garment – a hemline should be flexible; a V-neckline may need to be stabilized.

TWO-WAY STRETCHABLE KNITS must be used for swimwear and tight-fitting garments that require maximum stretch and recovery in both directions. Because Lycra® has been blended into the fabric, these knits have greater elasticity than regular knits. Special sewing techniques are necessary to retain maximum stretchability in the seams.

BEFORE CONSTRUCTION

As with woven fabric, knits may have to be straightened and preshrunk; see page 131. If tubular, split the fabric on one fold and press out the crease on the other. Occasionally, the crease will not press out. In that case you will have to refold your fabric so that the pattern layout avoids the crease. Make any necessary pattern alterations; do not use the stretchability of the fabric to compensate for minor figure variations. Fit is even more important for knits than wovens because of the tendency of the fabric to cling to the body.

Because many knits have a directional shading that is visible from certain angles, use a "with nap" layout. Mark the lengthwise grain with pins or thread tracing if the vertical ribs are not clearly discernable. Allow two-way stretchable knits to relax for at least 24 hours after being unrolled from the bolt and before you begin cutting.

Lay out your fabric on a large flat surface, being sure that none hangs off the edge to distort or stretch the knit. Pattern pieces that are to be cut on the bias can also be cut on the crosswise grain for maximum stretch. To prevent lightweight knits from curling, place pattern pieces on the wrong side of the fabric. For two-way stretch fabrics, place pattern so greatest stretch goes around the body. Always use ball-point pins or fine dressmaker's pins, and cut with very sharp shears to avoid snagging the fabric. Slippery or bulky knits should be cut one layer at a time. For stretchable knits, you may wish to cut 1" (25 mm) seam allowances on vertical seams to allow for any slight fitting changes in your garment.

Mark with tailor's tacks or chalk on stretchable knits and knits with a textured surface. A tracing wheel and dressmaker's carbon paper can be used for smooth, stable knits.

CONSTRUCTION POINTERS

Use a ball-point or stretch needle in a size appropriate to your fabric – ball-point needles are designed to separate rather than pierce the yarn loops. Dull or rough needle tips may cause snags or skipped stitches; insert a new needle if you experience stitching problems.

When sewing knits, use a thread that has some give – polyester or polyester-wrapped thread is recommended. A slightly shorter stitch length [12-15 stitches per inch (5-6 per cm)] has less tendency to break when the fabric is stretched than a longer stitch. Use a walking foot to keep the fabric from shifting and stretching

A plain seam can be used for most knits. Stretch the fabric very gently as it passes under the presser foot to add a little more stretch to the seams and to prevent puckering. Be careful not to pull the fabric or the seam will have a wavy appearance. However, narrow zigzag or special stretch stitches can also be used for seams. Seam finishes are seldom needed: only very loosely constructed knits have a tendency to unravel. For knits that have a tendency to curl, it may be necessary to staystitch ¼" (6 mm) from the fabric edge before stitching the seams. For knits with a loopy surface, such as stretch terry, you may have to wrap a piece of tape around the ends of the presser foot to prevent the small toes from catching in the loops or stitch over tissue paper.

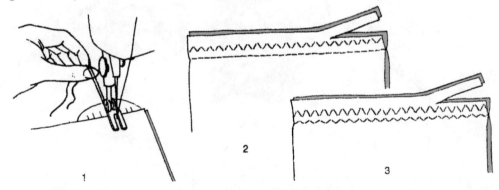

To prevent lightweight knits from being drawn down into the needle hole, use the straight stitch presser foot and needle plate, and hold both thread ends taut behind the presser foot when you begin to stitch. Lower the needle by hand for the first stitch (1).

To prevent seam allowances from curling or to eliminate bulk, you can double-stitch the seams with a row of straight or zigzag stitching. Trim away seam allowances close to stitching; press to one side (2). For two-way stretchable knits in swimwear or tight-fitting garments, combine a narrow zigzag seam with a wide zigzag stitch within the seam allowance, stretching the fabric slightly, to obtain maximum elasticity. Trim away seam allowances (3).

Although stretch may be desired in some seams, it may need to be controlled in others such as shoulder or waist seams – by using the taping technique discussed on page 209, Interfacing should be used in garment areas where stretch is not desired, such as a V neck-lines and buttonholes. Many interfacings, both regular and fusible, have been designed especially for use with knits to give soft shaping without added bulk. Refer to the Guide to Interfacings, page 163. If a lining is desired, select a lightweight, flexible fabric with the same care requirements. A lightweight tricot is often suggested.

When **PRESSING** knits, be wary of the tendency to overpress, as this causes irrepara-ble stretching and distortion. Always test press your fabric– some knits are composed of fiber types that may be damaged by heat. For lightweight knits, first press the seams closed and then open to obtain a smooth, flat seam. Place strips of brown paper under the seam allowances to prevent leaving an imprint on the right side. Use the press-and-lift method, as a back and forth motion will stretch the fabric

CLOSURES must be handled according to the stretchability of the knit. Bound, hand or machine buttonholes can be worked in almost any knit, but should have interfacing for sup-port. If your garment is not interfaced, use lightweight interfacing cut into ovals and catch-stitched or fused in place behind each buttonhole area (1). To avoid fabric distortion from too-heavy buttons, choose your buttons to suit the weight of the material. If your garment is not interfaced, reinforce button stitches with a small square of ribbon seam binding or fusible interfacing placed between the garment and the facing (2).

Choose a lightweight synthetic zipper for use with knits. Staystitch ½" (13 mm) from the fabric edge to stabilize the zipper area. For very stretchy knits, you may have to stitch rib-bon seam binding over the seamline before inserting the zipper.

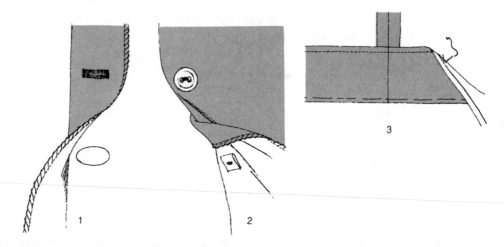

TRADITIONAL FINISHES on knits can be applied in a variety of ways at neck, sleeve, edges, and hems. Facings or bindings, in self-fabric or contrasting fabric, can be applied. Strip bands cut from a stretchable knit or purchased ribbing can also be used: see page 254.

Allow knit garments to hang for 24 hours before marking the hem. To hem most knits, simply turn up the hem allowance and stitch or fuse in place.

To ensure an invisible, hand-stitched hem, staystitch ¼" (6 mm) from the raw edge (3). Turn the edge back along the staystitching and blindstitch in place. Be sure to keep your stitches loose to prevent them from popping when the fabric stretches. Heavier weight knits may require a double-stitched hem (page 351). For lightweight stretchable knits, a nar-row topstitched hem (page 349) or a hand-rolled hem (page 461) give the best results.

Lingerie Fabrics

Elegant lingerie trimmed with lace is a wonderful addition to any wardrobe! Nightgowns, robes, slips, camisoles, and panties can be made of lightweight knits, crepe, satin, batiste, China silk, and crepe de chine. Tricot, a single knit available in several weights, is often used for lingerie because of its stretchability and run-resistant qualities.

BEFORE CONSTRUCTION

Woven fabrics may be cut on the bias for undergarments so that they will give and mold more closely to the body. Because tricot stretches most in the crosswise direction, place pattern pieces so the fabric will stretch horizontally on the garment. As for all knits, use ball-point pins and work on a large surface, being sure no fabric hangs over the edge. Because tricot is very strong despite its light weight, use very sharp shears or special lingerie shears to cut smoothly. It may be necessary to pin the fabric to your cutting board to prevent slipping. Mark with tailor's chalk.

CONSTRUCTION POINTERS

Refer to the section on Knit Fabrics, page 362, for complete information on sewing lightweight knits. Use a ball-point or stretch needle (size 9 or 11), polyester thread, shorter stitch length [12 to 15 per inch (5-6 per cm)], and a balanced tension; take care to prevent tricot from being drawn down into the needle hole. Incorporate "give" into the seam by gently stretching the fabric as you stitch, or use a narrow zigzag stitch or special stretch stitch. Never stitch over pins, as that may pull the fabric up and cause the seam to be uneven. Seams in tricot should be double-stitched, preferably with a row of zigzag stitching. Side seams can be finished with a very narrow French seam, if desired. Elasticized edges are often used as a substitute for casings to finish waist and leg edges; use lingerie elastic which is softer and more resilient.

To cut elastic, follow the pattern's cutting guide, or cut ½" to ¼" (13 mm to 20 mm) wide elastic 3" to 4" (7.5 cm to 10 cm) shorter than body circumference; cut ¼" to ⅜" (6 mm to 10 mm) wide elastic 2" (5 cm) shorter than leg circumference. Then join elastic in a ½" (13 mm) seam, reinforcing as shown (1).

To position, place elastic so seam allowances are away from the body. Then divide both elastic (2) and garment edge (3) into quarters; mark. Reduce the spaces between the marks on the fabric if it is greater than 6" (15 cm), dividing the elastic accordingly. Then pin to garment as suggested below.

EXPOSED ELASTIC FINISH: Place elastic on outside of garment with one edge along the seamline; match markings; pin. Stretch elastic and fabric as you stitch inner edge of elastic; use a zigzag or straight stitch. Do not stitch over pins (1). Trim seam allowance to ¼" (6 mm). Turn elastic to inside favoring garment edge, encasing raw edge of fabric. Stitch both edges of elastic to garment, stretching elastic and removing pins as you sew (2).

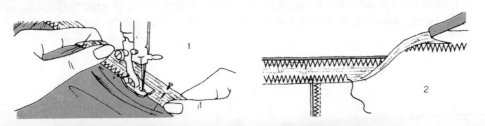

ENCLOSED ELASTIC FINISH: Place elastic on inside of garment with bottom edge along seamline or foldline; match markings and pin. Stretch elastic and fabric as you stitch inner edge of elastic, using a zigzag or straight stitch. Do not stitch over pins (1). Turn garment edge to inside enclosing the elastic, favoring garment edge. Stitch raw edge in place, catching remaining elastic edge and outer garment layer in the stitches (2). Note: Illustrations show a ⅝" (15 mm) seam allowance and ½" (13 mm) elastic. Cut wider seam allowances when using wider elastic.

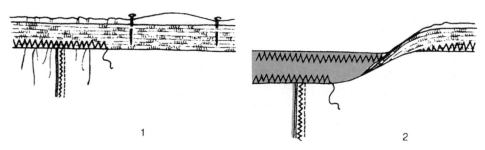

Lace adds an elegant finish to lingerie. It can be stitched to a hemmed edge, inserted with the fabric underneath trimmed away, or appliqued. Refer to Lace and Ruffles pages 468 and 469. Shell or scalloped tucks can also be used to finish an edge; see page 230.

Stretch Woven Fabrics

Gabardine, satin, denim, corduroy – these are just some of the many woven fabrics that have been developed with a certain amount of give. These fabrics have the appearance of traditional wovens, not "stretch" fabrics. However, their stretchability gives them the advantage of better shape retention and wearing comfort. Sewing techniques for stretch wovens include some of the same methods used for knits to maintain the stretchability of the fabric – yet they can be easily tailored like a regular woven fabric.

BEFORE CONSTRUCTION

Allow the fabric to "relax" on a flat surface before cutting, being sure that none hangs off the edge. Lay out pattern pieces so that the fabric will stretch in the direction desired. Use very sharp shears and avoid stretching the fabric as you cut, as this can distort the garment sections.

CONSTRUCTION POINTERS

Use a sharp regular needle or a ball-point needle in a size appropriate to your fabric, To provide stretchability in the seams, just as for knits, use a polyester thread, 12 to 15 stitches per inch (5-6 per cm), and a slightly looser tension. Always test the stitching on both the lengthwise and crosswise grain before you begin your garment. A tiny zigzag stitch or special stretch stitch can also be used.

Finish seams with overcasting or a double-stitched seam (page 223). Use interfacing to stabilize garment areas where stretch is not desired, such as buttonholes and V necklines. Many of the lightweight interfacings designed for knits can also be used to softly tailor stretch wovens.

A flexible hem finish must be used to allow the fabric to remain stretchable. Use overcasting, zigzag stitching, or stretchable lace seam tape, and be sure to keep your hemming stitches loose.

Fabrics that Flow and Float

Supple, drapable fabrics that glide and glow on your body – sheers, crepe and laces – deserve special attention. They may be cotton, wool, synthetic, even metallic; they can be firm or loosely constructed, soft or crisp, knits or wovens. Sheers can also have embroidered or flocked surface interests.

Complete your usual pattern adjustments and alterations. Sheer and lace fabrics should not be fitted tightly, as the tenuous nature of the fabric may not endure stress.

Sheer Fabrics

Crisp sheers – such as voile, organdy, and dimity – are quite durable and easy to manage. Softer sheers – chiffon, georgette, organza, or batiste – are airy and drapable, requiring greater care when cutting and stitching. Think sheer as you select the pattern; remember that sheers reveal all. If you're in great shape, why not show it? If you have some extra pounds, choose a style that will look well with sheer sleeves and underline the rest of the garment.

Sewing sheer fabrics requires extra care. Underfabrics may be necessary for certain parts of your garment, to provide support and to shield the see-through quality. The underfabrics should match sheer in both fiber type and care. Eliminate interfacing if possible. Self-fabric or underlining fabric is an appropriate substitute if interfacing cannot be entirely avoided. Use a lining only if the garment is entirely underlined. An underdress, underskirt, or camisole made from lining or other suitable fabric is an apt partner to any sheer garment.

BEFORE CONSTRUCTION

If your sheer has a nap, or sheen, use a "with nap" pattern layout. Nap does not have a grain and can be cut in any direction. The edges should be bound, as it is scratchy. Delicate sheers should be pinned to your cutting board or to a sheet that is fastened to your cutting surface. Use silk or ball-point pins and extra sharp scissors to prevent the fabric from becoming caught in the blades. Mark carefully using pins, chalk, or tailor's tacks; tracing wheel and/or dressmaker's carbon may permanently damage fabric. Handle gently to prevent stretching cut edges. Underlined garments should be marked on the underlining fabric only.

CONSTRUCTION POINTERS

The nature of the soft sheers makes seams hard to stitch. The threads tend to shift, so the crosswise fibers do not always remain perpendicular to the lengthwise fibers. To avoid mangled fabric, stitch seams with tissue paper or tear away stabilizer under seam between fabric and feed. Use straight stitch plate or cover the ends of zigzag stitch plate to help prevent fabric from being drawn down into the needle hole.

Use a fine needle (size 9 or 11) and a shorter stitch length—seams should be narrow and inconspicuous.

The most appropriate seam finishes for translucent sheers are French seam, French whipped seam with overcast or zigzag finish, mock French seam, or self-bound seam; see pages 221 and 222.

To finish sheers for a translucent look, omit facings at neck, sleeve, and opening edges, and substitute self or contrasting single or double binding, following procedures on pages 254 to 259. If you retain facings, trim seam allowances to about ⅛" (3 mm) wide. This holds true of collar seams, etc., without interfacing. Or use a hairline seam (page 222) for collars, cuffs, and facings.

PRESS with care using scraps of your sheer to test the heat, pressure, and steam of the iron. Enclosed seams should be pressed over a press pad or thick towel so no lumps or ridges will come through to the right side. Use a press cloth and press lightly, smoothing the seam flat with your fingers.

CLOSURES: Underlined sheers will usually support buttonholes, loops, or buttons. Translucent sheers must be able to support the button weight, with only hand or machine worked buttonholes. Zippers are usually too heavy for translucent sheers. Substitute a continuous bound placket (page 294) for loosely fitted sheers (1), using snaps, hooks, and thread eyes. For more fitted sheers, use dress placket (page 316).

For a zipper in a garment with an underlined bodice and an underskirt with a sheer overshirt, turn in the edges of the overskirt along seamline and narrow hem, matching finished edges to the seamline of the underskirt. Insert the zipper in the bodice section by hand or machine. Finish stitching the zipper to the underskirt only, keeping the hemmed edges of the overskirt free (2).

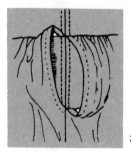

In a *layered sheer* garment, use four or more layers of one color for a "watered" look or each a different color for a moire´ look. Place the layers of fabric on your cutting surface, right sides up; pin together. With very lightweight thread and a sharp needle, "quilt" the layers together with long running stitches 6" to 12" (15 cm to 30.5 cm) apart. Proceed with cutting (3). Treat the bodice layers as one in construction; make and gather skirt layers separately; baste each skirt layer to the bodice in graduated levels. Stagger hems, making the outer layer the correct length and each following layer ¼" to ½" (6 mm to 13 mm) shorter (4).

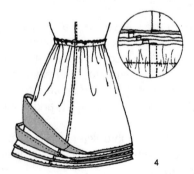

HEMS in translucent sheers that stand alone can be very narrow or very wide. Soft sheers are best hemmed with a hand-rolled narrow hem (page 461). Crisp sheers with a straight hem edge can have a very deep-up to 6" (15 cm) turned-up hem.

Lace Fabrics

Lace fabrics are unique because of their intricate nature. Once the product solely of hours of hand work, lace is now made mostly by special machinery.

Lace can be used for an entire garment or just a portion such as a bodice, sleeves, or inset, and it works equally well with velvet, sheers, crepe, taffeta, or even gingham. Choose a pattern with simple design lines as there is much beauty and elegance in a lace garment. A camisole and underskirt or slip of crepe, satin, or taffeta provide modesty and comfort for sheer or openwork lace. Opaque lace needs no underlining, but it can be added if you desire. Should you wish underlining, however, lightweight satin or taffeta, organdy, batiste, crepe, polished cotton, nude marquisette, tricot, or jersey are recommended. Sheer, fragile laces should never be interfaced, but the more substantial opaque, underlined laces may need it. Use interfacing that will suit the weight of your lace.

Check washability when purchasing lace–most laces made from synthetic fibers can be machine washed. Linen and silk laces, however, require either hand washing or dry cleaning.

BEFORE CONSTRUCTION

Most laces are designed with a net background, so no grain straightening is necessary. The main concern is the pattern of the lace and its direction, as lace can usually be cut either crosswise or lengthwise. Look at the lines of your pattern to determine if any lace motif can be used as a decorative edge, without facing or hem.

To use the lace design as a finished edge, cut out around the motif to create your own decorative edge (1). For straight edges, such as those found on a V neckline or at the hem of a sleeve or skirt, position the seamline or hemline at the outer edge of the motif as shown (2).

A *curved edge* as is found in an A-line skirt or bell sleeves requires several steps to achieve a completed garment edge. For an A-line skirt, fold fabric matching the scallops. Position the pattern hemline along the outer edge of the scallop. To raise the edge of the lace fabric to conform to the hemline curve, cut along a motif to form a lace strip as indicated. Raise strips, overlapping edges until pattern hemline curve is accommodated, making tiny clips between motifs if necessary so strip will lie flat. Baste strip in position and cut out skirt section. Applique′ strip to skirt by hand or machine. The results–a couture finish (3).

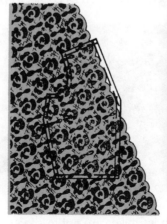

1   2   3

CONSTRUCTION POINTERS

Since lace is both sheer and delicate, apply the suggestions made for sheer construction or translucent and underlined garments. Translucent lace seams may require a self-finish such as a French seam, mock French seam, or double-stitched seam.

You may want to applique´ the seams and darts for an elegant finish. The edges are over-lapped, matching motifs, and sewn together by hand or machine. Before cutting out the garment sections, match the motifs along the seamlines. Cut one edge with a ⅝" (15 mm) seam allowance for the underlap (or wider for a larger design) and the other edge along the motif design for the overlapping layer. Match seamlines and design with overlap upper-most; pin, then baste, keeping overlap smooth. On the outside, applique´ the motif edges to underlap with tiny whipstitches or machine zigzag stitches (1). On the inside, trim away underlap close to the stitching (2). Finish darts in same manner, determining their depth before overlapping.

To retain the beauty of sheer or open-work lace, substitute a single or double binding instead of neck facings and hems for sleeve, skirt, or pant edges. Cut the bindings from satin, taffeta, crepe, or any other suitable fabric. Binding made from scraps of a companion slip-dress would be ideal. To make a successful binding, follow the directions on pages 254 to 259, or use self-trim instead of a facing to accent a scooped neckline or finish a hem edge. Cut along a line of motifs to form a lace strip. Place strip over garment with one edge along seamline or hemline; baste. Applique´ inner edge to garment same as for the seam above (3). For exceptionally curved edges you may find it necessary to make small clips between the motifs so the strip will lie flat. Overlap the motif edges and sew securely.

When the facings are retained, trim the seam allowances to about ⅛" (3 mm) in width. Do the same for other enclosed seams such as collars to preserve the sheerness.

When **PRESSING** lace fabrics, take care not to snag the lace pattern.

HEMS are the final touch in a lace garment. Use scalloped or decorative edge as hemline by cutting around the motif, or use self-trim for a decorative finish. For lightweight laces, use the same hemming techniques suggested for sheers. To face a hem in lace, use a doubled net strip in place of the bias facing suggested on page 351, or use horsehair braid for long gowns as described on page 462 (1).

To retain the beauty of a scalloped edge and still underline the lace garment, attach underlining in either of two ways: cut the under fabric with a straight edge level to the inner points of the design. Turn up the underfabric and whipstitch in place (2). Or trim the underfabric to match the shape of the scallops and staystitch ⅛" (3 mm) from the trimmed edge. Whipstitch shaped edge of underfabric to the lace (3).

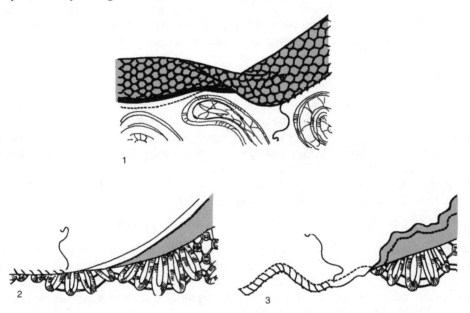

Crepe Fabrics

Choose your crepe according to the pattern style – light and mediumweight for draped – flowing designs and heavier, sturdier weaves for more tailored or fitted garments. Underlinings, if you use them, should be compatible with crepe, such as soft, uncumbersome batiste or organza. If you underline the crepe, omit interfacing, or substitute it with another layer of underlining. Do not use fusible interfacing.

Use the same cutting and marking techniques as for sheers. Since crepe can stretch and slip, use tissue paper or stabilizer between fabric and feed machine. It may be necessary to lengthen stitch and loosen tension slightly to avoid puckering. Very soft crepes may need the seams taped at stress points such as neckline and shoulder seams.

When **PRESSING,** test effect of heat and steam on fabric scraps. Some crepes may shrink or pucker from steam. Use a press cloth, and press on the wrong side to avoid shine. Crepes can usually support a zipper. Buttons and buttonholes are applicable too. See the closures section in sheers (page 368) for more sewing tips.

Allow your crepe garment to hang at least overnight before completing the hem.

Fabrics with Luster

Satin, taffeta, brocade, metallic, beaded, and sequined fabrics add dimensions of opulence to your wardrobe. Sewing these fabrics requires a knowledge of their nature, rather than special techniques.

For some garments you may want a soft, elegant look that can only be achieved with underlining. Choose an underlining fabric that will support your fashion fabric, as it will be used as a "hanger" for hems and facings so that no seam will leave an impression on the outside of the garment.

Make your normal adjustments and alterations. If your fabric is fragile and if fitting changes could leave permanent marks in the fabric, you may wish to make a test muslin. Follow the preliminaries before cutting, as explained on pages 131 to 134.

Satin and Taffeta

There was an era when satin was worn only for formal occasions-now it can go anywhere at any time of the day. Satin may be single-faced or double-faced, with a crepe or twill weave back so it can be used on either side. It varies from soft and drapable to a firm and crisp weight that will hold sculptured design lines. Some weights do not need interfacing, but use it if you are not underlining your garment.

Crisp, fresh-looking taffeta garments are a long-time fashion choice for day, evening, and lingerie wear. Taffeta is found in many weights and fibers.

BEFORE CONSTRUCTION

The sheen of satin comes from its weave – the lengthwise threads are caught by the crosswise threads after a longer space than usual, which creates "floats" on the right sides of the fabric. These "floats" reflect light and produce a shiny surface, which requires that satin garments be cut according to a "with nap" layout. Some taffetas, such as iridescent and moire, must also be cut using a "with nap" layout.

Use silk or ball-point pins and pin within the seam allowance only, because pin holes will show on the completed garment. Use very sharp shears to avoid snags: mark with tailor's tacks and silk thread within the seam or dart allowance.

CONSTRUCTION POINTERS

Handling the fabric is most important – use polyester, cotton or silk thread to avoid puckering. Set your machine for a medium stitch, 12 to 15 per inch (5-6 per cm), and hold the fabric taut during stitching to prevent sliding and bubbling. Stitch carefully as any removed stitches will leave holes in the fabric. Satin and taffeta ravel easily so the seams must be finished with machine or hand overcasting.

TO PRESS, test your fabric for heat and possible discoloration from steam; use a low temperature setting. For fabrics that water spot, use a dry iron. Press lightly with a press cloth, using brown paper or a seam roll to protect the fabric; folded edges should not be pressed flat.

For **CLOSURES,** zippers are suitable for most satins and taffetas with the exception of the very fragile – for better control, insert by hand with a prickstitch, page 458. Any type of button and buttonhole may be used, though buttons with rough edges may mar your fabric.

The final touch is an invisible **HEM** from the outside of the garment. Choose any of the standard finishes or one of the specialty hems described in the Couture section, pages 460 to 462.

Brocade Fabrics

At one time these luxurious fabrics were worn for only the most auspicious occasion, but with the advent of synthetics, beautiful brocades can now be worn anytime. These fabrics have a flat or raised woven-in design and are reversible; therefore, you have a choice. Use one side to make the entire garment, or make a portion of an ensemble from the reverse side – make pants and jacket from one side with a color-coordinated, contrasting vest from the other. Some may have metallic threads that require the same techniques as metallic fabrics in addition to those required for the surface interest.

Brocades are handled almost identically to satin and taffeta with the exception of pressing. Be sure to pad your ironing board with a towel so the design won't be flattened, and test heat endurance on scraps. Cover loose design threads with a press cloth to avoid accidentally pulling them.

Metallic Fabrics

Metallic fabrics is the name given to any fabrics that contain some metallic threads. They range from knits to wovens, soft to crisp, shiny lame´ to rich brocades.

Underlining is optional, but may be necessary to prevent the metallic threads from breaking at the seams. Many lightweight fusibles work well. Lining may be necessary to prevent the fabric from irritating the skin – use a soft but tightly woven fabric. Line garment to the edge, or cut facings from lining fabric to protect skin.

BEFORE CONSTRUCTION

Follow a "with nap" layout because the shiny threads cause a directional glow. Pin within the seam allowances and cut with old shears, since the metallic threads will dull the blades. Mark with tailor's tacks.

CONSTRUCTION POINTERS

Use polyester thread and a fine machine needle, which may have to be changed several times, lest it become too dull. If your fabric is sheer, use tissue paper when stitching seams. Test before stitching. Or, if the fabric is heavy, tape the shoulder, neck, and armhole seams to preserve the lines. Seam finishes may be necessary to avoid skin irritation.

PRESSING requires caution since steam may tarnish and discolor metallic threads. just as an iron that is too hot may melt some synthetic metallics or make them brittle. Press lightly – too much pressure may break the metallic threads. Or, finger-press seams open or edges in place, covering your finger with a thimble.

Most standard **CLOSURES** are acceptable for metallics. If you use a zipper, make sure the threads will not break when creased. Buttons and buttonholes are also appropriate, but do not make bound buttonholes on fabric that ravels.

The **HEMMING** methods are the same as for satin and taffeta if the fabric is nonirritating. However, if the fabric irritates, use the bias-faced hem, page 351.

Beaded and Sequined Fabrics

Found in many forms, beaded and sequined fabrics have some hidden characteristics – they can be attached with a continuous thread, secured with prongs, or sewn individually to a base of knitted or woven fabric. Beads or sequins may form an all-over design, may be sprinkled in random motifs, or used individually, adding glitter to brocades, lace, and other special fabrics.

Choose a pattern that will complement your fabric–simple lines without gathers, pleats, or buttonholes, and avoid set-in sleeves if possible. Consider a beaded or sequined bodice, sleeves, midriff section, or collar and cuffs to add sparkle to another fabric.

BEFORE CONSTRUCTION

Make your usual adjustments and alterations and do make a test muslin if expenditure is great and the silhouette unknown to you. Use an expendable pair of shears for cutting – beads are unavoidable and can easily dull the blades. Cut around the beads where it is impossible to cut through, cutting one layer at a time (1). Staystitch seam allowance edges immediately after cutting to prevent losing beads when attached continuously. Tailor's tacks usually work best for marking. Be sure to line the garment to protect your skin from the roughness of the fabric. Cut all facings from lining fabric.

CONSTRUCTION POINTERS

Use stitch length, tension, and needle size required by the base fabric. Remove beads from seam allowances and dart area, then sew with a zipper foot. Rest foot in seam allowance only, since beads would break under pressure. For beads or sequins attached by a continuous thread, fasten by hand or catch them in the seam (2).

Never use steam for pressing – it may cause the backing to curl and erase the sheen from the beads and sequins. Use a low heat setting as the beads could melt, then press along the seam or edges with the tip of the iron. When the garment is nearly finished, go over it and replace any missing or broken beads near seams or edges. Remove beads from hem allowance to prevent snagged hosiery or use a faced hem. Some garments may need an interfaced hem or a double-stitched hem. (See page 351.)

1

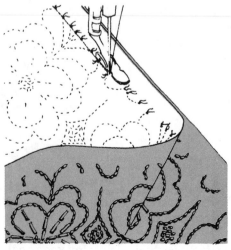

2

Fabrics with Surface Style

Intriguing surface interests make fabric selection even more diversified – from deep textured velvets and fake furs to smooth, shiny ciré's and vinyls. Woven or knitted, these fabrics can be made from a wide range of fibers. Some are very luxurious such as cashmere, camel's hair, and vicuna.

The most important feature to consider when using these fabrics is how they will look on you – will they complement your figure? The surface depth, the design (crosswise, lengthwise, floral, or geometric), and its brightness may work against you – creating an optical illusion, making you appear shorter or taller or thinner or heavier. Be realistic: select the fabric and the pattern that is just right for you.

Pile Fabrics

Plushy, luxurious pile fabrics come with many different faces–velvet, velveteen, corduroy (ribbed or uncut), plush, velour, terry cloth, boucle, melton, and fleece. All have many common characteristics. The most important is nap – stroke the surface with your hand, the smoother feel is the "run" or the direction of the pile or nap: the rough feel is caused when you brush the pile or nap in the opposite direction (1). This affects the color and texture of your garments; when the nap or pile runs up, the color is deeper, richer, and the textured surface is more visible.

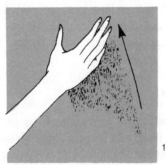

BEFORE CONSTRUCTION

Decide in which direction you want to place the nap or pile; use a "with nap" layout (see page 138), placing pattern pieces as they will be worn. Depending on the fabric weight and the pile depth, cut the pattern from either a single or double thickness of fabric. To avoid crushing the pile on velvets and velveteens, pin pattern to fabric within the seam allowance.

Mark with tailor's tacks and baste denser pile such as velvet with silk thread to prevent slippage. To reduce bulk, make facings from lining or other lightweight fabric. For knitted pile fabrics, apply appropriate cutting and marking methods: see page 362.

CONSTRUCTION POINTERS

Use 10 to 12 stitches per inch (4-5 per cm), matching needle size and thread to fabric weight. Stitch in direction of nap wherever possible. For velvet, use a fine needle and stitch carefully as removed stitches may leave holes in the fabric. It may be necessary to decrease pressure on presser foot and to hold fabric taut while stitching. To reduce bulk, slash darts and press them open.

PRESSING: All pile fabrics must be pressed carefully to avoid flattening the pile. If the pile is crushed on velvet, it can never be restored. Test-press a fabric scrap before you start. Place fabric, pile down, on a needle board; press carefully on the wrong side of the fabric. You can substitute a piece of self-fabric or a fluffy towel for a needle-board. Use low temperature setting for velvet.

When pile is exposed on both sides, use a self-fabric press cloth on the inside of the garment (1). Or, cover your iron with a damp cloth, then hold fabric lightly. Run the inside of the garment across covered iron to press seams open and steam out wrinkles (2).

1

2

CLOSURES should not present a problem. Select appropriate buttonhole, loop, or zipper application according to the weight of your fabric.

HEMS should be finished according to the weight and depth of the pile. Most pile fabrics can be hemmed like any mediumweight fabic. Because velvet can mar easily, a softly rolled hem is often used. Either interface the hem or add additional padding. The Hong Kong finish, using a strip of nylon net to encase the raw edge, may be used on velvet to finish the hem edge. For these techniques, refer to the couture section, pages 460 and 461.

Faux Fur Fabrics

Faux furs, available in a low-pile rayon fur and a longer pile, stiff-backed polyester type, add a dimension not found in the usual pile fabrics, although there are many fur-like fabrics that can be handled exactly like velvet. Follow the techniques suggested for pile fabrics, plus these additional tips. For long hairs, lay out fabric with nap running down. Cut one layer at a time, using a razor blade, and cutting only the backing. Baste seams firmly, pushing hairs back as you work. Stitch seams in the direction of the pile, using a size 14, 16, or 18 regular needle. Use a needle to work out hairs caught in the seam (1). Slash darts; press open. Shear hairs from seam allowance and exposed dart edges to reduce bulk using sharp scissors or a razor blade (2).

Never press the face of a fur—some are easily melted or the hairs may mat from the steam. Use a dry cool iron on the inside of the garment over a needle board on a short hair fur. Finger press only on long hair furs. Substitute snaps, hooks, and decorative closures for buttons and buttonholes. If unavoidable, some fabrics adapt to machine or bound buttonholes (substitute leather or other fabrics for the lips). For an attractive hem, use a double-stitched hem or a bias-faced hem; see page 351.

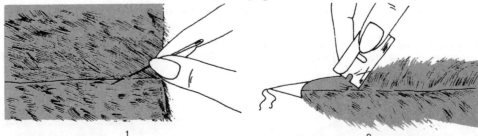

1

2

Cir'e and Vinyl Fabrics

Cir'e and vinyl fabrics require some special handling techniques. Cir'e is a very shiny finish applied to woven or knit fabics by a calendering process. Vinyls are plastic and can be single-ply or backed with a woven or knit fabric. The surface can be smooth and shiny or textured to simulate other materials. These fabrics are often semi water-repellent and somewhat windproof – ideal for sportswear and outerwear garments.

BEFORE CONSTRUCTION

Since pins leave permanent marks in cir'e and vinyls, pin only within the seam allowances or use tape to hold the pattern pieces in place when cutting.

Because coated fabrics are difficult to ease, you may need to reduce the fullness at the cap of a set-in sleeve. Make a tiny horizontal fold at the top of the sleeve pattern above the notches, taking out a total of ¼" (6 mm) (1). Be sure to make any other needed alterations in the pattern before cutting out the fabric.

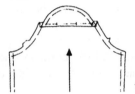

Mark the fabric on the wrong side with tailor's chalk.

CONSTRUCTION POINTERS

For lighter weight fabrics, use a size 12 or 14 needle and a longer stitch length [8 to 12 per inch (3-5 per cm)] to avoid puckering. For heavier weight fabrics, use a size 14 or 16 needle and 6 to 10 stitches per inch (2-4 per cm). A wedge-point needle is specifically designed for use on vinyls to help prevent splitting the fabric. However, a sharp-point needle can be used on vinyls backed with fabric. Hold the fabric slightly taut in front and behind the needle to help eliminate any seam puckering: do not pull the fabric through the needle. Sew carefully to avoid any later ripping, as needle marks show on the fabric.

Whenever possible, stitch with the right sides of the fabric together as the coated side has a tendency to stick to the machine foot. If you must stitch on the shiny side, use tissue paper or a roller foot to avoid sticking.

PRESS carefully with a warm, dry iron on the wrong side of the fabric. Be sure to test on a fabric scrap first. A press cloth must be used.

HEMS are best topstitched although some vinyls can be glued: refer to Leather, page 382. Buttonholes can be marked with tape to avoid marring the right side of the garment. Regular bound buttonholes or machine-worked buttonholes with a slightly wider stitch setting can be made on most cire's and vinyls. For other closure techniques, refer to the Leather section.

Ribbed Fabrics

Ribbed fabrics can be knitted or woven, soft or crisp, and the ribs can be lengthwise, as in corduroys, piqué, and Bedford cloth, or crosswise, as in bengaline, broadcloth, ottoman, and faille. Knits produce body-clinging, ribbed fabrics in crosswise velours or lengthwise sweater ribs. Treat your ribbed fabric according to its weight, stretchiness, drapability, and surface depth, choosing the special handling techniques from any of the preceding pages. For a couture touch, match the ribs if they are ¼" (6 mm) wide or wider.

Quilted Fabrics

Quilted fabrics – whether prequilted or do-it yourself – require no special sewing techniques except for eliminating bulk wherever possible.

BEFORE CONSTRUCTION

Always quilt your fabric before cutting out your pattern pieces as quilting draws up the fabric. Refer to the section on Quilting, page 481.

CONSTRUCTION POINTERS

Use a sharp needle (size 11-14) and a slightly longer stitch length [8 to 12 per inch (3-5 per cm)], depending on the thickness of your fabric. It may be necessary to loosen the tension slightly.

To eliminate bulk, trim away batting from the seam allowances and darts. Or slash the darts and press open. To eliminate bulky hems or edges on a quilted garment, you can use a bias facing or follow this special method. Trim the seam or hem allowance to ⅜" (10 mm); then stitch 1" (25 mm) from edge of fabric. Remove quilting stitches from outside the stitching line, pull thread ends to inside and knot. Trim batting close to stitching (1). Turn in edge of outside fabric and backing fabric along hemline and baste. Stitch close to the edge through all layers (2). PRESS quilted fabrics very lightly to avoid flattening the quilting.

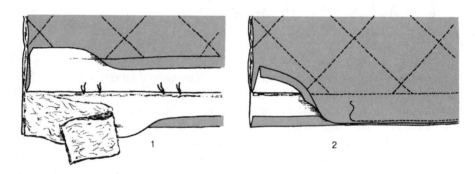

Double-Faced Fabrics

These fabrics combine two fabric layers that are held together with fine threads or bonding. There is no wrong side so, with the proper finishes, the garment can be reversible.

Choose a pattern with simple lines as the seams must be clean-finished so no raw edges are exposed. This fabric is usually too bulky for gathered styles and too firm for soft ones, classic or tailored garments with few details are best.

BEFORE CONSTRUCTION

Allow wider seam allowances for flat-fell seams and only 1" (25 mm) hems for sleeves and lower edges. Omit facing – interfacings are not used either. All markings must be made with tailor's tacks and thread tracings.

CONSTRUCTION POINTERS

Separate the layers by clipping the threads or pulling them apart. There are three ways to finish the seams. For a flat, plain finish, separate layers to a depth of 1½" (3.8 cm). Stitch the one layer in the usual ⅝" (15 mm) seam; press open. Trim remaining layer ¼" (6 mm), then turn in edges over the first seam, slipstitching folded edges together (1).

For a flat-fell seam, stitch the sections together along seamline. Separate the seam allowance layers, then trim and grade all but the uppermost layer. Turn in the edge and edgestitch in place (2).

For a strap seam, stitch the sections together along the seamline; press open. Separate the layers, then trim and grade. Cover the entire seam with a trim or a bias strip of the fabric. Separate the two layers so you have a single thickness. Make a bias strip as long as the seam and about 1⅞" (4.8 cm) wide. Turn in the edges ¼" (6 mm); press. Position over the seam and edgestitch through all layers (3).

EDGES for the hem, neck, and collar edges can be bound or the layers can be turned in and slipstitched together. Separate layers to a depth of 1½" (3.8 cm), turn in along seamline or hemline, and press lightly. Trim one edge ¼" (6 mm) and slipstitch or edgestitch together (4).

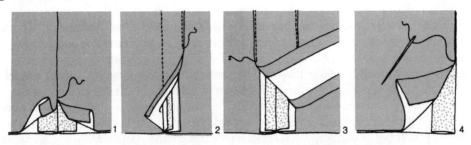

A *curved seam* is accomplished quite easily if all seam allowances fall in the same direction – the collar joining the garment is the most common example. Separate the inner curved edge to a depth of 1½" (3.8 cm); staystitch each layer. Clip curves to staystitching as you turn in these edges; baste. Press carefully, keeping the curve smooth. On the outer curve section, make clips about ¼" (6 mm) deep (5). Place the outer curved section between the turned-in seam allowances of the other section; match seamlines and symbols as you pin and baste. Slipstitch each side separately, or edgestitch close to fold through all layers (6).

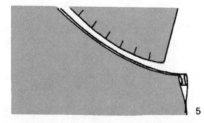 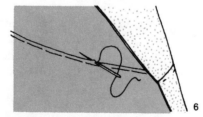

CLOSURES do not present a problem – use machine buttonhole and buttons or any decorative closure. Make one set of buttonholes, but sew on two sets of buttons for reversible garments – one in the normal position and the second set on the reverse side of the first. When the garment is reversed, the closure will be in the opposite direction.

Zippers can be inserted quite effectively. Separate the layers to a depth of 1½" (3.8 cm). For a slot zipper in a skirt, turn in the edges of each layer along the seamline; press lightly. Sandwich zipper between folded edges and stitch as usual. For an exposed separating zipper, turn in the edges beyond the seamline enough to clear the zipper teeth and allow the pull tab to move freely. Sandwich zipper tape between folded edges and edgestitch through all layers, catching the zipper tape in the stitching.

Leather and Suede

Leather and suede, with their luxurious beauty, are available in many weights, styles, and colors. Real leather is any animal skin that has been treated or tanned such as kidskin, chamois, reptile, calfskin, and buckskin. Suede is a type of leather that has been buffed to create a napped surface. The look of suede can also be obtained with synthetic suede, a very elegant fabric that is often featured by leading fashion designers. It has the look and feel of suede but can be handled like fabric.

For best results, select a pattern design with simple lines that will highlight the leather or suede. Avoid styles that require extensive easing because leathers and suedes – real or synthetic – do not ease well.

Leather

Leather, unlike cloth, is sold by the individual skin rather than by the yard (meter). Think of the pattern shapes as you calculate the number of skins needed. It may be necessary to add horizontal seams suggesting a yoke or vertical seams suggesting gores or princess lines-this adds to the individuality of your project. Use the chart on this page to convert the fabric yardage (metrage) specified for your size into leather square footage. Be aware that this formula does not give measurements of quantity that are as precise as the yardage (metrage) given: Since there are 13 square feet in one yard (meter) of 54" (140 cm) fabric, you must multiply the number of yards (meters) specified for this width in your size by 13. Allow additional footage for piecing and irregularities in the leather: 0.15 for a large skin or 0.20 for a small skin.

Specified yardage-metrage	4
Conversion figure	x 13
Converted yardage-metrage (square feet)	52
Piecing percentage (for large skin)	x 0.15
Piercing allowance (square feet)	7.80
Converted yardage-metrage (square feet)	+52
Total square feet needed	59.80

BEFORE CONSTRUCTION

Leathers crease easily – roll them in a tube until ready for use. Because stitching marks leave permanent holes in leather, letting out darts or seams can be disastrous. Make a test muslin if you are unsure of how the pattern fits, since alterations are generally impossible. Felt is a perfect substitute for muslin as it handles like leather and the seams can have the same treatment. Check leathers for irregularities and holes.

For suede, use a "with nap" layout. Smooth leathers and heavy buckskin types have no nap or bias to consider so a "without nap" layout can be used. However, lay out major pattern pieces in the lengthwise direction of the skin for greater stability (although leather has no grain, it does have greater crosswise stretch). Smaller pieces can be laid in any direction. Cut a single layer at a time, holding pattern pieces in place with tape or weights. Use very sharp fabric shears, single-edged razor blade, or another suitable cutting tool. Or, if you prefer, trace around the cutting line of the pattern pieces on the wrong side of the skin with tailor's chalk; remove the pattern and cut. Mark the wrong side with chalk or a smooth-edged tracing wheel and dressmaker's carbon paper.

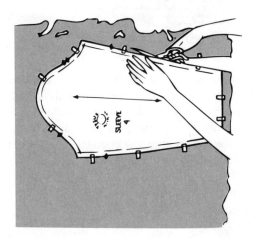

CONSTRUCTION POINTERS

Since seams are a focal point, especially on leather, your sewing machine must be clean and set up correctly. For best results, use a wedge-point needle in the size appropriate for the weight of the skin. Use 8 to 10 stitches per inch (3-4 per cm) and test the pressure on the presser foot; it may have to be reduced since leather is thicker and spongier than cloth. Stitch slowly, taking care not to pull or stretch the leather. Do not backstitch as it might tear the skin; knot thread ends securely. Hold regular seams together with tape (1) or paper clips (2). Overlapped seams can be held together with rubber cement before stitching (3).

Some seams may need to be reinforced with seam binding or twill tape to prevent stretching.

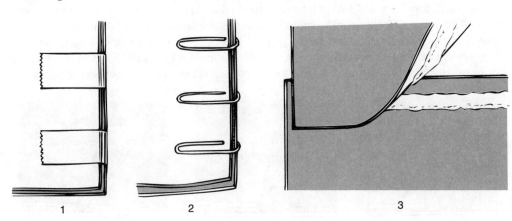

To reduce bulk in seams, grade the seam allowances. Bevel the edge of thicker leathers with a single-edged razor blade (4).

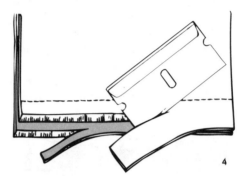

4

PRESS seams or flatten edges using a warm dry iron, with brown paper serving as a press cloth. Or, use a mallet or a hammer padded with cloth for pressing. Topstitch seams or apply rubber cement under each seam allowance to flatten (1). Pound cemented edges in place; when dry, lift seam allowances and peel away the rubber cement (2). Seams will stay open and flat, without leaving an impression on the outside of the garment. Darts are slashed open and flattened the same way as seams.

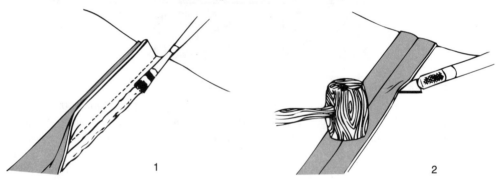

1   2

SEAM FINISHES can be modified for leathers. For a flat-fell seam, trim away one seam allowance: lap sections, matching seamlines. Hold in place with a thin line of rubber cement. Topstitch ⅛" (3 mm) from trimmed edge and again ¼" (6 mm) away (1). For a lapped seam, topstitch ⅛" (3 mm) from trimmed edge (2). For a slot seam, eliminate both seam allowances of sections to be joined, cut strips the length of the seam and twice the desired stitching width from the seam, plus ½" (13 mm). Center trimmed edges over the strip, cement in place. Topstitch each side of the trimmed edges, catching strip in stitching (3). Note: Rubber cement may be hard to remove, so do not cement beyond seamline.

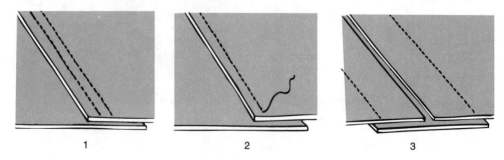

1   2   3

For details like collar, pocket, and facings, eliminate seam allowances from both layers. With wrong sides together, match cut edges; glue. Topstitch ⅛" (3 mm) from edge to match lapped seams (4) and again ¼" (6 mm) away to match flat-fell seams (5).

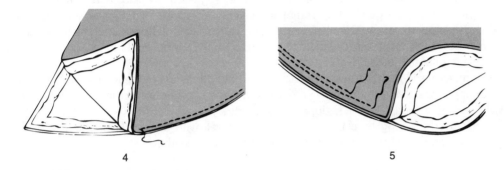

4   5

CLOSURES: The *buttonhole* method shown here is excellent for leathers.

Cut a rectangular opening the length of the buttonhole marking and ⅜" (10 mm) in width. For each buttonhole cut two strips ½" (13 mm) longer than the rectangle and 1½" (3.8 cm) wide. Fold strip lengthwise, grade edges, and flatten. Center strips over buttonhole opening, with folded edges meeting. Hold in place with a thin line of rubber cement. Then cement the facing in place smoothly over the buttonhole (1). On the outside, edgestitch the rectangle through all thicknesses to anchor the buttonhole lips and hold all layers in place (2). To complete the buttonhole, trim away facing inside the stitching (3).

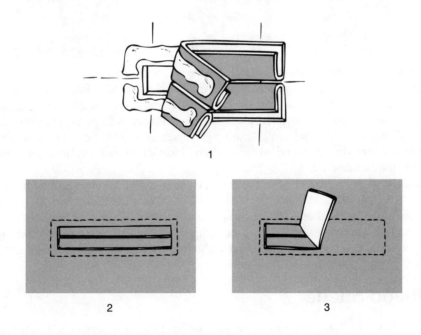

1

2   3

Zippers are inserted in the supple leathers in the same manner as fabric. Heavier leathers can use another approach when a flat-fell seam is used. Before stitching seam, make a ½" (13 mm) clip through zipper symbol on the underlapping layer and trim away ½" (13 mm) to upper edge. Tape zipper in place; edgestitch in place across the clip and along the trimmed edge (1). Lap remaining layer over zipper, matching seamlines; tape. Stitch ¼" to ½" (6 mm to 13 mm) from edge; start at top of zipper and stitch to end of seam through all thicknesses. Then stitch across end of zipper and along trimmed edge, completing flat-fell seam (2).

For an exposed zipper, trim away just enough of both layers of the leather so the zipper teeth are exposed and the pull tab works easily. Center zipper under trimmed edges; tape. Using a zipper foot, edgestitch zipper to garment (3).

Don't overlook toggles, clasps, etc., that work well with leather. Remember, too, that grommets and rawhide laces go with the rugged look of leather.

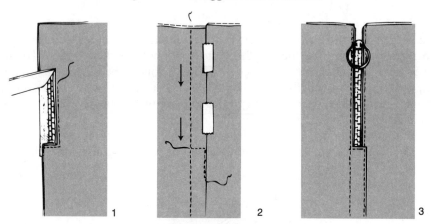

HEMS are simple for leathers and suedes – a 1" to 2" (25 mm to 5 cm) deep hem is adequate for most. Mark hemline with chalk. Apply rubber cement, fold up hem allowance, and flatten as required for the seams. Notch curved hems so they will lie flat. A topstitched hem is also a good finish for leather. Hold the hem in place with paper clips and use long stitches [6-8 per inch (2-3 per cm)]. One or two rows of stitching can be used. Press the hem with a warm dry iron and a press cloth. Heavier, firmer leathers can simply be trimmed at the hemline.

The final touch ... Some leathers and suedes spot easily, so avoid getting them wet. If any do get wet, allow to dry away from direct heat. Wipe smooth leathers first with a soft cloth. Suedes can be brushed when dry to restore the nap. When your leather needs to be cleaned, send it to a professional dry cleaner who specializes in leather cleaning. Store your leather garments in a cool spot and cover with cloth, never plastic, to prevent the leather from drying out.

Synthetic Suede

Synthetic suede has the fashion look of suede without the disadvantages. It is lightweight, wrinkle-resistant, colorfast, and machine washable. The fabric can be constructed with conventional seams or with lapped seams – or a combination of the two methods.

Interfacing is needed for most synthetic suede garments. Because the fabric can be pressed with steam, fusible interfacings are recommended. Use a fusible web to baste two layers of fabric together before stitching or to fuse one layer to another permanently. Refer to the section on fusibles, page 157. Jackets and coats should be lined to make them easier to slip on and off.

BEFORE CONSTRUCTION

Synthetic suede has a nap that gives a richer, darker appearance when the nap is running up on a garment. Because this luxurious fabric is very expensive, you may wish to pre-measure your pattern layout in order to determine the exact fabric that you will need. Be sure to make any alterations in your pattern, and if you are using the lapped seam construction method for any seams, to first trim away hem allowances before measuring your layout. If you are unsure of the pattern fit, you may wish to first construct the garment in felt or nonwoven interfacing that hangs like synthetic suede.

Use the "with nap" layout, although bias collars and cuffs can be cut on the crosswise grain. Facings and pieces that do not show can be tilted off-grain to save fabric (1). Pin marks will disappear when the fabric is steamed; however, it is best to place pins vertically within the seam allowances or to use tape to hold your pattern pieces in place. Use sharp scissors to achieve a clean-cut edge. Mark with tailor's chalk or a smooth-edged tracing wheel and dressmaker's carbon paper. Identify the wrong side of the fabric with pieces of tape.

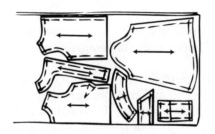

1

CONSTRUCTION POINTERS

Use 10 to 12 stitches per inch (4-5 per cm) and a fine needle (size 9 or 11). For top-stitching with silk or polyester topstitching and buttonhole twist thread, use a size 16 or 18 needle. When hand sewing, use a fine needle and a thimble as the fabric is strong and resilient. Use tape or paper clips to hold the fabric together as you stitch; see Leather, page 381. Or use basting tape placed ⅛" (3 mm) away from the seamline within the seam allowance. Be sure to remove the tape after stitching the seam.

To prevent puckering in seams, hold the fabric taut in front and behind the presser foot, feeding the fabric evenly through the machine. Do not stretch the fabric. Press on wrong side of fabric using a synthetic setting, lots of steam, and a press cloth. If it is ever necessary to press on the right side, use a piece of self-fabric as a press cloth.

To avoid puckers at the end of a dart, stitch to a very finely tapered point with the last four stitches just on the fold of the fabric. Slash the dart open to within 1" (25 mm) of the point. To press, slip strips of brown paper under the dart edges to prevent imprints on the right side.

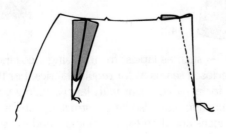

Seams can be constructed in either the conventional or lapped method.

For **conventional seams,** stitch seam and press open over a seam roll. Use a wooden clapper to help flatten the seam allowances. Or fuse them in place with a ¼" (6 mm) strip of fusible web under each seam allowance (1). The seams can also be topstitched (2) or double-topstitched (3).

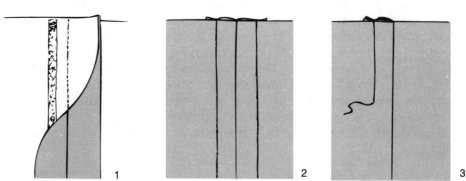

For best results, conventional seams should always be used for a set-in sleeve seam, neckline seam of a rolled collar with lapel, sleeve underarm seam, pants crotch seam, and pants inseam.

For **lapped seams,** you must carefully plan your garment and then trim or fold the overlapping allowance away: Side seams and shoulder seams lap front over back; yoke seams lap over both front and back bodice sections. This method results in lots of topstitching, which gives a sportier appearance to your garment. It also requires less fabric when the seam allowances are trimmed before cutting out the pattern pieces.

Trim ⅝" (15 mm) seam allowance away from the overlapping layer of fabric (4). Mark seamline with chalk on the right side of the under fabric. Place ¼" (6 mm) strip of fusible web between the two layers of fabric and press for 2 to 3 seconds just to "baste" in place. Or use basting tape along the outer edge of the bottom layer, being sure that it will not get caught into the stitching. Topstitch ¼" (6 mm) from the seamline and again close to the overlapping edge (5).

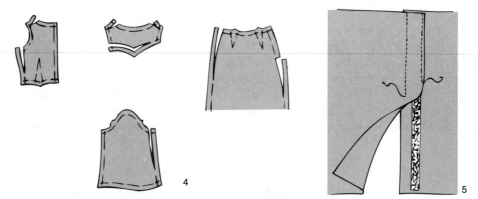

Collars and facing edges – such as lapels, front closings, collarless necklines, and cuffs- can be constructed with enclosed seams as for regular fabrics. For the best appearance, use the conventional method for a rolled collar with lapels; follow your pattern instructions. However, collars and facing edges can also be constructed using a flat method of trimming away all outer seam allowances and then topstitching around the edge, wrong sides of fabric together. The following illustrations and text describe this second method.

For a collar with stand, trim away all seam allowances except for the neck seam. Trim interfacing ¼" (6 mm) smaller than the collar and fuse to upper collar. Stitch collar sections, wrong sides together. Staystitch neck edge ½" (13 mm) from edge arid clip. Trim away all seam allowances from collar stands and interface both stands. Lap stands over neck edge of collar, encasing the collar in the stand, and topstitch along upper edges of stand (6).

Staystitch neck edge of garment and clip. Encase garment between collar stands and complete topstitching (7).

For a sleeve placket, cut placket facing and fuse to sleeve, wrong sides together. Slash through center of placket to point and stitch close to edge (8).

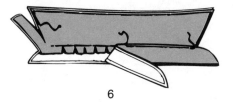

6

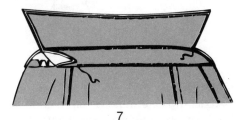

7

For a cuff, trim away all seam allowances and cut the cuff in half along foldline. Trim interfacing ¼" (6 mm) smaller than cuff and fuse to wrong side of upper cuff. Before attaching cuff, line sleeve if desired. Lap both cuff sections over seam allowance of sleeve and hold in place with tape or fusible web. Topstitch around entire cuff as desired (9). Cuffs can also be stitched following the conventional method.

For patch pockets, trim away ⅝" (15 mm) seam allowances. For an unlined pocket, cut

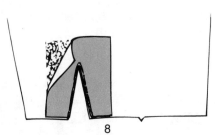

8

9

along foldline to separate self-facing; topstitch facing to pocket wrong sides together; topstitch to garment (10). For a lined pocket, trim ¾" (20 mm) from lining edge and stitch to pocket self-facing. Fold wrong sides together along foldline and topstitch across top of pocket. Topstitch pocket to garment (11).

For pocket flaps, cut two layers and trim away all seam allowances. Fuse wrong sides together. Topstitch sides and bottom edge; then topstitch top edge to garment (12).

10

11

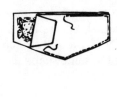

12

For waistband, trim away all seam allowances. Fuse interfacing to wrong side of outer waistband section, with top edge along foldline and other edge ¼" (6 mm) from edge of waistband. Lap waistband over waist seam allowance of garment and topstitch in place close to edge. Fold band to wrong side and topstitch ¼" (6 mm) from edge on outside of waistband through all layers. Continue topstitching around waistband, if desired.

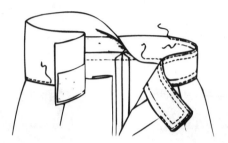

CLOSURES: Several different types of buttonholes can be made on synthetic suede – experiment to determine which method you like best.

For bound buttonholes, you can use the method shown for leather on page 383, except use fusible web instead of rubber cement to hold the buttonhole strips and the facing in place. Also insert a strip of web inside the buttonhole strips to hold the lips flat.

A regular bound buttonhole can be made conventionally using a patch method that does not require machine-basted markings.

Center a rectangle of self-fabric over the button area, right sides together. Stitch two rows of stitching the exact length of the buttonhole and slash diagonally to corners (1). Turn patch to wrong side of garment. To form buttonhole lips, fold patch over the opening so that the folds meet exactly in the center. Place strips of fusible web in each lip to hold lips flat (2). Fold back garment and stitch across ends of buttonhole (3).

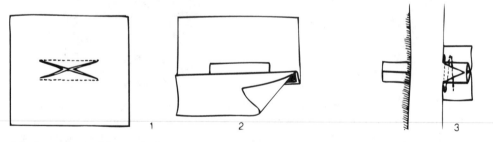

Machine-worked buttonholes can be made through all thicknesses after the garment is completed.

Zippers can be inserted with a centered application, or use the lapped application illustrated for leather; see page 384.

HEMS can also be finished on synthetic suede with different methods, depending upon your preference. For a conventional hem, turn up 1" to 1½" (25 mm to 3.8 cm), and fuse in place (1). For a more casual look, simply trim along the hemline and topstitch close to the edge to prevent stretching (2). Or face the hemline with a strip of ½" (13 mm) wide fabric cut the same shape as the hem. Topstitch to hem edge, wrong sides together (3).

The Elegance of Fur

From time to time, the experienced sewer needs a project that challenges her capability. Making a fur garment not only tests your skill, but also furnishes its own reward. Whether you choose to purchase new fur or remodel an old favorite, you can't go wrong if you follow the directions below closely.

You will need the following equipment for sewing with fur: single-edged razor blades, chalk pencil, safety pins, thumbtacks, or pushpins, heavy-duty needles (size 7 glover's needles are perfect), large board for blocking fur, button and carpet or heavy-duty waxed thread, ½" (13 mm) twill tape, interfacing, and heavyweight muslin for a test pattern.

BEFORE CONSTRUCTION

Choose your pattern carefully. A style with simple lines is best. Consider one with few pattern pieces, seams, or darts, and front opening edges that can be converted to extended facings. Make a test garment in muslin and try on as it will be worn: try on coats over another garment. Make any changes in muslin, then transfer changes to pattern. Since fur is sewn edge to edge, trim pattern away along seamlines and dart lines.

When working with old fur, pinch the skin side to test for suppleness and pliability. Wet a sample on the skin side and stretch it to test the skin's strength. Bend the fur hairs to be sure they are not too dry or brittle. To revive the fur side, dampen slightly, then gently brush it with the grain. Fluff against the grain and allow it to dry overnight before working with it.

Find the best parts of the pelts by placing your pattern pieces on the fur side first. To ensure similarity throughout the garment, place pattern pieces with respect to shading, spotting, and color of adjoining pelts. Outline pattern pieces with a sufficient number of safety pins so you will know where to place them on skin side of pelt. You may need to join pelts to get a fur area large enough to cut out a pattern piece.

Use a razor blade to cut fur. Cut from the skin side and raise the pelt to avoid cutting the hairs. Cut over a board. Place the pelts edge to edge, skin side up, or cut area needed to complete a section (1).

To piece pelts, use strong waxed thread and sew through skin only using an overhand stitch. Work out any hair from the seam with the point of a needle. Reinforce by sewing twill tape over the seam with running stitches along the taped edges (2).

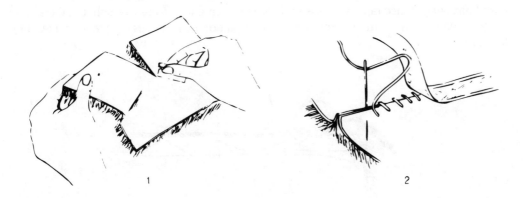

1

2

If there are worn spots in any of the pelts, mark them on the fur side with safety pins; place the pins in a triangle with one point toward the top of the garment (1). From the skin side, mark the triangle with tailor's chalk, drawing lines from pin to pin (2). Cut out the triangle and use it as a pattern for a replacement piece cut from leftover fur. Match texture, color, and grain of the fur carefully **before** you cut out the triangular replacement piece (3).

Use a small overhand stitch to sew the replacement piece (4).

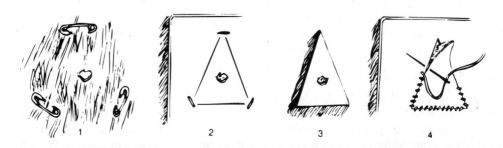

With your pelts atop the work board, place pattern pieces on the skin side and tack in place with thumbtacks or pushpins. For jackets and coats with collars, eliminate neck facings to reduce bulk. Chalk mark the pattern outlines and darts. Cut out pieces with razor blade without cutting fur. Do not cut out darts at this time.

Mark the outline of all the pattern pieces on the board. Using a brush, wet the skin side of each pelt, and place it fur side down over the pattern outline. Carefully matching the outline, tack each pelt in place and allow to dry thoroughly (at least 24 hours). This makes the skin easier to work with.

Remove the tacks when the pelts are dry. Pin the pattern pieces to the skins, check for stretching, and redraw the outline with a fine chalk pencil if necessary. Cut along the corrected outline and cut out the darts. Mark the notches but do not cut them. Also mark center fronts, foldlines, and hemlines.

CONSTRUCTION POINTERS

SEAMS: Sew twill tape to edges to be sewn in seams or darts with a hand zigzag stitch, keeping edge of tape flush with edge of skin. Join seams and darts with a close overhand stitch. Work with one skin side toward you and fur sides together (1). Keep edges even and push hairs away. Since tape is necessary for reinforcement, be sure to catch it in the seam. Smooth seams with warm, dry iron, being sure point of iron touches only taped edges, not the skin.

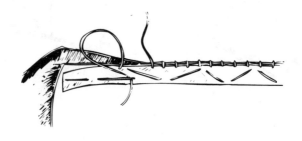

FINISHING EDGES: Hems or other edges that will become a finished edge of your garment must be finished with tape. The tape is then used to anchor linings. These edges are prepared after the seams and darts are sewn. Place the tape on the fur side and sew with small overhand stitches, mitering any corners (1). Finish all edges, then turn the tape to the skin side and sew it in place with long running stitches (2).

INTERFACING: Extended facings are interfaced to give the finished edge a soft rolled effect. Cut a strip of interfacing the length of the facing and twice its width. Place it ¼" (6 mm) from the facing edge on the skin side and sew along both long edges with running stitches. Attach hook for closure at this time (see Hooks and Eyes on next page). Turn facing to inside along foldline; sew the two layers of interfacing together halfway between the raw edges of the interfacing and the foldline (1). Then sew the same layers together close to the edge (2). For garments lined to the edge, slide one edge of interfacing under taped edge, and sew both long edges in place.

COLLARS: For a detachable collar, back the skin with flannel and lightweight interfacing. Sew both layers to the skin ¼" (6 mm) from edge with long running stitches. Prepare collar edges as you would finished edges (1). Make lining to fit; slipstitch to collar. Sew to garment (2).

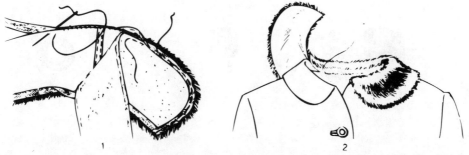

To make your fur collar easily removable as a separate accessory, simply sew a hook and eye to the ends before attaching the lining so they will meet at the neckline.

For a fur garment with a collar, finish edge of upper collar and undercollar as for seams. Sew them together. Then sew undercollar to garment. Shape the roll of the collar, then tack it loosely to the neck seam. This edge will later be finished with the garment lining.

BUTTONS and **BUTTONHOLES:** Using button and carpet thread, sew the button through the fur and interfacing, reinforcing the underside with a flat 1" (25 mm) button. Be sure to make the thread shank long enough to accommodate the thickness of the fur.

From skin side, make a slit the buttonhole size in facing and garment with razor blade. Finish edges with tape on skin side as instructed for seams. On fur side, place additional tape as described for finished edges (1). Turn tape on fur side through to skin side and sew together with running stitches (2). Join facing to garment, working overhand stitches around buttonhole openings.

1   2

POCKETS: The two types of pockets usually made in fur are in-seam pockets (page 312) and buttonhole pockets. For the latter type, follow the buttonhole instructions above. cutting the slit long enough for a pocket. Make pocket sections out of lining fabric and stitch together. Sew securely to twill tape on inside of garment.

HOOKS AND EYES: Use large hooks and eyes especially made for fur. For an opening edge with an extended facing, mark placement of hooks and eyes on skin side with chalk. Make a tiny hole through the interfacing and skin at the foldline to allow the bill of the hooks to extend from the fur side. Sew the remainder of the hook to the interfacing and skin (1). Work bill to fur side (2). On opposite side of opening, sew the ring eye (3). For other closures, sew the hooks and eyes to twill tape before attaching the lining.

1   2   3

LINING: For fur garments without neck facings. you will need to extend the lining up to the neck edge. Add neck facings to the lining pattern piece, overlapping seams and allowing for a back pleat before cutting. Cut and sew the lining with seam allowances according to pattern instructions. Slipstitch to the fur, covering taped edges.

7

Very Easy Vogue

Very Easy Vogue Concept

Very Easy Vogue patterns were launched in 1969, by then Design Director, Koko Beall, for the contemporary woman so she could achieve the "Vogue" look without complicated construction. These specially designed patterns beginning with a "One View" dress, combine high fashion styling with easy construction techniques-a concept that appeals both to the skilled sewer who desires to create a fashionable garment in a minimum amount of time, as well as to the beginner sewer who wants to make a fashionable garment while still perfecting her sewing skills. Garments have no more than five main pattern pieces and five minor ones.

However, the Very Easy Vogue concept goes beyond pattern design to include all phases of sewing-fabric selection, planning, cutting, marking, stitching, pressing, and finishing. It offers you alternative methods of sewing that are quick, easy, and fun to do. Which methods you choose depends upon the style of your garment, your fabric, the amount of time you have, and your own sewing experience and ability.

The following pages are filled with simplified sewing methods or "shortcuts" that reflect this concept of sewing. These ideas have come from dressmakers and sewing experts, who have learned through years of experience how to achieve professional results using time-saving techniques. The development of new fabrics, interfacings, notions, and equipment has made sewing easier and more pleasurable. Many traditional construction methods can be simplified or even eliminated. Machine stitching or fusing can replace hand sewing, even in tailoring.

Sewing is a very creative experience. Every project offers you a choice of styles and fabrics from which to choose. Now you also have a choice of sewing methods–simplified, traditional, or a combination of the two–that should be a part of your sewing repertoire. As with all creative arts, the final choice is up to you!

Very Easy PATTERNS

Easy-to-sew, fashionable clothes begin with your pattern selection. Choose a pattern that has a minimum number of seams, design details, and pattern pieces. The descriptive caption on the back of the pattern envelope and in the pattern catalogue will list the number of pattern pieces and describe the design and construction features of the garment. For example, a banded effect around the edge of a jacket can either be created simply with top-stitching or constructed with a separately applied band and facing.

To eliminate minor fitting adjustments, choose styles that are more loosely fitted. Flared or gathered skirts are easier to fit than straight skirts; blouson or body-skimming styles are easier than fitted bodices with darts or seams; raglan and kimono sleeves are easier than set-in sleeves. If your figure is two different sizes, such as a size 10 bodice and a size 12 skirt, try Vogue's Multi-size patterns, which include three sizes in one pattern. You can easily follow the cutting lines for whichever size you need without spending time altering various parts of the pattern. This is a great time-saver! If you are between sizes, simply cut between the two cutting lines.

Very Easy Vogue patterns are created for the contemporary woman with "too much taste and too little time." For more major alterations, always keep a record of the fitting corrections made on your basic pattern so that you can easily make the same alterations in any pattern that you are cutting out. This is much easier than having to fit and adjust as you sew.

Very Easy Vogue patterns are specially designed for easy construction. Each has a limited number of main pattern pieces such as front, back, sleeves, and collar. Details that require additional handling and sewing, such as cuffs, yokes, bands, pleats, tucks, and gathers, are kept to a minimum. Difficult-to-construct details such as complicated collars, welt pockets, bound buttonholes, mitered corners, gussets, and scallops are eliminated. Topstitching is done only on flat areas, and edgestitching is recommended only when it will make construction easier. If a lining is recommended, the garment is lined to the edge. Hand-stitching is kept to a minimum, and tailoring is not required.

The Sewing Guide for Very Easy Vogue patterns is clearly designed to show the garment, the diagram of all the pattern pieces, and the layout in one compact unit. Illustrations and descriptions of special construction terms such as layering, clipping, and interfacing are included in the Guide Sheet. Sewing instructions are concise and easy to follow, featuring flat construction where ever possible and many shortcut methods. Large, uncomplicated sketches help to make the construction of Very Easy Vogue patterns as easy as possible.

Very Easy FABRICS

Easy-to-handle fabrics that require little or no preparation and no lining or underlining are the best selection for easy construction. Choose a fabric that is firmly woven or knitted with body and resiliency. Learn to recognize quality – fabrics that are cheap, finished or printed off-grain, or contain flaws will cause sewing problems. Fabrics without a nap, a one-way design, or a matching pattern are easier to lay out; fabrics that do not ravel need no seam finishes.

Always check your pattern envelope for fabric recommendations. Some Very Easy Vogue patterns may include a separate fabric listing stating: "The following fabrics are also suitable but may be more difficult to handle." This alerts you to fabrics such as crepe, chiffon, and matte jersey, which require special handling techniques.

Your pattern envelope will also state whether plaids, stripes or diagonal fabrics are suitable for this particular design. All of these fabrics require special handling to match the fabric design. However, if you do choose a plaid or stripe, you can avoid matching detail areas such as collars and pockets by cutting those pattern pieces on the bias.

You may need to purchase a little extra fabric if you plan to use certain simplified construction techniques, such as a self-lined pocket or a waistline casing, which require an extension of the pattern pieces. Also, if you are like many women who sew, you may often purchase fabric before you purchase a pattern, planning to make a garment "someday." To avoid later disappointment, be sure to purchase ½ yard (½ meter) more fabric than the "average" pattern requires. Thus, you are usually assured of having enough fabric for whatever pattern you finally select.

Very Easy PLANNING

One of the secrets to easy, successful sewing is planning your project before you begin. Preplanning includes your fabric selection and preparation, cutting. and marking as well as organizing your materials, equipment, and sewing area.

When selecting a pattern and fabric, you may be unable to decide if the style, fabric, or color will be flattering to your figure and personality. This feeling is shared by many sewers, including professionals. For a very easy solution, turn to ready-to-wear! There you are certain to find a similar design in the same type of fabric that you can try on and analyze in front of a three-way mirror.

If you purchase your fabric before your pattern, make up a little notebook containing fabric swatches and yardages (metrages) to carry with you when you make your pattern selection. Use the swatches for choosing color-matched notions, such as thread, zipper, and buttons, so you can avoid a second shopping trip. To be superorganized, use your notebook whenever you shop to help you coordinate your entire wardrobe.

If your fabric requires preshrinking, this step can not be eliminated without disastrous results. However, most washable fabrics can be tossed right into your washing machine, along with any trimmings and lining, and laundered just as the finished garment will be. Follow the washing and drying directions, which are available on the fabric bolt or hang tag, recommended for your fabric. Washing also helps to remove finishes that sometimes cause stitching problems, especially on lightweight woven and knitted fabrics.

Organize

Next, organize your sewing area. Gather together all your supplies and keep them in a fabric-lined basket or fabric covered box. Many basic notions such as a variety of pins, needles, snaps, and hooks and eyes should always be kept on hand. Other notions that are color-coordinated with the fabric will have to be purchased for each specific garment.

Although only a needle and thread are needed to sew a garment, a wide variety of sewing tools and equipment can make sewing much easier and faster. Refer to Chapter 3 for information on such items as: special sewing machine feet and attachments for performing special tasks; different sized scissors for cutting, trimming, and clipping; tailor's ham for pressing curved areas; bodkin for threading elastic through casings; and basting and sewing tapes to simplify stitching. Many of these sewing aids are truly timesavers.

Keep your equipment in good condition. Scissors, pins, and needles need to be sharp and smooth without any nicks or burrs for easy cutting and stitching. Professionals replace their needles and pins frequently to avoid snags and skipped stitches. Many follow this rule: a new machine needle for every new project. By keeping your equipment together and in good condition, you will always be ready to begin sewing without any fuss.

Use a magnetic pin cushion to hold your pins. (It easily picks up pins scattered on the floor, too.) Tie a ribbon to your scissors to hang around your neck or chair back, so they are always accessible. Tape a small bag to the base of your machine or sewing table so you can sweep all threads and fabric trimmings into it as you sew and avoid a messy clean-up job afterwards.

If possible, set up your ironing board right next to your sewing machine to save extra steps, and to ensure that you always press as you sew. If this is not practical, then set up a small travel board or sleeve board which you can use to press all but the largest areas.

Layout and Cutting

Although there are many shortcuts to follow when laying out and cutting your pattern, always handle your fabric carefully. Accuracy in cutting and marking is truly your best guide and a "time-saver" when you begin sewing. An error of only ⅛" (3 mm) in cutting along the edge of a seam allowance can be multiplied into a 1" (25 mm) error for all four seams, Be sure your scissors are sharp. Dull scissors will only chew your fabric, causing inaccuracy, frustration, and a very tired hand! Use sewing scissors only for cutting fabric, never for other household tasks. A rotary cutter and mat is a valuable time saver particularly when cutting knits. Use sharp, new blades at all times.

Press your pattern pieces with a warm iron. Circle the correct layout on your cutting guide before you begin. Always lay out **all** your pattern pieces on your fabric before you begin to cut even one pattern piece. If you are a couple of inches (centimeters) short at the end, you can always move your pattern pieces closer together **before** you begin cutting.

Try using weights to hold your pattern in place the pinless way (1). Or you can use sewing tape or cellophane tape on some fabrics, testing the tape first for easy removal. If you do use pins, keep them on a magnetic pin cushion to prevent the frustration of spilling an entire box of pins. To prevent snagging your fabric, discard any pins that become dull or rough. With knits, use ball-point pins instead of sharps.

A prescaled cutting board can be an aid in straightening and aligning your fabric as well as for measuring. For easy and accurate placement of your pattern, be sure to use a long tape measure, not a short ruler. Never disregard the grainline on a pattern piece in order to save fabric—it will only result in later problems as you stitch, press, and fit your garment.

If you have to make minor fitting adjustments in your garment, plan ahead and cut 1" (25 mm) seam allowances on all side seams. Then if any seams have to be let out, you will have sufficient fabric to make the adjustment (2).

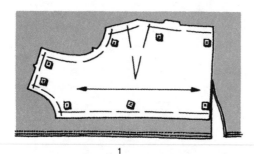

1

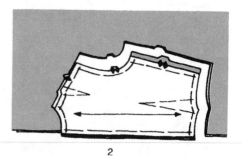

2

Certain construction techniques can only be used if you preplan and make the necessary changes when you are cutting out your fabric. Some garments with the center back seam on straight grain can be placed with the cutting line on the selvage for instant seam finishes (3). Clip the selvage at intervals to avoid puckering after washing (4).

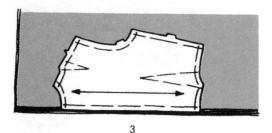

3

4

Waistbands, belts, ties, and straps can also be cut on the selvage to eliminate the added bulk of a seam allowance. Place your pattern piece so that the **stitching** line is even with the edge of the fabric (5).

Pockets can also be simplified by eliminating extra seams. In-seam pockets can be cut as part of the garment by overlapping the pattern pieces, matching stitching lines, and pinning or taping the pieces together (6). Pockets with a facing and separate lining can be easily converted to a self-lined pocket. Flip the pattern piece over along the foldline at the top of the pocket to create a "double" pocket (7).

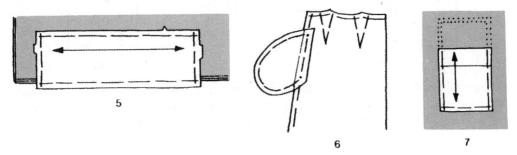

5   6   7

Plaids and stripes create special problems when laying out your pattern pieces. To help you match the fabric design at the **seamline,** not the cutting line, circle the match point in red on each pattern piece. If your pattern pieces do not have dots indicating match points, draw a line intersecting the seamline and the point of the notch to use as your match point for layout (8).

To make matching as easy as possible, lay out your pattern pieces side by side, or one above the other, exactly as they will be worn. Center front will always match horizontally if both sides are cut at one time from carefully folded fabric. The back should match the front horizontally along the side seams, below the bustline dart and vertically at the shoulder seams. Sleeves should match vertically at the shoulder seam and horizontally at the front armhole notch, the back notches usually will not match. For collars, match at center back, for detail areas, match to corresponding garment area (9).

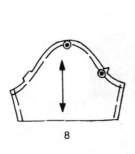

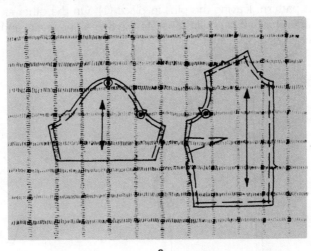

8   9

For the easiest method of handling plaids and stripes, cut all detail areas such as collar, cuffs, and pockets on the bias for "unmatched" construction. To change the grainline of a pattern piece from straight to bias, fold the pattern in half crosswise near the center of the grainline arrow (1). Bring the folded edge up to the arrow (2). Open out pattern and draw along one diagonal crease for bias grain of the pattern (3).

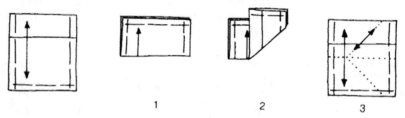

A special tip: When making calculations for changes or alterations in garments, you may find it easier to convert all measurements into eighths (millimeters) – ⅛, ²⁄₈ (¼), ³⁄₈, ⁴⁄₈ (½), ⁵⁄₈, ⁶⁄₈ (¾), ⅞ (3 mm, 6 mm, 10 mm, 13 mm, 16 mm, 19 mm, 22 mm).

Marking

Accurate markings on all your fabric sections will help you construct your garment more easily and quickly. Mark all your pattern pieces at one time, being careful not to overlook any important markings. It is very time-consuming to have to repin a pattern piece to your fabric to check a marking when you are sewing!

The marking method you choose depends upon your fabric and how soon you plan to construct your garment. Clips are clearly visible on firmly woven or knitted fabrics, but are lost in loosely constructed fabrics. Pins are simple to use but may fall out if the fabric will be handled several times before stitching. Try one or more of the following methods for quick and easy marking:

PINS: Many garments can be marked with pins if you plan to construct the garment immediately. Place pins through the pattern at all symbols and dots and carefully remove the pattern, leaving the pins in place (1). On the other side, insert additional pins at each marking. Then carefully separate the two fabric layers and secure the pins in each layer of fabric (2).

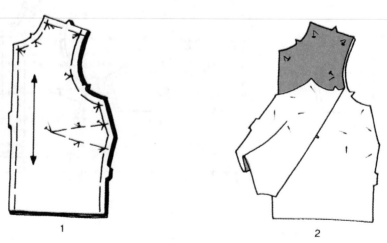

CLIPS: Tiny clips can be made in seams that you are certain will not be let out during fitting. Make ¼" (6 mm) snips in the seam allowances to mark notches, ends of darts, tucks, pleats, and foldlines; and the location of the zipper stop and top of sleeve (1).

PRESSING: Foldlines, tucks, and pleats can be marked by pressing the fabric with the pattern still attached. Pin along both sides of the foldline through the pattern and fabric (2). Fold the pattern and fabric together and press along the fold with a dry iron. (3).

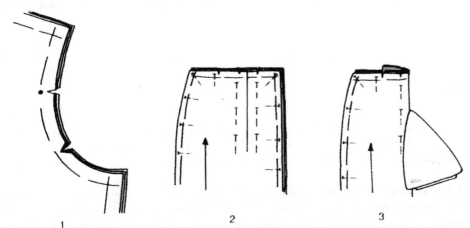

MACHINE-BASTING: The pivot point on a V neckline or yoke can be marked with machine basting, stitching two intersecting lines right on the seamline. Use the basting as a stitching guide when joining the two sections together to achieve a perfect point. Machine-basting can also be used on many fabrics to mark buttonhole and button placements (4).

CARDBOARD GAUGE: Instead of marking certain areas of a garment. you can make a cardboard gauge to use as your sewing or pressing guide. Simply notch a piece of lightweight cardboard the desired width of the garment area and use it for measuring pivot points, tucks and pleats, hemlines, and topstitching (5)

DRESSMAKER'S CARBON PAPER AND TRACING WHEEL: Both layers of fabric can be easily marked at the same time by folding the carbon paper in half and placing it under the pattern, making sure the carbon faces the wrong side of both layers of fabric. Use a ruler to help you make straight lines with the tracing wheel.

Some dressmaker's carbons on the market are water soluble. If your fabric is washable, you can mark details such as pocket or buttonhole placement on the right side of your fabric, and the markings will wash out.

A combination marking pen and remover also allows you to mark on the right side of the fabric. Use the "ink" tip of the pen to make your markings: use the "remover" tip to eliminate the ink marks after the garment has been completed. Be sure to test the ink and remover on a scrap of the fabric before marking.

Very Easy SEWING

Many basic sewing techniques, traditionally done by hand, can now be done entirely by machine stitching or fusing. Become familiar with your sewing machine, its attachments, and its variety of stitches so you can use it effectively. Experiment with fusibles--both fusible interfacings and fusible webs have created an entirely new approach to sewing. From preliminary basting to final hemming, new methods of construction have simplified many sewing tasks.

Basting

Traditional pattern construction methods always recommend basting fabric sections together before stitching. However, hand-basting can be very tedious and time-consuming. Instead, use pins, tape, machine-basting, or no basting at all for Very Easy Vogue construction.

PIN BASTING: Most sewing machine manufacturer's do not recommend sewing over pins for safety reasons. Insert pins about 1" to 4" (25 mm to 10 cm) apart with the heads far enough away from the seam so they will not be hit by the presser foot. For best control, reduce your sewing speed as you are about to reach a pin. Remove the pin just before stitching over it.

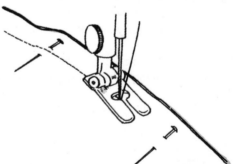

MACHINE-BASTING: Many sewing machines have a built-in basting stitch, which is very easy to remove after fitting or permanent stitching has been completed, However, your longest stitch length [6 to 8 stitches per inch, (2-3 per cm)] can also be used for basting. Clip the stitches about every inch (25 mm) so they will be easy to pull out later (1). Or use a contrasting color thread, especially in the bobbin, to identify the basting more easily.

For fabrics that must be carefully matched, such as plaids, use machine-basting to keep the fabric perfectly aligned as the seam is stitched. Place fabric right sides together, then fold back one seam allowance so you can match the fabric design. Machine-baste using a blind hemming stitch; press seam allowances together, and then stitch the seam (2).

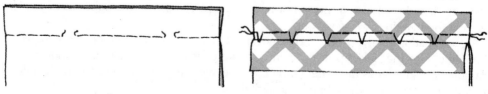

1   2

BASTING TAPE: For hard-to-handle fabrics or for fabrics that must be carefully matched, use basting tape or double-faced tape to hold the two fabric layers together. Place tape ¼" (6 mm) away from the seamline so it will not be caught in the stitching (1). Be sure to remove it after completing the seam.

NO BASTING: Seamstresses for garment manufacturers are able to sew seams quickly and evenly without any pinning or basting. Although this takes practice, the technique can be used for many fabrics. Match the top edges of your fabric and align the notches or markings. As you begin stitching, guide the fabric with your right hand in front of the needle and with your left hand in back of the presser foot. Keep the two layers of fabric even and anticipate any easing, You may have to stop occasionally to adjust the layers until you can eventually stitch a seam in one continuous operation (2).

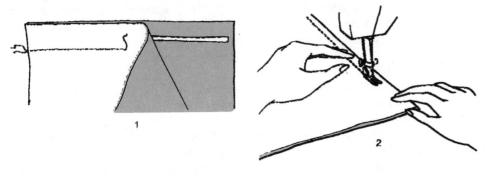

Machine-Stitching

The goal here, as with all steps of construction, is accurate stitching so that no time is spent ripping out stitches. A regular straight stitch can be used for most of the simplified techniques shown below: a zigzag stitch is needed for the others. However, if your machine has additional stitches, use them! Stretch stitches can "give" with knitted and stretch fabrics; overedge stitches can sew a seam and finish the edge at the same time: patterned stitches can be used for topstitching and a multitude of decorative trims.

Refer to Chapter 3 for information on needle and thread selection for all types of fabrics. If you have a stitching problem, first check your needle. A bent, blunt, nicked, or improperly inserted needle is usually the cause, so change your needle frequently.

CONTINUOUS STITCHING: Take a tip from assembly lines and stitch as many pieces together as possible without cutting threads until you are finished. Darts, facings. shoulder seams, collars, cuffs, sleeves, and pockets-sew from one piece right into the next. If a seam must be secured at the end, do it with your stitching instead of tying knots (page 404).

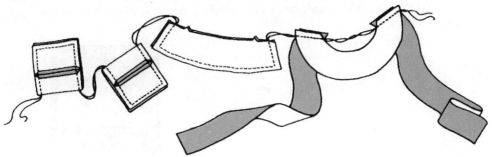

SEAMS: There are several different ways to secure the end of a seam without tying a knot. Either backstitch several stitches (1), use a lockstitch built into your machine at the end of the seam (2), or complete the seam using very small stitches (3).

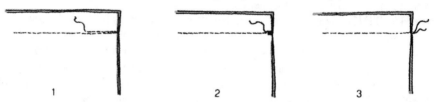

When stitching lightweight fabrics, you may have trouble with the fabric puckering or being pulled down into the needle hole as you stitch. Try placing tissue paper or tear-away stabilizer between the fabric and the feed; it can be easily torn away after the seam is completed. Use the straight stitch needle plate or place tape over the hole of the general purpose needle plate, and always hold both thread ends securely behind the presser foot as you begin stitching (4).

Curved edges should always be staystitched to prevent stretching and misalignment when stitching facings or seams. Use the staystitching as a clipping guide, so that the clips do not extend into or past the seamline (5).

Always reinforce corners such as collar points, V necklines, and sleeve plackets to prevent the frustrating experience of having fabric threads pull out as you are turning the seam. Use tiny stitches on either side of the corner, or reinforce the area with a piece of fusible interfacing before you stitch (6).

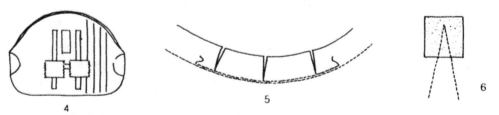

SEAM FINISHES: For most fabrics of light, medium or heavyweight, you can simply stitch the seam and trim and overcast the edges with your overlock machine. Pinking the edges also works to prevent raveling. Lightweight wovens and knits can be double-stitched and trimmed or a rolled edge can be applied with the serger for a narrow seam finish. If the seams allowance will show, clean-finish the edge by turning under ¼" (6 mm) and stitching.

DARTS: To achieve a smooth point at the end of a dart, gradually decrease the length of your stitches as you near the point. This secures the threads without having to tie a knot or backstitch, which can cause a bubble at the end of the dart (1).

TUCKS AND PLEATS: Rather than pinning or basting each tuck or pleat, use a special seam guide designed for tucks or make a cardboard gauge to keep tucks and pleats even as you stitch (2).

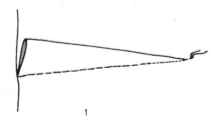

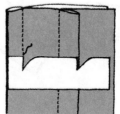

EASING: For areas that have only a moderate amount of ease, use your fingers to ease in the fullness as you stitch on a single layer of fabric. Press your index finger against the back of the presser foot, causing the fabric to pile up against your finger. This forces the fabric to ease in a little fullness under the needle. After stitching several inches (centimeters), release the fabric, then repeat until the entire area is eased (1). Pin the two layers of fabric together, and stitch the seam from the eased side.

For areas that have a lot of ease, such as a set-in sleeve, always use the longest stitch possible and loosen the tension so the bobbin thread can be pulled up easily without breaking. After distributing the fullness evenly, press the seam allowances flat to help prevent tucks from getting caught in the stitching as you sew the seam (2).

GATHERING: To help prevent the thread from breaking when you pull up gathering, use a heavy-duty thread or buttonhole twist in the bobbin and slightly loosen the upper tension. Another easy, fool-proof gathering method is to thread a narrow cord, gimp, or buttonhole twist under the back of your all-purpose presser foot and up and through the front for easy guiding. Using a wide zigzag stitch, stitch over the cord, being careful not to stitch into it. Pull up the gathers and stitch along the seamline just below the cord. Remove the cord when the seam is completed (3).

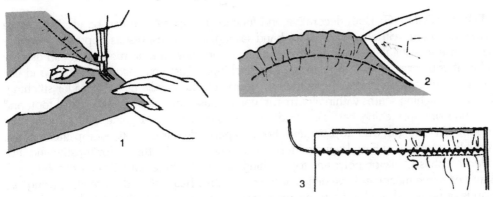

"STITCH IN THE DITCH": A clever name for a clever technique—"stitch in the ditch" can be used to hold layers of fabric together and to eliminate handwork. Stitch on the right side of your garment directly in the ridge or "ditch" of the seam with your edge stitch foot, using 10 to 12 stitches per inch (4-5 per cm). Be sure that the under layer of fabric is smooth and properly positioned before you begin stitching, Use this technique to finish facings, bindings, collars, cuffs, and waistbands; to hold cuffs in place on pants or roll-up sleeves; and to prevent elastic from twisting in a casing. For complete instructions, see the section on Very Easy Construction Techniques, page 410.

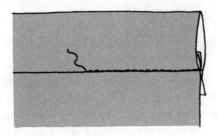

KEEPING STITCHING STRAIGHT: When stitching seams or topstitching sections of a garment, it is important to keep the stitching straight for appearance and accuracy. Here are several techniques to help you accomplish this.

Use the seam markings on the needle plate of your machine as your guide (1). If your plate is not marked, place a piece of white or colored tape exactly ⅝" (15 mm) away from the center of the needle hole. To aid you in turning a corner, place another piece of tape ⅝" (15 mm) in front of the hole. When the corner of the fabric is aligned with the intersecting tapes, it's time to pivot or turn your fabric (2). Or use an adjustable or magnetic seam guide, which is placed on the machine and can be adjusted both for distance from the needle hole and for curves (3).

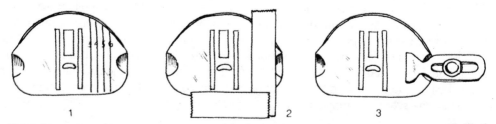

TOPSTITCHING: Both decorative and functional, topstitching can be used to secure facings and hems without any need for hand sewing. For easiest results, topstitch your garment while it is still flat. When topstitching along the edge of a garment, you can use the width of your presser foot for narrow edgestitching; adjust your needle position and use your edge stitch foot; or use the markings or tape on the needle plate for wider stitching. When topstitching seams within a garment, you can use your all-purpose presser foot, and a quilting or topstitching bar (1), or adhesive sewing tape as a guide. Stitch slowly but smoothly for straight, even topstitching. For two perfectly parallel rows of topstitching, use a double needle. Very Easy Vogue patterns recommend regular thread for topstitching. For added emphasis, silk or polyester topstitching and buttonhole twist thread can be used. However, some machines have difficulty stitching with a heavy thread; instead try using two strands of regular thread. If your machine does not have two spindles, wind thread on an extra bobbin and place on the same spindle under the spool of thread (2).

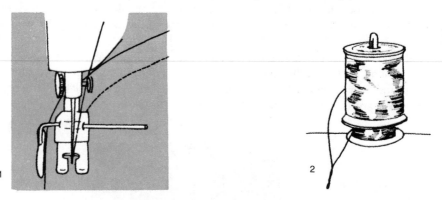

Machine stitching can also be used to finish many details which traditionally have always been done by hand. Hems, thread loops, bar tacks, buttonholes, buttons, and other fasteners can all be constructed or attached by machine; see pages 419 to 424. Your sewing machine can be a great time-saver for so many Very Easy Vogue techniques.

Pressing

"Always press as you sew"–this is one sewing adage that should not be bypassed. Careful pressing is vital to the final appearance of your garment. It is easy to press seams while your garment is still flat, but very difficult and sometimes impossible to press certain areas after the garment has been completed. However, the following techniques can help to simplify your pressing procedure.

Save time by not running back and forth between your sewing machine and ironing board. Organize your sewing construction so that you stitch as many darts or seams in different units as possible, and then press them all at the same time.

To be able to see what you are pressing, use a see-through press cloth or a special iron cover that is placed over the soleplate of your iron to prevent shine and scorching (1). To avoid making imprints of seam allowances on the right side of your fabric, use envelopes instead of brown paper strips. They don't have to be cut and are easy to slide along (2). To obtain a sharp seam edge on collars. cuffs, and lined pockets without using a point presser, preset the seam edge. Press the facing seam allowance back toward the facing before turning the fabric right side out (3). The seam edge will be smooth and even without having to tug or pull at the fabric.

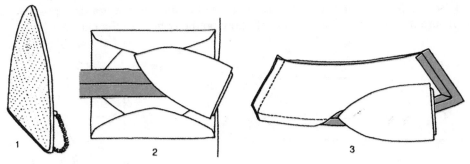

When pressing detail areas such as collars, lapels, facings, cuffs, and pockets, always "favor" the top layer of fabric. Press the outer seam so that it rolls slightly to the underside of the garment. This helps to prevent the facing side from curling or rolling up and becoming visible along the seamline (4).

Hems can be measured and pressed in one easy step by using a hem gauge or cardboard gauge. Place the gauge between the fabric and the hem allowance to prevent an imprint of the hemline from showing on the right side of the fabric (5).

To avoid crushing the pile on velvet, velveteen, corduroy, fake fur, and other pile fabrics, use a thick towel or a piece of self-fabric as a substitute for a needle board.

Occasionally use an iron cleaner to remove built-up fabric finishes, starch, detergent, and fusing agents from the soleplate of your iron. Your iron will glide more easily and smoothly.

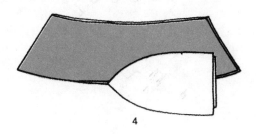

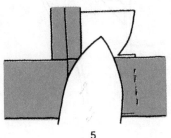

Fusing

Fusing has revolutionized many sewing procedures. Heat-sensitive fusibles-both interfacing and webs-can eliminate hand sewing, achieving professional results in just a fraction of the time. Your iron can also replace your sewing machine for basting, interfacing, and hemming applications.

Although fusing is quick and easy to do, **always** follow manufacturer's directions carefully to achieve the proper results. See page 157 for complete information on where and how to use fusibles. Always take time to pretest on your fabric before you begin fusing, checking the appearance and crispness of the fused fabrics. Although fusibles can be removed if you make a mistake, they cannot be reused and extra steps must be taken to remove any fusing agents remaining on the fabric.

For additional time-savers when working with fusibles, try these suggestions:

FUSIBLE INTERFACINGS: When cutting out sheer or lightweight fusible interfacings, place the interfacing over the pattern piece and trace along the seamline. Cut just inside the traced line and clip corners diagonally to eliminate the time-consuming task of trimming seam allowances separately (1).

Fuse interfacing directly to the facing instead of to the garment for easy positioning and to assure that no outline or imprint will show on the outside of the garment (2).

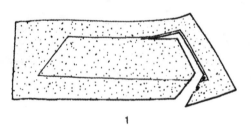

1

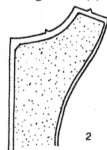

2

If you decide you need extra shaping or body in an interfaced area, fuse another layer of interfacing on top of the first. This method can be used for small areas such as the point of a lapel or the stand of a collar, as well as for an entire waistband or belt (3).

Detail areas such as individual buttonholes, plackets, and V-shaped slashes can be easily reinforced and stabilized by fusing a small piece of interfacing to the fabric before it is stitched or slashed. Pink the edge to help prevent an outline from showing on the right side of the fabric (4).

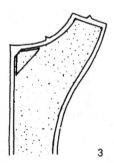

3

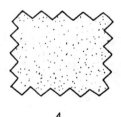

4

The use of a damp press cloth when fusing guarantees that enough steam is provided, even if you use a steam iron. The press cloth also prevents any fusing resins from touching the soleplate of your iron.

Fusible interfacings can be used to preserve a favorite pattern or a basic fitting pattern to use time and time again. Just press the inter-facing to the back of each pattern piece. Some fusibles are specially designed for just this purpose.

FUSING AGENTS: Use a narrow strip of fusible web or bonding agent to "baste" two layers of fabric together. Pockets, straps, tabs, trims, and applique's can all be positioned and held in place without shifting as you stitch. Many of these bonding agents are available in narrow widths from ⅜" to ⅞" (10 mm to 22 mm) for easy use.

When folding narrow strips of fabric together for buttonhole lips, belt carriers, and fabric loops, insert a narrow strip the of fusible bonding agent between the fabric layers. Pressing the fabric will fuse the layers together for a smoother appearance, adding body and a sharper edge.

When fusing a hemline, place the fusible bonding agent ¼" (6 mm) below the edge of the hem allowance to prevent any fusible particles from accidentally touching the soleplate of your iron and to make the outline of the hem less conspicuous on the outside of the garment. Always use a pres cloth.

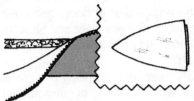

When cutting narrow strips of fusible web from a wide width, fold the fusing agent as many times as you can so that you only have to make one short cut.

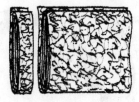

To mend a rip or burn in a garment, just fuse a piece of self-fabric behind the area for a no-stitch, invisible repair job!

Very Easy
CONSTRUCTION
TECHNIQUES

Before you begin the construction of any garment, always read the Guide Sheet completely. When you understand how a pattern is to be constructed, the procedure is always easier. Also, you can decide what shortcut methods will be applicable to your particular garment, as some methods necessitate a slightly different order of construction procedures. From collars and cuffs to buttonholes and belts, these simple construction techniques will ease your sewing efforts.

Flat Construction

Very Easy Vogue patterns feature flat construction techniques wherever possible. Flat construction means that you complete each section of a garment before you stitch the major seams together. Sleeves, zippers, pockets, facings, and bands can all be stitched much more easily when a garment is still "flat." Topstitching each area as it is constructed is easier than waiting until the entire garment is completed.

For *set-in sleeves,* stitch garment shoulder seams. Finish lower edge of sleeve unless it is going to be cuffed. Easestitch sleeve cap between notches, pin sleeve to armhole edge, and adjust gathers. With sleeve side up, stitch along seamline and again ¼" (6 mm) away (1). Trim close to stitching and press seam toward sleeve. Stitch back to front at side seams and sleeve edges in one continuous seam (2). Clip, if necessary, and press open.

For *raglan sleeves,* stitch neckline dart in sleeve and finish lower sleeve edge unless it is going to be cuffed. Pin sleeve to garment front and back, matching symbols, and stitch. Clip seams along underarm curve and press open. Stitch side of garment and sleeve in one continuous seam; press open (3).

For *armhole facing,* finish outer edge of facing and pin to armhole edge. Stitch, trim and understitch. Turn armhole facing to inside of garment and press. Open out facing and stitch side seams, including facing, as shown (4).

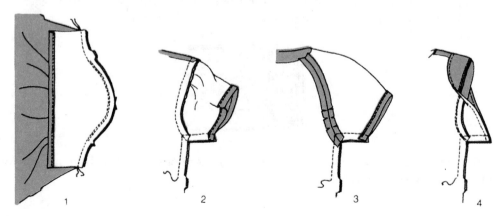

Insert a zipper before the facing or waistband is attached, using a centered application whenever possible. Stitch the center back or center front seam below the zipper opening. Insert zipper, (5) following directions on page 420 before the shoulder or side seams are stitched. For a neckline facing, stitch the shoulder seams and then apply the facing before the side seams are sewn. For a skirt or pants facing, stitch the facing sections separately to the garment front and back. Then stitch the side seams of the garment and facing in one continuous seam.

When applying a bias binding, banding, or decorative trim to a garment edge, leave one seam open for easier construction. Stitch the binding, band, or trim to the garment, then enclose the ends in the final seam (6).

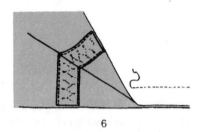

5   6

Facings and Other Edge Finishes

A smooth, even finish at the edge of a garment—whether it is a facing, banding, or bias binding—can often be difficult to achieve. Here are some easy methods to simplify your facing task, as well as alternative ways of finishing an edge.

FACINGS: Use the flat construction method when applying a neckline, armhole, or front edge facing. Not only is it easier to stitch the facing to the garment edge before the side seams are completed, but the tasks of trimming, pressing, and understitching are also simplified.

For a smooth, flat appearance, the seam allowances must be trimmed to eliminate any bulk. With light and mediumweight fabrics, you can grade both seam allowances at the same time by holding your scissors at an angle and cutting the facing seam allowance narrower than the garment seam allowance (1). Always press a facing seam, "favoring" the outside of the garment. Roll the seam slightly toward the facing side to help prevent the facing from showing along the garment edge (2). Then hold the facing securely inside your garment by using machine stitching instead of hand tacking (3). Either understitch through just the facing and the seam allowances, topstitch through all layers, or stitch in the ditch along another seam. You may also use a small piece of fusible web to hold the facings in place.

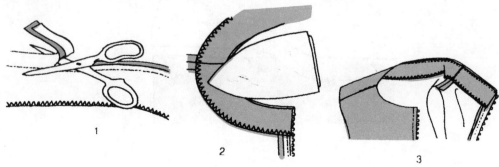

1

2

3

BINDINGS AND BANDINGS: Use the stitch-in-the-ditch method to eliminate any hand finishing when applying bias bindings, and fabric or knitted bands. Stitch binding or band to garment, right sides together; wrap over raw edges, and pin in place on inside of garment. On right side of garment, stitch-in-the-ditch to hold the binding or band in place. If your fabric ravels, finish the inside edge before you begin.

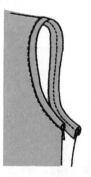

OTHER OPTIONS: For easy alternatives, try these methods for finishing edges. For armholes and necklines on casual knitted garments, such as T-shirts, just turn and topstitch the edge. Fold the fabric along the seamline; turn in raw edge ¼" (6 mm); and stitch close to the edge, as shown (1). For curved areas, first staystitch just inside the seamline to help the fabric fold smoothly to the inside of the garment.

For a casual appearance on sportswear, try trimming the seam allowances and stitching along the edge with an overlock stitch on your serger (2). Or for fabrics that do not ravel, simply trim or pink along the seamline and stitch ¼" (6 mm) from the edge to prevent stretching.

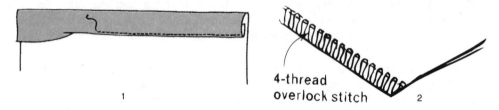

4-thread
overlock stitch

1   2

Fold-over braid is another option for edges. Be sure to trim away the seam allowances and preshape braid with a steam iron to match curved areas. As a guide for encasing curved edges, staystitch along fabric edge with the distance just slightly narrower than the width of the braid. Place braid over raw edge with widest side underneath and top edge covering staystitching. Machine-stitch close to edge of braid, catching underneath side (3).

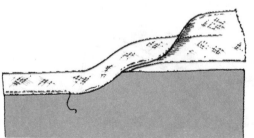

3

Collars

Because a collar frames your face it should always look well made. Symmetrical points, smooth edges, and a perfect roll can be easily achieved with these sewing tips.

For sharp points, always trim the interfacing away at the tip of the point before it is stitched or fused to the collar. When stitching your collar, use short reinforcement stitches for about 1" (25 mm) on both sides of the point to help prevent any fabric threads from pulling out when the collar is turned. To eliminate extra bulk at the point, make one or two diagonal stitches across the tip and trim close to the stitching, being very careful not to cut into the stitches (1). When turning the collar, you can use a pin to gently coax out the point on the right side; never use scissors to poke it out. "Favor" the upper collar when you press the outer edges to help keep the undercollar always hidden. For bulky fabrics that are not going to be topstitched, try understitching the collar just as you understitch a facing. From the right side, stitch through the undercollar and seam allowances from center back to as close to each point as possible. This helps to keep the undercollar out of sight (2).

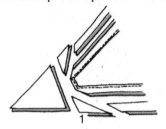
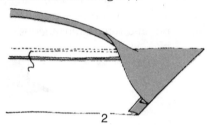

When attaching a collar, you have several shortcut options depending upon your fabric and style of garment. Many collars can be simply "sandwiched" around the neckline of the garment. Trim seam allowance of upper collar to ¼" (6mm) along the neck edge, and press to wrong side of collar at seamline. Stitch upper and undercollars together, trim, and turn right side out (3). Stitch undercollar to garment, right sides together, catching only the seam allowances of upper collar (4). Fold free edge of upper collar over seam allowances and topstitch in place (5).

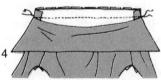
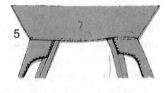

This method can also be used for a collar on a garment that has a front extended facing. Before the collar can be attached, complete the neck edge between the collar and the front foldline, and press the facing in place as shown (6). Sandwich the collar over the garment and facing seam allowances and stitch as described above, eliminating the back facing (7).

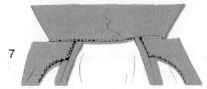

Or you can use the stitch-in-the-ditch method to eliminate a back facing. Before you begin, clip the upper collar at the shoulder markings almost to the seamline, and finish the neck edge between the clips with a ¼" (6mm) hem. Pin collar to garment and front facings, keeping finished back neck edge free; stitch, trim, and clip neck seamline (8). Pin free edge of upper collar along neckline, making sure that the collar rolls properly. Then stitch in the ditch along the neckline seam from shoulder to shoulder to secure the collar without any hand stitching (9).

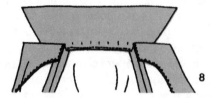 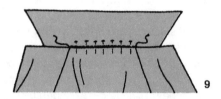

To easily make a stand-up or roll collar on a knitted garment, just pin both collar layers to the garment and stitch in place using an overedge stitch or a straight zigzag stitch. Trim close to stitching, and press seam allowances toward garment (10). If you own an overlock machine, trim and stitch simultaneously using a 3- or 4-thread stitch.

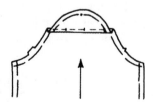

10

Sleeves and Cuffs

For easiest construction of set-in and raglan sleeves, use the flat construction method described on page 410. Many of the same techniques for collars can also be used for cuffs, making construction smoother and easier.

SLEEVES: If a set-in sleeve has a lot of ease, always use two or three rows of gathering stitches to help distribute the ease evenly and to act as security in case one thread breaks. If the sleeve cap has only moderate ease, try easing in the extra fullness with your finger as you stitch; see page 403. If you still need more ease because the sleeve cap is too large, use a pin to pull up several stitches. If the sleeve cap is too small, just clip the stitches every 2" (5 cm) or so.

Certain fabrics, such as heavy velvet, vinyl, leather, and synthetic suede can not be smoothly eased. Instead, take out a little fullness in the sleeve cap by pinning a narrow tuck

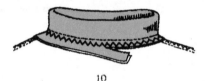

in the pattern above the notches before you cut out the fabric.

To help avoid any tucks in the sleeve cap when you stitch, be certain that the cut edge of the sleeve does not extend beyond the armhole. Then distribute any gathers evenly, and stitch accurately on the ⅝" (15 mm) seamline.

PLACKETS: Sleeve openings for cuffs need not be time-consuming. Many traditional plackets can be entirely machine-stitched instead of finished by hand. Or try these very easy openings, using a dart, seam, or facing.

For a dart opening, stitch a small dart beginning about 2" (5 cm) above the edge of the sleeve. Slash fabric to form opening, ending at stitching. Roll raw edges of opening to wrong side of garment and stitch (1).

For a seam opening, just end your stitching at the marking or about 3" (7.5 cm) above the sleeve edge, keeping the lower seam open. Machine-stitch or fuse seam allowance in place (2).

For an easy faced opening, reinforce the point or corners with small stitches; trim, clip, and turn. Fuse the facing in place, or turn under the raw edges and machine-stitch (3).

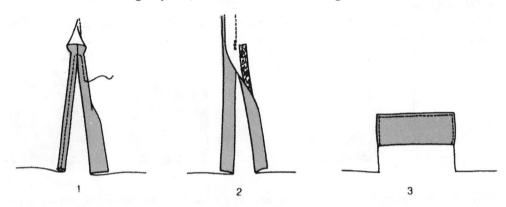

CUFFS: To complete a straight cuff with machine stitching, try this reverse seaming technique. Trim seam allowance of upper cuff to ¼" (6 mm), turn under and press. Stitch right side of cuff to wrong side of garment; trim. Fold cuff right sides together, complete ends, and turn cuff right side out. Pin upper cuff over seamline and topstitch in place (1).

Or use the stitch-in-the-ditch method to eliminate both bulk and hand sewing on the inside of the cuff. Finish raw edge of under cuff with ¼" (6 mm) hem or pinking. Stitch outer cuff to sleeve, trim seam allowance, and pin finished edge along seamline. Stitch-in-the-ditch along the seam from right side of garment (2).

For simple band cuffs and knitted cuffs, attach cuff to sleeve before underarm seam is stitched. Stitch cuff to sleeve edge using overedge seam or two rows of stitching. Trim close to stitching. Complete underarm seam, including cuff. To prevent the seam allowance from showing, fold corners under and machine-tack to the seam allowance (3).

Or eliminate cuffs entirely and finish sleeve with elastic casing! A special tip: To hold rollup sleeves in place, just stitch-in-the-ditch through all layers.

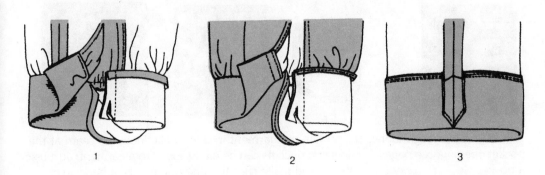

Pockets

Pockets can be easy to sew-whether decorative or functional, prominent or hidden in a seam. Choose patch or in-seam pockets and avoid difficult welt pockets. Some techniques depend upon special pattern layouts; others are done by machine stitching or fusing.

Patch pockets can be lined, topstitched, or stitched invisibly to your garment all by machine. For the easiest lined pocket, cut a self-lined or double pocket, page 399. Stitch pocket and lining, right sides together. Trim, clip and grade seam allowances (1). Preset edge of pocket by pressing seam allowance toward lining. Make a slit in the lining near the bottom of the pocket, and gently pull pocket right side out. Cover slit with a small piece of fusible interfacing (2).

For an unlined pocket, stitch just inside the seamline in the seam allowance to help the fabric fold smoothly to the inside. Trim and clip seam allowance to eliminate any bulk before the pocket is stitched. Machine-stitch or fuse upper edge of pocket in place (3).

1

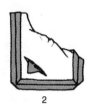
2

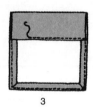
3

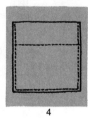
4

Whenever possible, topstitch patch pockets to garment before the side seams are sewn. Use fusible web to hold pocket in place and eliminate any problem of topstitching over pins. Place ¼" (6 mm) strip of web under side and bottom edges (not top) of pocket and fuse. Or you can use pieces of sewing tape or masking tape to position pocket. Use the inner or outer edge of your presser foot, depending upon desired width, as a guide for straight stitching (4). Machine bar tacks can be used to reinforce corners of pockets that will receive a lot of strain such as those of sportswear and children's clothes (5).

Large, curved patch pockets can be applied invisibly to a garment using this clever method. Machine-stitch or fuse pocket hem in place. Stitch around pocket on seamline, and press seam allowances under, rolling stitch slightly to the inside. Notch out fullness and pin pocket to garment (6). Machine-baste around pocket, barely catching pocket edge with long, narrow, zigzag stitches. On inside of pocket, stitch on top of first row of stitching, ending at the middle and beginning again from the other side until the stitching is completed (7). Remove zigzag basting. Or use a narrow blindhem stitch, invisible nylon thread and stitch your pocket in place on the right side (8).

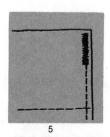
5

6

7

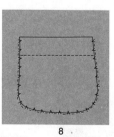
8

If you have enough fabric, cut pocket and garment in one to eliminate the seam at the pocket opening; see page 399. In-seam pockets can be easily added to a garment. Just use a pocket piece from another pattern, and make sure that the opening is at hand level.

Applied Trims

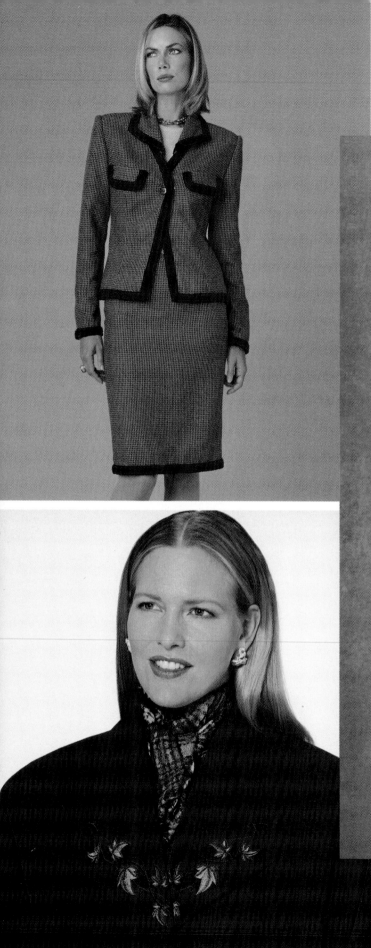

Ruffles and Bows

Ruffles and Bows

Tucks and Pleats

Tucks and Pleats

Sewing for Children

Waistlines, Waistbands, and Belts

Waistlines can be finished with a casing or a waistband, and further emphasized by many types of belts. All three details can be constructed easily and quickly by letting your sewing machine do all the work for you.

CASINGS: Whether along the edge or in the middle of the garment, a casing is one of the easiest ways to control fullness. To convert a pattern from a waistband to a self-facing, you must extend the pattern above the waistline seam twice the width of the casing plus a ¼" (6 mm) seam allowance. For a casing without a zipper, omit darts and redraw the side seams straight up from the hipline, as shown.

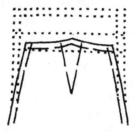

Mark foldline of casing with a clip at each seamline. Machine-baste (1) or fuse (2) seam allowances to garment in casing area to make it easier to thread the elastic or ties through the casing. Turn under the ¼" (6 mm) seam allowance and press. Stitch the casing in place along the top and bottom edges to help prevent rolling. With firmly woven fabrics and knits, you can eliminate some bulk by finishing the raw edge with zigzag stitching instead of turning the edge under.

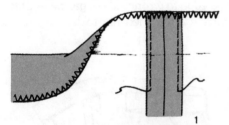

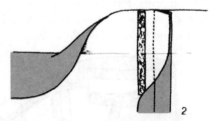

For easy insertion of elastic, be sure it is narrower than the casing, and try using a bodkin instead of a safety pin. To keep fullness adjusted evenly and to prevent elastic from twisting, stitch-in-the-ditch at each seam through all thicknesses (3).

Or, try stitching the casing with the elastic already inside. Measure elastic, including seam allowances, and mark into quarters. Leave one seam open and secure elastic ends in open seam allowance. Pin elastic along casing foldline, matching markings, with pins on outside of garment. Fold casing over elastic and stitch, stretching elastic so fabric lies flat. Complete final seam, catching in elastic ends (4).

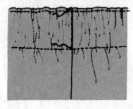

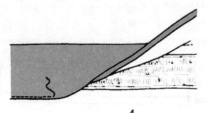

For an interior casing in a garment, use single fold bias tape. Fold in ends and stitch close to both long edges. Thread elastic or ties through casing (5). For an easier method, eliminate the casing and stitch the elastic directly to the garment. Measure elastic, mark into quarters, and pin to inside of garment between placement lines. Use one or two rows of stitching, depending upon width of elastic, stretching elastic as you sew (6).

5

6

WAISTBANDS: Try these alternative methods of constructing a waistband whenever you sew. Interfacing should be used to prevent rolling-for best results choose a special waistband interfacing or use a crisp fusible interfacing. For a simplified version of the straight waistband application, cut waistband with unnotched seamline, along edge of selvage to reduce bulk. Stitch waistband to garment; then stitch ends. Trim and press. Turn waistband to inside and pin or fuse selvage edge along seamline. From right side of waistband, topstitch close to seamline, catching in selvage.

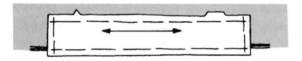

Or try the reverse seaming technique, the same one used for cuffs. Reverse the pattern piece when cutting waistband. Trim seam allowance on unnotched edge to ¼" (6 mm), turn under and press. Pin right side of notched waistband edge to wrong side of garment. Stitch, trim, and press seam toward waistband (1). Complete ends; then pin folded edge along seamline and topstitch in place (2).

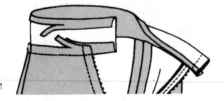

1

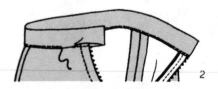

2

The stitch-in-the-ditch method is especially good for bulky fabrics because it gives a flatter appearance to the waistband seam. Cut waistband with unnotched edge along selvage so that the seam allowance is only ⅜" (10 mm) wide (3). Or trim the edge to ⅜" (10 mm) and finish with zigzag stitching. With right sides together, stitch waistband to garment, trim and press seam toward waistband. Stitch ends, trim, and clip seam allowances at center back underlap. Turn waistband right side out and pin finished edge along seamline, tucking in corners at ends. Stitch-in-the-ditch along the seamline from right side of garment (4).

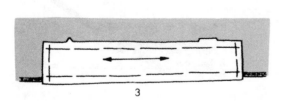

3

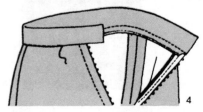

4

For knitted fabrics, you can attach the waistband using an overedge seam. If fabric is stretchy, you may wish to stay the seam by basting a piece of twill tape or seam binding along the seamline. With right sides together, stitch ends and underlap section of waistband; trim, turn, and press. Pin both edges of waistband to right side of garment. Stitch using an overedge or straight and zigzag stitch; trim close to stitching. Press seam toward garment.

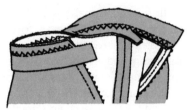

BELTS: Self-tie belts at least ⅜" (10 mm) wide are the easiest belts to make. For firmer fabrics or fabrics that are too bulky to turn, press under raw edges, fold belt in half and top-stitch in place (1). Soft or lightweight fabrics are best stitched right edges together and turned.

For a belt with buckle, use fusible web instead of stitching to hold the layers together. Cut belt with one edge along selvage. Form point at one end and fold in edges of fabric so that selvage slightly overlaps other edge. Fuse layers together with strips of fusible web (2). If extra stiffness is desired, insert a piece of interfacing or belting between the layers of fabric before fusing. Attach a no-prong buckle. Or leave both ends unfinished and attach an interlocking buckle.

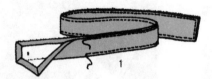
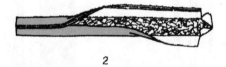

1

2

BELT CARRIERS: Both fabric and thread carriers can be easily made without any hand finishing. For fabric carriers, prepare one long strip using the selvage edge to reduce bulk. Stitch or fuse; then cut into the desired number of pieces when completed. If you plan to topstitch, cut fabric three times the desired finished width, fold strip lengthwise into thirds with selvage on outside, and press. Topstitch along both edges. If you plan to fuse the layers together, cut fabric twice the desired width plus ⅛" (3 mm). Center a strip of fusible web on wrong side of fabric. Fold in edges, overlapping ⅛" (3 mm) with selvage on top; fuse. To attach carriers, turn ends under and topstitch in place or enclose ends in seam.

Thread carriers can be made by machine or serger much faster than crocheting by hand. Twist several strands of thread together and hold taut as you stitch over them with a zigzag satin stitch (3). Another method for making thread carriers is to use the chain-stitch on your serger. Just chain off a length of threads. The threads knot together as they are serged. Pin the thread carriers in place before you sew the side seams of the garment.

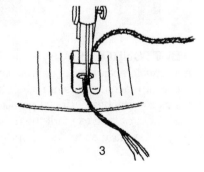

3

Fasteners

There are many different types of fasteners that can be used to secure garments-some of them can be easily adapted to shortcut methods.

ZIPPERS: Very Easy Vogue patterns recommend a centered zipper application whenever possible. For easiest construction, insert zipper before facings or waistband are attached and before side seams of garment are stitched.

Stitch seam below zipper, reinforcing end of stitching. Machine-baste zipper opening closed; clip basting stitches for easy removal; and press seam open.

Use basting tape or pieces of cellophane tape to hold zipper in place. Position top stop of zipper 1" (25 mm) below fabric edge. However, if you want to eliminate the need for a hook and eye above the zipper, place zipper stop ¾" (20 mm) below edge (1). Stitch on right side of garment, using sewing tape or cellophane tape placed ¼" (6 mm) from zipper seam as a guide for straight stitching (2), Always stitch from bottom to top along each side of zipper to prevent any distortion of zipper placket. Remove bastings.

To secure facing to zipper tape without hand sewing, try this easy method. Turn under ⅝" (15 mm) seam allowance of facing and pin in place from right side of garment. Use a zipper foot and stitch on the right side directly on top of the zipper stitching line for the width of the facing (3).

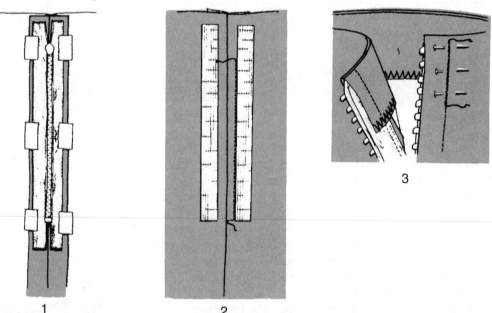

1   2   3

BUTTONHOLES: Very Easy Vogue patterns include only a limited number of buttonholes, which can always be machine-stitched for easiest sewing.

If your machine does not stitch buttonholes automatically, it is sometimes difficult to get the zigzag stitches perfectly parallel and the proper distance apart. An easy solution is to use pieces of tape to mark the dimensions of the buttonhole. Cut tape to exact buttonhole length and place about ⁵⁄₁₆" (8 mm) apart on outside of fabric to form a stitching guide (1).

Always test removing tape from a scrap of your fabric to be sure it is not too sticky; otherwise use machine basting as a guide.

When cutting buttonholes, place a straight pin at each end of the buttonhole so you will not cut through the stitches (2) or use a buttonhole cutter and block.

When interfacing dark colored fabrics, select dark interfacing so that you will not have to spend time trimming away white threads that may be visible when the buttonhole is cut open. If garment is not interfaced, use fusible interfacing to stabilize each buttonhole area. Cut out a small rectangle of interfacing and fuse to wrong side of fabric before marking buttonhole. If outline shows on right side of fabric, try pinking edges. Or stabilize the buttonhole with cording, guiding the cord as you stitch over it (3).

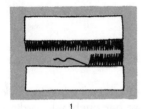 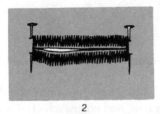 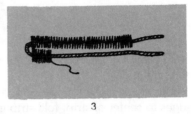

1   2   3

Although bound buttonholes are feared by many sewers, try these tips to help make their construction less difficult. Use fusible interfacing behind each buttonhole to stabilize the area and to prevent raveling when the fabric is slashed open. Place pieces of tape across the ends of each buttonhole to mark where stitching must stop (4).

For uniform results, always stitch all of your buttonholes at the same time. Use the production line method and complete each step for all buttonholes, before going on to the next step. This is faster than completing every buttonhole separately. If using fabric strips to form the buttonhole lips, make one long strip and cut into individual pieces. With bulky or very firm fabrics, try inserting a tiny strip of fusible web inside the buttonhole lips before they are stitched so they will lay flat after pressing.

Finishing off the back of a bound buttonhole can sometimes be tricky when you slash the facing and turn the edges under around the buttonhole. Stabilize the area with a piece of lightweight fusible interfacing pressed to the wrong side of the fabric. Or try the stitch-in-the-ditch method with firmly woven fabrics, knits, leathers, and synthetic suedes. Pin facing in place behind buttonhole, then stitch-in-the-ditch on right side of garment around buttonhole rectangle (5). On the facing side, trim away fabric close to stitching (6).

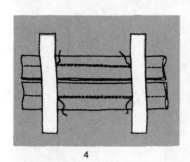 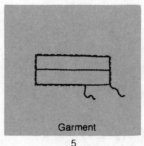 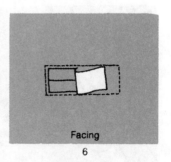

4   5   6

Garment   Facing

A special tip: To save you time when marking buttonholes, purchase the same size buttons as recommended on your pattern envelope. Your pattern pieces are already marked with the proper buttonhole position and length for this size button.

BUTTONS: Buttons can be stitched quickly and securely by machine, if you have a zigzag stitch. Hold the button in place with tape. Set width of zigzag to align with buttonholes and change stitch length to 0. Place a thick needle or toothpick on top of button to create a thread shank as you stitch. Pull threads to underside of button, and twist tightly around the stitches to form the shank. Many machines have a special adjustable button sew-on foot and stitch setting for sewing on buttons. The threads are locked at the end.

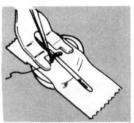

OTHER OPTIONS: Here are some other fastening ideas to substitute for buttonholes and buttons.

For easy-to-make fabric loops, cut a bias strip four times the desired finished width. Fold edges to center of strip, fold strip in half, and edgestitch (1). Or use narrow braid, cording, or ribbon for extra easy loops.

With casual shirts and jackets, consider using plain or decorative snap fasteners that can be applied with special pliers or applicators. Position fasteners at button and buttonhole markings on garment (2). Hook and loop fasteners can be machine-stitched to fabric, replacing snaps, hooks and eyes, or buttonholes. You can conceal the stitching on the outside of your garment with a button (3).

Or fasten a closure with fabric or grosgrain ribbon ties. Make fabric ties same as for fabric loops, except turn in one end when folding fabric. To attach ties, place raw edge over marking, stitch, and trim. Turn tie back over raw edge and stitch again through all layers. Cut ribbon ends diagonally or notch to prevent raveling (4).

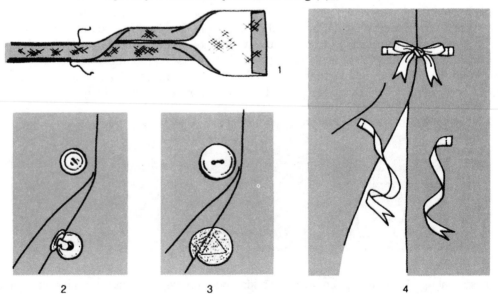

For a waistband, use a large hook-and-eye closure instead of several tiny hooks and eyes. Some types can be hammered onto the fabric before the waistband is completed.

Ready-made fasteners, such as frogs, toggles and loops, and special buckles, are both decorative and fun to use.

Hems

The final finishing detail of a garment is usually the hem. Take a tip from designers and utilize new methods of hemstitching for easy and decorative results. For an invisible hem, fusible webs will hold fabric layers together without machine or hand stitches. So if you are eager to complete your garment, just machine-stitch or fuse the hem in place, and you're ready to go!

Topstitching can be used to finish the hem and trim the garment at the same time. Use one, two, or more rows of stitches, taking care to keep them straight and parallel. If other areas of your garment are topstitched, the hem should be topstitched the same distance from the edge. Or you can duplicate a banded effect at the hemline to match a banded edge around the neckline or front of your garment. Finish by pinking close to the stitching.

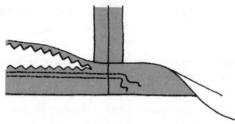

Narrow hems are ideal for sheer and lightweight fabrics. For woven fabrics, turn up ⅜" (10 mm) hem, fold in raw edge, and stitch. For knits, the hem can be stitched single thickness and then trimmed close to the stitching (1). Or you can use a special hemming foot that folds and stitches the hem in one operation. For best results, prefold an inch (25 mm) or so of your fabric so it will feed evenly into the foot (2).

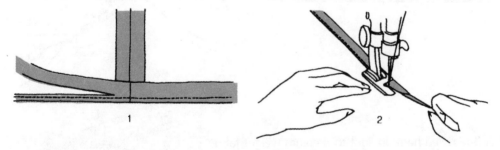

Mediumweight fabrics can be blindstitched by machine for a quick, invisible hem if your machine has the special stitch. Press up hem and turn under raw edge, if necessary. Fold back garment ¼" (6 mm) below hem edge. Align stitches so that straight stitches fall on the hem allowance and the single zigzag stitch just catches the garment along the folded edge.

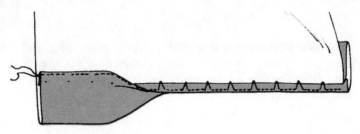

The blindstitch can also be used to create a shell edge on a hem. Trim hem allowance to ½" (13 mm) and fold under. Stitch along folded edge so that the zigzag stitch forms over the fold and scallops the edge.

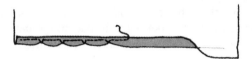

Other decorative hems, some created by designers, can also be done by machine. Jersey and double knits can be finished with a zigzag stitch. Sew along hemline with a small, narrow zigzag, then trim away hem allowance as close to the stitches as possible.

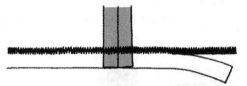

With mediumweight fabrics such as flannel and gabardine, try using a satin edge finish. Fold up hem and sew a row of narrow zigzag stitches (often called satin stitches) along the folded edge. Repeat with a second row on top of the first; trim away fabric close to stitching (1). Lightweight stretchable knits can have a special rippled or "lettuce" edge finish. Trim hem allowance to ½" (13 mm) and press up hem. Stitch along folded edge with a zigzag satin stitch, stretching fabric as you sew (2). Do not use if knit runs easily.

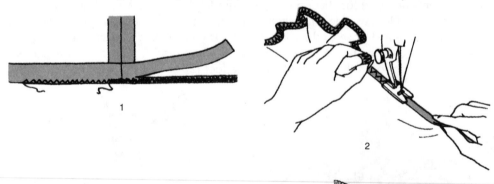

1

2

A fine rolled hem on light to medium weight fabrics can be accomplished on your overlock machine, trimming the edge and stitching at the same time. Using either a 2- or 3-thread configuration, this hem finish looks like a fine hand-rolled hem (3).

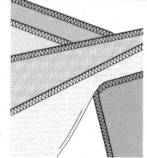

3

Fusing is one of the fastest ways to complete a hem. Always mark, trim, and press up hem before fusing. Also, cut web on each side of seam allowance for a smoother finish. See Fusing Agents, page 409. To alter a hem, press the area with steam until the two fabric layers can be gently pulled apart.

Tailoring

Tailoring is certainly not a fast or easy method of clothing construction. Yet there are many shortcuts for underlining, interfacing, padstitching, and lining that make tailoring less complicated and time-consuming. Professional results are still the goal in Very Easy Vogue tailoring, with machine stitching and fusing replacing traditional hand sewing wherever possible.

UNDERLINING: When stitching underlining and fabric sections together, zigzag along outer edge of fabrics to finish seam allowances at the same time.

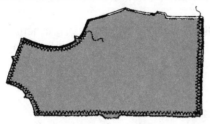

SEW-IN INTERFACING: Padstitch collars and lapels by machine rather than by hand. For collar, machine-baste interfacing to wrong side of undercollar ½" (13 mm) from edge; trim close to stitching. Using regular stitch and matching thread, padstitch stand of undercollar. Stitch first along roll line and then stitch parallel rows ¼" (6 mm) apart from roll line to neck seamline. For rest of collar, begin at center back and stitch toward collar seamline following grainline. Continue stitching parallel lines ½" to ¾" (13 mm to 20 mm) apart, pivoting near seamline and roll line as shown (1). Press with steam to shape.

For lapels, machine-baste interfacing in place, as for collars. Stitch parallel rows of padstitching from top of lapel down to seamline, starting near roll line. For extra body in lapel point, space rows more closely together. The roll line can be taped by zigzag stitching twill tape in place. Stitch through all thicknesses along the edge next to the lapel roll line. Shape lapels by steam-pressing over a pressing ham or tightly rolled towel (2).

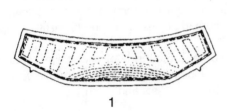

1

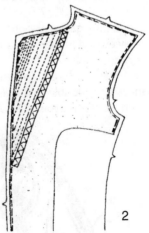

2

For hemlines, you can machine-stitch interfacing to hem allowance instead of catch-stitching by hand to wrong side of garment-a real timesaver!

FUSIBLE INTERFACING: Fusible interfacings have made tailoring easier than ever before. No catchstitching, no padstitching-just fuse interfacing to fabric. With the introduction of many different types and weights of fusible interfacings, you can achieve the exact amount of shaping desired. For collars, trim seam allowances and points of interfacing before fusing. For extra shaping in collar stand, cut a second piece of interfacing to fit between roll line and neck seamline, and fuse in place on top of first. Collar points can also be weighted with a triangular-shaped piece of additonal interfacing (1). Steam-press collar to shape.

For lapels, trim seam allowances and points before fusing. Lapel point can be weighted with another piece of interfacing just as for collar points. This will help to make the lapels lie smoothly against the garment (2). To tape roll line, zigzag stitch twill tape to garment; see page 501.

For hemlines, fuse interfacing directly to wrong side of garment, cutting at seamlines and fusing behind seam allowances (3). Or you can fuse the interfacing to the hem allowance.

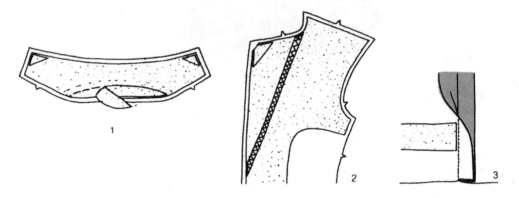

LINING: To insert a lining by machine, complete garment but do not tack facings to shoulders. Stitch lining pieces together, set in sleeves, and staystitch around curved neckline; clip to staystitching. With right sides together, pin lining to facings, matching center backs and shoulder seams. Starting 3" (7.5 cm) above lower edge, stitch from lining side around neckline, ending 3" (7.5 cm) from opposite lower edge. Press seam allowances toward lining and turn garment right side out. Tack lining to garment at underarm seams. Hem lining at sleeve and lower edge of garment by hand or use machine blindstitch; slipstitch front corners in place.

For an even faster finish, eliminate the lining. To finish the inside of your garment, bind seam allowances with double-fold bias tape or lace binding; or turn the seam allowances under and stitch; or lap narrow lace or trim over the raw edges and stitch.

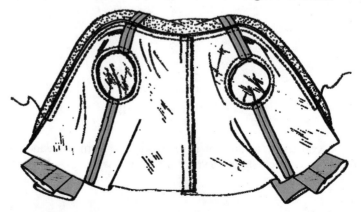

8

Impeccable
Tailoring

Creative Tailoring

If you want to make a tailored garment, be prepared to spend a reasonable amount of time and effort. Tailoring by its very nature is synonymous with difficulty to some people enough so that they are fearful of trying it themselves. Actually, tailoring is simply the additional pressing and hand-sewing techniques required to shape and stabilize the fabric to retain the precise look intended by the designer.

A tailored garment is molded and shaped by pressing and sewing with the aid of supporting inner fabrics and specialized hand stitches. Tailoring is not difficult once you realize there are no shortcuts to a professional finish. Develop good habits now and they will remain with you to polish every succeeding project.

Choose a style that will not go too far beyond your previous sewing experience, but also try to select one that will give you a real appreciation of what tailoring techniques actually add to a garment. Attempt to make yours a learning experience as well as an enjoyable challenge. If you already have some experience in the fine art of tailoring, treat any familiar information as a refresher course to recall important basic methods.

Tailoring can be divided into two categories by the degree of tailoring required. First there are tailored wool suits or coats that require special pressing and shaping techniques and special handling of the underlining, interfacing, and seams. The second category consists of garments that require tailoring techniques in certain areas, such as the collar and lapels of a soft dress, and of fabrics which require tailoring to achieve the proper molded look, such as limp, loosely woven, dressy, or washable fabrics. To be creatively tailored, garments of either type should have all these identifying characteristics:

- Pattern and fabric have been chosen to compliment your figure.

- Garment has smooth lines without wrinkles or sagging, and is molded to retain its shape without being stiff and uncomfortable.

- Buttons, flaps, pockets, and cuffs are positioned properly and are in the right proportion for the wearer.

- Collar rolls smoothly and evenly without seams showing at the outer edge and sits softly on garment without curling.

- All edges are pressed into soft or crisp edges as planned by the designer with seams at facing edges invisible.

- Hems are invisible with just the right amount of pressing.

- Lining does not pull or interfere with the hang of garment.

Tailoring will require some special equipment in addition to that needed for dressmaking. These tools, most of them pressing aids, will help give you a better-looking garment: tailor's ham or cushion, seam or sleeve roll, point presser or tailor's board, pounding block or clapper, pressing pad, pressing cloths, sleeve board, pointer and creaser, needleboard, and silk thread for basting.

When you approach tailoring, your preliminary decisions are the most important-style and fabric. For your first tailoring project, choose a style with basic lines that are flattering to your figure. To show off your skill, your garment should show fashion awareness as well as fashion longevity.

All Vogue patterns clearly state on the back of the pattern envelope what type of fabric may be used for each design along with all pertinent buying information. Purchase all notions and findings (dressmaker's tools) as suggested, to expedite your tailoring project once it is started. Choose a fabric that can withstand standard wearing and cleaning. All your materials, inside and out, should help maintain the built-in shaping of tailoring.

Vital Preparation

First prepare your fabric. Preshrink all underlining, interfacing, tape, and other notions that will be used in your tailored garment, as the great amount of steam used in tailoring will affect all fabrics and findings.

Make any adjustments or alterations in your pattern. You may wish to make the jacket or coat shell first in muslin. Jacket patterns allow an additional amount of wearing ease at the circumference of the bust, waist, and hip, plus style ease when needed. This will provide ample room for your jacket to move easily over a dress or blouse and skirt. Coats also have an additional amount of wearing ease so you have ample room to wear a suit underneath. Coat sleeves are made large enough to be worn over a jacket. Two notes of caution, however: first, do not confuse the top of a two-piece garment with a jacket, as these tops are made with the same measurements and ease as a one-piece dress; and second, you cannot wear a coat over a jacket that is a cutoff version of the same pattern.

CUTTING AND MARKING: Always cut your fashion fabric first and **cut the seam allowance wider** than marked on the pattern. They should be at least 1" (25 mm) wide on all edges that may require fitting over the bust, waist, and hip area of the garment, and on sleeve underarm seams, outer edges of upper collar, and lapel facings. Transfer all center markings before removing the pattern tissue.

Next, cut your underlining fabric, widening the seam allowances as for your fashion fabric. Transfer all seamlines, construction lines, grainlines, and symbols to your underlining with a tracing wheel and dressmaker's tracing paper.

Refer to Interfacing, page 432, before cutting your interfacing. Cut out the given lining pieces, using wide seam allowances as for your fashion fabric. Also refer to Skirt Lining, page 431, if your pattern does not include one. With your cutting complete and all fabric pieces stored on a flat surface, you are ready to do your first sewing.

BASTING: Pin the underlining to all of the fabric pieces, matching center lines and grainlines; review the marking section, page 149, and baste.

Some garment areas will require special attention as you baste to maintain their proper contour. Shape the undercollar, placing the underlining uppermost (1). The fashion fabric should be uppermost while you are shaping the upper collar (2) and sleeves (3).

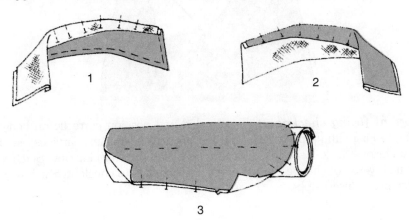

Turn jacket lapels along roll line as you baste, keeping the underlining uppermost.

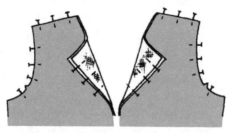

If your garment piece contains pleats, fold them, basting as you do to ensure smooth layering. Baste along foldline and roll lines, then turn fashion fabric along these markings in the direction they will fall.

Finally, baste along your traced seamlines. You will refer to these seamlines constantly during fitting. Then thread-trace along the lengthwise and crosswise grain of your fashion fabric on all major pieces. These markings will also be used as fitting guides.

First Stage: The Skirt

Since all tailored garments must be fit to move easily over one another, the skirt is the first unit to be constructed. Before you begin the actual construction, make a waistline stay to support the fabric during fitting. Cut a strip of 1" (25 mm) wide grosgrain ribbon your waist measurement plus 2" (5 cm). Position it around your waist, allowing ½" (13 mm) wearing ease; pin. Mark closing and centers.

You should prepare the skirt for fitting by first attaching the underlining; then, basting darts and pleats; flatten with fingertips. Baste seams or pin closely along the seamlines. Sew ease or gathering threads by hand. Lap skirt over waistline stay, matching centers, and adjust the ease or gathers. Pin and baste the waistline seam of the skirt along the edge of the stay.

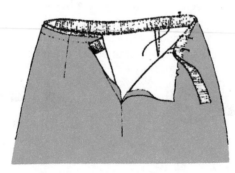

Important fitting checkpoint: Try on skirt and position correctly on body. Fit skirt according to First Fitting, page 121. Transfer any new seamlines, dartlines, etc. to underlining with tailor's chalk. Rebaste any adjustments. Remove waistline stay. Stitch any seams or darts that were not changed; press open. Try on again to check fit. Stitch together permanently; press. Insert zipper.

SKIRT LINING: The lining is constructed very much like the skirt. Most patterns do not include separate pattern pieces for a skirt lining; therefore, cut your lining from the skirt pattern pieces, allowing the same width seam allowances. To reduce bulk in a gathered or pleated skirt, cut your lining from a straight or A-line skirt pattern. Then baste the lining together as for the skirt, following the same alterations and leaving the appropriate seam open for the zipper. Pin lining to the skirt at the upper edge, wrong sides together; ease skirt to fit lining if necessary. Pin and baste attached skirt and lining to the waistline stay as before (1).

Important fitting checkpoint: Try on skirt and lining, positioning them correctly. Lining should hang free of skirt without bubbles or wrinkles in lining, or binding, or pulling in skirt. As with all circumferences, the outer layer (skirt) should be slightly larger than the inner layer (lining) for both layers to work together. Make any alterations by changing each seam minutely. A real problem will occur if the lining is considerably smaller than the skirt; it will be uncomfortable, the lining will wear out before the skirt due to strain, and you will not be able to complete the lining satisfactorily. When you have eliminated all fitting problems, stitch lining sections together.

Determine at this time whether you will hem your skirt and lining together or separately. If you are using a soft lining fabric, the two should be hemmed together; if you are using a crisp lining, they may be hemmed either way. The seam allowances will need to be finished only if your fabric is exceptionally ravelly or the hems are done separately.

Pin the skirt and lining together along the upper edge, slipstitch lining to zipper tape, and baste upper edges together. Pin hems to an approximate length, making the lining ½" (13 mm) shorter than skirt (2). The skirt hems should not be completed until you are prepared to sew the hem of the jacket or coat. The two hems must be in proportion to one another if you wish to achieve the most attractive results.

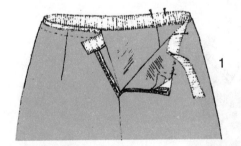
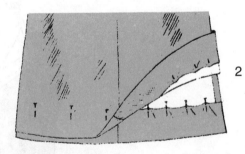

WAISTBAND: The final step is to attach the waistband. This permanently joins the skirt and lining at the waist. Use the waistband construction most suitable to your fabric (pages 317 and 318), adjusting it to your measurement. For a thick or bulky fabric, you may have to allow up to ½" (13 mm) more in the circumference of the waistband. Attach waistband and fasten with hooks and eyes.

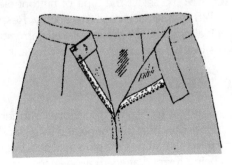

Tailoring Challenge: Jacket or Coat

The construction of a jacket or coat is the same in most cases; exceptions will be noted as they occur.

Construction Procedure

The first step is to construct and fit the **shell** of your garment, which consists of the front and back pieces only. Follow same procedure as for the skirt: prepare and attach underlining, baste and press darts, add ease or gathering threads by hand, and pin or baste sections together. Flatten seams with fingertips or creaser.

Important fitting checkpoint. Try on the garment shell over the skirt. Match the center front markings and pin. Position it correctly on your body. After fitting, transfer any new seamlines, dart lines, etc., to underlining. Stitch and press any darts and seams that were not changed. Baste along any new construction lines and flatten seams. Try garment shell on again with the skirt to check adjustments. Remember to allow enough room in a jacket for movement over a blouse or dress, and enough in a coat for over a jacket.

Stitch the shell together permanently, using your pattern's sewing guide for basic construction procedures. Press any remaining darts and seams.

BOUND BUTTONHOLES: To select the type of buttonhole you prefer, refer to the buttonhole section, pages 325 to 330, and read thoroughly. Respace buttonhole markings evenly if you have made any alterations. For man-tailored garments, you may wish to make corded keyhole buttonholes just before completing the garment.

Interfacing for Shaping

The degree of built-in shaping that highlights the tailored garment is dependent upon the proper use of interfacing. It must support the shape and with stand numerous wearings and cleanings without overwhelming the fabric's draping qualities. Interfacing also protects your fashion fabric from ridges being formed at seam allowances and darts during cleaning and

432

pressing. If you are in doubt as to the appropriate weight and type of interfacing for your fabric, refer to the chart on pages 163 to 167.

Lighter-weight interfacings, which have relatively little bulk, can be sewn into the garment seams, and their seam allowances trimmed away close to the stitching.

Heavier-weight interfacings, including hair canvases, are more rigid and should not be caught into the garment seams. Instead, all of the seam allowances except for the armhole are cut off before the interfacing is applied. Then the interfacing is catchstitched to the garment along the seamlines. The interfacing is stitched into the armhole seam, which is not pressed open to give further support to the shoulder area. The following tailoring techniques will illustrate this catchstitch procedure.

ADAPTING PIECES: Interfacing is necessary for support around the neck, shoulder, front, and armhole edges. If interfacing pattern pieces are not available, you will need,to adapt your existing pattern pieces. Except for armholes, eliminate all seam allowances, including style seaming details. Pin all front pattern pieces together to act as a unit. To draw your interfacing pattern, use a piece of tissue paper large enough to cover the desired interfaced area. Make the inner shaped edge ½" (13 mm) wider than the width of the front facing and draw a curved line from it across front, ending 2" (5 cm) below armhole seamline (1). For the back section, pin the pattern pieces together. Place tissue paper over them and draw pattern, starting 2" (5 cm) below the armhole and making it about 5" (12.5 cm) deep in the center back (2).

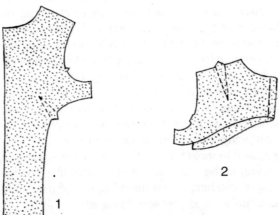

DARTS: There are three ways to make darts,in interfacing. The first two are to be used when darts do not correspond exactly to the garment darts. (They can also be used for lightweight interfacing when darts do correspond.) The third is best suited for darts that do correspond to those of the garment.

First method: trim along dart lines (1). Bring cut edges together, center a strip of underlining or ribbon seam binding over the edges, and stitch securely (2).

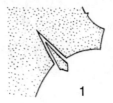

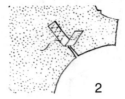

Second method: slash through the center of dart lines (3). Lap edges, matching dart lines, and stitch together; securely reinforce the point with additional stitches (4).

Third method: simply trim darts away along dart lines (5). Pin interfacing to garment and pull garment dart through cut edges; catchstitch edges to underlining (6).

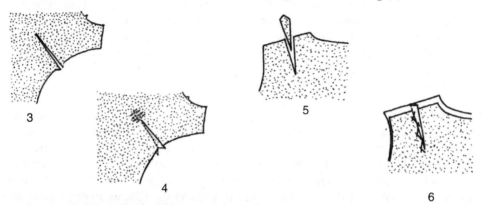

HAND STITCHES FOR TAILORED GARMENTS: In order to ensure that all layers of fabric will be stabilized, you will need to master two hand stitches. The firmness built in by these stitches will enable the layers to move as one through repeated wearing and dry cleaning. Both are variations of diagonal basting. Use a sharp needle and matching thread, coating a single unknotted thread with beeswax to eliminate possible snarls. Secure the thread end at the edge of the interfacing with backstitches; work in direction of the grain.

Diagonal Tacking is used to attach interfacing to the underlining only. Take a tiny horizontal stitch through interfacing, catching a thread or two of underlining; repeat directly below, placing stitches approximately ¾" to 1½" (20 mm to 3.8 cm) apart and forming a diagonal stitch on the interfacing side. Keep stitches long and loose and do not catch the fashion fabric as you sew (1). Cover surface of interfacing, shaping fabric as you sew to retain the garment contour. If you have not used underlining, omit this stitch and catch-stitch edges of interfacing to garment along seamlines.

Padstitching is used to mold and control undercollars and lapels (whether underlined or not) by actually sewing in the shape. It is done exactly like diagonal tacking except that you sew through all layers, catching only a thread or two of the fashion fabric, and holding the fabric in the desired position as you sew. Make stitches ¼" to ½" (6 mm to 13 mm) apart (2). Practice first on scraps of your fabric layers to get the feel of manipulating your fabric.

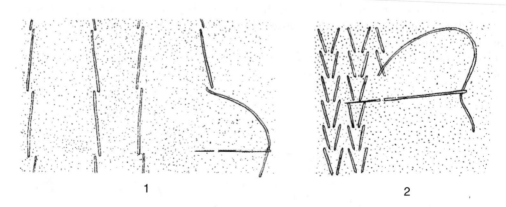

ATTACHING INTERFACING: You must first make sure the interfacing and garment shell will relate well to one another. Pin the two layers together, placing front, neck, and side edges along seamlines, and match armhole seamlines. Pin the interfacing to the garment and then baste shell along the center markings or seams only.

Important fitting checkpoint. Try on garment shell. If bubbles or ridges form in either interfacing or shell, they are not molding as one. If so, remove pins. With the right side of your shell uppermost, place both layers over a rounded surface similar to your body contour. Smooth the shell over the interfacing (with the grain as you did for the underlining), and pin where it falls inside the seamlines. Repin along foldlines and raw edges. Also make sure your lapels will roll smoothly; turn interfacing to outside along proposed roll, and pin along roll line and edges of interfacing as it falls in place (1). The interfacing should now relate to your garment shell and your body contour.

After any necessary adjustments and repinning, pin the interfacing securely on the inside. Examine interfacing edges along the seamline. They should be a scant ⅛" (3 mm) short of the seamline. If necessary, trim interfacing so it will not bubble when seams are pressed open or encased.

Baste interfacing to front along all edges. Sew it to the underlining along hemlines and any foldlines with long running stitches, and along the inner curved edge with catchstitches Cut out rectangular openings in the interfacing exactly behind each buttonhole. Pull raw edges of bound buttonholes through the cut openings in the interfacing (1).

Now attach the front interfacing to your underlining with diagonal tacking. If you are not using underlining, sew the interfacing edges to the seamlines with catchstitches and along the foldlines and hemlines with long running stitches (2).

For back interfacing, cut away shoulder darts along the stitching lines. Pull garment dart through cut edges; catchstitch edges to underlining along dart seamline. Baste neck, shoulder, and side edges in place and baste armhole edges together, retaining the garment's shape as you work. Catchstitch sides. Attach interfacing to underlining with diagonal tacking, or catchstitch the edges to the seamlines as you did for the front interfacing (3).

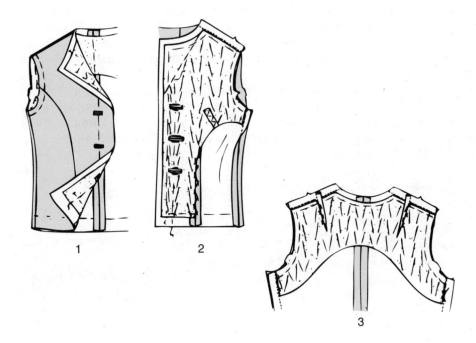

1

2

3

Important fitting checkpoint: Try on your garment shell and evaluate your work so far. If you notice a slight droop around the back of the armhole between the seam and shoulder blade or a slight indentation on the front between the armhole seamline and the apex of the bust, you need padding to get that impeccably tailored look.

TAILOR'S PADDING: Cut another layer of interfacing the width of the shoulder seamline less ½" (13 mm), using armhole shape on one edge and a curved shape on the remaining edges to extend to ½" (13 mm) beyond the end of the problem area. Then cut a piece of lamb's wool or heavy cotton flannel ½" (13 mm) less than the interfacing piece on all edges. To attach padding to garment back, sew lamb's wool to interfacing with long running stitches along all edges. Use diagonal tacking to hold the center area in place. Now place the additional interfacing layer over the lamb's wool and attach it to the main interfacing in same way (1). Attach the padding to the garment front section in the same manner (2).

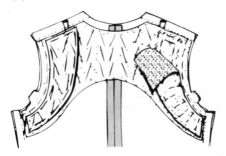

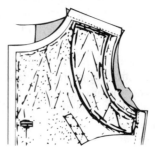

1

2

Undercollar and Lapels

Since many collar styles can be used on a tailored garment, turn to the collar section and review the introduction and the construction most closely related to your garment.

INTERFACING: To prepare interfacing for collar, trim away all seam allowances except the center back seam, if applicable (1). The interfacing sections can be joined in two ways for the center back seam. For the first method, you can lap the ends, matching seamlines, and stitch; trim both seam allowances close to stitching (2). For the second method, trim away center back seam allowances. Match edges, place a strip of underlining or seam binding over them, and stitch securely (3).

Then center the interfacing over the undercollar between the outer seamlines. Pin in place along the neck seamline. Shape the pieces as they will be worn. Make sure the interfacing is a scant ⅛" (3 mm) short of the seamline. If not, trim the interfacing so it will not bubble later when seams are pressed open or encased (4). Catchstitch the edges to the undercollar. Staystitch the neck edge if you haven't already done so.

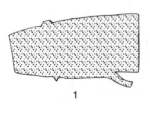

1

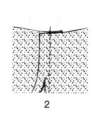

2

3

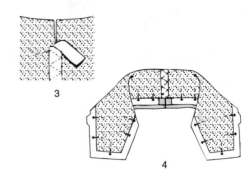

4

FIT AND SHAPE: Lap and pin undercollar neck edge over garment neck edge; match seamlines and markings. (If extended facings are to be used, they should be turned back at foldline, wrong sides together, and basted along neck edge at this time.) Baste collar in place, clipping the neck edge where necessary to lay flat.

Important fitting checkpoint: Try on garment or put it on a dress form to establish roll on collar and lapels. Lap and pin right front over left, matching centers and buttonhole markings. Begin rolling lapels at top buttonhole markings. The collar should lay as close to the neck as shown on the pattern illustration without riding high or low. The roll should be smooth, even, and unbroken from front to back. Be sure points of collar and lapels lie symmetrically against the garment.

The outer seamline of the collar should cover the back neck seamline. Adjust collar at the neck seamline until all features are correct. Transfer any seamline adjustments to both collar and lapels. Pin along roll line on both collar and lapels. This roll is very important in determining the finished shape. Thread-trace roll lines on collar and lapels and remove collar.

STABILIZE THE ROLL: Pin the undercollar to a tailor's ham. Using steam, hold iron over roll, never resting it on the fabric. Work from center back to center front, shaping each half separately but identically along your established roll. Never press the roll into a crease; use your finger to shape the roll. Allow undercollar to dry thoroughly. Now shape lapels in the same manner and allow to dry.

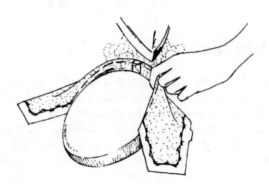

PADSTITCH UNDERCOLLAR: The area between the neck seamline and the roll line (called the stand) must have small padstitches placed close together –¼" (6 mm) or less to stabilize the stand. Hold the undercollar over your finger in the shaped position. Padstitch heavily from the neck edge to the thread-traced roll line; work along either the straight or crosswise grain (1). When you have completed the stand area, use larger stitches [about ¾" (20 mm) apart] to padstitch the remainder of the undercollar (2)

To blend the pad stitches into the undercollar, it must be pressed carefully. With the fashion fabric side up, press the outer curved area, placing a damp press cloth over the fabric. Press to the roll only (3). Do the same along the stand, always retaining the roll, and allow to dry thoroughly.

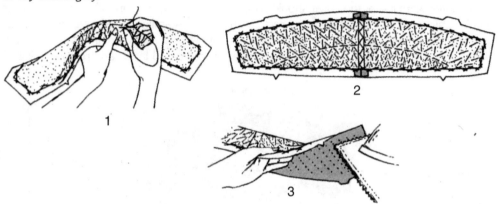

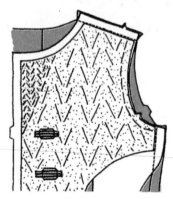

PADSTITCH LAPELS: Start at roll line and fill in area between thread tracing and seamlines, spacing stitches about ½" (13 mm) apart. Press the lapel area as for the under-collar and allow to dry.

Taping for Stability

According to traditional tailoring techniques, you should tape edges that will receive strain during wear and cleaning. Tape is especially needed along the front edge of your garment, around the neck seam, and on lapels because these areas have a tendency to pull or stretch out of shape. You may wish to tape other areas that might "give" with wear, such as shoulder or armhole seams, and foldlines of a seam pocket or vent openings.

Ribbon seam binding lends itself well to taping: it is thin, firmly woven, and usually preshrunk. Cotton twill tape, ¼" (6 mm) wide, is often used; be sure it has been preshrunk.

To apply seam binding, place it ⅛" (3 mm) over seamline (or foldline for an extended facing) with the larger portion within the garment area. This automatically grades the binding when the seam is completed. Baste the edge that will be caught in the seam and sew the inner edge to the interfacing with diagonal tacking. Make the stitches about ½" (13 mm) apart and catch a few threads of the interfacing with each stitch (1). Twill tape is applied in the same manner. Place one edge over the seamline just enough to be caught in the seam (2).

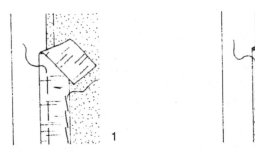

Begin by placing the tape along the front shoulder edge, extending it slightly beyond neck and armhole seamlines. Sew it to the seam along stitching with catchstitches. Sew the inner edge to the interfacing with diagonal tacking. Then tape front edges, extending tape slightly beyond the neck seamline and hemline. For lapel area, the tape must be placed from the shoulder seamlines to the point where the lapel begins to roll; placing tape just along roll line of lapel will not give enough support. Secure both edges to interfacing with diagonal tacking (3).

To tape foldlines, position tape the same as for a seamline; secure both edges by sewing it to interfacing along foldline with long running stitches and along the remaining edge with diagonal tacking.

To tape curved edges such as neck and armholes, seam binding is the best choice. Twill tape will add bulk to the seam, as it tends to roll when stitched in a curved seam. Make scant ¼" (6 mm) clips at even intervals, place unclipped edge ⅛" (3 mm) over seamline, and baste. Sew clipped edges to interfacing with long diagonal tacking stitches, placing the long stitch over the clipped edges (4). After mastering the techniques of taping, you may want to try a quicker method. If you are sure that your garment fits well, you may eliminate some handwork by machine-stitching tape to the interfacing before it is attached to your garment. Make sure the tape extends a generous ⅛" (3 mm) beyond the trimmed edge of the interfacing so the interfacing will not catch in the seam.

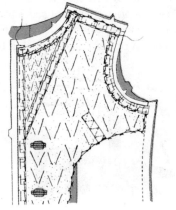

Collar and Facings

When you have completed taping, return to your collar. First pin undercollar to garment once again and check for all small, last-minute adjustments that may be needed.

PREPARE UPPER COLLAR: The upper collar will need additional handling to make sure it is large enough to hide the outer seam when the collar is completed. Make a minute tuck at the center of upper collar neck seamline, letting it taper to nothing at other edge. When released, it will automatically allow just enough fabric for you to favor the outer edge easily so any seams will fall on the undercollar side. Then pin upper collar to undercollar along neck edge, matching seamlines (1). Now shape collar as it will be worn with upper collar on top. Pin outer edges in place as they fall. To baste upper and undercollar together, follow seamline you thread traced on the undercollar previously (page 437). This maneuver will result in narrower seam allowances on your upper collar (2).

Stitch the collar sections together from the undercollar side, stitching along the thread-traced seamline. Use small stitches at points and end stitching ⅝" (15 mm) from neck edge. Trim, grade, and notch or clip seams as needed. Press seams open on point presser for easier turning. See Seams at Finished Edges on page 356 of the pressing section. Turn the collar and tailor-baste along the outer edges, using silk thread. Favor the upper collar at its outer edges so that the seam is on the undercollar side as you baste (3).

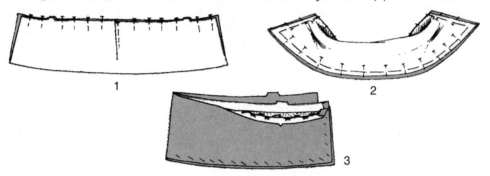

Press, using a damp press cloth to create a lot of steam. Then use a pounder or clapper to shape the edge to the desired effect (crisp or slightly rolled, depending on the style of your garment). Work with your fingers and the pounder to avoid shine or overpressing and allow to dry thoroughly. Staystitch the neck edges of the garment and facing pieces if you haven't already done so.

ATTACH COLLAR AND FACING: Pin undercollar to garment between markings (where collar ends and lapels begin). Baste, clipping garment seam allowance as necessary, and then stitch. Stitch neck and front facings together; press. Clipping facing seam allowance as necessary, pin, baste, and stitch upper collar to facing between markings.

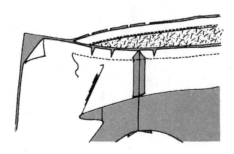

Make a minute pin tuck on lapel/facing, so you will have enough fabric to favor the lapel seam when garment is turned to right side (raw edges will not be even at this point). Pin the facing to the garment (1).

Baste facing to garment, following garment seamlines. Start stitching from the garment side where garment meets collar in order to eliminate bubbles that sometimes occur where the collar meets the lapels. (For bulky or heavy fabrics you rnay not be able to start exactly at the markings; leave thread ends long enough that you can complete that area by hand later.) Reinforce points and continue around lapel/facing. Clip seam at end of collar to stitching. Trim and grade lapel facing seams as needed. Trim only upper collar and facing neck seam, leaving the garment and undercollar seam ⅝" (15 mm). Clip both neck seams (2).

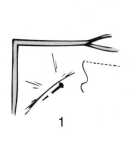

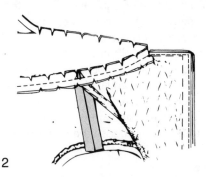

1

2

Press facing seams and both collar neck seams open on a point presser. Turn facing. Using silk thread, tailor-baste facing edges for pressing to within 5" to 6" (12.5 cm to 15 cm) of lower edge. Favor the lapels at the outer edge so the seam is on the undercollar and garment side; below the point where the lapel begins to roll, favor the garment so the seam is on the facing side. Press these edges with a damp press cloth, using a pounder to achieve the desired effect. Retain basting.

Try on jacket and re-establish roll. Remove jacket and pin about ¾" (20 mm) above the neck seam to hold the layers in place. Lift up facing and sew the neck seams together with long, loose stitches in a zigzag pattern, being very careful not to force the seams together if they don't meet. This holds the upper collar in place so it will not twist or pull during wearing or cleaning. Retain pins in facing.

At this time you should decide how to finish the underside of the bound buttonholes. The couture method, page 458, must be done at this time. The conventional methods, page 326, can be done before the buttons are attached. Sew inner edge of facing in place with long running stitches to within 4" to 6" (10 cm to 15 cm) of lower edge.

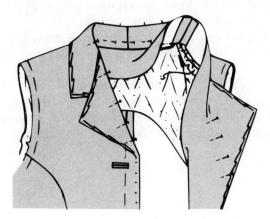

Pockets, Flaps, and Welts

Your most important consideration will be placement. Remember to reposition any pocket, flap, or welt placement lines if you have altered your pattern. There is nothing more frustrating than to end up with a beautifully made pocket that is too close to the jacket hem to be usable because the hem had to be sewn over it.

Pockets can be classified into two groups—utilitarian and decorative. Utilitarian pockets should be at a comfortable height for use, while decorative pockets should be placed as featured in the design. Both should add a balanced look to the total silhouette. To make sure that the pocket, flap, or welt placement is right for your garment, take the exposed portion and turn in the seam allowances along the seamline to simulate the finished item. Pin up garment hem along proposed hemline, then pin pockets, flaps, or welts to garment at placement lines. Try on garment (include skirt with jacket) and check position.

Experiment with the placement and size until you achieve the desired effect. Carefully analyze the position of the pockets, flaps, or welts in relation to the center front marking, and be sure they end an equal distance from the center marking and the lower edge of the garment. Transfer any necessary adjustments to the garment and individual pieces. You are then ready to construct and apply your pockets, flaps, or welts; refer to the instructions on pages 304 to 313 and choose the method that best suits your needs.

Sleeves

Tailored sleeves are basically the same as any other sleeve. The two-piece set-in sleeve is considered the classic tailored sleeve when its hem is interfaced appropriately to retain the shape. Since a poorly executed set-in sleeve will mar the appearance of a tailored garment, it would be wise to take the time right now to review all sections that will help you get a perfectly fitting sleeve. Then you will be able to insert your sleeve quickly, neatly, and easily. Turn to pages 92 to 95, 123 and 124, and 283 to 289.

Since the major alterations have already been done, your problem now will be adapting the fabric to your needs. Add the sleeve cap ease threads, using the stitch length appropriate for the fabric, and break the stitching at the seam so that you do not easestitch over the seam allowances. For extremely heavy fabric, add the ease threads by hand. Pull up ease threads the desired amount and secure them for fitting. Do not shrink the sleeve cap at this time. Baste the sleeve seams along the seamline, right sides together, and press seams open with fingertips or lightly with an iron so you do not leave an impression. Then baste the sleeve in the armhole.

Important fitting checkpoint. Try on garment with skirt to evaluate the sleeve lengths with the sleeve hems pinned in place. Allow enough room in a jacket sleeve to move freely over a long dress sleeve. Coat sleeves should be full enough to fit over a jacket sleeve. Place shoulder pads on shoulders if the sleeve needs support. Check sleeve lengths again. Stylized sleeve hems require careful planning before cutting so you will have only minute adjustments.

Check grainlines. Make any necessary adjustments and mark fabrics. Remove sleeve. To support heavy fabrics or to help retain the shape for loosely woven fabrics, apply tape to seams before stitching. If sleeve has a plain hem, stitch seams; press open, using sleeve board. If the sleeve has a vent opening or other stylized hem, stitch the seams necessary to complete hem.

SLEEVE HEMS: Interfacing applied correctly will protect your fabric so the imprints of hem and seam allowances will not show through to the outside during wearing, cleaning, or pressing. Choose an appropriate interfacing that will hold the curved line of the sleeve hem without "breaking."

Cut bias strips of interfacing equal in length to the circumference of the hem (allow additional fabric for lapping ends on a continuous sleeve hem) and equal in width to the depth of hem plus 1⅜" (3.5 cm).

Place one edge of interfacing ⅝" (15 mm) below hemline in hem area with the greater portion on the garment side; pin. For heavy or bulky fabrics, slash through interfacing along seamlines and tuck ends under seam allowances to prevent any imprint of the seam allowances. Sew interfacing to underlining along hemline with long running stitches and along the upper edge and ends with long catchstitches (1).

For hems that will be topstitched, cut interfacing ¾" (20 mm) wider than the hem depth and place one edge along the hemline. Baste hemline and foldline edges in place; catchstitch all other edges.

If you are not using underlining, the interfacing should still be attached in the same manner; be careful to catch only a thread of your fashion fabric so the stitches will not show on the right side of the fabric.

For a vent opening, cut a strip of straight-grain interfacing the length of opening plus ⅝" (15 mm) to extend beyond hemline, and wide enough to extend ½" (13 mm) beyond the end of the buttonhole on one side and ⅝" (15 mm) beyond foldline on the other. Place interfacing over vent buttonhole markings with one edge and end extending over foldline and hemline. Sew it to underlining along foldline and hemline with long running stitches and along upper end and edge with long catchstitches. Make bound buttonholes. (Make buttonholes through only the lightest weight interfacing; otherwise, apply interfacing after buttonholes are made.)

When interfacing is completed, pin hem in place and baste close to fold. (For a vent opening, the layers need to be graded to avoid ridges where several edges fall in the same place.) Trim away ⅝" (15 mm) from hem allowance edge of vent facing, ending at foldline. Sew hem to interfacing with long running stitches (2). For heavy or bulky fabric, blindstitch the hem in place. Stitch any remaining seams as directed in sewing guide; press. Do the same for the vent opening (3). Press hem over a sleeve board, using pounder or clapper and steam to get the desired edge.

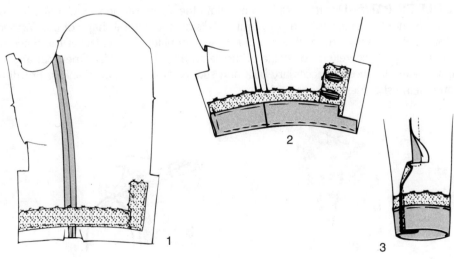

1

2

3

INSERT SLEEVE: Pin sleeve to garment. Adjust ease and baste. Important fitting checkpoint: Check position of armhole seam and ease distribution. Remove sleeve and shrink out fullness. Rebaste sleeve into armhole and then stitch. Between notches, add a second row of stitching over the first for reinforcement. Trim seam allowance to ¼" (6 mm) between notches.

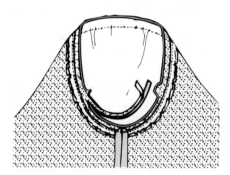

SLEEVE HEADING: This is used to support the weight of the sleeve cap fabric so it will not collapse. For padding, cut one bias rectangle of lamb's wool, polyester fleece, or heavy flannel, 3" (7.5 cm) wide and 4" to 6" (10 cm to 15 cm) long for each armhole. Make a 1 " (25 mm) fold on one long edge. Slipstitch folded edge of padding along seam at cap of sleeve.

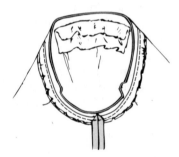

SHOULDER PADS: Use these to help maintain the shape of the shoulder line if needed. Be careful not to use too thick a pad, or it will distort the natural shape of the garment. Strive for a soft, fluid line rather than a rigid, raised shoulder. Try on jacket for exact pad placement. Pin pad securely on one side of the seam from the outside. Open out any facings at shoulders to avoid unnecessary bulk and sew pads to seam allowances. For directions on making shoulder pads, page 457.

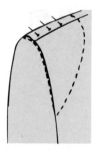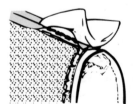

Final Fitting

Now it is time to determine the hem lengths for all the pieces of your tailored garment to ensure they are in proportion to one another. For help when measuring the hems, refer to page 348.

Important fitting checkpoint: Try on garment and skirt with the hems pinned in place. Wear the appropriate undergarments, shoes, and accessories. Lap fronts, matching centers, and pin. Be sure garments drape naturally and comfortably. Mark any necessary hem adjustments with thread tracing.

The right front must lap over the left front, concealing its lower edge. The inner folds of pleats should not show, nor should the underlap of a vent. Check your button placement markings once more for accuracy. Do you need a strategically placed snap, hook, or inner button to support the left front? Adjust any area that may need a final pinch of fabric removed or let out a bit. It is now the time to complete your hems.

Hems, Vents, and Pleats

You have already hemmed your sleeve successfully, so you are well on the way to finishing all of your hemming details. Work with the bulk of your garment on a table to avoid unnecessary wrinkles as you hem. Since you have already chosen the interfacing fabric for the sleeve hem, you should use the same type for the jacket hem.

Cut bias strips for the circumference of the hem and 1⅜" (3.5 cm) wider than the hem. Open out facings. Pin interfacing to garment with one edge ⅝" (15 mm) below hemline and lap ends over front interfacing. Trim and catchstitch ends to front interfacing. Then attach to garment hem as for sleeves (1).

For heavy or bulky fabrics, slash strip where it falls over seams and tuck edges under seam allowances. For a shaped or eased hem, preshape interfacing to fit contour of garment before applying.

Turn up garment along hemline and baste close to the fold; use silk thread (2). If necessary, add ease thread to hem edge before pinning it to interfacing.

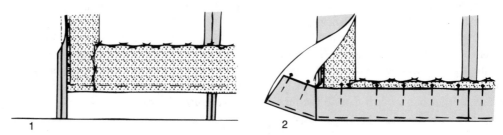

1

2

SMOOTH CORNERS: There are several ways to handle corners; select the one best suited for your fabric, design, and individual needs. The first, while probably the quickest and most popular method because the garment hem can be lengthened at a later time if necessary, does not give the best results for bulky fabrics. Prepare the hem as on previous page. The facing hem should taper up slightly, so it will not show on the outside. Trim ⅝" (15 mm) away from end of hem–between top and basting. Then trim ⅝" (15 mm) from top of hem to seam or foldline. Sew the hem to the interfacing with long running stitches or blindstitch in place for bulky fabrics (1). Press the hem, using steam and pounder or clapper to get the desired edge.

The completion of this type of corner depends upon your fabric. For lightweight fabrics, make a ¼" (6 mm) clip at the top of the hem and turn it in below the clip; pin (2). Slipstitch the facing below the clip and across the lower edge (3). For heavier fabrics, turn back the facing at the lower edge; blindstitch loosely to hem (4). Sew the raw edge of the facing securely to hem with hemming stitches (5). For both, sew remainder of facing in place above hem. Press, being careful to avoid shine on your fabric.

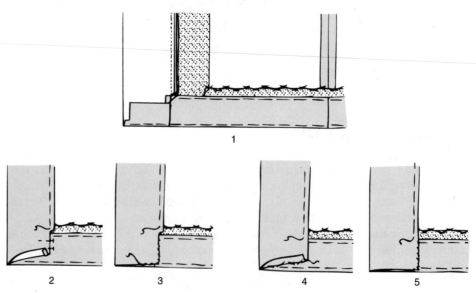

1

2

3

4

5

446

This alternate method will give you a flatter hem for bulky fabrics, but the hem **cannot be lengthened** later. Prepare hem as on previous page. Mark where facing edge will fall on hem. Open out facing. This method requires staggered trimming. First trim facing hem to ⅝" (15 mm), ending at seam or foldline. Then measure ½" (13 mm) from the marking toward the facing, and slash hem at this point to within 1" (25 mm) of hemline. From this point, trim across hem to seam or foldline. Clip alongside seam to first trimming line. Secure the trimmed edges with long, loose catchstitches (6). Sew hem in place and press, using steam and pounder or clapper to get desired edge. Turn facing to inside; press. Slipstitch lower edge together (7). Finish raw edge of facing with hemming stitch; press (8).

Excess fabric or extremely curved hems may be a problem also. Some openings work well with mitered corners, page 244. For handling an extremely curved hem, see page 461 of the couture technique section.

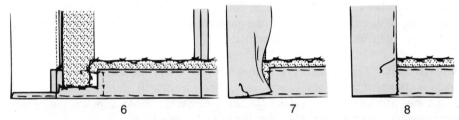

VENT or **PLEAT OPENINGS:** Jacket and coat vents or pleats differ only in length from those found in a sleeve hem. End the interfacing at the seamlines or extend it ⅝" (15 mm) beyond the foldlines, interfacing the outer layer the same as you would the hem. Be sure to support the foldlines with tape to stay the fabric (1). Use your sewing guide for the basic construction. Choose the corner finish appropriate for your fabric from the opposite page.

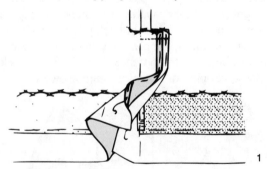

SKIRT HEM: If you are making a skirt as part of an ensemble, complete the hem and the lining hem at the same time as the jacket.

An Ultimate Pressing

Place the garment on a dress form or a well-padded hanger suspended from a wire so you can work around it. Look your garment over well-front, back, sleeves, collar, and pockets. Are there any creases or wrinkles that may need to be eliminated? Remember, once you have attached the lining there is little you can do to press some areas well. Use your press cloth or use the dress form as a pressing aid. Allow your garment to dry thoroughly on the dress form or hanger with the garment hanging free and the openings pinned in the proper position. Pad sleeves, collars, or other areas with tissue paper to help retain their shape.

Lining as a Finale

Lining a garment is the final construction step in tailoring. Lining fabric should complement fashion fabric in weight, wearability, and cleaning requirements. Be sure interior construction does not show through the lining. A smooth-fitting lining is absolutely essential for professional results and will greatly influence the total look.

The lining is the last layer to be applied. It demands the same careful attention to construction and detail as your actual garment shell. A lined garment must slide easily over another garment. Pleats and wearing ease should be placed where the garment must give with body movement at center back, above and below waistline, bust area, hem edges of sleeves, and hem of garment. Center back pleat should be ½" to 1 " (13 mm to 25 mm) deep from neck to hem. Adjust the pattern before cutting to allow for pleats or wearing ease if necessary. If warmth is a factor in the garment you are making, refer to Interlining, page 452, before you stitch the lining together.

CONSTRUCTION: Baste darts and seams together. Make the same seam adjustments as you did for your garment. Press seams, darts, and pleats with fingers or crease.

Slip lining into garment, wrong sides together. Lap lining over facings and pin or baste, matching seamlines around front, shoulder, neck, and armholes.

Important fitting checkpoint. Try on and test lining to make sure it does not interfere with the garment. Look for excessive wrinkles. The inner circumference of your lining should be just like the inner measurements of a cylinder, smooth and slightly smaller than the outside. Adjust lining, fitting as necessary. Mark any adjustments. Stitch only underarm bust darts. All waistline or shoulder darts, pleats, and tucks should be basted first, then anchored in place from right side of fabric with cross-stitches through all thicknesses. Place cross-stitches at neck, waist, and lower edges of back pleats. Stitch all major seams except shoulder seams. Press, using steam sparingly. Staystitch front, back shoulder, and neck edges, and across underarm between the notches. Turn in front, back shoulder, and neck edges along seamline. Baste, clipping or notching seam allowances so they will lie flat. Do not press edges.

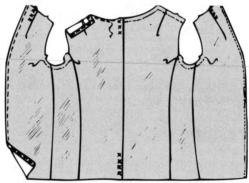

INSERTION: Work from center back to front opening edges. Pin lining to garment, matching center back. Then, matching any back seams first, sew the seam allowances together loosely by hand with long running stitches, ending the sewing 6" (15 cm) from lower edge. Sew any side or side front seam allowances together in the same manner. Now pin armhole, front shoulder, and front edges of lining in place. Sew front shoulders to back seam allowance with long running stitches (1). Slipstitch front turned-in edge to facing, ending 4" to 6" (10 cm to 15 cm) from lower edge. Place stitches about ⅛" (3 mm) apart and secure with backstitches at 3" to 4" (7.5 cm to 10 cm) intervals. Next, pin back shoulder and neck edges in place and slipstitch them to front lining at shoulders and to the back neck facing. Baste armhole edges together alongside seamline in seam allowance. Clip underarm of lining between notches every ½" (13 mm) (2). For vent openings, attach lining as directed on sewing guide.

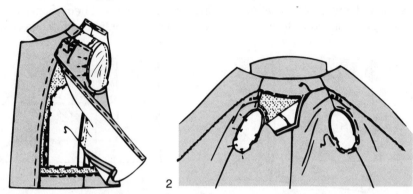

In man-tailored garments, the garment sleeves may not be sewn into the armholes until after this phase of the lining is completed. Then sleeve is sewn into armhole through all thicknesses. The sleeve lining is completed in the regular way.

Lining Hem

Now that the lining shell has been carefully sewn in place along facing and shoulder edges, you have only the lining hem to do. If you follow carefully the methods of handling your lining hem, you will have a better-fitting garment and the lining will not overwhelm the fashion fabric, causing pulling or distortion at the hem edges.

ANCHOR LINING: Work with garment on a dress form or on a padded hanger attached to a wire suspended from ceiling so you can work around the garment. This way the lining will drape well with the garment. From the outside, pin the lining to the garment 4" to 8" (10 cm to 20.5 cm) above hem, placing pins at right angles and at 2" to 3" (5 cm to 7.5 cm) intervals.

ATTACHED HEM: Begin by trimming the lining even with garment edge (1). Then add an ease thread ¼" (6 mm) from raw edge of the lining if the hem requires it. On the outside, make a ¼" (6 mm) wide tuck across the lining below the pin line, placing the pins parallel to the fold. Now turn in the raw edge ¼" (6 mm) and pin to hem where it falls (2). Slipstitch entire lower edge of lining to garment hem.

Remove pins from tuck. The lining will now smoothly fall down over the hem, forming a soft fold (3). Steam and pat into place with pounder. This fold allows for body movement and stretching during wearing without putting strain on garment hem. Slipstitch remaining turned-in-edges of lining to facings or any vent opening, continuing to edge of fold (4).

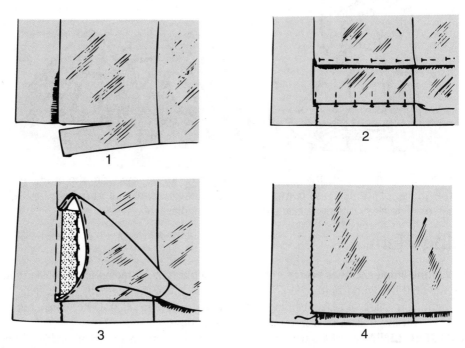

FREE HANGING HEM: Pin lower edges of garment and lining together as shown. Then turn up lining hem so the lining is ½" (13 mm) shorter than the garment and baste close to the fold. Now measure the depth of the lining hem and trim evenly if necessary. Use appropriate finish and method to complete lining hem. Press lightly (1). Slipstitch remaining turned-in lining edges to facing and hem or any vent openings (2). Sew lining hem to garment hem with 1" (25 mm) French tacks at seams (3).

Some garments will require a combination of these two methods of hemming a lining, such as a coat with a full pleat in the back. The front of the lining would be attached and the back would hang free to allow the pleat to drape naturally.

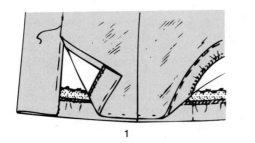

Sleeve Lining

This step will require additional molding. Baste seams and darts and adjust ease if necessary. Finger press seams. Wrong sides together, baste lining sleeves into armhole of garment lining along seamline, lapping edges and adjusting sleeve cap ease.

Important fitting checkpoint. Try on garment. Check fit of sleeve lining. Examine garment sleeve for wrinkles or bubbles. Shape sleeve cap lining inside garment. Mark adjustments on cap and seams; baste.

Stitch basted sleeve lining sections together and press seams open. Add new ease threads if sleeve cap was adjusted. Shrink out excess ease now, since this will be the last time you should press this part of the garment. Staystitch underarm between notches. Turn in armhole along seamline and baste; clip to stitching, if necessary, so underarm seam allowance will lie flat.

With wrong sides together, sew lining seam allowances to garment seam allowances with long, loose running stitches, starting and ending 4" (10 cm) from each end (1). Turn lining back over garment sleeve (2). Pin sleeve in armhole, matching seamlines and markings. Adjust ease and slipstitch, placing stitches ⅛" (3 mm) apart and backstitching at 1" (25 mm) intervals (3).

With garment on dress form or padded hanger, complete sleeve lining hem. Anchor hem first with pins as you did for the garment and then complete, using the attached hem method on page 450. You need the fold at the lower edge of the lining hem for movement and strain the same as you do in a garment hem (4).

Press all lining edges, using a light touch. Steam front and neck edges, patting lightly. Do the same for the fold formed at lower edge of an attached lining.

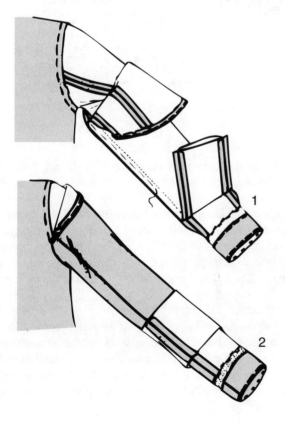

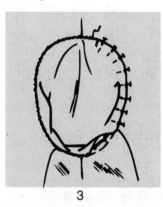

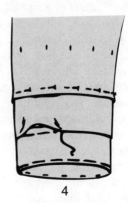

Interlining

A fourth layer of fabric called interlining can be added to your garment for warmth. For information about types and selection of interlinings, see page 163. Be sure to take interlining into consideration when fitting your garment, as it will use up needed wearing ease.

The easiest way to interline is to sew it as one with the lining. Cut interlining from lining pieces, omitting the back pleat. Cross-stitch the lining back pleat in place. Then baste the interlining and lining pieces together. Stitch darts and seams; slash darts and press open; trim interlining close to stitching. After staystitching front, shoulder, and neck edges, trim away interlining close to stitching. Attach the lining in the usual manner (1).

Final Touches

Now is the time to put all the small finishing touches on your garment. If you haven't already done so, finish the back of your bound buttonholes or add your machine or hand-worked buttonholes and attach your buttons.

Important fitting checkpoint: Try on garment. Does the front opening need a little support? Perhaps you will need a covered snap to hold the left front of a double-breasted garment in place (2). Check your convertible collar in both positions. To hold the lapel closed on a cold day, add a tiny thread eye on one lapel edge and a nearly invisible covered hook under the collar (3). Give the entire garment a detailed examination to double-check your workmanship. Did you miss a basting thread peeking out from a seam? If so, remove it with tweezers. You now have a garment which will retain, through many cleanings and wearings, the image you so carefully created. You will also find that as you become more experienced, many of the procedures emphasized in this chapter will become almost second nature to you. Some steps along the way can even be eliminated; once you know what changes needed to be made to fit your first tailored item, these changes can be transferred to each succeeding garment. Congratulations are definitely in order, for you have created a one-of-a-kind, impeccably tailored garment.

9

The Custom
Touch

Couture
Techniques

What transforms a dress into The Dress, immediately marks it with true quality and exquisite taste? Fashion is a splendid example of the axiom, "little things make a difference," for it is the little, but far from insignificant, finishing techniques known and followed by the world's most famous designers that will make the transformation work for you. This collection of couture techniques has been gathered for you from the greatest European and American houses of haute couture. They are dedicated to you, the Vogue woman, who delights in making and wearing clothes finished with the infinite touches of a couturier. They are the simple, yet irresistible, means of putting your signature on everything you sew.

Hidden Details

Most of these techniques are for the inside of the garment and may never be seen by others. Don't, however, let yourself be beguiled into believing that makes them in any way unworthy of the extra time and effort involved. There is nothing mysterious or awesome about any of these methods; without exception, they are actually quite simple and easy to do. And always remember that it is often the hidden details that are the true mark of quality. You cannot help but feel a personal sense of pride each time you see the inside of your professionally finished garment. And, of course, wearing lovely things next to your skin is like wearing exquisite lingerie; it envelops you with a priceless feeling of luxury.

In addition to giving your garments the fine finishing and beautiful detailing that are the mark of a couturier, these "extra somethings" above and beyond the actual construction also increase comfort, convenience, fit, and wearability. Using these techniques, you will always know that your garment will close neatly and easily; that everything you sew will hang and drape beautifully; that your garments will retain their precisely controlled shape; that you never need be embarrassed by the appearance of an open jacket or a dress on a hanger; and that you will be as proud of your creation on the tenth wearing as you were on the first.

Create your garments with the elegant expertise admired by all who appreciate the beauty and quality of the very finest couture. Then you will find that your wardrobe will help to give you the poise and assurance that comes with always being fashion-right.

The Inside Story

Lining and underlining are the hidden components of fine dressmaking that, although not immediately visible, are always reflected in the finished effect of your garment. Not only do they assist in creating and retaining the shape of your creations, but also give them a more luxurious look and feel. They are a "must" in all couture garments, and should be in yours as well.

UNDERLINING: If you intend to construct a garment in the manner of the fine designers, follow their example by **mounting** or underlining your garments to give it beautifully controlled shape and body. As an added bonus, underlining will prevent overhandling by keeping your handwork and markings from showing on the right side. Remember, however, that each and every construction mark must be transferred to the underlining, especially the seamlines and grainlines. This extra effort will provide you with a more faithful representation of the design lines and an accurate reference line for any necessary alterations. See pages 153 and 154 for further information and specific instructions.

LINING: Jackets and coats naturally require a lining to conceal their exposed inner construction, and your pattern instructions provide all the necessary guidance for these garments. But what about those other garments whose construction does not call for lining? This simple addition increases the comfort, durability, and aesthetic appeal of any garment and is really quite easy to do.

Cut lining from major garment pattern pieces and construct in same manner as garment, leaving appropriate seams open for closures. (For gathered or pleated skirts, cut your lining from a straight or A-line skirt pattern to reduce bulk.)

Baste the lining to the garment along the seamlines of the raw edges, treating the two layers as one. Turn under and slipstitch the lining edge to zipper tape (1). Apply either the facings (for dresses) or waistband (for pants or skirts). Blindstitch the facing edges to the lining. Refer to the tailoring section for further information.

Consider "show" value when lining your creations. Rather than discarding scarves that have already seen service in your wardrobe, use them to line a jacket. Use a large designer scarf with the famous signature at the lower front edge, then line the back and sleeves with color-matched crepe. You can also add impact to a lining by using a print, plaid, or contrasting color—perhaps lightweight remnants left over from a previous garment. There is no rule, written or unwritten, which says linings must be drab or inconspicuous. Just be sure your lining doesn't show through your garment fabric.

The Shapekeepers

Here are some additional couture touches to help you master the art of controlled shape. Use them to achieve that air of confidence that comes from the assurance that your garment is always hanging straight, draping beautifully, and not in constant need of adjusting to keep it from shifting.

CAMISOLES: Camisoles support skirts or portions of skirts to allow free swing to the design of the garment bodice. Use underlining or a lightweight taffeta for a camisole in order to keep fabric thickness to a minimum (1).

INSIDE WAIST STAY: This stay is suggested for stretchy fabrics, sheath or princess styles, or when skirt is heavier than bodice. Cut strip of ½" to 1" (13 mm to 25 mm) wide grosgrain ribbon to fit waist, adding 1" (25 mm) for finishing ends. Turn ends back and stitch. Sew hooks and eyes to ends, extending loops over edge. Tack stay at seams and darts, leaving at least 2" (5 cm) free on sides of zipper (2).

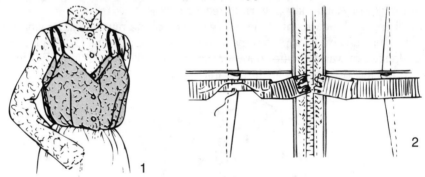

LINGERIE STRAP GUARDS: To prevent shoulder seams from shifting and keep lingerie straps from showing, use about 1 ½" (3.8 cm) of seam binding or a thread chain (page 334). Sew one end to shoulder seam near armhole. Sew a ball snap to free end of guard and a socket snap toward neck edge of garment.

FOUNDATION SUPPORTS: Make your foundation supports requiring feather boning from mediumweight taffeta or underlining fabric. The support takes the place of your undergarment and must, therefore, be made of materials sturdy enough to shape your body and to hold up the outer garment. Foundation supports are found most often in evening clothes, where underclothing could add bulk or detract from the sleek, smooth fit of the garment.

BONING: Boning is used to stiffen, mold, and maintain shape in garments such as strapless gowns, lingerie, and swimwear. Made of a firm but flexible nylon or other synthetic, it is usually covered with fabric for easy sewing by hand or machine. It is available by the yard (meter) or in prepackaged strips.

FABRIC STAYS: Fabric stays are made to control the fullness of an area of the garment and can be used effectively in skirts, bodices, or sleeves. They are constructed from lightweight lining or underlining fabric to make them invisible from the right side of the garment, but they must be firmly woven to retain the shape and drape as a stay is intended to do.

SHOULDER PADS: Shoulder pads can provide a smooth foundation from which the garment falls, camouflage round or sloping shoulders, or accentuate a broader-shoulder look in fashion.

Shoulder pads can be made of graduated layers of interfacing, polyester fleece, or foam rubber. Thickness can vary from ⅛" to 1" (3 mm to 25 mm). The designer's recommendations for shoulder pads are listed on the back of your pattern envelope. Thin pads are usually covered with a lining fabric for use in dresses and blouses. Thicker pads are used for jackets, suits, and coats. Choose wide pads to fill in the hollow between the shoulder and bustline.

Cut pads in a semicircular shape with a flat edge on one side approximately 8" to 9" (20.5 cm to 23 cm) long and a curved edge on the other. Pads should be approximately 3½" to 4½" (9 cm to 11.5 cm) wide at the shoulder seam. Cut one or more layers in decreasing size and tack the layers loosely together by hand. Using steam, press the pad over a tailor's ham, shaping it to fit easily into the armhole. Center pad at the shoulder seam, extending ⅜" (10 mm) beyond the armhole seam; pin. Try on garment and make any necessary adjustments in size and placement. Sew pads to seam allowances.

WEIGHTS: Weights are used to preserve the design lines of a garment and to prevent shifting during wear. They are also used to ensure the proper drape of a cowl neckline or to make a hem fall evenly. Select type and size by your fabric weight and desired use.

Flat Circular Weights, used in necklines and pleats, are enclosed in a pouch (1). Cut an underlining strip long enough to fold around weight, or allow extra fabric for a hanging mount. Stitch ¼" (6 mm) seams, turn, and insert weight. Pin in place and try on garment. Attach pouch with a French tack, or whipstitch through the extra fabric.

Lead Weight Strips consist of lead pellets enclosed in a fabric casing. Place them inside the hem of your garment as it is being placed into position so they will fall directly into the fold of the hemline (2). Begin and end the strip at the edge of your front facings, and tack the casing to the underlining with long running stitches. Never let the iron rest on your hem, as the weights will leave a noticeable impression.

Chain Weights are most frequently used in tailoring. They add the necessary weight to a coat or jacket hem and provide an attractive finish as well. Tack the chain directly below your lining, tucking the ends of the chain under the facing (3).

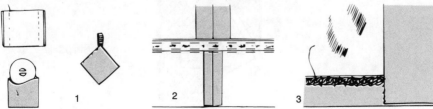

The Finest Fastenings

The master seamstress leaves nothing to chance. She will expertly insert a zipper by hand. She will not let the metallic glint of a snap or hook mar the look of her exquisitely finished garment, or an open jacket reveal any but the most perfect buttons and buttonholes. Follow these tips to make your closures as functional and yet unobtrusive as possible.

HAND APPLICATION OF A ZIPPER: Applying a zipper by hand is a custom technique. It is especially desirable on fine woolens, silks, and linens as well as on delicate and hard-to-handle fabrics. Follow the directions given for zipper placement in either the lapped or centered applications. Then use a tiny prickstitch (page 210) to complete the final stitching. Always sew with a fine needle and use a double strand of regular thread coated with beeswax for normal use, silk thread to match fabrics with sheen, or topstitching and buttonhole twist thread for added durability.

Use the prickstitch for the entire length of the zipper, always stitching from the bottom of the zipper to the top (1). There will be a space between the top stitches, but the understitches will be long and overlap to provide necessary strength. If your fabric is heavy, you may wish to make a second set of stitches, placing them between the first stitches for added strength.

ZIPPER UNDERLAY: To protect your skin and undergarments, place a piece of grosgrain ribbon (at least one inch longer than the opening) over the teeth. Hem the upper edge of the ribbon, ending the ribbon at the slider. Sew the long edge to one seam allowance of the opening with a backstitch. Catchstitch the lower end to the seam allowances. Fasten with a tiny snap (2).

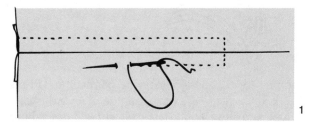

BOUND BUTTONHOLES: Long recognized as a couturier exclusive, beautifully worked buttonholes should become part of your own sewing repertoire. In the buttonhole section we gave you the construction methods. To complete the buttonhole as the great designers suggest, transfer the buttonhole markings to the facing and cleanly finish the facing with an organza patch, as directed for the garment in the organza patch method, page 328. Slipstitch facing to buttonhole for a professionally executed finish.

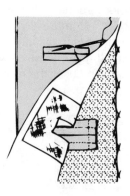

EXTENDED SNAPS: To fasten a collar or stand-up neckline with snaps, sew the ball section in position on the inside of the neckline or collar. Secure the socket section on the opposite side through only one hole, extending it from the edge as you would a hook (1). If your snaps might show, cover them as described above.

HANGING SNAPS: To fasten a neckline with snaps above a zipper, sew the socket section in position on the inside of the neckline. Attach the ball section on the opposite side by forming a thread loop using the blanket stitch, as described on page 334 (2).

1

2

COVERED SNAPS: For inconspicuous snaps, cover them with underlining or lining fabric. Cut two fabric circles about twice the diameter of the snap. Take a running stitch around edge of each circle. Place a snap section face down on each. Work ball of snap through center of fabric circle, snapping both sections several times to spread fabric apart. Draw up threads and fasten each section securely (3).

COVERED HOOK AND EYE: Make your hooks and eyes blend visually into your garment by covering them with a double strand of matching thread. Work from right to left, placing blanket stitches (page 213) very close together until the metal is completely covered. For larger hooks, use topstitching and buttonhole twist thread for quick and sturdy coverage (4).

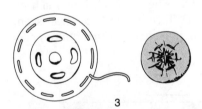

3

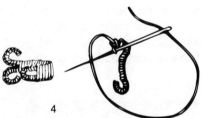

4

FINISHING BUTTONS: If you wish to cover the wrong side of a covered ring button (page 337), cut a circle of fabric the size of the inner diameter of the ring plus ½" (13 mm). Sew a gathering line around edge and adjust the gathers. Slipstitch to back of button (5).

COVERED BUTTONS: Individually decorated buttons can match or contrast with a garment. When using a small-scale print, center the motif on the button (6). Underline lace or eyelet with a matching or contrasting fabric (7). Use embroidery to monogram an initial, outline a motif, or stitch a simple design directly on the face of the button (8). Or stitch small beads to buttons for a sparkling effect (9).

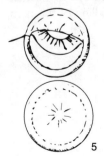

5

6

7

8

9

The Finishing Touches

The first things to catch your eye when you look at the inside of a couture garment are the beautifully finished seams and hems. It takes very little extra effort to impart the same custom touch and fine workmanship to your own garments.

LACE AND TRIMS: Lace can be an attractive and sturdy substitute for seam binding on your hems and facing edges, or you may wish to tack it on coats or jackets along the edge where the lining meets the facings. Select narrow, flexible lace for curves, and stretch lace for stretchy fabrics. Other trims (such as ribbon, braid, or rickrack) can also be very effective as long as they are relatively lightweight and flexible.

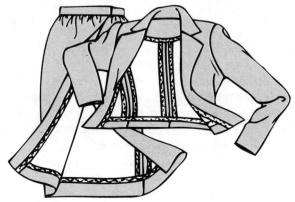

HONG KONG FINISH: This classic finish is used on underlined garments and is actually quite easy to do. Use 1" (25 mm) wide bias strips of your underlining or lining fabric, or press open double-fold bias tape. Matching edges, and using small stitches, stitch the bias strip to the garment raw edge in a ¼" (6 mm) seam (1). Turn bias to inside over seam. Stitch along line where binding and garment meet on the right side to catch bottom edge of binding and completely enclose the raw edge (2).

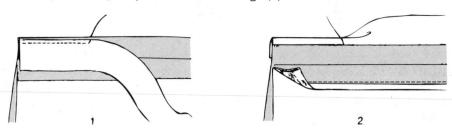

MACHINE-STITCHED HEMS: Some designers are featuring machine-stitched edges and hems on their couture garments, reflecting their innovative ideas and new techniques. For both woven and knitted fabrics, hems can be topstitched with one or two rows of stitching ¼" (6 mm) apart. Or an overlocked hem can be placed along the foldline of the hem, then the fabric trimmed away close to the stitching.

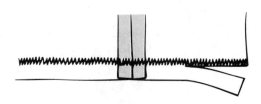

HAND-ROLLED NARROW HEMS: Use this hem to finish sheers, scarves, and lingerie. There are two popular methods, both time-consuming but well worth the effort. For the first technique, machine-stitch ¼" (6 mm) from raw edge; trim close to stitching. Roll approximately ⅛" (3 mm) of edge between thumb and forefinger, concealing stitching. Stabilize roll with third and fourth finger and slipstitch, taking a single thread at each stitch (1).

For the second method, stitch and trim as above. Turn edge about ⅛" (3 mm) and crease sharply. Pick up a thread along crease and carry thread over to raw edge diagonally and pick up a thread alongside the raw edge. Work in a zigzag pattern, making stitches ¼" (6 mm) apart. Repeat process for about 1" (25 mm), then pull thread to tighten stitches to create the roll (2).

1   2

SOFT HEM: A couturier rarely intends that the hem of a garment be pressed knife-sharp. The most common method is to simply interface the hem as directed on page 351.

Another method, used especially in very soft fabrics, is to insert additional padding along the hemline. First apply the interfacing; then, before completing the hem, place a 1" (25 mm) wide strip of lamb's wool, polyester fleece, cotton flannel, or soft cable cord on top of the interfacing at the hemline. Place approximately ⅓ of the strip below the hemline and ⅔ above it so that all the edges will be graded when the hem is turned. Sew to interfacing along hemline; use long running stitches for strips or long loose catchstitches for cord.

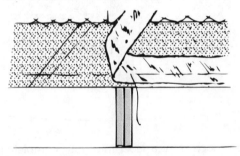

EXTREMELY CURVED HEMS: Some garments are so designed that the hem may have excess fabric or the hem edge circumference is not as wide as that of the garment. In such instances, the hem must be slashed at evenly spaced intervals, no deeper than 1" (25 mm) from the fold. As you adapt the hem, keep the garment free while sewing. To eliminate excess fabric, cut out narrow wedges and bring cut edges together. Hemstitch them shut. To add width to hem, insert small wedges of fabric and hemstitch them into place.

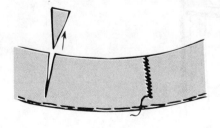
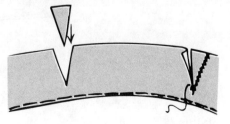

HORSEHAIR BRAID: This hem finish is most often used on full-length gowns, where extra stiffness is required in the hem without extra weight. Carefully mark the hemline. Steam braid to eliminate creases. The cut ends of the braid are very prickly and will require special treatment. To join them, lap ends ¾" (20 mm) and enclose both sides of braid with a fabric strip applied with a double line of stitching around all edges.

For a narrow braid, trim the hem allowance to ½" (13 mm). Place the braid on the right side of your fabric and match the edges. Stitch the braid and the hem allowance in a ¼" (6 mm) seam (1). Turn the braid up along the hemline. Baste close to the fold and complete the hem (2).

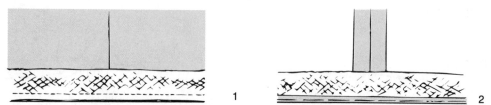

Wide braid usually has one prethreaded edge for easing; if not, run a gathering stitch along one edge. Place unthreaded edge along hemline; baste. Turn up and baste hem to check hemline. Sew basted edge of braid to underlining with long hemming stitch. Draw gathering thread to ease fullness on free edge. Sew this edge to underlining with long running stitches. Turn and complete hem (3).

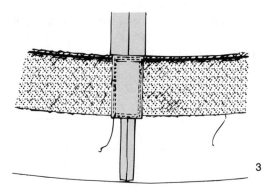

LABELS: For a custom touch, sew a label into your completed garment using small catchstitches or an embroidery stitch. Designer labels for Vogue patterns are available at the pattern counter. Personal labels can also be purchased or specially ordered.

Creative Trims

Trims add a new and exciting dimension to everything you sew. Apply them always with a tasteful hand, but don't let yourself be inhibited by traditional ideas. Use braid to outline design details as well as to finish the raw edges of a garment. Lace and ruffles always lend a romantic mood to an evening gown, but they also can add a subtle feminine touch to tweeds. The many decorative stitches, from topstitching to trapunto, can add crisp detailing or soft elegance.

Your trims should always be an integral part of your garment, coordinating with your design and fabric. Lavish beading, for example, would not only be inappropriate on a casual or tailored garment, but could possibly distract from an ornate brocade gown as well. A fashion rule of thumb is to coordinate elaborate trims with simple garments, simple trims with elaborate garments. Follow the lines of your garment or add lines to a simple style, but do not let your trimming destroy the balance of your garment by markedly interfering with the basic design. Permit your trims to enhance aesthetically and yet relate structurally by realizing their role in a total design concept.

And, as with everything you sew, relate the trim to yourself and your needs. If you love the rich look of quilting but fear the extra bulk on your frame, why not use it on just a collar or pockets? If you want your new creation for both daytime and evening wear, lace may be a better choice than beading.

If you can't find the perfect trimming in your fabric or notions departments, turn to the upholstery, drapery, or interior decorating departments. They often carry some stunning trims intended for use on furniture or draperies. Don't let this discourage you; they will work beautifully on your garments as well.

Even though there is a bewildering variety of trims, generally only two procedures are used for their application. They are either incorporated during the actual construction, or they are applied after the garment is completed. Always keep the method of application in mind while selecting your trim; don't wait until your garment is finished to discover that the trim should have been inserted during construction.

Armed with your good style sense, let your fancy lead the way. Change the look of last season's creation, give impact to a simple garment, or add the perfect finishing touch to a new dress-with trims, the mark of the creative seamstress.

Braid and Bands

If it's variety you're looking for, take a long look at braid and bands, which range from simple rickrack to gala beaded bands. Included in the galaxy of trims are embroidered bands, braid, lace, sequined bands, purchased fringe, and ribbon-all of them banded trims, in spite of their seeming diversity. Add the many possibilities in use and placement, and the variety totals great fashion excitement.

Whatever type of band you are using, be sure to mark accurately and measure frequently. Select an inconspicuous location to begin and end your application. Machine application, which produces a more casual appearance, is a rapid means of applying trim and may be necessary if the garment requires a very sturdy finish. Hand application with tiny invisible slipstitches will be strong enough to withstand the usual wear and cleaning and will allow increased control, a greater degree of manipulation, and a finer finish.

There are two basic methods of applying braid and bands. The most common method, direct application, is generally done after your garment is completed. Simply pin or baste the trim in place and apply by machine or hand. The second method, inset application, encloses one or both raw edges by sandwiching the trim between two fabric layers (such as the garment and a shaped or bias facing) and must be done during construction.

FLAT BRAID: Generally used to create a border effect or to highlight a specific garment area. Let braid add a touch of fashion or splash of color anywhere, from neckline to hemline. It is available in a wide range of colors, materials, weaves, and widths, making possible any number of effects. Do not limit yourself to only one row or one shade; braids are often best in combination.

Pin or baste to the garment and apply by hand or machine. Stitch along both edges in the same direction; do not pull the threads too tight or puckers will appear. Turn the ends in ¼" (6 mm) before sewing, overcasting them first if they tend to ravel (1).

SOUTACHE OR NARROW BIAS BRAID: Use this popular trim to outline a design with tracery or to emphasize an overall silhouette within a garment. Soutache is often used for a Spanish look on a jacket or dress.

Mark the design with chalk or thread tracing and pin the soutache in place. Ease the braid around corners; they will be slightly rounded, as soutache does not lend itself to sharp corners. Apply by hand with small, invisible stitches or apply by machine. Many machines have special braiding feet that will guide the trim while being sewn down (2).

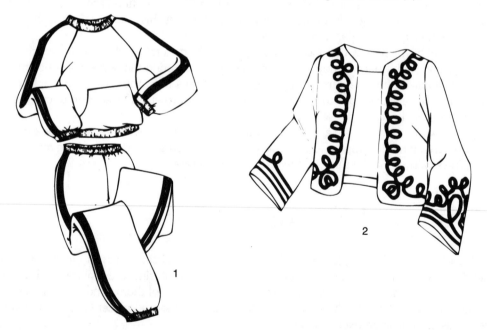

FOLD-OVER BRAID: Designed to trim garment edges, fold-over braid can also be utilitarian when used to finish raw edges such as a neckline or hemline.

Most braids are folded slightly off center, with the top side slightly narrower than the other to ensure catching the underside when stitching. For smooth application, shape the braid with a steam iron to achieve curves similar to those of your garment edge. For better control and a finer finish, apply the braid by hand. However, if you need an especially durable application, apply the braid by machine.

For a machine method with a minimum of visible stitching, first sew the upper half of the braid by hand. Then stitch on the right side of the garment with a zipper foot, as close as possible to the braid, to catch the bottom half. Baste the bottom half first if necessary to maintain control (1).

RICKRACK: There is such a large variety of sizes and materials available in rickrack-from baby rickrack to jumbo; from polyester to wool, to metallic-that you need not be traditional nor limited in your applications.

The zigzag shape makes rickrack very flexible for use around curves and corners. If you are using it on a corner, arrange the trim so an outside point is at the most conspicuous corner. Rickrack is often used at garment edges, exposing only the points after stitching; apply the trim by the inset method or machine-stitch along the edge of your garment with matching thread to secure the trim. Apply it within garment lines with a single line of machine stitching down the center or tiny handstitches at each point (1).

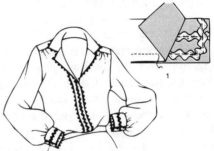

OTHER BANDED TRIMS: Embroidered bands and ribbons are available in any number of colors, patterns, and widths. Combine them with ruffles for ultrafrilly appeal, or use the provincial patterns for a charming Tyrolean look. For a touch of opulence, try tapestry or metallic embroidered bands on evening clothes. Combine ribbon with other trims, or team it with a matching bow. Apply these trims in the same manner as you would any banded trim. Special hints on beaded or sequined bands, purchased fringe, and flat lace are given on the following pages.

Fringe

Whatever the current trend, fringe and its related trims will always be present on the fashion scene. Purchased or made in a variety of materials and lengths, fringe has almost limitless uses for everything from clothes to home furnishings. Add rayon fringe to a shiny fabric for a jazzy effect, or several rows of wool fringe in various shades to accent the subtle colorings of a tweed. Mix fringe and tassels; combine different shades or outright contrasting colors. And remember that two rows (or three or four) are usually better than one. Easy to make or apply, fringe can create a multitude of effects.

KNOTTED FRINGE: Give your garments a mobile finish with knotted fringe. You may make it in any color and in a variety of yarns—wool, rayon, metallic threads. It works beautifully on the finished edge of any medium to loosely woven fabric. Experiment to determine the most appealing look; try several lengths, adjust the number of strands of yarn, change the distance between the groups, add more sets of knots. Generally, the fuller your fringe, the richer it will look.

Cut a cardboard strip the depth of the intended finished fringe plus ½" (13 mm) for each knot. Use the cardboard as a base and wrap your yarn around it. Cut through several strands at one end (1). With a stiletto or fine knitting needle, make a small hole about ½" (13 mm) from the finished edge of your garment and insert a crochet hook into the hole from the wrong side. Center the strands over the hook and pull them partially back through the hole. This will form a loop on the wrong side. Next, work the ends through the loop formed by the hook and pull the ends to tighten. Continue this process along the entire length of the edge. A second set of knots may be made by joining two halves of adjacent tassels with a single loop knot as shown (2). If you have made your strands long enough, several sets of knots may be made for an even more intricate, lacy appearance.

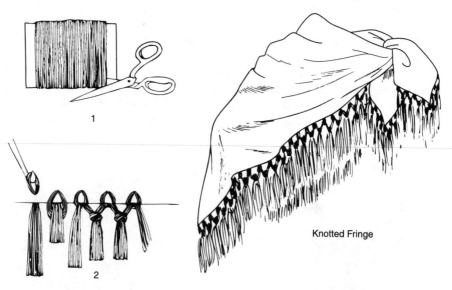

Knotted Fringe

PURCHASED FRINGE: Available in a vast assortment of materials, colors, and styles, all varieties of purchased fringe have a flexible braid heading for attaching the fringe. Just sew this heading to your fabric. Apply with an insert application or with a direct application using either a single row of matching stitching or invisible hand stitches.

SELF-FRINGE: This is a quick, easy trim that is a perfect match every time. It is particularly suited for soft, thick, heavy, or nubby fabrics. Do not feel you must limit your fringing to woolens, however, as most woven fabrics can be fringed with success; experiment first with a small scrap.

First straighten your fabric ends by cutting across the width along the grainline. Determine the desired depth of your fringe and pull out a crosswise thread from within the fabric to act as a guide. With small stitches, make a line of machine stitching along the pulled thread to anchor the fringe. Then remove all the threads beneath the stitching one at a time, always pulling them in the same direction.

Purchased Fringe

Self-Fringe

TASSELS: These are made in a manner similar to knotted fringe. Again cut a strip of cardboard the desired depth of the tassel to use as a base. Thread a needle with a double strand of your yarn and place strands at top of cardboard with the needle hanging at side. Wind your yarn around the cardboard and the strand of yarn until the proper fullness of the tassel has been achieved. Then tie your threaded strands very securely at the top and remove the cardboard (1). Wind the strand about ½" (13 mm) from top around the upper end several times; slip needle underneath the wound portion and bring out at top of tassel (2). Cut the lower loops and attach the tassel to your garment.

POM-POMS: The same operations are required for pom-poms and tassels except that pom-poms should be very, very full and have less depth. First, cut a strip of cardboard the desired depth. Then, using the cardboard as a base, put a separate strand at the top and wind the yarn around the cardboard. Securely tie the separate strand and cut across the other end (3). Remove the cardboard. Shake pom-pom gently to make a soft fluffy ball. To make a really full and lush pom-pom, repeat winding process. Then slip one wound cluster inside the other and tie the two together at the center, forming a cross. Cut all the ends and spread the strands to form a ball. For both methods, trim the strands of your pompoms into perfect spheres (4).

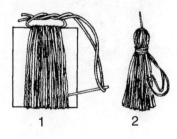

1

2

3

4

Lace and Embroidered Trims

So romantic, so fanciful, nothing can be more eye-catching than the perfect lace trim. Imagine the wistful beauty of delicate Val edging for a ruffled collar and cuffs, or the effect of heavy lace for a bodice insertion. Add lace to a velvet jacket for a choir-boy or Edwardian look. Combine laces with each other or with other trims—just think of all the possibilities.

Some of the well-known laces include Alencon, Battenberg, Bobbin, Breton, Chantilly, Cluny, Irish, Needlepoint, Spanish, and Valenciennes lace. Lace is made by hand with bobbins and pins, needles and hooks, or by machine. Lace is available in yardage (metrage) or as a trim.

Many charming varieties of lace trims have been produced commercially. Cotton, nylon, acetate, and wool are used, singly or in blends, to make the variety of lace trims available today. Many lace trims are re-embroidered, giving them an added dimension. The inherent fragility of lace calls for handling its open construction with special care. Let the fiber content, the openness of the lace, or the type and use of the lace on the design, guide you in deciding between hand or machine applications plus any necessary ironing and washing procedures.

Over the years, heirloom-sewing techniques have been translated successfully from hand to the sewing machine. If you apply your lace trim by machine, you may find an edging foot to be an indispensable tool. The guide or raised section on the foot keeps the lace in line while stitching. Spray starch is another necessary tool when sewing with fine cotton or linen batiste and laces. Lightly starch the fabric and lace prior to sewing on them for better control. Here are just a few techiques you will find helpful in working with lace or embroidered trims.

Joining Ends: The couturier method of joining lace ends is to appliqué along a motif. To appliqué by hand, lap the ends and trim around a motif on the upper layer. Whipstitch around the motif to join it to the under layer (1). Trim away the excess lace on the under layer. To appliqué by machine, lap the ends and trim around the motif on the upper layer. Using your embroidery foot, sew around the motif with a short, narrow zigzag stitch, and trim the excess lace from the under layer.

To join the end of Val lace (a flat lace made with the same thread forming the ground and pattern), a small French seam can be made. First stitch the ends of the lace wrond sides together with a scant ⅛" (3 mm) seam. Crease along the seam, bringing th eright sides together and stitch again ⅛" (3 mm) from the seam, encasing the raw edges (2).

1

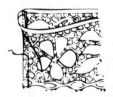

2

Mitering Corners: Pin the lace up to the corner, folding it to form a miter. Whipstitch or zigzag stitch from the inside corner to the outside corner. Trim the excess away.

FLAT LACE: There are many kinds of flat lace. One type has two finished edges and can be applied to the top of the fabric, inserted between strips of fabric, or rows of lace can be sewn to each other. To apply this type of lace directly to the fabric, stitch the straight edges by machine or hand. If the lace has scalloped edges, the lace is preferably sewn by hand with small invisible stitches or you can sew by machine with a short, narrow zigzag (1).

Another flat lace, often called insertion lace, can also be applied directly to the fabric and the underlying fabric trimmed away for a more airy, delicate look. Sew the lace to the fabric through the header; stitch again over the first line of stitches with a short, narrow zigzag then trim the fabric away from the back with sharp embroidery scissors or trim and whipstitch (2).

1

2

To sew rows of lace together creating "fancy bands", butt the edges of the lace together and whipstitch or sew with a short narrow zigzag (3).

3

Flat edging lace has one straight edge and the other edge is scalloped. It is used to trim the edges of sleeves, hems or collars. It can be applied to the edge of insertion lace as well as to create wider bands of lace. If applying edging lace to fabric by hand, for a more secure seam, trim the garment seam allowance to ¼" (6 mm) and roll the edge. Whipstitch the lace to the rolled edge (4).

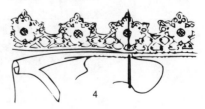

4

To stitch by a machine, trim the garment seam leaving approximately ⅛" (3 mm) on the edge. Layer the lace on the fabric with the ⅛" (3 mm) extending beyond the edge of the lace. Using a narrow zigzag stitch, sew the lace to the fabric edge. One swing of the needle will fall into the header of the lace and the other swing will fall off the edge of the fabric rolling the edge into the seam. For added strength, you can zigzag again from the right side over the rolled edge (1).

1

GATHERED LACE: You may purchase lace trims pre-ruffled or gather your own. To make a lace ruffle, you will need a piece of lace 2 to 3 times the finished length, depending on the desired fullness. Gather the lace by hand or machine by taking long stitches close to the straight edge of the lace, and distribute the gathers evenly. Use two rows of stitching if lace is 3" (7.5 cm) or wider (2). With Val lace, pull up the heavier thread found in the header along the straight edge of the lace to gather (3).

Apply your gathered lace to the edge of the fabric in the same manner as you would flat lace to fabric or baste it along the seamline for insertion into the seam on collars.

2

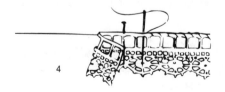

3

ENTREDEUX: This flat insertion looks similar to an embroidered ladder and is used "between two" pieces of lace or between fabric and lace. Entredeux edges may also be found along each side of embroidered fabric bands. To apply entredeux to lace by hand, trim one batiste edge from the entredeux. Butt the edges of the lace and the trimmed entredeux and whipstitch together (4). To stitch by machine, trim the edge from the entredeux and butt the edges of the lace and the entredeux together. Using a short, narrow zigzag, stitch having one needle swing go into the hole of the entredeux and the other into the header of the lace (5).

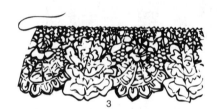

4

5

Stitch entredeux to fabric in the following manner. Trim one edge of the entredeux as described before. Sew a straight stitch very close to the edge of the fabric to stabilize the edge. Make a rolled hem along the same edge by hand or use a short, narrow zigzag stitch. With right sides together, place the trimmed entredeux over the rolled hem and whipstitch the edges. To apply by machine, zigzag having one swing of the needle fall into the holes on the entredeux and one stitch fall off the fabric.

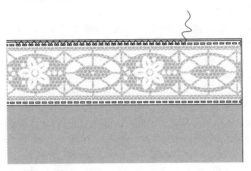

EMBROIDERED TRIMS: Swiss embroideries are lovely additions to many garments. The tone-on-tone or pastel-toned embroideries are stitched down the center of a batiste band of fabric. Both edges can be raw or one edge will be finished with a decorative satin stitch when purchased from the store. These embroideries can be sewn to entreudeux or lace bands. Apply the embroidered bands as you would lace to flat fabric, rolling the hem as you stitch.

To all lace insertions, entredeux, or embroidered bands to your pattern, it is recommended that you make the lace bands first. Add fabric sections before cutting out your pattern pieces to be sure the sections are large enough for the pattern, tucks and pintucks, puffing (gathered bands of fabric), rows of hand smocking, and ribbon rosettes can be added to complete the garment. Beading lace (flat lace through which ribbon is woven) is also a nice addition.

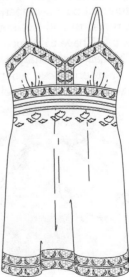

Beading

What can be more glamorous than a dress shimmering with the glitter of beading? Or top off your gown or cocktail dress with a jacket outlined with beaded tracery. The jeweled look is one you can always count on, for its appeal is perennial.

For more casual garments, select natural or colored beads of wood or clay, or the authentic look of multicolored Indian beads.

Beading is often a painstaking procedure, but one in which your patience is sure to be greatly rewarded. Following are some suggestions that will make your beading proceed faster and easier. You will, naturally, need a design. Outline a design in a printed fabric, trace one from another source, or create your own. When you have decided upon a design, transfer it to your garment with chalk and thread tracing.

Although beading is usually applied to a completed garment, you may wish to add an overall beading design in the process of construction. Cut out the garment section and back with a lightweight underlining. Mark all construction lines and transfer your beading pattern. Make sure that any fitting adjustments have already been made so that the beading will not interfere during construction. Stitch all seams with a zipper foot.

Use an embroidery hoop to hold the fabric taut for small motifs, and select a fine or special beading needle that will slip easily through the holes of the beads. Use matching thread coated with beeswax or transparent nylon thread. Keep your thread relatively short; a longer thread will tend to get tangled or knotted. Don't pull your stitches too tight or your fabric will pucker. Be careful when pressing; placing a hot iron on your beading may melt, scratch, or dull the beads. To press the garment around the beading, use a press cloth on the wrong side and press over a pressing pad or Turkish towel; avoid touching the beading.

Beads

You can attach your beads singly, in groups, or in a long strand. If you desire scattered beads, you will need to sew them individually (1). Start from the wrong side and use a back-stitch. For a straight line of several beads, take several beads on the thread at a time and use a modified running stitch from cluster to cluster (2). The number of beads you will be able to string at one time depends primarily on the size and weight of the bead; experiment on a scrap first to find out how many you can string without the cluster drooping. For curves, you will have to reduce the number of beads on each stitch, perhaps even sewing them individually on a sharp curve or with large beads. Use a double thread coated with beeswax or nylon thread when sewing beads in clusters. If you are applying prestrung beads, sew over the threads between beads at intervals (3).

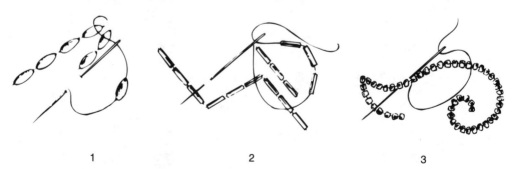

| 1 | 2 | 3 |

Bead Loops or Fringe dripping from a garment edge or within the garment lines for a scalloped effect is a look that is always elegant. Use nylon or a double strand of cotton thread coated with beeswax to prevent breaking. Count the number of beads on each strand to maintain uniformity.

For loops, pull the needle through from the wrong side, string several beads, and return the needle to the wrong side. Secure each loop singly for added security (4).

Do not pull the loops too tightly or they will appear stiff and rigid. For fringe, string smaller beads, a large bead, and an anchor bead, if necessary; return needle through the same or another series of small beads (5).

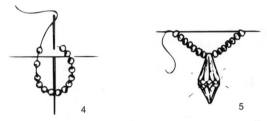

Prebeaded Bands and Appliqué are basted and then sewn. Ease the trim around curves as you baste. Sew with invisible slipstitches through the backing. To finish the ends, remove several beads from the backing, turn it under, and slipstitch securely in place. Be sure to firmly secure the last bead to prevent losing beads. Many sewing machines have special beading feet available for applying strings of beads using a wide zigzag stitch.

Sequins

Sequins can also be applied several ways. Apply single sequins with a backstitch from center hole to edge. For a finer finish, apply with a small coordinated bead. Bring the needle up through the hole, string a bead, and return through the hole (1). For sequin rows, bring needle through hole and take a backstitch over to edge. Bring needle forward in position for the next one, which will overlap the last and conceal the thread (2). Prestrung sequins are applied in the same manner as prestrung beads.

Paillettes, while larger than sequins, are applied in basically the same manner. The hole is located at the edge rather than in the middle. They may be applied with a backstitch from hole to edge, or with a bead. Rows are applied like sequin rows or individually if they are very large (3).

Sequin Bands and Appliqué can also be purchased. These trims generally have a series of thread chains or an elastic backing to act as a flexible foundation. Invisibly tack these strands to your garment. If you are using clusters, snip away the threads between the motifs and anchor the thread ends with a knot, clear nail polish, or glue to prevent raveling. Fold transparent tape over the cut ends to avoid unnecessary loss of sequins. Many sewing machines have beading or sequin feet available for applying strings of sequins. Read the presser foot manufacturer's instructions before stitching.

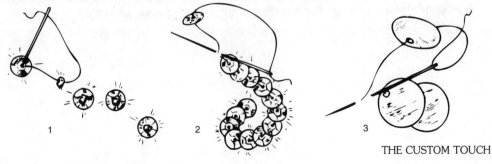

Feathers and Furs

Trimming with feathers or fur is a glamorous finale to any garment. Each has been adorning clothes for centuries, yet over the years neither one has lost its lush hypnotic appeal. Add a fur collar to a tweed coat and see how beautifully it frames your face. A full flourish of feathers at your hemline or an unexpected burst at the edge of a sleeve or neckline can be sensational. Don't be skimpy; use rows and rows for a lavish effect. Whatever you do with feathers and furs, don't overlook them!

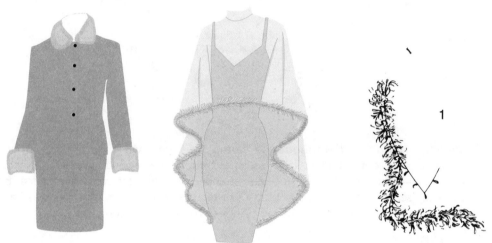

1

FEATHERS: Feathers are usually purchased in strips. The most common application is to sew an overhand stitch through the fabric edge and over the cord-like base of the trim. Keep the stitches fairly loose and far apart, but firm enough to support the trim. Conceal the threads and refresh the feathers by using a large blunt needle to work out each vane from underneath stitches (1).

To facilitate the removal of the feathers for cleaning, attach small thread loops to your garment edge. They should be several inches (centimeters) apart and large enough to accommodate the width of the trim. Then you can simply pass the feather strip through the loops as you would a belt. Close the ends of the strip with whipstitches and work out each vane from underneath the loops.

FUR: These trims are available in a variety of furs and in many widths and lengths. Usually in straight strips, some are already shaped for you to use on collars or lapels. The majority of fur trims are already neatly backed with lining fabric or grosgrain fabric. Therefore, joining the fur to your garment edge is just a simple matter of sewing the backing to the garment with firm but unnoticeable running stitches.

For cleaning ease, however, you may prefer to apply your trim by attaching large covered snaps to both the garment and the fur. Space the snaps according to the weight and width of the trim. Then you can merely snap the fur on and off at your own convenience.

For further information on the handling of fur, turn to pages 389 to 392.

Stitchery

The efficiency of the sewing machine has taken away the drudgery of hand sewing, but don't let it take away the enjoyable decorative role of hand sewing as well. Who would care to do without the marvelous custom effect of saddle stitching, or the richly seamed look of its machine-sewn version, topstitching? Decorative tacks can certainly add to a finely tailored appearance. If you have been limiting embroidery to tablecloths and pillowcases, you've been overlooking some great fashion ideas. A personal monogram can always add distinction to any garment. Embroidery floss, topstitching, and buttonhole twist thread, and yarn can be used to sew your finishing details. Just think of the wonderful fashion effects you can gain with a needle and thread and a small amount of time!

TOPSTITCHING: The most popular form of fashion stitchery, topstitching emphasizes the structural lines of your garment while working to keep the seams and edges flat and crisp. Although done by machine, it gives the same detailed look as fine hand sewing. Don't forget that it is often a construction procedure as well in such features as pockets, pleats, and man-tailored shirts.

The stitching can be done after the garment is completed, but it is often necessary or easier to stitch individual or large areas during construction. Make any fitting adjustments before you topstitch seams.

Use topstitching and buttonhole twist thread in the needle, and either topstitching thread or regular sewing thread in the bobbin. Use a size #90/14 or #100/16 needle, and 6 to 8 stitches per inch (2-3 per cm). You will probably have to adjust your machine tension before stitching; experiment first on scrap layers of your fabric and underlining. Stitch carefully, using a guide, such as the edge of the presser foot. Be particularly cautious at curves and pivot the fabric at corners; mark these tricky areas with thread tracing before stitching. Stitch two lines very close together on heavy fabrics. Leave thread ends long enough to be worked to the wrong side with a needle and tied.

SADDLE STITCH: This is a trimming stitch which, used with discretion, can be a charming subtle touch. The simplest of all stitchery techniques, it is usually added to a completed garment. Use topstitching and buttonhole twist thread, embroidery floss, or yarn-preferably in a contrasting color-and simply make continuous running stitches, evenly spaced and at least ¼" (6 mm) long.

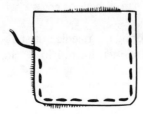

DECORATIVE TACKS: These are used on pockets and pleats on tailored clothes. First mark triangular shape. Secure thread for tack with small backstitches.

For the **Arrowhead Tack,** bring needle out at A and take a small horizontal stitch at B. Insert the needle at C and bring it out again just inside A. Continue until the entire tack is filled in (1).

For the **Crow's Foot Tack,** bring needle out at A and take a small horizontal stitch at B. Then make a small diagonal stitch at C and then across base to A. Continue until the entire tack is filled in (2).

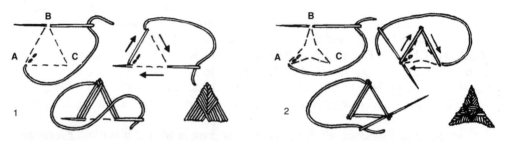

EMBROIDERY: Embroidery has become an indispensable addition to the design and style of many clothes. Whether embroidered by hand or with a computerized embroidery/sewing machine, the results are the same, you have personalized your garment fo ryourself. Used to embellish, embroidery stitches are seen on everything from home furnishing items to clotheing. The following hand embroidery stitches are just a few for your use. Many of the stitches can be duplicated on most sewing machines. Check your sewing machine manual for instructions and the correct presser feet to use.

The **Outline Stitch,** a slanting backstitch, is worked from the left to the right in a single line. Each stitch is followed by a short backstitch back to the right side very close to the previous stitch (1).

For the **Satin Stitch,** work close parallel stitches over an area padded first with tiny running stitches. For straight lines, the stitch is done on a slant; for curved lines, place the threads closer together on the inside of a curve, further apart on the outside (2).

For the **Cross-Stitch,** bring needle out at 1, cross over and take a stitch from 2 to 3, and then cross over and take a stitch from 4 to 5. Continue these diagonal stitches in same direction. Next, working in opposite direction, cross each stitch, keeping points together (3 on the following page).

For the **Herringbone Stitch,** bring the needle out at 1, cross over and take a stitch from 2 to 3. Cross over again, taking a stitch from 4 to 5. Repeat to finish row (4 on the following page).

For the **Blanket Stitch,** work from left to right between two lines. Bring needle up on lower line and hold thread down, insert needle a little to right on upper line, and bring up directly below on lower line. Draw needle through the loop formed and pull thread taut (5).

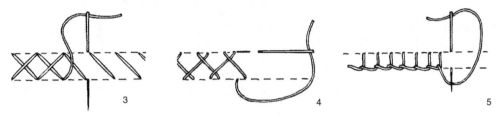

The look of the **Featherstitch** varies greatly based upon the angle of the needle and the length of the stitch. Keep the thread tension, your needle angle and the length of your stitch consistent for a pleasing result (6).

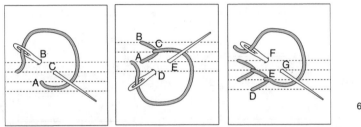

The **Cretan Stitch** is created by spacing the stitches farther apart. If the stitches are placed closer is makes a nice filling stitch (7).

The **Fly Stitch** is another type of blanket stitch. Bring thread out at A and work from left to right. Hold the thread down and stitch from B to C. Take a small stitch at 3 to secure the loop. Return to higher point for next V (8).

To make the **Chainstitch,** bring the needle to the right side, holding the thread down while taking the next stitch. As the needle crosses over the thread, it will form a loop (9).

The **Lazy Daisy Stitch** is an elongated, detached version of the chain stitch, grouped to form a daisy. Begin at the center of your flower, and return the needle to the pivot point after taking each stitch (10).

The **French Knot** is made by twisting thread around a needle. Bring the needle to the right side, hold thread taut, and twist the needle so the thread loops around it three or four times. Return the needle to the wrong side, very close to the point where it emerged, and pull the thread through the loops and fabric until a small knot remains (11).

The **Stem Stitch** is very similar to the outline stitch and is also known as the crewel stitch. The thread is alsways kept below the needle during the stitching (1).

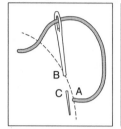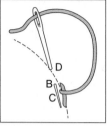

1

Couching is used for outlines or to fill in designs. A heavy or specialty thread is secured to the fabric with a finer second thread. Exquisite gold threads are often couched with tiny evenly spaced stitches on silk or satin fabrics (2).

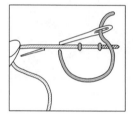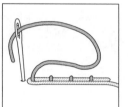

2

Many sewing machines have special presser feet designed to hold heavier threads for couching. Single or multiple cords can be sewn down using a variety of decorative stitches and novelty threads (3 & 4).

Many embroidery stitches are used on fine fabrics such as imported cotton batiste, china silk, or handkercheif linen to embellish or highlight other heirloom sewing techniques.

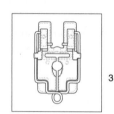

3

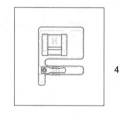

4

The **PIN STITCH or POINT de PARIS** is a delicate stitch often used for hemming or attaching laces to fabric. A larger needle, such as a tapestry needle, is used and tiny holes are created when the threads are pulled firmly together. This technique is sewn from the wrong side of the fabric (5). To acheive this same look by machine, use a single wing or a size #100 topstitching needle to create the holes. Many machines have a stitch built-in that duplicates the hand stitch.

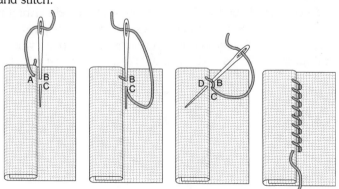

5

Shadow Work, an effect of shading on fine fabrics, is acheived using darker threads and a **Herringbone Stitch** on the wrong side. On the right side of the fabric, the design appears as an outline (6).

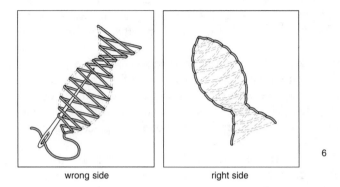

wrong side   right side

6

Ribbon Embroidery has become a very popular form of textural embellishment. This elegant technique has been part of our fashion culture since the Victorian era. First used on the fine gowns of the European royal courts, this technique has experienced a revival in recent years. Using beautifully-colored, narrow silk and organza ribbons, delicate flowers and leaves can enhance exquisite gowns, hats, shawls, or evening bags, to name just a few items. This embellishment technique can also be accomplished using your sewing machine.(7)

7

Fabric Manipulation & Embellishment

Those who sew enjoy the opportunity to create with fabric. The personal satisfaction of taking a flat piece of fabric and manipulating it into a well-fitting garment is an indescribable joy. The wonderful feel of fine wool or soft silk passing through your fingers is impossible to explain to another.

Besides employing fine stitching techniques, another aspect of sewing is the importance of making each garment truly your own. And that can be done by adding your own special touch—a unique trim, a clever applique, or a dramatic color-blocking scheme. When previewing patterns in the store, take an extra moment to consider a special embellishment that will make your next garment a one-of-a-kind piece to be proud of.

COLOR BLOCKING: First introduced in the early 1980's, fabric color blocking is reminiscent of a Mondrian painting. Large blocks of color are combined into one overall piece. This interesting color technique is a terrific way to add a dramatic attitude to your next garment without really doing anything extraordinary to the pattern. Simply, different colors of fabric are combined to create an overall, strikingly modern effect.

Rather than using one fabric for an entire garment, large sections are cut from a contrasting-colored fabric. Study the color wheel provided in the first section of color pages in this book to understand the primary, secondary and tertiary colors and their relationships to each other.

Complementary or contrasting colors are those colors opposite each other on the wheel—red and green, orange and blue, or yellow and violet. Used together, contrasting colors are almost electric. As you begin to work more and more with color, you will find the experience exhilarating. (See Color, pages 10 and 11.) Try bold combinations for a daring look on your next jacket or coat. Make the sleeves from one color and the body from another. A third color could be introduced for the front placket and collar.

As you begin to choose your color combinations, remember the effect color has on your size. Color blocking does not have to mean a constant use of the primary colors and their opposites but the technique can be as equally effective mixing white, black and brown or red, black, and white. For a more subtle effect, mix the hues (tints) or shades of the same colors together.

QUILTING: The term, quilting is often confused within today's sewing jargon with piecing or patchwork. Patchwork is the act of sewing small geometric-shaped pieces of fabric together into a larger piece thereby creating a design. Quilting is sewing two or more layers of fabric together with the middle layer often being a polyester or cotton fleece or batting. Like color blocking, quilting can be applied to any garment without actually changing the pattern.

For quilting, purchase more fabric than is called for on your pattern. As quilting can be done either by hand or machine it is best to test your stitching on a sample to see how much "shrinkage" of fabric you will experience. The quilting stitches will cause the fabric to draw in slightly and it is recommended that you quilt all your fabric prior to cutting out the pattern pieces.

Before beginning to quilt, it is important to understand the elements used. First, start with the batting. There are a variety of weights of batting, as well as suggested uses for each weight. As with the use of color, remember that quilted fabrics will add bulk to the chosen design and to your shape. Select your batting according to the effect you want – high-loft polyester batting for a puffier look or a thin cotton batting for a more subtle, textural effect. Silk batting tends to be puffier than cotton but is light in weight and should be used with silk fabrics. Wool batting provides warmth to any garment.

Refer to the thread chart on pages 176-178, for the appropriate quilting thread for machine or hand stitching and choose the correct size needle. Use matching or contrasting thread and experiment on a sample to determine the correct stitch length and tension for the fabric. For machine quilting, a walking foot is an indispensable tool. It helps feed the upper layer of fabric evenly through the machine avoiding any fabric shifting or slippage while stitching. A quilting guide that is attached to the foot or machine is also useful in keeping the rows of stitching straight.

The creative aspect of quilting is the actual stitching design you choose. To begin, layer your batting between the outer fabric and a lining fabric, right sides out, creating a "sandwich". The lining fabric may be the same fabric or the same weight as the outer fabric, lighter in weight, or just cotton muslin that will not show on the finished garment. The purpose of the lining is tol add stability to your stitching and make it easier to sew.

Pin the layers together approximately 2" (5 cm) apart across the entire piece of fabric. Baste around the edges to keep everything together. Using the appropriate marking tool (see Marking Tools, page 199), mark the quilting lines on the right side of the fabric. There are many simple linear quilting designs to choose from for stitching (see below).

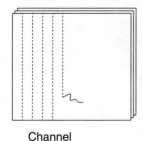

Channel

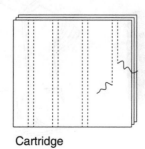

Cartridge

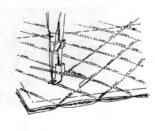

Diamond

TRAPUNTO: A form of quilting in which the background is left unpadded and only the design stands out in relief, trapunto is done after a garment section is cut out. The design is backed with a soft fabric (such as organdy) and padded with strands of yarn. Choose a design, determine its placement, and transfer it to the right side of your fabric with chalk or thread tracing. Baste the backing to the wrong side in the desired location. On the right side, stitch by hand or machine along the pattern with small stitches and tie the thread ends on the wrong side.

To pad the design, thread strands of matching or contrasting yarn through a blunt needle. Insert the needle through the backing, and carry the yarn between the fabric and backing from one stitching line to the other. Clip the ends of the yarn close to the stitching. Pass the needle as far as possible before bringing it up, and do not pull tightly. For large areas or angles and sharp curves, bring the needle out and back through the backing. When changing directions, leave some slack to fill out the angle. Continue until the entire area is padded. Slightly stretch the fabric around each section of the pattern to make the tiny yarn ends recede into backing. Press lightly on the wrong side over a Turkish towel or pressing pad.

CORDED QUILTING: A variation of trapunto, corded quilting consists of several parallel rows of stitching that are then padded with strands of yarn. The quilting is applied to a garment area, such as a neckband or hemband, before it is joined to the garment.

Stitch the band sections together along one long edge or fold a one-piece band along the foldline to create a double layer of fabric. If one end of the band will not be enclosed in a seam, fold the end seam allowances to the wrong side before stitching on the quilting lines. If several sections must be seamed together to create the band, leave open the inside portion of one seam to create an opening for inserting the yarn.

Baste the long raw edges of the band together along the seamline. To form the quilting, stitch through both layers of fabric in parallel lines spaced approximately ½" (13 mm) apart. To pad the design, thread several strands of yarn between the stitching lines to create the corded effect.

Baste along the seamline and trim the yarn out from the seam allowances before stitching ends into a seam. If ends are not to be enclosed in a seam, trim excess yarn and slipstitch the opening closed.

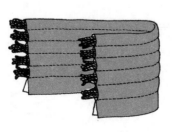

APPLIQUÉ: This embellishment technique consists of applying separate pieces of fabric as a decoration to a larger background. You may purchase a ready-made appliqué in a variety of forms (see Sequins and Beading, page 473) or make your own by cutting out a motif from your fabric or create a new design. Prints, contrasting solids, or fabrics with a definite texture lend themselves to appliqué. Try different weights of fabric together as well as textures for interesting effects.

Appliqué lends itself readily to sportswear, children's clothing and home decorating projects, but don't discount the elegant effect a lace or beaded appliqué can have on more formal wear.

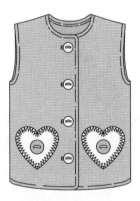

There are many new products available today to help make the appliqué process easier. Fusible webs and bonding agents have paper-backings to which the appliqué design is traced. These agents are bonded to the appliqué fabrics, the design traced and cut out, and then fused to the background fabric. If not pressed at this final stage many of the appliqués can be moved until you have them in the exact position desired. Investigate with all the different products on different types and weights of fabrics as some may make the background fabric too stiff after stitching. Be sure to select the type of fusing agent that can be used for sewing.

For **hand appliqué**, transfer the design to the appliqué fabric and machine stitch close to the design outline. Trim the excess fabric away to ⅛" (3 mm) outside the stitching line. Baste the appliqué to the garment. Attach with a small blanket stitch around edges, using matching or contrasting thread (1). Or if you prefer, turn and press the raw edges to the wrong side along the machine stitching and sew to garment with invisible slipstitches (2). Clip or notch any curves or corners.

1

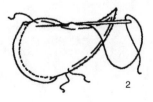

2

For **machine appliqué**, following the manufacturer's instructions, fuse the bonding agent or web to the wrong side of the appliqué fabric. Trace the design on the wrong side remembering to mirror image the design if necessary. Cut out the appliqué along the design lines and adhere to the garment. Match the thread to the appliqué (see Chart, page 176-178) and attach with a satin stitch, stitching slowly. Pivot as necessary to keep an even edge on inside and outside curves (1 and 2). Miter corners (3, 4) and points (5). If several appliqués are overlapped, begin with the bottom piece first. Stitch only the portions that will show as any heavy stitching lines may show through to the top or cause thread build up while stitching.

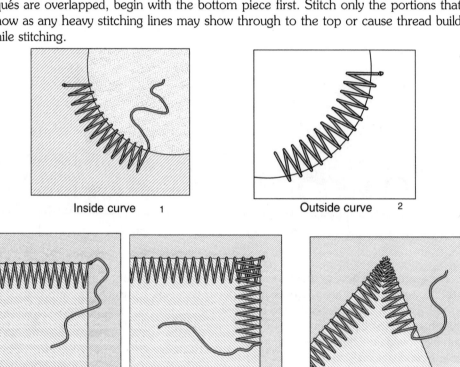

Inside curve   1   Outside curve   2

3   4   5

Most sewing machines have a variety of other stitches that are appropriate for appliqué. Built-in blanket stitches or other decorative satin stitches will also cover the edges of the appliqué pieces nicely. Experiment with your machine to create the effect you want.

There are numerous embellishment techniques that can be used on your garments. Carefully analyize the pattern before choosing a technique. Take into consideration the impact seam lines may have on any embellishment before starting. The adage "The simpler the better" applies more often than not.

Appendix

Stain Removal

Always read and follow the care instructions found on the end of the bolt or any warnings on the garment label. Carefully follow the directions on any stain removal product. Test any stain remover on a seam or edge for color fastness. Rinse all chemical dry cleaning solvents from fabric and air dry before laundering in the washer to prevent fires. Do no mix stain removal products, as some will produce noxious fumes (chlorine and ammonia).

ALCOHOLIC BEVERAGES & WINE

Launder with detergent in the hottest water safe for the fabric. Do not use soap (bar, flake or detergents containing natural soap) as it could set the stain permanently or make it more difficult to remove. Soak stain for 30 minutes in 1 quart of warm water and 1 tsp. of enzyme presoak product. If all the sugars are not removed a brown stain will appear when the fabric is dried in the dryer or ironed as the sugar carmelized.

BABY STAINS, FOOD, FORMULA OR EXCREMENT

First, scrape off whatever possible. Fresh protein stains can often be removed by soaking and agitating in cold water using a detergent or enzyme presoak for about 30 minutes before washing. If hot water is used it can set the stain making it more difficult to remove. Old stains may need to be soaked for several hours. Wash in warm water, rinse and inspect for any remaining stain, repeat if necessary. Launder in chlorine bleach if stain remains. Wash again to be sure all bleach is removed as baby's skin is sensitive.

BLOOD

Flush with cold water and scrape off any crusted material. Soak for 15 minutes in lukewarm water, 1 T. ammonia, and ½ tsp. liquid hand dishwashing detergent. Rub gently to loosen stain. If stain remains, wet the stain with hydrogen peroxide and a few drops of ammonia. Rinse with cool water. If stain is dried, pretreat with a prewash stain remover, liquid laundry detergent or a paste of granular laundry detergent and water. Bleach safe for fabric may be used.

CHOCOLATE

Apply a pre-wash spray or a pre-treat enzyme product. Rub with a heavy-duty liquid detergent and wash. Relaunder with bleach safe for the fabric if stain remains. For stubborn stains, treat as a Dye Stain.

COFFEE OR TEA

Saturate the stain with a pre-treat stain remover. Rub the stain with a heavy-duty liquid detergent and wash in the hottest water safe for the fabric. Do not use soap (bar, flake or detergents containing natural soap) as it could set the stain permanently or make it more difficult to remove.

DINGINESS, YELLOWING OR GRAYING

Wash in a permanent press cycle in hot water with a cool-down rinse and use 1 cup of water conditioner instead of detergent. If discoloration remains, repeat procedure or wash with correct amount of detergent and all-fabric or chlorine bleach safe for the fabric. White fabrics may be whitened with a "white wash" specialty product.

DYE STAINS, DYE TRANSFER (INCLUDES CHERRY AND BLUEBERRY STAINS)

Check fabric for color fastness. Soak in a dilute solution of all-fabric powdered bleach. If stain remains on color fast fabric, soak for no more than 15 minutes in a dilute solution of chlorine bleach and water. Chlorine bleach may change the color of the fabric so always check for color fastness first.

FRUITS AND JUICES

Launder with detergent in the hottest water safe for the fabric. Do not use soap (bar, flake or detergent containing natural soap) as it could set the stain permanently or make it more difficult to remove. Soak tough stains in 1 quart warm water and 1 tsp. of enzyme presoak product for 30 minutes.

GUM

Hold ice on the gum to harden; crack off with dull side of butter knife. Spray with aerosol pre-treat product and let stand for 5 minutes. Rub with heavy-duty liquid detergent and wash.

HAND LOTION, OIL-BASED MAKEUP, OINTMENT/SALVE

Saturate light stains with a pre-treat spray stain remover. Rub with a heavy-duty liquid detergent and wash. Treat for color fastness before using chlorine bleach on remaining stains. For heavy stains, place face down on folded paper towels. Apply dry cleaning fluid to back of stain. Following product instructions, replace towels frequently. Let air dry; rinse. Launder in hottest water safe for fabric.

INK (SOLVENT SOLUBLE)

Act fast to remove stain. Sponge area around stain with denatured alcohol and then apply directly to stain. Place stain face down on paper towels and apply alcohol to back of stain until no more ink is removed. Rinse thoroughly. Or use dry cleaning solvents (read instructions on product label first) instead of alcohol. Dye strippers may work on white fabrics.

INK (PERMANENT)

Treat immediately by forcing water through stain before it dries to remove ink. Allow to dry. Sponge the stain with dry cleaning solvent (follow instructions on product) and allow to dry. Rub liquid detergent into stain, rinse. Soak the stain in warm water and ½ T. ammonia. Rinse and repeat if necessary. Launder.

LIPSTICK

Place stain face down on paper towels. Sponge with dry cleaning solvent replacing towels as necessary. Let dry and rinse. Rub with heavy-duty liquid detergent and wash. Repeat using all-fabric bleach, if safe for fabric. Treat as Dye Stain if stain remains.

MILDEW

First brush off mildewed area. Rub area with heavy-duty liquid detergent. Launder in hottest water and bleach safe for fabric. Check for color fastness before using chlorine bleach. Dry in the sun. Badly mildewed fabric may be damaged beyond repair as mildew eats the celluosic fiber and can attack synthetic fibers too.

MUD

Scrap off all loose mud. Soak and agitate to remove any extra mud before washing. Soak tough stains for about 30 minutes in a detergent or enzyme presoak product. Launder normally. Repeat soaking and laundering for tough stains.

OILS, MARGARINE, BUTTER, MAYONNAISE

Spray light stains with pre-treat stain remover and rub with heavy duty liquid detergent, wash. Test for color-fastness before using all-fabric or chlorine bleach safe for the fabric. For tough stains, apply drycleaning solvent (follow instructions on product first) to the back. Rinse and air-dry before washing in hottest water safe for fabric.

PENCIL MARKS

Without damaging fabric, use soft eraser to remove any mark possible. Spray with a pre-treat product and rub area with heavy-duty liquid detergent. Rinse and wash as normal. Some pencil mark removers are available through notions suppliers.

PERSPIRATION

Frequent washing immediately after wearing may reduce damage from aluminum chlorides or zinc salts in antiperspirants. Rub light stains with liquid detergent. Treat tough stains with a prewash stain remover for about 5-10 minutes. Wash using an all-fabric bleach. Sponge fresh stain with ammonia and old stains with white vinegar.

SCORCH

If the damage is slight, gently brush the area to remove any residue. The heat has weakened the fabric. Rub liquid detergent into the area and wash. Treat with all-fabric bleach after testing for colorfastness.

TOMATO-BASED STAINS

Soak the area with a pre-treat stain remover. For tough stains, rub heavy-duty liquid detergent into stain and wash immediately. Test for color fastness before soaking in a dilute solution of all-fabric bleach or liquid chlorine bleach and water. For very tough stains, apply drycleaning solvent (read instructions on product first) to the back of stain. Let dry, rinse and wash.

To learn more about Vogue Patterns, to read recent sewing articles and to order patterns, visit *www.voguepatterns.com*.

Measurement Conversion Chart

Yards to Inches to Meters

Yards	Inches	Meters
⅛	4.5	.11
¼	9	.23
⅜	13.5	.34
½	18	.46
⅝	22.5	.57
¾	27	.69
⅞	31.5	.80
1	36	.91
1⅛	40.5	1.03
1¼	45	1.14
1⅜	49.5	1.26
1½	54	1.37
1⅝	58.5	1.49
1¾	63	1.60
1⅞	67.5	1.71
2	72	1.83

1 inch = 2.540 centimeters
1 yard = .9144 meters

1 centimeter = .3937 inches
1 meter = 3.281 feet/1.094 yards

Guide to Fabric Care Symbols

In 1998 the U.S. Federal Trade Commission approved the use of care symbols developed by the American Society of Testing and Materials (ASTM) allowing garment makers in the United States to dispense with written care instructions. This chart identifies these symbols and may be modified by the manufacturer to include more specific information.

WASH	MACHINE WASH CYCLES	NORMAL	PERMANENT PRESS		GENTLE CYCLE		HAND WASH
	WATER DEGREES — MAXIMUM	200F	160F	140F	120F	100F	65-85F
	SYMBOLS	∴·	∵·	∵	∵	··	·

BLEACH		ANY BLEACH WHEN NEEDED	ONLY NON-CHLORINE BLEACH WHEN NEEDED	DO NOT BLEACH

DRY	TUMBLE DRY CYCLES	NORMAL	PERMANENT PRESS	GENTLE CYCLE	LINE DRY/ HANG DRY	DRIP DRY	DRY FLAT
	SETTINGS	ANY HEAT	HIGH	MEDIUM	LOW	NO HEAT	

IRON	IRON-DRY OR STEAM	HIGH	WARM	LOW
	MAXIMUM DEGREES	390F	300F	230F

DRY CLEAN		ANY SOLVENT (A)	ANY SOLVENT BUT TRICHLO-ROETHYLENE (P)	PETROLEUM SOLVENT ONLY (F)	DO NOT DRY CLEAN
		REDUCE MOISTURE	SHORT CYCLE	LOW HEAT	NO STEAM FINISHING

A

Abdomen, altering, 107, 118
Accessories, defined, 23
Accordion pleats, 231
Acetate, 51
Acrilan, 51
Acrylic, 51, 52
Adjustment line, 68
Adjustments, 78–83. See
    also Alterations
    circumference, 81–83
    defined, 77
    length, 78–80
    pants, 113–116
    rules for, 78
Alcoholic beverage stains, 485
A-line, defined, 23
Allonger, defined, 23
Alpha olefin, 53
Alterations, 86–107. See
    also Adjustments
    abdomen, 107, 118
    back, 101–103
    bust, 96–99
    buttocks, 104–105, 120
    chest, 100
    defined, 77
    hips, 103–106, 119
    neckline, 86–87
    pants, 118–120
    shoulders, 88–90
    sleeveless armholes, 91
    sleeves, 92–95
Amincir, defined, 23
Analogous color scheme, 10
Anso-tex, 53
Anti-bacterial finish, 47
Anti-static finish, 47
Antron, 53
Applied band, 260–261
Applied design, 49
Applied and self-casings, 265
Appliqué
    defined, 23
    using, 483–484
Armholes, sleeveless
    altering, 91
    flat construction, 410
Arms, measuring, 59, 75
Arrowhead tack, 476
Ascot, defined, 23
Asymmetrical, defined, 23
Atelier, defined, 23
Attachments, sewing machine, 191
Au courant, defined, 23
Avant-garde, defined, 23

B

Baby stains, 485
Back, altering, 101–103

Backing, defined, 23
Backstitch, 210
Back waist length, measuring,
    59, 75
Balance, 9, 16
Balanced stripes, 145
Ball point needles, 187
Balmacaan, defined, 23
Band cuff, 298
Bands, 260–264
    applied, 260–261
    defined, 23
    knit, 264
    one-piece placket, 262
    topstitched, 261
    as trim, 463–465
    two-piece placket, 263
    Very Easy Vogue, 412
Bar tack, 213
Basket weave, 41
Basting, 208–209
    marking with, 401
    Very Easy Vogue, 402–403
    when tailoring, 429–430
Basting tape, 200
Basting tape marker, 200
Bateau, defined, 23
Batik, 49
Beaded fabrics, 374
Beading, 472–473
Beading needles, 173
Beeswax, 201, 207
Beetling, 46
Bell sleeves, 23
Belting, 185
Belts and carriers, 320–322, 419
Between needles, 173
Bias, defined, 23, 130
Bias-cut plaids and stripes, 147
Bias-cut seams, 219
Bias facings
    basic construction, 247, 252
    hems, 351
    ruffles, 242
Bias strips, cutting, 254–255
Bias tape, 184
Bindings, 254–259
    applying, 256
    cutting bias strips, 254–255
    defined, 23
    preshaping, 255
    special techniques, 257–259
    Very Easy Vogue, 412
BioFresh, 51
Bishop sleeves, 23
Blanket stitch, 213, 334, 476
Blind catchstitch, 211
Blind hems, 23
Blindstitch, 212
Blind tucks, 228
Blood stains, 485
Blouson, defined, 23
Blue jean zipper, 181

Bodice
    defined, 23
    measuring, 77
Bodkin, defined, 23, 200
Body measurements. See also
        Fit and fitting
    compared to pattern, 76–77
    for pants, 111–112
    pattern size charts, 62
    taking, 58–59, 74–75
Bolero, defined, 23
Bolt, defined, 23, 130
Bonding, 45
Boning, 23, 456
Border, defined, 23
Border prints, laying out, 148
Bouclé yarns, 39
Bound buttonholes, 325–330
    basic techniques, 325–326
    corded, 330
    couture technique, 458
    five-line patch method, 326–327
    one-piece folded method, 329
    organza patch method, 328
    two-piece method, 329
Bound edge seam finish, 221
Boutique, defined, 23
Box pleats, 231
Braid, 462–465
Braiding, 45
Brocade fabrics, 373
Brown paper, 203
Brushing, 46
Buckles, belt, 183, 322
Burnt-out printing, 49
Bust
    altering, 96–99
    measuring, 59
Butter stains, 486
Buttocks, altering, 104–105, 120
Buttonholes, 323–331
    bound, 325–330, 458
    in cuffs, 298
    in fur, 392
    hand-worked, 331
    machine-worked, 330
    placement, marking, 324
    pressing, 358
    seam, 330
    size of, 323
    symbols for, 68
    Very Easy Vogue, 420–421
Buttonhole scissors, 198
Buttonhole stitch, 212
Button-link cuff, 300
Buttons, 335–337
    couture techniques, 459
    for fur, 392
    placement of, 335
    size, 179
    symbols for, 68
    thread for, 336
    types, 179, 336–337

Very Easy Vogue, 422

C

Cable cord, 185
Caftan, 23
Calendering, 46
Camisoles, 23, 456
Cape, 23
Capima, 53
Caplana, 53
Caprolan, 53
Cap sleeves, 23
Captiva, 53
Cardboard gauge, 401
Cardigan, 23
Cartridge pleats, 23
Casings, 265–266
  sleeve, 293
  waistline, 315
Catchstitch, 211
Celanese, 51
Center back lines, 68
Center front lines, 68
Chainstitch, 213, 477
Chain weights, 457
Checks, matching, 144
Cheesecloth, 354–355
Chemise, defined, 23
Chenille needles, 173
Chest
  altering, 100
  measuring, 59, 75
Chesterfield, defined, 24
Chevron, defined, 24
Chewing gum stains, 485
Chez, defined, 24
Chic, defined, 24
Chinese ball buttons, 337
Chocolate stains, 485
Circular hems, 349
Circular ruffles, 241–242
Circumference adjustments, 81–83
Ciré, 46, 377
Clapper, 203
Cleerspan, 54
Clip, defined, 24
Clipping, seams, 217
Closures, 323–346. See also
Fasteners; Zippers; specific fabrics
  buttonholes, 323–331
  buttons, 335–337
  defined, 24
  fabric and thread loops, 296–297, 332–334
  fasteners, 345–346, 420–422, 458–459
  fitting, 123
Cloth beam, 40
Coatdress, 24
Coats. See Jackets, tailored

Coffee stains, 485
Coiled formation, 39
Collars, 267–282
  combining two patterns, 108
  cowls, 280
  detachable, 281
  flat (Peter Pan), 28, 268–269
  foldover bias, 277
  fur, 391
  rolled, 270–273
  shawl, 274–275
  with stand, 279
  standing (Mandarin), 276
  on tailored jacket, 440–441
  tie, 278
  Very Easy Vogue, 413–414
  well-made, 282
Collection, defined, 24
Color
  elements of, 10–11
  and fabric pattern, 48–49
Color blocking, 480
Colorfast, defined, 24, 47
Combination facings, 250
ComFortrel, 53
Complementary color scheme, 10
Complex yarns, 39
Construction basics, 205–246
  darts, 225–227
  gathering and shirring, 237–238
  hand stitches, 207–213, 434
  mitering, 243–244, 469
  pleats, 231–236
  ruffles, 239–242
  seams and seam finishes, 214–224
  tucks, 228–230
Construction techniques, 247–360.
See also specific techniques
  bands, 260–264
  belts and carriers, 320–322
  bindings, 254–259
  casings, 265–266
  closures, 323–346
  collars, 267–282
  cording and piping, 253
  cuffs, 298–303
  facings, 247–252
  hems, 347–353
  pockets, 304–313
  pressing, 354–360
  sleeves, 283–297
  Very Easy Vogue, 410–426
  waistbands, 317–319
  waistlines, 314–316
Continuous stitching, 403
Continuous strips, mitering, 243–244
Contour belts, 321
Contour darts, 227
Contour waistbands, 318–319
Contrasting, defined, 24
Conventional zippers, 181

Convertible, defined, 24
Corded buttonholes, 330
Corded quilting, 482
Corded seams, 224
Cording, 253
Cordura, 53
Corners
  binding, 257
  mitering, 244, 469
Cotton, 38, 50
Cotton darner needles, 173
Couching, 478
Courses, 43, 130
Couture, defined, 24
Couture techniques, 454–480
  fasteners, 458–459
  finishing, 460–462
  lining, 455
  shaping, 456–457
  trim, 463–480
  underlining, 455
Couturier, defined, 24
Covered buttons, 337, 459
Cover stitch hems, 349
Cowls
  constructing, 280
  defined, 24
Cravat, 24
Creme de Captiva, 53
Crepe fabrics, 371
Crepeset, 53
Creslan, 51
Cresloft, 51
Cretan stitch, 477
Crew, 24
Crimped formation, 39
Crocheting, 45
Cross dyeing, 48
Crossed seams, 218
Cross-stitch, 476
Cross-stitch tack, 213
Cross tucks, 230
Crosswise grain, 130
Crow's foot tack, 476
Cuffs, 298–303
  detachable, 303
  extended, 298–300
  placket opening for, 294–295
  turnback, 301–302
  Very Easy Vogue, 415
Culotte, 24
Cummerbunds, 24, 321
Curved hems, 461
Curved needles, 174
Curves, 15
Cut-in-one, defined, 24
Cutting, 135–137
  Very Easy Vogue, 398–400
  when tailoring, 429
Cutting guide, 70–71
Cutting lines, 68
Cutting tools, 198